WITHDRAWN FROM
MACALESTER COLLEGE
LIBRARY

Theater Law

Carolina Academic Press
Law Casebook Series
Advisory Board

❦

Gary J. Simson, Chairman
Cornell Law School

Raj K. Bhala
University of Kansas School of Law

John C. Coffee, Jr.
Columbia University School of Law

Randall Coyne
University of Oklahoma Law Center

John S. Dzienkowski
University of Texas School of Law

Paul Finkelman
University of Tulsa College of Law

Robert M. Jarvis
Shepard Broad Law Center
Nova Southeastern University

Vincent R. Johnson
St. Mary's University School of Law

Michael A. Olivas
University of Houston Law Center

Kenneth Port
William Mitchell College of Law

Michael P. Scharf
Case Western Reserve University Law School

Peter M. Shane
H. J. Heinz III School of Public Policy and Management
Carnegie Mellon University

Emily L. Sherwin
University of San Diego School of Law

John F. Sutton, Jr.
Emeritus, University of Texas School of Law

David B. Wexler
University of Arizona College of Law

Theater Law

Cases and Materials

Robert M. Jarvis
Professor of Law
Nova Southeastern University

Steven E. Chaikelson
Chair of the Theatre Arts Division
and Lecturer in Law
Columbia University

Christine A. Corcos
Associate Professor of Law
Louisiana State University Law Center

Edmund P. Edmonds
Director of the Schoenecker
Law Library and Professor of Law
University of St. Thomas

Jon M. Garon
Dean and Professor of Law
Hamline University

Shubha Ghosh
Professor of Law
State University of New York
at Buffalo

William D. Henslee
Associate Professor of Law
Florida A & M University

Mark S. Kende
Professor of Law
University of Montana

Charles A. Palmer
Professor of Law
Thomas M. Cooley Law School

Nancy L. Schultz
Professor of Law
Chapman University

Marin R. Scordato
Director of the Institute for
Communications Law Studies and
Associate Professor of Law
Catholic University of America

Libby A. White
Assistant Professor
of Legal Writing
Villanova University

Carolina Academic Press
Durham, North Carolina

Copyright © 2004
Robert M. Jarvis, Steven E. Chaikelson, Christine A. Corcos, Edmund P. Edmonds,
Jon M. Garon, Shubha Ghosh, William D. Henslee, Mark S. Kende, Charles A. Palmer,
Nancy L. Schultz, Marin R. Scordato, and Libby A. White
All Rights Reserved

Library of Congress Cataloging in Publication Data

Theater law : cases and materials / by Robert M. Jarvis ... [et al.].
    p. cm.
    Includes bibliographical references and index.
    ISBN 0-89089-246-6
    1. Theater—Law and legislation—United States—Cases.
    I. Jarvis, Robert M., 1959- II. Title.

KF4296.A7T48 2004
344.73'097--dc22

2004003705

Carolina Academic Press
700 Kent Street
Durham, North Carolina 27701
Telephone (919) 489-7486
Fax (919) 493-5668
www.cap-press.com

Printed in the United States of America

*For our families
and all those who love the theater*

Contents

Table of Cases	xiii
Preface	xvii
Acknowledgments	xviii

Chapter 1 Introduction — 3
- A. OVERVIEW — 3
- B. HISTORY — 3
  - Mason v. American Theatre Wing, Inc. — 3
  - Sacks v. Rubin — 7
  - Theater — 9
  - Theatre in New York: A Brief History — 13
  - Disney Plans 3 More Broadway Blockbusters — 19
    - Notes — 20
    - Problem 1 — 23
- C. PRACTICE — 23
  - People ex rel. Chicago Bar Ass'n v. Berezniak — 23
  - Chateau de Ville Productions, Inc. v. Tams-Witmark Music Library, Inc. — 27
  - Rodgers v. Sound of Music Company — 30
    - Notes — 33
    - Problem 2 — 37

Chapter 2 Playwrights — 39
- A. OVERVIEW — 39
- B. AUTHORSHIP — 39
  - Ntreh v. University of Texas at Dallas — 39
  - Jackson v. Universal International Pictures, Inc. — 42
  - Thomson v. Larson — 47
  - Ampersand Productions, Inc. v. Stahl — 58
    - Notes — 62
    - Problem 3 — 63
- C. CONTROL — 63
  - Barr v. Dramatists Guild, Inc. — 63
  - A Federal Recognition of Performance Art Author Moral Rights — 67
  - Mary Tyler Moore, Chided by Neil Simon, Quits His Play — 77
  - Found: A Twain Play Good Enough to Stage — 78
    - Notes — 80
    - Problem 4 — 81

Chapter 3 Rights Holders	83
A. OVERVIEW	83
B. SECURING RIGHTS	83
Lewys v. O'Neill	83
Outcault v. Lamar	95
Metro-Goldwyn-Mayer, Inc. v. Showcase Atlanta Cooperative Productions, Inc.	97
Presley's Estate v. Russen	106
Notes	112
Problem 5	114
C. GRANTING RIGHTS	114
Golding v. R.K.O. Pictures, Inc.	114
Burnett v. Warner Bros. Pictures, Inc.	119
Notes	120
Problem 6	121
Chapter 4 Producers	123
A. OVERVIEW	123
B. CAPITAL ACQUISITION	123
A Practical Guide to Theatrical Financing	123
Rosie the Producer, Navigating Broadway	131
Knapp v. Penfield	133
Classic Theater Corp. v. Amster	135
Elvin Associates v. Franklin	138
United States v. Altman	141
Theater Founders are Charged with Fraud	150
Notes	151
Problem 7	153
C. ADMINISTRATIVE RESPONSIBILITIES	154
Martin v. Commissioner	154
Theatre Guild Productions, Inc. v. Insurance Corp. of Ireland	159
Bates v. Select Lake City Theater Operating Co.	161
Russek Advertising, Inc. v. Hurst	164
Redgrave v. Stuart Thompson Productions	167
Notes	169
Problem 8	170
Chapter 5 Directors and Choreographers	171
A. OVERVIEW	171
B. DUTIES	171
Julien v. Society of Stage Directors and Choreographers, Inc.	171
Gennaro v. Rosenfield	173
Rodgers v. Logan	179
Notes	182
Problem 9	183
C. STAGE DIRECTIONS	184
New Clout for Stage Directors: Copyright Protection Available for Creative Work	184
Mantello v. Hall	184

Notes 192
Problem 10 192

Chapter 6 Cast 193
A. OVERVIEW 193
B. HIRING AND FIRING 193
    Mixing Law and Art: The Role of Anti-Discrimination Law
        and Color-Blind Casting in Broadway Theater 193
    New Star of 'Producers' is Replaced After 4 Weeks 195
    Redgrave v. Boston Symphony Orchestra, Inc. 197
    Pacitti v. Macy's 200
    Harry Rogers Theatrical Enterprises, Inc. v. Comstock 206
        Notes 207
        Problem 11 210
C. PAY AND BENEFITS 210
    In re Himes 210
    This Is Me, Inc. v. Taylor 215
    Miller v. Municipal Theatre Association of St. Louis 222
        Notes 226
        Problem 12 227
D. REPRESENTATION 228
    Actors in Ellis Island Show Vote, 7 to 1, to Join Union 228
    National Labor Relations Board v. Actors' Equity Association 229
    H. A. Artists & Associates, Inc. v. Actors' Equity Association 232
    Pawlowski v. Woodruff 238
    Personal Management 240
        Notes 243
        Problem 13 244

Chapter 7 Designers, Musicians, and Crew 245
A. OVERVIEW 245
B. BEHIND THE SCENES 245
    Lion's Den: Backstage at Broadway's Hottest New Musical 245
    Farce of Nature 247
    State ex rel. O'Brien v. Petry 251
        Notes 254
        Problem 14 255
C. EMPLOYMENT DISPUTES 255
    Ostertag v. The Historic Theater Group, Ltd. 255
    Anderson v. Long 257
    Carell v. The Shubert Organization, Inc. 258
    St. Louis Theatrical Company v. St. Louis Theatrical
        Brotherhood Local 6, IATSE 271
        Notes 274
        Problem 15 275
D. HAZARDS 275
    Eaves Brooks Costume Company, Inc. v. Y.B.H. Realty Corp. 275
    Artists' Embassy v. Hunt 276
    Donaldson v. Select Theatre Corporation 278

Mintiks v. Metropolitan Opera Association, Inc.	279
Notes	283
Problem 16	283

Chapter 8 Houses — 285
A. OVERVIEW — 285
B. BUILDING CODES — 285

Nemer v. Michigan State Board of Registration for Architects, Professional Engineers and Land Surveyors	285
Hart v. City Theatres Co.	288
Theatre Management Group, Inc. v. Dalgliesh	289
Notes	292
Problem 17	294

C. NAMING RIGHTS — 294

Booth v. Jarrett & Palmer	294
Southeast Bank, N.A. v. Lawrence	295
Cadillac on Marquee at Winter Garden	296
Notes	297
Problem 18	298

D. LEASES — 298

Theatre Party Associates, Inc. v. Shubert Organization, Inc.	298
Liza Co. v. Mark Hellinger Theatre, Inc.	302
A Theater Closing, A Hit Show in the Cold	306
Notes	307
Problem 19	308

E. HISTORIC PRESERVATION — 309

Friends of the Astor, Inc. v. City of Reading	309
Shubert Organization, Inc. v. Landmarks Preservation Commission of the City of New York	315
Fisher v. Giuliani	318
Notes	324
Problem 20	325

Chapter 9 Audiences — 327
A. OVERVIEW — 327
B. TICKETS — 327

Luxenberg v. Keith & Proctor Amusement Co.	327
Ex parte Quarg	332
Gold v. DiCarlo	334
Notes	337
Problem 21	338

C. SAFETY AND COMFORT — 339

Robbins v. Memphis Little Theatre Players Association	339
Ludwig v. Jefferson Performing Arts Society	343
Tantillo v. Goldstein Bros. Amusement Co.	345
Thielmier v. Louisiana Riverboat Gaming Partnership	346
Bloomberg Disconnects Cell Ban	349
Notes	350
Problem 22	352

Chapter 10 Critics — 353
A. OVERVIEW — 353
B. QUALIFICATIONS — 353
- Wanted: Theater Critic — 353
- Republican Publishing Co. v. American Newspaper Guild — 353
- Blanchard v. Northwest Publications, Inc. — 356
- Code of Conduct — 358
   - Notes — 359
   - Problem 23 — 361
C. IMMUNITIES — 361
- Merivale v. Carson — 361
- Adolf Philipp Co. v. New Yorker Staats-Zeitung — 364
- Phantom Touring, Inc. v. Affiliated Publications — 374
- Soul v. Wright — 379
   - Notes — 381
   - Problem 24 — 381

Chapter 11 Touring Companies — 383
A. OVERVIEW — 383
B. ECONOMICS — 383
- For Touring Shows, Rules of the Road Changing — 383
- On with the $how: Union Deal to Work for Lower Pay Lets '42nd Street' Get on the Road — 385
- It's Broadway. Well, Virtually: Slimmed-Down Shows Thrive on the Road — 387
   - Notes — 389
   - Problem 25 — 389
C. ARRANGEMENTS — 390
- Inge v. Twentieth Century-Fox Film Corporation — 390
- United States v. Shubert — 396
- Rapagnani v. Judas Company — 399
- Cuccioli v. Jekyll & Hyde Neue Metropol Bremen Theater Produktion GmbH & Co. — 403
   - Notes — 409
   - Problem 26 — 410

Chapter 12 Not-For-Profit Productions — 411
A. OVERVIEW — 411
B. FUNDING — 411
- Plumstead Theatre Society, Inc. v. Commissioner of Internal Revenue — 411
- Eychaner v. Gross — 417
   - Notes — 431
   - Problem 27 — 435
C. ARTISTIC FREEDOM — 436
- Boring v. Buncombe County Board of Education — 436
- DiBona v. Matthews — 442
- Linnemeier v. Indiana University-Purdue University Fort Wayne — 451
- Axson-Flynn v. Johnson — 457

Notes		463
Problem 28		464

Appendices 465
APPENDIX A	AGREEMENT TO JOINTLY WRITE A PLAY	465
APPENDIX B	AGREEMENT TO TURN A NOVEL INTO A PLAY	468
APPENDIX C	AGREEMENT TO PRODUCE A PLAY	471
APPENDIX D	AGREEMENT TO HIRE A DIRECTOR-CHOREOGRAPHER	483
APPENDIX E	AGREEMENT TO HIRE AN ACTOR OR ACTRESS	490
APPENDIX F	AGREEMENT TO RENT SCENERY	493
APPENDIX G	AGREEMENT TO LEASE A THEATER	495
APPENDIX H	AGREEMENT TO BOOK A ROAD SHOW	499
APPENDIX I	AGREEMENT TO ALLOW AN AMATEUR GROUP TO PERFORM A PLAY	503

Index 505

Table of Cases

Abrevaya v. Palace Theatre & Realty Co., 350
Adolf Philipp Co. v. New Yorker Staats-Zeitung, 364
Alderman v. Iditarod Properties, Inc., 325
Allied Sound, Inc. v. Neely, 254
American Theatre Press, Inc. v. Tax Commission of State of New York, 350
Ampersand Productions, Inc. v. Stahl, 58
Anderson v. Long, 257
Antonelli v. Majestic Theater, 352
Artists' Embassy v. Hunt, 276
Auditorium Theatre Co. v. Oregon-Washington R. & Nav. Co., 389
Axson-Flynn v. Johnson, 457

Barr v. Dramatists Guild, Inc., 63
Barry v. The Players, 381
Bates v. Select Lake City Theater Operating Co., 161
Belasco Theatre Corp. v. Jelin Productions, 308
Bell v. U-32 Board of Education, 464
Bishop v. Texas A & M University, 255
Blanchard v. Northwest Publications, Inc., 356
Board of Education of Independent School District No. 92 of Pottawatomie County v. Earls, 463
Board of Trustees of University of North Carolina v. Unknown and Unascertained Heirs of Prince, 434
Booth v. Jarrett & Palmer, 294
Boring v. Buncombe County Board of Education, 436
Boston Concessions Group, Inc. v. Criterion Center Corp., 309
Bourne Co. v. Speeks, 436
Boyer v. Commissioner, 410
Bristow v. Drake State Inc., 170
Burgess v. Chase-Riboud, 112
Burnett v. Warner Bros. Pictures, Inc., 119

Cabrera v. Teatro del Sesenta, Inc., 63
Carell v. The Shubert Organization, Inc., 258
Carlson v. WPLG/TV-10, Post-Newsweek Stations of Florida, 183
Century Paramount Hotel v. Rock Land Corp., 308
Charlotte Ampitheater Corp. v. NLRB, 275
Chateau de Ville Productions, Inc. v. Tams-Witmark Music Library, Inc., 27
Cheng v. Dispeker, 244
Cherry v. Des Moines Leader, 381
City of Fayetteville v. Phillips, 431
Classic Theater Corp. v. Amster, 135
Cleveland Leader Printing Co. v. Nethersole, 381
Comedy III Productions, Inc. v. Gary Saderup, Inc., 113
Community Drama Ass'n of Des Moines v. Iowa State Tax Comm'n, 431
Condell v. New School for Social Research, 275
Corto v. National Scenery Studios, Inc., 275
C.R. Theatricals, Inc. v. Concert Ass'n of Florida, Inc., 308
Cuccioli v. Jekyll & Hyde Neue Metropol Bremen Theater Produktion GmbH & Co., 403

Dailey v. Superior Court of the City and County of San Francisco, 23
Daniels v. State, 21

Denker v. Uhry, 112
Department of Revenue v. Louisville Children's Theater, Inc., 431
Diamond Circle Corp. v. Blocher, 227
DiBona v. Matthews, 442
Donaldson v. Select Theatre Corporation, 278
Downs v. Commissioner, 361

Eaves Brooks Costume Company, Inc. v. Y.B.H. Realty Corp., 275
Elvin Associates v. Franklin, 138
Ex parte Quarg, 332
Eychaner v. Gross, 417

Fisher v. Giuliani, 318
Fisher v. Washington Post Co., 381
Fox v. Chosen Co., 80
Friends of the Astor, Inc. v. City of Reading, 309
Front Row Theatre, Inc. v. American Manufacturers Mutual Ins. Co., 294

Gateway Theatrical of Bellport, Inc. v. Associated Musicians of Greater New York, 275
Gennaro v. Rosenfield, 173
Gershwin v. Whole Thing Co., 113
Gold v. DiCarlo, 334
Golding v. R.K.O. Pictures, Inc., 114
Greek Theatre Ass'n v. County of Los Angeles, 431
Groucho Marx Productions, Inc. v. Day and Night Co., Inc., 113
Guaranty Trust Co. of N.Y. v. New York Community Trust, 228

H. A. Artists & Associates, Inc. v. Actors' Equity Association, 232
Harry Rogers Theatrical Enterprises, Inc. v. Comstock, 206
Hart v. City Theatres Co., 288
Haviland v. Butz, 209
Horgan v. Macmillan, Inc., 192
Horton Plaza Associates v. Playing for Real Theatre, 464
Houlihan v. McCourt, 169
Huffman v. City of Poway, 227
Hughes v. Robinson, 308

In re Flying Squirrel Sports, LLC, 298
In re Himes, 210
In re Livent, Inc. Noteholders Securities Litigation, 153
Inge v. Twentieth Century-Fox Film Corporation, 390

Jack Hammer Associates, Inc. v. Delmy Productions, Inc., 227
Jackson v. Universal International Pictures, Inc., 42
Jacobs v. Felix Bloch Erben Verlag fur Buhne Film und Funk KG, 169
Jones Beach Theatre Corp. v. Commissioner, 254
Julien v. Society of Stage Directors and Choreographers, Inc., 171

Keep Productions, Inc. v. Arlington Park Towers Hotel Corp., 20
Kentucky Center for the Arts v. Handley, 275
Kirke La Shelle Co. v. Paul Armstrong Co., 121
Knapp v. Penfield, 133

Lacks v. Ferguson Reorganized School District R-2, 464
Lafayette Dramatic Productions v. Ferentz, 275
Lawrence v. Legitimate Theatre Employees Local No. B-183, 275
Lawrence v. Sun Printing & Publishing Ass'n, 381
Lewys v. O'Neill, 83
Linnemeier v. Indiana University-Purdue University Fort Wayne, 451
Litchfield v. Spielberg, 120
Little Theatre of Dallas v. City of Dallas, 431
Littlefield v. Superior Court, 36
Liveright v. Waldorf Theaters Corp., 308
Liza Co. v. Mark Hellinger Theatre, Inc., 302
Losch v. Marcin, 169
Ludwig v. Jefferson Performing Arts Society, 343
Lumley v. Wagner, 209

Luxenberg v. Keith & Proctor Amusement Co., 327

Makletzova v. Diaghileff, 210
Mantello v. Hall, 184
Martin v. Commissioner, 154
Mason v. American Theatre Wing, Inc., 3
Mawson v. Leavitt, 308
McIntosh v. Miner, 37
Memphis Development Foundation v. State Board of Equalization, 431
Merivale v. Carson, 361
Merrick v. Four Star Stage Lighting, Inc., 254
Metcalfe v. Bill Board Publishing Co., 381
Metcalfe v. Klaw, 381
Metro-Goldwyn-Mayer, Inc. v. Showcase Atlanta Cooperative Productions, Inc., 97
Metropolitan Opera Ass'n v. Wagner-Nichols Recorder Corp., 390
Miller v. Municipal Theatre Association of St. Louis, 222
Mintiks v. Metropolitan Opera Association, Inc., 279
MTIS Ltd. v. Corporacion Interamericana de Entretenemiento S.A. de C.V., 308
Murray Schwartz Enterprises Employee Pension Plan Trust v. Four Corners Productions, Inc., 153

National Labor Relations Board v. Actors' Equity Association, 229
Nemer v. Michigan State Board of Registration for Architects, Professional Engineers and Land Surveyors, 285
New Orleans Opera Guild, Inc. v. Local 174, Musicians Mutual Protective Union, 275
Ntreh v. University of Texas at Dallas, 39

Oakes v. Gaines, 283
Opera on Tour v. Weber, 275
Ostertag v. The Historic Theater Group, Ltd., 255
Outcault v. Lamar, 95

Pacifico v. Playwrights Horizons Theatre School, 463
Pacitti v. Macy's, 200
Paper Mill Playhouse v. Millburn Township, 431
Patterson v. Masem, 464
Pawlowski v. Woodruff, 238
People ex rel. Chicago Bar Ass'n v. Berezniak, 23
People v. Tryer, 36
People v. Weinberger, 82
Phalen v. Theatrical Protective Union No. 1, IATSE, 275
Phantom Touring, Inc. v. Affiliated Publications, 374
Plumstead Theatre Society, Inc. v. Commissioner of Internal Revenue, 411
Presley's Estate v. Russen, 106
Production Resource Group, L.L.C. v. Stonebridge Partners Equity Fund, L.P., 254

Rapagnani v. Judas Company, 399
Red Sail Easter Ltd. Partners, L.P. v. Radio City Music Hall Productions, Inc., 153
Redgrave v. Boston Symphony Orchestra, Inc., 197
Redgrave v. Stuart Thompson Productions, 167
Republican Publishing Co. v. American Newspaper Guild, 353
Ring v. Spina, 80
Robbins v. Memphis Little Theatre Players Association, 339
Roberts v. Atlantic Recording Corp., 183
Rochester Civic Theatre, Inc. v. Ramsay, 434
Rodgers v. Logan, 179
Rodgers v. Sound of Music Company, 30
Russek Advertising, Inc. v. Hurst, 164

Sacks v. Rubin, 7
Saginaw Stage Employees, Local 35, IATSE v. City of Saginaw, 275
Schacht v. United States, 22
Schenck v. United States, 293

Schuman v. State of New York, 21
S.E.C. v. Fox, 36
Seko Air Freight, Inc. v. Transworld Systems, Inc., 339
Seyfried v. Walton, 464
Shoptalk, Ltd. v. Concorde-New Horizons Corp., 114
Shubert Organization, Inc. v. Landmarks Preservation Commission of the City of New York, 315
Soul v. Wright, 379
Southeast Bank, N.A. v. Lawrence, 295
Southeastern Promotions, Ltd. v. Conrad, 22
St. Louis Theatrical Company v. St. Louis Theatrical Brotherhood Local 6, IATSE, 271
State v. Davis, 37
State ex rel. Fisher v. Warren Star Theater, 434
State ex rel. O'Brien v. Petry, 251
Stockton Civic Theatre v. Board of Supervisors of San Joaquin County, 431

Tantillo v. Goldstein Bros. Amusement Co., 345
Theatre Guild Productions, Inc. v. Insurance Corp. of Ireland, 159
Theatre Management Group, Inc. v. Dalgliesh, 289
Theatre Party Associates, Inc. v. Shubert Organization, Inc., 298
Theatre West of Lincoln City, Ltd. v. Department of Revenue, 431
Theodore v. Delaware Valley School District, 463
Thielmier v. Louisiana Riverboat Gaming Partnership, 346

This is Me, Inc. v. Taylor, 215
Thomson v. Larson, 47
Tillander v. Latin Quarter Cafe, Inc., 283
Today's Theatre, Inc. v. Ernest Co., 308
Tootle Theater Co. v. Shubert Theatrical Co., 308
Tulsa Theatrical Stage Employees Union, Local 354 v. Broadway Theatre League of Tulsa, Inc., 275

United States v. Altman, 141
United States v. Shubert, 396
United States v. West Productions, Inc., 152

Vernonia School District 47J v. Acton, 463

Walters v. National Ass'n of Radiation Survivors, 37
Washington Theatre Club, Inc. v. District of Columbia, 431
Webb v. Lake Mills Community School District, 464
Wells v. League of American Theatres & Producers, Inc., 21
Western Union Telegraph Co. v. Austlet, 389
Weston v. Boston & M. R. R., 389
William Morris Agency, Inc. v. Cambridge, 244
Woollcott v. Shubert, 381

Zal v. Steppe, 36
ZZYZX Studios v. Volvo Cars of North America, Inc., 434

Preface

Fueled by student demand, the number of law school courses focusing on entertainment law has skyrocketed during the past two decades. This, in turn, has led to a plethora of casebooks. While each differs in approach and arrangement, all share one basic trait: an emphasis on television and film and an almost complete absence of materials dealing with the theater.

Yet, as the oldest of the performing arts, theater has much to offer in the way of historical instruction. At the same time, it remains an important source of employment and enjoyment for millions of Americans. Indeed, at this very moment a play or musical is being performed—or planned—just a stone's throw from where you are sitting.

The value of studying theater as part of a well-rounded legal education has not gone completely unrecognized. Even before this book got underway in July 2001, Columbia University already offered a highly-respected theater law seminar, and while our work was progressing Professor Catherine Bigley McGovern at DePaul University began offering a course in theater law (January 2003). Also during this time Professor Rosalind S. Lichter at Yeshiva University (November 2001) and Professor John J. Cannon at Villanova University (April 2003) both organized theater law symposia. It is our hope that this book will spur even more law schools to embrace the subject.

A few procedural matters should be noted. First, the research for this book closed at the end of February 2004. Second, we have been liberal in our editing and normally have not indicated where text or footnotes have been deleted or repositioned. Third, the notes and problems that appear at the end of each section are an integral component of the book, and therefore should be given the same attention as the principal readings. Fourth, at various points in the notes you will be referred to one of the book's appendices, each of which reproduce a sample form of agreement. At such times you should turn to the indicated appendix and study it with care. Finally, for those without a stage background, Chapter 1 contains numerous suggestions for becoming better acquainted with the field. Of course, the best way to learn about the theater is to simply go to a show.

In closing, we hope you will enjoy using this book as much as we enjoyed writing it, and to that end we invite your comments and suggestions. All such thoughts can be sent to Professor Robert M. Jarvis, Nova Southeastern University Law Center, 3305 College Avenue, Fort Lauderdale, FL 33314-7721, telephone (954) 262-6172, telefax (954) 262-3835, e-mail jarvisb@nsu.law.nova.edu.

Acknowledgments

A number of institutions and individuals helped us in the long journey from having an idea to having a book. We are, of course, grateful to our respective law schools and the Publisher's Staff. We also are indebted to the following for specific contributions: Graham Atkins, Paul R. Baier, Kristine Calalang, Carolyn Casselman, June Chaikelson, Morris Chaikelson, Sherri D. Clarke, Christiane Clemens, Leigh Clemons, Cassie Coleman, Phyllis Coleman, Tim Colton, Diane Penneys Edelman, Kathy Fleming, Amy Fritz, Stacey Gordon, Michael Harnois, Elisa Hatlevig, Judith A. Jarvis, John Kernochan, Dwight King, Linda Lacy, Michael Landau, Wendy Lau, Ed LeClaire, Robert C. Lind, Emilia Pietrkiewicz, Amanda B. Rosen, Melinda Saran, Peter Schaub, Keith Sipe, Howard Stein, Lawrence J. Tabas, Terrie Tressler, Alan Wasserstrom, Brannon Wiles, Rachel Williams, Taylor Simpson-Wood, and Brian Zuccaro.

We also wish to thank the rights holders of the following materials:

American Theatre Critics Association, *Code of Conduct* (1997)

Elliot H. Brown & Daniel M. Wasser, *A Practical Guide to Theatrical Financing*, 16 Ent. & Sports Law. 6 (Fall 1998)

Tony Brown, *On With the $how: Union Deal to Work for Lower Pay Lets '42nd Street' Get on the Road*, Clev. Plain Dealer, Feb. 17, 2003, at C1

Bonnie Chen, Note, *Mixing Law and Art: The Role of Anti-Discrimination Law and Color-Blind Casting in Broadway Theater*, 16 Hofstra Lab. & Emp. L.J. 515 (1999)

Maureen Dezell, *For Touring Shows, Rules of the Road Changing*, Boston Globe, Apr. 27, 2003, at N1

Steven Greenhouse, *Actors in Ellis Island Show Vote, 7 to 1, to Join Union*, N.Y. Times, Aug. 15, 2002, at E1

David Johnson, *Farce of Nature*, Ent. Design, Mar. 1, 2002, at TCI (courtesy of PRIMEDIA Business Magazines & Media Inc.)

John Kenrick, *Theatre in New York: A Brief History*, at www.musicals101.com/bwaythhist.htm (2003)

Otto W. Konrad, *A Federal Recognition of Performance Art Author Moral Rights*, 48 Wash. & Lee L. Rev. 1579 (1991)

Alexander Lindey & Michael Landau, *Lindey on Entertainment, Publishing and the Arts: Agreements and the Law* (2d ed. 1980 & 2003 Supp.) (published by Thomson-West) (for the agreements that appear herein as Appendices A-F and H-I) (special additional thanks to Alvin Deutsch & Franklin R. Weissberg for Appendix D)

Gerald A. Margolis et al., *Personal Management*, 598 PLI/Pat 1149 (Mar. 2000)

Jesse McKinley, *Cadillac on Marquee at Winter Garden*, N.Y. Times, May 7, 2002, at E3

Jesse McKinley, *Found: A Twain Play Good Enough to Stage*, N.Y. Times, May 12, 2003, at E1

Jesse McKinley, *New Star of 'Producers' is Replaced After 4 Weeks*, N.Y. Times, Apr. 16, 2002, at E1

Jesse McKinley, *Rosie the Producer: Navigating Broadway*, N.Y. Times, Sept. 29, 2003, at E1

Richard C. Reuben, *New Clout for Stage Directors: Copyright Protection Available for Creative Work*, 81 A.B.A.J. 32 (Oct. 1995)

Michael Riedel, *Lion's Den: Backstage at Broadway's Hottest New Musical*, N.Y. Daily News, Nov. 16, 1997, at 1 (Sunday Extra)

Bernard Simon, *Theater Founders Are Charged With Fraud*, N.Y. Times, Oct. 23, 2002, at C2

Curtis L. Taylor, *Bloomberg Disconnects Cell Ban*, Newsday, Jan. 15, 2003, at A7

Theater, Wikipedia - The Free Encyclopedia (2004)

Wanted: Theater Critic, Juneau (Alaska) Empire Online, Sept. 9, 1999

Bruce Weber, *It's Broadway. Well, Virtually: Slimmed-Down Shows Thrive on the Road*, N.Y. Times, Mar. 18, 2003, at E1

Bruce Weber, *A Theater Closing, A Hit Show in the Cold*, N.Y. Times, Oct. 29, 2003, at E1

Frederick M. Winship, *Disney Plans 3 More Broadway Blockbusters*, United Press International Online, Dec. 17, 2003

Jason Zinoman, *Mary Tyler Moore, Chided by Neil Simon, Quits His Play*, N.Y. Times, Dec. 5, 2003, at E2

All the world's a stage,
And all the men and women merely players.
—*William Shakespeare (1564–1616)*

All the world's a stage and most of us are desperately unrehearsed.
—*Sean O'Casey (1880–1964)*

If all the world's a stage, I want to operate the trap door.
—*Paul Beatty (1962–)*

Theater Law

Chapter 1

Introduction

A. OVERVIEW

In the remaining chapters of this casebook, we will examine the various legal issues that regularly arise in connection with the creation, financing, and production of theatrical shows. Here, however, our focus is on more general matters: the history of the theater and the practice of theater law.

B. HISTORY

MASON v. AMERICAN THEATRE WING, INC.
627 N.Y.S.2d 539 (Sup. Ct. 1995)

CAHN, Justice.

Comedian Jackie Mason ("Mason") demands $75 million in compensatory and punitive damages—plus costs—for defendants' refusal to categorize his one-man topical comedy "Jackie Mason: Politically Incorrect," as a "play" eligible for a Tony award in the 1993-94 Broadway season. Politics aside, Mr. Mason is "Legally Incorrect." The motion of defendants American Theatre Wing, Inc. ("Wing"), The League of American Theaters and Producers, Inc. ("League"), and The Dramatists Guild, Inc. ("Guild") to dismiss the complaint or for summary judgment (CPLR 3211) is granted. By order of February 6, 1995, this court granted plaintiff's motion to discontinue the action as against defendants Actors Equity Association and United Scenic Artists. The remaining defendant, the Society of Stage Directors and Choreographers (sued as "Stage Directors and Choreographers"), was never served.

Background

The Antoinette Perry ("Tony") Awards are awarded annually for excellence in the theatre in certain categories of achievement. The presentation ceremony is administered by Tony Award Productions ("Productions"), which is a joint venture of League and Wing. Under Wing's Rules and Regulations ("the Tony Rules"), eligibility for nomination is determined by the Tony Awards Administration Committee ("the Committee"), a self-governing body established by Productions. The Committee is comprised of twenty-four individuals designated by Wing, League, Guild, Actors Equity Association, United Scenic Artists and the Society of Stage Directors and Choreographers.

Tony Rule 4(a) lists the categories in which "regular" Tonys may be awarded. Most category names specifically refer to either a "play" or a "musical," e.g., "Best Play," "Best Musical," "Best Performance by a Leading Actress in a Play," etc. A number do not contain those terms (e.g., simply "Best Costume Design," "Best Choreography"), but the omission is apparently not significant. Other rules also contain references to "plays or musicals," clearly implying that those are the only types of productions eligible for regular Tonys. However, Rules 4(c) and 4(d) provide for discretionary "Special Tony Awards," which may be granted to "a theatrical event...which does not fit into any existing Tony Award category," as well as for "lifetime achievement in the theatre."

Tony Rule 2 sets forth the six requirements a production must satisfy to be eligible in the "various categories." The Committee must determine that the entrant is "a legitimate theatrical production," but definitions of "play" or "musical" as used in the "various categories" are not provided. Also, as is relevant here, Rule 2(v) requires the producer of a production seeking consideration to invite and provide free tickets to all eligible Tony voters, and to certify in writing to the Committee that the invitations were extended in the manner and number prescribed by the Rules. The remaining eligibility requirements relate to minimum theatre size and opening date cut-offs.

Regardless of a show's eligibility, the Committee still retains discretion to determine "whether a sufficient number of eligible candidates exist in quality or quantity to merit the granting of an Award in the applicable category for the current season," Tony Rule 2(j)(A). Similarly, it has "sole discretion to reduce the number of nominees to fewer than four...in a particular category for the current season." Id. Finally, Rule 1(a) provides that "[a]ll decisions of the [Committee] concerning eligibility for the Awards and all other matters relating to their administration and presentation...shall be final."

Mason has presented one-man topical comedy performances on Broadway since at least the 1986-87 season, when he starred in "The World According to Jackie Mason." He accepted a Special Tony Award for "Excellence in the Theatre" that year, but the production was apparently deemed ineligible for a regular Tony because it was not considered a play or musical. Mason did not challenge that determination, nor a similar one made concerning his show "Jackie Mason: Brand New", in 1990.

"Jackie Mason: Politically Incorrect" opened on April 5, 1994. On April 7, 1994 the Committee met and determined that the show was not eligible for a Tony because, inter alia, like his previous productions, it was not a play or a musical. Mason did not object or take other action between that date and the presentation ceremony on June 12, 1994. The instant suit, for monetary damages only, was commenced on August 4, 1994.

The Complaint

The complaint seeks recovery under three theories. The first cause of action essentially challenges the disqualification as a corporate action and alleges that defendants "failed to apply objective and fair standards to allow plaintiff to be eligible for a Tony Award." In particular, defendants "did not consider plaintiff's one-man comedy show a proper Broadway production for a Tony Award...although several other one-man shows had been considered for a Tony Award in the past." Additionally, Mason complains that "defendants and their designees maintained rules and categories of eligibility which discriminated against one-man shows."

The second cause of action formalizes this latter claim of discrimination, relying on an unspecified section of the New York Human Rights Law to allege a "violation of [plaintiff's] civil rights." It alleges that "[t]he establishment of categories, which excluded [the] one-man show of plaintiff, was a form of discriminated [sic] against plaintiff who otherwise qualified for consideration for a Tony Award" and that defendants "wrongfully discrimination [sic] against plaintiff in his employment by eliminating his one-man show from fair consideration."

The third cause of action sounds in contract. Mason claims that the publication of defendants' eligibility rules "constituted an offer to the plaintiff and to other performers who were similarly situated for consideration for a Tony Award." Plaintiff asserts that his participation in the process was an "acceptance," and that defendants breached the agreement by wrongfully refusing to consider him as eligible for a Tony.

Discussion

The courts, of course, do not usually decide who is eligible to receive a Tony, or to whom one should be awarded. This suit could be dismissed out of hand if Mason were simply complaining that his show "deserved" to win a nomination or trophy on its merits. As noted in a related context,

> Most honors are alike in that some individual or committee must review what someone has accomplished and make a subjective judgment of whether that conduct is deserving of reward or recognition. Inherent in such a system is the possibility of error. If Paul Newman (The Verdict) "wins" the academy award instead of Dustin Hoffman (Tootsie), who is to say that he is really more deserving?

Karnstein v. Pewaukee School Board, 557 F.Supp. 565, 567 (E.D.Wis.); see also Dangler v. Yorktown Central Schools, 771 F.Supp. 625 (S.D.N.Y.).

The precise issue here, however, is one step removed from the highly subjective process of selecting a Tony winner. It concerns the corporate defendants' application of the internal, published threshold requirements regarding eligibility, not the ultimate determination of which shows are "better" or "best." Defendants' status as the conferrers of a highly publicized entertainment industry award does not immunize them from the normal rules of corporate or organizational governance, although the scope of judicial review of such private sector decisions is extraordinarily narrow.

Accordingly, while the court agrees that Mason's discrimination and contract claims are to be dismissed out of hand, patently frivolous, the challenge under the Tony Rules could arguably state a claim. Nevertheless, defendants are entitled to summary judgment dismissing the complaint because they complied with their rules, within the scope of their broad, discretionary authority.

The Challenge to Defendants' Corporate Action

The complaint does not specify the nature of this action, e.g., a derivative action or other civil suit. Primarily to advance a statute of limitations defense, defendants categorize it as an Article 78 proceeding. Although that procedure is more commonly applied to review challenges to public administrative agency decisions, it is also available to review the determinations of private, non-governmental organizations, Levandusky v. One Fifth Ave. Apartment Corp., 75 N.Y.2d 530, 554 N.Y.S.2d 807, 553 N.E.2d 1317 (corporate co-op board action); Susan M. v. New York Law School, 76 N.Y.2d 241, 557 N.Y.S.2d 297, 556 N.E.2d 1104 (private law school), and has been applied by at least one court in a dispute over whether a film warranted the "X" rating assigned to it by the Motion Picture Association of America, see Miramax Films Corp. v. Motion Picture Assn. of America, Inc., 148 Misc.2d 1, 560 N.Y.S.2d 730 (Sup.Ct.N.Y.Co.). It is doubtful whether that framework is appropriate here, as Mason does not request a reversal of defendants' decision, but only monetary damages not available under Article 78, CPLR 7806; Leisner v. Bahou, 97 A.D.2d 860, 469 N.Y.S.2d 255, appeal dismissed 61 N.Y.2d 985, 475 N.Y.S.2d 282, 463 N.E.2d 623; Rosario v. Blum, 80 A.D.2d 511, 435 N.Y.S.2d 596.

However, there is "no purpose in allowing the form of the action to dictate the substance of the standard by which the legitimacy of corporate action is to be measured," Levandusky, supra at 541, 554 N.Y.S.2d 807, 553 N.E.2d 1317. Any damage award would necessarily be premised upon a finding that defendants breached some duty created by the Tony Rules. Thus, a standard analogous to the business judgment rule should apply, see Levandusky, supra at 537, 554 N.Y.S.2d 807, 553 N.E.2d 1317, under which "the over-riding concern is whether respondent acted in good faith in furtherance of its own legitimate purpose," see Miramax, supra at 9, 560 N.Y.S.2d 730. This "more limited" standard of judicial review precludes the court from substituting its own judgment for the wisdom of the corporate governing body, Levandusky, supra at 539, 554 N.Y.S.2d 807, 553 N.E.2d 1317.

All that is left, then, is the question of whether defendants had authority to decide that Mason's production was not a play. They most certainly did. The power to make final determinations regarding all matters of eligibility was expressly granted to the Committee by the Tony Rules, as was the discretion to award no Tonys at all. Further inquiry as to the wisdom of their action is precluded.

In an effort to raise the specter of bad faith, Mason avers that Lily Tomlin received a regular Tony ("Leading Actress in a Play") in 1986 for "The Search for Signs of Intelligent Life in the Universe." That solitary example is insufficient to demonstrate that plaintiff was the victim of discriminatory enforcement of the Rules, see Miramax, supra at 8-9, 560 N.Y.S.2d 730 ("[t]hat over the course of more than two decades a handful of films may have been as sexually explicit as [petitioner's X-rated film] * * * and have obtained an 'R' rating is not inherently arbitrary and capricious or without rational basis"). In any event, plaintiff has made no showing that the Tomlin show was, in fact, a topical comedy show, or that the Tony Rules were the same in 1986 when Lily Tomlin was awarded a regular Tony (the current Rules "for the 1993-94 Season"). Moreover, defendants have provided numerous examples of comedy routines which were disqualified because they were not plays (Spaulding Gray's "Gray's Anatomy", 1993-94; Victor Borge, 1989-90; Robert Klein, 1988-89; Mort Sahl, 1987-88; Whoopi Goldberg, 1984-86) and musicians whose shows were not deemed musicals (Michael Feinstein, 1987-88, 1988-89, 1990-1991; Barry Manilow, 1988-89; Mandy Patinkin, 1989-90; Stephanie Mills, 1989-90; Harry Connick, Jr., 1990-91; Tommy Tune, 1992-93; Raffi, 1992-93; Tony Bennett, 1992-93; Jackson Browne, 1993-94), demonstrating a rationality and consistency that would pass muster regardless of the burden of proof or standard of review.

The Discrimination Claim

The flaws in Mason's theory that defendants discriminated against one-man shows are obvious. To begin with, a "one-man show" does not fall within any of the protected categories enumerated in the Human Rights Law, see Executive Law § 296, as the alleged discrimination relates to number ("one") rather than gender ("man"). Next, the statute protects only "individuals," not "shows." The proscribed activities relate only to employment, housing and credit, and it is not alleged that any defendant has employed, lodged or financed Mr. Mason. The argument that by failing to award him a regular Tony, the defendants damaged plaintiff's employment, is specious. Beyond all this, defendants have demonstrated that they do not discriminate against one-person shows so long as they qualify as plays (e.g., "Edmund Kean" with Ben Kingsley; "Tru," with Robert Morse; "Shakespeare for my Father" with Lynn Redgrave; "Twilight: Los Angeles 1992" with Anna Deveare Smith; "Miss Margarida's Way" with Estelle Parsons).

Mason's attempt to expand the realm of protected classes from human beings experiencing discrimination to Broadway shows suffering from Tony-deprivation seems more appropriate as a target for his act than as fodder for a lawsuit.

The Contract Claim

By way of either praise or disparagement, the parties label Mason's claims as "novel" or "of first impression." However, the contract claim is not. In Cinemateca Uruguaya v. Academy of Motion Picture Arts & Sciences, 826 F.Supp. 323 (C.D.Cal.), the Academy of Motion Picture Arts & Sciences revoked an Oscar nomination for Best Foreign Language Film upon discovering that the allegedly Uruguayan submission was primarily an Argentinean creation. The plaintiff argued that the Academy's acceptance of the film as an entry for nomination, together with the actual nomination, created a contract between the parties. In language equally applicable here, the court rejected that theory:

> This Court...agrees with the Academy that an Oscar is an award and not a contest where a contract arises between contest entrants and the sponsor. An award is retrospective in nature. While contests compel a particular act from the contestant, an award or nomination for an award (i.e., the Oscar) recognizes an achievement (i.e., a film) that was accomplished not for a contest, but for independent reasons. Courts have recognized that contracts arise between contest entrants and sponsors, but "the case [is] different if an award [is] made in recognition of past achievements...out of affection, respect, admiration, charity or like impulses." Therefore, Plaintiffs are not likely to succeed on their contract theory.

Cinemateca Uruguaya, supra at 325 (citations omitted).

The court also noted that even had the nomination created a "contract" under the contest theory, the Academy could not be found liable for a breach because the film did not qualify under the Academy's Special Rules. Id. Here, apart from the fact that Mason's show was never nominated and did not qualify as a play, Mason failed to comply with the Tony Rules in other respects. Although it appears, contrary to defendants' argument, that plaintiff complied with Rules 2(a) and 2(v) regarding the distribution of free tickets to Tony voters, his producer did not certify in writing as to that fact as mandated by Rule 2(a)(vi). Certification is one of six separate and distinct requirements of the eligibility process under Rule 2, and Rule 2(a) specifically provides that "all of the following six requirements must be satisfied".

Accordingly, it is ORDERED that the motion to dismiss is granted and the complaint is dismissed.

SACKS v. RUBIN
N.Y.L.J., June 15, 1990, at 21 (N.Y. Sup. Ct. 1990)

SAXE, Justice.

When is a theatre production "first-class" or a "workshop"? That is the issue raised on this motion for summary judgment.

INTRODUCTION

Defendant moves, pursuant to CPLR 3212, for summary judgment dismissing the complaint in the action, based upon a written agreement to pay for the rights to a literary property, on the ground that no issue exists as to the clear import of the clause in the contract that would relieve defendant of payment if the conditions in it were not met, as defendant contends they have not. Plaintiff cross-moves for summary judgment.

Plaintiff was a part owner of rights to a literary work entitled "A Valuable Property" that was proposed for production according to the agreement at issue dated June 2, 1986; defendant, a theatrical and film producer, entered into the agreement as producer of the show. By written agreement the plaintiff granted the defendant certain production rights and waived is rights to share in the royalties from the musical, in return for which he was to be compensated at future intervals.

Under paragraph 3.(c) of the contract, payment for plaintiff's rights was to be made as follows:

> 3. Upon the execution of this agreement, Producer shall pay the parties as follows:
>
> (c) $10,000 to Sacks upon the execution of this agreement. In addition, producer shall pay to Sacks $10,000 no later than October 2, 1986. Furthermore, provided and on condition that the musical shall be fully capitalized or shall commence rehearsals for a production (other than rehearsals for a "workshop" production) prior to full capitalization, Producer shall pay to Sacks the additional sum of $40,000 upon the earlier to occur of said events.
>
> In the event the Musical not be fully capitalized and shall not commence rehearsal for the first class production, producer shall have no further obligation to Sacks except for payment of the two $10,000 payments set forth above.

Rehearsals for the production (which was called MIKE, and was based on the life of the late theatrical producer Mike Todd) were held commencing March 1, 1988; the show opened on April 6, 1988 at the Walnut Street Theatre in Philadelphia and ran for at least 34 performances.

Payment of the first 2 $10,000 payments was made by the defendant, but she contends her liability ends there, because the Walnut Street Theatre production was not a "first-class" production but rather a "workshop" production, which was a "work-in-progress" in its development stage being readied for Broadway, in which changes were continually being made and the performances tailored to audience response. The defendant further alleges that the show was not staged in a "first-class" theatre and that since plaintiff was not to be paid in full until rehearsals would begin for a "first-class" production, the conditions precedent to the payment of the $40,000 as outlined in paragraph 3(c) of the agreement have not been satisfied and thus plaintiff is not entitled to this payment. A condition precedent is an act or event which must occur before a duty to perform a promised performance arises. If the condition does not occur the promised performance need not be rendered. Restatement, Second, Contracts § 225(2).

The defendant further offers as a definition of a "workshop" production: a production that is "unfinished, incomplete, unresolved and not set" in its final form; the definition offered of a "first-class" production is a production having a large budget and which is presented at a first-class theatre. She contends that the Walnut Street house does not meet this description, and that this theatre does not put on first-class productions. In addition, the defendant offers the opinion of her attorney, who is involved primarily in the practice of entertainment law, to the effect that the production that ran in 1988 was typical of a "workshop" production, which is put on to enable producers and authors to dictate changes and to determine whether adequate financing could be secured.

Finally, defendant contends that when the contract terms are read in accordance with custom and usage in the theatre industry and when these terms are applied to the production of MIKE the plaintiff has no claim for the $40,000 payment.

Plaintiff contends that he did not read the provisions of the agreement so analytically, but he nevertheless challenges defendant's characterization of the production and theatre. To this end, he presents the affidavit of a former business representative of Actors' Equity who is highly familiar with theatrical terms and contract provisions and who states that the Walnut Street Theatre meets the industry's qualifications of being "first class," being classified as a LORT [League of Resident Theatres] "A" theatre, which is the same designation given to the Vivian Beaumont Theatre in New York and the Mark Taper Forum in Los Angeles. He further asserts that all aspects of the production, such as the types of contracts used, the budget, admission prices, advertising and salary, point to the show having been a first class production, and thus the contract at issue is satisfied and the plaintiff became entitled to the $40,000 upon the start of rehearsals for the show, as agreed to in the contract.

The court sees that the most crucial fact, whether the production of MIKE was a "workshop" or a "first class" production, remains unresolved and is a triable issue. If material facts are in dispute or if different inferences may reasonably be drawn from facts themselves undisputed, a motion for summary judgment must be denied. Supan v. Mitchelfield, 97 AD2d 755, 468 NYS2d 384 (2d Dept. 1983). The court, therefore, denies both applications for summary judgment at this juncture, and the further material facts needed to determine what kind of production MIKE was, ultimately, will be at issue at trial.

The foregoing constitutes the decision and order of the court.

THEATER

Wikipedia - The Free Encyclopedia
en.wikipedia.org/wiki/Theater (2004)

"Theater" (American English) or "Theatre" (British English) is that branch of the performing arts concerned with acting out stories in front of an audience using combinations of speech, gesture, music, dance, sound and spectacle—indeed, any one or more elements of the other performing arts. In addition to the standard narrative dialog style, theater takes such forms as opera, ballet, mime, kabuki, Chinese opera, mummers' plays and pantomime.

Overview of Theater

"Drama" is that branch of theater in which speech, either from written text (plays or "dramatic literature") or improvised, is paramount. "Musical theater" is a form of theater combining music, songs, dance routines, and spoken dialogue. There is a particularly long tradition of political theater, intended to educate audiences on contemporary issues and encourage social change. Various creeds, Catholicism for instance, have built upon the entertainment value of theater and created (for example) mystery plays and morality plays.

There is an enormous variety of philosophies, artistic processes, and theatrical approaches to creating plays and drama. Some are connected to political or spiritual ideologies, and some are based on purely "artistic" concerns. According to Aristotle's seminal theatrical critique Poetics, there are six elements necessary for theater. They are Plot, Character, Idea, Language, Music, and Spectacle. The 17th-century Spanish writer Lope de Vega wrote that for theater one needs "three boards, two actors, and one passion." Others notable for their contribution to theatrical philosophy are Konstantin Stanislavski, Antonin Artaud, Bertolt Brecht, Orson Welles, and Jerzy Grotowski.

The most recognizable figures in theater are the playwrights and actors, but theater is a highly collaborative endeavor. Plays are usually produced by a production team that commonly includes a director, scenic designer, lighting designer, costume designer, dramaturge, stage manager, and production manager. The artistic staff are assisted by technical theater personnel who handle the creation and execution of the production.

Theater Buildings

A theater is also the building in which works and plays are performed. There are as many styles of performance space as there are styles of performance, but most theaters include a designated "stage" or playing space, a designated audience area or "house," and some sort of off-stage area for preparation and storage, called "backstage," which is typically concealed from the audience. Theaters range from ornate, cathedral-like structures to simple undecorated rooms or black box theaters. Some of these buildings are masterpieces of architecture. Others, often those known for opera, have become major cultural references and symbols.

The original Greek theater was semicircular in form and was normally built on a hillside, often overlooking the sea. These theaters also typically included a "raked" or sloped stage, with the back of the stage being higher than the front. Such theaters were often constructed with excellent acoustics, so that a player standing center stage could be clearly heard throughout the auditorium. The Romans copied this style of building, but tended not to be so concerned about the location, being prepared to build walls and terraces instead of looking for a naturally-occurring site.

During the Elizabethan era in England, theaters were constructed of wood and were circular in form, like the Globe Theater in London, home to William Shakespeare's troupe of actors.

Contemporary theaters are often non-traditional, such as very adaptable spaces, or theaters where audience and performers are not separated. A major example of this is the modular theater. This large theater has floors and walls divided into small movable sections, with the floor sections on adjustable hydraulic pylons, so that the space may be adjusted into any configuration for each individual play. As new styles of theater performance have evolved, so has the desire to improve or recreate performance venues. This applies equally to artistic and presentation techniques, such as stage lighting.

Specific designs of contemporary live theaters include proscenium, thrust, black box, theater in the round, amphitheater, and arena.

Additional Types of Theater

1. Vaudeville

Vaudeville is a style of theater, also known as variety, which flourished in North America from the 1880s through the 1920s. Its popularity rose in step with the rise of industry and the growth of North American cities during this period, and declined with the introduction of sound films and radio. The origin of the term is obscure, but the term is often considered a corruption of the expression "voix de ville," or "voice of the city." Another plausible etymology is that it is a corruption of the French Vau de Vire, a valley in Normandy noted for a style of songs with topical themes.

The first vaudeville theater was opened by impresario Tony Pastor in New Jersey in 1865. Vaudeville theaters featured performers of various types: music, comedy, magic, animal acts, novelty, acrobatics and gymnastics, and celebrity lecture tours. Many early film and radio performers, such as W. C. Fields, Buster Keaton, the Marx Brothers, Edgar Bergen and The Three Stooges, started in vaudeville.

There was no sharp end to vaudeville. The advent of radio and the cinema in the late 1920s started the decline, furthered in the early 1930s by the Great Depression. The closing of the prestigious Palace Theater in New York City in 1932 is regarded as an important marker in vaudeville's fading. The difficulties in civilian transportation during World War II and the subsequent rise of television helped end what was left of the old vaudeville circuits.

The advent of vaudeville in the U.S. marked the introduction of big business into the world of popular entertainment. Several circuits of theaters were built by Keith & Albee, Sullivan & Consodine, Alexander Pantages, Marcus Loew, and others. These businessmen hired full-time traveling performers, set strict rules about the kinds of shows allowed in their theaters, and competed fiercely among themselves for the best acts. Keith & Albee in particular tried to maintain high standards for their shows and did not allow anything bawdy or even suggestive on their stages. Even "legitimate" theater actors like Sarah Bernhardt sometimes supplemented their income with appearances in these shows.

2. Burlesque

Initially, burlesque referred to everything from comic sketches to dance routines, usually lampooning the social attitudes and entertainment venues of upper classes. Possibly due to historical social tensions between the upper classes and lower classes of society, much of the humor and entertainment focused on "low brow" and ribald subjects. Later, the humor and presentation focused almost entirely on sexuality.

The genre's origins are rooted in the 1840s, early in the Victorian era, a time of culture clashes between the social rules of established aristocracy and a working-class society. The genre often mocked such established entertainment forms as opera, Shakespearean drama, musicals, and ballet. The costuming (or lack thereof) increasingly focused on forms of dress considered inappropriate for polite society.

By the 1880s, the genre had created some rules for defining itself: 1) minimal costuming, often focusing on the female form; 2) sexually suggestive dialog, dance, plot lines and staging; 3) quick-witted humor, lacking complexity; and, 4) short routines or sketches, with minimal plot cohesion across a show.

In the 1930s a social crackdown on the burlesque shows led to their gradual downfall. The shows had slowly changed from ensemble ribald variety performances to simple performances focusing mostly on the strip tease. The advent of various forms of pornography gradually replaced titillation.

3. Improvisational Theater

Improvisational theater (also known as improv or impro) is a form of theater in which the actors perform without a script. There are several types of improvisation, including:

Short form improvisation, which consists of short, unrelated scenes; long form improvisation, in which the scenes are interrelated in such a way as to form a long narrative; improv games, in which the performers attempt to create a comprehensible scene while conforming to certain specified and possibly restrictive rules.

In all forms of improvisation, the actors invent the dialogue and action as they perform. Because of the unpredictable nature of such a performance and the unexpected events that occur, improvisation lends itself naturally to comedy, and the specific term "improv" usually refers to a form of high-energy comic entertainment.

It is also possible for improvised scenes to be emotionally dramatic, or experimental and non-narrative. Improvisation is also one of the primary tools used in actor training. It has also been used by many companies and artists as a means of generating text and content for later performance. This is sometimes referred to as "organic" theater, and is especially favored by creators of political theater, experimental theater, and practitioners of drama therapy.

4. Regional Theater

Regional theaters in the United States are theater companies outside of New York City and Broadway that produce their own seasons. While most U.S. cities have roadhouses that book in traveling productions of Broadway musicals and similar fare, most major U.S. cities often have one (or sometimes two) producing theaters of their own.

As the financial demands of producing a Broadway show can temper producers' desires to take risks with unpopular, controversial, or simply untried material and productions, regional theaters are regarded by some as the last bastion of the non-commercial American theater. Regional theaters vary widely, from the more traditional (e.g., The Cleveland Playhouse), to the more avant garde (e.g., The American Repertory Theater in Cambridge). Some regional theaters send their more successful productions on to Broadway.

5. Repertory Theater

Properly, repertory is a style of a number of repertory companies which rehearsed and performed plays in a fortnight. Originally a British idea, these were professionals, but due to time restraints and commercial restraints they played like amateurs. The largest repertory theater company was and still is in Liverpool.

There was a form of touring repertory called fit-up which involved carting round the set for about five different plays. The plays were shown on consecutive nights. Nowadays repertories perform just once or twice a year.

The term is used in the theater to refer to any number of two or more plays which are rotated within a season, usually alternating with different plays every night for a period of time. Plays are rehearsed at all once or in rapid succession, and often feature the same actors or company in several plays.

6. Summer Stock

A summer stock theater is a theater that generally produces plays only in the summertime. The name combines the seasonal aspect with a tradition of putting on the same shows each year and reusing "stock" scenery and costumes. Some smaller theaters still continue this tradition, and a few summer stock theaters have become highly-regarded theater festivals.

Summer stock theaters frequently take advantage of better weather by having their productions outdoors. The reliance on stock often leads summer theaters to specialize in a particular type of production, such as Shakespearean, musicals, or even opera. Some notable summer theaters include: Utah Shakespeare Festival, Santa Fe Opera, Oregon Shakespeare, Williamstown Theater Festival and Glimmerglass Opera.

THEATRE IN NEW YORK: A BRIEF HISTORY
John Kenrick
www.musicals101.com/bwaythhist.htm (2003)

Although it would eventually become the theatrical capital of the world, New York (called "New Amsterdam" until the British took over in 1664) had to wait more than a century to see its first professional stage production. Uptown movement was the mark of life in Manhattan from its earliest days until the mid-Twentieth Century, and where the populace went the theatre soon followed. The first theatres were located in extreme lower Manhattan, where the first Dutch colonists settled in 1624.

The city's earliest theatrical performances were makeshift amateur events staged in taverns. A crude, stable-like structure known as the Theatre on Nassau Street opened in 1732. New York's first formal performance space, it had no competition during its twenty-two year existence. The Theatre on Nassau Street housed its first professional production when a British touring company presented Shakespeare's Richard III on March 5, 1750. Actor-managers Walter Murray and Thomas Kean set up a resident company there for several seasons. Historians have had to resort to guesswork about this historic building, suggesting that it

> may have been either a warehouse or a brewery (or both)... probably fitted up with a stage at one end, benches in front of it, and a raised gallery at the rear for common folk. Murray and Kean made a significant addition to their New York playhouse—they added boxes along the side walls, not only to increase the seating (a sign that they attained a moderate success) but also to provide a special place for the elite of the city.

New Yorkers saw their first professional performance of a musical when the Lewis Hallam Company (from Williamsburg, Virginia) presented John Gay's The Beggars Opera in this same theatre in 1753. A year later, the building was taken over by an adjoining business and turned into storage space.

Over the next few decades, several theatres came and went. The Theatre on John Street appeared in 1767, and was colonial New York's premiere theatre for the next three decades. It was home to The Archers (1796), a native-born opera that some scholars point to as the first American musical. While that classification is debatable, it is clear that The Archers started no trends. Theatre had a hard time surviving in colonial Manhattan. There were no productions at all during the Revolutionary War years, and the city had to wait until the end of the 18th Century to see theatre develop real popularity.

The historic Park Theatre, built in 1798, was the city's most illustrious venue for several decades, welcoming a wide ranging audience.

> All kinds of performances were housed under one roof, so that audiences in the 1830s might see drama, circus, opera and dance on the same bill. New York's Park Theater, despite a reputation as an elite house, had a relatively large room that permitted the masses to govern the stage. Each class had its own part of the theatre, but all attended—mechanics in the pit, upper classes and

women in the boxes, and prostitutes, lower class men, and blacks in the balcony. The rowdy audiences often yelled, stamped, drank and smoked during the performance.

Over time, the Park was perceived as catering primarily to the upper classes. When the Bowery Theatre opened in 1826, it aimed at "mechanics" (i.e., the working class) by presenting action packed spectacles and super-sized stagings of Shakespeare. Over time, the Bowery became the center of all forms of working class entertainment, while Broadway catered increasingly to the rich. Resentment grew on both sides of the social divide, but few realized the stage was set for disaster when a group of wealthy patrons built the Astor Place Opera House at Astor Place and Broadway in 1847.

The Astor Place Riot

New York City's sense of social division came to a head in 1849, when two actors appeared in simultaneous productions of Macbeth. While American Edwin Forrest (at the Bowery) found his following among the working and lower classes, British actor William Macready (at the Astor Place) appealed to the upper classes. A dangerous combination of press ballyhoo and widespread anti-British sentiment incited Forrest's fans to disrupt some of Macready's performances at the Astor Place Opera House. On the night of May 10, 1849, the disruption spilled into the streets, where police fired into the crowd. At least twenty-two people died, and dozens more were wounded as the street fights stretched on for days.

After the Astor Place Riot of 1849 entertainment in New York City was divided along class lines: opera was chiefly for the upper middle and upper classes, minstrel shows and melodramas for the middle class, variety shows in concert saloons for men of the working class and the slumming middle class.

While festering class resentments would inspire unrest for decades to come, they would never again center around a theatrical event. In fact, during the mid-1800s, Broadway gradually became a place where all classes found entertainment to their taste.

In the eighteenth century, the few theatres permitted to arise in the face of lingering moral and religious opposition to theatrical activity were scattered throughout the city and were operated sporadically until the final years of the century. But in the nineteenth century, theatre was permanently established as an institution in the community, elegant theatres were built, and professionals followed the trend of the times by searching for an area in which to focus their activities. By mid-century, theatres had settled upon Broadway as their locale and they moved with the northward flow of the city.

The first native-born form of musical entertainment to thrive on the American stage was the minstrel show. According to The Encyclopedia of New York City, blackface acts were common features in circuses and traveling shows from the 1790s onwards. Thomas Rice brought his blackface performance of the song "Jump Jim Crow" to New York in 1832, and a troupe of four white men calling themselves the Virginia Minstrels presented the first recorded full length minstrel show at the Bowery Amphitheatre in 1843. Minstrelsy proved amazingly popular. By 1856, New York City had ten full-time resident companies, and twice that many a decade later.

Union Square

In 1829, impresario William Niblo supplemented his popular theatre and open air beer garden with a hotel and saloon. Located at Broadway and Prince Street, Niblo's

Garden quickly became one of New York's premiere night spots. The three thousand seat theatre presented all sorts of entertainments. Destroyed by fire in 1846, it was lavishly rebuilt. The new Niblo's had the best equipped stage in America. Niblo retired in 1858, but the theatre retained his name. Manager William Wheatley stumbled into theatrical history when he beefed up a weak melodrama with lavish sets and threw in a stranded French ballet company to create The Black Crook (1866). Considered by many to be the first Broadway musical, it ran for over a year and toured for decades, redefining the commercial possibilities of theatre in America. As for Niblo's, it remained one of the city's most popular venues for several more decades.

By the 1870s, "Broadway" and "theatre" were synonymous. Union Square (the area near Broadway at 14th Street) became New York City's first theatre district. A central hub for public transportation, this highly accessible neighborhood was soon packed with theatres, restaurants and fashionable shops. Countless producers and booking agents worked in the neighborhood, but not always in offices. One veteran of the period described the sidewalk negotiations one saw around Union Square.

> The most prominent players, including the stars and their respective managers and agents, could be found parading the sidewalks, their date books in their hands. Those were the days of the barn-stormer, when the "fly by night" manager was in his element. All classes of showmen congregated here, and here the plans of the most important stage providers were matured for many years.

Tony Pastor opened the first vaudeville theatre one block east of the square in 1881. The greatest Broadway musical talents of the age worked in Union Square venues, including Lillian Russell and George M. Cohan. Ned Harrigan and Tony Hart presented a series of musicals at the Theatre Comique, a converted synagogue. Although well south of Union Square, it was typical of the theatres in use in the 1880s:

> Inside, there was a smallish auditorium, attractively decorated in white, red and gold, with a seating capacity of 1,400. Conveniently abutting the orchestra level was a saloon; between the acts, thirsty patrons could obtain drinks by opening a window that connected the foyer with this establishment and yelling their orders through the gap...there were six evening performances a week, beginning at eight o'clock, and Wednesday and Saturday matinees, beginning at two.

Union Square included the central offices for two massive show business empires. B.F. Keith and Edward Albee took over the Union Square Theatre in 1893, extending their vast vaudeville circuit into the heart of New York. Their booking office controlled most of the major vaudeville houses across the US. In 1896, theatre owners Marc Klaw and A.L. Erlanger formed the Theatrical Syndicate, which gave them monopolistic control of almost every legitimate theater in the country. From offices near Union Square, the syndicate dominated the management of the American theatre for the next sixteen years.

Times Square

As the populated area of Manhattan stretched further to the north, new theatres sprang up to save ticket buyers the increasingly long trip downtown. By the mid-1890s, subway lines began to converge around Broadway at 42nd Street, the heart of an area then known as Longacre Square. For many years, it had been the city's main horse trading district, but increased accessibility attracted businesses, restaurants, hotels, theatres and upper-class brothels. By the time the British hit Florodora (1900) opened the new century with a smash hit run at the Casino Theatre, Longacre Square was becoming the new center of theatrical activity in New York. When the New York Times built its new headquarters there in 1904, the City Council renamed the district Times Square.

In the early 1900s, Oscar Hammerstein I (grandfather of the great lyricist/librettist) and brothers Lee and Jacob Shubert built major theatres in the Times Square area, as did some independent impresarios. The Erlanger syndicate built several houses in the neighborhood, with the magnificent New Amsterdam Theatre on 42nd Street as their flagship house. Many theatres built in this period had rooftop gardens where audiences could enjoy performances when the summer heat made indoor performances impossible. Union Square fell into a gradual decline, and Times Square began its long reign as the city's main theatre district.

During the first two decades of the 20th century, the concrete traffic island between Broadway and Seventh Avenue at 47th Street became a popular hangout for unemployed vaudevillians and actors, earning it the nickname "the beach." They would exchange false boasts about their latest engagements and keep an ear cocked for any hints of available work. This same stretch of sidewalk now draws greater crowds than ever as the location of the TKTS discount ticket booth.

Advances

Gaslight was too dull to be used with colored filters, so theatre district advertising was fairly dull through the 1890s. [But with the invention of electric light], new kinds of lighting effects [became] possible. The first animated electric billboard appeared in Times Square in 1903, when Victor Herbert's musical The Red Mill installed a sign with carbon lights that imitated the revolving arms of a windmill. Soon every show had some kind of electrified signage. Colored light bulbs were too unstable, so white light was standard. These electric signs kept the theatre district shimmering well into the night, [and the] glow that filled Broadway each evening earned it the nickname "The Great White Way." With the introduction of neon in 1927, bright colors became common in theatrical billboards.

Many Broadway producers treated their casts and crews like cattle. It was common practice to schedule extra performances on holidays without giving extra pay. Producers also fired people without notice, offered no pay during rehearsals, and could insist on actors paying for their own costumes. These abusive practices led to the formation of theatrical unions, which most producers tried to ignore. In August 1919, the Actors Equity Association called a strike, demanding that all professional productions offer a standard contract. When the stage hands and musicians refused to cross the picket lines, every show in Broadway was forced to shut down. After weeks of wrangling, the producers finally agreed to Equity's demands. Some producers continued to abuse the new contract, but the power of theatrical unions had been established.

Early Off-Broadway

Theatre in the 19th and early 20th centuries was not limited to the main theatre district. Vaudeville and burlesque venues thrived in every borough, and there was a so-called "subway circuit" of legitimate theatres in key neighborhoods. Now and then, a Broadway hit was launched from one of these theatres—the all-black revue Shuffle Along premiered at the 63rd Street Music Hall and remained there for 504 performances. But as a rule, these neighborhood theatres housed the post-Broadway tours of major hits.

In the 1910s, smaller off-Broadway theatre groups were established downtown with the express purpose of developing and promoting new experimental works. The Washington Square Players (later renamed the Theatre Guild), The Provincetown Players and The Neighborhood Playhouse were among the early pioneers in this field. Eva Le Gallienne headed a repertory company in the 1920s, and the next decade saw the Group Theatre present a series of socially challenging dramas. It would be some time before musicals became a regular part of the off-Broadway scene.

Best of Times, Worst of Times

By the 1920s, the Shubert Brothers had crushed the Erlanger syndicate, and were the most powerful figures in the American commercial theatre. Although the upper East and West sides of Manhattan filled with residential housing, the theatre district remained firmly centered in an around Times Square. The 1920s saw a final burst of theatrical construction, with more than thirty new venues appearing in the area. Most of the theatres the Shuberts built in New York and elsewhere were designed by architect Herbert J. Krapp.

> Krapp quickly won favor with the Shuberts because of his ability to crowd as many seats as possible into a theater, even if the public amenities had to be sacrificed. Often he had to work with odd-shaped sites, but he always came up with a workable solution. A Krapp-designed house is compact, intimate, and economical; its acoustics are generally excellent; and its sightlines range from satisfactory to very good. The facades are generally eclectic in a style that might be best described as Krapp Conservative. Of the forty theatres built in the immediate Times Square area, Krapp's playhouses have proven to be the most enduring. Most of them still fly the Shubert flag and have undergone periodic renovations that prolonged their existence.

The business of Broadway peaked in the season of 1927-28, when more than 70 legitimate theatres housed well over 250 shows. The proliferation of theatres in Times Square created a unique opportunity for producers as well as ticket buyers.

> At theater time, when many of the theatergoers were wearing evening dress, the combination of streetcars and taxis made the traffic sluggish. Most people walked. Theatres were built close together because pedestrians were accustomed to shop from theater to theater. Out for a good time, they provided some sort of audience for the plays that were not hits.... Theaters that had not sold out by six o'clock sent bunches of their tickets to Joe Leblang's shop to be sold at half price.

Within a few years, the Great Depression and the popularity of talking films took their toll, and the 1930s saw a perilous drop in the number of productions as well as attendance. When the Shuberts were forced to declare bankruptcy, Lee Shubert was the only man with money to bid when their theatres were auctioned off. So he bought back his most profitable properties at a fraction of their former value, and simultaneously put his brother Jacob in an inferior position. Some lesser theatres were sold off and demolished, and others were converted to use as film houses, but by and large Lee kept Broadway's key venues intact and in use.

World War II re-energized the American economy, and many great musicals appeared in the 1940s, particularly after Oklahoma (1943) redefined the genre. But theatre rents, union minimums and advertising costs rose, making it harder than ever for shows to turn a profit. So even as the American musical enjoyed what many have called its "golden age," the number of Broadway productions continued (with occasional exceptions) to gradually decline. The decades that followed saw their share of hits, but an increasing number of producers looked for a less expensive alternative to Broadway.

Off-Broadway Sings

Small downtown theatres in Greenwich Village and the lower East Side had been home to experimental theatre since the 1920s. The environment changed in the 1950s as musicals became part of the off-Broadway mix. An ongoing parade of profitable intimate revivals (Leave It to Jane), revues (Greenwich Village USA) and quirky new book shows (Little Mary Sunshine) began to prove that off-Broadway had unrealized commercial and artistic possibilities. The Fantasticks opened in 1960, its forty-plus year run marking a time when successful musical productions could emerge far beyond the bounds of Broadway. From the tiny Cherry Lane Theatre (Godspell, 1971) to the massive Brooklyn Academy of Music (Candide, 1974 revival), hit musicals kept emerging all over the city.

Several small to midsize musicals conceived for off-Broadway rank among the most popular works ever written, including Little Shop of Horrors (1982) and Nunsense (1985). Broadway hits as diverse as Bring in Da' Noise, Bring in Da' Funk (1996) and Urinetown (2001) were born off-Broadway, and every season brings new, innovative works to New York's smaller venues.

Resurrection

By the 1970s, Times Square was one of the tawdriest and most dangerous neighborhoods in New York. The [previous] quarter century [had seen] the demolition of dozens of old Broadway theatres, and the construction of only four new ones. The once glamorous theatres along 42nd Street (including the New Amsterdam) were all in varying states of disrepair, showing pornography and kung fu films. Many felt the decline of Times Square was irreversible.

> In 1975, the legendary entertainment and media district—whose name and glittering image still drew tens of millions of visitors each year—had degenerated in many places into a squalid, crime-ridden twilight zone of sex shops, strip clubs and seedy bars. New Yorkers themselves often took a kind of ironic civic pride in the fact that the crossroads of the world now looked more like Skid Row than the Great White Way, as prostitutes, drug addicts, alcoholics and swarms of men in search of sex patrolled 42nd Street and the storied side streets off Broadway and Times Square.

The 1980s saw Broadway dominated by imported megamusicals (Cats, Les Miserables), and the 1990s saw the rise of producing corporations like Disney (Beauty and the Beast, Lion King). These hits brought more theatergoers to Times Square, proving the neighborhood's potential. As several new hotels were built, and a series of major corporations (MTV, ABC, etc.) established a new presence there, tawdriness gave way to a renewed sense of high tech glamour.

> By the late 1990s, a new Times Square had emerged—cleaner, better lit, and more wholesome than it had been in half a century, and busier and more profitable than it had been in decades. Each night as the sun went down, the district was transformed into a glowing, shimmering diaphanous dish of light.

There were still causes for concern. As theatrical production costs continued to rise, so did the price of tickets. Orchestra seats that went for $8 in 1965 were $45 by 1985, and $100 by 2001—a far steeper rise than the overall increase in the cost of living. Theatre attendees became increasingly old and increasingly well-heeled. With the young and the poor effectively shut out, the once popular pastime of theatre was becoming a subculture for the select few who could either afford it or secure complimentary tickets.

But New York's theatre district is once again a prime tourist attraction, and the theatre remains a key factor in the city's financial well-being. According to the League of American Theaters and Producers, Broadway shows currently sell one and a half billion dollars worth of tickets annually. Figure in hotels, restaurants and stores, and it is estimated that theatergoers contribute four and a half billion dollars to the local economy. However skeptics may grumble about the future of New York City and the viability of commercial theatre, neither one is about to disappear.

DISNEY PLANS 3 MORE BROADWAY BLOCKBUSTERS
Frederick M. Winship
United Press International Online, Dec. 17, 2003

The Walt Disney Company has grossed an estimated $2.27 billion in the past decade on three Broadway musicals and their productions nationally and worldwide, and plans to follow up with three more shows on the Great White Way in the next four years.

The Hollywood film producer best known for its animated cartoon movies became a major player in the Broadway entertainment business in 1994 when it premiered a stage version of its fairy tale classic, "Beauty and the Beast," at the Palace Theater. Now in its 10th season, the show is showing no signs of slowing down at the Lunt-Fontanne Theater, having grossed $306 million in ticket sales to date, according to the Boneau/Bryan-Brown publicity firm representing Disney shows.

Disney entrenched itself on Broadway in 1997 by purchasing and renovating the long derelict New Amsterdam Theater on 42nd Street for the Tony Award-winning stage translation of its film "The Lion King," which cost Disney an estimated $20 million, a Broadway record, and has grossed $305 million to date.

In 2000 it opened "Aida," a knockoff of Giuseppe Verdi's opera without his musical score, at the Palace, where it has grossed $140 million to date.

Never a studio to rest on its laurels, Disney now has in production a musical staging of "Mary Poppins," its wildly popular 1964 film starring Julie Andrews.

According to Boneau/Bryan-Brown, the show already has begun casting in London and will open there in December 2004 and then come to Broadway. Also in the works are a musical version of Disney's 1999 "Tarzan," aimed for Broadway in 2005 or 2006, and another musical based on Disney's beloved 1989 blockbuster "The Little Mermaid," due in New York in 2007 with a score by Alan Menken.

This is of course good news for the theater industry, although Disney is not a member in as good standing as the Shubert Organization, Jujamcyn Theaters and other major Broadway production companies. It has kept aloof from the League of American Theaters and Producers, to which the other companies belong and which handles union negotiations for them.

Although Disney's failure to join the league would appear to weaken its negotiating position, most producers see Disney's presence on Broadway as a plus for the American theater in the long run.

"I wish they were part of the league, and I'd love to have them in on more of the industry promotional stuff, but all in all, I think they've been a positive addition," commented Rocco Landesman, president of Jujamcyn, which operates five Broadway theaters, none occupied by a Disney show.

However, there is a segment of the industry that feels Disney's shows based on stories for children and staged with Hollywood dazzle have pushed Broadway along the road to becoming a venue solely for spectaculars staged for the tourist trade, which already accounts for half of ticket sales. They fear Broadway will no longer be a place where new and original shows of serious dimension and new theater talents will be nourished as in the past.

Disney is sensitive to these fears concerning the "dumbing down" of Broadway and appears to have done its best to link up with top talents in the theater that are not connected in any way with the Disneyland world. It is producing "Mary Poppins" with British stage impresario Cameron Mackintosh, and Broadway veteran Bob Crowley will design and direct the show.

The Disney Company is notably tight-lipped about financing and profits, but the League of American Theaters estimates that "Beauty and the Beast" has grossed $1.2 billion in 22 productions around the world with another scheduled to open in Seoul next season. The league puts Disney's overall gross for "The Lion King's" 11 productions at $1 billion and at $270 million for "Aida's" five productions.

Disney is also the owner of the ABC TV network and Miramax, a major film producer, both of which also have invested in Broadway shows and produced them as well. Whatever the future of live entertainment on Broadway will be, it seems like a lot of Disney money is going into shaping it for the remainder of the 21st century.

Notes

1. As the *Mason* case demonstrates, agreeing on exactly what constitutes "theater" is a difficult, if not impossible, task. How would you have categorized Mason's work?

2. In reading this casebook, you will encounter repeated references to the phrases "first class theater" and "legitimate theater." As the *Sacks* case explains, "first class theater" is a term of art, although normally it refers to a full-dress production using professional actors and actresses in a theater of substantial size.

The term "legitimate theater" is even more nebulous. Once a convenient short hand for distinguishing between serious productions and burlesque, vaudeville, and some forms of musical comedy, *see* dictionary.reference.com/search?q=legitimate, the phrase today almost always is used to exclude adult entertainment. *See* Stephen Yagielowicz, *Is Pornography "Legitimate"?*, Oct. 1, 2002, at xbiz.com/articles/index.php?article_idp=341. For an interesting case in which a court was called on to decide whether an "alternative theater" qualified as legitimate theater, *see Keep Productions, Inc. v. Arlington Park Towers Hotel Corp.*, 364 N.E.2d 939 (Ill. App. Ct. 1977).

3. As the Wikipedia excerpt points out, yet another linguistic disagreement concerns whether one should use "theater" or "theatre." As has been explained elsewhere, however:

> The British forms are recognizable by Americans and occasionally found in American texts, though their usage may be considered an affectation. The British spelling that has perhaps gained the most currency in American English is theatre. However, theater is still more common in everyday use, and theatre is generally reserved for more formal settings.

American and British English Differences, at en2.wikipedia.org/wiki/American_and_British_English_differences. In this casebook we consistently use "theater."

4. In his bid for a Tony Award, Jackie Mason was seeking Broadway's highest honor. A complete list of Tony Award winners since the prizes' inception in 1947 can be found at www.tonyawards.com. For a further look at how the winners are chosen, *see Wells v. League of American Theatres & Producers, Inc.*, 706 N.Y.S.2d 599 (Sup. Ct. 2000). Of course, long-time viewers of the hit NBC sitcom *Seinfeld* probably will recall Episode 156 ("The Summer of George"), in which Kramer "won" a Tony simply by standing up at the right moment, then got to keep it after he agreed to fire the show's temperamental star (Raquel Welch), a task the actual producers were too afraid to undertake.

Although they are the best-known, the Tonys are not the only theater awards. Others include the Barrymore (Philadelphia theater), Carbonell (South Florida theater), Clarence Derwent (most promising New York performers), Critics Circle, Drama Desk, Drama League, Elliot Norton (Boston theater), Helen Hayes (Washington, D.C. theater), Jeff (Chicago theater), Lucille Lortel (Off-Broadway), OBIE (Off-Broadway), Olivier (London theater), Outer Critics Circle, Ovation (Los Angeles theater), Pulitzer (for drama), Star (Broadway tours), TDF/Astaire (Broadway dance), and Theatre World (New York stage debut). *See further* www.playbill.com/reference/awards.

5. Masks have been a part of theater from the beginning. Today, the universal symbol of the theater is two Greek masks—one happy and one sad—which denote comedy and tragedy are said to represent the two sides of Dionysus, originally the god of wine but now thought of as the god of theater:

> The symbols for [the] theater are the comedy and tragedy masks that were worn in ancient Greece [between] 500-300 BC, the first time that plays were written and performed. Plays were written in honor of the god Dionysus and were either Comedies or Tragedies. All the actors were male, and they all played multiple roles, so a mask was used to show [a] change in character or mood. Masks challenged the actors to portray their characters' feelings in more subtle ways, with voice and body language, since they couldn't use facial expressions. [In addition to now being the] universal symbol for drama, [the two masks] also represent the two sides of Dionysus, as well as the two effects of wine: joyous, Bacchic revelry, and a dark, sorrowful harvest.

History of Comedy Tragedy Masks, at byron.nysen.com/DramaHistory.html. To view different examples of the "comedy tragedy" masks, *see* www.angelfire.com/art/masks/menu.html.

6. In an effort to deter organizations like the Klu Klux Klan, a number of jurisdictions have enacted "anti-mask" statutes that prohibit the wearing of masks in public. Although all such laws permit the use of masks in theatrical productions, determining whether a particular "performance" qualifies occasionally has led to litigation. *See, e.g., Schuman v. State of New York*, 270 F. Supp. 730 (S.D.N.Y. 1967) (street theater), and *Daniels v. State*, 448 S.E.2d 185 (Ga. 1994) (one man improvisational act). For a further discussion, *see* Stephen J. Simoni, Note, *"Who Goes There?"—Proposing a Model Anti-Mask Act*, 61 Fordham L. Rev. 241 (1992).

7. The Astor Place Theater Riot of 1849, discussed by Kenrick, is a defining moment in Broadway history. For a detailed discussion of the causes of the melee and its aftermath, *see* Gretchen Sween, Note, *Rituals, Riots, Rules, and Rights: The Astor Place Theater Riot of 1849 and the Evolving Limits of Free Speech*, 81 Tex. L. Rev. 679 (2002).

8. As Winship points out, Disney (for better or worse) now is a major force on Broadway. As such, it has joined the ranks of the Shubert Organization, which controls 17 of Broadway's 40 theaters; the Nederlander Organization (nine theaters); and Jujamcyn Theaters (five theaters). For a complete list of Broadway theaters, including addresses, seating capacity, founding dates, and shows, *see* www.livebroadway.com/theaters_broadway.html.

9. Government officials (as well as polite society) historically have taken a dim view of theater. In addition to outright bans, lawmakers have imposed strict controls, in part to fight sin, in part to raise revenue, and in part to ensure patron safety. Depending on the era, these goals have been accomplished by means of obscenity prosecutions, licensing rules, and the Sunday "blue laws." *See further* George B. Bryan, *American Theatrical Regulation 1607-1900: Conspectus and Texts* (1993).

Today, theater enjoys a much wider latitude, and attempts to ban or censor stage works normally are rejected on constitutional grounds. *See, e.g., Southeastern Promotions, Ltd. v. Conrad*, 420 U.S. 546 (1975) (refusal to allow production of the musical "Hair" was unlawful restraint), and *Schacht v. United States*, 398 U.S. 58 (1970) (Congress could not punish an actor for wearing a military uniform while appearing in an anti-war street skit).

Outside the United States, however, censorship still occurs. In February 2004, for example, the Chinese government indefinitely postponed the premiere of Eve Ensler's "The Vagina Monologues" because officials felt the word "vagina" was too provocative. *See* Joseph Kahn, *Offended by the V-Word, China Mutes 'Monologues,'* N.Y. Times, Feb. 13, 2004, at A4.

10. For further readings on the development of theater, *see, e.g.,* Louis Botto, *At This Theatre: An Informal History of New York's Legitimate Theatres* (2002); John Russell Brown, *The Oxford Illustrated History of Theatre* (1995); Errol G. Hill & James V. Hatch, *A History of African American Theatre* (2003); John Bush Jones, *Our Musicals, Ourselves: A Social History of the American Musical Theater* (2003); Fellicia Hardison Londré & Daniel J. Watermeier, *The History of the North American Theater: The United States, Canada, and Mexico from Pre-Columbian Times to the Present* (1998); Don B. Wilmeth & Christopher Bigsby, *The Cambridge History of American Theatre* (1998-2000).

Theater-related web sites also are abundant. For links to many of them, *see McCoy's Guide to Internet Resources in Theatre and Performance Studies* (www.stetson.edu/csata/thr_guid.htm) and the American Society for Theatre Research (www.astr.umd.edu).

Lastly, numerous movies have been made about the theater, including: *42nd Street* (1933) (Ruby Keeler remains everyone's favorite understudy); *A Chorus Line* (1985) (based on the long-running play about Broadway dancers); *Author! Author!* (1982) (Al Pacino as a playwright coping with domestic travails); *Bullets Over Broadway* (1994) (Woody Allen's tribute to 1920s theater); *Deathtrap* (1982) (Ira Levin's black comedy about a felonious playwright); *Gypsy* (1962) (Rosalind Russell as the quintessential stage mother); *Kiss Me Kate* (1953) (a divorced couple resolve their differences while co-starring in a musical); *Noises Off!* (1992) (a rollicking look at a play in rehearsals); *Room Service* (1938) (the Marx Brothers become producers); *Shakespeare in Love* (1998) (Gwyneth Paltrow's Oscar-winning performance as the woman who inspired the immortal bard); *Summer Stock* (1950) (Judy Garland and Gene Kelly put on a show in the country); *The Dresser* (1983) (Albert Finney's Oscar-nominated portrayal of an aging actor); *The Muppets Take Manhattan* (1984) (Kermit struggles to get his musical to Broadway); *The Producers* (1968) (which in 2001 became a hit play, leading to plans for a second film version); *Stage Door* (1937) (life in a theatrical boarding house); *To Be or Not to Be* (1983) (Mel Brooks's poignant take on repertory theater); and *Waiting for Guffman* (1996) (Christopher Guest's wry send-up of community theater).

Problem 1

Based on his coverage of the pre-trial proceedings, a reporter wrote a play about a woman accused of a heinous murder. Just before opening night, the defendant moves to have the show shut down, arguing that its performance will make it impossible for her to receive a fair trial. Given these facts, should the court issue the injunction? *See Dailey v. Superior Court of the City and County of San Francisco*, 44 P. 458 (Cal. 1896).

C. PRACTICE

PEOPLE EX REL. CHICAGO BAR ASS'N v. BEREZNIAK
127 N.E. 36 (Ill. 1920)

DUNCAN, Justice.

An information to disbar respondent was filed at the April term, 1918, of this court by the Chicago Bar Association. Respondent filed his answer at the June term, 1918, and the case was referred to Charles C. Stillwell as commissioner to take and report the proofs and to make findings and recommendations. His report has been filed, and no exceptions thereto have been taken by either party. No evidence was transmitted with his report. The cause stands for decision upon the correctness of the legal conclusions drawn by the commissioner from the facts reported by him.

The commissioner has found the facts to be substantially as follows. Respondent was licensed in Illinois as an attorney at law about December 10, 1913, and has since that date been actively engaged in the practice of law in Chicago. He was born in Southern Russia in 1873, graduated at the Imperial University in Petrograd, and came to the United States in 1892 as the representative of Russian newspapers at the World's Fair. He was admitted to the Indiana bar in 1907 and practiced law in Indianapolis, Crown Point, and Hammond for nearly six years. After his admission in this state he began to specialize as a legal adviser of theatrical people, since which time his practice has been almost wholly confined to members of that profession. In January, 1916, he published and circulated among the members of that profession a diary and daily route book. The book contained a large number of blank pages, a calendar for 1916 and 1917, useful information, such as rates of postage, names of Presidents, and legal holidays in various states, and at the bottom of the blank memorandum pages were printed extracts from statements, letters, and testimonials laudatory of respondent and his services as an attorney. The title page contained the following:

<blockquote>
Published by Leon A. Berezniak
Attorney for the Profession
105 West Monroe Street
Chicago
</blockquote>

The second page had a likeness of the respondent, below which appeared the following:

Leon A. Berezniak
Lawyer to the Profession
105 W. Monroe St.
Chicago, Ill.

The preface or introduction to the book, signed by the respondent, contains the following:

'Of course, I have an object in distributing this little book, which only goes to the profession. I wish you to know me better in case you have need of me, and I wish to know you also. * * *

I know you will permit me a word or two about myself. I specialize largely in theatrical law; for there is such a thing, the outgrowth of the many unusual questions which have arisen because of the growth of the profession. I am also engaged in general practice, handling all matters requiring legal services in all its branches. As for my qualifications, I have been admitted to the bar of Illinois and Indiana and have practiced in both states over a considerable number of years and have also been admitted to practice in the several United States courts. * * *

As I said above, the primary object, upon my part, of this little book is to make your acquaintance, * * * and I wish further to assure you that when you are in need of the counsel of a lawyer you are perfectly free to call upon me, either personally or through correspondence, and consult me without charge or obligation to you. This is no fake offer. I wish to widen my already broad acquaintance in the theatrical field, since it is there that the bulk of my practice lies.

I wish your good will, knowing that it will mean your patronage in time of need, and knowing further that I shall acquit myself not only to your satisfaction, but to your high pleasure, whenever so employed.'

In September, 1917, the respondent caused to be printed and published a little book entitled 'The Berezniak Diary and Daily Route Book for 1917-18,' which he caused to be circulated and distributed in Chicago and throughout the United States generally, among the members of the theatrical profession only. It was gotten up upon the same general plan as his former book, and [in the] introduction is found the following printed matter:

'This is the second edition of what I am proud to call the Berezniak Diary and Route Book, and I hope it will prove an improvement over its modest predecessor. * * *

The theatrical profession, living largely in a world of its own, has most emphatically a body of law of its own. There are unusual contracts, pertaining almost wholly to this profession, to be drawn and construed. There is the domestic side of theatrical life to be considered. These are all things that require not alone a knowledge of this branch of the law, but a thorough familiarity with the profession itself, in order that the practitioner may specialize with the greatest degree of success in theatrical law. * * *

I specialize in theatrical law almost to the exclusion of all other branches of the practice, save those which are incidental to this specialty. * * * Therefore, while this little book is, in the main, offered for the purpose of giving something useful to the members of the profession from which I derive my livelihood and is intended to be a constant reminder of me to them, it has—I may as well admit it—also the purpose of bringing me to the attention of those who do not already know me and of further commending me to those who do.

I wish actor clients. I know I can serve them more intelligently than the average lawyer, and I am glad to be able to refer with confidence to a host of them whom I have already served. In these pages you will read some short and unsolicited testimonials from these.'

The following are a few of the printed extracts from statements and letters of other parties found in these two books in the nature of testimonials, the names of the authors being omitted:

'Berezniak is one of the few lawyers who look for the interest of the client first and the money second.'

'I consider that the theatrical artist who has Leon A. Berezniak as his attorney has already won half the fight.'

'His long and successful legal career has given Leon A. Berezniak well-deserved fame among theatrical artists.'

'Wrongs of theatrical artists are usually quickly righted if Leon A. Berezniak is their lawyer.'

'As the legal mentor to the people of the stage, Leon A. Berezniak is now above rivalry.'

'The artist whose lawyer is Leon A. Berezniak may count confidently on winning.'

'Berezniak is the legal Gibraltar of the theatrical profession.'

'No theatrical artist should ever sign a contract which attorney Berezniak disapproves.'

'Forehandedness' and 'preparedness' are synonyms, and they're both synonymous with 'Berezniak's advice.'

The respondent also caused to be printed and circulated through the United States mails to the members of the theatrical profession printed post cards containing photographic views on the back thereof, and on the face thereof a likeness of respondent and the following printed matter:

Here's a little remembrance of your engagement in Chicago. Take it with the sincere good wishes of Leon A. Berezniak, Lawyer to the Profession, 105 W. Monroe Street, Chicago, Telephone Central 5374.

He also caused to be printed and circulated among the members of the theatrical profession a book of 'I. O. U.'s,' containing on the back of each printed matter similar to that on the face of his printed post cards, and also inserted a card in certain papers, magazines, or publications which circulated among the members of the theatrical profession, as follows: In 1915 in 24 weekly issues of the Vaudville Breeze, published at Chicago; in 1918 in 5 issues of the New York Star, published in the city of New York; in 1916 in 22 issues of the Vaudeville, published at Chicago. This is the card so published:

Leon A. Berezniak
Lawyer to the Profession
1348 First National Bank Building
Telephone Central 5374
The Man Who Solves Your Troubles and Keeps Your Mind Easy.

When respondent was called before the grievance committee of the relator in reference to said advertisements, he stated that he approved [of] the canons of ethics of the

American Bar Association and of the State Bar Association of Illinois, but that he did not consider that obtaining a clientage through the means of advertising he had pursued was unlawful. He also stated that he had found advertising to be about the only means by which he could get a clientage. He has done no advertising since he was called before the grievance committee, except the advertisement in the New York Star. He states that he is willing to accept the judgment of the court on the question of advertising as to what is proper and what is improper, and that he is willing to cease advertising altogether and does not propose to continue it in any way.

[The respondent] has acquired as a specialty a practice among members of the theatrical profession. He is a man of good moral character and has established a good reputation for fair dealing with his clients.

The commissioner [found] that advertising for patronage of theatrical people, to be in the highest degree sucessful, must be similar in character to the advertising that they themselves employ—that is, gorgeous and self-laudatory advertisements; that there are from two to four lawyers in the city of Chicago, and a limited number in other cities in the United States, who are specialists and practice chiefly among members of the theatrical profession; [and] that it is the custom of such lawyers to advertise by means of unique advertisements, in a manner similar to that of respondent, their advertisements in legal newspapers and in entertainment programs and programs for church bazaars and like entertainments.

The commissioner further [found] that advertising of the character used by respondent has a tendency to lower the estimation in which the profession of a lawyer is held by the general public, even though it contains no misstatement of fact and is not resorted to for the purpose of misleading or victimizing the public, but only for the purpose of bringing business to the advertiser. His conclusion [is that the] advertisement of [the] respondent does not, of itself, amount to a violation by him of any law of this state or amount to malfeasance in his office as an attorney at law; that the facts do not call for the severe penalty of disbarment or the lesser penalty of suspension from practice, but that such facts do tend to show undignified conduct and have a tendency to lower the estimation of the profession of the lawyer in the eyes of the public and call for notice to respondent not to continue or repeat such advertisement.

The grant of a license to practice law is on the implied understanding that the party receiving it shall in all things demean himself in a proper manner, and that he will abstain from such practices as cannot fail to bring discredit upon his profession or upon the courts. This court has the power by express statute to grant a license to practice law, and has an inherent right to strike the name of an attorney from the roll for sufficient cause shown, upon information. People v. Goodrich, 79 Ill. 148. To constitute such sufficient cause the conduct of an attorney need not necessarily amount to a crime or a misdemeanor under our statute.

The advertisements of respondent are very obnoxious and disgusting, not only because they are gotten up after the manner of quack doctors and itinerant vendors of patent medicines and other cure-alls, but because of the fact that they contain statements that cast reflections upon the common honesty, proficiency, and decency of the profession generally of which he insists he is a distinguished member. Any one who is knowingly guilty of such conduct as a lawyer ought to suspect that he is laying himself open to the charge of unprofessional conduct, which, if persisted in, would lead to his disbarment.

[Nevertheless, we] are disposed to agree with the general conclusion of the commissioner that the severe penalty of disbarment or suspension ought not to be imposed upon respondent in this case, but we are moved to such conclusion by the extenuating facts and circumstances reported by the commissioner, and not because of the failure of [the Chicago Bar Association] to prove respondent guilty as charged. The proof is unquestioned that he was born in a foreign country, and that many others of the profession in Chicago are guilty of like misconduct in their profession. That is no excuse for any other attorney following a like guilty course, but it was perhaps the cause of his erroneous conception of what was right and proper in the manner of advertising for business, and inasmuch as he has expressed a willingness to accept the judgment of the court on the question of advertising as to what is proper and what is improper, and is willing to cease and has ceased his improper methods of advertising and bears a good reputation for honesty and fair dealing, we think the publicity with which he has been afflicted by this prosecution and the severe reprimand given him in this decision ought to be the full measure of punishment administered.

If respondent shall hereafter refrain from all improper methods of advertising as herein indicated, we will not take further cognizance of his actions, except to pronounce his conduct as very improper and as deserving very severe censure by this court.

Rule discharged.

CHATEAU DE VILLE PRODUCTIONS, INC. v. TAMS-WITMARK MUSIC LIBRARY, INC.
474 F. Supp. 223 (S.D.N.Y. 1979)

DUFFY, District Judge.

Plaintiffs, owners and operators of dinner theatres, stock theatres and musical playhouses, filed this action in June, 1976 charging defendant Tams-Witmark Music Library, Inc. (hereinafter referred to as "Tams-Witmark") with violations of the antitrust laws. Defendant has now moved for an order disqualifying plaintiffs' counsel on the grounds that a conflict exists because of such counsel's simultaneous representation of plaintiffs and a "co-conspirator" in the alleged antitrust violations.

Tams-Witmark is engaged in the business of licensing professional theatres to present stage presentations of musical plays on behalf of the copyright owners and controllers of the performance rights to such plays. Pursuant to contracts with these copyright owners, royalties are collected by Tams-Witmark and remitted to them. Plaintiffs, who proceed on their own behalf and seek to proceed on behalf of similarly situated professional theatres, charge that Tams-Witmark has conspired with the owners and controllers of the performance rights in musical plays to monopolize the licensing of musicals, to illegally fix fees and to unlawfully tie-in licenses with a requirement that music and textual material be rented from Tams-Witmark. Plaintiffs seek treble damages, an injunction against Tams-Witmark's allegedly illegal activities, a declaratory judgment declaring illegal and voiding Tams-Witmark's exclusive contracts with any owner of a musical and a dissolution of Tams-Witmark. Tams-Witmark has filed counterclaims against two of the named plaintiffs for alleged violations of their contracts with it. Tams-Witmark also sought and was given leave to join Music Fair Enterprises, Inc., the parent corporation of Westbury Music Fair, Inc., a named plaintiff herein, as an additional defendant to its cross-claims. Music Fair was the actual party to the licensing agreements with Tams-Witmark under which performances at Westbury Music Fair were permitted.

The instant motion for disqualification is based upon facts regarding Music Fair that have apparently only recently come to defendant's attention. According to plaintiffs' complaint, Tams-Witmark owns or controls the rights to an extensive number of musical plays. One of these musicals is a comedy entitled "Lorelei." Tams-Witmark has an agreement with the holders of the performance rights to Lorelei pursuant to which Tams-Witmark may license professional stock performances of Lorelei and must remit 40% of the net royalties it collects to The Lorelei Company, a limited partnership which is the producer of the play. Until recently, Tams-Witmark believed that the principals of The Lorelei Company, Leon Guber and Sheldon Gross, who are also officers, directors and principal stockholders of Music Fair, were involved in The Lorelei Company in their individual capacities only. Affidavit of Louis H. Aborn, ¶ 5, March 8, 1979. It now appears that Music Fair itself is a general partner in the limited partnership which formed The Lorelei Company and, according to its 1973 Form 10-k registration statement, was to receive 43.75% of any net profits, as well as one percent of the gross weekly box office receipts. The 1972 Offering Circular filed with Form 10-k provided that Music Fair may "(b)e associated as producer, director, or in any other capacity with the purchaser of subsidiary rights in (Lorelei) and retain any direct or indirect compensation paid for services as such." The Offering Circular also provided that upon the author's sale of its subsidiary rights, The Lorelei Company would retain a 40% interest in the net receipts therefrom

> if such rights are disposed of during the first 10 years after the close of the last first-class run of the Play and (such interest) decreases to nothing if such rights are disposed of during the next 8 years.

Exhibit G, Aborn Affidavit, March 8, 1979.

In 1974 Tams-Witmark entered into its agreement with the copyright owners of Lorelei. As indicated above by virtue of this agreement and a letter agreement between Tams-Witmark and The Lorelei Company, Tams-Witmark is to remit to The Lorelei Company 40% of the royalties it collects. In the letter agreement dated November 21, 1974, The Lorelei Company expressly consented to the license agreement and granted Tams-Witmark the right to use "the direction, ideas, stage business and choreography as used in the Broadway production." Exhibit A, Aborn Affidavit, April 9, 1979. It appears that Tams-Witmark paid The Lorelei Company $20,000 in consideration of its approval of the licensing agreement.

Music Fair is represented in this action by the same counsel which represents plaintiffs and the purported class. Since under the facts as developed above, Music Fair would have to be considered a co-conspirator with Tams-Witmark, the latter argues that a glaring conflict exists in violation of Canon 5, ABA Code of Professional Responsibility: "A lawyer should exercise independent professional judgment on behalf of a client."

The ABA Code of Professional Responsibility sets forth nine guiding principles of professional conduct. One of these basic tenets is that an attorney owes his client the duty of unimpaired loyalty. Thus, where a conflict of interest exists, as for example where the same attorney seeks to represent more than one client with adverse or potentially adverse concerns, disqualification will be required unless the attorney can show "that there will be no actual or apparent conflict in loyalties or diminution in the vigor of his representation." Cinema 5, Ltd. v. Cinerama, 528 F.2d 1384, 1387 (2d Cir. 1976); Estates Theatres, Inc. v. Columbia Pictures Industries, Inc., 345 F.Supp. 93 (S.D.N.Y. 1972). It is also necessary, however, when considering a disqualification motion, to be mindful of the recent spate of such motions and their use as "'tools of the litigation process.'" Allegaert v. Perot, 565 F.2d 246, 251 (2d Cir. 1977) (citation omitted). Our Court of Appeals has adopted a cautious approach to questions of disqualification, examining the problems sought to be met by the Code, the reality of those problems in practice and "'whether a mechanical and didactic application of the Code to all situations automatically might not be productive of more harm than good, by requiring the client and the judicial system to sacrifice more than the value of the presumed benefits.'" International Electronics Corp. v. Flanzer, 527 F.2d 1288, 1293 (2d Cir. 1975).

My concerns in this case are compounded by the fact that counsel for plaintiffs seek to represent a class and are thus obliged to exercise their fiduciary obligations with particular care. See generally Greenfield v. Villager Industries, Inc., 483 F.2d 824 (3d Cir. 1973). Because the proposed class members are absentees without an opportunity to partake in the proceedings, it is of paramount importance that their rights and interests be closely safeguarded. In a class action, even the appearance of divided loyalties should be avoided. Sullivan v. Chase Investment Services of Boston, Inc., 79 F.R.D. 246 (N.D.Cal.1978).

With all these considerations in mind, I turn to the instant motion. The issue before me is whether counsel for plaintiffs and a potential class may simultaneously represent one of defendant's co-conspirators in an antitrust action which seeks to nullify contracts between the co-conspirators. When so stated, I believe the answer becomes clear; such multiple representation is inappropriate. Permitting plaintiffs' counsel to proceed in this manner would expose them to competing influences and loyalties. Moreover, even if, as plaintiffs assert, no glaring conflict exists at this time, when adverse interests are at stake it is not possible to predict what conflicts might arise as the litigation proceeds. It is better to forestall such a potential danger early in the litigation than to wait until the parties are deep in the discovery process.

Coupled with this potential exposure to competing influences is the appearance of impropriety that follows from multiple representation in a case like this. If permitted to proceed, plaintiffs' counsel would have to bear two standards: one as champion of the class and the other as protector of Music Fair's integrity as a co-conspirator. Canon 9 provides that "a lawyer should avoid even the appearance of professional impropriety." Compliance with this tenet mandates that counsel be disqualified from representing both plaintiffs and Music Fair in the instant action.

It should be noted that plaintiffs do not dispute the basic facts underlying the joint representation. They do, however, denigrate their importance. In the first place, they argue that Music Fair did not control the granting of Lorelei performance rights by its authors to Tams-Witmark. However, even assuming the truth of this assertion, it does not vitiate the conflict that exists between a royalty recipient and the plaintiffs charging that such royalties are illegally collected. Nor does the representation that the royalties are "de minimis" detract from the basic proposition that where a conflict exists "the law will not inquire into the force of the impact or its potential damage." Estates Theatres, supra at 98. Plaintiffs also argue that the interests of plaintiffs and Music Fair are identical and thus joint representation is permissible. See Brown & Williamson Tobacco Corp. v. Daniel International Corp., 563 F.2d 671 (5th Cir. 1977). Unfortunately, plaintiffs make no effort to explain this so-called "identity of interest" and, other than the fact that Westbury Music Fair, a named plaintiff, is a wholly owned subsidiary of Music Fair, there appears to be no such identity. There are four other named plaintiffs and a host of potential class members and I have no reason to presume that they have anything in common with Music Fair.

The final contention in opposition to disqualification is that plaintiffs and Music Fair have consented to the use of the same counsel. This representation, made in counsel's affidavit, is hardly sufficient to constitute consent. See generally Rice v. Baron, 456 F.Supp. 1361, 1376 (S.D.N.Y.1978). Moreover, since plaintiffs still seek to proceed on behalf of a class, the consent of all would be required and this, of course, is not a practical possibility. Lastly, even if consent were acquired, it is doubtful whether it would suffice to cure the conflict since I do not believe it "obvious that (the same counsel) can adequately represent the interest of each" of the multiple clients. ABA Code of Professional Responsibility, DR 5-105(C).

The question left for my consideration is whether counsel must be disqualified from representing both plaintiffs and Music Fair, or whether they will be permitted to continue on behalf of one of these parties. Defendant contends that they may not represent any one in this action for to do so would condone a violation of Canon 4, which provides that "a lawyer should preserve the confidences and secrets of a client." Defendant relies upon cases which for the most part involve situations where an attorney seeks to represent an interest adverse to that of a former client in an action brought against that former client. See, e.g., Government of India v. Cook Industries, 569 F.2d 737 (2d Cir. 1978); NCK Organization Ltd. v. Bregman, 542 F.2d 128 (2d Cir. 1976); Emle Industries, Inc. v. Patentex, Inc., 478 F.2d 562 (2d Cir. 1973). See also Hull v. Celanese Corporation, 513 F.2d 568 (2d Cir. 1975), where in-house counsel for defendant sought to become a plaintiff in an action against defendant although she had worked on the very same action on defendant's behalf. In those cases, the defendants would have had their own confidences betrayed by the proposed representation. By contrast, in the case at bar, Tams-Witmark has no similar interest to protect. Nor do I believe that permitting counsel to continue representing one of the parties would create the appearance of impropriety since they will be obligated to sever all ties with the other if they are to do so.

Counsel has expressed a desire, if a choice must be made, to continue representing plaintiffs. This choice does not, of course, bind the Court. Estate Theatres, supra at 100. However, after careful consideration, I believe that it is, in fact, appropriate for counsel to proceed on behalf of plaintiffs and not Music Fair. Although this lawsuit has not moved rapidly along the discovery stages, it has generated a great deal of paper work and with it, presumably, an intimate familiarity with the case. This familiarity should not be lightly disregarded, particularly if this action does proceed on behalf of a class of plaintiffs. See generally Sullivan v. Chase Investment Services of Boston, supra. The hardship to Music Fair resulting from the disqualification of its counsel is not as apparent. Indeed, insofar as the aforementioned conflict is concerned, Music Fair is not a named party. Although it is a defendant as to contractual cross-claims and an antitrust suit brought by Tams-Witmark and consolidated herewith, I do not believe it will be difficult for Music Fair to retain counsel to defend these claims. Accordingly, Music Fair is directed to retain new counsel and counsel for plaintiffs are directed to submit an affidavit certifying that they have completely withdrawn from further representation of Music Fair and will not represent it again during the pendency of these actions.

It is SO ORDERED.

RODGERS v. SOUND OF MUSIC COMPANY
343 N.Y.S.2d 672 (Sup. Ct. 1972)

MARKOWITZ, Justice.

The 'Sound of Music', a play with music and lyrics by Rodgers and Hammerstein, book by Lindsay and Crouse, and produced by Hayward and Halliday, world famous for its words and its music, fantastically successful, and made into a movie about to be re-released, spawned this litigation.

Background

The play was produced under a contract dated July 20, 1959 between Hayward and Halliday and Rodgers and Hammerstein and Lindsay and Crouse. Exploitation rights to the play were eventually assigned to the Sound of Music Company, a limited partnership of which Hayward and Halliday were general partners.

As of May 31, 1961, Lindsay and Crouse and Rodgers and Hammerstein Pictures, Inc. granted 20th Century Fox Film Corporation a twelve year lease of the motion picture rights in the play. As of the same day, 20th Century Fox transferred the motion picture soundtrack album rights to Rodgers and Hammerstein Records, Inc., a Rodgers and Hammerstein controlled company.

The principals of the Sound of Music Company did not know of the contract concerning the motion picture sound track rights until late in 1965. When it finally came to their attention, the company instituted arbitration proceedings before the American Arbitration Association.

The arbitration took approximately a year, with 22 hearings, 1800 pages of testimony and 296 exhibits. Thirteen witnesses testified; sundry briefs were submitted. Eminent counsel represented the respective parties. In his award, dated August 20, 1967, the arbitrator found that the Sound of Music Company was entitled to share in the sound track album rights and that the making of the contract transferring these rights to Rodgers and Hammerstein Records, Inc., and its concealment from the Sound of Music Company, constituted wilful misconduct on the part of Rodgers and Hammerstein.

[The arbitrator] directed Rodgers and Hammerstein to pay the Sound of Music Company for sales in the domestic market as of March 1967, and for sales in the foreign market as of April 1967. For sales made thereafter, the Sound of Music Company was granted an award of 36.08% of stated royalty receipts or, where appropriate, of net profits from the manufacture, licensing, use or disposition of records, tapes or cartridges made from the sound track. The award will eventually result in total receipts by the Sound of Music Company of approximately $3,000,000, the largest sum ever awarded in a commercial case administered by the American Arbitration Association.

The award was confirmed by order of this court dated April 24, 1968. Upon appeal, the order was affirmed by the Appellate Division (Matter of Sound of Music Co. v. Rodgers, 30 A.D.2d 935). Leave to appeal was denied by the Court of Appeals (Matter of Sound of Music Co. v. Rodgers, 23 N.Y.2d 642, 297 N.Y.S.2d 1026, 244 N.E.2d 885).

Fitelson and Mayers, Esqs., represented the Sound of Music Company in the arbitration proceeding and in the courts. They acted under a written retainer agreement dated May 6, 1966, signed in behalf of the Sound of Music Company by Hayward and Halliday. In the retainer agreement the parties agreed that counsel be paid for their services a contingent fee based on the amount recovered by Sound of Music Company from the recording or sale of the sound track phonograph album of the motion picture and of the original stage cast phonograph album.

Character of the Action

In June of 1970, Rodgers and Hammerstein, as limited partners with a 25% interest in the Sound of Music Company, brought this action to rescind the contingent retainer agreement and to determine the value of the services of Fitelson and Mayers, Esqs., on the basis of quantum meruit.

The complaint in the main contended that by reason of Rodgers and Hammerstein's 25% beneficial interest in the Sound of Music Company and Lindsay and Crouse's 6% (actually 11%) interest in the company, recovery by the attorneys should be reduced by the extent of their interests as both 'debtors' and 'creditors'.

On motion, plaintiffs were granted a preliminary injunction against further payments to Fitelson and Mayers, Esqs. Defendants in turn were given the right to an immediate trial ten days after the filing by defendants of a note of issue and statement of readiness. Pursuant to the order, the case came before me for trial in March of 1972.

On March 28, 1972, counsel for plaintiffs, counsel for defendants Fitelson and Mayers, Esqs., and counsel for Sound of Music Company entered into a written stipulation of settlement, subject to the approval of the Court. By my order dated March 29, 1972, a hearing, pursuant to Section 115-a of the Partnership Law, on the fairness and adequacy of the proposed settlement was scheduled for April 12, 1972. Notice of the hearing, together with a copy of the stipulation of settlement, were mailed to all Sound of Music Company partners and participants. On April 12, 1972, testimony and exhibits were offered in support of the proposed settlement; no one appeared in opposition.

Consents to the Proposed Settlement

The settlement will result in the reduction of the contingent fee fixed by the parties by 10%.

Plaintiffs have consented to the settlement. Richard Halliday, the surviving general partner of defendant the Sound of Music Company, has also approved the settlement.

Mr. Halliday testified at the hearing. He stated that Mr. Hayward and he would not have retained Fitelson and Mayers, Esqs., to bring the arbitration proceeding other than on a contingent basis; that this is a common practice in the theatre. He also stated that the contingency in the retainer agreement met with the approval of Mr. Hayward, as well as his own.

Counsel who brought the action for plaintiff testified that there is little or no prospect of recovery in excess of that provided in the stipulation of settlement; and that under all the circumstances before the court, the settlement proposed was fair and reasonable.

Counsel for the Sound of Music Company stated that after investigation he could see no merit to plaintiffs' claim 'and certainly saw no basis upon which Sound of Music Company could in good faith, in good conscience, pick it up and assert it'. He concluded that he 'saw no basis upon which the Sound of Music Company could take any position that this fee had not been earned and should not be paid in any respect.'

This much is abundantly clear. The conduct of Fitelson and Mayers, Esqs., and of Halliday and Hayward in pressing the claim against Rodgers and Hammerstein was exemplary. They are to be commended for their efforts in retrieving the moneys due the Sound of Music Company. Any suggestion to the contrary is both unfair and unfounded.

Attorneys' Fees

Ordinarily an attorney's compensation is governed by the contract between the parties, express or implied (Judiciary Law § 474). Unless the retainer is unconscionable or illegal, the parties are bound by the terms they agree to (Rodkinson v. Haecker, 248 N.Y. 480, 162 N.E. 493; Greenberg v. Jerome H. Renuck & Co., 230 N.Y. 70, 129 N.E. 211; Ransom v. Ransom, 147 App.Div. 835, 133 N.Y.S. 173; see also Booth, Lipton & Lipton v. Cassel, 51 Misc.2d 853, 274 N.Y.S.2d 90, aff'd 27 A.D.2d 706, 278 N.Y.S.2d 178); and an attorney's contract with his client for compensation for future services is presumed to be fair until the contrary appears (Rodkinson v. Haecker, supra; Application of Peters, 271 App.Div. 518, 67 N.Y.S.2d 305, mod. 296 N.Y. 974, 73 N.E.2d 560; In re Sasson, 231 App.Div. 524, 248 N.Y.S. 125).

If, however, the contract is unreasonable or oppressive, the court will correct the abuse (Gair v. Peck, 6 N.Y.2d 97, 188 N.Y.S.2d 491, 160 N.E.2d 43, cert. den. 361 U.S. 374, 80 S.Ct. 401, 4 L.Ed.2d 380; Matter of Fitzsimmons, 174 N.Y. 15, 66 N.E. 554).

Approving or Disapproving a Settlement

Section 115-a of the Partnership Law sets forth no standard for passing on proposed settlements of derivative actions. Decisions in related fields, however, point the way (Zenn v. Anzalone, 17 Misc.2d 897, 191 N.Y.S.2d 840; Waterman Corp. v. Johnston, 106 N.Y.S.2d 813, aff'd 279 App.Div. 1073, 113 N.Y.S.2d 287; Silverstein v. Clarkson, 194 Misc. 1046, 88 N.Y.S.2d 67).

Eight guiding principles evolve from a study of the authorities: (1) The benefits in the agreement of settlement, as against the likelihood of recovery after trial. (2) The general rule that courts favor settlements. (3) Whether sharply contested and dubious issues are present, the determination of which would be obviated by the settlement. (4) The expense of going to trial. (5) The likelihood of success at the trial. (6) Whether the settlement is the result of good faith negotiation at arms length, or of collusion, chicanery or fraud. (7) The position of the parties to the litigation concerning the settlement; the opposition, if any, to the settlement. (8) Whether, in the court's judgment, the settlement is fair and reasonable under all the circumstances.

Conclusion

Judged in the light of these rules, the conclusion is inescapable that the proposed settlement should be approved.

The retainer under study was made with specialists in theatrical matters. The efforts of counsel were successful; the award they obtained for their client was full and abundant. For these efforts they are entitled to be paid.

All personally concerned in the case who have appeared before the court have approved the terms of the settlement and urged its acceptance. No one has urged its rejection; no one has opposed any of its terms or any of its provisions.

The settlement was hammered out by experienced attorneys of high standing. By the settlement all the parties have surrendered something; all have gained something; an extended trial has been avoided. The compromise reached is satisfactory to those who appeared at the hearing. No one has argued that it is not satisfactory.

Consequently, there is no purpose in further litigating the sharply-contested issues presented by the pleadings.

In this frame of reference I approve the stipulation of settlement, as modified at the hearing.

Notes

1. As the *Berezniak* case indicates, the "theater bar" in this country has long been a small and highly specialized one; the 2003 *Martindale-Hubbell Law Directory* lists less than two dozen theater lawyers. This fact, coupled with the tight-knit nature of the the-

ater industry, makes conflicts of interest, like those in *Tams-Witmark* and *Sound of Music*, quite common.

Of course, determining the actual size of the theater bar is impossible, for several reasons: (a) the lack of agreement as to what constitutes theater; (b) the malleability of the word "theater," which, depending on the context, can refer to stage, film, or adult entertainment; and, (c) the fact that surveys of the legal profession typically subsume theater law under such larger headings as "entertainment law" or "intellectual property law."

2. Lawyers who do specialize in theater law generally are found in New York City. However, opportunities to engage in theater law exist throughout the country. Two good ways to become involved in the field are by joining the Theatre & Performing Arts Division of the American Bar Association's Forum on Entertainment & Sports Industries (www.abanet.org/forums/entsports/theater.html) and participating in Volunteer Lawyers for the Arts (a local contact list appears at www.vlany.org/res_dir.html). You also will find it helpful to read William D. Henslee, *Entertainment Law Careers* (1998), and Gary Greenberg, *How to Build and Manage an Entertainment Law Practice* (2001).

3. If you decide to pursue a career in theater law, you will need to become familiar with the industry's operating structure. For example, in reading the *Tams-Witmark* case, it is helpful to know the following about the licensing of plays:

> In 1830 an [English] entrepreneur named Samuel French had what turned out to be a brilliant and highly profitable idea: he would license from the authors of plays of proven popularity the rights both to publish (as cheaply as possible) acting editions of those plays, so that each actor could have a full script to work from, and to sub-license the performing rights for those plays to amateur groups and provincial professional companies, keeping a healthy commission from the royalties collected for the authors. (Or, alternatively, buy the play outright from the author and keep all the royalties for himself.)
>
> By the time U.S. copyright law recognized British copyrights, and vice versa, Samuel French's company had established offices in London, Toronto, and New York (and eventually Los Angeles as well), and had the power and prestige that allowed it to charge commissions as high as fifty percent of the royalties on some of the plays the company published and licensed. Today the many authors represented by Samuel French range from Neil Simon and Jane Martin to Samuel Beckett and Agatha Christie. Two other play publishers founded in the nineteenth century—Baker's Plays (1845) and Dramatic Publishing Company (1885)—are also still active, concentrating heavily on the school and community theatre market.
>
> The American company M. Witmark & Sons, founded in 1870, followed this almost universal practice of having a print-for-sale and a rental library division. Eventually, Witmark Music Library became Tams-Witmark.
>
> As the middle of the twentieth century approached, changes in the theatrical marketplace help create new players in the publishing/licensing field. In 1936, dissatisfaction with Samuel French's policy of charging up to fifty percent in commissions prompted a group of Dramatist Guild playwrights and literary agents to form the Dramatists Play Service. [The shareholders of Dramatists Play Service initially included] Robert E. Sherwood, George S. Kaufman, and Moss Hart, and later, Arthur Miller and Tennessee Williams.

> The new musical theatre field was broad enough for individuals with highly successful shows to license for amateur production to enter the licensing/publishing market as well[, leading to the formation of] the Rodgers and Hammerstein Theatre Library in 1948 and Music Theatre International in 1952. Today, almost every major musical is licensed by one of these four organizations [i.e., Samuel French, Tams-Witmark, Rodgers and Hammerstein, and Music Theatre International].
>
> One of the most recent additions in the non-musical category is Broadway Play Publishing, Inc., founded in 1982 by Christopher Gould, former head of the musicals department at Samuel French. BPPI, now the third largest play publisher and licensing agency in New York, is primarily committed to contemporary playwrights [such as] Tony Kushner, Richard Nelson, and Eric Overmeyer[.]

Kevin N. Scott, *A Brief History of Copyright and Play Licensing*, 10 Teaching Theatre 6, 7–8 (Summer 1999).

Learning about the theater industry also means becoming conversant with its terminology. To do so, you should pick up one of the many theater dictionaries that exist, such as: Terry Hodgson, *The Drama Dictionary* (1990); Jonathan Law, *The Penguin Dictionary of the Theatre* (2001); Jonnie Patricia Mobley, *NTC's Dictionary of Theatre and Drama Terms* (1992); Joel Trapido, *An International Dictionary of Theatre Language* (1985). *See also Glossary of Technical Theatre Terms* at www.theatrecrafts.com. In addition, you should get into the habit of regularly reading the Arts & Leisure sections of *The New York Times* and your local newspaper to keep abreast of national and local theater developments.

4. Having been forced by the Illinois Supreme Court to abandon his "diary and daily route book," Berezniak in 1923 published what likely was the first treatise on theater law. Entitled *The Theatrical Counselor*, it is no longer in print, although copies still exist and can be found through used booksellers. Sadly, there is no modern day equivalent. As such, resort must be had to entertainment law treatises and encyclopedias that include coverage of the stage. The leading such work is 1 Alexander Lindey & Michael Landau, *Lindey on Entertainment, Publishing and the Arts: Agreements and the Law* (2d ed. 1980 & 2003 Supp.), at ch. 5 ("Plays"). It includes both commentary and sample theater contracts, a number of which are reproduced as appendices to this casebook.

5. Arbitration, discussed in the *Sound of Music* case, is the preferred method of resolving theater disputes, and normally is conducted under the auspices of the American Arbitration Association (www.adr.org). As compared to litigation, arbitration tends to be cheaper, quicker, and less formal; gives parties greater control over the process; employs decision makers who are experts in the field; and allows disputes to remain private. In addition to arbitration, theater lawyers also need (at a minimum) a strong grasp of agency law, anti-trust law, contracts, First Amendment law, intellectual property law, and labor and employment law; a working knowledge of tax law; and some familiarity with accounting.

The hardest thing about being a theater lawyer, however, is not how much law must be mastered. Rather, it is how willing one's clients are to do business while ignoring the legal niceties:

> By the time "Wonderful Town" opened last Sunday, lines had been memorized, sets built and money lined up. Everything was ready except one small detail: the producers hadn't signed a contract for the rights to the show. A week later the deal is still not final.

In most businesses, this situation might be cause for alarm. But on Broadway, where handshake deals are still typical business practice, it hardly raised an eyebrow. "I've worked on shows which have run for two years and closed and still don't have a contract," said the veteran producer Emmanuel Azenberg.

Jeffrey Seller, a producer of "Rent," said, "I've never worked on a show that didn't have the rights, but we opened 'Rent' without signing the lease [for the theater] and ran for over a year without doing it."

On "Wonderful Town," an unsigned written agreement was reached in early October, but the terms of royalties for road tours remain a sticking point, said Barry Weissler, one of the producers. He has been negotiating with representatives of Betty Comden, who wrote the lyrics with Adolph Green, as well as the estates of Green, the composer Leonard Bernstein and the book writers Jerome Chodorov and Joseph Fields.

"It's a little annoying to everybody," said Peter Franklin, the agent for Ms. Comden and the Green estate. "But it's just the vagaries of doing business in the theater."

Jason Zinoman, *On Stage and Off*, N.Y. Times, Nov. 28, 2003, at E1.

6. The fact that you are in law school, but reading about the theater, is not surprising, for law and theater have much in common. Indeed, many lawyers now take acting classes to enhance their courtroom skills. *See further* David Ball, *Theater Tips and Strategies for Jury Trials* (3d ed. 2003); Donald B. Fielder, *Acting Effectively in Court: Using Dramatic Techniques*, Champion, July 2001, at 18; Peter Morrison, *Lawyers Polish Up Their Acts*, Nat'l L.J., July 5, 1993, at 47; Bernadette Rappold, *Give My Regards to Camden: Law Professor Uses Improv to Teach Lawyering Skills*, Legal Intelligencer, Nov. 3, 1999, at S1.

The parallels between theater and law are many, and include the following: both are performed in public before an audience; both occur in designated places at prescribed times; both require minute preparation and rehearsal; both proceed according to well-known rules, procedures, and traditions; and both are populated by persons charged with specific responsibilities, as shown in this chart:

TASK	THEATER	LAW
Prepare story	Playwright	Plaintiff
Finance story	Producer or Public	Parties or Public
Oversee story	Director	Judge
Perform story	Cast	Witnesses
Support story	Crew	Attorneys
Watch story	Audience	Jury
Review story	Critics	Appellate Judges

For a further look at the connection between law and theater, *see, e.g., Zal v. Steppe*, 968 F.2d 924, 932 (9th Cir.), *cert. denied*, 506 U.S. 1021 (1992) ("In a courtroom, a lawyer without a client is like an actor without a part: he has no role to play, and no lines to deliver"); *S.E.C. v. Fox*, 855 F.2d 247, 253 (5th Cir. 1988) ("Like great plays, trials have their high moments and their lows."); *People v. Tryer*, 189 N.W.2d 226, 227 (Mich. 1971) ("A murder trial is to the lawyer what opening night is to the thespian[.]"); *Littlefield v. Superior Court*, 22 Cal. Rptr. 2d 659, 661 (Ct. App. 1993) ("Like an understudy in a play, [a standby lawyer's] task is to wait in readiness to play a role should the occasion arise."); *State v. Davis*, 607 N.E.2d 543, 548 (Ohio Ct. App. 1992) (Grey, J., concurring) ("[E]ach of the actors in the courtroom drama has a distinct part to play."); Luke Wilson, *Theaters of Intention: Drama and the Law in Early Modern England* (2000); Phillip E. Johnson, *Inherit the Wind: The Play's the Thing*, 13 Regent U. L. Rev. 279 (2000-2001). *See also* Roger I. Abrams, *This Is Not an Article, or Scholarship: The Greek Salad*, 13 Nova L. Rev. 33 (1988) (law review article written as a play); Carol A. Roehrenbeck & Gail L. Richmond, *Three Researchers in Search of an Alcove: A Play in Six Acts*, 84 Law Lib. J. 13 (1992) (same); Rodney A. Smolla, *The Trial of Oliver Wendell Holmes*, 36 Wm. & Mary L. Rev. 173 (1994) (same).

7. Ironically, the most famous connection between law and theater is also the most hotly disputed. In Shakespeare's *King Henry VI*, Dick the Butcher says, "The first thing we do, let's kill all the lawyers." To the public, the line is often understood as a plea to get rid of lawyers and their contentious ways; to attorneys, however, the line is proof that civilized society cannot exist without them:

> That function was, however, well understood by Jack Cade and his followers, characters who are often forgotten and whose most famous line is often misunderstood. Dick's statement ("The first thing we do, let's kill all the lawyers") was spoken by a rebel, not a friend of liberty. See W. Shakespeare, King Henry VI, pt. II, Act IV, scene 2, line 72. As a careful reading of that text will reveal, Shakespeare insightfully realized that disposing of lawyers is a step in the direction of a totalitarian form of government.

Walters v. National Ass'n of Radiation Survivors, 473 U.S. 305, 371 n.24 (1985) (Stevens, J., dissenting). Yet others have suggested that the line has little or nothing to do with lawyers. *See* Gerald T. Bennett, *Let's Kill All the Lawyers! Shakespeare [Might Have] Meant It*, 72 Fla. B.J. 58 (Dec. 1998).

Problem 2

An actor entered into a written agreement with a producer that guaranteed him work for "three seasons" at a rate of $1,000 per week. Two weeks later, however, the producer reneged. As the actor's lawyer, what is the maximum amount you can sue for? *See McIntosh v. Miner*, 65 N.Y.S. 735 (App. Div. 1900).

Chapter 2

Playwrights

A. OVERVIEW

The playwright is the author of the work that is to be performed. As the author, the playwright possesses numerous rights, including, of course, the right to be paid for his or her efforts. This leads to two important questions: 1) who may claim the title of "author"?, and, 2) to what extent can an author control how his or her work is presented to the public?

B. AUTHORSHIP

NTREH v. UNIVERSITY OF TEXAS AT DALLAS
2000 WL 1093233 (Tex. Ct. App. 2000)

MOSELEY, Justice.

In the second appeal in this case, appellant, Abraham Nee Ntreh ("Ntreh"), complains of an adverse judgment by the trial court in favor of appellee, the University of Texas at Dallas ("UTD"), on his claims of discrimination based on race or national origin and due process violations. On appeal, Ntreh raises four issues: (1) the trial court abused its discretion by denying Ntreh's motion for continuance; (2) the trial court violated Ntreh's due process rights by trying his case without Ntreh being present; (3) UTD violated Ntreh's due process rights by failing to allow him to waive a disciplinary hearing; and (4) the evidence was factually insufficient to support the trial court's findings of fact concerning allegations of academic dishonesty. For the reasons set forth below, we affirm the judgment of the trial court.

BACKGROUND

In 1991, Ntreh, a Ghanian national, was a legal resident alien and a student at UTD. During his senior year, Ntreh and his brother Joseph Ntreh ("Joseph") enrolled in the Nature of Theatrical Experience class taught by Ms. Coral Shafer ("Shafer"). To receive credit for the course, each student had to complete a final project consisting of either a research paper or a creative project. Options for the creative project included doing a performance of either already scripted material, or material written by the student, writing a script, or doing a design for a costume for a set. If the student chose to do a creative project, they were also required to write a two to three page paper placing the project within the context of the class. According to Shafer, Ntreh chose to do a creative project and write a script.

For his final project, Ntreh turned in a play entitled "A Return to Live" and the author of the play was designated as Abe Evan Nee, a name by which Ntreh is often referred. A two-page cover sheet was attached explaining the nature of the play. The language used in the cover sheet indicated that Ntreh wrote the play. Ntreh initially received a "B" grade for his project. Feeling that he should have received an "A" instead of a "B," Ntreh spoke with Dr. Linda Williamson ("Williamson"), the College Master for the College of Arts and Sciences at UTD, about the discriminatory manner in which "A" and "B" grades were assigned.

After reviewing Ntreh's play, Shafer questioned the play's authenticity. Williamson and Priscilla Ann Beadle, the Vice President for Administration and Student Affairs, testified at trial that when they questioned Ntreh about his play, he told them the play was his original work. Williamson and Shafer decided to conduct research to determine if Ntreh had plagiarized an existing work. Shafer conducted research at the Dallas Public Library where she discovered a play entitled "Resurrection" by Richard Rive. Except for some minor details, Shafer discovered that Rive's "Resurrection" and Ntreh's "A Return to Live," were verbatim. UTD initiated a disciplinary proceeding against Ntreh for alleged plagiarism. As a result of the proceeding, Ntreh was given an "F" in the class and expelled from the University.

Ntreh sued UTD in November 1993 alleging: (1) Ntreh was denied the equal protection of the law and was denied due process (both brought under 42 U.S.C. § 1983); (2) UTD discriminated against Ntreh (a black man) based on race or national origin in violation of Texas Civil Practice & Remedies Code section 106.001(a)(6); and (3) breach of contract. UTD filed a plea to the jurisdiction based on sovereign immunity. On April 20, 1994, the trial court granted UTD's plea to the jurisdiction and dismissed the case concluding that UTD was immune from suit on all of Ntreh's claims. On appeal, this Court concluded that the trial court correctly dismissed Ntreh's § 1983 claims. However, this Court further concluded that the trial court erred in dismissing Ntreh's claims for discrimination and breach of contract and remanded the case to the trial court. UTD appealed to the Texas Supreme Court concerning the remand of Ntreh's breach of contract claim. The supreme court concluded that the trial court properly dismissed Ntreh's breach of contract claim and modified this Court's judgment accordingly. Therefore, upon remand, the live cause of action was Ntreh's discrimination claim under section 106.001(a)(6) of the Texas Civil Practice & Remedies Code.

While this suit was pending on remand, on October 28, 1997, Ntreh and his wife were deported to England based on a conviction of perjury in an unrelated proceeding. On December 7, 1998, this Court reversed Ntreh's conviction for perjury and acquitted him of that charge.

On March 10, 1999, while Ntreh remained in England, Ntreh filed a motion for continuance in the present suit because of his inability to appear at the trial due to his deportation. The trial court denied Ntreh's motion and the case was called for trial on March 15, 1999. On April 13, 1999, the trial court rendered a take nothing judgment against Ntreh. Ntreh brings this appeal.

DISCUSSION

I. MOTION FOR CONTINUANCE

[This portion of the court's opinion is omitted.]

II. DUE PROCESS AT TRIAL

[This portion of the court's opinion is omitted.]

III. DUE PROCESS AT THE DISCIPLINARY HEARING

[This portion of the court's opinion is omitted.]

IV. FACTUAL SUFFICIENCY OF THE EVIDENCE

In his fourth issue, Ntreh argues that the evidence was factually insufficient to support the trial court's findings of plagiarism (Findings of Fact 5-10).

There is evidence in the record that as his final project in the class, Ntreh turned in a play entitled "A Return to Live"; he designated the author of the play as Abe Evan Nee, a moniker by which he was known. In a two-page cover sheet attached to his play, Ntreh described in detail how he had been inspired to write the play because of a personal experience he had had at a friend's aunt's funeral, how he developed the characters and dialogue, and how he envisioned the theatrical setting, scenery, lighting, and sound. The concluding paragraph in his cover sheet stated that, "[m]ost of the things we studied in class helped me considerably to explore the components of my story in relation to the components of my play. Things we studied also helped me in considering what was essential in my story to meet my objective in the play."

Beadle testified that Ntreh represented to her that he had written all of the two-page cover sheet and play he turned in as his final project. Ms. Veronica Davis ("Davis"), a former attorney with the Department of Education, also testified that Ntreh wrote the two-page cover sheet. There is also evidence and testimony in the record that Ntreh represented to Shafer, Beadle, and Williamson that the play was his own work.

Williamson testified that both she and Shafer questioned whether Ntreh's play was his original work because of the professional quality of the play, a quality that is not customary for student works. Williamson testified that she and Shafer both conducted research in various libraries to determine if a play existed that Ntreh could have plagiarized. Williamson further stated that based on the language used in the play, Shafer narrowed her search to Afro-American anthologies, which eventually led to Shafer's discovery of a previously published play entitled "Resurrection" by Richard Rives. Except for a few minor changes, Ntreh's play was the verbatim script of "Resurrection".

In her testimony, Williamson explained the search for "Resurrection":

> Q. How long did it take [Shafer] to locate this Rive play? How many hours did she put into it?
>
> A. I don't know the total number of hours, I know that she went solely for the—she went to the library looking for the play.
>
> Q. Looking for that particular play?
>
> A. Looking for any play that looked like it might be like—
>
> Q. How many plays are in the library?
>
> A. I don't know.
>
> Q. Probably thousands. Is that accurate?
>
> A. I would not think so.

Q. You would think there is less than a thousand plays in the UTD library?

A. She wasn't at the UTD library, she was at the Dallas County—Dallas Public Library.

Q. So it's your view that there is probably less than a thousand plays at the Dallas library?

A. Plays of this nature. I mean, when you are a professional you can read a play and get a sense of language, a sense of place and a sense of what the action is, and you even have a category to go to. Obviously, having his work, you wouldn't be looking under comedies you would be looking under—you would be looking for a needle in a haystack.

Q. Well, I mean, that's kind of what I am thinking.

A. Uh-huh.

Q. And I am trying to figure out how this needle was located in just a few hours, what—whether you had some kind of—

A. I had an idea—

Q. —informant who told you what the play was, or maybe Mr. Ntreh told you what the play was.

A. The—I am not aware of any of this other than the fact that the play was found.

Q. Did you think it was at all unusual that the play got found like that?

A. Yes. But I would have, and did do some searching on my own.

Q. And you found it as well, independently?

A. No.

Ntreh argues that Williamson's testimony that finding "Resurrection" was like looking for a "needle in a haystack," supports his argument that Shafer's expediency in finding this "needle in a haystack" is implausible without having prior knowledge of the play's existence. Ntreh argues that this is further supported by Joseph's testimony that Ntreh had informed Shafer that he was staging an existing work. Ntreh contends that, because the evidence demonstrates that he represented to Shafer that he was using an existing work for his project, the evidence does not support a finding of plagiarism.

UTD argues that the phrase "a needle in a haystack" meant that "conducting a search for the play in a library would have been like looking for a needle in a haystack without narrowing the search to a particular category of plays."

Having reviewed all of the evidence, including the evidence noted above, we conclude that the trial court's findings of fact [on the issue of plagiarism] are not so against the great weight and preponderance of the evidence as to be clearly wrong and manifestly unjust.

[The remainder of the court's opinion is omitted.]

JACKSON v. UNIVERSAL INTERNATIONAL PICTURES, INC.
222 P.2d 433 (Cal. 1950)

EDMONDS, Justice.

Frederick Jackson, the author of a play which was not a theatrical success, sued to recover damages assertedly resulting from the unauthorized use of its title. The principal ground relied upon as requiring a reversal of the judgment in his favor is that the evidence shows no acquisition by the title of a secondary meaning.

The first count of the complaint alleged that Jackson is the author of a play which he entitled 'Slightly Scandalous.' The play was rehearsed in Los Angeles and produced in Philadelphia and New York with publicity announcing the times of performance. The title thereby acquired a secondary meaning. Later, Universal produced a motion picture under the same title. Universal's distribution, advertising and showing of its picture misled the public and infringed upon Jackson's right in the title of his play. The second count of the complaint alleged that Universal had made a 'deliberate, wrongful and unfair misappropriation and use of plaintiff's name and title' in connection with the motion picture. Universal denied these allegations generally.

The evidence presented upon trial may be summarized as follows. Jackson is a writer with about 40 years of experience. He has written plays which were produced in New York and London and sold the motion picture rights to several of them. In 1943, he wrote 'Slightly Scandalous.' In the following year, while the play was being rehearsed in Los Angeles prior to production, a press agent was employed to publicize it. During the next two months about 40 stories concerning it were prepared and distributed to 550 metropolitan and suburban newspapers.

Only a small percentage of this material was published. A one-inch item appeared in the Hollywood Reporter, a trade journal. It stated that the play would open in Philadelphia and be presented in New York two weeks later with Janet Beecher in the leading role. The Los Angeles Evening Herald-Express, with a daily circulation of 325,000, reported that the author was adding final directorial touches to 'Slightly Scandalous' before its initial production in Philadelphia.

Variety, a theatrical magazine having a circulation of 600,000 and sold at newstands in the principal cities, included reference to the play in a section entitled 'Shows in Rehearsal.' The Los Angeles Times, which has a daily circulation in excess of 280,000, mentioned in a story concerning another play that the title of the one in which Janet Beecher was to be starred had been changed to 'Slightly Scandalous.' Rehearsal would commence in Hollywood immediately, it was said, preparatory to a New York appearance.

The play opened in Philadelphia as scheduled. It was advertised in newspapers there prior to and during its two weeks run, in space ranging from 10 to 60 lines. The producer also placed 20,000 'heralds' in hotels and restaurants and used outdoor advertising with '24-sheets' on 50 poster boards.

The play ran for almost two weeks in Philadelphia. The drama critics were uncomplimentary, and although the theater was nearly filled to its capacity of 1,500 persons at one performance, attendance at all of the others averaged about 200. The total of the audiences at the 15 performances did not exceed 3,000.

The New York opening followed, but the play closed after seven performances. Advertising was carried by 10 newspapers there in space varying from 12 to 50 lines. But, as in Philadelphia, the newspaper comments were critical and the public showed little interest. In a theater which seated 1,000 there was an average attendance of about 100 at each performance. The play has not since been presented.

A witness for Jackson, after qualifying as an expert, testified that 'Some of the most successful pictures have been made of plays that have been flops.' Examples were cited. This testimony was corroborated by other witnesses.

To establish a secondary meaning to the title of his play, Jackson presented the testimony of five witnesses. Three of them told the jury that they had seen reviews or advertisements of the play and thought that the picture was based upon it. The testimony of the other two was substantially to the same effect.

Other testimony showed that Jackson's agent requested Universal Pictures to 'cover' the eastern production of the play after it had been submitted to that company's West Coast story editor during the period of rehearsal in Los Angeles. A report concerning the play and its reception on Broadway was sent to the company's executive offices.

About two years later, Universal released and distributed throughout the country a motion picture by the same name. It was stipulated that three months before this picture was released, Universal knew of Jackson's play and referred to their attorneys the question as to whether the title 'Slightly Scandalous' should be selected for their production. The picture originally carried the title, 'Oh Say Can You Sing.' The attorneys for Universal were notified by Jackson's attorney that his client would sue for damages if the title to his play were used.

Jackson does not claim that there is any similarity whatever between the picture and the play. He bases his cause of action entirely upon the use of the title.

The evidence offered by Universal generally is to the effect that the public did not connect the motion picture with Jackson's play and only a handful of people had previously heard of the title. In the company's defense, its witnesses stressed the unsuccessful presentations in Philadelphia and New York.

As grounds for the reversal of the judgment, Universal asserts that the evidence is not sufficient to justify the conclusion that 'Slightly Scandalous' had acquired and retained a secondary meaning with relation to Jackson's play. The company also challenges an instruction as incorrect and prejudicially erroneous. Instructions offered by it were erroneously refused, it is asserted, and Jackson's damages in the amount of $17,500 are excessive. It is also claimed that the title was abandoned by Jackson's two year non-use of it. Finally, the appellant charges, Jackson's attorney was guilty of prejudicial conduct.

The position of Jackson is that the question as to whether a secondary meaning has attached to a literary or dramatic title is a question of fact. As substantial evidence sufficient to justify the jury's verdict, he refers to the testimony concerning prior use, advertising, and the general impression of the public in New York, Philadelphia and Los Angeles. He also relies upon the statements of his five witnesses that because of the title they associated the play with the motion picture. Nation-wide knowledge of a title is not essential to the acquisition of a secondary meaning, he declares, nor is success of the play a requirement. The correct test, as he analyzes the question, is whether an effect or reaction is created upon the public mind. He also contends that deliberate and unauthorized appropriation of a prior user's name, title or trademark is actionable.

As to the claimed procedural errors, the conduct of counsel was not prejudicial, he asserts, because it was promptly cured by an instruction to the jury. Moreover, the denial of the motion for a new trial was a determination that it did not influence the jury.

The points presented by amici curiae for Jackson are broader in scope. It is claimed that secondary meaning is established when the title is identified by the general public and it does not depend upon popularity. Although a play is unpopular or 'panned' by the critics, unfavorable comments, or any discussion of the play, fixes the title in the mind of the general public as the product of a particular playwright. Moreover, widespread publicity and advertising renders a title valuable and subject to protection entirely apart from rights derived from secondary meaning. The 'general public,' they say, need only be a substantial number of people not necessarily residing throughout the nation.

An author of a play has no inherent right in the title to his production. Paramore v. Mack, Sennett, Inc., D.C. 9 F.2d 66, 67; Martenet v. United Artists Corp., D.C., 56 F.Supp. 639, 640. Only when the title has acquired a secondary meaning identifying it in the public mind with the play is he entitled to its exclusive use. Warner Bros. Pictures v. Majestic Pictures Corp., 2 Cir., 70 F.2d 310, 311; Amusement S. Corp. v. Academy Pictures D. Corp., 162 Misc. 608, 294 N.Y.S. 279; see Nims, Unfair Competition and Trade Marks (4th Ed.1947), sec. 274-a. Therefore, regardless of any deliberate use by Universal of 'Slightly Scandalous' with knowledge of Jackson's prior use, he is not entitled to damages unless his literary product had acquired a secondary meaning.

There is no initial property right in household semantics or words which are merely descriptive, fanciful or geographic in nature. G. & C. Merriam Co. v. Saalfield, 6 Cir., 198 F. 369, 373. However, if words have been used by an author or manufacturer in such a manner that the public has learned to associate them with the product, book or play, they acquire a 'secondary meaning'. This principle, which was first applied in trademark cases, renders the words or symbols protectible and transferable because of that association. A play may become known to the public by its title, which thereby acquires a secondary meaning and attains a protectible status. Manners v. Triangle Film Corp., 2 Cir., 247 F. 301; Hemingway v. Film Alliance of the United States, Inc., 174 Misc. 725, 21 N.Y.S.2d 827.

In Johnston v. Twentieth Century-Fox Film Corp., 82 Cal.App.2d 796, 813, 187 P.2d 474, 484, the court stated, 'The question whether a title has acquired a secondary meaning is one of fact.' Other decisions to the same effect are International Film Service Co., Inc. v. Associated Producers, Inc., D.C., 273 F. 585; Bayer Co. v. United Drug Co., D.C., 272 F. 505, 509; Saland v. Monogram Pictures Corp., Sup., 67 N.Y.S.2d 436; Hemingway v. Film Alliance of the United States, Inc., 174 Misc. 725, 21 N.Y.S.2d 827. The Restatement of the Law of Torts, in stating this rule, adds: 'No particular period of use is required.' (Sec. 716b.)

There is substantial evidence in the record to support the implied finding of the jury that 'Slightly Scandalous' had acquired a secondary meaning. Jackson's play was publicized in three of the largest cities in this country. The rehearsal and production of the play were announced in dramatic and motion picture journals in Hollywood and New York. Although only about 3,750 persons attended performances of the play, there is no basis for a holding, as a matter of law, that they and the undetermined number who saw the advertising are not sufficient in number to provide a basis for secondary meaning. The precise size of this segment of the public is important in connection with the amount of damages which should be awarded, but it does not determine whether the title has acquired a secondary meaning.

This court, in speaking of the word 'public', has said that it "* * * does not mean all the people, nor most of the people, nor very many of the people of a place, but so many of them as contradistinguishes them for a few". Mary Pickford Co. v. Bayly Bros., Inc., 12 Cal.2d 501, 514, 86 P.2d 102, 108. The title of a play produced only in New York may acquire a secondary meaning which entitles it to protection throughout the United States. Aronson v. Fleckenstein, C.C., 28 F. 75; Hemingway v. Film Alliance of the United States, Inc., 174 Misc. 725, 21 N.Y.S.2d 827; Frohman v. Payton, 34 Misc. 275, 68 N.Y.S. 849. And the writer of a play recovered damages for the unauthorized use of its title although it was never produced in any city in the United States but had run for some weeks in Paris, France. Frohman v. Wm. Morris, 68 Misc. 461, 123 N.Y.S. 1090.

Popularity is not a requirement for secondary meaning because notoriety and adverse discussion may bring about widespread identification of the play by its title and may pique the public interest. Likewise, advertising, even of an unpopular play, may cause the public to identify it as one which has been a 'Broadway production'.

Although some decisions indicate that the word or phrase constituting the title must have been used '* * * long and * * * exclusively by one producer with reference to his article * * *', G. & C. Merriam Co. v. Saalfield, 6 Cir., 198 F. 369, 373, and, in some cases, the length of the use may be persuasive, the essence of the acquisition of secondary meaning is the impact upon the public mind. 'The duration of user required to create a secondary meaning can be measured by no accurate test. In the Yorkshire Relish case the time was twenty-five years, * * * in the Anatolia Licorice case, six weeks. From these instances it will be seen that there is no rule as to the length of time required.' Nims, Unfair Competition and Trade Marks (4th Ed.1947), vol. 1, sec. 38a, p. 162.

Judge Learned Hand has said in relation to trademarks that '* * * it is the priority of user alone that controls, even though, when the defendant comes into the field, it may not be fully established, or may not even be enough established to have become associated largely in the public mind with the plaintiff's make. * * * Were it not so, it would be of extreme difficulty to show at just what point in time the mark became associated with the maker in enough of his customers' minds to justify the inference that the defendant's use might have become confusing. Therefore, once his use begins, the rest of the public must avoid his fanciful mark.' Waldes v. International Manufacturers' Agency, Inc., D.C., 237 F. 502, 505.

Universal claims that, in order to gain secondary meaning, the title must be associated specifically with the author of the play rather than with the play. The contention is unrealistic and contrary to authority. 'Secondary meaning may exist between a name and the manufacturer or seller whose identity is not known to the buyer * * *. He (the buyer) does not know its (the manufacturer's) name, or its location, or whether it is a corporation or an individual.' Nims, Unfair Competition and Trade Marks (4th Ed.1947), vol. 1, sec. 42, pp. 169, 170.

In all probability only a very small percentage of persons who know something about plays can remember or identify the names of the authors. Usually, advertising and publicity are concentrated upon the title and the actors rather than the name of the playwright. There is no logical basis for holding that a public well acquainted with the title and the play could not confer secondary meaning upon that title merely because of unfamiliarity with the author's name.

The question of abandonment falls within the same category; it is one of fact to be determined by the jury upon substantial evidence. International Film Service, Inc. v. Associated Producers, Inc., D.C., 273 F. 585; Goldman v. R.K.O. Radio Pictures, Inc., 149 Misc. 226, 267 N.Y.S. 28. In Goldman v. R.K.O. Radio Pictures, Inc., supra, 267 N.Y.S. at page 29, the court stated: '* * * a lapse of thirteen years in the use of a title, under the circumstances of this case, raises a question of fact as to whether the title ('The Public Defender') still retains a secondary significance * * *.'

In the present case, there is evidence that several plays written by Jackson had been sold to motion picture producers, from two to ten years after they were produced in New York. It is also significant that in the United States, copyrights protect literary and dramatic properties for an initial period of 28 years with the right of renewal. The evidence, that Jackson had not produced his play for two years after it had closed in New York, does not compel a holding, as a matter of law, that he had abandoned his rights.

The instruction given at the request of Jackson and attacked as prejudicially erroneous refers to exhibits showing the extent of the advertising in the eastern cities at a total cost of $3,300. It is argued that although the court correctly directed the jury not to allow compensation for this expense, the cost of the advertising charges should not have been allowed in evidence. But the instruction directed the jury to limit its consideration to '* * * the value of the title in question and whether it had acquired a secondary meaning as hereinbefore defined, as a result of volume or extent of advertising.' Considering the instruction as a whole, it correctly presented the applicable rule of law.

The rejected instructions concerned the principle that there is not [a] property right implicit in the name or title of a literary work until a secondary meaning has attached to it. But in at least five different instructions, one of which was requested by Universal, the jury was told that the burden of proving a secondary meaning to the title of his play rested upon Jackson. Read together, they adequately covered the subject.

Considering the issue of damages, the sum of $17,500 does not appear to be excessive. The record includes testimony to the effect that other titles to unsuccessful plays have been sold for larger amounts. The value of property wrongfully taken is a matter for the determination of the jury and the evidence as a whole supports the award in Jackson's favor.

The conduct of counsel attacked as prejudicial was the cross-examination of an expert witness of Universal. He was asked whether he was prejudiced because his employer 'was just held for $25,000 damages in an action (of the same kind).' The objection of Universal was sustained, and the jury directed to disregard the whole incident. Another occurrence, cited as misconduct, involved a quarrel between counsel as to which of them submitted a certain document.

There is no showing that the reference to other litigation was untrue. Considering the record as a whole and the ruling upon the motion for a new trial, it cannot be said that the misconduct was prejudicial.

The judgment is affirmed.

THOMSON v. LARSON
147 F.3d 195 (2d Cir. 1998)

CALABRESI, Circuit Judge.

Plaintiff-appellant Lynn Thomson claims that, along with principal playwright Jonathan Larson, now deceased, she co-authored a "new version" of the critically acclaimed Broadway musical Rent. Since Thomson and Larson did not specify their respective rights by contract, this case raises two issues: (1) whether Rent qualifies as a statutory "joint work," co-authored by Thomson; and (2) whether, even if Thomson is not deemed a co-author, she automatically retains exclusive copyright interests in the material she contributed to the work. The first question is squarely answered by the nuanced co-authorship test announced in Childress v. Taylor, 945 F.2d 500 (2d Cir.1991), and, on that basis, we affirm the district court's conclusion that Thomson is not a co-author of Rent. The second question—ownership of a copyright (in the absence of any written contract) in a "non-co-author's" contribution to a work—was not addressed in Childress. Because Thomson did not plead infringement of any such putative copyright interest, however, this issue is not properly before us, and so we do not decide it.

BACKGROUND

The facts given below and found by the district court are essentially uncontested.

Rent, the Pulitzer Prize and Tony Award-winning Broadway modern musical based on Puccini's opera La Boheme, began in 1989 as the joint project of Billy Aronson and composer Jonathan Larson. Aronson and Larson collaborated on the work until their amicable separation in 1991. At that time, Larson obtained Aronson's permission to develop the play on his own. By written agreement, Larson promised that the title would always be "RENT a rock opera by Jonathan Larson. Original concept and additional lyrics by Billy Aronson." In return, Aronson agreed that he would "not...be considered [an] active collaborator or co-author of RENT."

From 1989-1991, the names of both Larson and Aronson appeared on the title pages of Rent drafts (in identical typeface). After their separation, Larson moved Aronson's credit from the title page to the final page of the Rent scripts. [Nevertheless,] Larson agreed that Aronson would be compensated at "the standard going rate" if the play ever made any money. Aronson later transferred his copyrights to the heirs of Jonathan Larson in exchange for four percent of the authors' share of royalties.

In the summer of 1992, Larson's Rent script was favorably received by James Nicola, Artistic Director of the New York Theatre Workshop ("NYTW"), a non-profit theater company in the East Village. Larson continued to develop and revise the "workshop version" of his Rent script. In the spring of 1993, Nicola urged Larson to allow the NYTW to hire a playwright or a bookwriter to help revamp the storyline and narrative structure of the play. But Larson "absolutely, vehemently and totally rejected [Nicola's] suggestion of hiring a bookwriter" and "was insistent on making RENT entirely his own project." Larson received a grant in the spring of 1994 to pay for a workshop production of Rent, which was presented to the public in the fall of 1994 in a series of ten staged performances produced by the NYTW and directed by Michael Greif. "[T]he professional consensus concerning the show, after the studio production, was that it was, at a minimum, very promising and that it needed a great deal of work." Artistic Director Nicola once again suggested to Larson that he consider working with a bookwriter, which Larson "adamantly and steadfastly refused, consistently emphasizing his intention to be the only author of RENT."

In May 1995, in preparation for Rent's off-Broadway opening scheduled for early 1996, Larson agreed to the NYTW's hiring of Lynn Thomson, a professor of advanced playwrighting at New York University, as a dramaturg to assist him in clarifying the storyline of the musical. Thomson signed a contract with the NYTW, in which she agreed to provide her services with the workshop production from May 1, 1995, through the press opening, scheduled for early February of 1996. The agreement stated that Thomson's "responsibilities shall include, but not be limited to: Providing dramaturgical assistance and research to the playwright and director." In exchange, the NYTW agreed to pay "a fee" of $2000, "[i]n full consideration of the services to be rendered" and to provide for billing credit for Thomson as "Dramaturg." The Thomson/NYTW agreement was silent as to any copyright interests or any issue of ownership with respect to the final work.

Dramaturgs provide a range of services to playwrights and directors in connection with the production and development of theater pieces. According to Thomson's testimony, the role of the dramaturg "can include any number of the elements that go into the crafting of a play," such as "actual plot elements, dramatic structure, character details, themes, and even specific language."

In the summer and fall of 1995, Thomson and Larson worked extremely intensively together on the show. For the most part, the two worked on the script alone in Larson's apartment. Thomson testified that revisions to the text of Rent didn't begin until early August 1995. Larson himself entered all changes directly onto his computer, where he kept the script, and Thomson made no contemporaneous notes of her specific contributions of language or other structural or thematic suggestions. Thomson alludes to the "October Version" of Rent as the culmination of her collaborative efforts with Larson. That new version was characterized by experts as "a radical transformation of the show."

A "sing-through" of the "October Version" of Rent took place in early November 1995. [O]n November 3, 1995, Larson signed a contract with the NYTW for ongoing revisions to Rent. This agreement identified Larson as the "Author" of Rent and made no reference to Thomson. The contract incorporated by reference an earlier draft author's agreement that set forth the terms that would apply if the NYTW opted to produce Rent. The earlier draft author's agreement gave Larson approval rights over all changes in text, provided that any changes in text would become his property, and assured him billing as "sole author." On November 30, 1995, Larson signed an option deal with the Broadway producers. This contract defined the royalty payments and other entitlements that would flow to Larson as "Author."

The final dress rehearsal was held on January 24, 1996. Just hours after it ended, Larson died suddenly of an aortic aneurysm. Over the next few weeks, Nicola, Greif, Thomson, and musical director Tim Weil worked together to fine-tune the script. All four agreed that they would not claim authorship in any of the material created during this time. Accordingly, before Rent opened off-Broadway, Nancy Dickmann, Managing Director of the NYTW, asked each of them to sign waivers disclaiming any copyright interest in the material they contributed. Thomson alone refused.

The play opened off-Broadway on February 13, 1996, to rave reviews. On February 23, Rent's move to Broadway was announced. Since its opening on Broadway on April 29, 1996, the show has been "an astounding critical, artistic, and commercial success."

Before the Broadway opening, Thomson, in view of her contributions to Rent, sought compensation and title page dramaturgical credit from the Broadway producers. [O]n April 2, 1996, she signed a contract in which the producers agreed to pay her $10,000 plus a nominal $50/week for her dramaturgical services. Around the same time, upon the producers' advice, Thomson approached Allan S. Larson, Nanette Larson, and Julie Larson McCollum ("Larson Heirs"), the surviving members of Jonathan Larson's family, to request a percentage of the royalties derived from the play. In a letter to the Larson family, dated April 8, 1996, Thomson stated that she believed Larson, had he lived, would have offered her a "small percentage of his royalties to acknowledge the contribution I made." In reply, the Larson Heirs offered Thomson a gift of 1% of the author's royalties. This offer was subsequently doubled (to 2%), according to the Larson Heirs, in response to Thomson's requests and her mention of health problems. According to the Larson Heirs, Thomson rejected this offer, and further communications ended after Thomson demanded the right to use the Rent libretto in a book that she planned to write.

After the parties failed to reach a settlement, Thomson brought suit against the Larson Heirs, claiming that she was a co-author of Rent and that she had never assigned, licensed, or otherwise transferred her rights. Thomson sought declaratory relief and a retroactive and on-going accounting under the Copyright Act. Specifically, she asked that the court declare her a "co-author" of Rent and grant her 16% of the author's share of the royalties.

Thomson's amended complaint alleges that "she developed the plot and theme, contributed extensively to the story, created many character elements, wrote a significant portion of the dialogue and song lyrics, and made other copyrightable contributions to the Work." Thomson claims that she seeks 16% of the proceeds "because of her respect for Larson's role as the principal creator of the work." Thomson derives the 16% figure in the following way: she alleges that 48% of the Rent script is new in relation to the 1994 Workshop version (prior to her involvement); as co-author, she is, therefore, entitled to 50% of this part (or 24% of the total revenues); but since there are three components to Rent (book, lyrics, and music) and she did not contribute to one (music), she is entitled to 2/3, or 16% of the total revenues. Thomson also [seeks] the right to quote freely from various versions of Rent in a book that she plan[s] to write.

A bench trial was held in the United States District Court for the Southern District of New York (Lewis A. Kaplan, Judge) from July 18-23, 1997. Judge Kaplan considered the testimony of over two dozen witnesses, as well as thousands of pages of documentary evidence, including Rent scripts, playbills, production notes, journal entries, and correspondence. In a decision rendered from the bench, Judge Kaplan concluded that Thomson was not a joint author of Rent and dismissed the remainder of Thomson's complaint.

On appeal, Thomson concedes that she has "virtually no disagreement with the District Court's findings with respect to what happened between her and Jon Larson, or with respect to the evidence of Larson's intent." Instead, the focus of Thomson's appeal is on whether the district court correctly applied the "Childress test of co-authorship," and, secondarily, whether the district court's declaration that Thomson is not a co-author nevertheless means that she retains exclusive copyright interests in any material that she contributed to the work.

DISCUSSION

The district court properly defined the principal question in this case as: "not whether Lynn Thomson made a great contribution to the show. It is not whether she has been or ought to be compensated differently than she has been compensated. It is about whether what happened between Lynn Thomson and Jon Larson met the statutory definition as it has been construed by the higher courts of a joint work." In analyzing this issue, the district court made numerous findings of fact and then applied the Childress test to these facts.

We review the district court's finding of facts for clear error. See Fed.R.Civ.P. 52(a); Anderson v. City of Bessemer City, 470 U.S. 564, 574-75, 105 S.Ct. 1504, 84 L.Ed.2d 518 (1985). And in this respect, the issue of intent is ordinarily a question of fact. See W. Alton Jones Found. v. Chevron U.S.A., Inc., 97 F.3d 29, 33 (2d Cir.1996). If, however, "a district court makes findings of fact predicated upon an incorrect legal standard such findings are not binding on an appellate court." Weissmann v. Freeman, 868 F.2d 1313, 1317 (2d Cir.1989). The "application of th[e] facts to draw conclusions of law," we review de novo. See FDIC v. Providence College, 115 F.3d 136, 140 (2d Cir.1997).

I. THOMSON'S CO-AUTHORSHIP CLAIM

A. Statutory Definition of "Joint Work"

Thomson's request for a declaratory judgment establishing her co-authorship under the Copyright Act of 1976, 17 U.S.C. §§ 101 et seq., requires us to interpret and apply the copyright ownership provisions of the Act. The Copyright Act defines a "joint work" as "a work prepared by two or more authors with the intention that their contributions be merged into inseparable or interdependent parts of a unitary whole." 17 U.S.C. § 101 (1994). The touchstone of the statutory definition "is the intention at the time the writing is done that the parts be absorbed or combined into an integrated unit." H.R.Rep. No. 1476, 94th Cong. 120, 121 (1976), reprinted in 1976 U.S.Code Cong. & Admin. News 5659, 5735.

Joint authorship entitles the co-authors to equal undivided interests in the whole work—in other words, each joint author has the right to use or to license the work as he or she wishes, subject only to the obligation to account to the other joint owner for any profits that are made. See 17 U.S.C. § 201(a); Childress, 945 F.2d at 508; Community for Creative Non-Violence v. Reid, 846 F.2d 1485, 1498 (D.C.Cir.1988) ("Joint authors co-owning copyright in a work are deemed to be tenants in common, with each having an independent right to use or license the copyright, subject only to a duty to account to the other co-owner for any profits earned thereby."), aff'd. without consideration on this point, 490 U.S. 730, 109 S.Ct. 2166, 104 L.Ed.2d 811 (1989).

B. Childress Requirements

In Childress v. Taylor, [945 F.2d 500 (2d Cir. 1991)], our court interpreted this section of the Act and set forth "standards for determining when a contributor to a copyrighted work is entitled to be regarded as a joint author" where the parties have failed to sign any written agreement dealing with coauthorship. 945 F.2d at 501. While the Copyright Act states only that co-authors must intend that their contributions "be merged into...a unitary whole," in Childress, Judge Newman explained why a more stringent inquiry than the statutory language would seem to suggest is required:

> [A]n inquiry so limited would extend joint author status to many persons who are not likely to have been within the contemplation of Congress. For example, a writer frequently works with an editor who makes numerous useful revisions to the first draft, some of which will consist of additions of copyrightable expression. Both intend their contributions to be merged into inseparable parts of a unitary whole, yet very few editors and even fewer writers would expect the editor to be accorded the status of joint author, enjoying an undivided half interest in the copyright in the published work.

Id. at 507.

The facts of Childress highlighted this concern with "overreaching" contributors. Actress Clarice Taylor wrote a script based on the life of legendary comedienne Jackie "Moms" Mabley, but Taylor was unable to get it produced as a play. Taylor convinced playwright Alice Childress to rescue the project by writing a new script. After Childress' completion of the script, Taylor took a copy of Childress' copyrighted play and produced it at another theater without permission. See id. at 503. Childress sued Taylor for copyright infringement, and Taylor asserted a defense of co-authorship. See id. at 504. Taylor alleged joint authorship, notwithstanding the fact that, as she conceded, her major role had been researching the historical background for the script. See Childress, 945 F.2d at 502.

The court concluded that there was "no evidence that [Taylor's contribution] ever evolved into more than the helpful advice that might come from the cast, the directors, or the producers of any play." Id. at 509. On that basis, the court upheld a grant of summary judgment for Childress. See id. The court stated that Childress had "always insisted upon her status as the sole author," noting that Childress had registered the copyrights in her own name and had refused to sign an agreement proposed by Taylor that provided that the play would be jointly owned.

The potential danger of allowing anyone who makes even a minimal contribution to the writing of a work to be deemed a statutory co-author—as long as the two parties intended the contributions to merge—motivated the court to set forth a two-pronged test. A co-authorship claimant bears the burden of establishing that each of the putative co-authors (1) made independently copyrightable contributions to the work; and (2) fully intended to be co-authors. See id. at 507-08. The court attempted to strike a balance between "ensur[ing] that true collaborators in the creative process are accorded the perquisites of co-authorship," id. at 504, while at the same time, "guard[ing] against the risk that a sole author is denied exclusive authorship status simply because another person render[s] some form of assistance," id.

1. Independently Copyrightable Contributions

Childress held that collaboration alone is not sufficient to establish joint authorship. Rather, the contribution of each joint author must be independently copyrightable. See 945 F.2d at 507. It noted that this is "the position taken by the case law and endorsed by the agency administering the Copyright Act." Id.; see Seshadri v. Kasraian, 130 F.3d 798, 803 (7th Cir.1997); M.G.B. Homes, Inc. v. Ameron Homes, Inc., 903 F.2d 1486, 1493 (11th Cir.1990).

Without making specific findings as to any of Thomson's claims regarding lyrics or other contributions, the district court concluded that Thomson "made at least some non-de minimis copyrightable contribution," and that Thomson's contributions to the Rent libretto were "certainly not zero." Judge Kaplan stated that "there are lines in Rent that originated verbatim with Ms. Thomson. I don't think they amount to 9 percent, and certainly not zero. There is probably enough there that it is not de minimis."

Once having said that, the court decided the case on the second Childress prong—mutual intent of co-authorship. It hence did not reach the issue of the individual copyrightability of Thomson's varied alleged contributions (plot developments, thematic elements, character details, and structural components).

2. Intent of the Parties

a. Mutual Intent Requirement

Childress mandates that the parties "entertain in their minds the concept of joint authorship." 945 F.2d at 508. This requirement of mutual intent recognizes that, since co-authors are afforded equal rights in the co-authored work, the "equal sharing of rights should be reserved for relationships in which all participants fully intend to be joint authors." Id. at 509. The court added that "[t]he sharing of benefits in other relationships involving assistance in the creation of a copyrightable work can be more precisely calibrated by the participants in their contract negotiations regarding division of royalties or assignment of shares of ownership of the copyright." Childress, 945 F.2d at 509 (citing 17 U.S.C. §201(d)).

The Childress court noted that "[a]n inquiry into how the putative joint authors regarded themselves in relation to the work has previously been part of our approach in ascertaining the existence of joint authorship." Id. at 508 (citing Gilliam v. American Broad. Cos., Inc., 538 F.2d 14, 22 (2d Cir.1976); Fisher v. Klein, 16 U.S.P.Q.2d 1795,

1798 (S.D.N.Y.1990); Maurel v. Smith, 220 F. 195, 198 (S.D.N.Y.1915), aff'd, 271 F. 211 (2d Cir.1921)). Moreover, the Childress rule of mutual co-authorship intent has subsequently been followed in this circuit and elsewhere. See, e.g., Erickson v. Trinity Theatre, Inc., 13 F.3d 1061, 1068-69 (7th Cir.1994) (adopting Childress, and noting that "reliance on collaboration alone...would be incompatible with the clear statutory mandate" that there be intent to create a joint work); Design Options, Inc. v. BellePointe, Inc., 940 F.Supp. 86, 90 (S.D.N.Y.1996) ("[B]oth parties must have intended, at the time of creation, that the work be jointly owned."); Papa's-June Music, Inc. v. McLean, 921 F.Supp. 1154, 1157 (S.D.N.Y.1996) ("The requisite intent to create a joint work exists when the putative joint authors intend to regard themselves as joint authors [and] [i]t is not enough that they intend to merge their contributions into one unitary work.").

Childress and its progeny, however, do not explicitly define the nature of the necessary intent to be co-authors. The court stated that "[i]n many instances, a useful test will be whether, in the absence of contractual arrangements concerning listed authorship, each participant intended that all would be identified as co-authors." Childress, 945 F.2d at 508. But it is also clear that the intention standard is not strictly subjective. In other words, co-authorship intent does not turn solely on the parties' own words or professed state of mind. See id. ("[J]oint authorship can exist without any explicit discussion of this topic by the parties."). Rather, the Childress court suggested a more nuanced inquiry into factual indicia of ownership and authorship, such as how a collaborator regarded herself in relation to the work in terms of billing and credit, decisionmaking, and the right to enter into contracts. See id. at 508-09. In this regard, the court stated that "[t]hough joint authorship does not require an understanding by the co-authors of the legal consequences of their relationship, obviously some distinguishing characteristic of the relationship must be understood for it to be the subject of their intent." Id. at 508.

Finally, the Childress court emphasized that the requirement of intent is particularly important where "one person...is indisputably the dominant author of the work and the only issue is whether that person is the sole author or she and another...are joint authors." Id. "Care must be taken...to guard against the risk that a sole author is denied exclusive authorship status simply because another person render[s] some form of assistance." Id. at 504; see also Erickson, 13 F.3d at 1069 ("Those seeking copyrights would not seek further refinement that colleagues may offer if they risked losing their sole authorship.").

Thomson intimates that Childress' stringent mutual intent standard is properly limited, by its facts, to cases involving claimants who have made "minimal contribution[s] to the writing of a work." And she asserts that her purported major contribution of copyrightable expression to Rent, by itself, is evidence of Larson's intent that she be a co-author. Indeed, Thomson goes further and claims that this proof is enough to give her relationship with Larson the "distinguishing characteristics" needed to establish co-authorship. But Childress makes clear that the contribution even of significant language to a work does not automatically suffice to confer co-author status on the contributor. Under Childress, a specific finding of mutual intent remains necessary. See 945 F.2d at 508. We therefore turn to an examination of the factual indicia of ownership and authorship relevant to this inquiry, as they are defined in prior cases.

b. Evidence of Larson's Intent

Under Childress, each putative co-author must intend to be a co-author in order to give rise to a co-author relationship. See 945 F.2d at 508. The Larson Heirs suggest that

"Thomson's lack of co-authorship intent provides a second and independent basis for affirming the decision below." The district court, having found that "Mr. Larson never regarded himself as a joint author with Ms. Thomson," stated that it had no reason to rule on this alternative basis for dismissal. (It noted that "arguments could be made both ways.") Because we affirm the district court's conclusion that Larson lacked co-authorship intent, we too will refrain from addressing Ms. Thomson's intent, except as it may seem to bear on Larson's.

i. Decisionmaking Authority

An important indicator of authorship is a contributor's decisionmaking authority over what changes are made and what is included in a work. See, e.g., Erickson, 13 F.3d at 1071-72 (an actor's suggestion of text does not support a claim of co-authorship where the sole author determined whether and where such contributions were included in the work); see also Maurel, 271 F. at 214-15 (claimant had a contractual right to control the contents of the opera).

The district court determined that Larson "retained and intended to retain at all times sole decision-making authority as to what went into [Rent]." In support of its conclusion, the court relied upon Thomson's statement that she was "flattered that [Larson] was asking [her] to contribute actual language to the text" and found that this statement demonstrated that even Thomson understood "that the question whether any contribution she might make would go into the script was within Mr. Larson's sole and complete discretion." There was also documentary evidence before the district court that confirmed the advisory nature of Thomson's role. Thus, a set of notes Thomson wrote to Larson began, "Please know that everything is intended as a question but might sound differently in the shorthand of the writing." And other notes, addressed to Nicola and Grief, read: "Usual disclaimer; the following is meant to generate discussion. Even when I offer 'solutions' what I mean is only to communicate a response by example...."

Moreover, as the court recognized, the November agreement between Larson and the NYTW expressly stated that Larson had final approval over all changes to Rent and that all such changes would become Larson's property. In this respect, the district court also credited a telephone interview Larson gave in October 1995 to a high school student, in which Larson "said, in substance, that he wrote everything in Rent and distinguished writers in the theater from writers in the other media by saying that in the theater the writer is the king." ("In theater, as opposed to film and television, dramatists retain copyright to their work, [and] are independent contractors....") The district court found this statement significant because it "evidences Mr. Larson's view that Rent in all respects was his, he was the king."

ii. Billing

In discerning how parties viewed themselves in relation to a work, Childress also deemed the way in which the parties bill or credit themselves to be significant. See 945 F.2d at 508 ("Though 'billing' or 'credit' is not decisive in all cases...consideration of the topic helpfully serves to focus the fact-finder's attention on how the parties implicitly regarded their undertaking."). As the district court noted, "billing or credit is...a window on the mind of the party who is responsible for giving the billing or the credit." And a writer's attribution of the work to herself alone is "persuasive proof...that she intended this particular piece to represent her own individual authorship" and is "prima facie proof that [the] work was not intended to be joint." Weissmann, 868 F.2d at 1320.

Thomson claims that Larson's decision to credit her as "dramaturg" on the final page of Rent scripts reflected some co-authorship intent. Thomson argues that this "unprecedented" credit on the copyright page of the script distinguishes her role from that of Larson's many other collaborators, including Artistic Director Nicola, Director Greif, the producers, and a previous dramaturg, none of whom was given similar credit. Thomson concedes that she never sought equal billing with Larson, but argues that she did not need to do so in order to be deemed a statutory co-author.

The district court found, instead, that the billing was unequivocal: Every script brought to [the court's] attention says "Rent, by Jonathan Larson." Similarly, both the Off-Broadway and the Broadway playbills identify Rent as being "by Jonathan Larson," while Thomson is listed as "Dramaturg."

In addition, Larson "described himself in the biography he submitted for the playbill in January 1996, nine days before he died, as the author/composer, and listed Ms. Thomson on the same document as dramaturg." And while, as Ms. Thomson argues, it may indeed have been highly unusual for an author/composer to credit his dramaturg with a byline, we fail to see how Larson's decision to style her as "dramaturg" on the final page in Rent scripts reflects a co-authorship intent on the part of Larson. The district court properly concluded that "the manner in which [Larson] listed credits on the scripts strongly supports the view that he regarded himself as the sole author."

iii. Written Agreements with Third Parties

Just as the parties' written agreements with each other can constitute evidence of whether the parties considered themselves to be co-authors, see Gilliam v. American Broad. Cos., 538 F.2d 14, 22 (2d Cir.1976) (written screenwriters' agreement between the parties indicate that they did not consider themselves joint authors of a single work); Erickson, 13 F.3d at 1072 (licensing agreement evidences lack of co-authorship intent); see also Maurel v. Smith, 271 F. at 214-15 (contracts evidence co-authorship relationship), so the parties' agreements with outsiders also can provide insight into co-authorship intent, albeit to a somewhat more attenuated degree.

The district court found that Larson "listed himself or treated himself as the author in the November 1995 revisions contract that he entered into with the NYTW, which in turn incorporated the earlier draft author's agreement that had not been signed." That agreement identifies Larson as Rent's "Author" and does not mention Thomson. It also incorporates the terms of a September 1995 draft agreement (termed "Author's Agreement") that states that Larson "shall receive billing as sole author." Another provision of the "Author's Agreement" explicitly reserved to Larson all rights in Rent not expressly granted to the NYTW. Such a reservation of rights clause is consistent with Larson's intent to be the work's sole author. See Gilliam, 538 F.2d at 22 (finding that a reservation of rights provision "suggest[s] that the parties did not consider themselves joint authors of a single work").

The district court commented, moreover, that "[t]he fact that [Larson] felt free to enter into the November 1995 contract on his own, without the consent of and without any reference to Ms. Thomson quite apart from whatever the terms of the agreements are, indicates that his intention was to be the sole author."

In addition to Larson's agreements with the NYTW (which were relied upon directly by the district court), on November 30, 1995, Larson agreed to an option deal with the commercial producers defining the royalty payments and other entitlements to flow to him as the "Author" of Rent. Like the November NYTW agreement, this option deal made no reference whatsoever to Thomson. (Indeed, Thomson engaged in no contractual negotiations with the NYTW or with the Broadway producers with respect to authorial rights.)

iv. Additional Evidence

Beside relying on evidence that Larson retained decisionmaking authority over the final work, that he was billed as sole author, and that he entered into written agreements with third parties as sole author, the district court found much other evidence that indicated a lack of intent on Larson's part to make Thomson a co-author.

Thus, at various times during the development of Rent (once shortly before Thomson was hired as dramaturg in the summer of 1995), Artistic Director Nicola suggested to Larson that he work with a bookwriter to assist him in the refinement of the script. Larson, however, "absolutely, vehemently and totally" rejected the idea of a bookwriter and was steadfast in his determination to make Rent "entirely his own project." The district court found that Larson's "rejection of a book writer...speaks to Mr. Larson's intent[ ]...[and] is part of a broader pattern that persuades me that Mr. Larson never intended the joint authorship relationship."

Moreover, the evidence before the district court established that Larson not only understood the concept of co-authorship, but that he had used the term "co-author" on two separate copyright applications for different versions of a screenplay he wrote in 1991 and 1992. Larson had also used the term "co-author" in the November 1993 written agreement with Billy Aronson, which provided that Aronson would "not...be considered an active collaborator or co-author of RENT." On the basis of this evidence, the district court found that, while Larson "understood that the phrase 'co-author' was one freighted with legal significance[ ]...there is absolutely no evidence whatever...that [Larson] ever regarded himself as a co-author with Ms. Thomson of Rent."

Finally, the court relies on "an explicit discussion on the topic of co-authorship" that Thomson claims she and Larson had. According to Thomson's written trial testimony, the conversation was as follows:

> I told him I was flattered that he was asking me to contribute actual language to the text. He responded by saying "Of course I want you to do that!"...He then told me the following: "I'll always acknowledge your contribution," and "I would never say that I wrote what you did."

The district court found that the alleged conversation was "entirely consistent with Mr. Larson's view that he was the sole author and that Ms. Thomson...was the dramaturg, which he conceived to be a different role."

c. Conclusion

Based on all of the evidence, the district court concluded that "Mr. Larson never regarded himself as a joint author with Ms. Thomson." We believe that the district court correctly applied the Childress standards to the evidence before it and hold that its finding that Larson never intended co-authorship was not clearly erroneous.

II. THOMSON'S ALLEGED COPYRIGHT INTERESTS

The Copyright Act declares that "[c]opyright in a work protected under this title vests initially in the author or authors of the work." 17 U.S.C. §201(a). Each author's rights in a joint work are non-exclusive, see id., whereas a sole author retains exclusive rights in his or her own work, see id. § 106.

The work-for-hire provisions are an exception to the rule that copyrights belong in the first instance only to creators. See 17 U.S.C. § 201(b). And in the case of specially ordered or commissioned works, the parties must "expressly agree[ ] in a written instrument" in order for the work to be considered a work for hire. See id.

In this respect, the instant case presents somewhat of a conundrum. "[M]ost dramaturgs work on play scripts as employees of the producing theater company, and even absent an employment agreement waiving ownership of copyrights, in the ordinary course they would not have any copyright interests, under the work-for-hire doctrine." Brief for Amici Curiae The National Writers Union and Literary Managers and Dramaturgs of the Americas, Inc. at 4-5. Thomson, however, independently contracted with the NYTW. (It is unclear whether the NYTW was Larson's agent, but this, seemingly, is of no significance.) Accordingly, there was no written agreement between Thomson and Larson. It is also undisputed that Larson never asked Thomson to state that her contribution would be work for hire, or that she would own no copyrights or transfer them to anyone. (We agree that "[o]ne of the salutary effects of [Thomson's] widely reported assertion of her rights has been in opening up discussions among playwrights and dramaturgs to clarify their respective understandings, and in understanding the advisability of reaching agreements and committing such agreements to writing." Brief for Amici Curiae The National Writers Union and Literary Managers and Dramaturgs of the Americas, Inc. at 19.)

Thomson argues that, if she is not deemed to be a joint author of Rent, then "she must have all of the rights of a sole author with respect to her own contribution." On appeal, she asserts for the first time that the only alternative to finding co-authorship is to split a co-created work into its components—i.e., she must be entitled to withdraw her purported contributions. The National Writers Union, a trade union of freelance writers, and Literary Managers and Dramaturgs of the Americas, Inc., a professional association, as amici curiae in support of Thomson, further suggest that Thomson has grounds to file an infringement suit relating to the same material on which her co-authorship claim is premised. Brief for Amici Curiae The National Writers Union and Literary Managers and Dramaturgs of the Americas, Inc. at 13 n.1.

The Larson Heirs contend that "[u]nder Childress, copyrightable contributions by an editor or other person retained to assist an author belong to the author, absent mutual co-authorship intent." They conclude that "[b]ecause she is not a joint author, Thomson has no rights." In the alternative, the Larson Heirs claim that "even if, despite Childress, the sole author is not the copyright owner of the materials contributed by others, the suggestions proffered by Thomson were impliedly or expressly licensed to Larson for use in Rent." Id. In a similar vein, The Dramatists Guild, Inc., a professional association of playwrights, librettists, composers, and lyricists, posits that "[g]iven the collaborative nature of theater, any 'contribution' of copyrightable material should be understood as conveying with it to the playwright a non-exclusive license to use the collaborator's material in the work, absent some other arrangement in writing." Brief for Amicus Curiae The Dramatists Guild, Inc. at 30.

Our circuit has not decided whether a person who makes a non-de minimis copyrightable contribution but cannot meet the mutual intent requirement of co-authorship, retains, in the absence of a work-for-hire agreement or of any explicit contractual assignment of the copyright, any rights and interests in his or her own contribution. This issue, however, was not presented to the district court by the parties. The only ground for relief asserted by Thomson was her purported co-authorship of Rent. Thomson's assertion that, if she is not deemed a co-author, she has exclusive rights with respect to the material that she contributed to Rent, is raised for the first time on appeal:

> [I]f it were to be affirmed that Rent is not a statutory joint work, [Thomson] then would be awarded rights which she never imagined, much less sought, and which she would be loathe to enforce. Under Section 106, she would have the right to enjoin any use of her contributions in any stage production, book, cast album, or motion picture.

Brief for Appellant at 44. In other words, she contends that "other than an argument of joint authorship between Thomson and Larson, there would be no defense to an infringement suit brought by Thomson." Brief for Amici Curiae The National Writers Union and Literary Managers and Dramaturgs of the Americas, Inc. at 13 n.1.

But Thomson has not brought such an infringement suit. Nor has she yet attempted to restrain any use of her allegedly copyrighted material. Accordingly, the district court had no occasion to rule on: (1) whether Thomson, if not deemed a co-author, nevertheless had copyright interests in the material that she contributed to Rent or, alternatively, (2) whether Thomson granted Larson a license to use the material that she purportedly contributed to Rent, and if so on what terms. Because these issues were not raised below and therefore are not properly before us, we express no opinion on them.

CONCLUSION

The district court found that Jonathan Larson lacked the requisite intent to accept Lynn Thomson as a co-author of Rent. We hold that the district court properly applied the Childress v. Taylor test of co-authorship and that its factual finding with respect to Larson's intent is not clearly erroneous. We therefore affirm the judgment of the district court.

AMPERSAND PRODUCTIONS, INC. v. STAHL
1986 WL 2449 (E.D. Pa. 1986)

NEWCOMER, District Judge.

This case arises out of a disintegrating business relationship between the two principals of a close corporation, Ampersand Productions, Inc. ("Ampersand"), and presents two distinct claims. First, the parties contest ownership of the copyright of the musical play "Philly's Beat." Plaintiff seeks injunctive and monetary relief for infringement of its copyright in the play; defendant seeks declaratory judgment of its ownership of "Philly's Beat." In the alternative, plaintiff contends that defendant Stephen Stahl usurped a business opportunity properly belonging to Ampersand, namely, the production of the play "Philly's Beat." For the reasons discussed below, I conclude that the defendant properly owns the copyright to the play "Philly's Beat," and therefore plaintiff's infringement action fails.

This Court has jurisdiction over the copyright infringement claim. 28 U.S.C. § 1338(a). Jurisdiction is also proper over the corporate opportunity claim on the basis of pendant jurisdiction. Venue is proper in this district. 28 U.S.C. § 1391(b).

FINDINGS OF FACT

I make the following findings of fact pursuant to Fed.R.Civ.P. 52(a).

Asher Hyman ("Hyman") and Stephen Stahl ("Stahl") began their business association in December 1984. Prior to their association, Hyman graduated from college in 1980 and worked as a bartender and in bar management. Stahl has worked in theater approximately twenty years, as a producer and director of plays.

In late 1984, Stahl and Hyman met at Ripley's, a nightclub in Philadelphia. At that time, Stahl was working there directing a play, and Hyman was tending and managing one of the bars.

As a result of their meeting, and some discussions, Stahl and Hyman formed Ampersand, a Pennsylvania corporation, in January 1985, with Stahl and Hyman as equal 50% shareholders. Hyman was appointed president and treasurer, Stahl the secretary of the corporation.

In addition to their duties as directors of Ampersand, both Stahl and Hyman were employed by the corporation, Stahl as "Artistic Director" and director of plays and Hyman as the producer, at salaries of $300 per week. Hyman was also responsible for managing the finances of the corporation, including handling the corporate checking account opened at Continental Bank. At the time of incorporation, Stahl and Hyman did not understand that Stahl's duties as an employee of Ampersand would include writing plays for the corporation to produce.

Following incorporation of Ampersand, Stahl negotiated a four-year lease of premises which Ampersand named "The Bank Street Theatre" in Philadelphia, which lease was executed by Ampersand. Ampersand spent approximately $15,000 to prepare the theater for use. The lease payments on the Bank Street Theater were $1300 per month.

Prior to their meeting, Stahl had acquired certain rights to produce a play known as "Sister Mary Ignatius Explains It All For You."

In March 1985, Ampersand produced the play "Sister Mary Ignatius" at the Bank Street Theatre, which play ran until the Memorial Day weekend of May 1985.

Prior to the closing of "Sister Mary Ignatius," Stahl and Hyman discussed their plans for the next play to be produced at the Bank Street Theater. Initially, they discussed use of a play called "Let's Twist Again," a history of rock and roll then being developed by Stahl, incorporating various best selling recordings.

In April 1985, Ampersand retained the services of Gracia, Francis & Associates ("GFA") to assist Stahl and Hyman in planning for their next play, paying a $400 monthly retainer in May and June 1985.

GFA conducted certain copyright searches of songs to be used in "Let's Twist Again," and inquired about possible use of Chubby Checker for a cameo role in the play. It was then determined that the costs and other problems associated with "Let's Twist Again" made that play unfit for production by Ampersand. As a result of this determination, Stahl never wrote "Let's Twist Again."

In mid-May 1985, Glenda Gracia of GFA and Stahl together developed the idea that the concept of "Let's Twist Again" be recast to focus on Philadelphia music and the history of rock and roll in Philadelphia.

On Thursday, May 23, 1985, Hyman drove Stahl to the Hacienda Inn in New Hope, Pennsylvania for the purpose of getting seclusion to write a story line and script for the Philadelphia-based musical play, later to become known as "Philly's Beat."

Stahl left the Hacienda Inn on Saturday morning, May 25, 1985, having completed writing a story line and script for "Philly's Beat."

Stahl registered at the Hacienda Inn as a representative of Ampersand in order to qualify for the discounted room and board rates given to corporations. Stahl, not Ampersand, paid for the expenses incurred during Stahl's stay at the Hacienda Inn. Ampersand did not reimburse Stahl for the expenses he incurred.

Hyman's testimony that Ampersand provided money to Stahl for his expenses while writing the play through checks written on the corporate account to the order of "Cash" or "Stephen Stahl," which checks were endorsed by Hyman either in his own name or in Stahl's, lacks sufficient credibility to establish that Stahl actually received the cash.

Stahl took with him to the Hacienda Inn some books on the history of rock and roll lent to him by GFA, then on retainer with Ampersand.

Stahl returned from New Hope [and] showed his handwritten manuscripts of "Philly's Beat" to Hyman. Shortly thereafter, Hyman, listening to Stahl's dictation, and reading from the handwritten manuscript, typed "Philly's Beat."

The cover page of the play manuscript typed by Hyman attributed authorship to Stahl. The word "copyright" followed only by the year 1985 appeared in the lower right corner. After the play was typed, several copies were made for Hyman and GFA.

GFA was also given a list of the pre-existing works in "Philly's Beat" in order to acquire rights to copyrighted songs for use in the play.

Sometime during the last week of May, 1985, Ampersand began work for the production of "Philly's Beat." Pre-production budgets were prepared, and GFA prepared a "concept proposal" and "Limited Partnership Agreement" for the production.

During June, 1985, Ampersand continued plans for production of "Philly's Beat," auditions were held and possible investors located. During this time, however, since Ampersand had no income, Hyman sought financial assistance from his parents, who lent the Corporation a total of $20,000 to pay salaries and expenses. Stahl arranged for and acquired an investor, Vincent Fortunato, who placed $20,000 in a separate corporate bank account with Mellon Bank to be used exclusively for "Philly's Beat."

During the latter part of June 1985, Stahl and Hyman began to experience friction in the production of "Philly's Beat." Unknown to Hyman, Stahl wanted to open the play at another theater, "Grendel's Lair," and Stahl began to hold discussions with that theater's owner. Also at this time, Hyman failed to come to work and otherwise perform his duties, disrupting the pre-production development of the play. On or about June 21, 1985, Hyman withdrew all remaining funds in the Ampersand account at Continental Bank, without the knowledge or consent of Stahl.

On June 25, 1985, the principal investor in the play, Vincent Fortunato, a friend and associate of Stahl, demanded that Ampersand return his $20,000 investment in "Philly's Beat." Ampersand complied with this demand, and returned the money.

Stahl delivered a letter to Hyman on June 27, 1985, purporting to resign his corporate positions and employment by Ampersand.

On July 1, 1985, Stahl signed a lease to open "Philly's Beat" at Grendel's Lair under the fictitious business name "Three Numbers Productions." Three Numbers Productions then produced and opened the play at Grendel's Lair.

As of the date of trial, "Philly's Beat" earned gross income of approximately $31,000. At the same time, the expenses from staging the show have been $9,000 per week for nine weeks, totalling approximately $81,000. The lease payments at Grendel's Lair were $1,400 per week.

On June 28, 1985, Ampersand registered and obtained a Certificate of Copyright Registration for "Philly's Beat" under Registration Number PAu 733-505, as a "work made for hire."

On July 26, 1985, Stahl registered and obtained a Certificate of Copyright Registration for "Philly's Beat" under Registration Number PAu 735-422.

CONCLUSIONS OF LAW

1. The Copyright Claims.

At the core of the competing claims of copyright ownership, as well as plaintiff's infringement claim, is a dispute over whether the defendant wrote "Philly's Beat" within the scope of his employment with Ampersand. Section 201 of the Copyright Act provides, in pertinent part:

> (a) Initial Ownership. Copyright in a work protected under this title vests initially in the author or authors of the work.
>
> (b) Works Made for Hire. In the case of a work made for hire, the employer or other persons for whom the work was prepared is considered the author for purposes of this title, and, unless the parties have expressly agreed otherwise in a written instrument signed by them, owns all of the rights comprised in the copyright.

Section 101 defines a work made for hire, again in relevant part, as "a work prepared by an employee within the scope of his or her employment." See, e.g., Roth v. Pritkin, 710 F.2d 934 (2d Cir.), cert. denied 464 U.S. 961 (1983) (finding authorship in employer, as work made for hire).

The parties do not dispute that Stahl was the sole author, in the sense in which that term is commonly understood, of the play "Philly's Beat." Rather, plaintiff asserts that Stahl wrote the play within the scope of his employment with Ampersand, thus affording Ampersand copyright ownership under section 201(b) as a work made for hire.

The Copyright Act does not define "employee" or "scope of employment," although it uses these terms. Rather, it applies the test used at common law to determine whether an individual working on behalf of another is an independent contractor or an employee. Aitken, Hazen, Hoffman, Miller, P.C. v. Empire Construction Co., 542 F.Supp. 252, 257 (D.Nebr.1982).

In making such a determination, a court must consider various factors. First the court must consider "whether the work was created at the employer's insistence and expense or, in other words, whether the motivating factor in producing the work was the employer who induced its creation." Murray v. Gelderman, 566 F.2d 1307, 1310 (5th Cir.1978) (citing Siegel v. National Periodical Publications, Inc., 508 F.2d 909 (2d Cir.1974)).

A second factor is whether the employer had the right—whether or not exercised—"to direct and to supervise the manner in which the work was being performed." Scherr v. Universal Match Corp., 417 F.2d 497, 500 (2d Cir.1969) (interpreting the parallel provision of the 1909 Copyright Act).

Finally, a court should consider the nature and amount of compensation, or the absence of compensation, received by the author for his work. Everts v. Arkham House Publishers Inc., 579 F.Supp. 145, 148 (W.D.Wisc.1984). In Everts, Richard Tierney submitted poems he had written to plaintiff for publication. Everts and Tierney agreed that

Everts would publish the poems, and the two of them would share the revenues produced by their sale. The court decided that Tierney retained the copyright, and yielded to Everts a license to publish the poetry. The court explained:

> Courts have found that the copyright belonged to the purchaser/employer and not the artist/independent contractor when the artist was paid a sum certain for the creation of a work according to the purchaser's specifications and the course of dealing between the parties established that the purchaser was buying the work and all the rights to it. Conversely, when the artist's compensation depended upon factors outside of either party's control, the artist created the work independently, and the course of dealing between the parties established that the artist would retain the copyright, courts have held that the work was not created for hire and the copyright accrued to the artist. (Citations omitted).

Id. at 148-49.

Assessing all of these factors, I conclude that "Philly's Beat" was not a work made for hire and that Stahl, as the author, owns the copyright. Plaintiff failed to establish by the requisite preponderance of evidence that it bore the expenses associated with the creation of the work. And while Stahl wrote "Philly's Beat" with the clear intention of producing it through Ampersand, neither Stahl nor Hyman envisioned at the time the show was written that Ampersand would own the copyright. Furthermore, there was no evidence that Ampersand had the right to direct or supervise Stahl in his creation of the show. This is true even though Stahl manifestly created "Philly's Beat" in the form it finally assumed because he intended Ampersand to produce the show. The informality with which responsibilities were defined within this close corporation as a practical matter blurs the distinction which the law attempts to draw clearly. But I do not believe that Ampersand possessed the right to control Stahl's creation of the work, despite its interest in the outcome. In addition, Stahl's compensation for the creation of "Philly's Beat" was entirely contingent on the success of Ampersand's production of the show, and the consequent profitability of the corporation. Under these circumstances, I must conclude that "Philly's Beat" was not created as a work for hire, and that Stahl owns the copyright.

Plaintiff strenuously advocated that, because Stahl did not expressly reserve his rights in the play with a writing, as required by section 201(b), the copyright necessarily belongs to Ampersand. This position is flawed, however, because it assumes a proposition which plaintiff failed to prove: that the play was written within the scope of Stahl's employment. Only if the work was created within the scope of Stahl's employment, thus qualifying as a work made for hire under section 101, would a written reservation of right, discussed in section 201, be required. Because I have concluded that "Philly's Beat" was not created within the scope of Stahl's employment, no written reservation is required for Stahl to maintain his ownership of the copyright.

[The remainder of the court's opinion is omitted.]

Notes

1. It can be argued that all four of the foregoing cases were wrongly decided: Ntreh, by first choosing and then making changes to Rive's play, however minimal they might have been, did display at least some "authorial judgment"; Jackson's coining of the phrase "Slightly Scandalous" was really too little to qualify him as an author; Thomson's contributions to "Rent" were such that without them the show would not have become

the Broadway hit it did; and Stahl had no right to keep for himself work so clearly done on Ampersand's time and in its field. So what accounts for the decisions coming out as they do?

2. In September 1998, three months after the Second Circuit handed down its ruling, the Larson heirs reached an out-of-court settlement with Lynn Thomson. *See* Jesse McKinley, *Another Claim Upon 'Rent,'* N.Y. Times, Sept. 18, 1998, at E1. This, however, was not the end of their troubles. Since February 1996, author Sarah Schulman had been contending that Larson had plagiarized her 1990 novel, *People in Trouble*, to write "Rent." Schulman went so far as to hire a lawyer, but eventually decided not to sue. Instead, she wrote a blistering book in which she laid out her charges against Larson. *See* Sarah Schulman, *Stagestruck: Theater, AIDS, and the Marketing of Gay America* (1998).

3. A sample playwrights' collaboration agreement appears in Appendix A of this casebook. For a further look at the issue of authorship in the theater, *see* M. Brannon Wiles, *Do Theatrical Collaboration Agreements Create a Joint Venture?*, 25 Colum. J.L. & Arts 219 (2002); Laura G. Lape, *A Narrow View of Creative Cooperation: The Current State of Joint Work Doctrine*, 61 Alb. L. Rev. 43 (1997); Faye Buckalew, Comment, *Joint Authorship in the Second Circuit: A Critique of the Law in the Second Circuit Following Childress v. Taylor and as Exemplified in Thomson v. Larson*, 64 Brook. L. Rev. 545 (1998); Paulette S. Fox, Note, *Preserving the Collaborative Spirit of American Theater: The Need for a "Joint Authorship Default Rule" in Light of the Rent Decision's Unanswered Questions*, 19 Cardozo Arts & Ent. L.J. 497 (2001); Susan Etta Keller, Comment, *Collaboration in Theater: Problems and Copyright Solutions*, 33 UCLA L. Rev. 891 (1986); Jane C. Lee, Comment, *Upstaging the Playwright: The Joint Authorship Entanglement Between Dramaturgs and Playwrights*, 19 Loy. L.A. Ent. L.J. 75 (1998).

Problem 3

A community theater group decided to write an original play and present it during its upcoming season. At first, nightly writing meetings were held at which everyone was present. Eventually, the number of regular participants dwindled to a half dozen, with most of the drafting being done by two specific individuals. When the play was half-finished, one of these individuals, having lost interest, stopped attending the meetings. As a result, the other individual finished the script herself. Given these facts, who is the play's legal author? *See Cabrera v. Teatro del Sesenta, Inc.*, 914 F. Supp. 743 (D.P.R. 1995).

C. CONTROL

BARR v. DRAMATISTS GUILD, INC.
573 F. Supp. 555 (S.D.N.Y. 1983)

WERKER, District Judge.

This action alleging violations of the antitrust laws was commenced by plaintiff Richard Barr, the president of The League of New York Theatres and Producers, Inc. (The League), against the Dramatist Guild, Inc. and three of its officers. The League is a trade association and multi-employer bargaining unit "whose members include producers of legitimate theatrical attractions and owners and operators of theatres in New York City" (Complaint ¶ 5). The Dramatists Guild is a not-for-profit corporation whose members include professional playwrights, composers and lyricists.

The case is presently before the court on the motion by the third party defendants and plaintiff Barr to dismiss or stay defendants' contingent counterclaim and third party complaint (collectively the counterclaim).

I.

The complaint alleges that the defendants, The Dramatists Guild and three individual playwrights—Peter Stone, Sheldon Harnick and Ruth Goetz—who are all among its officers, have violated Section 1 of the Sherman Act by conspiring "to restrain trade and commerce in the sale of authors' works for legitimate theatrical attractions" (Complaint ¶ 6). The complaint alleges, inter alia, that the defendants have conspired to fix the minimum prices and other terms on which they will deal with producers and have agreed among themselves that they will not license a play to producers except upon the minimum terms incorporated in a standard form contract—the Minimum Basic Production Contract (MBPC)—promulgated by the Guild (Complaint ¶¶ 17(a), 19(b)). Plaintiff Barr seeks a declaration that the alleged conspiracy is violative of Section 1 of the Sherman Act, 15 U.S.C. § 1, and an injunction against the "use of contracts containing minimum terms and conditions for the production of any author's work as a legitimate theatrical attraction" (Complaint ¶ 10). The complaint also seeks to enjoin the defendants from "involving themselves in any way, either directly or indirectly, in the negotiations between an author and a producer concerning the terms and conditions under which the right to produce any author's work will be licensed or offered for licensing for presentation as a legitimate theatrical attraction or in media other than legitimate theatrical attractions" (Complaint ¶ 11). No damages are sought by Barr.

Defendants filed an answer on September 16, 1982 which denied the material allegations of the complaint. The answer asserted eight affirmative defenses. On April 28, 1983, defendants, with leave of the court, filed an amended answer containing an additional affirmative defense premised on the doctrine of in pari delicto (Amended Answer, Ninth Affirmative Defense) and a contingent counterclaim and third-party complaint against Barr, The League, and The Shubert and Nederlander interests. The counterclaim alleges that the counterclaim defendants have violated Section 1 of the Sherman Act by conspiring to "fix, stabilize and/or maintain at artificially low and non-competitive levels the compensation received by playwrights" (Amended Answer ¶ 45(a)), and "to enforce unfavorable terms and conditions in the contracts that are offered to playwrights" by producers (Amended Answer ¶ 45(b)). The counterclaim is denominated contingent and is asserted by defendants only if and to the extent that any alleged conduct of defendants is found to violate the antitrust laws (Amended Answer ¶ 48).

Defendants argue that "if it is held that playwrights may not lawfully combine to negotiate with producers regarding the terms and conditions of their employment, it would surely follow that producers (who do not claim to be a labor organization) would not be entitled to combine to agree on the terms and conditions on which they would deal with those same playwrights." Defendants' Memorandum of Law at 9.

The counterclaim alleges that the Shubert and Nederlander interests are producers of plays (Amended Answer ¶¶ 25, 28). It alleges that they control about 70% of the first class theaters. The Shubert and Nederlander interests are alleged to have monopoly power in the market for ownership of first class theaters in New York City (Amended Answer ¶ 37). The counterclaim plaintiffs allege that the Shubert and Nederlander interests, by reason of their monopoly power in the market for theater ownership, dominate The League and dictate the terms on which they will produce playwrights' works (Amended Answer ¶¶ 30, 39).

The defendants and counterclaim plaintiffs contend that the minimum royalty terms of the MBPC have become maximum terms, and that this is the result of concerted action by the counterclaim defendants. They argue that the purpose and effect of the producers' negotiating the MBPC has been to impose a ceiling on the amounts producers pay playwrights.

The counterclaim alleges that the conspiracy complained of is "continuing and [is] causing and will cause irreparable injury to counterclaim plaintiffs and their business and property" (Amended Answer ¶ 47). The defendants seek injunctive relief and treble such damages as will be shown to have resulted from the conduct on which the contingent counterclaim is premised—but only in the event that the defendants' conduct is held to violate the antitrust laws.

The counterclaim defendants contend, among other things, that it is "factually untenable and legally impermissible for defendants simultaneously to (a) defend the past and continued use of their Minimum Basic Production Contract, the 'MBPC', as lawful, reasonable and necessary, and (b) argue that the same MBPC was coercively imposed on dramatists to their detriment and monetary injury." Counterclaim Defendants' Reply Memorandum of Law at 2. They state that in the event the court decides that dismissal of the counterclaim is inappropriate then the contingent counterclaim should be stayed and severed from the Barr suit.

II.

The contingent counterclaim states a claim. It alleges a conspiracy by producers to fix the price of the services they purchase "at artificially low and non-competitive levels" (Amended Answer ¶¶ 45-46). The counterclaim further alleges that the producers conspired through The League to establish and fix the economic terms on which they will purchase playwrights' services (Amended Answer ¶ 43), and that the purpose of the conspiracy was to reduce the compensation paid to playwrights and to remove competition among producers for the services of playwrights (Amended Answer ¶ 46). Conspiracies among buyers to suppress prices are unlawful under the antitrust laws. Mandeville Island Farms, Inc. v. American Crystal Sugar Co., 334 U.S. 219, 68 S.Ct. 996, 92 L.Ed. 1328 (1948); Mackey v. National Football League, 543 F.2d 606 (8th Cir.1976), cert. dismissed, 434 U.S. 801, 98 S.Ct. 28, 54 L.Ed.2d 59 (1977).

On a motion to dismiss, the well-pleaded allegations of the complaint must be taken as true and the complaint must be construed in the light most favorable to the plaintiff. A plaintiff is not required to provide detailed allegations tending to prove its case in its complaint. Speed Auto Sales, Inc. v. American Motors Corp., 477 F.Supp. 1193, 1195-96 (E.D.N.Y.1979).

The counterclaim defendants also contend that the counterclaim does not properly allege antitrust injury. The counterclaim adequately alleges that the defendants (as sellers) have dealt with the counterclaim defendants (as buyers) and that the counterclaim defendants have conspired to fix the prices they have paid for playwrights' services. A plaintiff in a price-fixing case is not required to allege facts beyond these to show antitrust injury. Illinois Brick Co. v. Illinois, 431 U.S. 720, 97 S.Ct. 2061, 52 L.Ed.2d 707 (1977).

The defendants' labor exemption defense also is challenged. The counterclaim adequately alleges that the Dramatist Guild is a labor organization (Amended Answer, Sixth Affirmative Defense) and that the MBPC was the result of collective bargaining between The Dramatist Guild and The League (Amended Answer, ¶¶ 40, 42). Whether a particular group of individuals is entitled to claim the labor exemption from the antitrust laws cannot be decided on a motion to dismiss. Bernstein v. Universal Pictures, Inc., 517 F.2d 976 (2d Cir.1975); Home Box Office, Inc. v. Directors Guild of America, Inc., 531 F.Supp. 578 (S.D.N.Y.1982), aff'd per curiam, 708 F.2d 95 (2d Cir.1983). In addition, a ruling by the court on the applicability of the per se rule to the conduct at issue here also would not be appropriate since there is no factual record upon which the ruling can be made.

The counterclaim defendants contend that "the Guild and its officers cannot simultaneously seek to uphold the legality of the MBPC and plead that Barr, who is seeking to enjoin its use, and the third party defendants are unlawfully injuring defendants by imposing the same MBPC on them" (Counterclaim Defendants' Memorandum at 15). This argument is without merit. The Federal Rules of Civil Procedure expressly permit "alternativ[e] or hypothetica[l]" pleading and also the assertion of "separate claims... regardless of consistency."

In this case, the defendants have denied that they engaged in any illegal conduct under the antitrust laws, but have alleged hypothetically that if they engaged in any illegal conduct then similar conduct of the counterclaim defendants is unlawful as well. The counterclaim is properly framed as a hypothetical pleading.

The counterclaim defendants invoke the doctrine of judicial estoppel as an additional bar to the counterclaim. Judicial estoppel is a "doctrine of rather vague outline" that "is limited to change of position in judicial proceedings." 1B J. Moore, Federal Practice ¶ 0.405[8], at 239 (2d ed. 1982). Judicial estoppel is not applicable because pleadings framed in an alternative or hypothetical manner do not involve a change of position. The contingent counterclaim does not involve a change of position by the defendants.

The counterclaim defendants have moved to stay or dismiss the contingent counterclaim contending that adjudication of the counterclaim together with the main action would be uneconomical and impose needless burden and expense on the parties. They argue that trial of the main action together with the counterclaim would burden the Barr action with the adjudication of many additional, complex and irrelevant issues.

The original claim asserted by Mr. Barr challenges the lawfulness of the MBPC under the antitrust laws. Defendants contend that the MBPC is lawful and have set forth a number of affirmative defenses which the counterclaim defendants have not moved to strike and which will have to be tried by the court in any adjudication of the original claim. The Fifth Affirmative Defense alleges that the negotiation of the MBPC in 1955 and 1961 "and the related contract practices of the Dramatists Guild are reasonable and have facilitated the presentation of first class productions" (Amended Answer ¶ 14). The Eighth Affirmative Defense alleges that acts complained of by Mr. Barr: "are reasonable, have redeeming virtue, and do not unreasonably restrain trade and commerce, in light of the economic realities and unique conditions which characterize the business of presenting legitimate theatrical attractions—including, inter alia, (i) monopolistic ownership of theaters, (ii) vertical integration of theater ownership and production of legitimate theatrical attractions, (iii) the dominant position of the theater-owner producers in The League, (iv) the absence of coercion by defendants, and (v) collective bargaining between The League and organizations representing actors, directors, scenic designers, musicians, writers and other individuals who provide personal services for the first-class production of a play." (Eighth Affirmative Defense).

Defendants' Ninth Affirmative Defense of in pari delicto asserts that "[p]laintiff and the other producers in The League have conspired to use their vastly superior bargaining power to establish the terms of the MBPC and to compel the adherence of playwrights to those terms." There is an overlap between the issues raised by the defendants' counterclaim and their in pari delicto defense.

A stay or severance would be inappropriate because the discovery necessary for both the main claim (including defenses to it) and the counterclaim appears to be basically the same. As noted by the defendants, trial of both the main claim and the counterclaim will involve similar proof—including the negotiations leading to the adoption of the MBPC, the role of The League and the Shubert and Nederlander interests in its adoption, the comparative bargaining power of the parties, and the effect of the MBPC.

Further, both the original claim and the counterclaim involve nearly identical legal issues. In one case, the issue is the legality of concerted action taken by sellers (the dramatists) with regard to the terms of their employment by buyers (producers). In the other case, the issue is the legality of concerted action by buyers with respect to the same sellers in the same transaction. A severance would not result in judicial economy.

Finally, the counterclaim defendants contend that the Dramatist Guild does not have standing to sue under the antitrust laws. The contingent counterclaim asserts claims for injunctive relief and damages on behalf of four plaintiffs. The three individual playwrights have standing to sue for damages and injunctive relief, and the counterclaim defendants do not argue otherwise. The Dramatists Guild is an organization composed of playwrights who write for the first class theater and who represent the common interests of playwrights. The defendants note that while an association may not sue for treble damages under Section 4 of the Clayton Act, 15 U.S.C. § 15, where the only injury alleged is to its members, Hawaii v. Standard Oil Co., 405 U.S. 251, 262-65, 92 S.Ct. 885, 891-92, 31 L.Ed.2d 184 (1972); Nassau County Ass'n of Insurance Agents v. Aetna Life & Casualty Co., 497 F.2d 1151, 1153-54 (2d Cir.), cert. denied, 419 U.S. 968, 95 S.Ct. 232, 42 L.Ed.2d 184 (1974), associations have been allowed to sue for injunctive relief on behalf of their membership under Section 16 of the Clayton Act, 15 U.S.C. § 26. The reason for this is because of the differences between Section 4 actions and Section 16 actions. The Dramatists Guild is entitled to represent its members on its claim for injunctive relief.

For the foregoing reasons, the motion by the counterclaim defendants to dismiss or stay the contingent counterclaim and third party complaint is denied.

SO ORDERED.

A FEDERAL RECOGNITION OF PERFORMANCE ART AUTHOR MORAL RIGHTS
Otto W. Konrad
48 Wash. & Lee L. Rev. 1579 (1991)

A young playwright, enrolled in a college graduate program, writes a two act play and directs and produces the initial performance of his work for the annual college theater festival. Funny, energetic, and a bit weird, his play is the hit of the festival. Subsequently, the playwright agrees to a more elaborate and "fully realized" production of his script, directed and produced by a fellow graduate student. Halfway through the rehearsal period, the playwright visits a rehearsal. He is shocked to discover that his eccentric, funny work has been twisted into a turgid, overly serious "soap-opera." The playwright protests and demands that the director stage his play in accordance with the manifest intent contained in the playwright's script. The director refuses, claiming the right to interpret and stage the author's play as the director sees fit. On opening night, prior to the commencement of the play, the playwright disavows the production to the discomforted audience.

Another example of college art students taking themselves too seriously? Perhaps; however, the incident graphically illustrates a conflict between the authors and interpreters of performance art that extends well beyond the academic environment. Indeed, the conflict between authors and interpreters of performance art at one time or another has affected much of the professional performance art community.

One of the most dramatic manifestations of this conflict began in 1984 when the Boston American Repertory Theater (Boston ART) purchased the rights to produce Samuel Beckett's "Endgame." Pursuant to these rights, the Boston ART staged a production of "Endgame" that allegedly made significant departures from Mr. Beckett's script. Instead of setting the play in a bare, cell-like room, as specified in Mr. Beckett's script, the Boston ART set the play in an abandoned subway tunnel with a bombed out subway car extending halfway across the stage. The Boston ART also cast two black actors to perform characters specifically described as white in Mr. Beckett's script. At one point during the play these actors froze silently in place while their lines were spoken out over an amplified sound system emanating from the rear of the theater. Finally, instead of the specified silence preceding the play's beginning, the Boston ART added an overture that Phillip Glass composed. Beckett asserted that these changes violated his rights as the author of "Endgame."

Mr. Beckett is not the only notable professional playwright to object to novel interpretations of his works. Playwrights Sam Shepard and Edward Albee strenuously have objected to certain productions of their respective plays.

The above described incidents all involve a conflict that pits performance art authors—playwrights, composers and choreographers—against the interpretive artists—directors, conductors and choreographers—who stage the authors' works. The authors of performance art are asserting a right to control the use of their work to protect the artistic vision they have imbued in their work, while the interpretive artists are claiming the right to control the author's work to communicate their own artistic vision.

DEFINING THE PERFORMANCE ART AUTHOR'S "MORAL RIGHT"

Because all artists have impressed their thoughts and feelings, their inner being, into their art, artists want to control the presentation of their work. Artists are not the only creators who materialize themselves in their creations, but because the artistic mediums are subject to relatively few constraints of economy, efficiency, and physical environment, artists can inject more of their personalities into their creations than can the creator of a drill press.

The artist's freedom to inject his personality into his art is a double-edged sword, however. Because an artist's art largely is free from the constraints of economy, efficiency and physical environment, individuals other than the artist can easily distort or change the art. If an individual distorts or changes the artist's art, then the individual changes the artist's manifestation of his personality, and thereby wounds the artist's feelings. Thus, the plethora of personality in art, in concert with the fragility of its manifestation, explains why artists attempt to control the presentation of their art and justifies recognition of the unique right of artists to protect the manifestations of their personalities from distortion by others: an artist's moral right.

Theorists have broken the moral right into a multiplicity of subparts, but for the purposes of this article, the moral right will be divided only into rights of paternity and integrity. Such a subdivision accords with the terms of the Berne Convention (Berne), which the United States Congress adopted in part on October 12, 1988. The paternity right encompasses the artist's right to be known as the author of his work. Commentators further subdivide the paternity right into the artist's right to prevent others from being named the author of his work, and conversely, the right to prevent others from falsely attributing authorship to the artist of art that the artist has not created. The right of integrity encompasses the artist's right to prevent others from making deforming changes to his work.

PROTECTING THE MORAL RIGHTS OF PERFORMANCE ART AUTHORS—THE SUFFICIENCY OF AMERICAN ANALOGUES

Europe and a large part of the Third World long have incorporated into their respective common-law and legislative schemes some form of moral rights protection for artists, including the authors of performance art. Within America, however, legal recognition of the moral rights doctrine has been much more recent and limited in scope. State and federal courts never have recognized artists' moral rights. State legislatures have recognized the doctrine, but they have limited its reach to the creators of visual art. [In the Visual Artists Rights Act of 1990 (VARA), 17 U.S.C. § 106A] Congress followed the lead of these state legislatures and limited its recognition of moral rights to the creators of visual art. Thus, within the United States, a performance art author finds no explicit, legal recognition of his moral rights.

When Congress enacted the Berne Convention in 1988, it had the opportunity to institute the kind of inclusive moral rights protection that would have encompassed the moral rights of performance art authors. Specifically, Congress could have given full effect to the complete text of Berne, including section 6bis(1), the moral rights provision protecting the paternity and integrity rights of all artists. Instead Congress chose to adopt Berne without giving effect to section 6bis(1), stating that section 6bis(1) did not expand or reduce any right of an author to assert attribution or integrity rights. Congress justified its limitation on its enactment of Berne with the rationale that existing American statutory and common-law already accorded moral rights protection equivalent to that accorded by section 6bis(1).

The limitations that Congress placed on its enactment of Berne have forced authors of the performing arts to find moral rights protection in the statutory and common-law that Congress described as analogues to moral rights. These moral rights analogues include causes of action for breach of contract, libel, invasion of privacy, unfair competition and copyright infringement. Despite Congress' apparent belief in the sufficiency of these analogues, commentators uniformly have found them ill-equipped to properly protect artists' moral rights. Because unfair competition, breach of contract and copyright infringement actions particularly are prevalent in the context of the performance arts, the ability of these analogues to protect the personality interests of performance art authors deserves closer attention.

In general, of all artists, performance art authors have the closest approximation to a contractual form of moral rights when they contract with interpretive artists and producers. At least some performance art authors, as a group or individually, have the bargaining power to reserve expressly in the assignments or licenses for their works the right to prevent distortion or truncation of their works—a contractual right analogous to the performance art author's right of integrity. Courts have long recognized and enforced such express reservations.

An example of such an express reservation is the prohibition against distortion or truncation contained in the "Approved Production Contract" (APC), a contract used by playwrights belonging to the Dramatist Guild. The APC is a mandatory contract between the playwright and the producer that governs the first production of the playwright's script. The contract provides that no interpretive artist or producer can make changes to the playwright's script without the playwright's prior approval. Further, the APC specifies that the playwright does not have to be reasonable in refusing to make such changes to his script. Similar to the playwright's APC provisions, choreographers often enter into contractual agreements with producers and interpretive artists that reserve quasi-integrity and paternity rights. For instance, these choreography contractual agreements typically reserve the choreographer's right to forbid any alteration to his work without his prior approval.

While the above described contractual provisions appear to protect the personality interests of the performance art author, at best, reliance on contract is a chewing gum and bailing wire approach to protecting these interests. The principal difficulty with the contractual analogue is that economic forces compel even the authors of performance art to waive their personality rights, and the courts consistently have upheld such waivers. In addition the entrepreneurs of the performance art industry have a decided bargaining advantage that performance art authors find hard to counter. Organizations such as the Dramatist Guild may provide effective contractual protection for the artist's personality interests, however, these protections are only available to Dramatist Guild's members. Additionally, the vast majority of choreographers and composers do not belong to any comparable organization. Thus, most performance art authors are placed in an unequal bargaining position with respect to protecting their personality interests and, as a result, are forced to waive their rights.

Even if a performance art author manages to secure contractual provisions protecting his personality interests, the author still faces the difficulty of protecting his personality interests from the virtually unlimited number of wrongful acts falling outside the specific terms of the contract. For example, absent an express contractual provision prohibiting a particular form of modification, the courts will follow one of two equally nonbeneficial courses. They either will rely on the custom prevailing in the performance art industry to evaluate liberally the suitability of modifications falling outside the contractual terms, a determination that obviously will favor the interpretive artist, or the courts simply will allow the modification because the contract does not expressly prohibit that particular type of change.

To further illustrate, a licensing agreement between the author and a producer may prohibit modifications to the dialogue of a play, the choreography of a ballet or the score of an orchestral work. However, a skillful artist performing the work could make dramatic interpretive changes that would not modify the "text" of the work in any way. For instance, an interpretive artist could turn a tragic work into a farce merely by exaggerating the emotional range of his performance or by speaking his lines with an unintended irony. While the "modifications" might harm the author's personality interests, the changes may be beyond the purview of contract law, due to the omission of an express prohibition against changing the tone of the work.

Assuming that performance art authors do have the bargaining power and the legal acumen to draft effective contractual provisions to protect their personality interests, the enforcement of these contractual rights will continue to remain difficult for most authors. First, the cost of pursuing a breach of contract action prevents most artists from enforcing what contractual protections they do have. Second, the remedies available to a performance art author for breach of a contract are limited and possibly ineffective. The typical award for breach of contract is compensatory damages based on some kind of lost profits analysis. In many cases, a paternity or integrity rights violation causes serious harm to the author's personality interests but results in little or no quantifiable lost profits for the author. While injunctive relief may be available, such relief could create serious First Amendment difficulties and could be extremely destructive for the fragile entrepreneurial aspects of the performance art industry.

Similar to the illusionary protections of contract law, federal copyright law initially appears to afford substantial protection to the performance art author's personality interests. These protections basically take the form of two copyright privileges: the exclusive rights to do and authorize the (1) public display and performance of the copyrighted work and (2) derivative works based on the copyrighted work. In addition to these two basic statutory rights, commentators have suggested that [there is] a third "integrity type" right that authors have in their copyrighted works—the right to prevent unauthorized mutilations to their works.

Commentators have argued that, in a number of fashions, these statutory and common-law copyright protections approximate moral rights protection for authors of performance art. First, an author who has granted a performance license can bring an action for copyright infringement if the licensee performs such a modified version of the author's work that it constitutes a derivative version of the author's work. In effect the licensee would be infringing on the author's right to perform derivative versions of his work. Second, significant mutilations to the author's work, not rising to the level of a derivative version, might be prohibited as exceeding the scope of the performance license. Finally, where an author has granted a license to perform a derivative version of his work, modifications beyond those necessary to make a derivative version could constitute a violation of the author's right to prevent mutilation to his work.

While these theories of copyright infringement appear to be powerful analogues for moral rights, in practice their protections are problematic. Most notably, the weak economic position of many performance art authors may force them to sell their copyrights. Obviously, without the copyright to their work, authors will not have access to the protections of the copyright laws. In addition to assigning their copyrights, performance art authors may also forgo the protections of the copyright laws by failing to register their works, a common event in some areas of the performance arts. In part these performance art authors fail to register because they are skeptical about the usefulness of copyright registration. The United States has conceived and formulated its copyright law primarily to protect a creator's economic interests in his intellectual property. Where intellectual property has little economic potential, as does most performance art, its authors have little motivation to seek out copyright protection for their property.

Another reason why performance art authors have not sought copyright protection for their works hinges on copyright law's historical biases against certain types of performance art. Congress' slow recognition of choreography as an independent art form, one that could be registered under the federal copyright laws, illustrates this bias. Congress did not consider dance an independent art form, copyrightable under federal law, until 1976 when Congress enacted the 1976 Copyright Act. Prior to 1976 federal copyright law treated dance as a subspecies of drama. This inaccurate classification prevented choreographers from registering their works unless their choreography depicted some story or emotion. Because much dance lacks such elements, many choreographers could not register their works. Though choreography eventually was afforded its own distinct niche within the federal copyright laws, choreographers, particularly those outside the mainstream, remain suspicious of current law and have been reluctant to register their works.

Regardless of whether an artist has registered and retained his copyright, the use of copyright laws to protect the personality interests in a work may be difficult. Similar to the inadequacies of contractual moral rights analogues, copyright is a clumsy legal mechanism for redressing the multitude of personality rights violations that a performance art author can suffer. For instance, as previously mentioned, where the performance art author grants a performance license for his work, and the interpretive artist performs such a modified version as to constitute a derivative work, the author may be able to sue for copyright infringement under title 17 of United States Code section 106(2). However, to constitute a derivative work under section 106(2), the interpretive artist might have to make gross modifications to the author's work, modifications that rise to the level of an adaptation rather than a distortion or mutilation of the author's work. Because most changes to an author's work will be isolated deviations, not rising to the level of an adaptation, many actions brought pursuant to section 106(2) will not redress severe violations to the author's personality rights.

Those personality right violations that fall through the cracks of section 106 might be caught by a suit brought pursuant to Gilliam v. American Broadcasting Co., Inc., 538 F.2d 14 (2d Cir.1976), a case that commentators have suggested stands for the proposition that artists have a right to prevent mutilations to their work, whether or not the mutilations rise to the level of a derivative work. However, Gilliam is too indiscriminate a tool to redress personality right violations. First, in the fifteen years since the United States Court of Appeals for the Second Circuit issued the Gilliam opinion, no other court ever has used Gilliam to redress personality rights violations. Second, the copyright portion of the Gilliam opinion simply may be a contract case, in which the plaintiff's victory hinged solely on its explicit reservation of the right to approve all subsequent edits. Finally, even if Gilliam does stand for the proposition that an author has an absolute right to prevent mutilations to his work, the facts of Gilliam may limit the meaning of "mutilation" to the kind of gross editing that the defendant in Gilliam performed on the plaintiff's work. Obviously, such a conception of mutilation does not begin to encompass the multitude of personality rights violations that an interpretive artist can inflict on the work's author.

Besides copyright and contract, potentially the most significant American moral rights analogue for performance art authors is embodied in unfair competition under state common law and particularly section 43(a) of the Lanham Act, 15 U.S.C. § 1125(a). These two doctrines originally were conceived as a means to prevent false advertising in the sale of goods or services. However, commentators and a number of court opinions have suggested that unfair competition and section 43(a) of the Lanham Act could encompass an author's rights of paternity and integrity.

Simply put, a successful cause of action for unfair competition brought under the common-law or under section 43(a) of the Lanham Act requires the plaintiff to demonstrate that "a representation of a product, although technically true, creates a false impression of the product's origin," and that the representation harms the plaintiff's reputation. Theoretically, a production of a performance art author's work could so significantly diverge from the author's intent that the production could be termed as not being the author's work. To avoid criticism or prevent the production from diverging from the author's work, the author could bring either a common-law unfair competition claim or a federal Lanham Act action, claiming that crediting authorship of the work to the author constitutes a false impression of the work's origins.

Despite the apparent suitability of unfair competition as a moral rights analogue, the doctrine in both its state and federal forms inadequately protects the personality interests of performance art authors. As in the case of contract and copyright, unfair competition primarily focuses on protecting the author's economic interests by protecting the author's personal and business reputation. More specifically, the underlying theory of unfair competition is that an individual should not get economic benefit by falsely presenting his work as that of another. Conversely, a creator should not have his business or personal reputation harmed by false attributions that he has authored shoddy work.

These underlying rationales suggest that a successful state or federal unfair competition claim depends on the performance art author having some kind of professional or personal reputation that has economic value for the author. Most performance art authors have no such reputation. Thus, while a production of a performance art author's work may severely harm the author's personality interests, unfair competition will provide little recourse for the relatively unknown author.

In addition to unfair competition's basic incompatibility with the personality interests of performance art authors, the doctrine's ability to protect performance art author's moral rights often is limited by the author's contractual arrangements with the producer of the author's work. If the author expressly or implicitly has contracted away a personality right attached to his work—the right to forestall editing, for instance—then the artist cannot bring an unfair competition action that arises out of the licensee's valid exercise of that waived right. Because of the disparate bargaining power between performance art authors and performance art entrepreneurs, the interdependence of unfair competition and contracting especially is detrimental to the doctrine's usefulness for the performance art author.

In addition to the difficulties afflicting the general unfair competition doctrine, the federal form of unfair competition, section 43(a) of the Lanham Act, has several unique limitations of its own that limit the doctrines usefulness as a moral rights analogue. First, no court, including the Gilliam court, explicitly has held that the Lanham Act encompasses an author's integrity or paternity rights. Second, a producer of a performance art author's work may be able to cure a Lanham Act violation simply by not attributing the author's work to the author. Such a tactic would avoid the misdescription that is basis of a Lanham Act violation.

In view of [the foregoing], effective recognition of moral rights for performance art authors only can come from cohesive federal legislation....

BALANCING THE INTERESTS—DEVELOPING SPECIFIC PROVISIONS FOR FEDERAL MORAL RIGHTS LEGISLATION FOR PERFORMANCE ART AUTHORS

Any federal recognition of the performance art author's moral rights should encompass the two components of the moral right: the author's right of paternity and the author's right of integrity.

Implementing paternity rights into the present framework of American law would be [] simple. Because correctly attributing authorship is easy and inexpensive, performance art author paternity rights would not intrude on the financial interests of interpretive artists or performance art entrepreneurs. Further, attributing correct authorship to a work has little to do with the performance of the work. Thus, a right of paternity for performance art authors would have little effect on the expressive interests (First Amendment or otherwise) of entrepreneurs or interpretive artists.

Because a paternity right fits comfortably within existing American law and the performance art industry, the ancillary provisions effectuating the right should be strong and effective. For instance, because recognition of the performance art author's paternity right is neither onerous nor expensive and because it does not implicate the First Amendment, monetary damages and injunctive relief would be appropriate means to enforce the right. Congress' previous enactments support such enforcement mechanisms. When Congress accorded paternity rights to visual art artists in 1990, with the exception of criminal penalties, Congress afforded visual artists the full panoply of legal and injunctive remedies available under the federal copyright laws. Because paternity rights in the context of visual art and performance art essentially have the same impact, Congress' paternity right damage provisions for visual art artists are suitable equally for performance art author paternity rights.

The comfortable fit between paternity rights, American law and the performance art industry also argues for federal legislation prohibiting any form of an inter vivos transfer of an author's paternity right. Absent such a provision, the weak bargaining position of most performance art authors would allow interpretive artists and entrepreneurs to coerce authors into contracting away their paternity rights. Performance art authors' lack of bargaining power also should make the paternity right nonwaiveable. Finally, because attribution of authorship is both easy and inexpensive and does not implicate the expressive interests of the participants in performance art to any great degree, Congress, consistent with the durational limitations of the copyright clause, could promote the useful arts by extending the duration of the author's paternity right to a period coextensive with copyright.

While implementing a paternity right for performance art authors would be a relatively simple matter, implementing a performance art author right of integrity would be much more difficult. Central to such an implementation is determining exactly what constitutes an integrity rights violation. Once the scope of the integrity right is delineated, one can define ancillary provisions to the integrity right that will effectively balance the disparate interests involved. Essentially, there are two approaches to defining an integrity rights violation. The first approach defines the concept as those distortions, mutilations or other modifications that harm the artist's "honor or reputation." Both the Berne Convention and Congress' 1990 visual artists moral rights enactments use this approach.

The "honor or reputation" approach (Berne approach) uses a two part analysis to identify an integrity rights violation. First, the interpretive artist must modify the author's work. Second, the interpretive artist's modification must harm the author's professional honor or reputation. Both prongs of the test essentially are objective in that neither prong exclusively relies on the author's testimony to determine whether either prong is satisfied. Rather, a court applying the Berne approach would look to independent evidence to determine if the interpretive artist has modified an author's work in a manner that harms the authors's honor or reputation.

The advantages and disadvantages to the Berne approach primarily reside in the second prong: an integrity rights violation must harm the author's professional honor or reputation. The American judicial system is familiar with this reputational standard, having applied it in the context of libel for years. However, other than the American judicial system's familiarity with the second prong of the Berne approach, the approach has serious disadvantages. First, the second prong of the Berne Approach is resoundingly pro-interpretive artist. Because many performance art authors lack a public reputation, in many cases it would be very difficult for authors to demonstrate that a modification to their work has harmed their professional reputations. Further, even if an author has a reputational interest, the public may perceive the distortion to the author's work as benefitting the author's reputation rather than harming it.

The Berne approach's bias towards the interpretive artist is symptomatic of the test's more fundamental flaw—the test does not directly protect the personality interests of the author. Instead of focusing on the performance art author's psyche, the Berne approach ultimately protects the artist's economic interests, an interest many artists do not have. Thus, the second prong of the Berne approach effectively forestalls the performance art author's recovery for many serious violations to the author's personality interests.

Another approach to defining an integrity rights violation is the German approach which defines an integrity violation as a distortion or mutilation to an author's work that "prejudice[s] [the author's] lawful...personal interests" (German approach). Like the Berne approach, the German approach has a two part test that has the same first prong: the author must demonstrate that the interpretive artist has modified the author's work in some fashion. As in the Berne approach, this prong is essentially an objective test, not requiring the court to rely solely on the author's belief that the interpretive artist has modified the author's work. The German approach breaks with the Berne approach, however, in the second prong wherein the author must demonstrate that the modification prejudices his personal interests.

The second prong of the German approach is a much more subjective test than the "honor and reputation" prong of the Berne approach, and herein lies the strength and weakness of the German approach. By divorcing the author's integrity interests from the author's economic interests, the "prejudice" prong of the German approach defines an integrity violation much more accurately. However, the "prejudice" prong also runs the risk of becoming a completely subjective standard that inordinately favors the performance art author. [This] raises the specter of countless numbers of successful integrity right claims based solely on the whims of the performance art author.

If these easy judgments for the author were coupled with monetary and injunctive remedies, the chill to the performance art industry could be overwhelming. While performance art producers are wealthy compared to performance art authors, the vast majority of producers nonetheless operate in a fragile economic environment. A single monetary judgment or injunction could put a producer permanently out of business. Such an outcome would harm every interest involved in the performing arts. The performance art author permanently would lose a means of communicating his message to the public as well as a potential source of income. The entrepreneur and interpretive artist would lose money and the opportunity to express themselves, and the public would see less performance art. Further, the mere prospect of authors obtaining monetary or injunctive relief solely on the basis of their personal whims would discourage many interpretive artists from exercising their free speech rights when performing an author's work of performance art. Indeed, such a subjective approach to defining an integrity rights violation might even discourage individuals from even attempting to perform performance art.

Clearly then, the German approach's ability to accurately define an integrity violation carries with it the potential to seriously harm the performance art industry. Thus, its use in any federal legislation protecting the integrity rights of performance art authors is problematic. Nonetheless, a legislative scheme could use the German approach to define a moral rights violation and effectively accommodate all of the disparate interests in the performance art industry if two provisos were added. First, legislation using the German approach must direct the courts to strictly apply the first prong of the German approach. Specifically, courts must ascertain whether an interpretive artist has modified an author's work solely by comparing the particular performance at issue to the "four corners" of the author's work of performance art. The author's "work of performance art" encompasses the author's fixed expression, including a script or a musical score, provided that the author intended the fixed expression to be a "blueprint" from which interpretive artists could create a fully realized work of performance art. Only when an interpretive artist modifies an ascertainable element of the author's fixed expression could a court find an actionable integrity violation.

This strict approach to identifying actionable modifications to a performance art author's work ensures that the law only would hold interpretive artist's responsible for real diversions from an author's expression, as opposed to holding them liable for bad interpretive choices. Where the author's work is silent, an interpretive artist's expressive conduct within those areas cannot violate the author's integrity rights, and thus, receives First Amendment protection. The "four corners" rule is the first step to a balanced application of the German approach to defining an integrity violation.

However, by itself, the "four corners" rule would never create a balance among all of the involved interests. The subjective nature of the second prong to the German approach would still permit a multiplicity of integrity right actions that would overwhelm the performance art industry. Thus, to reach an effective balance of interests, another legislative limitation on the German approach is necessary. Limiting the author's remedy for an integrity right violation to a "labeling" remedy, in conjunction with the "four corners" rule, would create the appropriate balance among all of the involved interests within the performance art industry.

A labeling remedy for an integrity right violation would involve a court ordering the producer and/or the interpretive artist to indicate in the performance's credits and/or advertisements that the interpretive artist has modified the author's work against the wishes of the author. Such a remedy in large part would avoid both economic and expressive chill to the performing arts, while still protecting the integrity interests of performance art authors. For the producers of performance art, compliance with a labeling order would be a relatively inexpensive task. Further, while compliance with a labeling order might be inconvenient for the producer, it might actually increase the production's profits through the public controversy that labeling tends to engender. Most importantly, a labeling remedy does not prevent the producer or the interpretive artist from proceeding with their intended performance.

In addition to serving the interests of the performance art entrepreneur and the interpretive artists, the labeling remedy also serves the interest of the public in that both the author's message and the interpretive artist's message reach the public. Indeed, because the labeling remedy increases dialogue and the amount of information that enters the market place of ideas, the remedy actually would promote the public's First Amendment interests.

As for the author, while labeling does not stop the integrity rights violation from occurring, the remedy does allow the author to communicate his message to the public and disassociate himself from the performance without destroying a future means to perform his works. Further, the labeling approach allows the author to maintain some control over the personality interests contained in his work. Finally, the labeling approach has the added benefit of allowing more latitude for pro-author ancillary provisions within performance art author moral rights legislation. For instance, inalienable performance art author integrity rights would be much more onerous for the performance art industry if moral rights legislation did not limit the remedy for an integrity rights violation to labeling.

CONCLUSION

With the enactment of VARA, Congress took the first significant step towards a cohesive system of federal moral rights laws. Federal recognition of performance art author moral rights could be the next step. Current moral rights analogues for performance art authors are inadequate, and a real need exists for a system of federal law protecting the personality interests of performance art authors. While interfacing such protection into our present legal and commercial systems would be a complex task, as this article has demonstrated, it is not an impossible one.

MARY TYLER MOORE, CHIDED BY NEIL SIMON, QUITS HIS PLAY

Jason Zinoman
N.Y. Times, Dec. 5, 2003, at E2

Hurt by harsh criticism from the playwright Neil Simon, Mary Tyler Moore has withdrawn from his latest comedy, "Rose's Dilemma," which was to open at the Manhattan Theater Club on Dec. 18.

Ms. Moore was seen storming out the backstage door minutes before the 2 p.m. curtain on Wednesday. Several sources close to the production said she had just received a brusque letter written by Mr. Simon and delivered by his wife, the actress Elaine Joyce, reproaching her for not knowing her lines. Ms. Moore had received prompting through a microphone in her ear, the sources said.

Ms. Moore, who played the title role of a novelist, was replaced by her understudy, Patricia Hodges, on Wednesday and yesterday. Producers said Ms. Hodges would perform at least through the weekend.

"Mary was devastated and completely debilitated personally and professionally," said her publicist, Mara Buxbaum, in a prepared statement. "Mary has been working tirelessly for months but feels pushed out of this production."

Mr. Simon declined to comment.

What seemed like a match made in theater heaven—Broadway's favorite comic playwright and America's television sweetheart—has become the latest subplot in a season beset by failed productions and revolving-door casts.

Manhattan Theater Club has had a particularly difficult time holding onto actresses. Laura Benanti was replaced in its production of "The Violet Hour" after a few rehearsals, and Jasmine Guy left the play in the middle of a preview, citing medical reasons.

Ms. Moore's departure follows reports that jokes were falling flat and that there was tension between Mr. Simon and the cast. "Neil gets nervous when he doesn't get laughs in a show," said a source close to the production, speaking on condition of anonymity. "Inevitably, the actors get blamed."

FOUND: A TWAIN PLAY GOOD ENOUGH TO STAGE
Jesse McKinley
N.Y. Times, May 12, 2003, at E1

Politely put, Mark Twain was not known for his skills as a dramatist. Despite one early commercial success and many subsequent attempts, most of Twain's output as a playwright is, as one scholar puts it, "well worth burying."

This fall, however, the University of California Press is publishing a three-act play it says is not only worthy of Twain's legacy as America's greatest humorist but that also has already been optioned by a Broadway producer.

The play, a comedy titled "Is He Dead?," was unearthed by Shelley Fisher Fishkin, a professor of American studies and English at the University of Texas and a noted Twain scholar. Ms. Fishkin says she came across the script in October 2001 in the course of researching a book about Twain and race at the Bancroft Library at the University of California at Berkeley, which holds the world's largest archive of Twain's papers.

She didn't expect much. "I knew most of them were totally awful," Ms. Fishkin said of the Twain theatrical canon. "But I felt I needed to become as familiar with them as I could, as bad as they were."

But what she found surprised her. The manuscript of "Is He Dead?," its edges still marked with corrective notes in Twain's handwriting, was well thought out, well structured and, most important, funny.

"I think it has a lot of Twain's characteristic humor in it," she said. "It has some really intriguing characters and sets up complicated situations that he also knows how to unravel."

Written in January 1898 while Twain was living in Vienna, "Is He Dead?" tells the story of a group of destitute painters outside Paris who, in a desperate effort to deal with their debts, fake the death of one of their friends to try to drive up the worth of his paintings. Along the way, Twain takes jabs at artists, art dealers, art buyers and art journalists, as well as at Frenchmen, Irishmen, Germans and Americans.

Several scholars had read "Is He Dead?," elements of which are based on an earlier Twain short story, "Is He Living or Is He Dead?," without making much note of it. But Ms. Fishkin said she found herself laughing out loud.

"I thought, 'Am I crazy?'" she recalled. "But in my mind's eye, I could see it onstage."

Ms. Fishkin, however, didn't trust her theatrical taste. So she began seeking out other opinions, one of them from—who else?—the actor Hal Holbrook, who has been playing Twain in various incarnations and in various mediums for half a century.

Mr. Holbrook read the script and liked it. (In promotional material for the play, he calls the piece "another gold nugget.") Then, on the advice of a mutual friend, Ms. Fishkin sent the script to Bob Boyett, a former television producer who has produced several shows on Broadway in recent years. Mr. Boyett read the script in July 2002 and said he, too, was surprised that Twain seemed to understand how to write for the stage.

"The first time I read it, I almost read it as literature," Mr. Boyett said. "But I thought this could absolutely be staged today and work."

Twain no doubt would be happy to hear it. He had a lifelong interest in the theater, working as a critic and attending shows regularly.

Robert H. Hirst, general editor of the the Mark Twain Project in Berkeley, said Twain traveled to Vienna in late 1897 in part to try to master the art of playwriting, spending time "essentially apprenticing himself to several local playwrights," working on translations and trying to learn German.

There were a couple of reasons for Twain's sudden interest in playwriting, Mr. Hirst said.

"He's fed up with the way in which the works of fiction have failed to earn him much money," he said. "And he's also looking for a project to do fast."

Ms. Fishkin said Twain had reason to believe the theater could be his ticket out of the stifling debt that he had incurred after several bad investments. In the 1870's he had made a nice profit on a stage version of his book "The Gilded Age," featuring the exploits of a rakish character named Colonel Sellers. There were also adaptations during his lifetime of his novels "Tom Sawyer," "Pudd'nhead Wilson" and "The Prince and the Pauper."

That said, Twain's own later efforts as a playwright, like the obscure "Ah, Sin," and the even lesser known "Death Wafer," were largely "boring, unreadable plays," Ms. Fishkin writes in the foreword to "Is He Dead?"

Unlike those failures, "Is He Dead?" was written in a flash, probably in less than a month. (Twain was famous for writing some on a project, then dropping it, only to pick up with a new idea months or years later.) His speed is especially surprising, Mr. Hirst said, considering his money woes and that he was still struggling with a depression brought on by the death of his daughter, Susy, in 1896.

"He manages to knock it off fast, and he doesn't labor over it," he said. "There's a newness to it."

Twain was enormously optimistic during the writing of "Is He Dead?," writing to friends that his wife had read the script and found it "very bully." That hope, however, would soon curdle.

Shortly after finishing the script, Twain sent it to his London-based agent, Bram Stoker (author of "Dracula"), who was unable to find a producer. Twain then turned to a friend, the industrialist H. H. Rogers, who tried to find an American producer, to no avail.

By August 1898 Twain was done with "Is He Dead?" and, to a large extent, playwriting as a whole.

"Put 'Is he dead?" in the fire," Twain wrote to Rogers. "God will bless you; I too."

Now, however, a mere 105 years later, there are plans afoot to allow American audiences to see the play at last. Mr. Boyett said yesterday that he had obtained the rights this spring, and that he planned to give the play two "kitchen table" readings over the summer to get a feel for the piece.

As indicated by Twain's notes on the original manuscript, it still needs work. With three acts and 23 characters, "Is He Dead?" will probably require some pruning, Mr. Boyett said, and may also require some sort of polishing by a present-day playwright.

Still, he said, no major changes would be made. "If you're presenting a play by Mark Twain," he said, "people want to hear Mark Twain's voice."

It's exactly that voice, Ms. Fishkin said, that first had her laughing in the Twain archives. "I sensed that there was just a lot of energy, and a lot of exuberance and wit," she said. "Especially coming at a time when we tend to think of Twain as being very cynical and very gloomy."

Notes

1. For a further discussion of the moral rights of playwrights, *see* John M. Kernochan, *Moral Rights in U.S. Theatrical Productions: A Possible Paradigm*, 17 Colum.-VLA J.L. & Arts 385 (1993).

2. As *Barr* and the excerpt from Konrad explain, the Dramatists Guild of America (www.dramaguild.com) has sought to enhance the bargaining power of playwrights by setting minimum standards and promulgating model agreements for use by its members (respectively known as the "Approved Production Contract for Plays" and the "Approved Production Contract for Musical Plays.") *See further Fox v. Chosen Co.*, 1988 WL 140810 (S.D.N.Y. 1988) (analyzing the APC in a dispute between a composer and a producer).

The Guild's contracts do not have the force of law, however, and playwrights must still strike their own deals with producers. Because producers typically have the upper hand in these negotiations, the Guild long has wanted to engage in collective bargaining but cannot do so—as a trade association rather than a labor union, its activities are not shielded from the federal anti-trust laws. *See further Ring v. Spina*, 148 F.2d 647 (2d Cir. 1945). To overcome this fact, in December 2001 Representatives Barney Frank (D-Mass.) and Henry Hyde (R-Ill.) introduced the "Fair Play for Playwrights Act of 2001" (H.R. 3543). In April 2002, Senators Orrin Hatch (R.-Utah) and Charles E. Schumer (D.-N.Y.) followed their lead and proposed the "Playwrights Licensing Relief Act of 2002" (S. 2082), which reads as follows:

A BILL

To modify the application of the antitrust laws to permit collective development and implementation of a standard contract form for playwrights for the licensing of their plays.

Be it enacted by the Senate and House of Representatives of the United States of America in Congress assembled,

SEC. 1. SHORT TITLE.

This Act may be cited as the 'Playwrights Licensing Relief Act of 2002'.

SEC. 2. NONAPPLICATION OF ANTITRUST LAWS.

(a) IN GENERAL—Subject to subsection (c), the antitrust laws shall not apply to any joint discussion, consideration, review, action, or agreement for the express purpose of, and limited to, the development of a standard form contract containing minimum terms of artistic protection and levels of compensation for playwrights by means of—

(1) meetings, discussions, and negotiations between or among playwrights or their representatives and producers or their representatives; or

(2) joint or collective voluntary actions for the limited purposes of developing a standard form contract by playwrights or their representatives.

(b) ADOPTION AND IMPLEMENTATION—Subject to subsection (c), the antitrust laws shall not apply to any joint discussion, consideration, review, or action for the express purpose of, and limited to, reaching a collective agreement among playwrights adopting a standard form contract developed pursuant to subsection (a) as the participating playwrights sole and exclusive means by which participating playwrights shall license their plays to producers.

(c) AMENDMENT OF CONTRACT—A standard form of contract developed and implemented under subsections (a) and (b) shall be subject to amendment by individual playwrights and producers consistent with the terms of the standard form contract.

SEC. 3. DEFINITIONS.

In this Act:

(1) ANTITRUST LAWS—The term 'antitrust laws' has the meaning given it in section (a) of the first section of the Clayton Act (15 U.S.C. 12) except that such term includes section 5 of the Federal Trade Commission Act (15 U.S.C. 45) to the extent that such section applies to unfair methods of competition.

(2) PLAYWRIGHT—The term 'playwright' means the author, composer, or lyricist of a dramatic or musical work intended to be performed on the speaking stage and shall include, where appropriate, the adapter of a work from another medium.

(3) PRODUCER—The term 'producer'—

(A) means any person who obtains the rights to present live stage productions of a play; and

(B) includes any person who presents a play as first class performances in major cities, as well as those who present plays in regional and not-for-profit theaters.

At present, it is uncertain when, or even if, these bills will become law. For a further discussion, *see* Jesse McKinley, *Legislation to Help Playwrights Negotiate*, N.Y. Times, Apr. 11, 2002, at E1.

3. To what extent should playwrights be able to control how their work is presented? Obviously, highly-successful living playwrights generally exercise considerable control, as Neil Simon's run-in with Mary Tyler Moore makes clear. Samuel Beckett fared less well in his battle with the Boston American Repertory Theater, but even he was given space in the program to disavow the production and explain why he objected to the changes. Would a lesser known playwright have been accorded the same opportunity?

Of course, there always is the possibility that changes will make a play better—or at least more commercially successful. In this regard, what do you think of Boyett's plan to do "some pruning" before presenting "Is He Dead?" Indeed, what do you think of the whole idea of staging "Is He Dead?," given that Twain told his friend that if he burned the script, "God will bless you; I too."? For a further discussion, *see* Jon Garon, *Director's Choice: The Fine Line Between Interpretation and Infringement of an Author's Work*, 12 Colum.-VLA J.L. & Arts 427 (1988).

Problem 4

Mortified by a new play, local authorities brought criminal obscenity charges against everyone associated with the production. The play was performed exactly as the playwright wrote it, except that the cast was totally naked throughout the show. If the playwright moves to have the charges against him dismissed on the ground he neither contemplated nor authorized such nudity, how should the court rule? *See People v. Weinberger*, 146 N.E. 434 (N.Y. 1925).

Chapter 3

Rights Holders

A. OVERVIEW

If one decides to use another's property (e.g., a novel) as the basis for a play, permission to do so must be obtained. The same is true if one wishes to use an existing play as the basis of a new work (e.g., a movie). In certain instances, authorization is granted by operation of law; otherwise, actual permission from the rights holder is required.

B. SECURING RIGHTS

LEWYS v. O'NEILL
49 F.2d 603 (S.D.N.Y. 1931)

WOOLSEY, District Judge.

The complaint herein is dismissed with costs, which will include an allowance for counsel fees to all the defendants, as hereinafter fixed and allocated among them.

I

This is a suit in equity based on alleged infringement of copyright, whence arises the jurisdiction of this court.

The plaintiff's book is in the form of a novel called by her The Temple of Pallas-Athenae, with a subtitle Posterite, and will be hereinafter referred to as The Temple. The plaintiff claims and states underneath the notice of copyright that her book was written in 1917; the printing was begun in April, 1923, and was finished in April, 1924. It was not published but—as stated on the title page—was privately printed for subscribers only. It was copyrighted in May, 1924. There were not any copies sent to reviewers.

The defendant Eugene O'Neill's alleged infringement is by a play called Strange Interlude, copyrighted in February, 1928, first produced on the stage by the defendant Theatre Guild, Inc., and published through ordinary trade channels, first by the defendant Boni & Liveright, Inc., and then by its successor, the defendant Horace Liveright, Inc.

II

A few days before the case was tried, at the request of both parties, I read first The Temple and then Strange Interlude.

At the opening of the trial a motion was made by the defendants jointly and severally for a dismissal of the complaint on the ground that, under the decision handed down November 10, 1930, by the Circuit Court of Appeals for this Circuit in Nichols v. Universal Pictures Corporation, 45 F.2d 119 (C.C.A. 2), all that was necessary in a case of this kind was to read the two books and record the resultant impressions made on the court.

I denied the motion to dismiss at that stage of the proceeding, because it seemed to me that the plaintiff was entitled to have an opportunity of presenting her case outside the mere text of the two books as far as she properly could be allowed to do so in conformity with the suggestions to trial courts made by the Circuit Court of Appeals in the Nichols case.

Neither the evidence of the plaintiff nor the argument and brief of her counsel, nor a careful analysis of the two books since the trial, has in any way tended to decrease my first impression that there is not any possible ground for the contention that Strange Interlude is an infringement of the plaintiff's book The Temple.

On the contrary, my reflection in regard to the case and a reading of the relevant authorities and text-books has ripened my first impression into a conviction that the plaintiff has made herein a wholly preposterous claim.

A study of this case, however, is not without its usefulness, I think, because it illustrates how claims of this kind arise and are fostered.

III

The plaintiff testified that she was born in 1898 in Los Angeles, California, and that she wrote The Temple in 1917, when she was nineteen years old—seven years before it was printed and copyrighted.

The Temple was heralded to the waiting world of subscribers for what are known in the booksellers' catalogues as curiosa, in a circular sent out with the plaintiff's approval from Los Angeles, California, in March, 1924, by those interested in its sale.

This circular is entitled: "The Temple of Pallas-Athenae (Posterite) by Georges Lewys—Edition Limited to 995 Copies, Signed By the Author, in De Luxe Art Format, Large Octavo Size, Privately Printed and Distributed to a Restricted Number of Subscribers Only." It reads as follows:

> A house of "pleasure" wherein women of easy virtue are kept—this subject is as old as history. But the subject of a house of impregnation where males are incarcerated for the benefit not of female lust, but generation is a new development in literature.
>
> The male house of assignation in ancient Greece was "The Temple of Pallas-Athenae" in the Acropolis. Transfer this to modern Paris and you have the motif of Georges Lewys' powerful romance of the same name, now being privately circulated among subscribers and members of La Societe des Arts et des Illuminati. In announcing publication of "The Temple of Pallas-Athenae," Georges Lewys offers a masterpiece of literature dealing with posterity or the mission of the unmarried father in social life.

The author's rhythm of language, intense causticism of theme and amiable sophistication supplant much of the salacity of the usual book of this kind; Lewys offers an arraignment of the abuses of the married state, coloured with satirical dialogue on the most indulged in and least discussed practice of the human race—namely, offspring.

[The] work is perfectly scientific, lending itself to a new treatment under the form of fiction. The subtlety of its humor and freshness of its theme will appeal to cognoscenti wearied with the eternal intrigues of passion as the motif in literature, and craving original text swathed in the orthodoxy of pure English.

This is a work of art and a strictly limited edition, each volume being numbered and registered. After these are sold, no further copy can be obtained.

The book caters to the Illuminati. If you belong to this discerning class of readers whose standing is assured among exclusive gatherings where high-class literature is freely and boldly discussed, we know we may entrust to you a book of the type of "The Temple of Pallas-Athenae" with full confidence in the chaste motive, if voluptuous treatment, of the author, and Lewys' power to intrigue you.

In the summer of 1924, after The Temple had been printed and copyrighted, the plaintiff and her mother came from California to live in New York. During the summer she met Mr. T. R. Smith, of Messrs. Boni & Liveright, Inc., gave him a copy of her book, and had a talk with him about the promotion of its sales.

On February 2, 1925, plaintiff wrote to Mr. Courtney Lemon, the reader for the Theatre Guild, sending him, under separate cover, a copy of The Temple which had folded in it a typewritten manuscript which she had entitled a "Resume of Plot or Stage Play or Spectacle based on Georges Lewys' novel 'Posterite' or 'The Temple of Pallas-Athenae.'"

In her letter to Mr. Lemon she described The Temple as a satire and also as a somewhat idealistic or humorous work. She mentioned the source of the basic idea of her story and urged that it be accepted for dramatization by the Theatre Guild because it would "make a distinct departure for your Guild from the realism of the present stage school."

IV

The impression made on me throughout by the examination of the plaintiff was that she had become so obsessed with the idea that Mr. O'Neill had dramatized the plot of her book that, when challenged, she would seek by every means possible to bolster up her case, even to the extent of attempting recklessly to deny the authorship of letters or papers which she had obviously written.

At the commencement of the trial when the plaintiff was being examined in chief she endeavored to introduce into evidence as the document which she had sent to the Theatre Guild with her book a typewritten manuscript called "A Synopsis of Dramaturgy for The Temple of Pallas-Athenae (or Posterite) The Novel by Georges Lewys, Outlined for a Psycho-romantic Drama in Five Acts (and Prologue)."

This synopsis of dramaturgy was temporarily accepted as an exhibit for the plaintiff, subject to a motion to strike out, and the attorney for the Theatre Guild was allowed to cross-examine the plaintiff regarding it.

When the letter of February 2, 1925, and the resume above referred to were first shown to her, the plaintiff claimed that they were forgeries, and had to be reminded by me that an attitude of candor was advisable in court, especially for a party plaintiff in equity. Finally she was forced to admit that the letter of February 2d to Mr. Lemon and the resume which accompanied it were written by her.

These documents were thereupon marked as exhibits for the defendants and a motion to strike out the synopsis of dramaturgy was granted. The latter, however, remains in the record, for it is part of the plaintiff's bill of particulars and will be referred to hereafter.

The case made by the defendant O'Neill and the witnesses called in his behalf and in behalf of the other defendants was in pleasing contrast with the plaintiff's case, although, of course, after the lapse of time which had intervened between the events described and the trial, it was natural some of the witnesses, being busy men, should make some mistakes in unimportant details.

V

In a case of alleged literary larceny like this, previous decisions can do little more than point out the technique of approach to the decision of the question of fact on which alone such cases usually turn.

But there is a necessary background involving the theory of the growth of literature which has seldom been better discussed than by Dr. Samuel Johnson, who never touched on any subject without measurably adding to the store of common sense concerning it.

On Tuesday, October 2, 1753, in The Adventurer, No. 95, Dr. Johnson wrote an essay on plagiarism in which he called attention to the fact that the common field in which authors necessarily have to work is comparatively small, and that as a consequence similarities are often observable between them when they come to deal with similar or cognate subjects. He wrote:

> The allegation of resemblance between authors, is indisputably true; but the charge of plagiarism, which is raised upon it, is not to be allowed with equal readiness. A coincidence of sentiment may easily happen without any communication, since there are many occasions in which all reasonable men will have the same sentiments, because they have in all ages had the same objects of speculation; the interests and passions, the virtues and vices of mankind, have been diversified in different times, only by unessential and casual varieties; and we must, therefore, expect in the words of all those who attempt to describe them, such a likeness as we find in the pictures of the same person drawn in different periods of his life.
>
> It is necessary, therefore, that before an author be charged with plagiarism, one of the most reproachful, though, perhaps, not the most atrocious of literary crimes, the subject on which he treats should be carefully considered.

Among his Seven Lectures on the Law and History of Copyright in Books, Mr. Augustine Birrell, K.C., M.P., the well-known English barrister, statesman, and man of letters, has a lecture entitled "Literary Larceny" [in which he explains]:

> The literary larcenist must do more than filch ideas, imitate mannerisms, repeat information, borrow phrases, utilize quotations; you must be able to attribute to him the felonious intention of appropriating without independent

labour a material part of a protected work. To do this is, in the eye of the law, to infringe copyright—to misuse your brother author.

These quotations indicate better than anything which I have been able to find elsewhere the background against which courts have to act in cases of alleged plagiarism, and the zone, fortunately narrow, within which law impinges on letters.

VI

Functioning within that narrow zone, the courts find that the first question in a case of alleged literary larceny is whether there is any direct evidence of access by the defendant to the plaintiff's book.

In this case there is a categorical denial by Mr. O'Neill, who was examined by a written commission in Paris on August 12, 1930, that he ever heard of the plaintiff's book, The Temple, until he read in the Paris Herald in early June of the year 1929 that the present suit had been brought on May 27th of that year.

About a month after this suit was brought a copy of the book, sent by Mr. Weinberger, his attorney, reached Mr. O'Neill, who, on Mr. Weinberger's insistence, read it for the first time. This was in the early summer of 1929.

Mr. O'Neill says in his commission that before he wrote Strange Interlude he never saw, or read, or had any synopsis, or any outline for any dramatization, or scenario, of The Temple, or any outline or synopsis of its characters, dialogue, detail, or arrangement of the plot, or settings of background, or any part thereof. He says that neither Mr. Lawrence Langner nor Mr. Courtney Lemon, nor any one else, directly or indirectly, connected with the Theatre Guild ever had any conversation with him at any time with reference to The Temple, its plot, scenario, or outline for dramatic purposes. He says he never had been talked to or written to about The Temple, its plot, scenario, synopsis, or outline by Thomas Smith, or Horace Liveright, Inc., or Boni & Liveright, Inc., or any one connected with Horace Liveright, Inc., or Boni & Liveright, Inc. The statements by Mr. O'Neill that he did not receive any information whatever about The Temple from Mr. Langner, Mr. Lemon, or Mr. Smith is confirmed by the evidence of those gentlemen at the trial. Counsel stipulated on the record that Mr. Horace Liveright, if called, would give identical evidence.

I do not see any reason whatever for disbelieving the essence of their testimony which entirely disproves any access through them by Mr. O'Neill to the plaintiff's book, although, of course, as above noted, busy men such as they might possibly make mistakes in minor details.

The plaintiff has put great emphasis on the fact that Mr. O'Neill did not come over himself for the trial of the case and expose himself to cross-examination. Of course the decision to come or not to come rested entirely on Mr. O'Neill's own judgment and that of his counsel. They probably thought that the plaintiff's case was so weak that Mr. O'Neill need not interrupt his life in France and his work there in order to come over for the trial. The event has proved that their judgment was correct.

It must be remembered, moreover, that Mr. O'Neill's position is not limited to a flat denial. He particularizes with regard to his early notes as to Strange Interlude. He annexes to his commission photostat copies of the notebooks in which these notes were contained, and exhibited at the trial the originals, the authenticity and dates of which I have no reason to doubt.

Mr. O'Neill says that the first written record he has of the underlying idea of Strange Interlude was made in the autumn of 1923 at Ridgefield, Conn. It was entitled Godfather, and a photostat of it is annexed to the commission as an exhibit in this case. Mr. O'Neill says that he is able to fix the date of this note because he remembers that he made it in the autumn of 1923 at the time when he was writing the scenario for his play Desire Under the Elms, and because it was during the previous summer of 1923 at Provincetown, Mass., that he heard from an aviator, formerly of the Lafayette Escadrille, the story of a girl whose aviator fiancé had been shot down just before the armistice, with the result that the girl had gone to pieces from the shock, had become neurotic and desperate, and had started drinking and having promiscuous sex affairs. Finally she married, not because she loved the man whom she was marrying but because she wanted to have a child and hoped through motherhood to win back a measure of contentment in life.

It is Mr. O'Neill's habit, when one of his notes eventually grows into a play, to write the name of the play across the note. The name Strange Interlude and the date 1926 is written diagonally across the note headed Godfather of which the story just detailed was the basis.

Mr. O'Neill then describes the growth of this idea in his mind. He has in the same notebook a photostat which was an exhibit annexed to the commission, of a detailed scenario of Strange Interlude with notes of possible other titles for it. This scenario follows in the notebook the scenario of The First Man and covers four pages, written in his minute handwriting which is quite difficult to read. It is followed by the scenario of Desire Under The Elms.

Mr. O'Neill points out that the names of the characters in the scenario of Strange Interlude were changed later when he actually wrote the play—that some were left out and others added. In addition to the notebook, the original longhand script of the play, on deposit in a safe deposit box here, was tendered for production, but I did not require it. Mr. O'Neill says that the scenario of Strange Interlude was written in 1925 at Nantucket, Mass.; that he started the play at Bermuda in the spring of 1926, and wrote the next four acts at Belgrade Lakes, Me., in the summer of 1926, and the final four acts in the winter of 1926-1927, at Bermuda, finishing it finally in February, 1927, at Bermuda.

Mr. O'Neill frankly admits that he discussed the germ of the idea, which developed into the play—an idea for a series of psychological plays depicting the outer and inner life of a woman from the age of young womanhood until forty-five—with George Jean Nathan in the spring of 1923, after he had finished writing Welded. Mr. Nathan, when called, confirmed this.

While Strange Interlude was being written he says that he discussed its psychological aspect with Dr. G. V. Hamilton, and the technique of the use of spoken thoughts, which he so effectively employs, with Professor George Pierce Baker, of Yale University, when in New Haven at the time he was given his degree of Doctor of Letters at the Yale Commencement of 1926.

He also says that he discussed what he had written up to that time with Kenneth MacGowan when the latter visited him at Belgrade Lakes, Me., in 1926.

Mr. O'Neill says that he did not receive any suggestions from others during the writing of Strange Interlude, and that it was written out in his own handwriting before it was typed. He denies explicitly that either Mr. Liveright or Mr. Smith of that firm, or any one directly or indirectly connected with Boni & Liveright, Inc., gave him any ideas or made any suggestions to him concerning the writing of the play. He makes the same denial also regarding Mr. Langner and Mr. Lemon, of the Theatre Guild.

Eventually Strange Interlude was produced by the Theatre Guild in January, 1928, and published by Boni & Liveright, Inc., predecessors of Horace Liveright, Inc., in March, 1928.

Mr. O'Neill states that he did not make any changes in the play except some cuts during the rehearsal thereof when he trimmed it down so that the time of playing it could be somewhat reduced, and, consequently, that the book is slightly longer than the acting script, but that the book is the original complete version.

Mr. Nathan, the well known dramatic critic, stated that he had known Mr. O'Neill since 1919, when he was editor of Smart Set in which some of Mr. O'Neill's shorter plays were published. He says that Mr. O'Neill often discussed his short plays with him. Mr. Nathan thinks that he first heard of the idea of Strange Interlude when they were walking up Sixth Avenue, probably in February, 1923. At that time Mr. O'Neill was working on a play called Welded which Mr. Nathan did not like. Mr. O'Neill then told him that he wanted to write a play dealing in great detail with a woman's emotional life from young womanhood until forty-five, taking a young woman who had lost her idealism and was attempting to recapture it. Mr. Nathan says he has made very few suggestions of any kind to Mr. O'Neill and had not made any suggestions whatever about Strange Interlude.

Mr. Nathan testified that he had never heard of the plaintiff's book before this suit. Much was made of the fact that he used the phrase "A Temple of Pallas-Athene" in a humorous criticism of a motion picture in a copy of Judge, dated August 20, 1927. This inconsequential fact, however, did not make any impression whatever on me for, of course, the phrase "A Temple of Athene," by the confession of the plaintiff's own resume, is as old as the heroic age in Greece, and has, therefore, been in the public domain more than two thousand years.

I found Mr. Nathan the most acute and competent of witnesses and I accept his evidence in toto.

Mr. Peter Mulligan, who was called by the plaintiff to attack the credibility of Mr. T. R. Smith, is now in the restaurant business at Freeport, Long Island. At one time he worked for Macmillan & Co., and then became a publisher's agent. He seems to have been well acquainted with Mr. Smith since some time shortly after the war, and at one time shared Mr. Smith's apartment with him.

He stated that he tried to interest Mr. Smith in The Temple in the summer of 1924, first showing him the circular mentioned above and then bringing him a copy of the book which he had been reading himself. He does not know what became of that copy, but did see a copy of the book in Mr. Smith's library.

Mr. Mulligan agreed to take over the selling agency of The Temple for Miss Lewys and had several hundred copies, both of The Temple and another book by Miss Lewys called Merry-Go-Round. They were sent by express from California in 1924, apparently after The Temple had been excluded from the mails.

Miss Lewys, on being recalled and with her memory refreshed by the evidence given by Mr. Mulligan and Mr. Smith, says that Mr. Mulligan telephoned her apartment asking if he might bring Mr. Smith to see her, that he had done so, and they had discussed books in general, and The Temple in particular. She admitted, on cross-examination, that she does not claim that Mr. Smith had sent a copy of The Temple to Mr. O'Neill. In fact she stated that once she planned to go into business with Mr. Smith, but that the arrangement was not consummated.

The plaintiff's great surprise witness Mulligan, therefore, added nothing of value to her case.

The suggestion adumbrated during the trial that Mr. O'Neill might have got access to the plaintiff's book whilst it was in possession of Mr. Lemon or Mr. Smith, because charwomen had keys to their respective offices, is wholly unworthy of consideration, and, if it were not on a parity with most of the plaintiff's contentions in this case, I should not have mentioned it.

Under these circumstances I find that the plaintiff has entirely failed to make out by any direct evidence that Mr. O'Neill had any access to her book before he wrote, or whilst he was writing, Strange Interlude.

VII

Inasmuch as there is not any direct evidence of access by Mr. O'Neill to her book, the plaintiff is thrown back necessarily on the question of a comparison between her book The Temple and Mr. O'Neill's play Strange Interlude.

The plaintiff contends that the denials as to any direct access to her book made by Mr. O'Neill and the other defendant witnesses called in that regard must be deemed to have been overcome by a comparison of the books in respect of the words used, the characters portrayed, and the arrangement of the scenes.

Consequently, she claims that from the alleged resemblances in these respects I should infer that Mr. O'Neill and the witnesses who testified at the trial in defendant's behalf have perjured themselves, and to find that Mr. O'Neill read a copy of The Temple which had been at the office of Boni & Liveright in the possession of Mr. Smith, or at least was informed by some one in detail about the book. A comparison of the books as the test of the truth of the denials of the defendant witnesses does not in any way shake my belief in their evidence. A few samples of the plaintiff's processes of comparison will suffice for illustration of their fantastic nature without going into any great detail.

The plaintiff has certain points which she refers to as "finger prints" which, she claims, show that Mr. O'Neill must have read her book, that he dramatized part of it, and that he wrote Strange Interlude from it. One of these is that she has a doctor in her book called Dr. Cramwell who comes of a good family in Philadelphia and went to Munich in his youth where he sowed his wild oats. The defendant, she says, has a doctor named Darrell who also comes from Philadelphia and goes to Munich for what she describes in her bill of particulars as his "capers." The fact that the names of the two men each end in "ell" is regarded by the plaintiff with suspicion as are the excursions to Munich.

She also makes a great point of the fact that Mr. O'Neill did not on his examination on commission specifically deny that Darrell was copied from Cramwell. Neither as characters nor as names are the two doctors alike, and I venture to guess many doctors from Philadelphia have been to Munich.

The second of the so-called finger prints reaches more fantastic heights. There is an instance in the plaintiff's novel when Adonais, one of the young men who is kept at stud as a professional father in the palace of the Russian princess, Gortacheff, in Paris, goes to the roof and looks at the stars in the spirit which is described as one of exaltation and reflects on the number of the descendants through whom his blood would flow.

The plaintiff regards it as of the most profound significance that, at the end of the first act of Strange Interlude, the father of the heroine, who is a professor at a New

England university, after his daughter has determined to leave him, crosses his library, turns for comfort to his books, pulls down a volume which he opens at random and reads a Latin quotation of somewhat obscure provenance, which turns out to have been from lines 95 to 98 of the fourth book of Astronomica—a poem in five books—by the Latin poet Manilius, of whom it is said that he was neither quoted nor mentioned by any ancient writer, but of whom several editions have been published since the first in 1579. The quotation refers to the not uncommon phenomenon of a man on a high place at night looking with wonder at the stars and endeavoring to read his fate in them.

I think it is incredible that, if Mr. O'Neill wanted to plagiarize the passage of the plaintiff's book to which she refers, he would have had to take the trouble to seek a quotation from a little known Latin author to conceal the fact that he was copying a passage from the plaintiff's book, when he might have easily dealt with such a comparatively usual emotion in English words which would have been equally effectual in covering his theft.

Another instance of alleged plagiarism which the plaintiff emphasizes greatly reaches the borderland where sense gives place to nonsense. She claims that the name Gordon Shaw, used as the lost fiancé of Nina Leeds in Strange Interlude, was secured thus:

> In The Temple there is a Russian princess named Gortacheff, of horrible aspect but limitless wealth, who has an altruistic interest in sex, and, hence, finances the temple. There is a statute of Athene in the temple; there was a sculptor named St. Gaudens; Adonais was the leader of the stud in the temple; Shelley wrote a poem called Adonais and was a friend of Lord Byron, whose middle name was Gordon. I do not recall, at the moment, just where the name of Shaw came in. But this is another "indelible finger print" on Mr. O'Neill's play.

Absurdity could not rise to greater heights. What I have just been mentioning is within what the plaintiff calls the category of paraphrase and which she claims constitutes plagiarism. Plaintiff makes in all four hundred and fifty-five comparisons of words and phrases, of which she emphasizes twenty-one in the list given in defendant's Exhibit O put in on her cross-examination.

She even goes so far as to claim plagiarism because a character in The Temple, at page 272, refers to his uncle as "an old fox," and, at page 23 of Strange Interlude, Marsden uses the expression "old fox" in connection with Nina's father.

More examples of claims of this kind would be merely tedious. It suffices to say that, inasmuch as the plaintiff cannot claim a copyright on words in the dictionary, or on usual English idioms, or on ideas, the alleged paraphrasing comes to naught as an attack on the denials of the defendant and his witnesses.

VIII

The next category of similarities which plaintiff emphasizes is the similarity between the characters in her book and in Mr. O'Neill's play. It is true that there are old and young people in both plots. It is true that there are fathers and mothers and daughters and sons. But after having carefully read both [works] more than once, I think it is fair to say that in the plaintiff's book the characters are merely types—the socially ambitious mother and daughter, the obtuse but successful American business man, the dissipated foreign nobleman, the middle aged English philanderer, and the fabulously rich Russian princess. None of these types is individualized sufficiently to make the characters of the defendant any possible infringement of the plaintiff's copyright.

In the defendant's [play], on the other hand, the characters are individualized and are perceptible in the round, as it seems to me, to a very extraordinary degree.

The plaintiff cannot copyright a type any more than could Miss Nichols in the case of Abie's Irish Rose, by taking for her characters stock figures, such as a low comedy Jew or a low comedy Irishman. Cf. Nichols v. Universal Pictures Corp., 45 F.2d 119, at 121-22. We may, therefore, dismiss the question of any possibility of infringement of the plaintiff's types in The Temple by the defendant's characters in Strange Interlude.

IX

After having unsuccessfully attempted to palm off the synopsis of dramaturgy taken from her bill of particulars as the document which she submitted to Mr. Courtney Lemon as a basis for a dramatization of her book for the Theatre Guild, the plaintiff was—as above noted—forced to admit that what she sent to him was the so-called "resume."

When this is compared with a summary of Strange Interlude, it effectually disposes of the plaintiff's third contention—a copying of the scenes, structure, and story of her book by the defendant.

The resume sent by the plaintiff to the Theatre Guild for dramatization of her novel is as follows, quoted verbatim:

> The story is basically designed as a satire. Characters are adapted from life among social leaders in France, England and America. The story rests on a scientific foundation: the Greek custom of "specimen reproduction" or selective parenthood. Scientific reproduction of the human species was incorporated in a Greek ritual, practiced in the ancient Temple of Pallas-Athenae in the Athenian Acropolis. The words "Pallas Athene" mean "Phallus the Serpent."
>
> A house is built in Paris in the present day for the same purpose, six male specimens are incarcerated there, and the handsome American and European women who are married to senile, awkward, or debauched husbands ("marriages de convenience") visit this house without the knowledge of their husbands in order to obtain beautiful children and to improve the human race.
>
> The book is divided into three parts. The first traces the ancestry of all the actors in the drama, including the principal male inhabitant of the Parisian Temple of Pallas-Athenae, called Adonis (Adonais). The second part is inside the Temple, describing the furnishings and life of the male specimen, the actual ritual of the Temple, and contrasts this sublime beauty with morbid conditions of marriage and debauchery in the so-called normal relationships outside. The third part of the book takes up the generation following—the descendants of these male specimens and follows out their life stories, dwelling principally on the two chief actors....

A summary of the defendant's play follows:

> 1. The first act of Strange Interlude opens in the library of Professor Leeds' home in what is described as a small university town in New England on an afternoon in the late part of a summer subsequent to the Great War.
>
> Marsden, a middle aged Anglicized New England gentleman, who is an intimate of the family, and, though many years older than Nina, the professor's daughter, is secretly in love with her, comes in, having just returned from Europe.

Professor Leeds enters, Marsden greets him and asks for Nina. He gets the impression that the professor is anxious about her, and when he is told that she dreams about Gordon Shaw, her fiance who was killed in an airplane during the war, he feels that things have somewhat changed during his absence. The Professor explains that, though on the surface matters go on much as usual, Nina is haunted by Gordon, and that Nina's condition is such that her mind seems to confuse the real and the unreal; that her mind dwells perpetually on her lost lover.

Nina enters the room and at first does not see Marsden. Finally she welcomes him somewhat coolly for an old friend, and she then says that she has made up her mind to leave her father's house that evening. This, apparently, is the first time that the subject of her leaving him has come to any definite decision, and the professor is evidently much upset by it.

Finally Nina, emphasizing what she calls her treachery to Gordon in not having married him before he left for the war, states that she is going to pay for the sex deprivation which she caused Gordon and, for his sake, is going as a nurse to a soldiers' hospital and there enter into sex relations with the wounded men as a kind of expiation for her failure to marry Gordon.

Her blunt statement of her regrets and of her purpose results in the confession by Professor Leeds that he had suggested to Gordon that he and Nina should not marry until he returned from the war.

2. Act 2 is also Professor Leeds' study on a night in early autumn a year later. Professor Leeds has died and Nina has returned for the funeral. She comes in dressed in a nurse's uniform and brings with her Dr. Darrell from the hospital where she has been during the past year.

Marsden is in the room and Nina greets him. They are then joined by Sam Evans, a college friend of Gordon Shaw, who is in love with Nina and wants to marry her. Evans is sent on an errand by Darrell.

Nina goes upstairs to her father's room and Darrell tells Marsden about Nina's relations with the wounded men at the hospital and says that in his opinion the only way to rescue her from the promiscuous affairs in which she had been indulging is to have her marry. He suggests Sam Evans who is much in love with her and whom Darrell knows well and likes.

3. Act 3 is seven months later. Nina and Sam Evans [are] on a belated honeymoon to the Evans home in Northern New York where Marsden joins them. During this visit Sam Evans' mother sees that Nina is [pregnant] and tells her that there is a strain of insanity in Sam's father's family, that Sam's father died in an asylum, and that an insane aunt lives with her at the family homestead. Mrs. Evans suggests to Nina that she should get rid of her impending baby, and in order to have happiness for her husband, and for herself, should seek outside of her marriage another child who would not have a taint in its blood.

4. In act 4, we return to Professor Leeds' study. There is a sense of uneasiness between Evans and Nina who is not well. Evans is trying to carry on with his work, but there seems to be something wrong, although Nina tells him that she loves him and suggests a renewal of their marital relations, having in the interval between this act and the last disposed by abortion of their impending child.

Into this household full of unrest Darrell returns in his capacity of doctor to advise on Nina's health. When he and Nina are alone Nina tells him of the insanity in her husband's family and suggests that Darrell should become the father of a child by her for the sake of her husband and also to gratify her own desire for motherhood. Darrell is astonished at the suggestion, but finally agrees.

[5. The remainder of the play focuses on the child fathered by Darrell.]

Thus the defendant's play tells the life of a woman and shows her sexual vagaries induced by various emotions, some normal and some pathological. It centers about her feelings for a man who was killed in the war for whom desire had been thwarted. It is an intensely personal theme, and her desire for a healthy child is not to improve the race, or entirely to avoid her husband's heredity, but to produce a child who would be worthy of her dead lover.

The plaintiff's book purports to be propaganda for eugenics. Its plea, if any, is racial rather than personal, and it shows the limitations necessarily placed by eugenics as a practice under our present prejudices when a popular stud-father is involved. Two young folks, patterns of perfection, become engaged, but have to part when their mothers find out at the last moment that they have the same stud-father. There is a Latin motto opposite the last page of the book, "Abuses Non Tollit Usum," which carries the supposed moral of the book: misuse of a good idea does not argue against its proper use.

One looks in vain for the parallelism between the plots in respect of any matter not long in the public domain. The idea of stud-fathers is, by the plaintiff's own confession, as old as the Greeks; hereditary taint in a family has been the subject of many books, and the expression of a desire to avoid perpetuation of such taint certainly was not new with the plaintiff, nor is the idea new of secret extramarital relations for any purpose which may interest those involved....

XI

The question now remaining is to determine the amount which I should allow as attorneys' fees to the defendants in a wholly synthetic case like this. In her complaint, in addition to praying for the usual injunction, the plaintiff claims damages in the sum of $1,250,000 for which she seeks recovery, and she also alleges that the defendants have realized profits, for which she craves an accounting, of over $1,000,000 up to the commencement of the suit.

The plaintiff, therefore, has played for high stakes and lost. The expense of their success will necessarily bear heavily on the defendants. Fortunately in copyright cases Congress has seen fit to leave the courts free to adopt the wise English practice of throwing a large part of the expense of litigation on the unsuccessful party. Section 40 of the Copyright Act of March 4, 1909 (now title 17, U.S. Code, Sec. 40), provides: "In all actions, suits, or proceedings under this title, except when brought by or against the United States or any officer thereof, full costs shall be allowed, and the court may award to the prevailing party a reasonable attorney's fee as part of the costs."

In determining what is a reasonable fee for an attorney, the elements to be considered, among others, are the amount involved, for that measures the attorney's responsibility; the amount of work necessary; the amount of work done; the skill used, and the result. [Calculating] my allowances for fees to the defendants by these considerations, I fix as reasonable fees for the attorneys of the several defendants the following amounts which I hereby award severally to the defendants: to Eugene O'Neill, as the principal defendant, on whom the heaviest burden fell, the sum of $7,500; to Boni & Liveright, Inc., and Horace Liveright, Inc., together, as they were represented by one firm of attorneys, the sum of $5,000, to be allocated between them as they see fit; and to the Theatre Guild, Inc., the sum of $5,000, making in all $17,500.

Settle orders and decrees on two days' notice.

OUTCAULT v. LAMAR
119 N.Y.S. 930 (App. Div. 1909)

LAUGHLIN, Justice.

[From a judgment dismissing the complaint, plaintiffs appeal.]

The plaintiffs allege, in substance, so far as material to the questions to be decided, that the plaintiff Outcault is a cartoonist, and is the author, inventor, and designer of a series of sketches or prints entitled "Buster Brown" and "Buster"; that the hero and protagonist of the sketches is a fictitious character, the creation of the cartoonist for which he adopted the fanciful and arbitrary name and title of "Buster Brown"; that the sketches or prints represent the fictitious character as a young male child, about five years of age, with blonde hair, dressed in bloomers and a pink coat extending a little above the knees, around which he wears a belt, and with his feet encased in socks and slippers, with the knees exposed, and a large white collar and a large bow, and wearing or carrying a sailor hat; that the character is represented in pictorial illustrations invented by the cartoonist in connection with different situations, characters, objects, and scenes, and particularly with his playmate, a dog, which the cartoonist arbitrarily named "Tige"; that the pictorial illustrations are a narrative of the adventures, experiences, and exploits of the fictitious character familiarly called "Buster" and his dog "Tige"; that on the 15th of April, 1902, the cartoonist granted to the New York Herald Company the right to print, publish, and vend the cartoons and prints entitled "Buster Brown" in connection with its Sunday issue of the New York Herald, and that the cartoons were duly copyrighted, but that the cartoonist "reserved to himself all other rights in said series, including the sole and exclusive right to dramatize said series of sketches or prints"; that the cartoons or prints illustrating the exploits and adventures of the fictitious character have since been published in each successive issue of the newspaper, extending over a period of about four years, and have been reproduced in numerous other papers in different parts of the United States and Europe through the Herald; that since about the 1st day of January, 1906, the cartoonist granted to the New York American the right to print, publish, and vend a continuation of said series of prints or sketches and the same have been duly copyrighted, likewise reserving to himself the exclusive right to dramatize the same, and that since that date the sketches or prints have been and are now being published by the New York Sunday American and other papers, with its consent, under the title of "Buster"; that the sketches or prints have been extensively advertised and have since been published in book form by the cartoonist under the title "Buster Brown"; that the prints or cartoons were the sole, exclusive, and original creations of the cartoonist, and acquired a great popularity and reputation with the public, both through their intrinsic merit and through his reputation; that in 1902 the cartoonist, in collaboration with one George Totten Smith, dramatized the sketches or prints in the form of a musical drama, based on the sketches depicting the scenes, characters, adventures, and exploits of "Buster Brown" and his dog "Tige" for public performance, and adapted the same for use upon the public stage, and for the purpose of identifying the play as his and indicating the origin of the same to the public, and indicating to theater-goers that the play is a dramatization of his famous sketches or prints entitled "Buster Brown," adopted and used and now uses as the title of the play the name "Buster Brown"; that in the year 1909 said Smith assigned his rights in the play to the individual plaintiffs, who are now the exclusive owners of the play, including the title and name, as well as the manuscript; that on the 25th day of September, 1903, the plaintiffs copyrighted the play under the title "Buster Brown," and certificates of copyright were duly issued to them under said title by the Librarian of Congress; that the individual plaintiffs granted to one Melville B. Raymond the right to produce the play upon the public stage under the title "Buster Brown," and he caused it to be continuously produced upon the public stage by a number of theatrical companies throughout the United States since on or about the 25th day of December, 1903, until the 1st day of June, 1906; that the plaintiff corporation was incorporated under the laws of this state on the 6th day of January, 1906, for the purpose of producing this play among others, and thereafter acquired the exclusive right to produce the play, and has since the 15th day of August, 1906, presented it to the public by several theatrical companies; that the play and its principal character, known as "Buster Brown," familiarly called "Buster," and his dog "Tige," acquired great popularity through their intrinsic merits with the public and especially with children, as they "deal with the pranks of a mischievous boy and his dog"; that the play became and was successful and profitable, and the individual plaintiffs have realized in royalties from its production more than $50,000; that the press and public have associated and continue to associate the name "Buster Brown" or "Buster," "as he is usually known by the children," with the plaintiffs' play and leading character; that the play, as well as the title thereof, is the sole and exclusive property of the individual plaintiffs, and that the name "Buster Brown" has never before been used as the title of a play or the name of any character in a play, and is used by the plaintiffs to designate the play and the hero and leading character thereof; that, with full knowledge of these facts, the defendants, without the consent of the plaintiffs, and in violation of their rights, "and in pursuance of a deliberate design to cheat and defraud the plaintiffs and the public," have since on or about the 3d day of August, 1908, produced upon the public stage "at the Brighton Beach Music Hall, Brooklyn, N.Y., and still continue to do so, a play or dramatic sketch advertised and announced to the public in posters, placards, and newspapers, under the title 'Buster Brown,' and simulated and colorably imitated the plaintiffs' said title," and are still producing the play upon public stages throughout the United States, and charging admission fees therefore, and are booking their play throughout the country, and threaten and intend to have it performed in each city wherein the plaintiffs' play is to be performed; that the defendants fraudulently and wrongfully appropriated and used the title and name "Buster Brown" in connection with their play to falsely lead the people to believe that it is the play owned by the plaintiffs and based upon said cartoons or prints, and have conveyed that impression to the public by press notices and announcements and otherwise; that the profits of the plaintiffs from the play arise from its production and from royalties or percentages of the receipts of the performances paid by others for the right and privilege of producing it, and the individual plaintiffs have at all times reserved to themselves the exclusive right to license others to produce the play; that the defendants have deceived and misled many persons and induced them to attend the production of their play, believing it to be the play of the plaintiffs, and have thus obtained large profits, to the great injury and damage of the plaintiffs, and, unless they are restrained from the use of the title and name of the plaintiffs' play, they will destroy its value and will cause irreparable injury to the plaintiffs, who have no adequate remedy at law; that the plaintiff corporation has incurred large cost and expense and liability in causing two independent performing companies, with the necessary scenery, costumes, printing matter, and accessories to produce the play in various cities of the United States and has obtained bookings therefore; that the unlawful acts of the defendants will seriously interfere with the booking of the plaintiffs' play, and will result in the cancellation of their bookings to their great loss, injury, and damage.

The relief demanded is that the defendants and their agents and servants be enjoined from using the title or name "Buster Brown" or "Buster" as the title or part of the title of any play or dramatic sketch, and from using the names "Buster Brown," "Buster," or "Tige," or imitations thereof, in connection with any dramatic play or in any advertisement thereof, and that the defendants account for all profits realized by them from the public performances of their play under the title "Buster Brown" or "Buster," with the usual prayer for other and further relief.

Upon the trial the plaintiffs gave evidence tending to establish the material allegations of the complaint. The defendants by their answer claim that the Herald Company, by virtue of copyrighting the cartoons, obtained the right to dramatize the incidents depicted thereby, and that they have been duly authorized and licensed by the Herald Company to use the title "Buster Brown" and "Buster" and those names and the name "Tige," and to dramatize and present a play based on the incidents depicted by the cartoons.

It thus appearing by the answer that the defendants claimed under rights derived from the Herald Company, the plaintiffs anticipated the defense, and showed on their affirmative case, not only that, when Outcault conferred upon the Herald Company the right to copyright the cartoons, he reserved to himself the right to dramatize them, but for the purpose of showing, also, that the Herald Company recognized that it had not obtained the dramatic rights, they proved two letters from the Herald Company to him under date of October 1, 1902, the first reciting that the Herald Company was the owner of the copyright in the cartoons, and would transfer to Outcault at any time its rights therein in order to enable him to protect himself against infringement, also "all dramatic rights in this series," and the second, which was written because he did not like the phraseology of the first, purports to transfer to him, in consideration of a dollar and other valuable considerations, all of the Herald Company's rights in the copyright and "all dramatic rights in this series."

The learned counsel for the [defendants] argues that this evidence changed the pleading, and that the plaintiffs should now be conclusively held to have based their claim to relief on the trial on the assignments of the copyright from the Herald. We are of opinion, however, that there was no intention by the introduction of this evidence to change the theory of the plaintiffs' action. The plaintiffs might well have waited to introduce it on rebuttal to show, if necessary, merely that the Herald Company had no dramatic rights to assign to the defendants since any assignment to them was after the Herald Company thus formally recognized the agreement under which it had received from Outcault merely the naked right to copyright and publish the cartoons. It should be, for the purpose of determining whether or not the pleading was changed, regarded as if introduced on rebuttal.

It follows, therefore, that the judgment should be reversed and a new trial granted, with costs to the plaintiffs to abide the event. All concur.

METRO-GOLDWYN-MAYER, INC. v. SHOWCASE ATLANTA COOPERATIVE PRODUCTIONS, INC.
479 F. Supp. 351 (N.D. Ga. 1979)

EVANS, District Judge.

The present action, involving alleged copyright infringement, claims of unfair competition and alleged violation of the Anti-Dilution Statute and the Uniform Deceptive Trade Practices Act is before the Court on Plaintiffs' Motion for a Preliminary Injunction.

Plaintiffs have various respective rights or interests in Margaret Mitchell's copyrighted novel, "Gone With The Wind," and works derived from that novel: Metro-Goldwyn-Mayer, Inc. owns the screen rights and copyright for the film, Gone With The Wind; The Macmillan Company, Inc. is the holder of the copyright for the novel Gone With The Wind; [and] Stephens Mitchell and Trust Company Bank in their capacity as Trustees for certain heirs of Margaret Mitchell own certain residual interests in the copyrighted works and derivatives thereof, including the stage rights. Defendants are the respective owners/producers/creators of a musical production entitled "Scarlett Fever," which was originally scheduled to begin public performance in Atlanta on September 21, 1979.

Scarlett Fever is a three-hour-long three-act play based on Gone With The Wind (primarily on the film Gone With The Wind). It opens, just as the movie does, with the scene at Tara on the day before the Wilkes' barbecue, with Scarlett talking to the Tarleton twins. It moves in sequence through the major episodes of Gone With The Wind, though in condensed form and omitting certain scenes, and ends as Rhett leaves Scarlett. Interspersed throughout the various scenes are original songs and dance routines.

Although modern vernacular has been employed in certain scenes in Scarlett Fever, the script on a scene by scene basis is largely faithful to that of the film. The play also utilizes backdrops depicting scenes reminiscent of the major settings in the film, for example, the plantation house at Tara and the train depot in Atlanta with flames in the background. However, the names of the major characters have been changed so that they are, for example, Shady Charlotte O'Mara, Brett Studler, Melody Hampton, Ansley Mall, and so forth. Further, Shady Charlotte's plantation is dubbed Tiara; Ansley's home, Thirteen Elms. In the original works the equivalents are, of course, Scarlett O'Hara, Rhett Butler, Melanie Hamilton, Ashley Wilkes, Tara, and Twelve Oaks.

As its name implies, Showcase Cabaret provides "cabaret" entertainment, which is predominantly light, musical entertainment in a fairly intimate setting (approximately 150 to 200 seats). The major characters in Scarlett Fever are played by a small cast, with most of the actors portraying more than one role in an intentionally obvious way. On the whole, the production is humorous, entertaining and skillfully performed by the cast.

The central issue presented here is whether Scarlett Fever, asserted by defendants to be a spoof or parody of Gone With The Wind, infringes upon plaintiffs' copyright interests in the novel (and the film) Gone With The Wind. The resolution of this issue primarily lies in a determination of whether defendants are entitled to invoke the so-called "fair use" defense afforded by 17 U.S.C. § 107, Copyright Act of 1976, which has been a recognized source of protection for such forms of comment upon copyrighted works.

Having viewed Scarlett Fever and the film Gone With The Wind at the invitation of the litigants, considering the evidence presented at a hearing on October 1, 1979, and having had the benefit of the excellent arguments and briefs of counsel for both sides, the Court concludes that Scarlett Fever falls short of entitlement to the fair use defense. In reaching its conclusion, the Court finds that Scarlett Fever taken in its entirety is not the sort of original critical comment meant to be protected by the fair use defense, but rather is predominantly a derivative or adaptive use of the copyrighted film and novel Gone With The Wind; additionally, that to the extent the production contains critical comment in the form of parody or satire, defendants have drawn on the copyrighted work far more extensively than is permissible to "conjure up" the subjects or characters parodied. These issues, together with others, are more fully discussed below.

A. The showing required by plaintiffs

In a copyright case, as in all others, a plaintiff seeking preliminary injunctive relief must demonstrate that there is a substantial likelihood of plaintiff's success on the merits at trial, that irreparable injury will be suffered unless the injunction issues, that the threatened injury to the movant outweighs the damage which the injunction may cause the opponent, and that the injunction would not be adverse to the public interest. Dallas Cowboys Cheerleaders v. Scoreboard Posters, 600 F.2d 1184 (5th Cir. 1979). As indicated below, plaintiffs have very little difficulty in this case making out a prima facie case of copyright infringement. The heart of the case lies in an affirmative defense raised by defendants, namely that Scarlett Fever is saved from copyright infringement by the fair use defense, 17 U.S.C. § 107. On a motion for preliminary injunction, plaintiffs must demonstrate a likelihood of success on the merits at trial as to asserted affirmative defenses, as well as to the elements of plaintiffs' prima facie case.

B. Plaintiffs' prima facie case

In order to obtain injunctive relief for copyright infringement, the movant must show ownership of a valid, existing copyright and copying of the copyrighted material by the defendant. See Uneeda Doll Co. v. Regent Baby Products Corp., 355 F. Supp. 438 (E.D.N.Y. 1972); Walco Products, Inc. v. Kittay & Blitz, Inc., 354 F. Supp. 121 (S.D.N.Y. 1972).

The parties have stipulated to plaintiffs' ownership of valid, existing copyrights in the film and novel Gone With The Wind. This automatically establishes that plaintiffs have the exclusive right to prepare derivative works based on the copyrighted work, 17 U.S.C. § 106(2); and that plaintiffs are entitled to prevent any unauthorized "musical arrangement, dramatization...or any other form in which the work may be recast, transformed or adapted," 17 U.S.C. § 101.

What remains for plaintiffs to establish a prima facie case is to prove copying by defendants of the copyrighted material. One method of doing so is to show "substantial similarity" between the copyrighted and the infringing works. See Walt Disney Productions v. Air Pirates, 581 F.2d 751 (9th Cir. 1978); Berlin v. E. C. Publications, Inc., 329 F.2d 541 (2d Cir.), cert. denied, 379 U.S. 822 (1964). When dramatic works are at issue, this method involves more than the mere quantitative analysis of dissecting the two works and matching the similarities and differences. It also requires the intrinsic test of the response of an ordinary reasonable person, a form of qualitative analysis. Sid and Marty Krofft Television Productions, Inc. v. McDonald's Corp., 562 F.2d 1157 (9th Cir. 1977). This can be thought of as the "ordinary observation or impression" test. There must appear to be substantial similarity to the ordinary observer, so that the alleged copy comes so near to the original as to give the audience the idea created by the original. Costello v. Loew's, Inc., 159 F. Supp. 782 (D.D.C. 1958).

It is clear that there is "substantial similarity" between Scarlett Fever and the copyrighted works, especially the film Gone With The Wind, in both quantitative and qualitative terms. The foundation, materials of locale, settings, characters, situations and relationships are basically the same in Scarlett Fever, the film Gone With The Wind and the novel Gone With The Wind. The other foundation elements of theme and characterization are also very similar, although the treatment of these elements is at times more comical in Scarlett Fever than in the film Gone With The Wind or in the novel Gone With The Wind. The story line in Scarlett Fever is nearly identical to that in the film Gone With The Wind, although it is somewhat condensed. The dialogue in Scarlett

Fever is often near-verbatim of the dialogue in the film Gone With The Wind, though again in a condensed manner and at times inserting modern vernacular in the characters' speech. Not only is a substantial quantity of the film Gone With The Wind and the novel Gone With The Wind used in Scarlett Fever, but the impression that Scarlett Fever undoubtedly gives to anyone viewing it or reading the script is that it is a version of Gone With The Wind, invoking in the audience images of the copyrighted works.

The Court notes that defendants do not deny that Scarlett Fever is quantitatively or qualitatively "substantially similar" to the film Gone With The Wind or the novel Gone With The Wind. In fact, the defendants basically agree that Scarlett Fever is a comic version of the film Gone With The Wind and the novel Gone With The Wind, and argue strongly that the nature of their comedy is parody or satire and therefore protected by the "fair use" defense to copyright infringement, 17 U.S.C. § 107. Having determined that there is the "substantial similarity" between Scarlett Fever and the film Gone With The Wind and the novel Gone With The Wind required for a finding of infringement, the Court now turns to the defenses asserted by the defendants in this case to decide if there is a substantial likelihood of plaintiffs' success on the merits as to each of the asserted defenses.

C. Defenses raised by defendants

1. Fair use

The first and foremost defense asserted by the defendants in this case is that Scarlett Fever is a parody or satire of the film Gone With The Wind and the novel Gone With The Wind and therefore protected as a "fair use" under 17 U.S.C. § 107. That provision of the Copyright Act of 1976 states that the "fair use of a copyrighted work...for purposes such as criticism, comment, news reporting, teaching..., scholarship, or research, is not an infringement of copyright." Although the "fair use" provision does not mention parody or satire, many courts have recognized that parody or satire may be protected as "fair use," including the Fifth Circuit. See Dallas Cowboys Cheerleaders v. Scoreboard Posters, supra; Walt Disney Productions v. Air Pirates, supra; Berlin v. E. C. Publications, Inc., supra.

In the discussion of the applicability of "fair use" to Scarlett Fever, the Court first recognizes that the Court is not an expert on literature, drama or comedy, and makes no pretense as to being a dramatic or literary "critic." However, the Court also recognizes that Scarlett Fever is to be judged and evaluated on the basis of its overall effect. Counsel for both sides agreed at the hearing on the preliminary injunction that the Court is to look at the work Scarlett Fever as a whole in deciding the threshold question of whether it is a parody or satire before the issue of "fair use" can be addressed. In looking at the play as a whole, the Court finds that Scarlett Fever is neither a parody nor a satire. Rather, Scarlett Fever is a musical adaptation of the film Gone With The Wind and the novel Gone With The Wind, generally in the nature of comedy, with some elements of parody but also with some elements of tragedy or straight drama.

The underlying rationale for applying the "fair use" doctrine to parody and satire is that these art forms involve the type of original critical comment meant to be protected by § 107 of the Copyright Act of 1976. The defendants have put forward the following definition of parody and satire, taken from an opinion in a trademark violation case, Dallas Cowboys Cheerleaders v. Pussycat Cinema, 467 F. Supp. 366 (S.D.N.Y. 1979), in which the court discussed the application of "fair use":

> A parody is a work in which the language or style of another work is closely imitated or mimicked for comic effect or ridicule. A satire is a work which holds up the vices or shortcomings of an individual or institution to ridicule or derision, usually with an intent to stimulate change; the use of wit, irony or sarcasm for the purpose of exposing and discrediting vice or folly.

Id. at 376.

This Court accepts this definition, with the caveat that in order to constitute the type of parody eligible for fair use protection, parody must do more than merely achieve comic effect. It must also make some critical comment or statement about the original work which reflects the original perspective of the parodist thereby giving the parody social value beyond its entertainment function. Otherwise, any comic use of an existing work would be protected, removing the "fair" aspect of the "fair use" doctrine and negating the underlying purpose of copyright law of protecting original works from unfair exploitation by others.

In applying this view to Scarlett Fever, it is clear that the play is not a parody or satire, although it contains some such elements, because the work as a whole is not a critical commentary on either the film or the novel Gone With The Wind. Therefore, Scarlett Fever is not protected by the "fair use" doctrine, although the Court does recognize that the songs in Scarlett Fever appear to be original and therefore may be protected and not an infringement of plaintiffs' copyrights. It is the inconsistent use of parody and satire in Scarlett Fever that deprives the play of the overall effect or impression of parody or satire, as shown by the following examples.

Perhaps the best example of consistent satire in Scarlett Fever is the character Melodie, through which the playwright critically comments upon the gentle ("insipid") nature of the character of Melanie ("Melodie"). Similarly, Chaz Hampton is a satiric character (described as being "like a suckling pig"). The name of the play and the names of some of the characters are satiric.

An example of the inconsistent use of satire is the character of Charlotte, based on the central character Scarlett O'Hara. At times Charlotte comically exaggerates traits of Scarlett, thereby critically commenting upon them, while at other times Charlotte is treated strictly comically (no comment on the character of Scarlett, just for laughs) or very dramatically, thereby denying an overall impression of satire.

The characters of Mammy and Sissy (the latter being the counterpart of Prissy, the character played in the film Gone With The Wind by Butterfly McQueen) in Scarlett Fever, although comical, are examples of imitating what was a comical characterization, or comic relief, in the film Gone With The Wind and therefore involve no comment upon the original characters. The character Aunt Kitty Kat is an example of a character varied from the original, but not in a manner which reflects comment on the original character Aunt Pitty Pat, who may be recalled from the film Gone With The Wind as a highly nervous but lovable old maid possessing corkscrew curls, lace handkerchiefs and continually fluttering hands—definitely a comic relief character. Aunt Kitty Kat in the play incorporates the basic features of Aunt Pitty Pat; the original touch is that she is played by a male actor, whose purposely ill-concealed male identity is not parody or satire but rather pure comedy.

There are also several highly serious or dramatic sequences in Scarlett Fever, perhaps the most lengthy of which is the return to Tiara in Act II involving Charlotte's contact with her insane father and learning of her mother's death and the ruin of her home by the Yankees. Further, the character Brett Studler did not appear to add any new dimension or comment on the original character Rhett Butler, but rather seemed to be a non-comic imitation.

Even if Scarlett Fever was a parody or satire in its overall effect, the Court finds that the play is still not protected by "fair use" because Scarlett Fever incorporates more material from the film Gone With The Wind and the novel Gone With The Wind than "fair use" allows. The four factors or guidelines enumerated by 17 U.S.C. § 107 to be "considered" in determining whether "fair use" applies are the following: (1) the purpose and character of the use, including whether such use is of a commercial nature or is for nonprofit educational purposes; (2) the nature of the copyrighted work; (3) the amount and substantiality of the portion used in relation to the copyrighted work as a whole; and (4) the effect of the use upon the potential market for or value of the copyrighted work.

The first factor, the purpose and character of the use, is assumed to be parody or satire, which is generally a recognized "fair use." The second factor, the nature of the copyrighted work, is a novel and a film and any derivative uses of such works, including any non-parodic or non-satirical form of theatrical production. The other two factors, the amount and substantiality of the portion used and the effect upon the plaintiffs' potential market, are more significant and are really the factors at issue once the assumption of parody or satire is made.

Several cases from the Second and Ninth Circuits have developed rules to be applied when analyzing the amount and substantiality of the original work used in the alleged infringing work. There is a threshold test, the so-called Benny test, which holds that exact or "near-verbatim" copying of a copyrighted work prevents application of a "fair use" defense, even if the infringing work is a parody or satire. This test arose in Benny v. Loew's Incorporated, 239 F.2d 532, 536 (9th Cir. 1956), aff'd by an equally divided court, 356 U.S. 43 (1958), in which the Ninth Circuit said: "The fact that a serious dramatic work is copied practically verbatim, and then presented with actors walking on their hands or with other grotesqueries, does not avoid infringement of the copyright."

Although the court in Benny referred to substantial similarity in applying this test, it is recognized that the court intended "near-verbatim" to be the standard. See Walt Disney Productions v. Air Pirates, supra. Otherwise, the test for finding infringement and the test for disallowing "fair use" would be the same, effectively eliminating the "fair use" standard. Although there is "near-verbatim" copying by Scarlett Fever of the dialogue and other elements of the film Gone With The Wind, there is enough originality in Scarlett Fever, particularly the songs, so that it passes the Benny test, albeit barely.

However, Scarlett Fever incorporates much more of Gone With The Wind than is necessary to "recall or conjure up" the original works and therefore no "fair use" applies. The "recall or conjure up" test was fully articulated by the Second Circuit in Berlin v. E. C. Publications, Inc., supra, and more recently applied by the Ninth Circuit in Air Pirates. In Berlin, the court devised this test from two earlier district court cases from California: Loew's, Inc. v. Columbia Broadcasting System, 131 F. Supp. 165 (S.D. Cal. 1955) (the Benny case), and Columbia Pictures Corp. v. National Broadcasting Co., 137 F. Supp. 348 (S.D. Cal. 1955) (the "From Here to Obscurity" case), both decided by Judge Carter.

In holding that there was "fair use" in Berlin, the court found the disparities in theme, content and style between the original lyrics and the alleged infringements could hardly be greater. While brief phrases of the original lyrics were occasionally injected into the parodies, this practice [was deemed] necessary if the defendants' efforts were to "recall or conjure up" the originals.

Scarlett Fever clearly fails the test developed by the court in Berlin. Scarlett Fever closely follows the general plot of the film Gone With The Wind, copies specific incidents and details extensively, and reproduces significant portions of the dialogue in a nearly identical manner. Furthermore, the disparities in theme, content, and style between the works, where they do exist, are not very significant. Also, much more than "brief phrases" of the original works are more than "occasionally injected" into Scarlett Fever. Given the fact that the characters, plot, and dialogue of Gone With The Wind are well-known to the public, it appears that such extensive copying of the original works was not necessary to "conjure up" or "recall."

Defendants argue that such an extensive incorporation of material from Gone With The Wind is not only justified but required under the test of "recall or conjure up" as applied in Air Pirates, supra. This Court finds that such an interpretation of Air Pirates is in error. In Walt Disney Productions v. Air Pirates, 581 F.2d 751 (9th Cir. 1978), the court recognized the Benny test as a threshold test eliminating near-verbatim copying but chose not to apply it because the court felt that the defendants took more than allowed by the Berlin test with regard to both the conceptual and physical aspects of the copyrighted cartoon characters. In applying the Berlin test, the court in Air Pirates stated:

> In evaluating how much of a taking was necessary to recall or conjure up the original, it is first important to recognize that given the widespread public recognition of the major characters involved here, such as Mickey Mouse and Donald Duck, in comparison with other characters very little would have been necessary to place Mickey Mouse and his image in the minds of the readers.

Id. at 757-58.

That court also found it significant that the infringing parody focused on the personalities of the characters and not merely their physical appearances. In discussing this factor, the court (in dicta relied upon by defendants herein for their theory of a "close parallel" requirement) said:

> Thus arguably defendants' copying could have been justified as necessary more easily if they had paralleled closely (with a few significant twists) Disney characters and their actions in a manner that conjured up the particular elements of the innocence of the characters that were to be satirized. While greater license may be necessary under those circumstances, here the copying of the graphic image appears to have no other purpose than to track Disney's work as closely as possible.

Id. at 758.

The meaning of the "close parallel" language in Air Pirates is not at all clear, and such language is neither binding nor persuasive in the present case. If a parody or satire is to warrant "fair use" protection, then it should parody that part of the original work which it copies. Therefore, if a parody or satire "closely parallels" an entire original work, it should parody at least a majority of those parts or elements of the original work which it parallels. Scarlett Fever failed to parody or satirize even a significant portion of the elements of Gone With The Wind which it parallels.

This Court has found that even if Scarlett Fever was assumed to be a parody or satire, it clearly incorporates more material from the original works than is allowed under the third factor of § 107 and the Berlin test and therefore "fair use" does not apply. However, the Court feels that its analysis would be incomplete without addressing the fourth factor, which is the effect of the use upon the potential market for or value of the copyrighted work. The defendants in this case have argued that Scarlett Fever will not harm the existing or potential markets for either the film Gone With The Wind or the novel Gone With The Wind, but is more likely to enhance the demand for those works. Defendants have also claimed that a prior authorized stage version of Gone With The Wind was a failure and that no authorized stage production is planned for the immediate future, and therefore Scarlett Fever does not harm the existing or potential market for such a derivative use of the original works. The Court does not agree with this analysis and finds that Scarlett Fever is likely to harm the potential market for or value of the derivative use of Gone With The Wind in the form of a theatrical adaptation.

The Court first recognizes that a non-parodic or non-satiric stage version of Gone With The Wind is a protected derivative use of the original works which only the holders of the valid, existing copyrights in such works have a right to exploit. Harm to the potential market for or value of such a derivative use is more difficult to specify than it is to conceptualize. Defendants argue that since a previous authorized stage version of Gone With The Wind was a failure, no future productions are likely to be attempted by local producers, and therefore Scarlett Fever can in no way harm the potential market for or value of a future production since no such market or value exists. This logic is persuasive only if the Court assumes that any future production of Gone With The Wind would be the same as or very similar to the past failure. This would be an unreasonable assumption to make, especially in light of the highly positive audience response to the production of Scarlett Fever viewed by the Court. The potential for success of Scarlett Fever indicates that a future stage production of Gone With The Wind superior to the earlier failure is likely to succeed and therefore Scarlett Fever could harm a potential market for or value of a stage version of Gone With The Wind.

The Court acknowledges that this type of analysis is speculative, but that is inherent in the nature of a "potential" market for a future derivative use. This analysis is aided by what Nimmer calls the "functional test." He states that in determining the effect of the defendants' use upon the potential market for or value of the plaintiffs' work, a comparison must be made not merely of the media in which the two works may appear, but rather in terms of the function of each such work regardless of media. 3 Nimmer, The Law of Copyright § 13.05(B) (1978). Nimmer describes this test as follows:

> If both the plaintiff's and defendant's works are used for the same purpose, then under the functional test the defense of fair use should not be available since the defendant's work serves the same function as that of the plaintiff's.
>
> The scope of fair use is then constricted where the two works in issue fulfill the same function in terms of actual or potential consumer demand, and expanded where such functions differ.

Id. at 13-57 and 13-58.

It can be said that the overall function of both the film Gone With The Wind and the novel Gone With The Wind is to entertain. The overall function of Scarlett Fever is also to entertain. Having found that Scarlett Fever is not a parody or satire, its overall function is not criticism, comment, reporting or teaching. Using the "functional test," "fair use" cannot be applied to Scarlett Fever because its function is identical to the functions of the film Gone With The Wind and the novel Gone With The Wind and any potential derivative use of Gone With The Wind as a stage adaptation. As Nimmer notes, similarity of medium is not relevant to application of the functional test. As to defendants' claim that a prior failure of an authorized stage production destroys the potential market for and value of another authorized production, Nimmer's comments concerning Meeropol v. Nizer, 361 F. Supp. 1063 (S.D.N.Y. 1973), seem appropriate:

> The Meeropol court was further moved by the fact that plaintiffs' copyrighted work containing such letters had been out of print for almost 20 years. The fact that a work is out-of-print surely cannot mean that the copyright therein is vitiated. Works out of print are published in new editions when the demand becomes sufficient. Such demand may never arise if competitors may freely copy the out-of-print work.

Nimmer, supra, n. 51, at 13-57.

In summing up the foregoing discussion of "fair use," the Court holds that Scarlett Fever is neither a parody nor a satire with respect to "fair use" protection, and further holds that even if Scarlett Fever was a parody or satire, Scarlett Fever would not be protected by "fair use" because it copies more of Gone With The Wind than is allowed by the Berlin test. Also, Scarlett Fever does not warrant "fair use" protection because it has the same function as Gone With The Wind under the "functional test" and therefore is likely to harm the potential market for or value of the copyrighted work.

2. Other defenses

Defendants also argue that Scarlett Fever is protected by a First Amendment privilege even if it is found not to be a "fair use," relying upon Triangle Publications v. Knight-Ridder Newspapers, 445 F. Supp. 875 (S.D. Fla. 1978). There, the publisher of "TV Guide" sought an injunction to prevent a newspaper from displaying TV Guide in a "comparative" advertisement placed by a competitor. The District Court held that although "fair use" did not protect defendant's copying, the First Amendment did allow depiction of TV Guide in the ad and that when the First Amendment and the Copyright Act operate at cross-purposes, the Free Speech Guarantee of the First Amendment takes precedence.

Even if Triangle has implications as broad as the holding would indicate, it still has no relevance to the present case in light of the finding made above that Scarlett Fever is not a parody or satire. Thus, it does not constitute the sort of critical comment which might draw First Amendment protection of the fair use defense into play.

Finally, defendants assert that plaintiffs have either abandoned, or are estopped to assert, any copyright protection against parodies or satires of Gone With The Wind, citing certain other spoofs of Gone With The Wind as to which no legal action was taken by plaintiffs. Of course, this defense is foreclosed by the Court's finding that Scarlett Fever is not predominately a satire or parody. But additionally, it should be noted that abandonment can only be shown by proving that the copyright owner intended to surrender his rights. Imperial Homes Corp. v. Lamont, 458 F.2d 895 (5th Cir. 1972). Estoppel requires both intent and knowledge on the part of the one to be estopped, plus the other party's right to rely. Hampton v. Paramount Pictures Corp., 279 F.2d 100 (9th Cir. 1960). No evidence was presented which would indicate the existence of plaintiffs' intent to abandon, or any conduct of plaintiffs which might furnish the basis for justifiable reliance by defendants....

E. Conclusion

Based upon the foregoing, the Court holds that plaintiffs have established a substantial likelihood of success on the merits. [Accordingly,] plaintiffs' Motion for a Preliminary Injunction is hereby GRANTED and pending trial on the merits, defendants are hereby enjoined from further production of Scarlett Fever.

PRESLEY'S ESTATE v. RUSSEN
513 F. Supp. 1339 (D.N.J. 1981)

BROTMAN, District Judge.

During his lifetime, Elvis Presley established himself as one of the legends in the entertainment business. On August 16, 1977, Elvis Presley died, but his legend and worldwide popularity have survived. As Presley's popularity has subsisted and even grown, so has the capacity for generating financial rewards and legal disputes. Although the present case is another in this line, it presents questions not previously addressed. As a general proposition, this case is concerned with the rights and limitations of one who promotes and presents a theatrical production designed to imitate or simulate a stage performance of Elvis Presley.

FINDINGS OF FACT

Plaintiff

Plaintiff is the Estate of Elvis Presley (hereafter the Estate) located in Memphis, Tennessee, created by the Will of Elvis Presley and is, under the laws of the State of Tennessee, a legal entity with the power to sue and be sued. The Estate came into being upon the death of Elvis Presley on August 16, 1977.

During his career, Elvis Presley established himself as one of the premier musical talents and entertainers in the United States, Europe and other areas of the world. He was the major force behind the American Rock and Roll movement, and his influence and popularity has continued to this day. During Presley's legendary career, his talents were showcased in many ways. He performed in concert, setting attendance records and selling out houses in Las Vegas and other cities in which his tour appeared. He starred in numerous motion pictures, made records which sold over one million copies, and appeared on television programs and in television specials made from his tour programs.

Although Elvis Presley exhibited a range of talents and degrees of change in his personality and physical make-up during his professional career, he, in association with his personal manager, Thomas A. (Col.) Parker, developed a certain, characteristic performing style, particularly as to his live stage shows. His voice, delivery, mannerisms (such as his hips and legs gyrations), appearance and dress (especially a certain type of jumpsuit and a ring), and actions accompanying a performance (such as handing out scarves to the audience), all contributed to this Elvis Presley style of performance.

One particular image or picture of Presley became closely associated with and identifiable of the entertainment provided by Elvis Presley. This image (hereafter referred to as the "Elvis pose") consisted of a picture or representation of Elvis Presley dressed in one of his characteristic jumpsuits with a microphone in his hand and apparently singing.

Elvis Presley exploited his name, likeness, and various images during his lifetime through records, photographs, posters, merchandise, movies, and personal appearances. As a result of Presley's own talent, as well as of the various promotional efforts undertaken on his behalf, the popularity of Elvis Presley and his entertainment services, as identified by certain trademarks and service marks, reached worldwide proportions. Elvis Presley productions achieved a reputation for a certain level of quality and performance. Goodwill attached to Presley's performances and the merchandise bearing his name and picture.

The Estate and its licensees and sub-licensees, and during his lifetime Elvis Presley and his representatives and those with whom he had contracts or licenses, have taken actions to protect the rights of the Estate and of the licensees.

Defendant

Defendant Rob Russen d/b/a THE BIG EL SHOW (hereafter Russen) is the producer of THE BIG EL SHOW. THE BIG EL SHOW is a stage production patterned after an actual Elvis Presley stage show, albeit on a lesser scale, and featuring an individual who impersonates the late Elvis Presley by performing in the style of Presley. The performer wears the same style and design of clothing and jewelry as did Presley, hands out to the audience scarves as did Presley, sings songs made popular by Presley, wears his hair in the same style as Presley, and imitates the singing voice, distinctive poses, and body movements made famous by Presley.

Russen charges customers to view performances of THE BIG EL SHOW or alternatively charges fees to those in whose rooms or auditoriums THE BIG EL SHOW is performed who in turn charge customers to view THE BIG EL SHOW.

THE BIG EL SHOW production runs for approximately ninety minutes. The show opens with the theme from the movie "2001—A Space Odyssey" which Elvis Presley also used to open his stage shows. The production centers on Larry Seth, "Big El," doing his Elvis Presley impersonation and features musicians called the TCB Band. The TCB Band was also the name of Elvis Presley's band; however THE BIG EL SHOW TCB Band does not consist of musicians from Presley's band.

From the inception of THE BIG EL SHOW, the star was Larry Seth. Seth, who is under a long-term contract with THE BIG EL SHOW, recently "retired" from the show; but he may return. THE BIG EL SHOW has continued its performances by using replacements for Seth.

THE BIG EL SHOW was first presented in 1975 and has been performed in the United States and Canada. For example, performances have been given in cities and towns in Connecticut, Maryland, New Jersey, Pennsylvania, and Nevada (one engagement at a hotel-casino in Las Vegas). In addition, Larry Seth as the star of THE BIG EL SHOW has appeared on television talk shows in Philadelphia and Las Vegas, and on the David Suskind Show, a nationally syndicated program.

Russen has advertised the production as THE BIG EL SHOW and displayed a photograph of the star, Larry Seth, or an artist's rendering of Seth dressed and posed as if in performance. The advertisements make such statements as "Reflections on a Legend... A Tribute to Elvis Presley," "Looks and Sounds LIKE THE KING," "12 piece Las Vegas show band."

Although the various pictures and artist's rendering associated with THE BIG EL SHOW are photographs of Larry Seth, or based on such photographs, a reasonable viewer upon seeing the pictures alone would likely believe the individual portrayed to be Elvis Presley. Even with a side-to-side comparison of photographs of Larry Seth as Big El and of certain photographs of Elvis Presley, it is difficult, although not impossible, to discern any difference.

On October 18, 1978, Russen applied to the United States Patent and Trademark Office to register the name THE BIG EL SHOW and the design feature of that name, i.e., an artist's rendition of Larry Seth as Big El, as a service mark. Plaintiff did prepare and timely file its Notice of Opposition in the United States Patent and Trademark Office to contest the defendant's right to register the mark. The proceeding before the Trademark Trial and Appeal Board has been stayed by the Board pending the results in the suit before this court.

Russen has produced or had produced for him records of THE BIG EL SHOW (including two albums and three 45 RPMs). Only a limited number of these records were pressed, and they were made for sales and promotional purposes. One record album, entitled "Viva Las Vegas," has on the cover of the jacket only the title and an artist's sketch which upon reasonable observation appears to be of Elvis Presley. It is only on the back of the jacket in a short blurb and in the credits that the name BIG EL SHOW appears. It is also indicated that the show stars Larry Seth as Big El and features the TCB Band. The other album is entitled BIG EL SHOW "In Concert" and also features an artist's drawing, ostensibly of Big El, but which looks like Elvis Presley, with microphone in hand, singing. Only one of the 45s has been presented to this court. THE BIG EL SHOW insignia appears on both sides. The artists are designated as Larry Seth and TCB Orchestra, on Side I, and Larry Seth and PCB [sic] Orchestra on Side II.

In addition to selling records at performances of THE BIG EL SHOW, Russen sold Big El pendants and a button with the picture of Larry Seth as Big El.

Russen began to produce THE BIG EL SHOW and to use his certain identifying marks, such as THE BIG EL SHOW logo, after Presley had become famous as one of the premier performers in the world and had used and established certain marks as strongly identifying his services and the merchandise licensed or sub-licensed by him.

Russen has never had any authorization from, license or contractual relation with Elvis Presley or with the Estate of Elvis Presley in connection with the production of THE BIG EL SHOW.

CONCLUSIONS OF LAW

In the present case, we are faced with the following issues:

> 1. Does a right of publicity and the concomitant cause of action for its infringement exist at common law in New Jersey?; if so, does this right descend to the estate at the death of the individual?

> 2. Assuming the existence and inheritability of a right of publicity, does the presentation of THE BIG EL SHOW infringe upon the plaintiff's right of publicity?

1. Right of Publicity in New Jersey

Although the courts in New Jersey have not used the term "right of publicity," they have recognized and supported an individual's right to prevent the unauthorized, commercial appropriation of his name or likeness. In the early and widely cited case of Edison v. Edison Polyform Mfg. Co., 67 A. 392 (N.J. 1907), Thomas Edison sought to enjoin a company which sold medicinal preparations from using the name Edison as part of its corporate title or in connection with its business and from using his name, picture, or endorsement on the label of defendant's product or as part of the defendant's advertising. In granting the requested relief, the court concluded that:

> If a man's name be his own property, as no less an authority than the United States Supreme Court says it is…it is difficult to understand why the peculiar cast of one's features is not also one's property, and why its pecuniary value, if it has one, does not belong to its owner rather than to the person seeking to make an unauthorized use of it.

Id. at 394.

This idea that an individual has a property right in his name and likeness was reemphasized in Ettore v. Philco Television Broadcasting Corporation, 229 F.2d 481, 491-92 (3d Cir.), cert. denied, 351 U.S. 926 (1956) (interpreting New Jersey law), and Canessa v. J.I. Kislak, Inc., 235 A.2d 62 (N.J. 1967). Cf. Palmer v. Schonhorn, 232 A.2d 458 (N.J. 1967).

Judge Lynch in his thoughtful opinion in Canessa initially found that "in the concept of 'right of privacy' there is implicit the right of property, at least in the instance of an appropriation by defendant of another's likeness." 235 A.2d at 69. After a comprehensive examination of a number of cases occurring prior to Canessa, Judge Lynch decided that:

> Entirely apart, however, from the metaphysical niceties, the reality of a case such as we have here is, in the court's opinion, simply this: plaintiffs' names and likenesses belong to them. As such they are property. They are things of value. Defendant has made them so, for it has taken them for its own commercial benefit.

Id. at 76.

New Jersey has always enjoined the use of plaintiff's likeness and name on the specific basis that it was a protected property right. It is as much a property right after its wrongful use by defendant as it might be before such use.

We therefore hold that, insofar as plaintiffs' claim is based on the appropriation of their likeness and name for defendant's commercial benefit, it is an action for invasion of their "property" rights and not one for "injury to the person." We thus determine that during his life Elvis Presley owned a property right in his name and likeness which he could license or assign for his commercial benefit.

In deciding whether this right of publicity survived Presley's death, we are persuaded by the approach of other courts which have found the right of publicity to be a property right. These courts have concluded that the right, having been exercised during the individual's life and thus having attained a concrete form, should descend at the death of the individual "like any other intangible property right." Factors Etc., Inc. v. Creative Card Co., 444 F. Supp. 279, 284 (S.D.N.Y. 1977). As Chief Justice Bird of the California Supreme Court has explained:

> granting protection after death provides an increased incentive for the investment of resources in one's profession, which may augment the value of one's right of publicity. If the right is descendible, the individual is able to transfer the benefits of his labor to his immediate successors and is assured that control over the exercise of the right can be vested in a suitable beneficiary. There is no reason why, upon a celebrity's death, advertisers should receive a windfall in the form of freedom to use with impunity the name or likeness of the deceased

> celebrity who may have worked his or her entire life to attain celebrity status. The financial benefits of that labor should go to the celebrity's heirs.

Lugosi v. Universal Pictures, 603 P.2d 425, 446 (Cal. 1979) (Bird, C.J., dissenting).

Following the line of reasoning in the above cases, we hold that Elvis Presley's right of publicity survived his death and became part of Presley's estate. Since we are not directly faced with the issue of whether there should be a durational limit on the right of publicity after it is inherited, we will not decide this question. However, the court suggests that a length of time should be set by the New Jersey State legislature. The Federal Copyright Act, 17 U.S.C. §§ 302, 305 provides guidelines which may be informative in this situation.

2. Theatrical Imitations and the Right of Publicity

Having found that New Jersey supports a common law right of publicity, we turn our attention to a resolution of whether this right of publicity provides protection against the defendant's promotion and presentation of THE BIG EL SHOW. In deciding this issue, the circumstances and nature of defendant's activity, as well as the scope of the right of publicity, are to be considered. In a recent law journal article, the authors conducted an extensive and thorough analysis of the cases and theories bearing on media portrayals, i.e., the portrayal of a real person by a news or entertainment media production. Felcher & Rubin, Privacy, Publicity, and the Portrayal of Real People by the Media, 88 Yale L.J. 1577 (1979) [hereinafter "Portrayal"]. They concluded that "[t]he primary social policy that determines the legal protection afforded to media portrayals is based on the First Amendment guarantee of free speech and press." Id. at 1596. Thus, the purpose of the portrayal in question must be examined to determine if it predominantly serves a social function valued by the protection of free speech. If the portrayal mainly serves the purpose of contributing information, which is not false or defamatory, to the public debate of political or social issues or of providing the free expression of creative talent which contributes to society's cultural enrichment, then the portrayal generally will be immune from liability. If, however, the portrayal functions primarily as a means of commercial exploitation, then such immunity will not be granted.

After careful consideration of the activity, we have decided that although THE BIG EL SHOW contains an informational and entertainment element, the show serves primarily to commercially exploit the likeness of Elvis Presley without contributing anything of substantial value to society. In making this decision, the court recognizes that certain factors distinguish this situation from the pure commercial use of a picture of Elvis Presley to advertise a product.

In the first place, the defendant uses Presley's likeness in an entertainment form and, as a general proposition, "entertainment...enjoys First Amendment protection." Zacchini v. Scripps-Howard Broadcasting Co., 433 U.S. 562, 578 (1977). See, e.g., Southeastern Promotions, Ltd. v. Conrad, 420 U.S. 546, 557-58 (1975) (the musical play "Hair"); Joseph Burstyn, Inc. v. Wilson, 343 U.S. 495, 501 (1952) (the motion picture "The Miracle"); Goldstein v. Town of Nantucket, 477 F. Supp. 606, 608 (D. Mass. 1979) (public performance of Nantucket's traditional folk music). However, entertainment that is merely a copy or imitation, even if skillfully and accurately carried out, does not really have its own creative component and does not have a significant value as pure entertainment.

In the second place, the production does provide information in that it illustrates a performance of a legendary figure in the entertainment industry. Because of Presley's immense contribution to rock 'n roll, examples of him performing can be considered of public interest. However, in comparison to a biographical film or play of Elvis Presley or a production tracing the role of Elvis Presley in the development of rock 'n roll, the information about Presley which THE BIG EL SHOW provides is of limited value.

This recognition that defendant's production has some value does not diminish our conclusion that the primary purpose of defendant's activity is to appropriate the commercial value of the likeness of Elvis Presley. Our decision receives support from two recent cases. In Price v. Worldvision Enterprises, Inc., 455 F. Supp. 252 (S.D.N.Y. 1978), aff'd without opinion, 603 F.2d 214 (2d Cir. 1979), the court found that the protection of the right of publicity could be invoked by the widows and beneficiaries, respectively, of Oliver Hardy and Stanley Laurel to enjoin the production or distribution of a television series entitled "Stan 'n Ollie," wherein two actors would portray the comedians Laurel and Hardy. Although the facts bearing on the content of the program are not entirely clear, it appears that the show was to be based on old Laurel and Hardy routines which the comedy team performed during their careers and was not a biographical portrayal of the lives of the two men. In this regard, the court can be deemed to have decided that an inherited "right of publicity" can be invoked to protect against the unauthorized use of the name or likeness of a famous entertainer, who is deceased, in connection with an imitation, for commercial benefit, of a performance of that famous entertainer.

In Zacchini v. Scripps-Howard Broadcasting Co., 433 U.S. 562 (1977), the Supreme Court addressed a situation which implicated both a performer's right of publicity and the First Amendment. The Court held that the First Amendment did not prevent a state from deciding that a television news show's unauthorized broadcast of a film showing plaintiff's "entire act," a fifteen second human cannonball performance, infringed plaintiff's right of publicity.

In reaching its conclusion, the Court reasoned that "[t]he broadcast of [the] film of petitioner's entire act poses a substantial threat to the economic value of that performance," id. at 576, [and] that

> the broadcast of petitioner's entire performance, unlike the unauthorized use of another's name for purposes of trade or the incidental use of a name or picture by the press, goes to the heart of petitioner's ability to earn a living as an entertainer. Thus, in this case, Ohio has recognized what may be the strongest case for a "right of publicity"—involving, not the appropriation of an entertainer's reputation to enhance the attractiveness of a commercial product, but the appropriation of the very activity by which the entertainer acquired his reputation in the first place.

Id.

In the present case, although the defendant has not shown a film of an Elvis Presley performance, he has engaged in a similar form of behavior by presenting a live performance starring an imitator of Elvis Presley. To some degree, the defendant has appropriated the "very activity [live stage show] by which [Presley initially] acquired his reputation," id. at 576, and from which the value in his name and likeness developed. The death of Presley diminishes the impact of certain of the court's reasons, especially the one providing for an economic incentive to produce future performances. However, through receiving royalties, the heirs of Presley are the beneficiaries of the "right of the individual to reap the reward of his endeavors." Id. at 573. Under the state's right of publicity, they are entitled to protect the commercial value of the name or likeness of Elvis Presley from activities such as defendant's which may diminish this value.

We thus find that the plaintiff has demonstrated a likelihood of success on the merits of its right of publicity claim with respect to the defendant's live stage production. In addition, we find this likelihood of success as to the defendant's unauthorized use of Elvis Presley's likeness on the cover or label of any records or on any pendants which are sold or distributed by the defendant.

[The remainder of the court's opinion is omitted.]

Notes

1. The foregoing cases are distinguishable. In *Lewys*, the plaintiff lost because she was unable to prove that famed playwright Eugene O'Neill had copied her novel. Instead, both authors independently came up with stories that involved some of the same ideas. In contrast, the defendants in *Outcault* admitted using the plaintiff's creation, but claimed they had sought and received permission from the *New York Herald*. However, the *Herald* did not own the right to dramatize "Buster Brown" and "Tige." Thus, the defendants needed to negotiate with Outcault before putting on their plays. Of course, the *Herald* might be liable in an indemnity action, depending on the representations it made to the defendants regarding its authority.

The third and fourth cases are examples of defendants consciously deciding not to seek permission (to their later regret). In *Showcase Atlanta*, the defendant claimed it did not need authorization because it was satirizing Margaret Mitchell's famous novel, while in *Presley's Estate* the defendant argued the entertainer's heirs had no cognizable property rights.

The lesson from these cases should be clear: determining whether permission is needed, and from whom, can be quite tricky. On the one hand, paying someone who does not own the subject property makes no sense; on the other hand, not paying may result in a messy lawsuit that ends up costing more than it would have taken to obtain the plaintiff's permission in the first place. *See further Burgess v. Chase-Riboud*, 765 F. Supp. 233 (E.D. Pa. 1991).

2. As Judge Woolsey points out in *Lewys*, it is not uncommon to run across a litigant who simply will not accept the idea that his or her work has not been improperly appropriated. *See, e.g., Denker v. Uhry*, 820 F. Supp. 722 (S.D.N.Y. 1992), *aff'd mem.*, 996 F.2d 301 (2d Cir. 1993) (plaintiff insisted that his novel had been used by the defendant to create the hit play "Driving Miss Daisy," even though the two works' themes, concepts, plots, and characters bore no similarity). Some of these parties can be satisfied by paying a token amount of money or giving them a small credit in the playbill. Of course, Georges Lewys was not willing to be brought off so easily (recall she was suing for more than $1 million). Suppose, however, that she had been more reasonable, and had been willing (prior to filing her lawsuit) to accept an acknowledgment in all future copies of "Strange Interlude" that it was partially based on her novel. If you had been O'Neill's lawyer, would you have recommended the offer? Why or why not?

3. How does one ever know he or she is negotiating with the actual rights holder? For example, what else could the defendants in *Outcault* have done to protect them-

selves? If you had been advising them, would you have suggested they contact Outcault directly, to see what rights he believed he still owned? Why might this be a dangerous strategy to pursue?

4. Going ahead without permission in the hope that if litigation arises a judge will decide no permission was needed (as in *Showcase Atlanta* and *Presley's Estate*) is not a course of action most lawyers would recommend. Nevertheless, business people, who are much less risk-adverse, proceed in this fashion every day. Can a lawyer go along with a client's decision to not seek permission, or is there an ethical problem in doing so? If there is, what options are open to the lawyer?

5. The issue of whether the estates and heirs of deceased celebrities have rights came to a head in a case involving a play about the Marx Brothers. *See Groucho Marx Productions, Inc. v. Day and Night Co., Inc.*, 689 F.2d 317 (2d Cir. 1982). Although the district court sided with the plaintiffs, the Second Circuit reversed and held that a celebrity's right of publicity terminated at death. In response, the California legislature in 1984 passed a landmark statute extending the right of publicity to deceased celebrities. *See Comedy III Productions, Inc. v. Gary Saderup, Inc.*, 21 P.3d 797 (Cal. 2001), *cert. denied*, 534 U.S. 1078 (2002) (tracing the evolution of what is now the "Astaire Celebrity Image Protection Act"). Following California's lead, a number of other states have enacted similar laws. Despite these steps, many commentators continue to call on Congress to provide a uniform solution. For a further discussion, *see* William H. Binder, *Publicity Rights and Defamation of the Deceased: Resurrection or R.I.P.?*, 12 DePaul-LCA J. Art & Ent. L. 297 (2002).

6. One of the most common types of rights that must be acquired are so-called "grand rights," which authorize the grantee to use music in a play. In *Gershwin v. Whole Thing Co.*, 1980 WL 1182 (C.D. Cal. 1980), the defendant had obtained from music publishers the "small" or non-dramatic rights to various songs written by Ira and George Gershwin. When it sought to use these pieces in its play, the Gershwins were able to obtain an injunction:

> Mr. Gershwin argues that Whole Thing is required to have a license from Mr. Gershwin even though Whole Thing has a license from music publishers. The copyright laws permit an owner of a copyright to transfer some or all of the rights comprised in a copyright, 17 U.S.C. §201(d)(2), and Mr. Gershwin had previously transferred some rights to certain music publishers. In general, the publishers have been granted small performing rights (or non-dramatic rights) to certain Gershwin songs. Mr. Gershwin contends that he generally retains grand performing rights (also known as grand rights or dramatic rights).
>
> There are two basic tests to determine whether grand rights are required. Grand rights are required if: (1) a song is used to tell a story, M. Nimmer, Nimmer on Copyrights §10.10(G), at 10-92 (1979); or (2) a song is performed with dialogue, scenery, or costumes, Finkelstein [ASCAP's former general attorney], The Composer and the Public Interest-Regulation of Performing, 19 L. & Contemp. Prob. 275, 283 n. 32 (1954). See also Robert Stigwood Group Ltd. v. Sperber, 457 F.2d 50, 56 (2d Cir. 1972) (preliminary injunction issued against defendants from performing any songs "accompanied by dramatic action, scenic accessory or costumes" where defendants possessed only non-dramatic rights and did not have grand rights).

Id. at *4.

7. A sample rights agreement between a novelist and a playwright appears in Appendix B of this casebook. For a further look at the acquisition of dramatic rights, *see* Elliot H. Brown, *Screen to Stage: Hollywood Movies Sing on Broadway*, 21 Ent. & Sports Law. 1 (Fall 2003).

Problem 5

After seeing a movie about a man-eating plant, a playwright decided to turn it into a Broadway musical. Not wishing to be sued, he entered into a licensing agreement with the film's owner. Subsequently, the copyright on the movie expired. Given these developments, does the playwright have to continue paying royalties? *See Shoptalk, Ltd. v. Concorde-New Horizons Corp.*, 168 F.3d 586 (2d Cir.), *cert. denied*, 527 U.S. 1038 (1999).

C. GRANTING RIGHTS

GOLDING v. R.K.O. PICTURES, INC.
221 P.2d 95 (Cal. 1950)

EDMONDS, Justice.

In an action for the infringement of literary property, the producers of a motion picture appeal from a judgment awarding the authors of the assertedly plagiarized stage play damages in the sum of $25,000. The sufficiency of the evidence to support the judgment is the principal question presented for decision.

Samuel R. Golding and Norbert Faulkner, both well-established writers, collaborated in writing a play entitled, "The Man and His Shadow." They neither published nor dedicated it to the public and it was not copyrighted. The Pasadena Playhouse produced the play in December, 1942. After the authors made some revisions, they submitted it to R.K.O. Radio Pictures, Inc. and Val Lewton, a producer. Lewton retained the manuscript for about six weeks. At that time, according to the evidence, Lewton was looking for a story with the action on board a ship in order to utilize an old set which was available. The appellants admit access to the play in that a copy of it was in the custody of Lewton for some time.

In August, 1943, the appellants released the motion picture entitled "The Ghost Ship" and this action followed. Upon the trial, the play was read to the jurors and the motion picture was shown to them. After they returned a verdict for damages in the amount of $25,000, a motion for judgment notwithstanding the verdict was denied. The appeal is from the judgment and from the order denying the motion.

The central dramatic situation or core in which the plaintiffs claim property is as follows: The action takes place on board a ship. Only one person aboard, a passenger, suspects the captain of being a murderer. He accuses the captain who neither admits nor denies the accusation; in fact, to his crew and passengers the captain clearly implies that his accuser is either guilty of hallucinations or desires to kill him. The accuser knows that he is subject to the captain's whims and is in a position where he can be killed or imprisoned. The captain, sure of his authority, informs the accuser that he is free to try to convince any one on board ship of the truth of his suspicions. The passenger tells his story to the first mate and to others on the ship but they refuse to believe him and instead suspect the passenger of hallucinations or malice. Finally, however, the captain becomes aware that he is suspected by at least one other person and he threatens to kill, or does kill that person as an intermeddler. Knowledge that his murders are about to be uncovered causes him to lose his mind and brings about his own undoing and death.

In the plaintiffs' play this basic dramatic core was filled out by placing the passengers and crew upon a pleasure cruise and making the captain an imposter who has come to show his superiority to the man in whose shadow he has worked for years; this man is the person throughout who knows the captain's true identity. There are various other sub-characters who give body and filling to the central plot, but as testified to by both Golding and Faulkner, this matter was all superficial and could be changed in innumerable ways without affecting the literary property and its value.

The moving picture "Ghost Ship" has its captain as the dominant figure of the story. The locale of the drama is on a freighter with members of the crew having the subordinate roles. The ship carries no passengers and, to that extent, the minor characters are quite different from those in the play. However, the captain and his obsession with authority and the fact that no one aboard can successfully challenge his position is found in the picture, as is the dramatic struggle between the captain and his adversary, the one person who knows his true nature. Basically, the psychological situation is that described by the plaintiffs as the dramatic core of their work.

The producers contend that the evidence does not support the finding of plagiarism. The correct standard for making a comparison between the play and the picture, they assert, is that of an ordinary observer; if dissection, rather than observation, is necessary to determine the question of similarity, a finding of infringement is unwarranted. They also claim that the evidence is insufficient to support the award of damages. In answer, the respondents argue that "whether or not similarities are apparent to an 'ordinary observer' and support a finding of copying is a question of fact upon which the jury's unanimous determination is conclusive."

The rights asserted in this case are not based upon statutory copyright but stem from the so-called common-law copyright. Cal. Civ. Code § 980. Upon such a cause of action, to recover for infringement, or piracy, of literary property, three elements must be established: (1) ownership by the plaintiff of a protectible property interest; (2) unauthorized copying of the material by the defendant; and (3) damage resulting from the copying.

Literary property in the fruits of a writer's creative endeavor extend to the full scope of his inventiveness. This may well include, in the case of a stage play or moving picture scenario, the entire plot, the unique dialogue, the fundamental emotional appeal or theme of the story, or merely certain novel sequences or combinations of otherwise hackneyed elements. It is, however, only the product of the writer's creative mind which is protectible. If only a portion of the play or story is original and the remainder is but an orthodox collection of filler comprising matters in the public domain, the property right must be fully analyzed and closely defined, because in the subsequent determination of the issue of copying, it is necessary to make a comparison of the two works, and such comparison is of value only if it is based upon a correct determination of the issue as to the extent and nature of the plaintiff's protectible interest.

The question as to whether the claimed original or novel idea has been reduced to concrete form is an issue of law. The determination of it must be made as a condition precedent to the vesting of any rights stemming from the common law copyright. The plaintiff must establish, as the subject of the cause of action, a right in the nature of property which is capable of ownership. Certainly, if the only product of the writer's creative mind is not something which the law recognizes as protectible, that is, an idea not reduced to concrete form, no right of action for infringement of literary property will lie even if the idea assertedly infringed is original and the result of his independent labor.

After a plaintiff has established a protectible property right, the further issue, common to all copyright cases, statutory or common law, is: Was the plaintiff's material copied by the defendant? There will seldom be direct evidence of plagiarism, and necessarily the trier of fact must rely upon circumstantial evidence and the reasonable inferences which may be drawn from it to determine the issue. An inference of copying may arise when there is proof of access coupled with a showing of similarity. Where there is strong evidence of access, less proof of similarity may suffice. Conversely, if the evidence of access is uncertain, strong proof of similarity should be shown before the inference of copying may be indulged.

It is particularly important to keep clearly in mind, insofar as the question of similarity is concerned, that it is only similarity as to the plaintiff's protectible property which is relevant. Thus, if the property interest entitled to protection extends only to certain sequences or characters, similarity of the plaintiff's and the defendant's works as to other phases of the play or scenario is wholly irrelevant.

If it is established that the plaintiff has a protectible property in his literary work, and there was copying, the elements of liability for infringement or piracy are established and all that remains is the determination of damages. On this latter issue, the rules are the same with regard to literary property as apply to any other form of personal property.

The plaintiffs do not claim that their entire play, or any particular sequence or dialogue, was directly or totally pirated. Their insistence throughout has been that the thing of value in their play is the central dramatic situation and the interplay of the dominant and secondary characters upon each other. All other characterizations and dialogue are admittedly nothing more than hackneyed filler which could be added or subtracted without affecting the value or substance of the plaintiffs' literary property.

Golding testified that when Lewton became reluctant to purchase the play, he told the producer that a moving picture of "The Man and His Shadow" could be based upon very simple lines, and the action need not necessarily take place on a pleasure yacht. The story might well be played in all its dramatic aspects on a freighter, having an ordinary captain and an ordinary crew. There is one important dramatic figure in this play and only one, he said; that is the captain, with his insane lust for power, driving to carry out his sadistic objectives. And as the production on the Pasadena stage was summarized by the witness, "the sub-story of the other characters seemed very must warped and almost trivial as compared to the figure of the captain who dominated the scene when he appeared."

The first question presented for decision is whether this basic dramatic situation constitutes protectible literary property. On the subject of the use of such plots Faulkner, who formerly had been a story editor at a studio, testified that

> the basic duty of (the story editor) is to read a book or play and condense the story theme into two or three pages. This material is then used for conferences with producers and executives of the studios so they don't have to read the whole book or play. You have in studios a great problem of budget. That means the studio gives a producer an assignment and says, "Here is a story, but we don't want you to spend more than this amount of money for

the production." Now in such cases, the story editor goes in and talks over the story with the producer, he says, "You can do this story for the lower budget cost because you can eliminate certain incidents, certain persons, certain settings, so that you can create the same basic theme and powerful story."

According to this evidence, the real value of a story or play may have little to do with specific dialogues or sequence of scenes or locale and there is ample evidence tending to prove that the basic dramatic core of the plaintiffs' play constitutes the truly original and valuable feature of it. Further, there was testimony to the effect that this particular psychological drama, with its emphasis upon the captain's controlling monomania for authority and power, was particularly well timed with the early days of the war and, therefore, of unusual value at that time. Nor was it a mere abstract idea. It had been reduced to the form of a full stage play. Its creators had embellished it with much of the trappings that give form, if not substance, to such literary work.

The fact that a plan or theme of the plaintiffs' story is similar to the plots of prior stories does not defeat the claim of originality within the meaning of that word for copyright purposes. "It is not essential that any production, to be original or new within the meaning of the law of copyright, shall be different from another...the true test of originality is whether the production is the result of independent labor or of copying." Drone, Copyrights, cited with approval in Fred Fisher, Inc., v. Dillingham, 298 F. 145, 151; to same effect, Amdur on Copyrights, sec. 3, pp. 69, 70. It is of no consequence that R.K.O. could have obtained the story from another source, when there is strong evidence from which the jury has reasonably concluded that the scenario of "Ghost Ship" was copied from the plaintiffs' play. Or, as stated by Justice Holmes: "Others are free to copy the original. They are not free to copy the copy." Bleistein v. Donaldson Lithographing Co., 188 U.S. 239, 249.

Concerning the issue of copying, and its subsidiary determinations of access and similarity, the evidence as to access is strong. The producers of the motion picture have conceded access, but because the inference of copying must rest upon both access and similarity, it is necessary to examine, to a certain extent, the nature of the evidence of access.

It appears without conflict that the plaintiffs' play was submitted to Lewton to read and consider. Both Golding and Faulkner testified to conversations with Lewton regarding the acceptability of the story for moving picture purposes. In one of the discussions of it, according to Golding, Lewton stated: "Well, Golding, I don't have to buy my stories. I don't have to lay out money for originals; I get my idea and I call in a couple of writers in the lot and I make my stories that way." It was a few days later that the manuscript was returned to plaintiffs. The evidence of opportunity and, indeed, inclination to pirate plaintiffs' literary property is therefore clearly supported by the evidence.

Proof of access, however, establishes no more than the opportunity to copy and not actual copying. And liability for damages must rest upon substantial evidence of similarity between plaintiffs' literary property and the moving picture produced by the defendants. The play was read to the jury and the picture was viewed by them. There was no other evidence of similarity offered or received, and whether such evidence is sufficient to sustain the jury's implied finding of similarity is a question which can only be determined upon appeal by reading the play and seeing the moving picture, which have been done by this court.

In support of the appellants' contention that there is not sufficient evidence of the value of the damages sustained by the authors of the play, it is argued that all of the evidence concerning the value of the motion picture rights is found in the testimony of the respondents, and that no person with experience in the determination of the value of such property was called to testify on their behalf. But the testimony of Faulkner, who stated his opinion in regard to the value of the play, was not necessary as an expert for both he and his co-author testified as owners of the property. Each of them told the jury that the value of the play before the infringement was between $25,000 and $50,000 and that it had no value after the production and distribution of the picture. It is a well recognized rule that the owner of property is competent to testify as to its worth:

> Literary property is not distinguished from other personal property and is subject to the same rules and is likewise protected, Palmer v. De. Witt, 47 N.Y. 532, 538, 7 Am. Rep. 480. California has held that plaintiffs may testify to the value of an unpublished manuscript prior to misappropriation in Barsha v. Metro-Goldwyn-Mayer, 32 Cal. App. 2d 556, 90 P.2d 371. See Yadkoe v. Fields, 66 Cal. App. 2d 150, 151 P.2d 906; Nathan v. King Features Syndicate, 32 N.Y.S.2d 519.

Universal Pictures Co. v. Harold Lloyd Corporation, 9 Cir., 162 F.2d 354, 369. The testimony of the appellants' experts that the play contained no material of value for motion picture purposes merely created a conflict in the evidence.

The judgment and the order denying the motion for judgment notwithstanding the verdict are affirmed.

TRAYNOR, Justice, dissenting.

I cannot agree that a comparison of defendants' picture with plaintiffs' play reveals evidence of similarity not attributable to the use of a common idea, theme, or plot in the public domain and therefore not subject to exclusive appropriation by any author. I would therefore reverse the judgment.

SCHAUER, Justice, dissenting.

As I view the film, if it possesses any quality at all which may be said to give it character, originality or any element of literary protectiblity, that quality would seem to be a combination of details in production, an imprint of the artistries of director and actor. But insofar as plot or, as the majority denominate it, "central core," is concerned, I am satisfied that neither the story told by plaintiffs nor that pictured in the film can be said to possess in this decade any element of originality qualifying it to be the subject of exclusive literary property rights and protectibility. In some aspects each plot is at least as old as Shakespeare and, since Polti, the whole substance of each has been but a published formula. And if either work does possess originality in substance, structure or form sufficient to make it protectible as literary property, then, measured by an equal standard, it surely follows that the film is so different from plaintiffs' story as to preclude plaintiffs' recovery for plagiarism.

The Ghost Ship sailed but I think neither it nor its author was engaged in piracy; and I think upholding the judgment in this case supports a result which approaches closer to piracy than did any act of the defendants. Certainly the individual writer should have ample protection for his literary enterprise but zeal to protect him should not lead to strait-jacketing producers against what appears here to have been but a legitimate exercise of their own freedom of enterprise in an open field.

BURNETT v. WARNER BROS. PICTURES, INC.
493 N.Y.S.2d 326 (App. Div. 1985),
aff'd mem., 492 N.E.2d 1231 (N.Y. 1986)

MEMORANDUM DECISION.

Order of the Supreme Court, New York County entered January 28, 1985, which granted defendants-respondents-appellants' cross motion for summary judgment dismissing the complaint without prejudice, for lack of subject matter jurisdiction, is unanimously modified on the law, to the extent of granting to defendants summary judgment dismissing the complaint, with prejudice, for failure to state a cause of action, and the order is otherwise affirmed, without costs and disbursements. 127 Misc.2d 553, 486 N.Y.S.2d 613.

In 1941 plaintiffs wrote a play entitled "Everyone Comes to Rick's." On January 12, 1942, plaintiffs assigned their rights to the unproduced play to defendant Warner Brothers, Inc., in exchange for $20,000. The agreement entitled "Assignment of All Rights" states that plaintiffs

> give, grant, bargain, sell, assign, transfer and set over all now or hereafter existing rights of every kind and character whatsoever pertaining to said work, whether or not such rights are now known, recognized or contemplated and the complete and unconditional and unencumbered title in and to said work for all purposes whatsoever.
>
> 2. I further give...the absolute and unqualified right to use said work in whole or in part, in whatever manner said purchaser may desire, including (but not limited to) the right to make, and/or cause to be made, literary, dramatic, speaking stage, motion picture, photo play, television, radio, and/or other adaptations of every kind and character, of said work, or any part thereof; and for the purpose of making or causing to be made such adaptations or any of them the purchaser may adapt, arrange, change, novelize...add to and subtract from said work, and/or title....

In 1942 Warner Brothers released the motion picture "Casablanca" which was based on plaintiffs' play. Later, in 1955, Warner Brothers produced a television series entitled "Casablanca" which was essentially a sequel to the movie and set in the 1950's. Plaintiff Burnett, although aware that the television series had been produced, made no protest to Warner Brothers of infringement of character or sequel rights. Warner Brothers then obtained a copyright registration for another adaptation of plaintiffs' play, which was produced for television in 1983. This production was a "prequel" story set in 1940, one year prior to the action of both plaintiffs' play and the movie "Casablanca." The weekly series was broadcasted from April 10 to May 7, 1983.

Plaintiff learned that the new "Casablanca" television series was being planned but raised no objection until June 21, 1983, after the series had been aired. Plaintiffs' attorney complained to the National Broadcasting Company, Inc. (NBC), which broadcast the series, that the television series, based on the characters plaintiffs had created, violated their rights to those characters. Plaintiffs followed this complaint by commencing the instant action in July 1983, seeking a declaratory judgment that the defendants had no rights under the contract to use the characters of his play except for the use in the movie "Casablanca." Plaintiffs sought $10,000,000 in compensatory and $50,000,000 in punitive damages. Defendants Warner Brothers and NBC answered, asserting five affirmative defenses, including failure to state a cause of action and lack of jurisdiction over the subject matter due to federal preemption under 17 U.S.C. §301, the federal copyright law.

Justice Bradley granted defendants' motion to dismiss the complaint on the ground that the court did lack subject matter jurisdiction to determine the controversy because of federal preemption. The court, therefore, dismissed the complaint, but without prejudice, to enable plaintiffs to bring an action in federal court.

Plaintiffs argue on appeal that the court erred in finding that their causes of action concerning their rights to their characters were preempted by the federal copyright law. Defendants argue, inter alia, on their cross-appeal, that plaintiffs' complaint should have been dismissed with prejudice because plaintiffs contracted away any and all rights they had in their play.

We need not determine whether plaintiffs' causes of action are preempted by the federal copyright law, for it is beyond question that plaintiffs failed to retain any rights, copyrightable or otherwise, which defendants could infringe, and have consequently failed to state a cause of action, thus requiring dismissal with prejudice.

The very words of the agreement between plaintiffs and Warner Brothers unequivocally demonstrate plaintiffs' intent to assign all their rights "of every kind and character whatsoever pertaining to said work, whether or not such rights are now known, recognized or contemplated...for all purposes whatsoever." Moreover, plaintiffs granted Warner Brothers the absolute right to use the work in any manner or medium they desired and to add to or subtract from the work. The assignment of rights agreement contains no clauses specifically enumerating any rights retained by plaintiffs or enumerating any rights excluded to Warner Brothers. Rather, it contains only general clauses assigning all imaginable rights to defendant Warner Brothers. The explicit wording of the clause belies plaintiffs' allegation that the assignment "contains no grant with respect to characters, continuation or sequel rights." The assignment was very obviously designed to grant the assignee the broadest of rights with respect to plaintiffs' play. In instances where the assignment clauses were drafted in the broadest of terms, courts have concluded that had the plaintiff intended to retain certain rights, specific clauses to that effect should have been included in the agreement. See Bartsch v. Metro-Goldwyn-Mayer Inc., 391 F.2d 150; Landon v. Twentieth Century-Fox Film Corporation, 384 F.Supp. 450. Inapposite to these cases and the instant appeal is Warner Brothers Pictures, Inc. v. Columbia Broadcasting System, Inc., 216 F.2d 945, where, unlike the language in Burnett's assignment, the contract there contained specifically enumerated rights granted to Warner Brothers and specifically enumerated rights reserved by the author Hammet. Since plaintiff retained no rights in his play which could be infringed, the complaint below fails to state a cause of action and is dismissed with prejudice.

Notes

1. Are you at all troubled by how the foregoing cases come out? Do you think the plaintiffs in *Golding* received an unjustified windfall? What about the defendants in *Burnett*? Assuming either of them did, is there anything a court could (or should) have done about it?

2. In *Litchfield v. Spielberg*, 736 F.2d 1352 (9th Cir. 1984), *cert. denied*, 470 U.S. 1052 (1985), playwright Lisa Litchfield claimed that Steven Spielberg used her 1978 one-act musical, entitled "Lokey from Maldemar," as the basis for his hugely successful 1982 movie "E.T.—The Extra Terrestrial." Like the district court, the Ninth Circuit disagreed,

finding that although both stories involved aliens coming to earth and being befriended by children, these similarities were outweighed by the differences:

> Whereas E.T. concentrates on the development of the characters and the relationship between a boy and an extra-terrestrial, Lokey uses caricatures to develop its theme of mankind divided by fear and hate. No lay observer would recognize E.T. as a dramatization or picturization of Lokey. See Bradbury v. Columbia Broadcasting System, Inc., 287 F.2d 478, 484 (9th Cir.1961); Kustoff v. Chaplin, 120 F.2d 551, 559 (9th Cir.1941).

736 F.2d at 1357.

Problem 6

A playwright authorized a movie studio to make a film out of his play, as well as "whatever sequels may be commercially justified." Because the movie turned out to be an enormous hit, the studio, through one of its wholly-owned subsidiaries, rushed a video game into production. When the playwright objected, the movie studio took the position that the game was a "sequel" to the movie. If the case ends up in court, who is likely to win? *See Kirke La Shelle Co. v. Paul Armstrong Co.*, 188 N.E. 163 (N.Y. 1933).

Chapter 4

Producers

A. OVERVIEW

Producers primarily are responsible for raising the money needed to stage a show. While a few use their own funds, most seek out backers (because of past abuses, federal and state securities laws now strictly regulate such investments). As funds are acquired, producers turn their attention to negotiating rights deals; making hiring decisions; signing venue and merchandising agreements; and arranging for publicity.

B. CAPITAL ACQUISITION

A PRACTICAL GUIDE TO THEATRICAL FINANCING
Elliot H. Brown & Daniel M. Wasser
16 Ent. & Sports Law. 6 (Fall 1998)

> "Don't forget the checkie!
> Can't produce plays without checkie!"
>
> —Max Bialystock, The Producers (1968)

Lots of people know how money is raised for the theater. A well-dressed group of prospective "angels" gathers at twilight in a chic Manhattan apartment in the East 60s. The composer sits down at a grand piano and, perhaps joined by the lyricist and a few attractive, young, out-of-work actors and actresses, plays the score of the new musical. The book writer chimes in with notes on her story. The costume designer displays color sketches of the costumes and the set designer manipulates a working model of the sets. The producer makes an enthusiastic speech and the 30 or 40 attendees put down their champagne glasses long enough to applaud and write out their checks.

The problem with this scenario, of course, is that finding substantial investors at a soiree of this nature has become immensely difficult, especially because theatrical investment is quite risky compared to other investment opportunities and because purchasing a substantial share of any show requires a significant investment.

There was a day when it worked, apparently. In the fall of 1944, Michael Todd produced "Up in Central Park" for $150,000, paid off the show (and the opening night party!) in nine weeks, and "netted over $20,000 a week during the first year's capacity run." Today, with musicals costing $6,000,000 to $12,000,000, a payoff in one year is considered a miracle, and a payoff in eighteen months is considered spectacularly successful. A show which can "net" $100,000 a week would be a gift from heaven, and very few producers would close a show clearing the $20,000 a week which Todd and his investors apparently saw.

In this article we will describe the securities law considerations affecting theatrical financing, as well as the practical considerations producers face as they raise money.

Who Invests?

Given the risks, who invests in the theater today? Broadway investors can be broken down into two broad categories: the old-fashioned "angel" and the flinty-eyed investor.

The "angel" is the extremely wealthy person who has decided that he or she likes the producers, likes the play, and likes the stars. Likes them so much, in fact, that, even with the knowledge that a return of his or her investment is a long shot, he or she still wants to be a part of it. This investor is enamored, perhaps, by the idea of a credit in the playbill, a pair of tickets for opening night, and years of cocktail party conversations with friends.

The flinty-eyed investor is an individual who has reasons to invest in a play or musical beyond the possibility of the New York run of the show turning a profit. This category of investors includes the following: theater owners, road producers and presenters, booking agents, general managers, merchandising companies, cast album companies, and motion picture and television companies.

1. Theater Owners

With the rental of a Broadway theater now running at over $30,000 per week plus a percentage of the gross, and a guaranteed rental of four weeks required in advance, it is not difficult for a theater owner to determine that it is in his or her best interests to help fund a production which will play in his or her theater, particularly if the alternative is for the theater to be "dark," that is, unrented. Not only do theater owners collect rent, they also generate income streams from their share of merchandise receipts and from the sale of drinks and candy, both of which heighten the potential return on their investment.

2. Road Producers and Presenters

To some extent, Broadway has become a loss leader for the "road" (all of the U.S. outside New York City and Canada), where a show with a Broadway reputation can be opened and run at much lower production and operating costs than on Broadway and potentially sell out in theaters larger than the largest Broadway theaters. Road producers and presenters need "product" to keep their pipeline of hit shows flowing, and for that reason they often invest heavily in New York City productions. Of course, investments are designed to position such entities to acquire (on arm's length terms) the road rights in a play or musical.

3. Booking Agents

The entities that "sell" plays on the road to local presenters also need a product to sell, and consequently often will invest in anticipation of being appointed tour booking agent.

4. General Managers

The parties who manage shows (the equivalent of motion picture "line producers") make money on a weekly basis, whether or not there is money available to repay capitalization or to pay net profits. Thus, for the same reasons as theater owners, they often find it advantageous to invest in a production prepared to engage them.

5. Merchandising Companies

While not a crucial source of Broadway financing, merchandising companies have invested in shows in exchange for merchandising rights.

6. Cast Album Companies

In days gone by, when cast albums were more popular with the record-buying public, most musicals could count on a cast album company investing in the show and simultaneously acquiring cast album rights. There appears to be a rebirth of interest in cast albums, and thus a rebirth in cast album company investment in shows with the proper pedigree.

7. Motion Picture and Television Companies

Motion picture and television companies have an interest not only in the potential motion picture or television rights in a show (which could range from an HBO-type live or taped telecast of the show itself to a feature length motion picture version of a play or musical), but also appear to regard Broadway investment as a valuable device for increasing the prestige of the company and signifying its commitment to the arts.

* * *

Groups of theatrical professionals with complementary interests often invest in one another's shows on a regular basis, particularly on the road. In that way, each party knows that it will acquire the rights which initially drove its investment. For example, a theater owner will require that the show play in its theater, a road presenter will require that it have the right to present the play in "its" cities (that is, the cities where it normally presents), a booker will require that it have the right to book the show, and the general manager will require that it have the right to general manage the show.

The traditional "angels" and the theater professionals who invest in new productions tend to have an "accredited" investor status in common. In general, "accredited" investors, as defined in Rule 501 of Regulation D, promulgated under the Securities Act of 1933, 15 U.S.C. §§ 77a-77aa, are investors of significant net worth. In the case of individuals, an accredited investor is defined as an individual with a net worth in excess of $1 million, or who, in each of the last two years, has earned income in excess of $200,000 per year (or $300,000 with spouse), with a reasonable expectation of reaching that amount in the current year. To the extent any of the investors described above might not technically qualify as "accredited" investors, they presumably are financially sophisticated. As will be seen below, limiting offerings to accredited investors and a small number of financially sophisticated unaccredited investors ease the process of raising funds for new theatrical productions.

An additional category of investors is the family and friends of the producer and playwright. Nonprofessional investors of this sort typically appear when an author or producer without a reputation first ventures into theatrical production, and a large percentage of such investors often turn out to be unaccredited. Usually, the budget will be considerably less than the Broadway-type budgets discussed above. In fact, an off-Broadway nonmusical (or "straight") play might be financed for as little as $400,000, and an off-off-Broadway production in a 99-seat theater might involve considerably less. Ironically (and distressingly for the producer trying to get started in the business of theatrical production), despite the limited amount of funds to be raised, the presence of unaccredited, unsophisticated investors actually complicates the task of complying with relevant securities laws and results in legal fees which are disproportionately large in the context of the proposed capitalization.

Financing Structures

There are several ways in which theatrical productions are financed, including self-financing, coproduction or joint venture, and syndication.

1. Self-financing

Self-financing is rare, since it violates one of the cardinal principles of the entertainment industry: spend only other people's money. Nevertheless, this is the manner in which Disney and Livent, for example, are now financing their productions.

2. Coproduction or Joint Venture

Coproductions or joint ventures are particularly common in connection with touring productions, and generally involve a handful of sophisticated parties which finance and manage the production together. Joint ventures do not involve the sale of passive investment interests, and therefore do not implicate securities laws. To avoid exposure to potential liability beyond the assets of the production, coproducers or joint venturers often associate themselves through a limited liability company (LLC).

3. Syndication

The syndication of theatrical investment interests, typically via a limited partnership or an LLC, is the most common method of financing theatrical productions. Until the 1990s, limited partnerships were the only practical way to structure theatrical syndication financing arrangements. However, the adoption of state legislation during the 1990s authorizing LLCs created a viable alternative financing structure.

In general, the desired result—limited liability and partnership tax treatment—can be achieved either through a limited partnership or an LLC. However, if the producer is an individual, and not an incorporated entity, the producer becomes personally liable for the obligations of the partnership by serving as the general partner of a limited partnership, a risk not faced by the manager of an LLC. If the producer is incorporated, the issue of personal liability for the producer disappears, and either the limited partnership or the LLC will serve equally well. Note, however, that due to state income tax considerations, some theatrical accountants recommend limited partnerships over limited liability companies for touring productions. Moreover, in New York, quirks in the law make the formation and maintenance of an LLC more expensive than that of a partnership, although the amount involved is unlikely to be of any consequence for Broadway productions of the sort described above.

Securities Law Considerations

The sale of limited partnership or LLC interests to investors constitutes the sale of securities, and therefore, state and federal securities regulation must be taken into account. Under authority granted in the New York Arts and Cultural Affairs Law, the New York Department of Law has developed an extensive regulatory scheme governing the issuance of theatrical investment interests. Subject to the superseding effect of federal law discussed below, the New York theatrical syndication financing regulations pertaining to offerings of theatrical investment interests from or to New York generally require advance filing and review of offering papers by the Department of Law in a manner similar to the way public offerings are reviewed by the Securities and Exchange Commission. In addition to New York State regulation, if applicable, producers need to consider the securities laws (or "blue sky" laws) of other states in which investors are located and, of course, federal securities law.

Overlapping state and federal securities regulation has long been identified as a factor in increasing the cost and time involved in raising capital. In 1996, Congress addressed this concern with the passage of the National Securities Market Improvement Act (the NSMIA). A principal feature of NSMIA is the federal preemption of state securities laws in connection with offerings of securities which comply with the requirements of Rule 506 of Regulation D. Thus, theatrical offerings which qualify as Rule 506 offerings are no longer subject to substantive state regulation (although it may be necessary to make certain state filings and fee payments). Given the extensive substantive review procedures adopted by the New York Department of Law, adoption of NSMIA constituted a major innovation for New York producers.

Regulation D describes different types of private offerings in Rules 504, 505, and 506. A private offering made pursuant to Regulation D which involves the sale of investment interests in excess of $5 million must satisfy the requirements of Rule 506. Since the budgets of Broadway musicals now routinely exceed $5 million, such financing, if privately raised, must be raised pursuant to Rule 506. If less than $5 million is to be raised, the offering could be characterized as a Rule 506 offering if the applicable requirements are met: potential investors must be furnished with a thorough disclosure document (unless all the investors are accredited, in which event no particular type of information is stipulated); and there may be no more than 35 unaccredited investors, all of whom must demonstrate that alone, or together with a purchaser representative, they have the financial knowledge and experience necessary to evaluate the merits and risks of the offering.

If an offering of theatrical securities does not qualify as a Rule 506 offering, producers must comply with substantive state securities regulations. Particularly in the case of an offering to or from New York, compliance with state law could significantly increase the time and cost of completing the offering. Not surprisingly, the vast bulk of the recent theatrical financings with which these writers are familiar are Rule 506 offerings.

Basic Financial Structure

The deal traditionally offered to theatrical investors is as follows. Initially, all operating profits (the excess of income from ticket sales, merchandise, and so forth, over operating expenses such as authors' royalties, actors' salaries, light rentals and theater costs) are paid to investors until the amount of operating profits equals the amount invested. Thereafter, the investors are deemed to have "recouped," and any additional operating profits (now referred to as net profits) are split 50 percent to the investors and 50 percent to the producers. Better deals are available, but generally only for those who take greater risks or who are investing large enough amounts to demand their own terms.

The customary limited partnership or LLC structure contrasts with the joint venture structure in which each of the parties commits to a certain proportion of the capitalization, receives that proportion of the profits, and bears that proportion of losses. While it is possible that there may be an "edge" for a managing joint venturer, it would not be uncommon for all profits and losses to be shared in direct proportion to the financing.

Who gets a better deal? As in every context, money talks, and the investor in a position to furnish a substantial portion of the financing generally will find himself or herself negotiating terms with a flexible producer. Investors accepting an increased risk may also get an enhanced deal. One type of high-risk investor is the "front money investor," who puts up the seed money needed by the producer to secure rights, hire attorneys, and pay other preproduction expenses before offering papers are prepared. A second type of high-risk investor permits her investment to be utilized by the producer prior to the point of full capitalization, risking that her money will have been spent in vain if the producer ultimately fails to raise the funds necessary to launch the production. Other high-risk investors fund developmental productions from which there is no possibility of a profit, but the possibility, if the developmental production is well-received, of a full-scale commercial production.

To understand the special deals described below which may be offered to theatrical investors, it is necessary to identify what the producer is entitled to from the production, since additional consideration will be at the expense of the producer, not at the expense of other investors. The producer's financial remuneration consists of a share of the profits of the production, a weekly royalty of 2-to-3 percent of the gross weekly box office receipts, and a cash office charge (which might be $2,000 per week for a Broadway musical) designed to cover the producer's out-of-pocket costs.

A form of non-cash consideration under the producer's control is billing credit, which is accorded great value by theatrical investors. When a Playbill lists six names above the title and eight below, you can be sure that most of the persons named are major investors or high risk investors rather than actual producers.

Finally, the producer, through management of the production, controls the selection of parties contracting to perform services for, or lease equipment or facilities to, the production or which will be licensed to exploit rights such as merchandising, cast album, or touring privileges. The producer has an obligation to investors to enter into arm's length deals with these third parties. However, the producer can potentially use the power to select the general manager or to grant touring rights as leverage to secure investments for the production.

Precapitalization Money

A substantial outlay of funds is normally required before producers make a final decision about how a play or musical will be financed. Early costs include: advances for options on underlying rights and/or rights in the play or musical; payments to attorneys to prepare rights agreements, production contracts and offering papers; payments to general managers to begin to negotiate deals and to prepare budgets; and other preliminary costs such as sums required to secure the commitment of a director or star. Money used prior to preparing formal offering documents is commonly referred to as "front money."

While a producer can, of course, use his or her own money for front money, the laws of the state of New York permit front money to be raised from up to four people and to be used for all categories of expenses which would normally be included in the production budget of a play. In view of the preemption of state law by federal law under the NSMIA discussed above, it could be argued that, even in New York, front money could be accepted from an unlimited number of accredited investors, even in the absence of offering documents, as a Rule 506 offering. Nevertheless, most New York-based theatrical practitioners remain likely to continue to advise their clients to abide by the four-person limitation, especially since, at the early point when front money is most needed, it may not be possible to predict whether the offering ultimately will fall under Rule 506.

Offering papers typically include a production budget which corresponds to the capitalization sought by the producer. In the offering documents, producers will agree to hold all investments in a special account and not to spend those funds for production or preproduction purposes until they have raised the full amount of the capitalization. Since the producer will need the full budgeted amount to launch the proposed production, it is understandable for most investors to refuse to permit their funds to be spent unless all funds have been raised; otherwise, individual investors' funds could be spent on a potentially worthless effort for which there will not even be an opening night party.

Notwithstanding the foregoing, producers typically will be in desperate need of money to meet the production schedule. Thus, producers will approach investors about furnishing written authorization to utilize their funds for preproduction and production purposes prior to full capitalization. In fact, producers often will request that investors not only authorize such use, but that they also agree to waive any right of refund (i.e., any personal obligation on the part of the producer) if the full capitalization is not raised and the production is abandoned. Needless to say, any investor authorizing precapitalization use of her investment is taking a significant risk and is entitled to an enhanced return for doing so.

Front money investors and investors authorizing precapitalization use of their funds normally receive substantial "rewards" for putting up this risky money. These "rewards" could include an enhanced financial participation in the production, billing credit and other benefits, such as the right to participate in meetings or have access to house seats.

Most commonly, the high-risk investor will receive an enhanced participation in the net profits of the production. For example, a front money investor who puts up $100,000 may insist that, beyond the percentage of profits he would receive as a "mere" investor (for example, 1 percent if the full capitalization is $5 million), he or she also receives a 50 percent share of that profit participation out of the producer's profits (so that, in our example, the investor would end up with a 1.5 percent profit participation). Since the producer shares not only in net profits, but also in the weekly cash office charge and the weekly producer's royalty, an important front money investor may also attempt to negotiate a share of the producer's royalty and, less frequently, the cash office charge.

Getting an extra 1/2 percent of profits is, of course, only an example. Deals may be as low as 1/4 percent or, when the going gets really tough and money is very difficult to raise, as high as 1 percent from the producer side for each 1 percent purchased as an investor. The problem with a one-to-one deal for a producer, of course, is that it leaves the producer with nothing.

Financing Developmental Productions

In addition to front money investors and investors authorizing precapitalization use of their funds, there is a different type of high-risk investing which has become more common as the cost of mounting full-scale productions has risen. Rather than risk $5 million or more on a Broadway production of a musical, a producer may opt to spend $400,000 to mount a private "workshop" or $800,000 to "enhance" a regional theater production in exchange for the opportunity to see the production professionally produced and to better assess its chances of commercial success. To fund the workshop or to furnish "enhancement" money, producers sometimes organize developmental financing entities. Investors who invest therein know there is no possibility of a return on the developmental production. Their reward for investing in the developmental production is that if a commercial production occurs, they may have any combination of the following rights: a first priority right to invest in the commercial production; recognition of their investment in the developmental production as part of the capital of the commercial production (so that they secure an interest therein without further investment); an enhanced financial return, payable out of the producer's entitlements; billing credit; and any additional benefits they can negotiate.

Additional Benefits for Large Investors

Investors who make substantial financial contributions towards the full capitalization of a production may also get special deals. Generally, an investor who contributes 20 percent or more towards the total capitalization could expect to receive an advantage over a smaller investor. As noted above, this advantage would come out of the producer's share, not at the expense of other investors.

Most producers, faced with the prospect of countless nerve-racking, expensive and uncertain backers auditions, are content to give away a substantial piece of their producer's share of net profits to make the money-raising process smoother, quicker, and easier.

Conclusion

Theater remains a high-risk investment. A motion picture, for example, at least results in a tangible product, allowing home video and television to serve as a safety net when all else has failed. When a Broadway show fails, that's normally the end of the story. An investment of $8 million can, quite literally, evaporate overnight.

However, when a Broadway show hits, the potential profits are phenomenal. In 1995, the New York Times reported that "Phantom of the Opera" had grossed $1.5 billion "out-earning even the most successful movie ever made, 'Jurassic Park.'" At that point, according to the New York Times, "Cats" had made even more money than "Phantom of the Opera." The potential for profit in shows with that degree of success is unlimited and, to an investor with interests beyond the investment in the show itself—such as a theater in which the show could play for ten or twelve years, or a local presenter with a list of subscribers across the United States who want the show to come to their city year after year—the reason for investing is clear.

But even the old-fashioned reason for investing—that an investor really loves a show and wants to be associated with it—cannot be totally discounted in the theater of today, nor should it be. Investing in a play or musical, after all, should be viewed as at least as praiseworthy as making donations to an art museum or symphony orchestra. Investing in theater can carry the same amount of prestige, give the same amount of personal intellectual pleasure and, if the stars align properly, could result in a truly admirable return on investment.

ROSIE THE PRODUCER, NAVIGATING BROADWAY
Jesse McKinley
N.Y. Times, Sept. 29, 2003, at E1

Last Monday morning Rosie O'Donnell put on her favorite yellow jacket and went on "The View," ABC's popular morning chat show, to do what she does better than almost anybody in America: sell a Broadway show.

The scene was familiar. From its debut in 1996 to last year, when it went off the air, "The Rosie O'Donnell Show" was one of Broadway's most potent marketing tools, providing national exposure for dozens of shows dying for television time, a rarity for theater productions.

But last Monday Ms. O'Donnell was not on television selling someone else's production. She was selling her own: "Taboo," a new musical with songs by the 1980's pop star Boy George, in which Ms. O'Donnell is the sole investor, putting up $10 million of her fortune to produce it.

While that alone would make her involvement remarkable—most shows on Broadway get their money from dozens of smaller investors—Ms. O'Donnell has also taken the risky step of casting herself as the principal draw for "Taboo," using her brassy image and her reputation as an arbiter of suburban taste to lure audiences.

The campaign combines two of Ms. O'Donnell's abiding passions: big-time showmanship and small-time arts and crafts. The show's radio advertisements, for example, feature Ms. O'Donnell boldly predicting that the show will win a Tony Award. On Friday she went to Los Angeles to promote "Taboo" on "The Tonight Show With Jay Leno," part of a preopening television blitz that will also include appearances on "The Today Show," "Dateline NBC" and "Access Hollywood." Ms. O'Donnell, who has never produced a Broadway show, has also made it clear that she has little use for traditional methods of Broadway marketing, preferring to use e-mail messages, for example, rather than direct mail. (A recent one featured Ms. O'Donnell modeling the show's cast jacket.)

Despite hiring one of Broadway's biggest advertising firms, Serino Coyne, Ms. O'Donnell has taken it upon herself to design and make thousands of promotional stickers on her personal computer, many featuring images from some 2,000 paintings she has done at home since quitting her show.

"For six years I sold everyone else's shows with great success," Ms. O'Donnell said. "So I think the fact that I'm producing this and putting my money in it speaks volumes to people who for six years went to see Broadway shows based on my enthusiasm."

That attitude has inspired more than a little skepticism from other Broadway producers, many of whom believe today's audiences, no longer enthralled by the reputations of legendary producers like David Merrick and Cameron Mackintosh, will not go go see a show simply because of its producer.

"The only producing entity that has ever sold a ticket on name alone is Disney, and Rosie is not Disney," said one producer, who like many in the superstitious, fishbowl world of Broadway would speak only on condition of anonymity. "She's not in it, and she doesn't necessarily represent quality in the theater. She certainly attracts press attention, but I don't know if that translates to sales."

Advance sales for "Taboo," which opens Nov. 13 at the Plymouth Theater, have been weak, though this week there were signs that ticket-buyers were beginning to believe

Ms. O'Donnell's pitch. What is certain is that Ms. O'Donnell has, by sheer force of her personality, made "Taboo" the show to watch this fall, whether it becomes a megahit, a colossal bomb or something in between.

"Rosie is obviously not someone afraid to take risks," Jed Bernstein, president of the League of American Theatres and Producers, said. "And as much as the theater world takes comfort in its traditions and ways of doing things, it's pretty exciting when someone comes along to challenge those assumptions. But with any risk you can both fly high or crash hard."

"Taboo" is not an easy sell. The story of the wild excesses of the 1980's club scene in London, replete with sex, drugs and glam rock 'n' roll, the musical was a marginal hit in London during a 15-month run in 2001 and 2002. In addition to being its composer, Boy George also appears in the musical, as a character (played by Euan Morton) and as an actor, in the role of Leigh Bowery, the real-life fashion provocateur who died of AIDS in 1994.

In London "Taboo" played at a 300-seat theater, equivalent to a midsize Off Broadway theater. (One of the British producers, Adam Kenwright, is credited as a producer here, although he has little involvement in the New York production.) In New York Ms. O'Donnell is staging the show in the 1,078-seat Plymouth, with a top ticket price of $101.25. She says she has no fear about her bigger ambitions for the show.

"You know, it sounds so cocky to say I know it's great, but I know it's great," she said. As for the show's subject matter, she likes to compare it to Broadway smashes like "Rent" and "Cabaret."

Besides Serino Coyne, the advertising agency, and the show's press agent, the Barlow/Hartman company, Ms. O'Donnell has hired several established talents to translate the show to American audiences, including Charles Busch, who wrote downtown camp classics like "Vampire Lesbians of Sodom" and the recent Broadway hit "The Tale of the Allergist's Wife." New songs have been added and other characters enhanced, including Big Sue (Liz McCartney), a stocky hanger-on who watches as Mr. Bowery self-destructs.

As that suggests, Ms. O'Donnell's connection with the piece seems intensely personal. Shortly before her show ended last year, Ms. O'Donnell came out publicly as a lesbian—she and her partner, Kelli, have four children—and one of the ongoing refrains in "Taboo" is the question of sexual identity. (The song "Sexual Confusion" is a centerpiece of the first act.)

She also seems completely in awe of Boy George, who is 42 and whose band, Culture Club, broke up in 1986.

"My need for him to love me is pretty absurd, and unlike anyone I've ever worked with," said Ms. O'Donnell, who is 41. "I remember being 18 and watching him and he was 18, too. It's very odd to have such reverence for him and have him be a contemporary."

Boy George, whose real name is George O'Dowd, speaks highly of Ms. O'Donnell, though perhaps not as obsessively as she does of him. "I wouldn't be very good at pretending to be her friend if I wasn't," he said. "At the end of the day, God bless her, because she brought the show to New York."

Ms. O'Donnell's outspoken and sometimes blunt manner, however, has led to some tabloid reports of her meddling in the creative process, an assertion the show's director, Christopher Renshaw, denies.

"She has a lot of creative input," Mr. Renshaw said. "Probably more than most producers. But it's her enthusiasm that has been the main drive for the show."

There are some concrete signs, however, that her unorthodox approach initially backfired, including the response to the show's first advertising campaign, which depicted an overweight, heavily made-up Mr. Bowery posed in front of a man urinating in a dirty restroom. The ad, which was blown up as a giant billboard in Times Square, was released in August and generated scant advance sales for the show. A more recent and more traditional ad depicting Boy George's face has done better.

"Broadway is conservative," said one prominent Broadway press agent not connected with the show. "One show on its own can't build a new audience. Somewhere in there you have to have the traditional theatergoing audience."

Some in the industry also wonder whether Ms. O'Donnell's reputation is still sound enough to sell tickets. Since Ms. O'Donnell, who was once known as the Queen of Nice by her fans, shut down her show in May 2002, her image has been buffeted by several negative episodes.

Last year, for example, she unamicably exited Rosie, the magazine that bore her name, a decision that led to dueling—and still pending—lawsuits between her and her publisher, Gruner & Jahr USA.

Some of the industry's skepticism can be chalked up to its conflicted feelings about Ms. O'Donnell, who was an Emmy-winning host of the Tony Awards twice in the late 1990's, appeared in several Broadway shows and was a tireless booster of the industry, particularly of shows she felt had gotten a raw deal from critics. But she also gained a reputation for being bossy and demanding to producers during her television show's later years, as well as endorsing theatrical shows that had little artistic merit. "She'd become a shoe salesman," one press agent said. "She liked everything."

That love-hate relationship was evident at one of the first public events for "Taboo," on Sept. 7 at "Broadway on Broadway," a free annual concert in Times Square. At that event Ms. O'Donnell appeared onstage to introduce her cast and mouthed along with the lyrics as the troupe performed.

To some, this display illustrated the central problem of Ms. O'Donnell's producing strategy: she is not the star anymore, but still wants to be.

Others, however, saw something else.

"You've got to admire her passion, and you've got to admire her courage, and you've got to admire that she's willing to put her money where her mouth is," Mr. Bernstein, the theater league president, said. "And hopefully in the array of unorthodox methods she's employing, she'll pick out the right combo."

KNAPP v. PENFIELD
256 N.Y.S. 41 (Sup. Ct. 1932)

HAMMER, Justice.

This action is by plaintiff, an actress, for damages, compensatory and punitive or exemplary, for interference by the defendants with her contractual status resulting in her discharge. In 1923 the plaintiff was the winner of a national beauty contest for young women and awarded the title Miss America. Previously she had won a preliminary contest in this State and was awarded the title Miss New York. Miss America, a full figure statue in the nude, was sculpted by Howard Chandler Christie. Plaintiff "in bathing costume" was the model. Professionally her beauty has been exploited by advertisement and press agent in the reference to her as "the most beautiful girl in the world." Concededly, she is fair of face, form and figure.

Although so advertised and exploited, plaintiff does not give an impression of sophistication or calculating worldliness, but that of education, culture and refinement. Plaintiff testified that she had been featured in several sketches, but admitted she had never before starred or played a leading part in a musical show, nor as an actress had she done more than ordinary dancing, the singing of a mediocre number, or the speaking of a few lines in a feature act. It appeared that whatever she did as an actress was merely incidental to and afforded an opportunity for the exhibition of her attractiveness as a professional beauty.

The defendant Penfield, who has died since the trial of this action, an elderly lady over eighty years of age, of high social position, great wealth, and culture, the widow of a former United States Ambassador, was desirous of aiding the defendants Bagby and Johnson in promoting their reputations as musical composers. Through and in the name of her agent and alter ego, defendant Evelyn Hubbell, she entered into a contract with the defendant Earl Carroll, the theatrical producer, to prepare, develop and produce the defendants Bagby and Johnson's musical compositions, among them the theme song to be sung by the heroine in the musical theatrical play "Fioretta."

There were then four parties to the contract: the financier, the two authors and the producer. The contract provided that Mrs. Penfield would advance $250,000 to finance the preparation, development and production by Carroll. This amount with five per cent interest was to be repaid from, but only in the event of, net profits. Carroll received a salary of $1,000 per week. Bagby and Johnson were to receive royalties. The net profits, if earned, were to be divided in equal quarterly shares. Carroll's corporation, the defendant Vanities Producing Corporation, of which he was president but in which the others were neither officers, directors nor stockholders, was the agency, although not a party to the contract, used for the production of "Fioretta." Under a standard run-of-the play Actors Equity Association contract, plaintiff was employed by Vanities Producing Corporation, through Carroll, at a salary of $1,000 per week to play Fioretta Pepoli, the star role or leading part.

Plaintiff was not equal to singing the theme song or dancing as the heroine's part was originally cast and the part was recast by Carroll to exhibit her physical attraction and beauty. Leading parts which were played by other stars at large salaries were accordingly required to support the recasted part of the heroine and were limited in the exhibition of their own talents. The defendant Hubbell, acting for Mrs. Penfield, protested that the role required a star who could sing and dance, and that plaintiff could not sing, dance or act up to the part and demanded that plaintiff be replaced by such star and other stars provided with appropriate parts.

Carroll did not comply with the demand and Mrs. Penfield, through the defendant Hubbell, brought an action against Carroll for an injunction requiring him to replace the plaintiff by an artist equal to the part, alleging that for the purpose of serving his own personal ends and those of the said Dorothy Knapp he so constructed the whole performance that she might be featured in said play to her advantage, exploitation and glorification, and thus seriously impaired and jeopardized said Hubbell's (Penfield's) investment in the play. Thereupon Carroll discharged plaintiff but paid the balance of her salary under the contract and obtained another actress for the part. The play was not a financial success and there were no net profits.

A party to a contract ordinarily has the right to perform and to have same performed without interference by a non-party or stranger. Such interference, unless privileged, justified or excusable, is an actionable wrong arising out of the invasion of the party's right to freedom from interference with the contract and performance thereunder. [However, p]ersons acting for the protection of contract rights of their own which are of an equal or superior interest to another's contractual rights may invade the latter with impunity.

Mrs. Penfield's interest was equal and superior to the interest of the plaintiff. Her large financial investment provided not only the common enterprise of the four parties to the original contract out of which came their respective rights and obligations but also the employment of and benefit to plaintiff and other stars and numerous other persons. The continuance of the enterprise and of the benefits depended upon the success of the play without which the Penfield investment was lost. The right of the plaintiff was subordinate to that of said defendants, whose contract was paramount to plaintiff's. Without defendants' contract plaintiff would not have the employment under her contract with Vanities Producing Corporation. The very money which paid her agreed compensation arose out of defendants' prior agreement with Carroll. The performance or breach of the terms of the prior contract by the defendants imposed no obligation on and gave no rights to plaintiff. Any she had came from her contract of employment. The employment by Carroll, however, of an artist not equal to the heroine's role or part would be a breach by him of his prior agreement with the other individual defendants.

The plaintiff's interest in her contractual status and her right to freedom from interference with her performance of the contract, therefore, were invaded with impunity by the defendants in protecting contract rights of their own which were of an equal or superior interest.

CLASSIC THEATER CORP. v. AMSTER
148 N.E. 651 (N.Y.),
reargument denied, 150 N.E. 534 (N.Y. 1925)

CRANE, Judge.

The plaintiff sued the defendant on a written agreement to recover his share of the losses on a theatrical venture. The courts below have interpreted this agreement as creating no such liability. As we have come to a different conclusion it is necessary to set forth this agreement and then state the meaning which we give to it:

> Agreement made and entered into this 10th day of April, 1923, by and between Nathan L. Amster of the City of Boston, State of Massachusetts, party of the first part, and Classic Theatre Corporation, a corporation created and existing under and by virtue of the laws of the State of New York, party of the second part.
>
> Whereas the party of the second part is the owner of the scenery used in connection with the production of the play called 'Anathema,' and is about to produce the said play upon the English speaking stage, with Maurice Schwartz as star or leading actor; and is the owner of the right to produce said play in English, the repertoire and stock rights, and a one-half interest in the motion picture rights of said play, subject to the payment of a five per cent royalty in the gross receipts;
>
> It Is Now Agreed by and between the said parties hereto as follows:

1. The said party of the first part has paid to the party of the second part, at or before the signing and delivery of this instrument, the receipt whereof is hereby acknowledged, the sum of Three thousand ($3,000) dollars, in payment for a one-quarter or twenty-five (25%) per cent interest in and to the rights to produce said play in English and to any and all profits that may be earned in the production of the said play upon the English speaking stage as aforesaid, and one-quarter of the receipts for stock and repertoire rights, and also in payment of a twenty-five per cent interest in the scenery now used in said production, and in any new costumes or fixtures that may be used in said production; which is hereby transferred, assigned and set over to the party of the first part, and it is agreed between the parties hereto that the said party of the first part shall be entitled to have a one-quarter or twenty-five (25%) per cent share of any and all profits that may accrue in the production of said play upon the English speaking stage, and in the leasing for stock and repertoire productions, and he shall also bear any losses that may occur in the production of said play upon the English speaking stage, in the same share or part and to the extent of twenty-five (25%) per cent or one-quarter of any and all of said losses, it being expressly agreed between the parties hereto that in the event that the run of the said play upon the English speaking stage is not longer than four weeks, or that the run of said play is limited to four weeks, and if the gross receipts for said play during said fourth week does not amount to Nine thousand ($9,000) dollars, then and in either of said events the party of the second part must return to the party of the first part, the sum of Five hundred ($500) dollars of said Three thousand ($3,000) dollars, paid in as aforesaid.

2. It is further agreed between the parties hereto that the salary of the said star or leading actor during the production of said play upon the English speaking stage, shall be Five hundred ($500) dollars per week, which sum shall be considered an expense incidental to the production of said play upon the English speaking stage.

3. It is further agreed that the party of the first part shall have twenty-five (25%) per cent or a one-quarter interest of the fifty (50%) per cent interest in the motion picture rights of said play, now held by the said party of the second part; namely, the said party of the first part shall be entitled to one-eighth, or twelve-and-a-half (12 1/2%) per cent of any profits that may be made by or from motion pictures of said play.

4. It is further agreed between the parties hereto that the party of the first part contributes the sum of Five hundred ($500) dollars, and the party of the second part contributes the sum of Fifteen hundred ($1,500) dollars, which combined sum shall be used as a working capital for the carrying on of the business for the production of the said play upon the English speaking stage, and the said sum of Two thousand ($2,000) dollars, contributed as aforesaid, shall remain as the working capital of said enterprise; and said respective sums shall be returned to said respective parties at the termination of the said enterprise; or in the event of a loss, the proportionate share of said respective sums shall be returned to said parties; and that all receipts or income during the production of said play upon the English speaking stage and all receipts for stock and repertoire rights, shall be deposited in a bank account in the joint names of Martin Schwartz and Joseph Lawren, and checks and drafts upon the said account shall be signed by both of said par-

ties jointly, and the profits of said enterprise shall be divided on Monday of each week.

The party of the first part [Amster] is the defendant in this action. The party of the second part [Classic Theater Corp.] is the plaintiff.

Analyzing the agreement we find that the defendant paid to the plaintiff the sum of $3,000 for which he received one-quarter interest in the play called "Anathema," and in the profits to be earned upon its production. This is not all. He also received one-quarter of the receipts for stock and repertoire rights, and a one-quarter interest in the scenery used in the production and in the new costumes and fixtures. By the agreement these property rights were transferred and assigned to him.

What were the defendant's privileges and obligations? He was to have one-quarter share in all profits to accrue in the production of the play upon the English speaking stage "and he shall also bear any losses that may occur in the production of said play upon the English speaking stage, in the same share or part and to the extent of twenty-five (25%) per cent or one-quarter of any and all of said losses." In other words, for $3,000 he got one-quarter interest in the play called "Anathema" together with scenery and costumes and was to share to the extent of twenty-five (25%) per cent in the profits or losses of the production upon the English speaking stage.

A concession was made however; the parties added this clause: "it being expressly agreed between the parties hereto that in the event that the run of the said play upon the English speaking stage is not longer than four weeks, or that the run of said play is limited to four weeks, and if the gross receipts for said play during said fourth week does not amount to Nine thousand ($9,000) dollars, then and in either of said events, the party of the second part [the plaintiff] must return to the party of the first part [defendant] the sum of Five hundred ($500) dollars of said Three thousand ($3,000) dollars, paid in as aforesaid."

Notice should be taken here of the omission to state anything in this clause regarding a loss. The clause does not refer to a loss or to a profit. In the event that the play did not run for longer than four weeks or was limited to four weeks and the gross receipts in the fourth week did not amount to more than $9,000, then the defendant was to get back $500. He would be entitled to a reduction of $500 in the purchase price even if there had been a profit in a three weeks' run.

The courts below have construed this clause to mean that if there were a loss in the production of the play for less than four weeks, no matter how great the loss was, the defendant would lose $2,500 of the amount he had put in and no more. But he put in $3,000. Would the plaintiff be obliged to pay him back $500 besides standing all the loss? If this is what the parties had in mind, why did they say that the defendant was to share one-quarter of the losses? If one-quarter of the loss was to be limited to $2,500 of the amount he put in, it would have been very easy and simple to have so expressed it. What, we may ask, becomes of the defendant's one-quarter interest in the play rights and stage property? We read this agreement as one of a theatrical venture wherein the defendant bought a twenty-five (25%) per cent interest not only in the profits, but in the property, and was to be liable for 25 per cent of the losses. If the play only ran four weeks or less he was to be allowed $500 out of his purchase price. This would be added to his profits, if there were any, and taken out of his share of the losses, should the venture be unsuccessful.

By this interpretation we give effect to every clause in the agreement according to the terms and words used by the parties. It is a formal agreement apparently drawn up with some care. The courts are asked to construe it. The parties differ as to its construction. The plaintiff has paid a loss alleged to be over $13,000. Naturally the defendant wants to pay as little of this as possible. He construes this agreement one way, the plaintiff another. When such differences have arisen, and the events have occurred which require the courts to determine between such parties the share of loss which each must pay, it is wise as well as reasonable to follow closely the words and phrases used by the parties in making the agreement before the event happened and to give to those words and phrases their natural meaning limiting them to the conditions expressed.

For these reasons the judgments below must be reversed, with costs in all courts and the motion for judgment on the pleadings denied, with costs.

McLAUGHLIN, Judge, dissenting.

The plaintiff and the defendant, about to enter into a theatrical venture, executed a written contract, a copy of which is set forth in the prevailing opinion, by which the respondent Amster sought to limit, in case of the failure of the venture, his loss. The intent to do so is so clearly expressed that it is difficult to see how there can be the slightest doubt about it. After providing that the respondent was to contribute, which he did, towards the venture $3,000, it was expressly stated that his loss if such occurred was limited to $2,500 and in event of such loss $500 of the $3,000 was to be returned to him. If language means anything this is precisely what the parties intended. This is the provision in the contract, viz., "it being expressly agreed between the parties hereto that in the event that the run of said play upon the English speaking stage is not longer than four weeks, or that the run of said play is limited to four weeks, and if the gross receipts for said play during said fourth week does not amount to Nine thousand ($9,000.00) dollars, then and in either of said events, the party of the second part [the plaintiff] must return to the party of the first part [the respondent] the sum of Five hundred ($500.00) dollars of said Three thousand ($3,000.00) dollars, paid in as aforesaid."

The run of the said play upon the English speaking stage did not continue for four weeks. The gross receipts for said play during said fourth week did not amount to nine thousand ($9,000) dollars. The play only ran three weeks. Therefore, according to the express provisions of the contract quoted, the respondent's loss incurred by the venture was limited to twenty-five hundred ($2,500) dollars, and it cannot by a forced and unwarranted construction make the respondent liable for twenty-five per cent of the loss. If it can be done then the court makes a contract which the parties themselves did not intend to make.

ELVIN ASSOCIATES v. FRANKLIN
680 F. Supp. 121 (S.D.N.Y. 1988)

KNAPP, District Judge.

In this action, plaintiff Elvin Associates, whose principal is Ashton Springer ("Springer"), alleges that defendants Aretha Franklin and Crown Productions, Inc. breached a contract under which Franklin was to star in a New York musical production entitled "Sing Mahalia Sing" ("Mahalia"), which plaintiff was to produce and manage. Defendants have denied that they entered into the contract upon which plaintiff is suing and have asserted a counterclaim alleging breach by plaintiff of a second contract relating to the same production.

The case is before us on defendants' motion (a) for leave to amend their answer to assert as an affirmative defense that the alleged contract, even if proven, would be unenforceable as against public policy, and (b) for summary judgment dismissing the complaint on the basis of that defense. For the reasons stated below, we deny leave to amend, and, of necessity, summary judgment. Plaintiff's cross-motion for summary judgment dismissing the counter-claim due to the lack of factual basis for the damages alleged on that claim is also denied.

BACKGROUND

The facts pertaining to defendants' instant motions are that on or about September 22, 1982, the Attorney General of the State of New York brought suit against Springer alleging that he had engaged in unlawful and fraudulent activities with respect to the handling of funds invested by former limited partners in his production of the musical "Eubie." Springer responded by consenting to the entry of a judgment of permanent injunction and by agreeing to make an offer of full restitution of $123,745.95 to his former limited partners in "Eubie." The judgment was entered in the Supreme Court, New York County, on September 27, 1982, stating that its purpose was to permanently enjoin and restrain Springer from the issuance, offering for sale, sale, promotion, negotiation, advertisement and distribution of syndication interests in any theatrical production to the public within and from the State of New York pursuant to Article 26-A of the General Business Law of this State.

The judgment provides, inter alia, that Springer

> is restrained and enjoined permanently from directly or indirectly engaging or attempting to engage in the issuance, offering for sale, sale, promotion, negotiation, advertising and distribution of any offering of syndication interests in any live-staged dramatic plays or dramatic musical production which hereafter are intended to be shown to the public for profit, and are financed wholly or in part by the offering or sale in or from this State, directly or through agents or distributors, of investment agreements, evidences of interest, limited partnerships, producer's shares, equity or debt securities, pre-organization subscriptions or any other syndication participation when any persons are offered, solicited to purchase or sold directly or indirectly such syndication interests for money or services within or from the State of New York unless and until [Springer has] complied with Article 26-A of the General Business Law including the filing of certified financial statements with the Department of Law for [the shows] 'Daddy Goodness,' and 'Whoopee'... [and has made] an offer of full restitution to all investors in the Eubie Company who have not executed a waiver of their right to receive full restitution....

Defendants contend that Springer's plan for financing the production of "Mahalia" violated the September 1982 injunction. Defendants claim that, notwithstanding the injunction, Springer sought to finance the musical show at issue in this action ("Mahalia") by soliciting funds from potential limited partner investors throughout the country, including the Nederlander Organization, Irwin Meyer, Steven Friedman, Ronald Avis, Sam L'Hommedieu, Greg Reed and Moe Septee. They assert that Springer circulated an investment agreement in the form of a proposed Limited Partnership Agreement to most of the prospective investors, seeking a capitalization of $500,000-$600,000. They further contend that Springer spent approximately $93,000 of his own money on the production of "Mahalia," instead of paying restitution to the "Eubie" investors, and that he failed to make the filings called for by the consent judgement.

Plaintiff admits that he has not entirely complied with all the requirements of the injunction, but denies that his financing of "Mahalia" violated the injunction. Plaintiff first argues that the correct interpretation of the injunction is that it only prevents him from attempting to solicit funds from "the public." He claims he is permitted under the terms of the decree to finance a theatrical production with his own funds or those of private investors. In support of this claim, plaintiff argues that the safeguard and enforcement provisions of Article 26-A of the General Business Law and its successor statute Article 23 of the Arts and Cultural Affairs Law of New York are intended to protect members of the general public who lack the expertise and familiarity with the entertainment industry necessary to evaluate the risks inherent in investing in legitimate stage productions.

Plaintiff further contends that he did not finance "Mahalia" with funds solicited from the public, but instead sought financing entirely from sources within the entertainment industry who were to co-produce "Mahalia" with him. These sources included Irwin Meyer and Steven Friedman, who are experienced Broadway producers of such productions as "Annie," and the Nederlander Organization, which owns or controls legitimate stage theatres throughout the United States and which co-produced "La Cage Aux Folles." Plaintiff also intended to approach for funds local promoters or presenters in other cities who would also be co-producers, including Sam L'Hommedieu, Moe Septee and Greg Reed. In addition, plaintiff claims he borrowed money from various private sources in order to keep the production of "Mahalia" going.

At oral argument, it was learned that the Attorney General of the State of New York has been alerted by defendants to plaintiff's conduct in financing "Mahalia," and that the Attorney General has thus far taken no steps to bring contempt proceedings against Springer.

DISCUSSION

Defendants assert that the contract Springer alleges to have entered into with Franklin is unenforceable as against public policy because his ability to perform the contract depended upon his violation of the injunction. Defendants rely primarily on Reiner v. North American Newspaper Alliance (1932) 259 N.Y. 250, 181 N.E. 561, the so-called "Graf Zeppelin" case, in arguing that a court may not aid a wrongdoer or lawbreaker by enabling him to recover on a contract that derives from or depends upon his unlawful conduct. Defendants also rely on Anabas Export Ltd. v. Alper Industries (S.D.N.Y.1985) 603 F.Supp. 1275, and on McConnell v. Commonwealth Pictures Corp. (1960) 7 N.Y.2d 465, 199 N.Y.S.2d 483, 166 N.E.2d 494.

In the case at bar, the alleged contract itself violates no third party's rights, because Springer's entry into the alleged contract with defendants did not of itself violate the injunction. Furthermore, in performing under the contract, Springer did not engage in plain or undisputed illegality. Neither the correct interpretation of the injunction's provisions, nor the lawfulness of the plaintiff's activities in gathering financing for "Mahalia," are clear. Resolution of these issues would involve a commitment of extensive judicial resources to collateral and potentially prejudicial inquiries.

Moreover, even if it were clear that Springer had violated the injunction in assembling his financing, we would still bar this affirmative defense as inappropriate. It is significant that in response to a question posed at oral argument of these motions, defendants responded by letter that they had been unable to locate "any case in which a court had ruled a contract unenforceable as against public policy because it derived from or depended upon the promisee's contempt of a court order." Letter of Thomas S. Howard, November 12, 1987. The absence of such precedent is not surprising. It is primarily the province of the party in whose favor an order is entered—here, the Attorney General of the State of New York—to determine what, if any, remedies to pursue in response to a perceived violation of such order.

In our view, a federal jury trial is not an appropriate forum for determining whether or not any actions by plaintiff in carrying out the alleged contract intentionally or unintentionally violated an injunction issued by the New York Supreme Court and, if so, what sanctions should be applied. Such a determination should be made by the court that issued the injunction upon application of the Attorney General of the State of New York. It seems to us that, assuming the New York Supreme Court should find the injunction to have been violated, it could react in at least three possible fashions: (a) it might conclude that the violation did not call for sanctions at this time; (b) it might enjoin the plaintiff from pursuing the instant law suit; or on the other hand (c) it might direct the plaintiff to vigorously pursue this action and to use all or some of its proceeds to make restitution to investors in the earlier production. It would be inappropriate for us to preclude the first or last possibility.

UNITED STATES v. ALTMAN
48 F.3d 96 (2d Cir. 1995)

MINER, Circuit Judge.

Defendant-appellant Melvyn Altman appeals from a judgment of conviction and sentence entered on February 1, 1994 in the United States District Court for the Southern District of New York (Knapp, J.), following a jury trial, convicting him of four counts of mail fraud, in violation of 18 U.S.C. §1341, one count of witness tampering, in violation of 18 U.S.C. §1512(b)(3), five counts of making false statements on bank loan applications, in violation of 18 U.S.C. §1014, and two counts of subscribing to false federal tax returns, in violation of 26 U.S.C. §7206(1). Grouping the mail fraud convictions with the witness tampering and false bank application convictions for sentencing purposes, the district court sentenced Altman to a prison term of 41 months, to be followed by a supervised release term of three years. The court also ordered payment of restitution and a special assessment of $500. On the income tax counts, the court sentenced Altman to a concurrent prison term of 16 months as well as a concurrent supervised release term of one year, and ordered the payment of restitution and a $100 special assessment.

On appeal, Altman challenges his conviction on the mail fraud counts as based on insufficient evidence, contends that the Sentencing Guidelines were applied erroneously in regard to those counts, asserts that reversal of his mail fraud convictions inevitably leads to reversal on the other counts, and argues that the district court should have departed downward on account of his medical condition and because his criminal conduct was aberrant. The government cross appeals for the purpose of challenging the district court's denial of sentence enhancements for obstruction of justice and violating a court order. For the reasons that follow, we reverse the convictions on the mail fraud counts, affirm the convictions on the remaining counts and remand for resentencing, with instructions.

BACKGROUND

I. Of "Brazil En Fete"

This is the story of a lawyer who fancied himself an impresario. Melvyn Altman, whose previous show business experience consisted of a limited practice in entertainment law, became deeply involved as financial backer, producer and counsel in a dancing and variety show that originated in Brazil. This production, known variously as "Rio By Nite," "Brazil En Fete" and "The Great Brazil Show," never made it to Broadway. After a brief run in Miami, the show opened on May 20, 1985 at the Palais des Sports in Paris. It played to sparse audiences there for a brief period and then closed for good, due to lack of funds, in early June, 1985. The show was a financial disaster, and Altman lost substantial sums of money that he had invested in the production—his own funds as well as funds that he had embezzled. The funds that were embezzled to prop up the faltering production were entrusted to Altman in a fiduciary capacity—as executor of the estate of his friend, David Haber, deceased, and as court-appointed conservator of the person and property of Armando Corsini, a mentally handicapped person.

II. Of the Haber Estate

Altman was appointed executor of the Haber estate on December 9, 1983. The estate assets totaled approximately $1.2 million dollars, and Altman, as sole executor, was responsible for collecting the estate's assets, paying its expenses, making distributions to the beneficiaries and keeping proper records. At the time of his appointment, Altman had been involved for more than a year in the production and promotion of the show, having already invested several hundred thousand dollars of his own money in the expectation of receiving 10-20% of the show's profits. By early 1984, Altman was aware that his investment was in jeopardy, because the company responsible for securing financing for the production, LRC Inc., was running short of cash. Altman was a director of LRC and, in October of 1984, Barry Kaplan, the president of the company, advised him in writing that an infusion of money was necessary to avoid a total loss.

Commencing in July of 1984, Altman embarked on a course of looting the Haber estate and transferring the funds into the bottomless pit that the show had become. He went about the removal of the funds by liquidating the estate's certificates of deposit and treasury bills, depositing the proceeds into the estate bank account and then drawing checks for the use of the show. In July and August of 1984, Altman converted $115,000 of estate funds. After hearing in January of 1985 from Marvin Krauss, the show's general manager, that the entire investment would be lost if additional funds were not forthcoming, Altman converted an additional $380,000 between February and April of 1985. Of the total amount embezzled from the estate, approximately $125,000 was passed through Altman's personal bank account and the balance was passed principally to the producer and director of the show and to the wire-transfer company that paid the show's expenses.

Edith Haber, widow of David Haber and principal beneficiary of the Haber estate, was represented by attorneys Arthur Brown and Dean Braslow. Between 1985 and 1989, the attorneys repeatedly called upon Altman to make distributions to their client, who was ill, elderly and in need of funds. Altman falsely represented to them that the estate money was tied up in certificates of deposit and treasury bills and that an IRS audit was pending. In 1986 and 1987, Altman disgorged four $50,000 payments to Edith Haber after her attorneys threatened to take action against him in the Surrogate's Court. Edith Haber died in January of 1988, and her attorneys pressed Altman for further information and for distributions to her estate. Continuing to receive unsatisfactory answers to their inquiries, the attorneys in late 1988 petitioned the Surrogate's Court for an accounting. That court ordered Altman to account for his actions as executor.

After some delay, Altman submitted an accounting to Braslow on April 10, 1989. Braslow signed the receipt that Altman had prepared, acknowledging that he had received "Melvyn Altman's First Intermediate Accounting For The Estate of David Haber." Included in the accounting was a statement that the estate had made loans in the aggregate amount of $495,000 to a "theatrical production company in Europe," with interest accruing at 10% per annum. Also included was a representation that the balance of the principal remaining due on the loans, $93,500, together with interest in the total sum of $91,528.48, would be paid on August 1, 1989. There never were any "loans" as such and, even if there were, the production company could not repay them, having ceased to exist four years earlier. Altman had taken $37,000 in executor's commissions and secured Braslow's consent to credit himself with $20,000 more. It was not until November of 1990, however, that Altman raised the money to provide the Edith Haber estate with the final payment due from the David Haber estate.

The accounting was false in another respect, because it failed to reveal the repayment of a $50,000 loan that Altman had received on behalf of the David Haber estate from Richard Gamsu, a friend of David Haber. Gamsu had executed to Haber a promissory note, with a due date of January 28, 1984, as evidence of the debt. Altman received full payment on the note in January of 1984 and deposited it in his own account. He never returned the money to the estate and never listed it as an estate asset at any time. When reviewing the accounting with the attorneys who had pressed him to provide it, Altman represented that the debt had been repaid before Haber's death and was omitted from the accounting for that reason. In January of 1992, during the course of an FBI investigation, Gamsu stated that he owed no money to the Haber estate but that Altman had borrowed $50,000 from him, an amount still unpaid. Later, Gamsu admitted that he owed Haber the $50,000 at the time of Haber's death, that he had never loaned the money to Altman and that he had lied because Altman, who was a close friend, asked him to do so.

III. Of the Corsini Conservatorship

By order of the New York County Surrogate's Court dated January 9, 1985, Altman was appointed Conservator of the Person and Property of Armando Corsini. Armando's father, Andrea Corsini, had died on July 26, 1984 leaving an estate then valued at approximately $106,000. Armando was the sole distributee of the estate. He also was the beneficiary of nine Totten Trust bank accounts established by his father having a total value in excess of $246,000. Carlos Agosto, with whom Armando lived, filed a petition to be appointed conservator, but a guardian appointed by the court testified that Mr. Agosto did not have the necessary skills to discharge the duties required. Accordingly, the court appointed Altman as conservator for Armando Corsini and later appointed him administrator of the estate of Andrea Corsini.

Although a conservator is required by New York law to file a sworn accounting in January of each year describing the condition of his stewardship, Altman did not file his 1985 accounting until March 2, 1987. This filing came only in response to threats by a referee that a removal proceeding would be instituted if Altman failed to account. The referee was appointed by the court to review each annual accounting, and his recommendations were reported to a special referee, who acted in a supervisory capacity on behalf of the Appellate Division of the New York Supreme Court. In his accounting,

Altman stated that he had made loans totaling $206,400 to E. Belle-M. Santos Productions, Inc. during the period May 3 to May 23, 1985. E. Belle-M. Santos was, of course, the production company for Brazil En Fete. According to the accounting, the money was to be repaid within 24-36 months of the last advance, with interest at 15% and a 10% share in any net income generated by the production. Altman noted that he had guaranteed repayment by executing a promissory note.

After examining Altman's report, the referee submitted his own report to the special referee. In it, the referee was critical of the theatrical investment, noting that the conservator, without court approval, had placed the corpus of the conservatee's estate in a high-risk venture in which the conservator had a personal interest. The referee recommended that the conservator make application for leave to file an intermediate accounting within thirty days and further recommended that, when the accounting was filed, the court consider whether Altman should be removed as conservator and compelled to reimburse the estate for the monies loaned plus accrued interest. The referee noted that the $250,000 bond posted by Altman appeared to be sufficient for the protection of the estate. The special referee thereafter issued an order on behalf of the court confirming and adopting the report of the referee in all respects and directing payment to the referee from the estate for his services and disbursements.

Except for the direction to pay the referee for his services and disbursements, Altman failed to comply with the order. The referee assumed that the case had been terminated and closed his file in June of 1989, at which time he solicited Altman's confirmation that there had been a judicial settlement of his accounts. Altman did not respond to the inquiry or take any further steps in regard to the repayment of the alleged loans. He also made no claims on the $250,000 bond, which by then was insufficient to cover the money stolen from the estate. The embezzlement was not discovered until 1991, when the FBI conducted a search of Altman's office. It was not until 1992 that Altman was removed as conservator by the Surrogate's Court. At that time, there was $12,596 remaining in the Corsini account, and Altman requested a $15,000 fee for his services. When Altman filed his 1985 account in 1987, the production was defunct, there was no way in which any investments in the show could be recovered or any profits realized, and the embezzlement already was a fait accompli.

IV. Of the Contentions on Appeal

Altman was convicted of one count of mail fraud upon the Haber estate. The nature of the mailing described in that count was a letter bearing the signature of Attorney Braslow, acknowledging receipt of Altman's Haber Estate accounting of April 10, 1989, which was mailed from Braslow to Altman at the latter's request. Altman also was convicted of three counts of mail fraud upon Armando Corsini, with the nature of the mailings as follows: letter dated August 12, 1987 to Altman from the referee enclosing an order signed by the special referee; letter dated August 20, 1987 to Altman from the referee enclosing a copy of the report of the referee to the special referee in accordance with Altman's request; and a bank account statement for May, 1989 in the name of Altman as conservator, mailed by Manufacturers Hanover Trust Company to Altman in June of 1989. Altman contends on appeal that the evidence was insufficient to sustain mail fraud convictions in either the Haber matter or the Corsini matter.

With respect to Altman's remaining counts of conviction, the counts charging false statements on bank loan applications stemmed from his failure to list the debts to the Corsini and Haber estates in the applications. The tax counts charged that Altman's personal returns for 1987 and 1989 were false in that they omitted income received from a certain receivership unrelated to the Corsini and Haber estates. The convictions on the witness tampering count related to Haber's instructions to Richard Gamsu to give false information regarding Gamsu's $50,000 payment to the estate. Altman's contention with regard to these remaining counts boils down to a claim that there would be no conviction on these counts if they were prosecuted separately from the mail fraud charges. He states that "if the mail fraud counts were removed from this case, the trial of the remaining allegations would have been put in an entirely different light, a light which would have allowed a fair resolution of these charges."

Attacking the sentence, Altman contends that the district court erroneously calculated his sentence for mail fraud by applying the 1991 version of the Sentencing Guidelines and, because the money was not fraudulently obtained, by counting the loss to include the $495,000 from the Haber estate that went into the show. Also, Altman argues that he is entitled to resentencing because the district court did not understand its authority to depart downward and because his health was poor and because his conduct was aberrant.

In its cross appeal, the government challenges the district court's refusal to apply the obstruction of justice enhancement, contending that the conduct giving rise to Altman's convictions for witness tampering warranted application of that guideline. The government also challenges the district court's refusal to enhance the sentence for violation of the judicial order requiring the filing of an intermediate accounting. The government contends that the authorities would have learned about the missing funds if the order were complied with and argues that "it is difficult to conceive of a court order whose violation would be more central to a fraud scheme."

DISCUSSION

I. Of the Elements of Mail Fraud

Whoever, having devised or intending to devise any scheme or artifice to defraud, or for obtaining money or property by means of false or fraudulent pretenses, representations, or promises...for the purpose of executing such scheme or artifice or attempting so to do, places in any post office or authorized depository for mail matter, any matter or thing whatever to be sent or delivered by the Postal Service, or takes or receives therefrom, any such matter or thing...

is guilty of mail fraud. 18 U.S.C. § 1341. Accordingly, the elements necessary to establish the offense are: 1) a scheme or artifice to defraud 2) for the purpose of obtaining money or property (or of depriving another of the intangible right of honest services, see 18 U.S.C. § 1346) and 3) use of the mails in furtherance of the scheme. See United States v. Wallach, 935 F.2d 445, 461 (2d Cir.1991). Proof of fraudulent intent is required. Id.

II. Of the Scheme to Defraud

The Supreme Court early on gave the scheme to defraud element a broad interpretation, construing it to "include[ ] everything designed to defraud by representations as to the past or present, or suggestions and promises as to the future." Durland v. United States, 161 U.S. 306, 313, 16 S.Ct. 508, 511, 40 L.Ed. 709 (1896). In the Durland case, the Court specifically rejected the contention that "the statute reaches only such cases as, at common law, would come within the definition of 'false pretenses,' in order to make out which there must be a misrepresentation as to some existing fact and not a mere promise as to the future." Id. at 312, 314, 16 S.Ct. at 510, 511. Despite its expansive reading of the scheme to defraud element, the Court drew the line in a case where the mails were used to obtain money by threats of murder or bodily harm. See Fasulo v. United States, 272 U.S. 620, 47 S.Ct. 200, 71 L.Ed. 443 (1926). Although the words "scheme or artifice to defraud" were considered to include a "great variety of transactions," the Court held that "they do not include threat and coercion through fear or force." Id. at 628, 47 S.Ct. at 202.

By embezzling the estate funds with which he was entrusted as a fiduciary, Altman effectuated a scheme to defraud within the meaning of the mail fraud statute:

> The concept of "fraud" includes the act of embezzlement, which is "'the fraudulent appropriation to one's own use of the money or goods entrusted to one's care by another.'" Grin v. Shine, 187 U.S. 181, 189 [23 S.Ct. 98, 101, 47 L.Ed. 130] (1902).

Carpenter v. United States, 484 U.S. 19, 27, 108 S.Ct. 316, 321, 98 L.Ed.2d 275 (1987). Clearly, Altman appropriated funds for his own use from time to time from the estates that were entrusted to his care and that he was charged with administering. He used the funds to bolster a show in which he had a substantial personal interest. It is a general rule that the intentional conversion of funds held in a fiduciary capacity to the personal use of the fiduciary is a fraud upon those for whom the funds are held. See United States v. Buckner, 108 F.2d 921, 926 (2d Cir.), cert. denied, 309 U.S. 669, 60 S.Ct. 613, 84 L.Ed. 1016 (1940). Altman is guilty of that fraud.

Altman is guilty of fraud in another respect. The Supreme Court over seventy years ago determined that the words "to defraud" commonly "signify the deprivation of something of value by trick, deceit, chicane, or overreaching." Hammerschmidt v. United States, 265 U.S. 182, 188, 44 S.Ct. 511, 512, 68 L.Ed. 968 (1924). Overreaching on the part of a fiduciary includes concealment under certain circumstances:

> [T]he concealment by a fiduciary of material information which he is under a duty to disclose to another under circumstances where the non-disclosure could or does result in harm to the other is a violation of the [mail fraud] statute.

United States v. Bronston, 658 F.2d 920, 926 (2d Cir.1981), cert. denied, 456 U.S. 915, 102 S.Ct. 1769, 72 L.Ed.2d 174 (1982).

Aside from the frequent misrepresentations by Altman to Edith Haber's attorneys regarding the condition of the David Haber estate, the estate accounting filed on April 10, 1989 by Altman as Executor failed to disclose several items of material information: that the loans supposedly made to a "theatrical production company in Europe" were not evidenced by any writing; that there was no possibility that the balance of principal or interest on the loans could be paid because the production company had been non-existent for four years; and that the $50,000 loaned by David Haber to Richard Gamsu had been repaid to the estate. It cannot be gainsaid that the failure to disclose resulted in harm to Edith Haber, the principal beneficiary of the estate, who was ill, elderly and in need of funds for living expenses. Had she or her estate representatives been aware of the true facts, appropriate action against Altman could have been taken.

Altman's accounting in the Corsini conservatorship likewise failed to disclose material information. The accounting was filed in 1987 and was the annual accounting for 1985. It came about only after threats were made by the referee to remove Altman as conservator. The accounting listed $206,400 in loans made to the production company between May 3 and May 23, 1985, when the company was in its last throes in Paris. By the time the accounting was filed in 1987, however, the production company had expired and there was no way in which the loan could be repaid. Altman failed to disclose this fact in the accounting, never filed another accounting of his stewardship, as required, and never repaid the stolen funds. The harm to Altman's ward, Armando Corsini, who was living with a friend in reduced circumstances, is readily apparent. Had there been a proper disclosure, appropriate action could have been taken to recover the stolen funds from Altman, who had substantial assets at the time. Also, recovery might have been sought upon the bond posted by Altman for the protection of the conservatee.

The evidence is overwhelming that Altman's "object was to filch from [the estates their] valuable property by dishonest, devious, reprehensible means. That is to 'defraud', for 'the law does not define fraud; it needs no definition; it is as old as falsehood and as versable as human ingenuity.'" Abbott v. United States, 239 F.2d 310, 314 (5th Cir.1956) (quoting Weiss v. United States, 122 F.2d 675, 681 (5th Cir.), cert. denied, 314 U.S. 687, 62 S.Ct. 300, 86 L.Ed. 550 (1941)).

III. Of the Mailing Element

With respect to the mailing element, the Supreme Court has written:

> The federal mail fraud statute does not purport to reach all frauds, but only those limited instances in which the use of the mails is a part of the execution of the fraud, leaving all other cases to be dealt with by appropriate state law.

Kann v. United States, 323 U.S. 88, 95, 65 S.Ct. 148, 151, 89 L.Ed. 88 (1944). The scheme to defraud need not contemplate the use of the mails as an essential part of the scheme as long as the mailing is "incident to an essential part of the scheme." Pereira v. United States, 347 U.S. 1, 8, 74 S.Ct. 358, 363, 98 L.Ed. 435 (1954). The government must establish that the defendant caused the mailing, i.e., "act[ed] with knowledge that the use of the mails will follow in the ordinary course of business, or where such use can reasonably be foreseen, even though not actually intended." Id. at 8-9, 74 S.Ct. at 363.

A mailing cannot be said to be in furtherance of a scheme to defraud when it occurs after the scheme has reached fruition. See Kann, 323 U.S. at 94, 65 S.Ct. at 150. Obviously, such a mailing cannot be considered even as incident to an essential part of the scheme. In the Kann case, the defendants cashed fraudulently obtained checks at various banks, knowing that the checks would be forwarded to a drawee bank for collection. The court held that the mailing was not material to the consummation of the scheme, and therefore concluded that there was no mail fraud. Id. To the same effect was United States v. Maze, 414 U.S. 395, 401-02, 94 S.Ct. 645, 649-50, 38 L.Ed.2d 603 (1974), in which the Court determined that the mailing element was not satisfied by the mailing of credit card invoices for payment following the use of a stolen credit card to obtain goods and services. See also Parr v. United States, 363 U.S. 370, 80 S.Ct. 1171, 4 L.Ed.2d 1277 (1960) (mailing element not satisfied either by mailing of credit card statements by oil company to school district defrauded by unauthorized use of card or by mailing of checks in payment of the statements). It is clear that proximity to a mailbox sometime before or after the execution of a scheme to defraud simply does not fill the bill.

The "mailing in furtherance" requirement found its farthest reach in Schmuck v. United States, 489 U.S. 705, 109 S.Ct. 1443, 103 L.Ed.2d 734 (1989). The defendant in that case was a used-car distributor who purchased used cars, rolled back their odometers and sold the vehicles to retail dealers at prices he was able to inflate by reason of the low-mileage readings. The dealers, unaware of the fraud, resold the automobiles to their customers, who also paid inflated prices. The Court, in a 5-4 decision, held that the mailing element was satisfied by the dealers' mailings of title application forms to the state of Wisconsin on behalf of the customers:

> [A] rational jury could have found that the title-registration mailings were part of the execution of the fraudulent scheme, a scheme which did not reach fruition until the retail dealers resold the cars and effected transfers of title.

Id. at 712, 109 S.Ct. at 1448. Finding that the scheme would have come to an end if the dealers had lost faith in the distributor or were unable to re-sell the cars, the Court concluded:

> Thus, although the registration-form mailings may not have contributed directly to the duping of either the retail dealers or the customers, they were necessary to the passage of title, which in turn was essential to the perpetuation of Schmuck's scheme.

Id.

None of the mailings relied upon by the government in the prosecution of Altman was incident to any essential part of his scheme to defraud the estates. None of the mailings was necessary to avoid jeopardizing a "relationship of trust and good will" as was the case in Schmuck. Id. at 714, 109 S.Ct. at 1450. None was a "part of the business of processing a claim or transaction" as was the case in United States v. Bortnovsky, 879 F.2d 30, 40 (2d Cir.1989). The mailings were insufficiently related to Altman's scheme to be said to be in furtherance of it. See United States v. Dick, 744 F.2d 546, 552 (7th Cir.1984); United States v. Tackett, 646 F.2d 1240, 1244 (8th Cir.1981). By the time Attorney Braslow mailed to Altman an acknowledgment of the receipt of Altman's Haber Estate accounting of April 10, 1989, the looting of the estate was long past and the fraudulent accounting was completed. The mere mailing of an acknowledgment that the accounting was received could no longer further the scheme.

In the Corsini Estate situation, the three mailings relied upon by the government likewise were too remote from the scheme and were insufficiently related to it to support mail fraud convictions. The mailing of the letter dated August 12, 1987, forwarding an order signed by the special referee, did nothing to advance the scheme. That order only confirmed the report of the referee that was critical of Altman's stewardship and effectuated the referee's recommendation that Altman file an additional accounting. The looting had already taken place and the fraudulent annual accounting had already been filed. The mailing of the letter on August 20, 1987 enclosing the referee's report certainly did nothing to advance the scheme. Finally, the mailing of the bank statement from Hanover Trust Company in June of 1989 cannot by any stretch of the imagination be considered to further the scheme to defraud the Corsini Estate. That statement merely reflected the barren condition of the bank account. The mail fraud charges must be dismissed.

IV. Of the Remaining Counts

Altman contends that the reversal of his convictions on the mail fraud counts should result in a reversal of his convictions on the remaining counts. Altman does not make it clear why this should be so. He says only that "the remaining counts are charges which most probably would never have been prosecuted alone and, if prosecuted alone, would most probably not have resulted in conviction." We reject the contention, in the absence of any showing of "compelling prejudice." See United States v. Novod, 927 F.2d 726, 728 (2d Cir.), cert. denied, 500 U.S. 919, 111 S.Ct. 2018, 114 L.Ed.2d 104 (1991); see also

United States v. Warner, 690 F.2d 545, 554 (6th Cir.1982). The trial judge instructed the jury to consider each count separately, and the convictions on the remaining counts were independently supported by overwhelming evidence, which included evidence relevant to the mail fraud counts. Gamsu's testimony was sufficient to convict Altman for witness tampering; documentary evidence supported the convictions for false bank loan statements, Altman having failed to list his indebtedness to the Haber and Corsini Estates on those statements; and the tax count convictions were fully supported by documentary and other evidence that Altman failed to include as income on his 1987 and 1989 personal tax returns certain income he received in connection with a receivership. There is no basis for reversal of Altman's convictions on the remaining counts.

V. Of Sentence

Because we remand with instructions to vacate the mail fraud convictions, Altman must be re-sentenced. His challenges to his sentence on the mail fraud counts—that the district court erroneously calculated his sentence for mail fraud by applying the 1991 version of the Sentencing Guidelines and by erroneously calculating the loss in the Haber Estate—are moot. Likewise moot is the government's challenge on cross-appeal to the district court's refusal to enhance the sentence for violation of the order requiring an intermediate accounting. The government's claim on cross-appeal that the district court erred in refusing to apply the obstruction of justice enhancement also must be rejected. With the elimination of the mail fraud convictions, the obstruction of justice enhancement now applies only to the witness-tampering count. Under the circumstances, the two-level enhancement the government seeks for obstruction is prohibited. See U.S.S.G. §3C1.1, comment. (n. 6).

The parties dispute whether Altman's claim for a downward departure in his sentence for health reasons was waived in the district court, but the claim fails in any event. Section 5H1.4 of the Sentencing Guidelines restricts departures based on physical condition to defendants with an "extraordinary physical impairment," such as those which render a defendant "seriously infirm." The defendant here claims that the district court did not recognize its power to depart, but the record does not support that claim. The health problems cited by the defendant simply need monitoring, and Altman does not challenge the district court's finding that the Bureau of Prisons would be fully able to monitor his health. We can conclude that the district court did not consider Altman to have an extraordinary physical impairment. The district court will be free, however, to consider the current state of Altman's health on re-sentencing.

We reject Altman's claim that the district court did not understand its authority to depart downward on the ground that Altman's crimes constituted a "single aberrant act." Section 3553(a)(1) of Title 18 directs sentencing courts to consider "the nature and circumstances of the offense and the history and characteristics of the defendant," and some courts have construed this to include aberrational acts. See, e.g., United States v. McCarthy, 840 F.Supp. 1404, 1407 (D.Colo.1993). While this court has not yet confronted the issue of "single aberrant act," the repeated and long-lasting criminal conduct involved here cannot under any circumstances be considered a "single aberrant act."

CONCLUSION

We reverse the convictions on the mail fraud counts and affirm the convictions on the remaining counts. We vacate the sentence and remand to the district court for re-sentencing in accordance with the foregoing.

THEATER FOUNDERS ARE CHARGED WITH FRAUD
Bernard Simon
N.Y. Times, Oct. 23, 2002, at C2

After a four-year investigation, the Canadian police today charged the two founders of a Toronto theater group that staged hits like "Showboat" and "Ragtime" on Broadway with defrauding investors and creditors of $325 million.

The Royal Canadian Mounted Police said it filed 19 charges of fraud against the two men, Garth H. Drabinsky, 52, and Myron I. Gottlieb, 59, who started the theater group, Livent Inc., in the late 1980's.

In addition, the police charged two other former Livent executives—Gordon Eckstein, 50, the senior vice president for finance, and Robert Topol, 47, senior executive vice president—with taking part in schemes to defraud investors and creditors.

The police said the four men had falsified financial statements for nine years in an effort to misrepresent the financial health of the company.

Through his lawyer, Edward Greenspan, Mr. Drabinsky, 52, the producer of shows including "Phantom of the Opera," reiterated that he was innocent. Mr. Greenspan said in a statement that Mr. Drabinsky would vigorously defend himself.

"Our courts are a place where the presumption of innocence is not a Hollywood catch phrase, but a place where evidence, facts and truth prevail," Mr. Greenspan said. Mr. Gottlieb's lawyer issued a similar statement.

The four executives surrendered to the police this morning and later appeared briefly in a Toronto court. They were released on bail and will appear again on Dec. 3. Mr. Drabinsky's bail was set at 150,000 Canadian dollars ($95,920).

Livent was started in the late 1980's after Mr. Drabinsky failed in a bid to take over the Cineplex Odeon Corporation, a cinema chain that he helped start in 1979. Livent grew rapidly through the 1990's to become one of North America's biggest theater companies, with properties in New York, Chicago, Toronto and Vancouver.

A group led by Michael Ovitz, the Hollywood agent, bought Livent in early 1998 but within a few months the new owners said that they had uncovered accounting irregularities. The company collapsed that year.

Mr. Drabinsky and Mr. Gottlieb have been considered fugitives in the United States since the United States attorney's office in Manhattan indicted them in January 1999 on 16 counts of fraud and conspiracy. Federal prosecutors charged the two men and the other two executives with taking kickbacks from contractors working on Livent's theaters and hiding losses of more than $60 million.

Mr. Drabinsky and Mr. Gottlieb have denied the American charges and have not shown up for court appearances in the United States.

The Securities and Exchange Commission has also filed a civil complaint against the two men, and the Ontario Securities Commission filed a statement containing accusations in July 2001. The Ontario commission is expected to consider the matter again on

Nov. 1, but a spokesman said today that the matter might be delayed pending the outcome of the criminal case.

In the earlier statement, the Ontario Commission accused Livent of modifying its computer system so that financial statements could be altered without leaving a trail that auditors could follow.

Outside companies were also said to have filed false invoices to Livent and received payments from the company, the commission said. Part of the payments were passed to Mr. Drabinsky, the commission said.

Mr. Drabinsky is currently working as a marketing consultant to the Toronto Argonauts football team. As part of his efforts to attract fans, he arranged for Muhammad Ali, the former boxing champion, to appear at Toronto's SkyDome stadium last Sunday.

Mr. Drabinsky has also been inching his way back to the stage, starting with a production last year of an Athol Fugard play, "The Island," in Toronto. Though he cannot enter the United States without risking arrest, he announced plans this year for a Broadway comeback with a revival of the 1980 backstage London drama "The Dresser."

In the last year, Mr. Drabinsky has also been hired to stage cultural weekends promoting Muskoka Sands, a luxury resort and condominium development north of Toronto.

Notes

1. Raising money for a Broadway show requires compliance with the "New York Theatrical Syndication Financing Act" (except to the extent that federal securities laws preempt its operation). The New York State Attorney General's Office has promulgated detailed regulations to carry the Act into effect, and these can be viewed at www.oag.state.ny.us/investors/investor/part50.html and www.oag.state.ny.us/investors/investor/part51.html.

2. As Brown and Wasser point out, producers normally set up a limited partnership or limited liability company and then offer third parties an opportunity to buy into it. A sample limited partnership agreement appears in Appendix C of this casebook.

Although the number of investors can run anywhere from one to 300 or more, most producers prefer to keep the number small enough to be manageable but large enough to avoid giving any one participant too much say:

> The producers of "The Producers" constitute a list of no less than 14 individuals and groups, all of whom recruited dozens of investors to raise the $10 million needed to get the show up and running. One of the principals is Steve Baruch of the Frankel-Baruch-Viertel-Routh Group. And two of the investors Baruch recruited were his acquaintances, Kay and Dexter Brooks (no relation to the renowned Mel).
>
> "We [the Brooks] evidently had a demographic profile (we go to a lot of shows, subscribe to ballet, etc.) which led (Steve) to inquire whether we would be interested in investing with his group in future shows. We thought it would be fun. When 'The Producers' offer came along we jumped at it because we had seen and loved the original movie."
>
> To spread the risk, and to dilute possible disillusionments, Broadway producers tend to prefer a lot of smallish investors to a few big spenders. "We were not allowed to invest much money," the Brooks [explained], "so the show's fi-

nancial success won't change our lives, but the investment is a great conversation piece."

Joe Adcock, *Sweet 'Failure': Despite the Odds, 'The Producers' Can't Help But Be a Winner*, Seattle Post-Intelligencer, Jan. 31, 2003, at 3.

3. In November 2003, Rosie O'Donnell's "Taboo" opened to decidedly mixed reviews—*The New York Times*, for example, called the production "dazed and confused," "a disastrously overcrowded tableau of a show," and "a crazy, mixed-up mess in tone, structure and rhythm." See Ben Brantley, *Flagrantly Stylish, Outrageously Sexy*, N.Y. Times, Nov. 14, 2003, at E1. By December 2003, the show was the weakest on Broadway, filling just 42% of its seats, and in January 2004 it announced it would close. See Jesse McKinley, *Box Offices on Broadway Feel the Chill*, N.Y. Times, Jan. 15, 2004, at B1.

At least, however, "Taboo" ran for a little bit, something many shows now are routinely failing to do. Just four days after "Taboo" opened, the play "Oldest Living Confederate Widow Tells All," starring Ellen Burstyn, closed after just one performance. See *'Widow' Closes After One Night*, N.Y. Times, Nov. 19, 2003, at E1. Incredibly, the shows of five other stars suffered similar fates during the same month: Farrah Fawcett ("Bobbi Boland"—closed in previews), Mark Hamill ("Six Dances Lessons in Six Weeks"—closed after 30 performances), Barry Manilow ("Harmony"—closed in rehearsals), Jackie Mason ("Jackie Mason's Laughing Room Only"—closed after 14 performances), and Stephen Sondheim ("Bounce"—closed out of town). See Jesse McKinley, *Confirmed: No 'Bounce' to Broadway This Season*, N.Y. Times, Nov. 19, 2003, at E1; Jesse McKinley, *Manilow's Musical Shuts Down Production*, N.Y. Times, Nov. 14, 2003, at B3; Jesse McKinley, *Mason's Broadway Revue Will End Run on Nov. 30*, N.Y. Times, Nov. 22, 2003, at B14; Jason Zinoman, *Farrah Fawcett Play Closes in Previews*, N.Y. Times, Nov. 11, 2003, at B1; Jason Zinoman, *Weak at Box Office, 'Six Dance Lessons in Six Weeks' Closes*, N.Y. Times, Nov. 25, 2003, at E6.

Although no one reason accounts for all of these failures, the soaring cost of staging a Broadway production, coupled with the increasing price-sensitivity of audiences (even as they demand ever more elaborate sets and special effects), are clearly important contributing factors. *See further* Jesse McKinley, *'Dance of the Vampires,' a $12 Million Broadway Failure, is Closing*, N.Y. Times, Jan. 16, 2003, at B1 (noting that the show, one of Broadway's biggest financial flops, employed an array of expensive and technically-demanding stage tricks). In response, producers are shying away from new shows, preferring instead to stage revivals of previous hits; increasingly casting television and films stars in the hope that audiences will be drawn in by the novelty of seeing such actors and actresses perform live; relying more heavily on British imports and non-Broadway shows; experimenting with less elaborate sets to keep costs down; and, when all else fails, slashing ticket prices. *See further* Stephen Kinzer,…*Starring the Original Houston Cast*, N.Y. Times, June 11, 2002, at B1; Jesse McKinley, *2 Shows Illustrate Broadway Volatility*, N.Y. Times, Mar. 31, 2003, at E1; Robin Pogrebin, *Movie Stars Onstage: Big Daddy Speaks Out*, N.Y. Times, Nov. 25, 2003, at B1; Robin Pogrebin, *The Show That Ate the Original Cast*, N.Y. Times, Oct. 20, 2003, at B1; Robin Pogrebin, *Spare Revival of 'Town' Could Be a Long Shot*, N.Y. Times, Nov. 11, 2003, at B1; Bruce Weber, *For Musicals, Big and Brassy Gives Way to Small and Affordable*, N.Y. Times, Jan. 25, 2002, at E1.

4. The *Knapp* case is a good example of the control that large investors can have on a show. It also demonstrates the fiduciary responsibilities that parties engaged in a theatrical venture have to one another. For a further look at these duties, *see, e.g., United States v. West Productions, Inc.*, 168 F. Supp. 2d 84 (S.D.N.Y. 2001) (tax liabilities), and

Red Sail Easter Ltd. Partners, L.P. v. Radio City Music Hall Productions, Inc., 1993 WL 287620 (Del. Ch. 1993) (profit maximization).

5. In thinking about the *Knapp* case, are you convinced that Carroll did anything wrong when he decided to revise the script, rather than hire a new leading lady, once it became clear that Knapp could not act? Would your answer change if it was discovered that Carroll either was having an affair with Knapp or wanted to? In fact, Carroll and Knapp were long-time lovers, but broke up as a result of the problems encountered during the staging of "Fioretta." Carroll then began seeing another beauty, Beryl Wallace, who died with him in a 1948 plane crash. *See further* www.geocities.com/welkerlots/beryl.htm. For a picture of Knapp, *see* www.markreubengallery.com/1111.html.

6. Judges Crane and McLaughlin obviously could not have disagreed more over how to interpret the contract in *Amster*. Unfortunately, such disputes are common in the theater world, for once the glow of opening night has passed, investors often are shocked to discover just how hard it is to make back their money. *See further* Alexander Lindey & Michael Landau, *Lindey on Entertainment, Publishing and the Arts: Agreements and the Law* § 5:46, at 5-246 (2d ed. 1980 & 2003 Supp.) ("Ordinarily a musical requires a run of at least 300 performances, a straight play 200, to return a profit. But a play can have a good run and still wind up in the red.").

7. If you had been the New York State Attorney General, would you have sought to have Springer held in contempt for trying to produce "Sing Mahalia Sing" before paying back the investors of his previous show "Eubie"? Is pursuing such suits a good use of taxpayer dollars?

8. *Altman* and the Livent scandal are examples of the fraudulent practices that some producers have resorted to (and that the play "The Producers" is built around). While waiting for the criminal case against Drabinsky and Gottlieb in Toronto to be resolved, investors in the United States have filed numerous lawsuits against Livent's outside directors, accountants, auditors, bankers, and underwriters. Although some of the claims have been dismissed, most remain pending. *See In re Livent, Inc. Noteholders Securities Litigation*, 78 F. Supp. 2d 194 (S.D.N.Y. 1999), 148 F. Supp. 2d 331 (S.D.N.Y. 2001), 151 F. Supp. 2d 371 (S.D.N.Y. 2001), and 174 F. Supp. 2d 144 (S.D.N.Y. 2001).

Problem 7

A pension fund lent money to a borrower, who invested it in a company that was getting ready to stage a play. The fund soon began hearing rumors that the company was going over budget and, concerned about repayment, asked the borrower to look into the matter. When he failed to report back, the fund sued the company for an accounting. Given these facts, does the company have any obligations to the fund? *See Murray Schwartz Enterprises Employee Pension Plan Trust v. Four Corners Productions, Inc.*, 741 N.Y.S.2d 35 (App. Div. 2002).

C. ADMINISTRATIVE RESPONSIBILITIES

MARTIN v. COMMISSIONER
50 T.C. 341 (1969)

ATKINS, Judge.

Certain concessions having been made by the respondent, the issues remaining for decision are (1) whether the amount received in 1955 by the limited partnership, Guys and Dolls Production Co. (of which the petitioners were the general partners), representing a portion of the proceeds from the sale of motion-picture rights to the story 'The Idyll of Miss Sarah Brown,' constituted ordinary income or capital gain; (2) whether petitioners derived capital gain or ordinary income in 1955 and 1958 from the sale in 1955 of the motion-picture, radio, and television rights to the musical play 'The Boy Friend'; (3) whether they derived capital gain or ordinary income in 1956 and 1957 from the sale in 1956 of their rights in the novel 'Stay Away Joe'; and (4) whether [one of] the petitioner[s] is entitled to deduct for 1958 a greater amount on account of expenses of operation of a yacht and depreciation thereon than the amount allowed by the respondent, and whether petitioner is entitled to deduct a loss sustained upon the sale of the boat.

FINDINGS OF FACT

Since 1947 the petitioners, Ernest H. Martin and Cy Feuer, have been associated together in the production of musical plays on Broadway. They have produced nine shows, namely, 'Where's Charley,' 'Guys and Dolls,' 'Can-Can,' 'The Boy Friend,' 'Silk Stockings,' 'Whoop-Up,' 'How to Succeed,' 'Little Me,' and 'Skyscraper.'

The operations of the petitioners were similar to those of producers generally. They would obtain the rights to produce a play and then transfer all such rights to a limited partnership which undertook to manage and produce the play and to exploit and turn to account all rights in connection therewith. The petitioners as general partners performed the actual duties of production and presentation of the play, and others as limited partners furnished the necessary financing. The petitioners as general partners would rent a theater, assemble the cast, hire a director, supervise rehearsals, arrange for advertising publicity, etc.

Generally the petitioners obtained from the author of a novel or literary work, commonly referred to as the story, the right to produce a musical play based upon the underlying work. Very few musical plays are original. The owner of the underlying work would grant and assign to them the right to write and compose a musical play based upon the underlying work, to produce and present such musical play on the speaking stage, to own and dispose of the musical play and any subsidiary rights with regard thereto, such as motion-picture, radio, and television rights, and to authorize or permit others to do any of the foregoing. As consideration the petitioners agreed to pay the author a percentage of the box-office receipts and of the proceeds from the sale of the subsidiary rights.

The petitioners would then enter into contracts with a librettist to write the play, commonly referred to as the libretto or book, with a composer to compose the music and with a lyricist to write the lyrics. All librettists, composers, and lyricists are members of the Dramatists Guild of the Authors League of America, Inc., and the contracts which the petitioners entered into with them were prescribed by such guild, some modifications being made in individual cases. These contracts are referred to as dramatic-musical production contracts. Therein the petitioners are referred to as managers and the librettist, lyricist, and composer are referred to as author. By such contracts the petitioners 'authorized' the authors to write the book, lyrics, and music, and it was provided that such authors should be vested with the legal and equitable title to the musical play and all subsidiary rights therein. By the same contracts the authors granted the petitioners the right to produce and present the musical play, the authors to receive a royalty consisting of a percentage of the box-office receipts.

Such contracts further provided that the petitioners would be entitled to a share of the proceeds, usually 40 percent, from any sale by the authors of any subsidiary rights, such as motion-picture, radio, and television rights in the play, provided petitioners timely produced and presented the play according to certain standards and for a specified number of times. A successful stage play usually results in a lucrative sale of the motion-picture rights to such play. The dramatic-musical production contract recognizes this by stating that a 'successful run also publicizes the play and adds materially to the value of the subsidiary rights.'

When a musical play is to be based on an original literary work such as a novel, the producer generally obtains from the author of such underlying work all subsidiary rights therein, including the motion-picture rights. This is necessary in order to insure no conflict of interest between the holder of the motion-picture rights to the play and the holder of the motion-picture rights to the underlying literary work. The contract provides for a 'merger' of the motion-picture rights to both the play and the motion-picture rights to the underlying work. Thus, all the motion-picture and other subsidiary rights generally pass to the petitioners and then to the play authors.

If, as is sometimes true, the author of the underlying story has already transferred the motion-picture rights to the story to a third party, generally a motion-picture company, before the producer enters into negotiations for the acquisition of the dramatization rights, the producer attempts to obtain from such third party the motion-picture rights to the underlying work for the play authors. Sometimes such motion-picture rights to the underlying work can be bought from the third party, but generally such third party will agree with the producer and the play authors to convey its motion-picture rights to the underlying work to the person who eventually buys from the play authors the motion-picture rights to the play. In such case it is provided that such third party shall receive a percentage of the total consideration paid upon a subsequent disposition of all the motion-picture rights. Sometimes such third party is willing to buy the motion-picture rights from the authors of the play at a lesser price than such rights are offered to others. In some instances the third party is unwilling to enter into any agreement with the producer or the play authors, in which case it is impossible for the play authors to sell the motion-picture rights to the play.

With respect to the musical plays which the petitioners produced, in only one instance, namely, 'Skyscraper,' was it impossible to obtain the motion-picture rights to the underlying work. In that instance the authors of the play were therefore precluded from selling any motion-picture rights to the play and hence the petitioners obtained no income from that source. In all other instances motion-picture rights were sold either by the petitioners or by the musical play authors, with the result that the petitioners derived income from that source.

'The Idyll of Miss Sarah Brown'

Damon Runyon was the author of a short story entitled 'The Idyll of Miss Sarah Brown,' hereinafter called 'Idyll.' On January 20, 1934, Runyon executed an agreement with Paramount Productions, Inc., hereinafter referred to as Paramount, by which he granted and assigned to that company all the motion-picture rights to that story.

On October 1, 1949, the Chase National Bank, executor of the Estate of Damon Runyon, hereinafter referred to as the bank, entered into a contract with the petitioners, granting and assigning to them the exclusive right to compose, produce, and present on the stage a musical play based upon 'Idyll' together with the right to 'use, sell, lease or otherwise dispose of and deal in the Musical Play and any dramatic, motion picture, radio, television, or other version and adaptation thereof, * * * and to authorize and permit others so to do.' The petitioners were also granted the right to use the title 'Guys and Dolls' or any variation thereof. In the contract the petitioners agreed to produce and present the musical play upon the stage in the United States or Canada not later than a specified date. It was provided that if petitioners produced the play within the times specified 'then and in such event all rights of every kind and nature in and to the Story and the title 'Guys and Dolls' shall be deemed merged in the Musical Play as part thereof, to the same extent as though the said Story and the Musical Play were one single work (together with the title 'Guys and Dolls'), and the Producer or the Dramatists, as their respective interests may appear, shall have the same rights in the Story and the title 'Guys and Dolls' as are acquired hereunder by them in the Musical Play.' This, however, was made subject to the rights which Paramount owned in the story.

On April 5, 1950, petitioners as 'Manager,' entered into a dramatic-musical production contract with Jo Swerling, as 'Author,' whereby they authorized Swerling to write the book of a dramatic-musical work to be known as 'Guys and Dolls.' It was provided that the contract would be subject and subordinate to the agreement entered into by petitioners and the bank, and would be governed thereby. The contract provided that Swerling 'hereby leases to the Manager the sole and exclusive right to produce and present the Book of said play on the speaking stage,' but it was provided that unless the play was produced and presented on or before December 31, 1950, the rights granted by Swerling should automatically terminate. [T]he petitioners [further] agreed to pay Swerling 2 1/2 percent of the gross weekly box-office receipts against which they would immediately make an advance to him of $1,000.

On April 5, 1950, the petitioners, as managers, [also] entered into a dramatic-musical contract with Frank Loesser, as author, whereby they authorized him to write both the music and lyrics for the play 'Guys and Dolls.' In all essential respects the contract with Loesser was the same as the contract which the petitioners had entered into with Swerling. The petitioners agreed to pay Loesser 5 percent of the gross weekly box-office receipts. As in the case of the contract with Swerling, the contract with Loesser provided that the author retained complete title, both legal and equitable, in all rights with respect to the music and lyrics, 'other than those specifically leased to the Manager.' It was specifically provided that it was the intention of the parties that the manager 'shall have no right, title or interest, legal or equitable, in the motion picture rights, other than the right to receive the Manager's share of the proceeds of the motion picture rights.'

On April 28, 1950, Swerling, Loesser, and the petitioners entered into an agreement with Paramount, whereby Swerling and Loesser agreed to write the book, music, and lyrics and petitioners agreed to produce the play. Therein it was agreed that the motion-picture rights to the musical play should be offered for sale to Paramount before being offered to others. It was provided that if Paramount should not purchase such rights, then if such rights were sold to another, Paramount would convey to the purchaser all its right, title, and interest in the motion-picture rights to the story 'Idyll' which it had acquired under the agreement with Runyon in 1934, and receive in consideration a specified sum or a specified percentage of the total price to be paid by the purchaser.

On May 15, 1950, a limited partnership was formed, under the firm name of Guys and Dolls Co. by the petitioners, who were the general partners, and others, who were limited partners, for the 'purpose of managing and producing the play, and for the purpose of exploiting and turning to account the rights at any time held by the partnership in connection therewith.' The petitioners, as general partners, agreed to contribute to the partnership 'all of the rights in the play held by them.' They also agreed 'to render, in connection with the play, services customarily and usually rendered by theatrical producers' and they were to 'have complete control, in their discretion, both of production of the play and the exploitation of all rights therein.' The petitioners, as general partners, were to receive 50 percent of the net profits of the partnership, and the limited partners were to receive the remaining 50 percent.

The show 'Guys and Dolls' opened on Broadway on November 24, 1950, and ran in New York until October 21, 1953. The road show closed on May 22, 1954.

On March 16, 1953, Paramount, in consideration of the receipt of $75,000, transferred to Loesser [and] Swerling the worldwide motion-picture rights in and to 'Idyll' which it had acquired from Runyon in 1934. On the same date the above agreement of April 28, 1950, was canceled and terminated.

On June 28, 1954, Loesser [and] Swerling entered into an agreement with Samuel Goldwyn Productions, Inc. (hereinafter referred to as Goldwyn), whereby they sold and assigned all their right, title, and interest in the motion-picture rights with respect to 'Idyll' which they had acquired by the above contract of March 16, 1953. In consideration thereof Goldwyn agreed to pay $200,000 upon execution of the agreement and $265,000 on January 3, 1955. By a contract of the same date, Loesser [and] Swerling granted, conveyed, and assigned to Goldwyn the sole and exclusive motion-picture rights to the play 'Guys and Dolls.' In consideration thereof, Goldwyn agreed to pay $465,000 ($25,000 upon execution of the agreement, $340,000 on January 3, 1955, and $100,000 on January 3, 1956), plus 10 percent of the gross receipts in excess of $10 million from all motion-pictures produced under the agreement. The bank as executor of the Runyon Estate was also a party to this contract and transferred to Goldwyn any motion-picture rights to 'Idyll' and to certain Damon Runyon characters to the extent, if any, not theretofore transferred by its contract with Paramount and its subsequent contracts with the petitioners.

The partnership return of Guys and Dolls Co. for the taxable year ended October 31, 1955, reported $103,209 received by it with respect to 'Idyll' as a long-term capital gain, and it reported $131,399 received with respect to the Guys and Dolls motion-picture rights as ordinary income.

The petitioners each reported his distributive share of the above amount reported by the partnership as capital gain which for the taxable year 1955 amounted to $4,644.42 for the petitioner Martin and $5,676.52 for the petitioner Feuer.

In the notices of deficiency the respondent determined that the gain from the sale of the motion-picture rights to 'Idyll' constituted ordinary income and not long-term capital gain as reported by the partnership Guys and Dolls Co., and therefore determined that the above amounts of $4,644.42 and $5,676.52 constituted ordinary income, rather than long-term capital gain, to the petitioners Martin and Feuer, respectively.

OPINION

The petitioners contend that the amount received by the partnership, Guys and Dolls Co., in its taxable year ended October 31, 1955, as its share of the proceeds from the sale of the motion-picture rights to 'Idyll,' was long-term capital gain, and that hence their distributive shares thereof as general partners (namely, $4,644.42 to petitioner Martin and $5,676.52 to petitioner Feuer) for their taxable year 1955 constituted long-term capital gain. See sec. 702(a)(2) and (b), I.R.C. 1954. The respondent, on the other hand, contends that the amount received by the partnership, and hence the partners' distributive shares thereof, constituted ordinary income.

Section 1222(3) of the Internal Revenue Code of 1954 provides that the term 'long-term capital gain' means 'gain from the sale or exchange of a capital asset held for more than 6 months.' Section 1221 provides that the term 'capital asset' means 'property held by the taxpayer,' with certain exceptions. The petitioners contend that the partnership's share of the proceeds constituted capital gain 'because its interest in those proceeds was a capital asset under Section 1221.' It is the position of the respondent that neither the petitioners nor the partnership sold or exchanged any asset (whether capital or not), that the authors of the play sold the motion-picture rights to both the play and the story, and that the partnership's share of the proceeds was obtained in the ordinary course of its trade or business of producing the play and deriving income in part from the sale of the ancillary rights.

We think that the respondent properly determined that the amount in question received by the partnership constituted ordinary income. We agree with his view that there was no sale or exchange by the partnership of any asset, which, of course, is one of the prerequisites to capital gains treatment. Neither the petitioners nor the partnership ever acquired the motion-picture rights to the underlying story, 'Idyll.' The authors of the play acquired them from Paramount. In the contract between the petitioners and the authors of the play, it was specifically provided that such authors would retain complete title, both legal and equitable, and that the petitioners should have no title or interest in such rights, other than the right to receive a share of the proceeds from the sale of the rights.

We think it clear that the amount in question constituted ordinary income derived by the partnership from the conduct of its business of producing the play, 'Guys and Dolls.' We have described in some detail in the Findings of Fact the manner in which the petitioners, through limited partnerships, carried on the business of producing Broadway shows. The production of the play 'Guys and Dolls' and the realization of income from the exploitation of the subsidiary rights therein is typical of their customary activities. They, through the partnership, produced and presented the play under a contract with the play authors whereby, in consideration of their timely production of the play in a first-class theater in a first-class manner with a first-class cast and director, and upon the presentation of the play for a minimum number of performances within a specified time, were entitled to a percentage of the proceeds from the sale of the motion-picture and subsidiary rights therein. The contract between the petitioners and the play authors provided that the motion-picture rights to both the play and the original story 'Idyll' would merge and be subject to a combined sale and that the petitioners would receive a percentage of the proceeds of the sale. Thus, the income in question was ordinary income from the partnership's business of producing and presenting the musical play and thereby benefitting from the exploitation of the subsidiary motion-picture rights in both the play and the underlying literary work. It follows that, as determined by the respondent, the petitioners' distributive shares of the gain in question constituted ordinary income. See Commissioner v. Ferrer (C.A. 2) 304 F.2d 125, affirming in part and reversing in part 35 T.C. 617, in which it was clearly indicated that had the taxpayer in that case produced the play and received an amount representing a percentage of the proceeds from the sale of motion-picture rights such amount would have constituted ordinary business income.

[The remainder of the court's opinion, as well as the dissenting opinions of Judges Fay, Raum, and Tannenwald, is omitted.]

THEATRE GUILD PRODUCTIONS, INC. v. INSURANCE CORP. OF IRELAND
267 N.Y.S.2d 297 (App. Div. 1966),
aff'd mem., 225 N.E.2d 216 (N.Y. 1967)

McNALLY, Justice.

This is an appeal from an order and judgment granting plaintiff's motion for summary judgment in the sum of $166,704.51. The question presented on stipulated facts is the scope of coverage of five policies of insurance.

Plaintiff was the producer of the play entitled 'Dear Me, The Sky Is Falling'. Gertrude Berg was the star performer. The show opened March 2, 1963. Defendants issued the policies effective January 26, 1963 and expiring July 26, 1963. The relevant provisions thereof are:

> 1. This insurance is to pay the insured in the event of the inability of the insured artist [Gertrude Berg] to appear in the insured production, directly in consequence of her suffering any personal accident or sickness or in the event of the occurrence of her death or total disability during the period of insurance.
>
> 2. The amount of insurance payable hereunder is $1,500 per performance and the Underwriter's liability shall be limited to an aggregate of $50,000 for the period of insurance.

On July 11, 1963 Gertrude Berg became ill and disabled within the meaning of the policies. By reason of such disability the show closed on July 22, 1963. The disability continued until and existed on October 15, 1963, at the commencement of this action. Defendants concede liability to July 26, 1963, the expiration date of the policies, at the rate of $1,500 for each nonappearance of Gertrude Berg less the deductible sum of $1,500. Plaintiff contends for additional payment for nonappearances subsequent to July 26, 1963 and has been awarded judgment accordingly by the learned Justice at Special Term.

Plaintiff's insurable interest derived from its employment of Gertrude Berg as the star of the production. (Insurance Law, §§ 146, subd. 2.) The economic success of the production depended on the effective appearance and performance of Gertrude Berg. Towards the end of insuring against the economic loss consequent on her nonappearance, plaintiff sought and obtained the policies herein providing for stipulated indemnity for the nonappearance of Gertrude Berg due to specified causes during the priod of insurance.

The production of the show might terminate because it was unprofitable and a financial failure or other reasons unrelated to the nonappearance of the star. In that event, the subsequent disability or death of the artist would not be of financial concern to the plaintiff. The insurance contemplated a going production dependent on the services and appearance of the artist. It was intended to indemnify against financial loss in the course of 'the insured production' resulting from 'the inability of the insured artist to appear' during the period of insurance.

The relevant intent is that expressed in the policies of insurance. The surrounding circumstances at the inception of the policies serve to define that intent within the framework of the content of the policies. 'Our guide is the reasonable expectation and purpose of the ordinary business man when making an ordinary business contract. It is his intention, expressed or fairly to be inferred, that counts.' (Bird v. St. Paul Fire & Marine Ins. Co., 224 N.Y. 47, 51, 120 N.E. 86, 87, 13 A.L.R. 875.)

The primary and excess cover notes' captions describing the coverage as 'non appearance coverage' are to be read and given effect in ascertaining the scope and intent of the coverage. (13 Appleman, Insurance Law & Practice, § 7387.)

The event insured against was the nonappearance of the star in the production. Her inability to appear under the terms of the policies must be directly in consequence of personal accident or sickness or the occurrence of her death or total disability, during the period of insurance. The insurer's liability in the event of the nonappearance of the star is limited to $1,500 a performance and to an aggregate of $50,000 'for the period of insurance'. Every clause or word in an insurance contract is deemed to have some meaning. (Finery Silk Stocking Co. v. Aetna Ins. Co., 227 App.Div. 39, 42, 237 N.Y.S. 36, 39.)

We construe said provisions to provide coverage for the nonappearance of the insured artist in the insured production during the six-month term of the policies.

The policies clearly and unambiguously limit the indemnity to $1,500 for each nonappearance of the star at a performance occurring during the period of insurance. Thereby the insured was to be paid in the event of the inability of the star to appear in the insured production because of certain specified conditions including accident, sickness, death or disability occurring after the effective date and while the policies were in full force and effect. The insured event was the star's nonappearance; her health was not insured. Sickness was one of the specified factors giving rise to indemnity in the event it caused nonappearance.

The insurance here involved is not to be confused with a policy providing an assured indemnity for loss resulting from disability because of illness or accident. In such case the illness per se occurring during the policy period affects the assured so long as it persists and the contract is one for indemnity during the illness even though it extends beyond its termination date. (See Greiper v. National Casualty Co., 1 A.D.2d 806, 148 N.Y.S.2d 778.) Here, the nonappearance of the artist could affect the plaintiff only during the course of its production of the show. The six-month term represented the parties' estimate of the duration of the show or the agreed period of exposure. The parties might have provided for indemnity arising from nonappearance during the run of the show, but they did not, and there are no circumstances supporting the intent to so do. In short, the coverage here involved is for nonappearance 'in the insured production * * * during the period of insurance' and not for disability of the artist by reason of sickness or accident.

There may be no recovery under this policy unless the illness of the artist, which brought the liability of the insurer into play, occurred some time between January 26, 1963 and July 26, 1963. There is no dispute about that—it is conceded. Accordingly, the words 'during the period of insurance,' as they appear in paragraph 1 of the policy, mean during the period beginning January 26 and ending July 26, 1963. Paragraph 2 also contains the words 'for the period of insurance' and it is the construction to be given to those words in that paragraph that brings this lawsuit. It seems to be clear that we must construe the words 'for the period of insurance,' as appears in the second paragraph, in the same manner as it is construed in paragraph 1, and hold that payments are to be made only up to July 26, 1963. We test this conclusion by reading paragraph 2 as though the sentence were terminated after the figure $50,000, i.e., by striking from paragraph 2 the words 'for the period of insurance.' Reading it in this manner would give to the plaintiffs everything they now claim they are entitled to receive, i.e., all payments until the $50,000 maximum is reached. However, the words 'for the period of insurance' are added. Being added they must be given some meaning, and the only meaning that can be given would be one of limitation, as is given to the same words as written in paragraph 1. If we do not give it that meaning, they are meaningless.

The order and judgment should be modified, on the law, to the extent of directing judgment in the sum of $24,000, with costs and interest, pursuant to paragraph 23 of the stipulation of admitted and agreed facts, and, as so modified, affirmed, with costs to defendants-appellants.

All concur.

BATES v. SELECT LAKE CITY THEATER OPERATING CO.
397 N.E.2d 75 (Ill. App. Ct. 1975)

SIMON, Presiding Justice.

Plaintiff Bates, a patron of the Shubert Theater, was injured when she slipped and fell on an icy stair as she was leaving the theater. She sued the theater operator (Theater), which sought to shift liability by way of a third-party complaint to the producers (Producers) of the show being performed. The Theater relies in its third-party action on an indemnity clause in the licensing agreement between the Theater and the Producers governing the presentation of the performances at the Shubert.

The licensing agreement provided most of the details for the production of a modern legitimate musical show in the Theater, for the apportionment of costs and for the division of receipts. Among its provisions were the following:

> (a) During the engagement Producer shall carry and pay for (workmen's compensation), Public Liability (Personal Injury and Property Damage) Insurance, and (fire insurance) of all scenery, costumes, electrical and sound equipment, literary and musical material, and all other properties and materials owned, rented or brought into Theatre by Producer. * * * All liability policies shall name Theatre as an insured. * * * Upon the failure of Producer to carry and pay for such insurance, Theatre shall have the right, but not the obligation, to take out and pay for the same and charge Producer for all expenses incurred thereby.
>
> (b) Notwithstanding anything contained in subparagraph (a) hereof, Producer agrees to release, indemnify and/or hold Theatre safe and harmless with

respect to any claim or demand for any loss, damage and/or injury to any property, person, or thing owned, rented or brought into Theatre by Producer.

The Theater was given exclusive control over the sale of tickets and admission to the performances. A separate provision of the licensing agreement required the Producers to accept the Shubert Theater "as is." They were not allowed to make any alterations to or repairs of the physical premises.

The third-party complaint by the Theater against the Producers alleged, in one count, a breach of the agreement to buy liability insurance and requested indemnity as relief, and, in the second count, a breach of the indemnity agreement itself. The circuit court granted summary judgment in favor of the Producers on both counts. The only issues raised by the Theater's appeal are the construction of the indemnity agreement, its validity and the breach of the promise to purchase insurance.

Summary judgment is proper where there are no material issues of fact and the moving party is entitled to judgment as a matter of law. (Ill.Rev.Stat.1977, ch. 110, par. 57.) Here, there is no dispute concerning the language or formation of the licensing agreement. Only its construction and validity are at issue, so summary judgment was a proper procedure. Simone Corp. v. Builders Architectural Products (1975), 28 Ill.App.3d 595, 597, 328 N.E.2d 723.

The meaning of written agreements must be determined from the words used by the parties. (Westinghouse Electric Elevator Co. v. LaSalle Monroe Building Corp. (1946), 395 Ill. 429, 70 N.E.2d 604.) In construing an agreement to indemnify, the agreement must be given a fair and reasonable interpretation based upon consideration of all the language and provisions. (Tatar v. Maxon Construction Co. (1973), 54 Ill.2d 64, 294 N.E.2d 272, 274.) Indemnity agreements are not void, but are sufficiently disfavored that they must be strictly construed. (DeTienne v. S. N. Nielsen Co. (1963), 45 Ill.App.2d 231, 233, 195 N.E.2d 240, 242.) The Theater here is asking the court to construe the licensing agreement so that it is indemnified for its own negligence in maintaining the theater exits. The rule in such situations was stated in Westinghouse:

> It is quite generally held that an indemnity contract will not be construed as indemnifying one against his own negligence, unless such a construction is required by clear and explicit language of the contract, * * * or such intention is expressed in unequivocal terms.

Westinghouse, 395 Ill., at 433, 70 N.E.2d at 607.

In Westinghouse, the operator of a building was seeking indemnity against losses "arising out of" work performed by the elevator company. The language of the indemnity clause was held to be too general to support a construction of the agreement which would indemnify the building operator for its own negligence. Later cases confirmed the rule that broad and general language cannot be used to indemnify one from one's own negligence. Davis v. Marathon Oil Co. (1976), 64 Ill.2d 380, 1 Ill.Dec. 93, 356 N.E.2d 93 ("attributable directly or indirectly to the operations" held too broad); Zadak v. Cannon (1974), 59 Ill.2d 118, 319 N.E.2d 469 ("arising out of such work" held too broad); Tatar v. Maxon Construction Co. (1973), 54 Ill.2d 64, 294 N.E.2d 272 ("arising out of or connected with" held too broad).

The licensing agreement called for indemnity "with respect to" any loss or damage to items or persons "brought into" the Theater by the Producers. The parties could have drafted an agreement explicitly calling for indemnification from the Theater's own negligence [and] in one provision of the agreement the Producers actually did release the

Theater from liability for any fire loss even if the fire "* * * shall be due to the negligence of Theatre." As noted in Barger v. Scandroli Construction Co. (1976), 38 Ill.App.3d 348, 349, 347 N.E.2d 207, 208, it required no extraordinary skill in draftsmanship to bind the Producers "* * * in words or phrases of absolute certainty as to require (them) to indemnify (the Theater) for (its) own negligence." The language employed in the licensing agreement was too general and too broad to be construed as indemnifying the Theater for its own negligence which resulted in Bates' injury. See Kerulis v. Tatera (1977), 55 Ill.App.3d 428, 13 Ill.Dec. 342, 371 N.E.2d 37.

Even if that language were explicit enough to cover the Theater's acts of negligence, the agreement still did not cover the injury to Bates. The object of the parties' venture was to draw patrons, such as Bates, to the Shubert Theater to see the performance, but the circumstances of the entire licensing agreement preclude the interpretation that patrons were "persons brought into" the theater by the Producers. The production scheme made the Producers generally responsible for what went on behind the curtain, while the Theater was generally responsible for what went on in front of it. We note that under the licensing agreement the Theater had veto power over the admission of anyone into the audience; likewise, the Producers alone were responsible for the conduct of the company putting on the play. But Bates was not an actress, a member of the production crew, or a friend of the cast or company, was not an instrumentality of the Producers and was not under their control. She was, simply, a theater-goer. Because we construe the indemnity agreement to cover only those persons brought into the theater by the Producer to further the production, we decline to adopt the Theater's version of the clause, which would make the Producers responsible for anyone and everyone who came into the Theater. Because Bates was a patron, she was not covered by the indemnity clause.

The policies which allow indemnification support this interpretation of the agreement. As the Theater has argued, Patent Scaffolding Co. v. Standard Oil Co. (1966), 68 Ill.App.2d 29, 215 N.E.2d 1, 3, noted that when businesses allocate losses through indemnity contracts, the incentive to minimize safety risks usually remains. The indemnitor, upon whom any loss will fall, will find it in his interest to take steps to insure public safety. But if the licensing agreement's indemnity clause were read to cover Bates' injury, the policy of fostering public safety would be frustrated. Even though the Producers bore the risk of Bates' slip and fall, they could nevertheless do nothing to prevent the accident. By the express terms of the licensing agreement, they were forbidden from doing anything to correct the Theater's negligent maintenance. It would not be reasonable for the parties to provide that the loss would fall on one who did not control the means of accident prevention.

The circuit court correctly construed the licensing agreement as not applying to the Theater's act of negligence to Bates, and properly granted summary judgment on Count II against the Theater. Because the licensing agreement as construed did not cover the injury in question, it is unnecessary to reach the issue of the validity of [the] indemnity clause under Ill.Rev.Stat.1977, ch. 29, par. 61.

The only question remaining is the circuit court's granting of summary judgment on Count I. The Theater alleged that the Producers breached the licensing agreement by failing to purchase liability insurance as required, and asked for indemnity as relief. Similar contracts to buy insurance (which the Theater here argued would provide a fund for the indemnity agreement) existed in Zadak v. Cannon (1974), 59 Ill.2d 118, 319 N.E.2d 469; Tatar v. Maxon Construction Co. (1973), 54 Ill.2d 64, 294 N.E.2d 272;

and Westinghouse Electric Elevator Co. v. LaSalle Monroe Building Corp. (1946), 395 Ill. 429, 70 N.E.2d 604. In each of these cases, the indemnification which was sought as relief was denied because the contract to purchase insurance failed to explicitly state that it was the "indemnitee's" own negligence which was being insured. (Zadak, 59 Ill.2d at 121-122, 319 N.E.2d 469; Westinghouse, 395 Ill. at 434, 70 N.E.2d 604.) The contract to purchase insurance here similarly failed to pass the Westinghouse test. (See Svenson v. Miller Builders Inc. (1979), 74 Ill.App.3d 75, 88, 29 Ill.Dec. 931, 392 N.E.2d 628, 638.) Thus, summary judgment was also properly granted against the Theater on Count I.

Judgment affirmed.

RUSSEK ADVERTISING, INC. v. HURST
1992 WL 98807 (S.D.N.Y. 1992)

FRANCIS, Magistrate Judge.

The plaintiff, Russek Advertising, Inc., brought this action charging the defendant Howard Hurst with breach of contract and related claims. The defendant answered the complaint but then failed to cooperate in discovery. The plaintiff moved for relief pursuant to Rule 37 of the Federal Rules of Civil Procedure, and the Court granted that motion by Memorandum and Order dated February 4, 1992, striking the defendant's answer and entering a default judgment against him. The action was then referred to me for an inquest on damages. Although I notified the defendant of the hearing date, he did not appear, and the following findings are therefore based on the evidence presented by the plaintiff.

Background

Russek Advertising, Inc. ("Russek") is an advertising agency based in New York. One of its clients was Howard Hurst, a Canadian citizen who produced a Broadway play called "Truly Blessed." Mr. Hurst engaged Russek to place advertisements in connection with the production. According to the agreement, Russek would purchase advertising in the media at a fifteen percent discount from normal rates, and Mr. Hurst, doing business as The Blessed Company or The Truly Blessed Company, would then reimburse Russek at the full undiscounted rate.

Russek prepared and placed advertising pursuant to the contract. From February 20 through June 5, 1990, Russek invoiced The Truly Blessed Company for a total of $275,994.77. By April, 1990, Mr. Hurst had paid $54,888.42 toward the outstanding invoices. At that time, however, there was still a balance owing, and on May 9, 1990, Mr. Hurst executed a personal guaranty for all media expenditures made on behalf of The Blessed Company.

From April 30 to mid-May, 1990, Mr. Hurst delivered five personal checks to Russek in partial payment of the outstanding balance. All of these checks were returned for nonsufficient funds, but Russek did not learn of this until sometime after May 17, 1990, when its bank sent notice that the first of the checks had bounced. Thus, Russek continued providing services to Mr. Hurst throughout this period based on his representation that the invoices had been or would be paid.

At the inquest, James Russek, the president of Russek Advertising, testified about the effects on his agency of Mr. Hurst's failure to pay the outstanding debt. Company personnel were diverted from their usual tasks in order to perform cash management responsibilities. Payments to Russek's vendors had to be delayed or compromised, resulting in a loss of the agency's good will and potential harm to its credit rating. Finally,

Merrill Lynch rejected Russek's application to participate in a small business checking program.

Russek now seeks payment of the amount due and owing, consequential damages for the harm to its business, punitive damages, interest, and attorneys' fees for time spent making the Rule 37 motion.

Discussion

A. Jurisdiction

Because the defendant is a foreign citizen while the plaintiff is a citizen of New York and the matter in controversy exceeds $50,000, the Court has diversity jurisdiction pursuant to 28 U.S.C. § 1332. Further, there is personal jurisdiction in this forum based on Mr. Hurst's transacting business here out of which the plaintiff's claims arise. Mr. Hurst engaged Russek, a New York company, to place advertising in the New York media in connection with a Broadway play. N.Y.Civ.Prac.L. & R. §§ 302.

B. Liability

Following a default, all factual allegations of the complaint, except those relating to damages, must be accepted as true. See Au Bon Pain Corp. v. Artect, Inc., 653 F.2d 61, 65 (2d Cir.1981); Meehan v. Snow, 494 F.Supp. 690, 695 (S.D.N.Y.1980), rev'd on other grounds, 652 F.2d 274 (2d Cir.1981); 10 C. Wright & A. Miller, Federal Practice and Procedure §§ 2688 at 444 (1983). Here, the allegations of the complaint establish that Mr. Hurst was contractually obligated to pay the full amount of the invoices and that he failed to do so. He is personally liable both because he operated The Truly Blessed Company as a personal business and not as a corporation, and because he personally guaranteed the company's debts.

C. Damages on the Contract

The evidence establishes that the undisputed invoices presented by Russek to Mr. Hurst total $275,994.77. Of this, Mr. Hurst paid $54,888.42. He is therefore liable on the contract for $221,106.35.

D. Interest

Russek seeks an award of pre-judgment interest on the amount of the debt. Because federal jurisdiction is based on diversity, the right to interest, a substantive right, is governed by state law. Adams v. Lindblad Travel, Inc., 730 F.2d 89, 93 (2d Cir.1984). New York law requires such an award in an action based on breach of contract. Id. Therefore, Russek is entitled to interest at the statutory rate of nine percent per year. N.Y.Civ.Prac.L. & R. §§ 5004.

Technically, interest should be calculated individually with respect to each invoice, running from a date some time after the invoice date to allow for a reasonable time for payment. However, since the unpaid invoices are dated from April 3, 1990 through June 5, 1990—a relatively brief period—and are fairly evenly distributed over that time, it is more efficient and no less just to choose a single date for the calculation of interest. The midpoint of the invoice dates is May 4, 1990. A reasonable time to allow for delivery of the invoices and for payment is two weeks. Therefore, interest should be calculated from May 18, 1990 for the entire outstanding balance of $221,106.35.

E. Consequential Damages

The evidence presented by the plaintiff is insufficient to justify an award of consequential damages. It is true, as the plaintiff contends, that damages should not be denied merely because they cannot be calculated with precision. See Novelty Textile Mills, Inc. v. C.T. Eastern, Inc., 743 F.Supp. 212, 219-20 (S.D.N.Y.1990); S. Leo Harmonay, Inc. v. Binks Manufacturing Co., 597 F.Supp. 1014, 1030 (S.D.N.Y.1984), aff'd mem., 762 F.2d 990 (2d Cir.1985). Here, however, the difficulty is not with the calculation, but with the lack of proof that any quantifiable damages flowed directly from the defendant's breach. Mr. Russek testified about the need to devote energy to cash management, but he failed to specify how this affected his company economically. He talked in general terms about the loss of good will, but he did not cite a single specific example of a vendor declining to do business with Russek. He failed to present any proof to show that Merrill Lynch's refusal to accept Russek into a new program was based on the outstanding debt owed by the defendant. Finally, although Mr. Russek expressed concern about the company's credit rating, he introduced no evidence that it had, in fact, been adversely affected. This is not a case where such proof was solely within the control of the defendant. Cf. Whitney v. Citibank, N.A., 782 F.2d 1106, 1118 (2d Cir.1986) (permitting estimation of damages where difficulty in calculation due to defendant's misconduct); RSO Records, Inc. v. Peri, 596 F.Supp. 849, 862 (S.D.N.Y.1984) (estimating damages where proof in hands of defaulting defendant). Rather, it was within the plaintiff's power to demonstrate that it was harmed in specific ways by the defendant's conduct. It did not do so, and consequential damages should therefore not be awarded.

F. Punitive Damages

A court may award punitive damages where it finds that the defendant engaged in a transaction with the clear intent to defraud. See Ostano Commerzanstalt v. Telewide Systems, Inc., 880 F.2d 642, 649 (2d Cir.1989). That is the case here. As demonstrated by the fact that Mr. Hurst submitted five worthless checks to Russek, it is clear that he knew both when he wrote the checks and when he executed the personal guaranty that he did not have the funds to make good on his promises. Instead, he consciously shifted the risk for the theatrical venture from himself to Russek. This is the type of wanton conduct that justifies an award of punitive damages. In light of the magnitude of the actual damages suffered by Russek as well as the fraudulent behavior of Mr. Hurst, an award of $50,000 is appropriate.

G. Attorneys' Fees

In granting the plaintiff's Rule 37 motion, the Court found the defendant liable for attorneys' fees, and referred to me calculation of a reasonable fee. Plaintiff's counsel has submitted copies of original time records showing that 8.5 hours were spent on the motion. From a review of the papers submitted in support of the motion, it appears that this was a reasonable expenditure of time.

Plaintiff's counsel did not specifically identify the rate at which he seeks reimbursement. However, it can be inferred that he seeks to be compensated at the rate of $200 an hour, since he requests a total of $1,700. Plaintiff's counsel also did not set forth his qualifications, though it appears from the firm letterhead that he is an associate rather than a partner. Under these circumstances, the requested rate of $200 is excessive. Two recent cases in this district awarded fees to associates at rates ranging from $105 to $130 per hour. See Caruso v. Peat, Marwick, Mitchell & Co., 779 F.Supp. 332, 334 (S.D.N.Y.1991) ($125); Novelty Textile Mills, Inc. v. Stern, 136 F.R.D. 63, 77 (S.D.N.Y.1991) ($105 and $130). In the absence of any proof by plaintiff of prevailing rates, $125 per hour is more in line with fees awarded in other cases and will be utilized here. For 8.5 hours of work, then, an attorneys' fee of $1,062.50 is appropriate.

Conclusion

For the reasons set forth above, I recommend that judgment be entered in favor of the plaintiff and against the defendant for $221,106.35 on the contract claims, pre-judgment interest on that amount at nine percent per year from May 18, 1990, punitive damages of $50,000, and attorneys' fees of $1,062.50. Pursuant to Rule 72 of the Federal Rules of Civil Procedure, the parties shall have ten (10) days to file written objections to this Report and Recommendation. Such objections shall be filed with the Clerk of the Court, with extra copies delivered to the chambers of the Honorable Lawrence M. McKenna, Room 626 and to the chambers of the undersigned, Room 633.

McKENNA, District Judge.

[This] action was referred to Magistrate Judge James C. Francis IV for an inquest on damages. Defendant has not filed objections to his Report and Recommendation dated April 15, 1992, and the Report and Recommendation is accepted.

SO ORDERED.

REDGRAVE v. STUART THOMPSON PRODUCTIONS
2002 WL 32001232 (N.Y. Sup. Ct. 2002)

SHAFER, Justice.

In this personal injury action, plaintiff actor Corin Redgrave seeks damages for facial injuries allegedly sustained on May 12, 1999, at the Circle in the Square Theatre (the theatre), while he was performing in the Broadway play, "Not About Nightingales" (the play). Defendant Australian American Arts Corporation d/b/a Stuart Thompson Productions, s/h/a Stuart Thompson Productions, seeks dismissal of the Complaint, pursuant to CPLR 3212.

At the time of this incident, plaintiff was employed by nonparty Nightingales Limited Liability Company (Nightingales), a New York limited liability company. Defendant provides general managerial services to theatrical productions through its President, Stewart Thompson, and was retained as General Manager of the play by Nightingales.

The facts surrounding plaintiff's accident are not in dispute. Near the end of the play, plaintiff's character was killed, and his body tossed out of a window into the ocean. The stage was darkened, so the character could exit the stage unnoticed by the audience. On the incident date, as plaintiff exited the stage, he tripped on the rails of an electronic door that had been used in a previous scene and had not been fully retracted. Nightingales prepared a Performance Report, which stated that plaintiff tripped and landed on his face when the "Klondike door jammed into the center door again and was left upstage off the track." Kremen Aff., Exhibit A.

Carole Shorenstein Hays Enterprises, Inc. (Shorenstein), the sole Managing Member of Nightingales, joined with several other parties and entered into a Limited Liability Company Agreement (the Agreement) on December 23, 1998, in order to produce and present the play. The Agreement listed defendant as the General Manager of the play and gave Nightingales' principal place of business as c/o Stuart Thompson, Stuart Thompson Productions, 1501 Broadway, New York, New York. At section 5.4 of the Agreement the parties agreed that defendant could be listed on billboards as a co-producer of the play.

Section 5.9(a) stated that Nightingales "intends to enter into a Theatre License Agreement (TLA) with the Circle in the Square Theatre, where the play would be presented."

On November 16, 1998, Nightingales, as Producer, entered into a TLA with Thespian Theatre, Inc., the owner of the theatre. Section II.(A) of the TLA stated that the "Producer will furnish and pay for all other personnel, services, properties and material not herein specifically agreed to be furnished and paid for by [Thespian] necessary to take in, present, and take-out the play...including, but not limited to, complete cast, scenery, costumes, electric and sound equipment...." Thespian Theatre, Inc., Theatre License Agreement, Kremen Aff., Exhibit C. Section II.(C) provided that the Producer would "furnish, pay for and present the play as a complete theatrical production including, but not limited to, complete cast, scenery, costumes, electric and sound equipment,...and all other properties, materials and services not herein specifically agreed to be furnished by Thespian, necessary for the presentation of the Play." Id. Paragraph XIII.(A) of the TLA recited that all "wages, payroll taxes and miscellaneous union benefits of all employees of the Theatre will be paid for by Producer...." Id.

The Complaint alleges that defendant's negligence in its maintenance and operation of the door, among other things, caused plaintiff's injuries. Defendant seeks summary judgment dismissing the Complaint, pursuant to CPLR 3212, contending that it owed no duty to plaintiff.

Stewart Thompson, defendant's President, testified that, pursuant to a verbal agreement with Nightingales, defendant's services for the play were limited to drafting budgets and negotiating contracts with the estate of the play's author, with the theatres where the play originated, and with the people or companies that built and set up the stage. Thompson stated that defendant was listed as a co-producer of the play on the playbill, and possibly on the marquee, merely as a courtesy, and that defendant was not responsible for the management or maintenance of the theatre or the stage and did not supervise the work crew. Thompson testified that he visited the theatre from time to time, to check on the crew, which he usually did by speaking to the stage manager or to the technical supervisor. He stated that he had an associate, Florie Seery, who assisted him with his managerial responsibilities during the play's run, but could not recall whether Seery was defendant's employee or Nightingale's.

Defendant claims that it did not provide, set up, or maintain the scenery or the sets for the play, or contract with anyone else to do so. According to defendant, Nightingales employed the persons engaged to provide and install the scenery, while the sets were built and maintained by unionized stagehands, who were employed by the theatre or by Nightingales. The stage hands answered to the stage managers, who bore ultimate responsibility for the condition of the stage. Nightingales had hired the stage manager, who answered to the producer and director of the play. Defendant claims that Nightingales either owned the door in question, or had leased it from one of the play's originating theatres, and that employees from Nightingales or the theatre were responsible for the door's placement and operation. Defendant maintains that it was only present at the theatre sporadically, and that it had no notice of the door's alleged defective condition. Defendant contends that the note in the Nightingales Performance Report, which stated that the door had "jammed again" did not establish that defendant was on notice of the door's condition.

Plaintiff alleges that there are issues of fact as to whether defendant was a co-producer of the play, with responsibility for the condition of the door that caused his accident, pursuant to the terms of the Agreement and the TLA. Plaintiff points out that, according to the Agreement, defendant had dual roles as General Manager and co-producer of the play, which rendered defendant responsible for the condition of the stage generally and of the door particularly. Plaintiff also points out the TLA charged the play's Producer with responsibility for the cast and the stage's props and scenery. Plaintiff opines that Thompson's testimony, that he checked on the stage crew occasionally, and that he questioned the stage crew about plaintiff's accident, and about remedial action necessary to fix the door, establish defendant's responsibility for the door's condition. Plaintiff asserts, too, that the Performance Report, which indicated that the door had malfunctioned before plaintiff's accident, establishes that defendant was, or should have been, on notice of the door's alleged defective condition.

On the evidence presented, plaintiff has established that there is an issue of fact about defendant's responsibilities for the door's alleged dangerous condition, precluding an award of summary judgment in defendant's favor. See Sillman v. Twentieth Century-Fox Film Corp., 3 N.Y.2d 395, 165 N.Y.S.2d 498, 144 N.E.2d 387. A fact finder should determine the credibility of defendant's testimony that it was billed as a co-producer in the play's credits merely as a courtesy, and that it was only responsible for the play's budgets and contract negotiations. See Hajder v. G & G Moderns, Inc., 13 A.D.2d 651, 213 N.Y.S.2d 880. A fact finder needs to determine if Thompson's post-accident communications with the stagehands and the stage manager evince defendant's control of, and responsibility for, the door. Id. Although, as defendant contends, the Agreement specified that Shorenstein was the only Managing Member of Nightingales, which signed the TLA with the theatre, questions remain about defendant's role in the play. Thompson testified both that defendant had no say "over how the scenery or the sets or the props were to be laid out or set up" for the play and that, after the play's official opening, he "would visit the theater from time to time...[to] check on the company of actors, the crew...." Deposition of Stewart Thompson, at 21, Beth Rex, Affirmation in Support of Motion, Exhibit F. When asked if he had undertaken an investigation of plaintiff's accident, Thompson testified, "It's most likely I would have gone to the stage hands and stage managers who run the show to...inquire about what was wrong and have them explain it to me and have them explain what steps were taken to correct it." Id. at 33. Thompson's testimony raises questions about whether his company's work for the play went beyond budget preparation and contract negotiation.

Viewing the evidence in the light most favorable to plaintiff, defendant has not established the parameters of the alleged verbal general managerial contract entered into with Nightingales, either in principle or as performed, during the play's presentation. See Szczerbiak v. Pilat, 90 N.Y.2d 553, 664 N.Y.S.2d 252, 686 N.E.2d 1346. Therefore, defendant's motion for summary judgment dismissing the Complaint must be denied.

Notes

1. As the *Martin* case indicates, after capital acquisition the task of negotiating rights is a producer's single most important job. But as *Theatre Guild*, *Bates*, and *Russek* demonstrate, a hundred other details also require attention on an on-going basis.

2. Normally, rights disputes pit producers against playwrights or authors. *See, e.g.,* Houlihan v. McCourt, 2002 WL 1759822 (N.D. Ill. 2002); *Jacobs v. Felix Bloch Erben Verlag fur Buhne Film und Funk KG,* 160 F. Supp. 2d 722 (S.D.N.Y. 2001); *Losch v. Marcin,* 167 N.E. 514 (N.Y. 1929). But producers also can find themselves up against other producers. In November 2001, for example, Scott Rudin and Stephen Sondheim went to

court to determine who had the right to produce "Gold!" Although Sondheim had been working on the script since 1952, Rudin had helped finance a workshop production of the play in New York in 1999. Sondheim finally gave in and agreed to pay Rudin $160,000 for the rights. *See* Jesse McKinley, *Accord in Legal War Over Sondheim Musical*, N.Y. Times, Feb. 2, 2002, at B7.

A short time late, a similar dispute broke out when it was announced that Benjamin Mordecai planned to star Whoopi Goldberg in a revival of August Wilson's "Ma Rainey's Black Bottom," which had debuted on Broadway in 1984. The news led Robert Cole and Frederick Zollo, two of the original producers, to threaten legal action unless they were included. After several tense weeks, a settlement was reached that gave Cole and Zollo financial and theatrical credit. *See 'Ma Rainey' Advances*, N.Y. Times, Nov. 29, 2002, at E1.

3. The *Redgrave* case is a good example of what can happen when one insists on receiving a "producer's credit." Assuming the case gets to a jury, do you think it will believe Thompson's claim that he played only a modest role in the staging of "Not About Nightingales"? Having read Justice Shafer's opinion, what advice would you give to a client regarding seeking or accepting a producer's credit?

4. Despite all the headaches, many people still want to be producers. In part, this is due to the popular perception that producers are rich, live in mansions, and lead glamorous lifestyles. This belief is so widespread, in fact, that in the CBS sitcom *The Nanny*, Fran Drescher's character went to work for, and eventually married, Maxwell B. Sheffield (played by Charles Shaughnessy), a Broadway producer who *was* rich, lived in a mansion, and led a glamorous lifestyle. Of course, having Fran's love interest be a successful Broadway producer made it easy for the writers to work in the series's numerous guest stars (such as Celine Dion, Elton John, Elizabeth Taylor, and Ben Vereen), and also led to Fran's memorable comment about Max's work: "Your plays are much better than [Andrew Lloyd Webber's] 'cause you can always get tickets for yours and his are sold out for months!"

For those who are serious about becoming producers, a number of useful books exist, such as Donald C. Farber, *Producing Theatre: A Comprehensive Legal and Business Guide* (2d ed. 1997), and Charles Grippo, *The Stage Producer's Business and Legal Guide* (2002). In addition, since 1982 the Commercial Theater Institute, part of the Threatre Development Fund (www.tdf.org), has hosted two annual programs (an open three-day seminar and a by-invitation 14-week course) specifically designed to teach people how to break into producing. *See* Jesse McKinley, *No Biz Like This Biz*, N.Y. Times, Apr. 25, 2003, at B1.

For a further look at producers, see the web sites of the League of American Theatres and Producers (www.broadway.org) and the League of Off-Broadway Theatres and Producers (www.offbroadway.org).

Problem 8

Needing help with an upcoming play, a producer hired an associate producer and gave her a two-year contract, the expected length of the play. After 18 months, however, the show closed. If the associate producer sues for the last six months of her pay, should the court award it to her? *See Bristow v. Drake State Inc.*, 41 F.3d 345 (7th Cir. 1994).

Chapter 5

Directors and Choreographers

A. OVERVIEW

The director is the person who melds the efforts of the playwright, cast, and crew into an integrated whole. Indeed, it is the director's vision that brings the play to life. In a musical, the director is joined by a choreographer, who designs and arranges the production's dance sequences.

B. DUTIES

JULIEN v. SOCIETY OF STAGE DIRECTORS AND CHOREOGRAPHERS, INC.
1975 WL 957 (S.D.N.Y. 1975)

STEWART, District Judge.

Plaintiff Julien, a producer of stage plays, has brought this action seeking damages and injunctive relief for alleged violations of Section 1 of the Sherman Act, 15 U.S.C. §1. Defendant, Society of Stage Directors and Choreographers, Inc. ("SSDC"), is an industry-wide organization of directors and choreographers. In 1962 and again in 1972, SSDC entered into a collective bargaining agreement ("Agreement") with the League of New York Theatres, Inc. ("League"), a group which represents the producers of first class theatrical productions. It is this Agreement which plaintiff challenges as violative of the antitrust laws. The Agreement requires that any director engaged by a producer be a member of the SSDC. It further provides for minimum basic wage scales and working conditions, including pension and welfare contributions, a no-strike, no-lockout clause, and compulsory arbitration.

While such an industry wide agreement, providing among other things for minimum fees, is in violation of the Sherman Act, as plaintiff argues, defendant claims that the agreement comes within the labor exemption provisions of the Clayton and Norris-LaGuardia Acts. (Sections 6 and 20 of the Clayton Act, 15 U.S.C. §17; 29 U.S.C. §52; and Section 1 of the Norris-LaGuardia Act, 29 U.S.C. §101). Plaintiff argues, however, that defendant is not entitled to claim the labor exemption since SSDC members are independent contractors and therefore not in the necessary employer-employee relationship with the producers which is required to claim such an exemption. See e.g., Los Angeles Meat & Provision Drivers Union v. U.S., 371 U.S. 94 (1962); American Medical Ass'n v. U.S., 317 U.S. 519 (1943); Columbia River Packers Ass'n v. Hinton, 315 U.S. 143 (1942); Taylor v. Local No. 7, Int'l Union of Journeymen Horseshoers, 353 F.2d 593 (4th Cir.), cert. denied, 384 U.S. 969 (1965).

We now conclude, for the reasons set forth below, that directors are employees of producers and not independent contractors. Defendant therefore comes within the labor exemption and plaintiff's case must fail.

While there are numerous factors which courts and commentators have considered in determining whether an independent contractor or employee status exists (Restatement, Agency § 220(2) (2d ed. 1958)), the general test is found in an analysis of "the nature and amount of control reserved by the person for whom the work is done." Taylor v. Local No. 7, 353 F.2d at 596. If the employer has no right to control the manner in which the work is performed, then the worker's independent contractor status is clear. See NLRB v. United Insurance Co., 390 U.S. 254 (1968); Bernstein v. Universal Pictures, Inc., slip op. 535 (2d Cir. May 27, 1975); Herald Co. v. NLRB, 444 F.2d 430, 432-33 (2d Cir.), cert. denied, 404 U.S. 990 (1971). Even if an employer exercises complete control over the result contemplated by the parties, however, the worker's independent contractor status may remain. Taylor v. Local No. 7, supra; NLRB v. Steinberg, 182 F.2d 850 (5th Cir. 1950). Even some reservation of control to supervise the manner in which the work is done, or to inspect the work during its performance, does not destroy the independent contractor relationship where the contractor is not deprived of his judgment in the execution of his duties. Taylor v. Local No. 7, 353 F.2d at 596. Thus, the degree of employer control necessary to establish an employer-employee relationship must be determined upon the peculiar facts and circumstances of each case.

In the instant case, the decision is an especially difficult one to make because of the nature of the theatrical production industry. A few courts, however, have been called upon to consider similar problems within the industry. In Ring v. Spina, 148 F.2d 647 (2d Cir. 1945), an antitrust action was brought against the Dramatists' Guild of the Authors' League of America ("Guild"), a nation-wide association of playwrights. Plaintiff alleged violations of the Sherman Act in the Guild's requirement that producers sign an agreement with its members providing for compulsory arbitration, minimum fees and exclusive dealing with Guild members. As a defense, the Guild asserted the labor exemption contained in 15 U.S.C. § 17. The Second Circuit found that the playwright members of the Guild were not "employees" of theatrical producers and were not, therefore, entitled to claim the labor exemption.

> An author writing a book or play is usually not then even in any contractual relation with his producer. If and when he does contract, he does not continue in the producer's service to any appreciable or continuous extent thereafter.... The minimum price and royalty provided by the Basic Agreement, unlike minimum wages in a collective bargaining agreement, are not remuneration for continued services, but are the terms at which a finished product or certain rights therein may be sold. And no wages or working conditions of any group of employees are directly dependent on these terms.

148 F.2d at 652.

Recently, a class action suit was brought by members of the Composers and Lyricists Guild of America ("CLGA") charging antitrust violations by 15 motion picture and television producers. Bernstein v. Universal Pictures, 379 F.Supp. 933 (S.D.N.Y. 1974), rev'd, slip op. 535 (2d Cir. May 27, 1975). The district court dismissed the action citing exclusive National Labor Relations Board jurisdiction over the dispute which the court perceived to be a refusal to bargain by the producers. National Labor Relations Act §8(a)(3). The Second Circuit reversed, holding that the district court was required to determine whether the composers were independent contractors or employees hired by the producers. "Antitrust jurisdiction cannot be declined simply because independent contractors masquerade as a union." Slip op. at 3710. The Court took notice of "substantial evidence" in the record which indicated that the composers were not employees.

> [The] record suggests that the composers contract for a specific output, work at their own pace at home, and are not subject to day-to-day supervision by the producers. It may be, consequently, that the producer has no right to control the manner in which work is performed, so that... the composers are independent contractors.

Slip. op. at 3710-11.

In sharp contrast to the playwrights in the Ring case and the lyricists in the Bernstein case, we think that defendant here demonstrated at trial that directors are employees of producers. It became clear to us during the course of the trial that the producer has the right to and does exercise control over all facets of a production and of the director's work. The testimony revealed that the producer attends auditions and has final authority, with the playwright, in the selection of the cast. (Richards, tr. at 164-67; DaCosta, tr. at 206-10). The producer may add or delete scenes, overruling any objections raised by the director. (DaCosta, tr. at 201-02; Feuer, tr. at 283-88, 258-63; Aaron, tr. at 310-13, 326-28). That authority is just part of the producer's pervasive control over the artistic direction of the play. (See e.g., Traube, tr. at 228-29; Feuer, tr. at 257-58, 266-68; Forde, tr. at 300-03; Aaron, tr. at 344; Schneider, tr. at 349-50, 361-65).

The witnesses cited testified that producers, by redesigning sets, choosing costumes, changing the cast and even altering individual cast members' performances, are deeply involved in the artistic direction of the production. In addition, by governing the budget, the producer determines the length of rehearsal time, the theatres in which the show will be performed, and the locations for out-of-town runs. The producer, therefore, has final control over every aspect of the director's job, unless such control is specifically delegated to the director in his or her contract. To the extent that the testimony of David Merrick, a witness for plaintiff, differed from the findings here and was not discredited upon cross-examination, we do not find that testimony to have been credible.

Since we find the overwhelming credible evidence in the record establishes that directors are employees of producers, we must deny plaintiff's prayer for relief.

So Ordered.

GENNARO v. ROSENFIELD
600 F. Supp. 485 (S.D.N.Y. 1984)

GOETTEL, District Judge.

The plaintiffs, Peter Gennaro, and his company, Geannie Productions, Inc., allege that Mr. Gennaro has contracted to choreograph the proposed Broadway production of "Singin' In The Rain" for the defendant, Maurice Rosenfield. The plaintiffs claim that the defendant has breached this contract and, therefore, seek damages for breach of contract and defamation. Presently before the Court is the plaintiffs' motion for a preliminary injunction which, in essence, would prevent the defendant from engaging any other choreographer pending the outcome of the litigation. The Court must deny this motion for the reasons stated below.

The individual plaintiff, Peter Gennaro, is a choreographer and dancer. He has choreographed a number of well-known Broadway musicals, including "Fiorello," "The Unsinkable Molly Brown," and "Annie" (for which he won a Tony Award). Mr. Gennaro is also the president of the corporate plaintiff, Geannie Productions, Inc. The defendants, Maurice and Lois Rosenfield, are husband and wife. Mr. Rosenfield is a Broadway producer. Among his credits are the 1980 Broadway musical "Barnum" and the 1983 revival of Tennessee Williams's "The Glass Menagerie." In 1980, Mr. Rosenfield acquired the right to adapt "Singin' In The Rain" for stage presentation from Metro-Goldwyn-Mayer and Robbins Music Company. Rosenfield subsequently granted a license to Harold Fielding for the London production of "Singin' In The Rain."

The events giving rise to the instant controversy commenced in November 1980, when Ian Bevan, a British theatrical agent and manager, contacted Mr. Gennaro's agent and attorney, Robert M. Cavallo. According to Mr. Cavallo, Mr. Bevan said that Mr. Fielding wanted Peter Gennaro to choreograph the London production. Mr. Cavallo relayed this offer to Mr. Gennaro, who allegedly said that he would agree to choreograph the London production only on the condition that he also receive the option to choreograph any first-class stage production of "Singin' In The Rain" in the United States, including any Broadway production. Mr. Gennaro alleges that Mr. Bevan proceeded to negotiate with Mr. Cavallo for Mr. Gennaro's services and with Mr. Rosenfield to obtain the desired option. The plaintiff further alleges that an agreement was reached on both counts and that the option agreement was embodied in a January 20, 1983, letter signed by both Bevan and Rosenfield. Complaint para. 8.

On February 2, 1983, Mr. Fielding forwarded a copy of the January 20 letter to Mr. Gennaro along with his own letter confirming an agreement between himself and Mr. Gennaro. According to this letter, Mr. Bevan had "negotiated conditions for [Mr. Gennaro to choreograph] the American and other first-class productions of 'Singin' In The Rain' which [would] be separately confirmed to [Mr. Gennaro] by the American producer, Mr. Maurice Rosenfield." Affidavit of Robert M. Cavallo, Exhibit A. On April 5, 1983, Ronald Taft, Mr. Rosenfield's attorney, forwarded a draft contract to Mr. Cavallo and requested Mr. Cavallo's comments. According to Mr. Rosenfield, this contract concerned both the London and American productions. Mr. Gennaro maintains that the April 5 draft only concerned the London production. For unknown reasons, Mr. Cavallo informed Mr. Taft that he would not comment on the draft. At the same time, Mr. Cavallo was negotiating with Mr. Fielding. On April 14, 1984, Harold Fielding, Ltd. and Geannie Productions, Inc. entered into a written agreement with regard to Mr. Gennaro's role in the London production. Mr. Gennaro alleges that this agreement formalized the January 20 letter with respect to the American production. Complaint para. 8.

In early June, Mr. Rosenfield visited Mr. Cavallo in his New York office. Precisely what transpired at that meeting is unclear. Soon thereafter, Mr. Cavallo sent Mr. Taft a letter commenting on the April 5 draft. There were no further discussions about that document.

The London production opened on June 30, 1983, and is still running. Mr. Gennaro has met twice with Mr. and Mrs. Rosenfield since the opening, once in June 1983, and again in December 1983. Precisely what was said at those meetings is also in dispute.

During the summer of 1984, Mr. Cavallo heard that the American production of "Singin' In The Rain" was being planned and that the plans did not involve Peter Gennaro. On September 17, 1984, Mr. Cavallo sent a mailgram to Mr. Rosenfield advising him that Mr. Gennaro had elected to exercise the option to choreograph the American production. On September 20, 1984, Mr. Taft responded for Mr. Rosenfield in a letter that stated, "Mr. Rosenfield has not asked Mr. Gennaro whether he would like to choreograph the production of 'Singin' In The Rain' which Mr. Rosenfield plans to produce in New York." Affidavit of Robert M. Cavallo, Exhibit D. The plaintiffs then brought the instant action by order to show cause seeking, inter alia, a preliminary negative injunction enjoining the defendants and their agents from

> (a) producing any American first-class stage production of the musical "Singin' In The Rain" (the "American production") with choreography by any choreographer other than Peter Gennaro;
>
> (b) entering into any contract for choreography of the American production with any choreographer other than Peter Gennaro;
>
> (c) advertising, promoting or otherwise publicizing the American production, in print or any other media, whereby the actual or prospective choreography is represented as by any choreographer other than Peter Gennaro....

A court will grant preliminary injunctive relief if a plaintiff can show (a) irreparable harm and (b) either (1) likelihood of success on the merits or (2) sufficiently serious questions going to the merits to make them a fair ground for litigation and a balance of hardships tipping decidedly toward the party requesting the preliminary relief. Lawe v. New York State Public Employment Relations Board, 689 F.2d 378 (2d Cir. 1982). Even if the plaintiffs have established irreparable harm, they have shown neither a likelihood of success on the merits nor a balance of hardships tipping decidedly in their favor.

A. Irreparable Harm

An inadequate remedy at law is a necessary prerequisite to a showing of irreparable harm. Buffalo Forge Co. v. Ampco-Pittsburgh Corp., 638 F.2d 568, 569 (2d Cir. 1981). Mr. Gennaro argues that he will continue to suffer two wrongs for which money damages will not compensate: harm to his reputation and erosion of his professional skills. While it may be that the harm to the plaintiff's reputation constitutes irreparable harm, we do not believe that erosion of his skills constitutes such harm.

Although courts recognize that atrophy of professional skills could constitute irreparable harm, Dos Santos v. Columbus-Cuneo-Cabrini Medical Center, 684 F.2d 1346, 1350 (7th Cir. 1982), we are aware of only one case finding that, under the facts established, such atrophy constitutes irreparable harm. In that case, Neeld v. American Hockey League, 439 F. Supp. 459 (W.D.N.Y. 1977), the court found that a young hockey player would suffer irreparable harm were he denied the right to play professional hockey during the pendency of his lawsuit challenging certain league restrictions that would have prevented him from playing. The district court noted that

> the denial to plaintiff of an opportunity to play professional hockey in the AHL will result in the possibility of irreparable harm to plaintiff's professional hockey career. A young athlete's skills diminish and sometimes are irretrievably lost unless he is given an opportunity to practice and refine such skills at a certain level of proficiency. Therefore, plaintiff has shown the possibility of irreparable harm if an injunction pendente lite is not granted.

Id. at 461.

Mr. Gennaro argues that the alleged breach of contract will limit his opportunities for work, thereby denying him the chance to develop and refine his skills. The plaintiff's situation, however, differs markedly from the young hockey player's in Neeld. The plaintiff, an established choreographer with a first class reputation, will not be denied the opportunity to embark on a promising artistic career. Nor are his skills likely to diminish or atrophy. Since he has already choreographed the London production, the Broadway production represents less than a unique opportunity to develop his skills. In addition, as a top flight choreographer, he is likely to gain other work during the time he would be choreographing "Singin' In The Rain." Thus, we decline to follow Neeld. The plaintiff has not established that his skills will diminish so as to cause him irreparable harm.

Mr. Gennaro also asserts that his reputation has been irreparably harmed. In his words,

> The world of theatre is small, and its every event is illuminated by the bright spotlight of public curiosity. Reputations which have been built up over many years can be torn apart overnight when it appears that other artists are more desirable. Colleagues have been asking me why I was "replaced" as choreographer for the American production. The situation is painfully embarrassing to me and is severely damaging the first-class reputation and professional credibility I have worked so hard to establish over so many years. I have no traditional monetary remedy, since no amount of money can fully compensate me for this injury; indeed, its subtle effects can never be fully known.

Affidavit of Peter Gennaro in Support of Order to Show Cause Seeking Preliminary Injunction at para. 10.

Several cases from this circuit establish that damage to reputation often constitutes irreparable injury and justifies injunctive relief. Peter Gennaro has worked for many years to establish a reputation as a first class choreographer. His reputation is of great commercial value to him. The apparent replacement of the plaintiff could damage his reputation in the theatre community. Those who had thought Mr. Gennaro would choreograph the production may now hold him in lower esteem. As the plaintiffs correctly point out, such damage to reputation is difficult if not impossible to measure in money terms.

On the other hand, show business arrangements often take into account considerations other than artistic merit. One bad review cannot tarnish the image of an established artist such as Peter Gennaro. Theatre people may well find fault with Mr. Rosenfield in this situation—particularly in light of the success of the London production. This situation resembles that where a baseball manager replaces the starting pitcher in the late innings despite the fact that he is pitching a shut out and has a comfortable lead. If the relief pitcher fails, the manager looks terrible.

B. The Likelihood of Success on the Merits

Setting aside the question of irreparable harm, we next consider whether the plaintiffs have demonstrated a likelihood of success on the merits. We conclude that they have not.

The nub of this case is a dispute over whether Mr. Rosenfield ever contracted with Mr. Gennaro. In determining whether a contract exists, the objective intent of the parties as manifested by their expressed words and deeds at the time of the alleged contract controls. Brown Brothers Electrical Contractors, Inc. v. Beam Construction Corp., 41 N.Y.2d 397, 399, 393 N.Y.S.2d 350, 352, 361 N.E.2d 999, 1001 (1977). If the parties' expressions and conduct would lead a reasonable person to determine that they intended to reach a binding agreement, their agreement will be enforced. Phillip v. Gallant, 62 N.Y. 256, 263 (1875).

Mr. Gennaro asserts that the January 20 letter from Ian Bevan to Maurice Rosenfield countersigned by Mr. Rosenfield, standing alone, constitutes a binding contract. That letter states, in part:

> I write to record the heads of agreement I have reached on your behalf in negotiations with Mr. Robert M. Cavallo...for the services of Mr. Peter Gennaro as choreographer for the above production [("Singin' In The Rain")].
>
> His services have been engaged by Harold Fielding Ltd. for the London production....Subject to that production running not less than 100 consecutive performances, you undertake to offer Mr. Gennaro a contract to choreograph the first American and/or Broadway production.
>
> * * *
>
> This letter is to record in "heads of agreement" style the basic terms agreed between you and Mr. Gennaro, which terms will now be converted into a formal document or documents in such form as shall be to the approval of your respective legal advisers. By our respective signatures to this letter we confirm to each other and to Mr. Gennaro that the basic terms to be incorporated into the formal documentation are those outlined in this letter.

Order to Show Cause, Affidavit of Robert M. Cavallo, Exhibit A. The letter further specified Gennaro's fee and his share of the royalties. No other terms were detailed.

Acknowledging that this letter contemplated more formal documentation, the plaintiffs nevertheless contend that it constitutes a binding agreement. They rely on authority to the effect that a letter containing the essential terms of a contract may create a binding obligation although the parties may have contemplated executing a more formal agreement at a later date. V'Soske v. Barwick, 404 F.2d 495 (2d Cir. 1968), cert. denied, 394 U.S. 921, 89 S.Ct. 1197, 22 L. Ed. 2d 454 (1969); Sommer v. Hilton Hotels Corp., 376 F. Supp. 297 (S.D.N.Y. 1974).

The plaintiffs argue that the evidence conclusively establishes that the parties intended the January 20 letter to be a contract. The plaintiffs point out that the letter contained the material financial terms of the deal and that Mr. Gennaro's agent made it known to Mr. Fielding that Mr. Gennaro would not choreograph the London production unless he had an option to choreograph the Broadway production. To buttress this position, Mr. Cavallo and Mr. Gennaro also offer their recollection of several conversations with Mr. Rosenfield allegedly confirming the agreement. The plaintiffs also submit a letter from Mr. Bevan that purports to support their position. Standing alone, their evidence might establish the likelihood of success on the merits.

However, the defendants make a number of points in rebuttal. They thus make clear that whether the January 20 letter is a contract is, at most, a serious question going to the merits and a fair ground for litigation.

The defendants first argue that the behavior of the parties subsequent to January 20, 1983, indicated their intention not to be bound by the January 20 letter. They also take issue with the plaintiffs' characterization of the January 20 letter. According to the defendants, "the January 20 letter is not a contract because it expressly provides that it is to be followed by a detailed agreement to be crafted and approved by counsel and to contain additional terms." Defendants' Reply Memorandum at 15. "[Such] an agreement...does not bind the parties until such documentation and approval are accomplished." Id. at 17. They cite C.H. Rugg & Co. v. Street, [1962] 1 Lloyd's List L.R. 364, 369 (Q.B.); Reprosystem B.V. v. SCM Corp., 727 F.2d 257 (2d Cir.), cert. denied, 469 U.S. 828, 53 U.S.L.W. 3237, 83 L. Ed. 2d 54, 105 S.Ct. 110 (1984); and Read v. Henzel, 67 A.D.2d 186, 415 N.Y.S.2d 520, 523 (1979), to support this proposition. However, these cases turned not on the law, or on any hard and fast rule of contract interpretation, but rather on the particular intentions of the parties to the alleged contract. Similarly, the dispute about the January 20 letter turns not on the law but on the facts. Whether the parties intended to contract is a serious question for the factfinder.

The defendants also claim that the January 20 letter is not sufficiently definite to constitute a binding agreement. Under the general principles of contract law, there can be no contract if the parties fail to agree on all the essential terms. The January 20, 1983, letter specifies only the fee and royalty terms. Mr. Cavallo asserts that this accords with industry practice, an assertion that the defendants vigorously dispute. We are not sure who has the better of this dispute, but we are certain that the plaintiffs have not demonstrated that they are likely to prevail.

The plaintiffs also argue that, even if the January 20 letter is too indefinite to constitute a contract, the April 14 long form agreement between Geannie Productions, Inc. and Harold Fielding Ltd. is sufficiently definite. This detailed agreement contains the essential terms necessary for a binding contract. However, the defendants argue that Fielding lacked actual or apparent authority to bind Rosenfield. In rebuttal, the plaintiffs argue that, even if Fielding lacked actual authority, he had apparent authority.

The Restatement (Second) of the Law of Agency §8 defines apparent authority as "the power to affect the legal relations of another person by transactions with third persons, professedly as agent for the other, arising from and in accordance with the other's manifestations to such third persons." Restatement (Second) of the Law of Agency §8. According to Mr. Gennaro, Mr. Rosenfield manifested Mr. Fielding's authority in his January 20 letter. The defendants, of course, reject this contention. They claim that the plaintiffs have alleged no act by Mr. Rosenfield whereby he conferred authority upon Mr. Fielding to act as his agent or whereby he communicated that authority to Mr. Gennaro or Mr. Cavallo. Again, the facts are so vague that to draw any conclusion with regard to the likelihood of either side prevailing on the authority issue is impossible.

The foregoing discussion leaves no doubt that the plaintiffs have not established the likelihood of success on the merits. There exist too many unresolved factual questions to justify any such conclusion.

C. The Balance of Hardships

Given our conclusion regarding the likelihood of success on the merits, we may grant the requested relief only if the plaintiff can "show that the harm which he would suffer from the denial of his motion is 'decidedly' greater than the harm which [the defendants] would suffer if the motion was granted." Buffalo Forge Co. v. Ampco-Pittsburgh Corp., 638 F.2d 568, 569 (2d Cir. 1981). In this case, the balance of hardships does not tip decidedly in favor of the plaintiffs. We therefore decline to grant the requested relief.

If the motion is denied, the plaintiffs may suffer some additional irreparable harm. However, even if we accept Mr. Gennaro's assertion of irreparable harm, most of the damage to his reputation has already been done. No doubt, if we grant the requested relief, a group of individuals who would otherwise learn of Mr. Gennaro's alleged dismissal will remain uninformed (assuming the defendants choose to go ahead with the production). A denial of injunctive relief will harm the plaintiff's reputation among this group. However, the plaintiff's primary concern is his reputation among those in the theatre industry. That group is well informed, and has by now learned of this controversy. Thus, the denial of injunctive relief will do little to mitigate the total harm the plaintiff will suffer as a result of his alleged replacement.

On the other hand, should we grant the requested relief, the defendants will have two choices. They may hire Mr. Gennaro, or abandon the production. Abandonment, while not unrealistic—given the assertions to this effect in Mr. Rosenfield's papers—would constitute self-inflicted harm. We do not believe such harm is cognizable or relevant to our determination. Assuming Mr. Rosenfield opts to have Mr. Gennaro choreograph his production, Mr. Rosenfield would find himself in the uncomfortable position of working closely with someone whom he allegedly had replaced, had litigated against, and had no desire to work with. In addition, Mr. Rosenfield would be forced to abandon any discussions or contract into which he might have already entered with another choreographer. He would then suffer the obvious consequences of such an action. In our view, the defendants will suffer at least as much if not more harm from a grant of injunctive relief than the plaintiffs will suffer from a denial.

Although our judgment about the relative harms each party would suffer is subjective, we think it clear that the plaintiff has failed to show that the balance of hardships tips decidedly in his favor. Therefore, we decline to grant the requested prohibitive injunctive relief.

Given our holding, we need not decide if and when negative injunctive relief will issue to force an employer to abide by a personal services contract. See generally Restatement (Second) of the Law of Contracts § 367, Illustration 2.

The plaintiffs' motion for preliminary injunctive relief is denied.

RODGERS v. LOGAN

503 N.Y.S.2d 36 (App. Div. 1986)

MEMORANDUM DECISION.

Order and judgment (one paper) of the Supreme Court, New York County (Ira Gammerman, J.) entered October 11, 1985, which granted petitioners' application for a permanent stay of arbitration, is reversed, on the law, and the motion to stay arbitration denied, without costs.

Respondent-appellant Joshua Logan appeals from the above order of the Supreme Court which granted the motion of petitioners-respondents, the personal representatives of the estates of Richard Rodgers and Oscar Hammerstein, for an order permanently staying arbitration. By demand, dated April 15, 1985, Logan had sought arbitration of petitioners' alleged failure to pay him royalties arising from the production of the musical play "South Pacific."

On or about July 1, 1948, Rodgers and Hammerstein, as "author," entered into a contract with Surrey Enterprises as "manager," for the production and presentation of the play "South Pacific" for the period of time defined in the "Minimum Basic Agreement," which was incorporated by reference into the production contract. Rodgers and Hammerstein were president and secretary, respectively, of Surrey Enterprises, as well as its stockholders and directors.

On February 2, 1949, Surrey Enterprises entered into a "Director's Contract" agreement with Logan. Under that agreement Logan was engaged as the stage director of "South Pacific." This agreement provided for various payments and royalties to Logan. Paragraph 3(a) of the agreement set forth Logan's payment for the rehearsal of the "original New York company" production of "South Pacific." Paragraph 3(b) provided for a royalty payment to Logan from any Surrey Enterprises production of the play performed by the original company in the United States, Canada or Great Britain. Paragraphs (c) and (d) established rehearsal fees and royalty payments, respectively, for Logan's direction of any additional "first class company" performing the musical play in any English speaking country under Surrey Enterprises' management or authority. Finally, paragraph (e), the basis for Logan's claim to royalties in this action, provides for

> [a] royalty of One Percent (1%) of the gross weekly box office receipts derived by each first-class company not directed by you performing the said play in the United States of America, Canada and Great Britain, or in any other English speaking company [sic].

Unlike the other provisions for payments and royalties, this paragraph did not limit the royalty payments to a production of the play by Surrey Enterprises.

On May 3, 1950, Surrey Enterprises elected to dissolve. Its certificate of dissolution was filed on July 17, 1950. Hammerstein died on August 23, 1960. Rodgers died on December 30, 1979.

On April 15, 1985, Logan served his demand for arbitration on petitioners-respondents as successors in interest to Surrey Enterprises, claiming royalties due him under paragraph 3(e) of the Director's Contract. The demand for arbitration was based on paragraph 10 of the Director's Contract which provided that "[a]ny and all disputes arising hereunder out of or in connection with or in relation hereto or in breach hereof, shall be subject to arbitration in New York City...." In their petition for a permanent stay of arbitration respondents argued that Surrey Enterprises was not a predecessor to respondents and that in any case Surrey Enterprises and its successors, if any, no longer had any right to produce the musical play. Special Term granted the petition, concluding that petitioners were not parties to Logan's agreement with Surrey Enterprises and were not shown to be successors to the dissolved corporation and that Logan had not shown that he was a creditor of Surrey Enterprises before dissolution.

At the time of the dissolution of Surrey Enterprises, General Corporation Law § 29, which is now repealed and which was a source for present Section 1006(b) of the Business Corporate Law (BCL), provided that:

> [u]pon the dissolution of a corporation..., its corporate existence shall continue for the purpose of paying, satisfying and discharging any existing liabilities or obligations... [and] the directors shall have full power to settle its affairs and to distribute to the persons entitled thereto the assets remaining after the payment of debts and necessary expenses.

Stock Corporation Law § 105(8), also now repealed and also a source for BCL § 1006(b), similarly provided that:

> [s]uch corporation shall continue for the purpose of paying, satisfying and discharging any existing liabilities or obligations, collecting and distributing its assets and doing all other acts required to adjust and wind up its business and affairs....

Currently, BCL § 1005(a)(1) and (3) state that upon dissolution the corporation continues to exist for the purpose of "winding up its affairs," which includes "paying or adequately providing for the payment of its liabilities...."

BCL § 1006(b) states that "[t]he dissolution of a corporation shall not affect any remedy available to or against such corporation, its directors, officers or shareholders for any right or claim existing or any liability incurred before such dissolution...." Thus, a corporation undergoing dissolution continues to exist for the purpose of and for as long as is necessary to satisfy and provide for its debts and obligations and it may sue or be sued on these obligations until its affairs are fully adjusted. Matter of Ehrlich, Inc., 5 N.Y.2d 275, 279, 184 N.Y.S.2d 334, 157 N.E.2d 495; City of New York v. New York and South Brooklyn Ferry and Steam Transportation Co., 231 N.Y. 18, 22, 131 N.E. 554. Included as corporate liabilities are contractual obligations and contingent claims. Matter of Ehrlich, Inc., supra, 5 N.Y.2d at 279-280, 184 N.Y.S.2d 334, 157 N.E.2d 495; United States v. Oscar Frommel & Bros., 50 F.2d 73, at 74 (2nd Cir.1931).

Until dissolution is complete, title to the corporate assets remains in the corporation. BCL § 1006(a)(1). After dissolution, the shareholders to whom are distributed the remaining assets of the corporation are said to "hold the assets which they received in trust for the benefit of creditors [citation omitted]." Plastic Contact Lens Co. v. Frontier of the Northeast, Inc., 324 F.Supp. 213, 220 (W.D.N.Y.1969) aff'd 441 F.2d 67 (2d Cir.1971) cert. denied 404 U.S. 881, 92 S.Ct. 196, 30 L.Ed.2d 162; see also United States v. Oscar Frommel & Bros., supra, at 74. As a result, the shareholders remain jointly and severally liable to existing creditors of the corporation.

In actions by a creditor to satisfy or enforce a corporate liability it has been said that a creditor must ordinarily exhaust his remedies at law by obtaining a judgment against the corporation and by the return of an execution unsatisfied. However, where it is impossible or futile to obtain such judgment, the creditor can maintain an action directly against the directors or shareholders, even though no judgment has been obtained. Sherill Hardwood Lumber Co. v. New York Bottle Box Co., 118 Misc. 636, 638, 195 N.Y.S. 22; see also United States v. Oscar Frommel & Bros., supra, at 74. Thus, in Sherill Hardwood Lumber Co., the directors, who had dissolved the corporation without ascertaining, providing for, or paying corporate liabilities, were allowed to be added as defendants in an action for recovery of damages for breach of a contract by the defendant corporation.

Surrey Enterprises underwent dissolution more than thirty years ago, making it futile for appellant to even attempt to sue it directly on his breach of contract claim for payment of royalties due him. Accordingly, this is one of those instances when the creditor may directly sue the trustees of the corporate assets, the shareholders, who in this case are the now deceased Rodgers and Hammerstein. Another factor indicating the appropriateness of suing the shareholders directly is the fact that appellant apparently seeks to pierce the corporate veil, as Surrey Enterprises did not appear to have any existence separate from Rodgers and Hammerstein, who were its directors, officers and shareholders, and who formed Surrey Enterprises to produce their musical play "South Pacific." However, Rodgers and Hammerstein now being deceased it is their personal representatives, as the successors in interest to their assets, who are the proper defendants in this breach of contract claim.

While it has been said that "[a] corporation cannot by divesting itself of all property leave remediless the holder of a contingent claim...." (United States v. Oscar Frommel & Bros., supra, at 74), which is what appellant argues he is here, a substantial question is, nevertheless, presented as to whether our law contemplates that the obligations under a contract, including an agreement to arbitrate any contractual disputes, survives so many years after dissolution, especially when it appears in this case that at the time of dissolution no further productions of the play were even contemplated. What is clear, however, is that a valid and broad agreement to arbitrate was entered into in 1949. This being the case, "issues relating to subsequent acts which may affect a cancellation or termination of the prior contract are properly within the arbitrator's jurisdiction to decide." Matter of Riccardi v. Modern Silver Linen Supply Co., 45 A.D.2d 191, 195-196, 356 N.Y.S.2d 872; see also, Matter of Vann v. Kreidler, 78 A.D.2d 255, 434 N.Y.S.2d 365. Accordingly, we direct that the motion to stay arbitration be denied.

All concur.

Notes

1. As *Julien* points out, directors are highly unionized and most belong to the Society of Stage Directors and Choreographers ("SSDC") (www.ssdc.org). The SSDC defines the duties of directors as follows:

> advising with respect to casting, script revisions, sets, costumes, props and similar matters; consulting with the various designers; and attending, conducting and directing all auditions, rehearsals, tryouts (out-of-town or otherwise), previews and invitational performances, if any, prior to the official New York City opening.

Director Agreement for SSDC 1st Class Performance (Broadway). In reality, however, a director's responsibilities are determined by the needs of the individual production:

> Like many tasks, the director's role keeps changing. It changes not only because our view of theatre and the related performing arts change, but because it is different with each new production. Each cast, each script, each theatrical space, each evolution of a production style will bring new roles for the director. He will need to let go of some of his previous practices and develop new ones for every effort he undertakes.

John Ahart, *The Director's Eye: A Comprehensive Textbook for Directors and Actors* 23 (2001). A sample director's contract appears in Appendix D of this casebook.

2. Actor Peter Ustinov once said that "while the French is a playwright's theatre [and] the English [is] an actor's theatre, the American is a director's theatre." *See* Harold Clurman, *On Directing* 3 (1997). Yet as *Julien* makes clear, directors often labor under severe restrictions: the playwright typically has veto power over the script as well as consultation rights on casting while the producer has total control over the budget and a large say in creative decisions. Nevertheless, when things go wrong it usually is the director who takes the fall. In Episode 180 of the NBC sitcom *Frasier*, entitled "The Show Must Go Off," for example, the Cranes suddenly realized the play they were producing was going to be a flop. When Niles frantically asked what they should do, Frasier responded, "We do what all good producers do—we shut down and blame the director!"

3. Although full-time university faculty are not required to sign a contract approved by the SSDC, those who are guest directors/choreographers, part-time directors/choreographers, or employed to direct or choreograph a specific project must enter into a SSDC agreement. For those part-time individuals who are both teaching and directing, the test is whether more than 50% of their time is spent directing.

Many colleges and universities are barred from negotiating with the SSDC as a result of state laws limiting collective bargaining or requiring exclusivity among bargaining units. As a result, the University/Resident Theatre Association has been created. It signs the SSDC agreement and then "loans" the employee to the production, thereby allowing a director or choreographer to meet his or her obligations to both the union and the school. The SSDC reports that approximately 100 of these arrangements currently exist.

4. *Gennaro* and *Rodgers* are examples of directors and choreographers fighting for a slice of a show's financial pie. Another is *Roberts v. Atlantic Recording Corp.*, 892 F. Supp. 83 (S.D.N.Y. 1995). The musical arranger of the play "Smokey Joe's Cafe" sought a temporary restraining order when he discovered his name was going to be left off the cast album. In an earlier proceeding, however, he had obtained an injunction barring the producer from using his name in connection with the play (due to a falling out between the two). Given this fact, the court refused to enjoin release of the album:

> In plaintiffs' April 24 letter, they state that "Payment of the invoice and inclusion of appropriate billing credit on all album materials will resolve this matter." If the album dispute is decided in plaintiffs' favor and defendants pay the invoice amount, the only remaining injury to Roberts would be a lack of billing credit. Defendants agreed at oral argument of the request for a TRO to credit Roberts on any future CD's or cassettes. Defendants cannot, however, change the credits on the 18,000 units which have already been manufactured and shipped. Roberts' injury, therefore, would ultimately be the lack of billing credit on the 18,000 CD's and cassettes already manufactured.
>
> However, Roberts did not receive billing credit for the 18,000 units because of his own actions. As noted above, Justice DeGrasse granted Roberts' motion for a preliminary injunction on July 22, 1994. This injunction enjoined defendants from using his name "in connection with" the Play. Roberts claims that irreparable injury flows from defendants' failure to display his name on the cast albums. Plaintiffs, however, sought and received an injunction prohibiting defendants from using his name "in connection with" the Play. For plaintiffs now to claim that he is irreparably harmed by defendants' failure to use his name amounts to unclean hands. See Johanna Farms, Inc. v. Citrus Bowl, Inc., 468 F.Supp. 866, 874 (E.D.N.Y.1978). As a restraining order is a form of equitable relief, Roberts' previous request that his name not be used precludes him from claiming irreparable harm as a result of defendants' failure to use his name.

Id. at 88.

Problem 9

As part of her ongoing obligation to revisit a long-running play, the original director determined it was time to recast the lead actor and actress. The pair had starred in the production since its opening a decade before and each was now 44 years old. If their replacements both turn out to be 32 years old, can the former leads sue for age discrimination? *See Carlson v. WPLG/TV-10, Post-Newsweek Stations of Florida*, 956 F. Supp. 994 (S.D. Fla. 1996).

C. STAGE DIRECTIONS

NEW CLOUT FOR STAGE DIRECTORS: COPYRIGHT PROTECTION AVAILABLE FOR CREATIVE WORK
Richard C. Reuben
81 A.B.A.J. 32 (Oct. 1995)

Stage directors and choreographers now can obtain copyright protection for their creative work, thanks in part to a 1992 ruling by the U.S. Copyright Office and to changes in theater contracts.

"This isn't about greed, it is about getting one's fair share of compensation for one's creative intellectual property," said Kathryn Haapala, acting director of the New York-based Society of Stage Directors and Choreographers, an independent trade union.

Previously, stage directors and choreographers received credit but no protection for their creativity under so-called "work for hire" contracts, she said. Under today's collective bargaining agreements, they retain copyright ownership.

A few stage directors and choreographers have gone even further, registering the copyright on their works under a precedent set in 1992. That year, lawyer Evan Katz persuaded the U.S. Copyright Office to grant a copyright on a client's stage production.

The claim presented "a new issue," said James Vassar, who heads the performing arts section of the U.S. Copyright Office's examining division. "And we took a direction that, based on our prior practices,...we feel is right."

At least two factors were influential in the decision, Vassar said. First, Katz's client had an express grant of the copyright from the producer. Second, the copyright claim included a videotape of the production, so there literally was a "fixed" work to register as a copyright.

Despite the ruling, few have sought such protection. "A huge tree fell in the copyright world, but no one was around to hear it," said Katz, of Monroe Partners International in New York City.

Still, the availability of the copyrights has had an impact. Earlier this year, director Gerald Gutierrez settled a lawsuit against a Chicago producer and director for their 1994 production of "The Most Happy Fella." The suit alleged Gutierrez's artistic innovations in a 1992 Broadway revival of the production had been appropriated without consent, royalties or credit.

MANTELLO v. HALL
947 F. Supp. 92 (S.D.N.Y. 1996)

MUKASEY, District Judge.

Joe Mantello sues Michael Hall and Caldwell Theatre Company for false representation in violation of the Lanham Act, 15 U.S.C. §1125(a), copyright infringement in violation of the Copyright Act, 17 U.S.C. §101 et seq., "reverse passing off" in violation of plaintiff's common law rights, and unjust enrichment. Defendants move to dismiss on various grounds including lack of personal jurisdiction. For the reasons stated below, defendants' motion to dismiss for lack of personal jurisdiction is granted. The other grounds accordingly need not be considered.

I.

Plaintiff is a stage director and a citizen of New York. (Compl. ¶ 3) Caldwell Theatre is a regional theater and not-for-profit corporation located in Boca Raton, Florida. (6/6/96 Hall Aff. ¶¶ 2, 3, 5) Michael Hall is Caldwell's president, chief executive officer and artistic director, and a citizen of Florida. (Id. ¶ 1)

In 1994, plaintiff was employed by the Manhattan Theatre Club, located in New York, to direct a play written by Terrence McNally and entitled "Love! Valour! Compassion!" ("the Play"). (Compl. ¶ 6) The Play ran at the Manhattan Theatre Club until February 1995 when it moved to the Walter Kerr Theatre in New York City. (Id.) The Play received "favorable reviews" and acclaim and won several awards, including a Tony. Plaintiff personally won the Outer Critics Circle and the OBIE awards for his direction as well as the Joe A. Calloway award. (Id. ¶ 8)

Plaintiff is a member of the Society of Stage Directors & Choreographers ("SSDC") which has entered collective bargaining agreements with Leagues of off-Broadway and Broadway producers. (Id. ¶ 3; Mantello Aff. ¶ 3; 7/24/96 Shechtman Aff. ¶ 2) In connection with the off-Broadway production of the Play at the Manhattan Theatre, and the Broadway production at the Walter Kerr Theatre, plaintiff entered into contracts which incorporated those collective bargaining agreements. (7/24/96 Shechtman Aff., Ex. B, C) Each collective bargaining agreement included a clause that granted to the director all property rights in and to the direction of the Play. Although the parties dispute the scope of that grant of rights, that dispute need not be resolved to decide this motion. (Id. ¶¶ 4-5)

After plaintiff's successful production of the Play, defendants presented the Play, directed by Hall, at defendant Caldwell's theater in Boca Raton over a seven-week period from February 11, 1996 through March 31, 1996. (6/6/96 Hall Aff. ¶ 7) Defendants negotiated with McNally's agent and obtained a license to produce the Play from Dramatists Play Service, Inc., a New York company which licenses the rights to produce plays. (6/6/96 Hall Aff., ¶ 9, Ex. A)

Plaintiff claims that Hall and Caldwell, in their production of the Play, intentionally recreated his "unique direction and staging" including "the replication of the stage movement, design, lighting and sound." (Compl. ¶ 12) Plaintiff alleges that Hall and his collaborators attended the New York production of the Play and took notes to help copy plaintiff's staging, that defendants obtained literature describing the New York production, that Hall cast actors who had seen the New York production to obtain information about it, and that Hall instructed the designers of his production to attend the New York production to obtain information. (Compl. ¶ 11)

Plaintiff learned about the Caldwell production when a cast member from his production called him from Florida in February or March 1996. (Mantello Aff. ¶ 6) Plaintiff then flew to Florida on March 3, 1996 and saw the Caldwell production. (Id.) Plaintiff describes specific scenes in the Caldwell production which he claims duplicated his stage directions and conceptions. (Mantello Aff. ¶¶ 8-11)

Plaintiff filed suit on April 10, 1996. Defendant now moves to dismiss for lack of personal jurisdiction, for improper venue, for transfer under the doctrine of forum non conveniens, for lack of subject matter jurisdiction because plaintiff lacks standing, for failure to state a claim upon which relief can be granted, and finally for a more definite statement pursuant to Fed.R.Civ.P. 12(e).

II.

Defendants move first to dismiss based on lack of personal jurisdiction pursuant to Fed.R.Civ.P. 12(b)(2). In a diversity case, or a case arising under federal law which does not provide for service of process on a party outside the state, personal jurisdiction is based on the law of the forum state. See, e.g., Omni Capital Int'l. v. Rudolf Wolff & Co., 484 U.S. 97, 108, 108 S.Ct. 404, 411-12, 98 L.Ed.2d 415 (1987); Savin v. Ranier, 898 F.2d 304, 305 (2d Cir.1990). [Hence, we look to New York state law.]

A. CPLR § 301—Doing Business

Plaintiff argues first that defendants are subject to the jurisdiction of this court pursuant to § 301 of the New York Civil Practice Law and Rules ("CPLR"). N.Y.C.P.L.R. 301 (McKinney 1990). CPLR § 301 confers on New York courts general personal jurisdiction over any non-resident or foreign corporation "engaged in such a continuous and systematic course of 'doing business' here as to warrant a finding of its presence in this jurisdiction." A party subject to general personal jurisdiction in New York may be sued in New York on any claim, whether or not the claim arose in New York or from any of the defendant's contacts with New York.

The test to determine whether a corporation or individual is subject to jurisdiction pursuant to § 301 has been called a "simple and pragmatic one...which is necessarily fact sensitive because each case is dependent on its own particular circumstances." The issue is whether a defendant's contacts with New York "show a continuous, permanent and substantial activity in New York." The traditional indicia which courts rely upon in deciding whether a foreign corporation is doing business in New York include: 1) the existence of an office in New York; 2) the solicitation of business in New York; 3) the existence of bank accounts or other property in New York; and 4) the presence of employees of the foreign defendant in New York. Hoffritz for Cutlery, Inc. v. Amajac, Ltd., 763 F.2d 55, 58 (2d Cir.1985). Accordingly, a defendant is doing business such that jurisdiction pursuant to § 301 is appropriate if it does business in New York "not occasionally or casually, but with a fair measure of permanence and continuity."

Plaintiff asserts that "[i]t is virtually impossible to be legitimately involved in the professional theater business and not do regular, consistent and purposeful business with the New York theater community" and "by the very nature of their business, Defendants systematically conduct business in and with the New York theater community." (Pl.Mem. at 26, 27). Plaintiff relies on defendants' following alleged business dealings in New York to support § 301 jurisdiction: 1) Hall regularly comes to New York to see plays and decide which ones Caldwell wants to produce, and to meet with members of the professional theater community; 2) defendants regularly negotiate and execute licenses to produce plays from licensing services and agents in New York, and regularly make payments to those agencies; 3) Caldwell is a member of the League of Resident Theatres ("LORT"), a New York based organization of regional theaters which negotiates on behalf of regional theaters with various unions, including Actors Equity Association, United Scenic Artists and the Society of Stage Directors and Choreographers (7/9/96 Shechtman Aff. ¶ 6); 4) pursuant to the agreements entered into by LORT, grievances and arbitrations are conducted in New York and Caldwell contributes money to the actors unions' health and pension funds; 5) Caldwell regularly advertises for actors in New York and employs a New York casting agent; and 6) Caldwell regularly solicits contributions and ticket subscriptions from New York foundations, organizations and individuals. (Def.Mem. at 26-27)

Plaintiff does not assert that defendants show the traditional indicia of doing business in New York—an office, solicitation, property or employees in New York. In a sworn affidavit, Hall states that neither he nor Caldwell solicits business or advertises in New York or has an office, mailing address, agent or telephone line in New York. (6/6/96 Hall Aff. ¶3) Further, Hall asserts that "all negotiations, discussions and correspondence in connection with Caldwell's association with [LORT] takes place from Caldwell's office in Florida" and Caldwell executes an individual contract with each person employed for a theatrical performance. (Id. ¶8) Hall claims also that "Caldwell does not and has not regularly solicited support or contributions in New York" and does not "regularly communicate with New York residents." (Id. ¶4)

Most of the cases in which courts base jurisdiction over foreign corporations on CPLR §301 feature one or more of the traditional indicia of doing business. However, in Erving v. The Virginia Squires Basketball Club, the Court held that the defendant was subject to jurisdiction pursuant to §301 based on: a) the defendant's connections with the American Basketball Association which was headquartered in New York; b) defendant's regular and continual visits to New York "for the business purpose of playing professional games for profit"; and c) defendant's "dealings with New York business concerns...in furtherance of the business purpose in New York." 349 F.Supp. 709, 714-15 (E.D.N.Y.1972). To find the defendant subject to general personal jurisdiction pursuant to CPLR §301, Erving relied on Hawkins v. National Basketball Ass'n., 288 F.Supp. 614 (W.D.Pa.1968), in which the Court denied a motion by defendant basketball clubs to change venue, stating that "[t]he only business a corporation-owned professional athletic league team could engage in profitably is to systematically play games with other member teams...." Id. (citing Hawkins, 288 F.Supp. at 619). Thus, Erving reasoned that the playing of games is the business of a professional sports team, and by playing games professional sports teams are doing business. Thus, a defendant who lacks the traditional indicia of doing business nevertheless does business in New York when it engages in its principal corporate activity within New York on a systematic and continual basis.

Here, Caldwell's business is the presentation of plays. Plaintiff has not alleged that defendant presented the Play or any other play in New York. Indeed, plaintiff has alleged, and defendants have not denied, only three systematic and ongoing contacts defendants have with New York: that Caldwell regularly enters into licensing agreements with New York entities or individuals for the rights to produce plays, that defendants regularly hire New York actors for their productions and deal with their New York-based unions, and that Caldwell is a member of LORT and participates in its activities. Plaintiff also alleges that Hall regularly travels to New York to see plays.

Those activities do not constitute "doing business." Hall's visits to New York to review current theater, even if for the purpose of determining which plays Caldwell should produce, is not "doing business." Hiring New York actors for productions in Florida and obtaining licenses is not "doing business." Through these activities, defendants, in essence, merely secure the goods and services they need—plays, actors and licenses—to do their business in Florida, i.e., produce plays. See Agency Rent A Car System, Inc. v. Grand Rent A Car Corp., 916 F.Supp. 224, 228 (E.D.N.Y.) ("[T]he purchase of goods from New York by a Defendant, even if on a large scale, would not, in and of itself, amount to 'doing business' within the state."), rev'd on other grounds, 98 F.3d 25 (2d Cir.1996).

Also, defendants' association with LORT is not "doing business" such that defendants are subject to the general personal jurisdiction of New York courts. "The mere existence of a business relationship with entities within the forum state is insufficient to establish presence." Insurance Co. of Penn. v. Centaur Ins. Co., 590 F.Supp. 1187, 1189 (S.D.N.Y.1984). Indeed, in Agency Rent A Car System, the Court refused to find the defendants subject to jurisdiction under §301 absent the traditional indicia of doing business, despite the defendants' connections with business organizations that serviced their needs in New York. 916 F.Supp. at 228. General jurisdiction over a foreign corporation may be based on its relationship to an entity which is "definitively 'present' in New York" only in two circumstances: "when the local corporation has no actual, independent existence from the foreign corporation,...and when the local corporation acts as the foreign corporation's agent to the extent that it 'does all the business which [the foreign entity] could do were it here by its own officials.'" Mayatextil v. Liztex U.S.A., Inc., No. 92 Civ. 4528, 1995 WL 131774 (S.D.N.Y. March 23, 1995) (brackets in original, citations omitted).

Here, plaintiff does not claim that either Hall or Caldwell participates in any way in the business or affairs of LORT, other than by being a member theater and, presumably, incorporating into Caldwell's employment contracts the agreements LORT enters into with the actors unions. Cf. Erving, 349 F.Supp. at 714 (noting that the defendant "participated in the management and revenues" of the ABA which it termed a "joint business enterprise"). Plaintiff states merely that "upon information and belief" defendants participate in the business of LORT. (7/9/96 Shechtman Aff. ¶6) That allegation alone is insufficient. See Agency Rent A Car, 916 F.Supp. at 228 (holding plaintiff failed to make a prima facie showing of jurisdiction, "notwithstanding that certain executives of some Defendants hold positions" in the New York entities with which defendants were associated). Also, plaintiff does not claim that LORT serves as defendants' agent for all purposes in New York. Rather LORT serves Caldwell and other regional theaters as an agent for one discrete aspect of their business—entering into collective bargaining agreements with theatrical unions. Accordingly, plaintiff has not presented a prima facie case that defendants, through their association or membership in this consortium, actually did business in New York such that they should be considered generally present in New York. Here, it is important to remember that if CPLR §301 applied, defendants would be subject to the general personal jurisdiction of New York courts and could then be sued on any claim, not just one arising out of the production of allegedly infringing plays.

Finally, plaintiff admits that his argument for finding defendants subject to the general personal jurisdiction of New York courts would apply as well to nearly all of the regional theaters in the nation that obtain licenses to produce plays from New York entities, hire New York actors, review Broadway and off-Broadway productions and are members of LORT: "[t]he reality is that most of the LORT theaters around the country regularly do business in New York." (7/9/96 Shechtman Aff. ¶8) Although plaintiff embraces that extreme result, these defendants are unlike basketball teams, who actually engage in their business when they travel into New York and play a game. Defendants and others similarly situated, who lack the traditional indicia of doing business, do not subject themselves for all purposes to the jurisdiction of New York courts merely because they travel to New York to "exploit the synergy between New York City's unique theatrical resources and the work of regional theaters." (Id.)

B. CPLR 302(a)—New York's Long-Arm Statute

Plaintiff also argues that defendants are subject to the personal jurisdiction of this court pursuant to New York's long-arm statute, CPLR §302(a). In particular, plaintiff argues that defendants satisfy either §302(a)(1) or §302(a)(2).

CPLR §302(a)(1) permits a court to exercise jurisdiction over a non-domiciliary who, in person or through an agent "transacts any business within the state...." N.Y.C.P.L.R. 302(a)(1). To justify the exertion of personal jurisdiction over a defendant based on §302(a)(1) two conditions must be met: "first, the nondomiciliary must 'transact business' within the state; second, the claim against the nondomiciliary must arise out of that business activity." To "transact business," a nondomiciliary must "purposefully avail[ ] itself of the privilege of conducting activities within [New York], thus invoking the benefits and protections of its laws." McKee Elec. Co. v. Rauland-Borg Corp., 20 N.Y.2d 377, 382, 283 N.Y.S.2d 34, 37-38, 229 N.E.2d 604 (1967) (quoting Hanson v. Denckla, 357 U.S. 235, 253, 78 S.Ct. 1228, 1239-40, 2 L.Ed.2d 1283 (1958)). The factors a court considers to determine whether an out-of-state defendant transacts business in New York include: 1) the existence of an ongoing contractual relationship; 2) whether the contract was negotiated or executed in New York; 3) if there are any choice-of-law provisions in the contract; and 4) whether the contract requires franchisees to send notices or payments into New York. Agency Rent A Car System, Inc. v. Grand Rent A Car Corp., 98 F.3d 25, 29-30 (2d Cir.1996). Because a court must examine "the totality of circumstances," other factors may also be considered. Id.

Plaintiff has alleged that the following contacts with New York constitute transaction of business and demonstrate that defendants availed themselves of New York's laws: 1) Hall's trips to New York to see the Play and determine whether Caldwell should produce it; 2) defendants' negotiations with Dramatists Play Service to obtain the license to produce the play and defendants' sending royalty payments in connection with that license into New York; 3) defendants' auditions in New York to cast actors; 4) defendants' filing the actors' contracts in New York with Actors Equity Association; 5) defendants' meeting in New York with backstage personnel from the New York production to obtain technical information; and finally, 6) defendants' payments to the actors union's benefit funds in New York. (Pl.Mem. at 18-20) In reply, Hall claims that all negotiations to obtain the rights to the Play were conducted from Florida and not in New York, and that no one from Caldwell met with backstage personnel or inspected the set of the New York production of the play. (6/6/96 Hall Aff. ¶ 8; 6/17/96 Hall Aff. ¶ 7)

Of the above contacts, only defendants' license with Dramatist Play Service and its employment contracts and connections with New York actors and their unions arguably constitute transaction of business in New York. Transaction of business does not include viewing a Broadway production which is open to the public, or meeting with technical people to obtain information about the Play. Those actions may very well have been blameworthy in the sense that defendants were attending the Play not merely to enjoy it but to copy its presentation so they could produce their allegedly infringing play. However, simply because conduct may be blameworthy does not make it transaction of business.

Even if defendants transacted business with the actors, their unions and Dramatist Play Service, they are not subject to personal jurisdiction in New York courts pursuant to §302(a)(1) unless plaintiff's claims for relief arise out of that business. See, e.g., Agency Rent A Car, 98 F.3d at 30-31. "A claim 'arises out of' defendant's transaction of business in New York 'when there exists a substantial nexus between the business transacted and the cause of action sued upon.'" Id. (citations omitted).

Here, plaintiff has claimed that defendants misrepresented the source of the staging and direction of the Play in violation of the Lanham Act and plaintiff's common law rights, that defendant infringed plaintiff's copyright, and that defendant was unjustly enriched. Plaintiff's claims all sound in tort and do not arise out of defendants' transaction of business in New York. For a tort claim to arise out of transaction of business in

New York, the connection between the transaction and the claim must be direct. Here, plaintiff claims that defendants intentionally copied his unique staging of the Play. The business which defendants transacted in New York included holding auditions in New York and hiring New York actors whose contracts were filed with unions in New York, sending benefits payments to the actors unions in New York, entering into a licensing agreement with Dramatists Play Service, and sending royalty payments to the Play Service. None of these activities resulted directly in an injury to plaintiff. The torts alleged here, all stemming from the wrongful misappropriation of plaintiff's stage directions, do not arise out of defendants' hiring of New York actors and dealing with New York unions, or defendants' agreement with Dramatist Play Service. Each of these alleged transactions was with a third party and not with plaintiff. Plaintiff has not made a prima facie showing that his claims arise out of defendants' transaction of business in New York. Therefore, CPLR § 302(a)(1) does not confer jurisdiction here.

Plaintiff argues next that New York courts may exercise personal jurisdiction over defendants pursuant to CPLR § 302(a)(2) which grants jurisdiction over a nondomiciliary who "commits a tortious act within the state...." N.Y.C.P.L.R. 301(a)(2).

To satisfy § 302(a)(2), in cases involving copyright infringement and violations of the Lanham Act, the offering, display or sale of the allegedly infringing product must occur in New York. That is to say, the conduct that occurs in New York must be the infringer's misrepresentation of the source of the product or his unauthorized presentation of the product. See, e.g., Imagineering, Inc. v. Van Klassens, Inc., 797 F.Supp. 329 (S.D.N.Y.1992) (unfair competition in violation of the Lanham Act); Dave Guardala Mouthpieces, Inc. v. Sugal Mouthpieces, Inc., 779 F.Supp. 335 (S.D.N.Y.1991) (trademark/trade dress infringement); Business Trends Analysts v. Freedonia Group, Inc., 650 F.Supp. 1452 (S.D.N.Y.1987) (copyright infringement). In addition, plaintiff's state law claim of "reverse passing off" is a tort encompassed within a claim of "unfair competition." See Grupke v. Linda Lori Sportswear, Inc., 921 F.Supp. 987, 996 (E.D.N.Y.1996). "Under New York law the 'essence' of an unfair competition claim is 'the bad faith misappropriation of the labors and expenditures of another, likely to cause confusion or to deceive purchasers as to the origin of the goods.'" Id. (citing Milstein v. Greger, Lawlor, Roth, Inc., 58 F.3d 27, 34 (2d Cir.1995)); see also American Movie Classics Co. v. Turner Entertainment Co., 922 F.Supp. 926, 932 (S.D.N.Y.1996) ("[T]he essence of [passing off] is false representation of origin."). Accordingly, to commit the tort of reverse passing off within New York, a defendant must pass off goods in New York—offer some products, goods or services within New York which he misrepresents as his own. See Business Trends, 650 F.Supp. at 1456 (finding jurisdiction over an unfair competition claim based on evidence that the defendant attempted to sell his product in New York); Imagineering, 797 F.Supp. at 331 ("For each of plaintiff's claims [including common law unfair competition] the cause of action is deemed to arise where the allegedly infringing sales were made."). An actual sale of an infringing product "is not necessary to establish personal jurisdiction" Business Trends, 650 F.Supp. at 1456; merely offering one copy of an infringing product through distribution of a catalog within the state is sufficient. Honda Assocs., Inc. v. Nozawa Trading, Inc., 374 F.Supp. 886, 889 (S.D.N.Y.1974).

Here, plaintiff claims that defendants passed off their infringing play in New York by soliciting ticket sales, subscriptions and contributions from New York residents. Plaintiff claims first that defendants obtained contributions from Chemical Bank and the IBM corporation, two New York-based organizations, and to solicit these contributions, "undoubtedly...sent promotional material and other information to New York in which Defendants passed off Plaintiff's work as their own." (Pl.Mem. at 22) Plaintiff bases that claim on the program for the Caldwell production of the Play, which lists Chemical Bank and IBM as major contributors. (7/9/96 Shechtman Aff. ¶ 7). Defendants state that they obtained contributions in the form of used computer equipment and donations from IBM and Chemical Bank, but that those contributions were solicited from IBM's and Chemical Bank's local offices in Boca Raton, Florida. (7/17/96 Hall Aff. ¶ 4) Defendants' explanation thoroughly refutes plaintiff's allegation; other than that bare allegation, plaintiff has offered no evidence that defendants solicited foundations or companies in New York or that defendants sent promotional material into New York. Plaintiff merely surmises both that defendants solicited Chemical Bank and IBM in New York, and that in doing so defendants sent to New York promotional material in which they passed off the Play.

Plaintiff argues next that "based on the dual residence of many members of Defendants' audience [Florida and New York], Defendants have likely solicited ticket sales or subscriptions for the infringing play in New York." (Pl.Mem. at 22) Plaintiff's argument, that defendants "must have" solicited ticket sales or subscriptions to the Play, is not factually based or intuitively apparent. Rather, plaintiff is merely making an inference from the fact that many residents of Florida also are residents of New York that defendants must have solicited business in New York. In two sworn affidavits, Hall states that "the Caldwell production of the Play was promoted, marketed and advertised exclusively in the State of Florida" (6/6/96 Hall Aff. ¶ 22), and "Caldwell does not and has not regularly solicited support or contributions in New York from New York residents." (7/17/96 Hall Aff. ¶ 4)

Although on a motion to dismiss I must resolve all doubts and construe all documents in favor of plaintiff non-movant, plaintiff has failed to present a prima facie case that the alleged torts took place in New York. Plaintiff merely surmises that defendants solicited or sold tickets in New York. Even if I took judicial notice of the fact that many residents of Florida are also residents of New York, the conclusion that defendant solicited ticket sales in New York does not follow. Indeed, absent specific evidence—and there is none here—it is implausible that a Florida business whose product—plays— can be consumed only at its theater in Florida and is unlikely itself to provide the reason or focus for a trip to Florida, would solicit business in New York. In plain terms, these defendants run a regional theater, not Disneyworld.

Finally, Plaintiff's allegation that defendants came to New York to spy on his production of the Play, i.e., to view the Play and take notes on the direction and staging may, as noted, constitute blameworthy behavior. However, those acts do not constitute the torts which plaintiff alleges defendants committed. Each tort plaintiff alleges—copyright infringement, unfair competition under the Lanham Act, and common law reverse passing off—requires the sale or the offering for sale of the allegedly infringing product or service in New York. It is important to remember that "CPLR 302 does not extend jurisdiction as far as may be constitutionally permitted." Interface Biomedical Labs. Corp. v. Axiom Medical, Inc., 600 F.Supp. 731, 734 n. 3 (E.D.N.Y.1985). The issue here is whether the statute permits the exercise of personal jurisdiction, not whether the Constitution does. Plaintiff has failed to make a prima facie showing that defendants committed a tort in New York by offering or promoting the Play in New York and CPLR § 302(a)(2), therefore, does not confer jurisdiction.

III.

For the reasons stated above, defendants' motion to dismiss based on lack of personal jurisdiction, Fed.R.Civ.P. 12(b)(2) is granted. Defendants' other motions need not be decided.

Notes

1. Even before the Copyright Office's 1992 decision, it was clear that protection existed for certain types of stage directions:

> Several witnesses at the hearings recommended the specific enumeration of additional categories of works in section 102, including...works of stage directors.... The committee concluded, however, that to the extent these works constitute "original works of authorship" under the statute, they are already included in section 102's list.

Copyright Law Revision, H.R. Rep. No. 2237, 89th Cong., 2d. Sess., at 45-46 (1966).

2. At present, *Mantello* is the only case addressing the copyrightability of stage directions. There are, however, a number of law review articles, each with its own take on the subject. *See* David Leichtman, *Most Unhappy Collaborators: An Argument Against the Recognition of Property Ownership in Stage Directions*, 20 Colum.-VLA J.L. & Arts 683 (1996); Talia Yellin, *New Directions for Copyright: The Property Rights of Stage Directors*, 24 Colum.-VLA J.L. & Arts 317 (2001); Richard Amada, Note, *Elvis, Karaoke, Shakespeare and the Search for a Copyrightable Stage Direction*, 43 Ariz. L. Rev. 677 (2001); Beth Freemal, Note, *Theatre, Stage Directions & Copyright Law*, 71 Chi.-Kent L. Rev. 1017 (1996). *See also* Patrick T. Perkins, *"Hey! What's the Score?": Copyright in the Orchestrations of Broadway Musicals*, 16 Colum.-VLA J.L. & Arts 475 (1992).

Problem 10

A publishing house is planning to release a book containing photographs of the dance routines that appear in a new Broadway musical. Because there are so many pictures, anyone looking at them will be able to figure out exactly how each routine is done. Given these facts, can the choreographer who devised the steps obtain an injunction? *See Horgan v. Macmillan, Inc.*, 789 F.2d 157 (2d Cir. 1986).

Chapter 6

Cast

A. OVERVIEW

Night after night, it is the performers that the audience comes to see. For no matter how good the script, how polished the direction, or how breathtaking the sets, the success of any show ultimately depends on its cast.

B. HIRING AND FIRING

MIXING LAW AND ART: THE ROLE OF ANTI-DISCRIMINATION LAW AND COLOR-BLIND CASTING IN BROADWAY THEATER
Bonnie Chen (Student Author)
16 Hofstra Lab. & Emp. L.J. 515 (1999)

In 1989, Miss Saigon, a musical written by the creators of Les Miserables, opened in London and was brought to Broadway in 1990 by producer Cameron Mackintosh. In London, British actor Jonathan Pryce played the half-French and half-Vietnamese role of "the Engineer." [C]ontroversy began when Actors' Equity ("Equity"), a union representing American stage actors, rejected Mackintosh's application to allow Jonathan Pryce to repeat his role in the Broadway production. In response, Mackintosh canceled the show. Because Miss Saigon was a great source of employment (offering 182 jobs, which were mostly minority roles), Equity reversed its vote and allowed Pryce to play the part of the Engineer.

David Henry Hwang and B.D. Wong, Tony award winners for M. Butterfly, were the ones who brought the controversy to Equity's attention. Their major concern was the lack of roles available to Asian actors. Equity's initial decision was celebrated by the Asian-American theater community, but also sparked a national debate on the issue of color-blind casting. Another concern was that casting Pryce would condone the "offensive and demeaning" practice of "yellow face." Similar to the "black face" practices of the minstrel shows, yellow face uses makeup in a grotesque and exaggerated manner to parody and degrade the physical characteristics of an Asian.

However, Equity's original decision to prohibit Pryce from performing as the Engineer in Miss Saigon was also criticized as contradictory and hypocritical. This decision seemed to stress that minority-specific roles be performed by an actor of the same race.

The few available racial minority roles would be preserved for minority actors. Equity also encourages color-blind casting, a practice which allows actors to play any role, regardless of race, unless race is germane to the character or play. Thus, roles that are traditionally cast for Caucasians should be open to minority actors, giving them more employment opportunities. Equity's approach to color-blind casting seemed inconsistent, implementing it only when it was favorable to minorities. Critics have argued that, "[y]ou can't encourage the casting of an African-American as a Caucasian and forbid a Caucasian to play an Asian."

The controversy spurred Equity to reverse its original position and allow Pryce to play the part of the Engineer. Alan Eisenberg, Equity's executive secretary, apologized on behalf of the union and termed Equity's position on color-blind casting as "distorted and misconstrued." In the end, the show went on, and Miss Saigon employed many Asian-American actors. In this instance, color-blind casting prevailed. However, almost a decade later, the debate continues as more minority actors enter the theater and as racial discrimination law evolves.

The Civil Rights Act of 1964

Congress passed the Civil Rights Act of 1964 to remedy the racial discrimination that had long shamed this nation. Congress passed Title VII of the Act to deal with employment discrimination. The congressional intent behind Title VII is to provide formal procedures to eliminate employment discrimination based on race, color, religion, or national origin. In Griggs v. Duke Power Co., 401 U.S. 424 (1971), the Supreme Court examined the legislative objective of Title VII, stating that Title VII was not designed to guarantee employment for minorities. Instead, Title VII was meant to "remov[e] artificial, arbitrary, and unnecessary barriers to employment when the barriers operate invidiously to discriminate on the basis of racial or other impermissible classification."

The relevant section [of Title VII] states:

> It shall be an unlawful employment practice for an employer (1) to fail or refuse to hire or to discharge any individual, or otherwise to discriminate against any individual with respect to his compensation, terms, conditions, or privileges of employment, because of such individual's race, color, religion, sex, or national origin....

In applying this statute to Broadway theater, casting actors according to their race seems blatantly violative of this rule. A decision to reject an actor based on race seems discriminatory on its face. However, refusing to audition an actor because the part requires the actor to be of a certain race exists in the theater world. The casting director selects actors that have a certain look, and race is often part of that consideration. This brings up the issue of whether casting an actor according to race qualifies as a Bona Fide Occupational Qualification ("BFOQ").

The BFOQ exception, found in Title VII of the Act, reads as follows:

> it shall not be an unlawful employment practice for an employer to hire and employ employees...on the basis of his religion, sex, or national origin in those certain instances where religion, sex, or national origin is a bona fide occupational qualification reasonably necessary to the normal operation of that particular business or enterprise....

[During the congressional debate over Title VII,] Senators Joseph Clark and Clifford Case explained that a casting director does not need the BFOQ exception to hire someone who fits the physical characteristics of a role. They stated that:

[a] director of a play or movie who wished to cast an actor in the role of a Negro could specify that he wished to hire someone with the physical appearance of a Negro—but such a person might actually be non-Negro. Therefore, the act would not limit the director's freedom of choice.

The senators went on to say that if a movie company was making a movie about Africa, it could hire extras of a certain race or color to make the movie more authentic. This statement seems to imply that discriminating according to appearance while casting actors may not violate Title VII.

[In addition to the legislatively-created BFOQ defense, there also is a judicially-created "business necessity" defense, which] evolved from the Supreme Court's decision in Griggs v. Duke Power Co. The Griggs court held, "[t]he Act proscribes not only overt discrimination but also practices that are fair in form, but [are] discriminatory in operation. The touchstone is business necessity. If an employment practice which operates to exclude Negroes cannot be shown to be related to job performance, the practice is prohibited."

In Miller v. Texas State Bd. of Barber Examiners, 615 F.2d 650, 654 (5th Cir. 1980), the Fifth Circuit discussed, in dicta, the possibility that business necessity would be a valid defense for a director engaging in race-specific casting. "For example, it is likely that a black actor could not appropriately portray George Wallace, and a white actor could not appropriately portray Martin Luther King, Jr."

[To date,] the issue of discrimination in the theater has not been decided by the courts. Even though it has not been brought before the courts, the issue of racial discrimination continues to percolate in the theater world. As society approaches the brink of the twenty-first century, the debate continues to grow.

NEW STAR OF 'PRODUCERS' IS REPLACED AFTER 4 WEEKS
Jesse McKinley
N.Y. Times, Apr. 16, 2002, at E1

In the first major crisis of a charmed Broadway run, the producers of "The Producers" have fired the acclaimed British actor Henry Goodman from the lead role of Max Bialystock and replaced him with his understudy, Brad Oscar.

Mr. Goodman's dismissal, after only 30 performances as Nathan Lane's replacement in the hit musical, occurred just after the Sunday matinee at the St. James Theater. Mr. Goodman was informed backstage via telephone by his London agent; the producers, including Rocco Landesman and Richard Frankel, who had helped cast Mr. Goodman, were not in attendance.

Mr. Goodman had been in the show for just four weeks since taking over from Mr. Lane, who originated the role of Max and won widespread acclaim and a Tony Award for his performance.

Stepping into the role next is Mr. Oscar, who was nominated for a Tony in the supporting role of Franz Liebkind, the demented, pigeon-loving Nazi playwright, and was Mr. Lane's longtime understudy. He will take over the role on Tuesday and will be offered Max on a permanent basis, Mr. Landesman said.

The news of Mr. Goodman's dismissal, which was first reported yesterday in The New York Post and Variety, quickly spread across Broadway as the producers of the musical scrambled to explain how they could have miscalculated so badly on a such a critical piece of casting. (Steven Weber, who replaced Matthew Broderick in the role of Leo Bloom, Max's nebbish sidekick, is staying in the show.)

Mr. Landesman said the decision to release Mr. Goodman was made late last week after it became apparent to the producers that he was not charming audiences as Mr. Lane had.

Mr. Goodman's performance, Mr. Landesman said, was less comic and broad than Mr. Lane's.

"I think the feeling was that it was the right actor in the wrong role," Mr. Landesman said. "The chemistry with Steven and the integration with the show was not what we would have liked."

For his part Mr. Goodman said that while he respected the producers' decision, he believed he was doing a good job.

"I think they've made a mistake," he said. "I think they should have let the critics see me."

The producers had set May 1 as the date for critics to attend the post-Lane show and, in accordance with Broadway tradition, reviewers were respecting that schedule.

"But I think you're dealing with the pressure of Broadway, dealing with an industry where just giving a good performance isn't enough," Mr. Goodman said. "I respect that they're dealing with an industry of millions of dollars on the line, and when you are, you start dealing with people as commodities, not as people."

He added, "This is as much about the boardrooms as it is about the boards."

While the producers said they understood Mr. Goodman's feelings, they were unapologetic about their decision.

"The bottom line," Mr. Landesman said, "is that it's going to be a better show on Tuesday than it was on Sunday."

Susan Stroman, the show's director, who cast Mr. Goodman, said she had hoped to give him time to grow into the role but was informed last Thursday that the producers intended to replace him.

"He gave an incredible audition, but it just didn't work out," Ms. Stroman said, adding that Mr. Goodman hadn't been able to establish the comedic tone the show required. "As the director, always give the actor the benefit of the doubt. We all have to immerse ourselves into the world of Mel Brooks, and that's where he fell short."

Based on Mr. Brooks's screwball 1968 movie about two scheming New York producers who intend to bilk their investors by putting their money into "a sure-fire flop" and pocketing the proceeds, "The Producers" has been the hottest ticket on Broadway since its opening in April 2001.

Last June it dominated the Tony Awards, winning 12, a record. And in November the production surprised Broadway again by introducing "premium" $480 tickets, the highest price ever charged on Broadway. Several other productions have since followed suit with their own high-priced seats.

Since Mr. Lane and Mr. Broderick left the show on March 19, however, the demand for tickets has cooled somewhat, a factor that probably influenced the producers' decision to dismiss Mr. Goodman.

John Barlow, a spokesman for the show, said Mr. Brooks, a producer of the musical still deeply involved with its casting and management, was on a long-planned European vacation.

The dismissal came as a shock to Mr. Goodman, 51, one of Britain's most accomplished stage actors, who won that country's most prestigious acting award, the Olivier, in 1999 for his portrayal of Shylock in "The Merchant of Venice" at the Royal National Theater.

"I saw Mel at a restaurant on Saturday, and he said, 'I love you,'" Mr. Goodman said. "I thought we were flying."

Mr. Landesman conceded that Mr. Goodman had been given no indication that his job was in jeopardy.

"I think he has every reason to feel rather shocked and miffed because he had nothing but assurances that everything was O.K.," Mr. Landesman said. "The feeling was, as you start to voice concerns that seriously it starts to affect the performances."

Mr. Landesman said the producers did not break the news to Mr. Goodman themselves, choosing instead to call him after Penny Wesson, his London-based agent, had spoken to him after the matinee.

The dismissal also surprised some of Mr. Goodman's peers. Jeffrey Denman, a longtime cast member, said only that he learned of the change yesterday morning, when he was called by Ms. Stroman.

"The decision was made pretty quick and pretty quietly, which I think was the right thing to do," Mr. Denman said. "The stakes are so high with this show, and I think that's why the decision was made."

Others outside the production, however, voiced more angry opinions.

Brian Cox, an actor and friend of Mr. Goodman who had seen "The Producers" on Saturday night, said he was disgusted by the manner—and the speed—of the dismissal.

"Unlike the original cast that has previews to get it right, replacements are playing to 1,800 people straight away," Mr. Cox said. "And in my opinion, Henry was doing a great job. He got a standing ovation for his number in the second act. It was a very detailed, very focused performance."

But it may have been that very intensity, and Mr. Goodman's classic British approach, that turned off the show's producers, Ms. Stroman said.

"There are iconic moments—American moments—in 'The Producers' that just weren't in his bones," she said.

Despite his dismissal, Mr. Goodman will be compensated for the remaining eight months of his contract, which paid him approximately $15,000 a week.

REDGRAVE v. BOSTON SYMPHONY ORCHESTRA, INC.
855 F.2d 888 (1st Cir. 1988) (en banc),
cert. denied, 488 U.S. 1043 (1989)

COFFIN, Circuit Judge.

The plaintiffs, actress Vanessa Redgrave and Vanessa Redgrave Enterprises, Ltd. (hereinafter Redgrave), brought suit against the Boston Symphony Orchestra (hereinafter the BSO) for cancelling a contract for Redgrave's appearance as narrator in a performance of Stravinsky's "Oedipus Rex." The cancellation occurred in the wake of protests over Redgrave's participation because of her support of the Palestine Liberation Organization. She sought recovery both for breach of contract and for violation of her civil rights [under the Massachusetts Civil Rights Act ("MCRA")].

A jury awarded Redgrave $100,000 in consequential damages caused by the BSO's breach of contract; sitting in an advisory capacity on Redgrave's MCRA claim, the jury found for the BSO. On the BSO's motion for judgment notwithstanding the verdict on the consequential damages issue, the district court held that the evidence of consequential damages was sufficient but that Redgrave could not recover these damages because of First Amendment limitations. The court also held that the MCRA does not impose liability on a party for acquiescence to third party pressure. Redgrave appealed from these rulings, and the BSO cross-appealed, arguing that the evidence of consequential damages was insufficient.

We conclude that the district court erred in reversing the jury's award of consequential damages, but that Redgrave has presented sufficient evidence to prove only $12,000 in consequential damages, minus certain expenses. We therefore affirm the judgment for the BSO on the MCRA claim and remand for entry of a reduced judgment for consequential damages on the contract claim.

THE CONSEQUENTIAL DAMAGES CLAIM

Redgrave's consequential damages claim is based on the proposition that a significant number of movie and theater offers that she would ordinarily have received in the years 1982 and following were in fact not offered to her as a result of the BSO's cancellation in April 1982.

To the extent that Redgrave may have experienced a decline in film offers received subsequent to April 1982, that decline could have been the result of Redgrave's political views and not the result of the BSO's cancellation. Even if the cancellation highlighted for producers the potential problems in hiring Redgrave, it was Redgrave's burden to establish that, in some way, the cancellation itself caused the difference in film offers rather than the problems as highlighted by the cancellation. Redgrave produced no direct evidence from film producers who were influenced by the cancellation. Thus, the jury's inference that the BSO cancellation had caused Redgrave consequential damages was one based more on "conjecture and speculation," than on a sufficient factual basis.

Redgrave also claims that the BSO's cancellation caused a drop in her offers to perform on Broadway. Bruce Savan, Redgrave's agent, testified regarding all offers to perform in American theater that had been made to Redgrave prior to April 1982. The offers averaged from two to four plays in the years 1976-1980. Redgrave accepted only one of the offers made during this time period, appearing in Lady From the Sea in off-Broadway's Circle in the Square in 1976. There was no evidence of any offers to perform on Broadway made to Redgrave in 1981, the year immediately preceding the BSO cancellation.

Redgrave contends that, as a result of the BSO cancellation, she no longer received offers to appear on Broadway. She testified that in April 1983 she was appearing in a successful English theater production of The Aspern Papers and was led to believe by the producers that the show would move to New York. Although it was Redgrave's opinion that the reason the play did not move to Broadway was because of the "situation" caused by the BSO cancellation, there was no testimony from the producers or others as to why the production did not go to Broadway.

Redgrave also testified that in August 1983 she was asked by the Jujamcyn producers to appear in The Abdication, but that the play was never produced. Again, there was no testimony from the producers or others as to why the production did not materialize.

In addition, Redgrave testified that Lillian Hellman had wished Redgrave to portray Hellman in a theater production on Broadway, but that Hellman was concerned about the BSO incident.

Finally, Redgrave testified that Theodore Mann had considered offering her a role in Heartbreak House at Circle in the Square, but decided not to extend the offer because of the ramifications of the BSO cancellation.

Theodore Mann was the one producer who testified regarding his decision not to employ Redgrave in a Broadway production. He explained that

> the Boston Symphony Orchestra had cancelled, terminated Ms. Redgrave's contract. This had a—this is the premier or one of the premier arts organizations in America who, like ourselves, seeks support from foundations, corporations, individuals; have subscribers; sell individual tickets. I was afraid... and those in my organization were afraid that this termination would have a negative effect on us if we hired her. And so we had conferences about this. We were also concerned about if there would be any physical disturbances to the performance.... And it was finally decided... that we would not hire [Redgrave] because of all the events that had happened, the cancellation by the Boston Symphony and the effects that we felt it would have on us by hiring her.

The evidence presented by Redgrave concerning her drop in Broadway offers after April 1982, apart from Mann's testimony, is not sufficient to support a finding of consequential damages. We do not, of course, question Redgrave's credibility in any way. Our concern is with the meager factual evidence. Redgrave had to introduce enough facts for a jury reasonably to infer that any drop in Broadway offers was proximately caused by the BSO cancellation and not by the fact that producers independently were concerned with the same factors that had motivated the BSO. Mann's testimony itself reflects the fact that many producers in New York may have been hesitant about hiring Redgrave because of a feared drop in subscription support or problems of physical disturbances. Apart from Mann's testimony, Redgrave presented nothing other than the fact that three expected offers or productions did not materialize. This type of circumstantial evidence is not sufficient to support a finding of consequential damages.

In addition, we note that it would be difficult for any assessment of damages resulting from the lack of Broadway theater offers to meet the standard that damages must be "capable of ascertainment by reference to some definite standard, either market value, established experience or direct inference from known circumstances." John Hetherington & Sons, Ltd. v. William Firth Co., 210 Mass. 8, 21, 95 N.E. 961, 964 (1911). The three specific performances to which Redgrave referred, other than Mann's, were never performed on Broadway and there is no indication of the compensation Redgrave would have received. In addition, Redgrave had accepted only one Broadway offer among the many she had received over the years because, according to Redgrave, the scripts were not good enough for her first Broadway appearance. There was no evidence that Redgrave would necessarily have accepted any Broadway offer made in 1982.

Mann's testimony regarding the production of Heartbreak House is the one piece of evidence from which reasonable factfinders could draw conflicting inferences and upon which a reasonably ascertainable damage award could be granted. We therefore defer to the inferences drawn by the jury from that testimony and grant Redgrave damages on that basis.

Mann's testimony reveals that, in considering whether to hire Redgrave, he and his partners were concerned about losing support from foundations and subscribers, having difficulty selling tickets, and dealing with possible physical disruptions. These are factors that result from the community response to Redgrave's political views. They are the same factors that apparently motivated the BSO to cancel its contract with Redgrave and are not the result of that cancellation. Thus, one possibly could infer from Mann's testimony that the BSO cancellation was not a proximate cause of the damage suffered by Redgrave in being denied the part in Heartbreak House.

Mann also testified, however, that he and his partners were affected by the BSO cancellation because the BSO was a premier arts organization and was dependent on the same type of support as Circle in the Square. A jury reasonably could infer that the BSO's cancellation did more than just highlight for Mann the potential problems that hiring Redgrave would cause but was actually a cause of Mann's decision, perhaps because Mann's theater support was similar to that of the BSO or because Mann felt influenced to follow the example of a "premier arts organization." Because this is a possible inference that a jury could draw from Mann's testimony, we defer to that inference. We therefore find that Redgrave presented sufficient evidence to prove consequential damages of $12,000, the fee arrangement contemplated by Mann for Redgrave's appearance in Heartbreak House, minus expenses she personally would have incurred had she appeared in the play.

[The remainder of the court's opinion, as well as the dissenting opinion of Circuit Judge Bownes, is omitted.]

PACITTI v. MACY'S
193 F.3d 766 (3d Cir. 1999)

ALITO, Circuit Judge.

Stella and Joseph Pacitti, on behalf of their daughter, Joanna Pacitti ("plaintiffs"), appeal the District Court's grant of summary judgment in favor of Macy's East, Inc. ("Macy's") on their state-law contract and tort claims arising from Macy's role as promoter and host of "Macy's Search for Broadway's New 'Annie'" (the "Search"). For the reasons that follow, we reverse on both grounds and remand for further proceedings.

I.

In May 1996, the producers of "Annie," the Classic Annie Production Limited Partnership (the "producers"), and Macy's, a retail department store chain, entered into an agreement under which Macy's agreed to sponsor the "Annie 20th Anniversary Talent Search." Specifically, Macy's agreed to promote the event and to host the auditions at its stores in the following locations: New York City, Boston, Atlanta, Miami, and King of Prussia, Pennsylvania. The producers agreed to select one finalist from each regional store to compete in a final audition at Macy's Herald Square store in New York City. The producers also agreed to offer the winner of the final audition "a contract for that role to appear in the 20th Anniversary Production of Annie..., subject to good faith negotiations and in accordance with standard Actors' Equity Production Contract guidelines" (the "standard actors' equity contract").

The Actors' Equity Association requires producers to attach its standard "Agreement and Rules Governing Employment under the Production Contract" to "all contracts where production is bonded as a Bus and Truck Tour." As we discuss below, that contract provides, among other things, that the producer retains the authority to replace the actor at any time so long as the actor is compensated through the term of the contract.

Macy's publicized the Search in newspapers and in its stores in the five regional locations. All of the promotional materials referred to the event as "Macy's Search for Broadway's New 'Annie.'" Plaintiffs learned of the Search from an advertisement in the Philadelphia Inquirer that stated, in pertinent part:

> If you are a girl between 7 and 12 years old and 4'6" or under, the starring role in this 20th Anniversary Broadway production and national tour could be yours! Just get your hands on an application...and bring it to the audition at Macy's King of Prussia store.... Annie's director/lyricist...will pick the lucky actress for final callbacks...at Macy's Herald Square. Annie goes on the road this fall and opens on Broadway Spring 1997.

In June 1996, Joanna, then eleven years old, and her mother picked up an application at the King of Prussia store. The application form announced:

> Annie, America's most beloved musical[,] and Macy's, the world's largest store, are conducting a talent search for a new "Annie" to star in the 20th Anniversary Broadway production and national Tour of Annie....

The reverse side of the application form contained the "Official Rules [of] Macy's Search for Broadway's New 'Annie.'" In addition to explaining the two-part audition process, the official rules provided, in relevant part:

> 1. All participants must be accompanied by a parent or legal guardian and must bring completed application forms to one of the Macy's audition locations...and be prepared to audition....
>
> 2. The "Annie" selected at the "Annie-Off-Final Callback" will be required to work with a trained dog. The tour commences in Fall 1996, with a Broadway opening tentatively scheduled for Spring 1997, [and] with a post-Broadway tour to follow....
>
> 6. [Y]ou and your parent or legal guardian are responsible for your own conduct, and hereby release Macy's...and the Producers...from any liability to or with regard to the participants and/or her parent or legal guardian with respect to the audition(s)....
>
> 8. All determinations made by the Producers or their designated judges are being made at their sole discretion and each such determination is final.

Unlike Macy's contract with the producers, neither the official rules nor any of the promotional materials included a provision informing the participants that the winner of the Search would receive only the opportunity to enter into a standard actors' equity contract with the producers.

Joanna and her mother signed the official rules and proceeded to the initial audition at the King of Prussia store. Macy's publicized the event by placing balloons, signs, pins, and other promotional materials advertising "Macy's Search for Broadway's New 'Annie'" throughout the store. After auditioning hundreds of "Annie" hopefuls, the producers selected Joanna as the regional finalist. In a press release, Macy's announced Joanna's success to the public: "One in Ten She'll Be a Star!!! Macy's Brings Local Girl One Step Closer Towards 'Tomorrow' to Become Broadway's New 'Annie.'" The press release further provided:

> Philadelphia's own, twelve year-old Joanna Pacitti, will join nine other talented girls for a final audition to cast the title role in the 20th Anniversary produc-

tion of the classic Tony Award-winning musical, Annie, coming to Broadway this season.... Ten finalists, most of whom were selected from over two thousand "Annie" hopefuls..., will vie for the chance to become Broadway's new "Annie."

At the producers' expense, Joanna and her mother traveled to New York City for Joanna to participate in the "Annie-Off-Final Call Back" at Macy's Herald Square store. After auditioning for two days, the producers selected Joanna to star as "Annie" in the 20th Anniversary Broadway production. Again, Macy's announced Joanna's success to the public, referring to her as "Broadway's New 'Annie.'"

Joanna and her mother met with the producers and signed an "Actors' Equity Association Standard Run-of-the-Play Production Contract." Consistent with the Actors' Equity Association's rules governing production contracts, the producers retained the right to replace Joanna with another actor at any time as long as they paid her salary through the term of her contract.

For nearly a four-month period, Joanna performed the role of "Annie" in the production's national tour. In so doing, Joanna appeared in over 100 performances and in six cities. In February 1997, approximately three weeks before the scheduled Broadway opening, the producers informed Joanna that her "services [would] no longer be needed," and she was replaced by her understudy.

On March 21, 1997, plaintiffs filed suit against Macy's in Pennsylvania state court, alleging breach of contract and the following tort claims: (1) fraudulent misrepresentation, (2) equitable estoppel, (3) public policy tort, (4) breach of implied covenant of good faith and fair dealing, and (5) punitive damages. In particular, plaintiffs alleged that Macy's failed to deliver the prize it had offered, i.e., the starring role of "Annie" on Broadway, and that Macy's knew it could not award this prize but promoted its ability to do so nonetheless. Macy's subsequently removed the suit to federal district court based on diversity.

Macy's then moved for summary judgment, contending that it did not deprive Joanna of any prize she had been promised and that her rights were limited by the terms of her contract with the producers. In support of its motion, Macy's proffered, among other things, its contract with the producers, which, as explained above, specified that the successful contestant would receive only the opportunity to enter into a standard actors' equity contract with the producers.

The District Court granted summary judgment in favor of Macy's. See Pacitti v. Macy's, No. Civ. A. 97-2557, 1998 WL 512938 (E.D.Pa. Aug.18, 1998). Addressing plaintiffs' breach of contract claim, the District Court concluded that the contract was unambiguous and capable of only one reasonable interpretation—i.e., that Macy's offered only an audition for the opportunity to enter into a standard actors' equity contract with the producers for the title role in "Annie." Therefore, the Court rejected plaintiffs' contention that Macy's offered Joanna a guaranteed Broadway opening, and the Court concluded:

> Plaintiffs received the benefit of their bargain by being offered a contract with the Producers for the "Annie" role, in exchange for Ms. Pacitti participating in "Macy's Search for Broadway's New Annie." When the Producers offered a contract to Plaintiffs consistent with the terms of the Official Rules[,] any possible obligation Macy's had to Plaintiffs was fully met.

After rejecting plaintiffs' breach of contract claim, the District Court turned to their tort claims. Reasoning that each cause of action was predicated upon the assertion that

Macy's offered Joanna the role of "Annie" on Broadway, and concluding that Macy's made no such representation, the District Court granted Macy's motion for summary judgment on these claims as well. Plaintiffs then took this appeal.

II.
A.

We turn first to plaintiffs' argument that the District Court erred in granting summary judgment in favor of Macy's on the breach of contract claim. We exercise plenary review over a grant of summary judgment and apply the same legal standard used by the District Court. See Hullett v. Towers, Perrin, Forster & Crosby, Inc., 38 F.3d 107, 111 (3d Cir.1994). In so doing, we evaluate the evidence in the light most favorable to the nonmoving party and draw all reasonable inferences in that party's favor. We conclude that the District Court erred.

Under the law of Pennsylvania, "[t]he promoter of a [prize-winning] contest, by making public the conditions and rules of the contest, makes an offer, and if before the offer is withdrawn another person acts upon it, the promoter is bound to perform his promise." Cobaugh v. Klick-Lewis, Inc., 385 Pa.Super. 587, 561 A.2d 1248, 1249 (Pa.Super.1989) (quoting Annotation, Private rights and remedies growing out of prize-winning contests, 87 A.L.R.2d 649, 661).

Here, the parties entered into an enforceable contract under Pennsylvania law. Macy's offered girls the opportunity of becoming "Broadway's New 'Annie'" by participating in and winning the auditions, and Joanna participated in and won the auditions. Therefore, the dispute in this appeal relates to the parties' interpretation of that contract and, in particular, to the question whether the District Court properly found that the contract is unambiguous.

A contract is ambiguous if it is capable of more than one reasonable interpretation. If the contract as a whole is susceptible to more than one reading, the factfinder resolves the matter. On the other hand, where it is unambiguous and can be interpreted only one way, the court interprets the contract as a matter of law.

In determining whether a contract is ambiguous, the court reads the contract in the context in which it was made. Therefore, to determine the parties' intentions, the court may consider, among other things, "the words of the contract, the alternative meaning suggested by counsel, and the nature of the objective evidence to be offered in support of that meaning." Hullett, 38 F.3d at 111.

In this case, the District Court concluded that the contract was unambiguous and capable of only one reasonable interpretation—i.e., that Macy's offered only an audition for the opportunity to enter into a standard actors' equity contract with the producers for the title role in "Annie." See Pacitti v. Macy's, No. Civ. A. 97-2557, 1998 WL 512938, at *3-4 (E.D.Pa. Aug. 18, 1998). In reaching this conclusion, the Court noted that the official rules repeatedly referred to the promotion as an "audition," as opposed to a "contest," and vested "sole discretion" in the producers to make final determinations. Hence, the District Court found that "Plaintiffs could not reasonably have relied upon Macy's as the selector of 'Annie' or as a controller of the Producers," id., and that "it was obvious that Macy's was promoting auditions for the benefit of the Annie Producers." Id. at *4. The District Court also found that plaintiffs "knew that while Macy's was promoting the search, it was not the entity that would be contracting with the new 'Annie.'" Id. at *3. Rather, the District Court noted, plaintiffs "wholly expected" to sign a standard actors' equity contract with the producers and, according to the Court, their expectation is evidenced by the fact that they executed such a contract after Joanna won the Search. See id. The Court explained further:

> The contract which she signed with the Producers did not guarantee her that she would open on Broadway, but instead considered her to be like every other actor in "Annie" who had won their role through an audition process but could be replaced at the Producers' discretion pursuant to the standard equity contract.

Id. Therefore, the District Court rejected plaintiffs' contention that Macy's offered Joanna a guaranteed Broadway opening, see id. at *4, and the Court concluded:

> Plaintiffs received the benefit of their bargain by being offered a contract with the Producers for the "Annie" role, in exchange for Ms. Pacitti participating in "Macy's Search for Broadway's New Annie." When the Producers offered a contract to Plaintiffs consistent with the terms of the Official Rules[,] any possible obligation Macy's had to Plaintiffs was fully met.

Id.

Applying the standards discussed above, we conclude that the District Court erred in determining that the contract was capable of only one reasonable interpretation. Plaintiffs' interpretation— that Macy's offered the prize of performing as "Annie" on Broadway for at least some period—is a reasonable alternative to that of the District Court.

The official rules and promotional materials referred to the promotion as "Macy's Search for Broadway's New 'Annie.'" The official rules provided that the producers and Macy's were "conducting a talent search for the new 'Annie' to star in the 20th Anniversary Broadway production," and the advertisement in the Philadelphia Inquirer promised that "[t]he starring role in this 20th Anniversary Broadway Production and National Tour could be yours!" From these assertions, one reasonably could conclude that Macy's offered the winner of the Search the prize of starring as "Annie" on Broadway. In addition, the use of the word "audition," as opposed to "contest," in the official rules does not make plaintiffs' interpretation unreasonable. As plaintiffs assert:

> [T]he word 'audition' refers to the process a contestant must undergo before she can 'win' the prize.... It follows, one would think, the girl selected after the 'final audition' has won something more than an 'audition.'

Moreover, it is not unreasonable to conclude that Macy's had the ability to offer the winner of the Search the starring role on Broadway. The official rules provided that:

> Annie, America's most beloved musical[,] and Macy's, the world's largest store, are conducting a talent search for a new "Annie" to star in the 20th Anniversary Broadway production and national Tour of Annie....

That passage suggests that Macy's and the producers jointly promoted and hosted the Search. It does not indicate any relative imbalance of authority in favor of the producers. Nor do we believe that the clause vesting "sole discretion" in the producers supports only the interpretation that the producers were "the sole determiners of the Annie role." Pacitti, 1998 WL 512938, at *3. Rather, that clause can be interpreted more narrowly as only restricting Macy's from selecting the winner of the auditions.

Further, Macy's at no point revealed—either through its printed materials or other means—that the winner of the Search would receive only the opportunity to sign a standard actors' equity contract with the producers. Nor do the facts suggest that plaintiffs—none of whom was a member of the Actors' Equity Association—had any knowledge greater than that provided by Macy's. We do not believe that Macy's role was so "obvious" that it need not have limited its offer to public, and we find it telling that Macy's contract with the producers contained qualifications on the prize to be offered. Therefore, we conclude that it was reasonable for plaintiffs to believe that Macy's offered the starring role of "Annie" on Broadway.

We reach this conclusion even though plaintiffs executed a standard actors' equity contract with the producers. Courts may consider the subsequent actions of the contracting parties to ascertain the parties' intentions and resolve any ambiguities. See Department of Transp. v. Mosites Constr. Co., 90 Pa.Cmwlth. 33, 494 A.2d 41, 43 (Pa.Commw.1985); see also In re Estate of Herr, 400 Pa. 90, 161 A.2d 32, 34 (1960). Joanna's contract with the producers, however, does not demonstrate plainly and unambiguously that when plaintiffs contracted with Macy's, they "wholly expected" to execute a standard actors' equity contract with the producers.

For these reasons, we hold that the contractual language is ambiguous, and its interpretation should be left to the factfinder for resolution. Accordingly, the District Court erred in concluding that Macy's is entitled to judgment as a matter of law.

B.

Macy's also contends that plaintiffs' claims are barred by the express release in the official rules. The official rules provide, in pertinent part:

> [Y]ou and your parent or legal guardian are responsible for your own conduct, and hereby release Macy's...and the Producers...from any liability to or with regard to the participants and/or her parent or legal guardian with respect to the audition(s).

That paragraph simply releases Macy's from liability "with respect to the audition(s)." It does not allow Macy's to escape liability arising from this action. We therefore reject Macy's contention.

C.

With respect to the tort causes of action, plaintiffs maintain that the District Court erred in granting summary judgment. As noted above, the District Court dismissed these claims because it had rejected the predicate upon which each claim was based, i.e., that Macy's offered the successful participant the role of "Annie" on Broadway. See Pacitti, 1998 WL 512938, at *4. Because we conclude that the contract reasonably may be interpreted to make such an offer, we reverse on these claims as well and remand for further proceedings.

STAFFORD, Senior District Judge, dissenting.

I cannot agree that the district judge erred in granting summary judgment in favor of Macy's. Macy's offered Joanna Pacitti the opportunity of starring in the 20th Anniversary Broadway production and national tour of "Annie." Joanna Pacitti received that opportunity. She auditioned for the part of Annie; she was selected by the show's producers to play the part of Annie; and she, in fact, played the part of Annie, performing in over one hundred performances in six cities during the production's national tour. She did not, however, appear on Broadway because the producers decided to replace her before the Broadway opening.

The district court concluded, and I agree, that Joanna Pacitti received the benefit of her bargain with Macy's. Because I do not believe that her contract with Macy's was subject to the interpretation urged by Plaintiffs, I must respectfully dissent.

HARRY ROGERS THEATRICAL ENTERPRISES, INC. v. COMSTOCK

232 N.Y.S. 1 (App. Div. 1928)

FINCH, Justice.

The question presented by this appeal is the right to an injunction pendente lite enjoining a theatrical performer from rendering services to another than his employer and enjoining the third party from so employing him. The injunction was denied at Special Term.

The plaintiff corporation or its assignor had a five-year contract, starting in 1923, with the defendant Comstock, professionally known as 'Billy House.' Before this contract expired and in 1927, a new contract for four years, or until 1931, was entered into by the plaintiff with the defendant Comstock. Defendant Shubert and defendant Shubert Theatrical Corporation wished to obtain the services of Comstock for a musical show which was in preparation. Defendant Shubert, together with one Lyons, the booking agent of Shubert, saw Rogers for the purpose of obtaining a release of Comstock or a transfer of Rogers' contract to Shubert. After various negotiations, the proposed deal fell through, and then Shubert engaged Comstock. Shubert now attempts to justify this action and urges various grounds of defense.

The defendants urge as their first ground of defense that no written contract existed between the plaintiff and the defendant Comstock. The record shows that the existence of the written contract is clear, and the attempt to raise an issue as to its existence is wellnigh ludicrous.

The principal item of the second ground of defense urged by the defendants is an alleged estoppel, based upon a written offer by the plaintiff's predecessor to release Comstock upon certain terms. This offer was declined, and it is elementary that no estoppel can be based thereon. Moreover, the making and declination of this offer, together with other evidence in this record, afforded ample notice to the defendants that the defendants were not proceeding in accordance with the rights of the plaintiff, but in direct violation thereof.

The third ground of defense urged by the respondents is that there was nothing unique, special, or extraordinary about the services of the defendant Comstock, but that said services were ordinary and could easily be replaced. Therefore, urge the respondents, these services fall within the principle that ordinary contracts for personal services are not enforceable in equity (Lawrence v. Dixey, 119 App. Div. 295, 104 N.Y.S. 516), and that damages at law afford an adequate remedy. The record is replete with the usual conclusory opinion affidavits, pro and con, alleging and denying the uniqueness of the services. Facts when present, however, are always more persuasive than opinions.

In the case at bar the contract whose existence is attacked admits the services of Comstock to be unique and extraordinary. While such recital is not controlling, it reflects upon the affidavit later made by Comstock, when his interest was to the contrary, swearing that his services were not unique. Next we have the uncontroverted fact that the ability of Comstock is regarded as unique upon the Albee-Keith circuit and that a substitute will not be accepted. Hence in this well-known vaudeville office Comstock cannot be replaced. Again, Comstock is now admittedly receiving a salary of $1,000 a week, which, in his work, is very large and compares most favorably with that received by the leaders in the scientific, artistic, and political world. In Winter Garden Co. v. Smith, 282 F. 166, where two plaintiffs were to receive a joint salary of $1,100 a week, the Circuit Court of Appeals of the Second Circuit said: 'When, therefore, actors such as these have been successful for many years because of individual characteristics, and command salaries of a size rarely known in the liberal arts and sciences, their peculiar ability in the field in which they perform is almost res ipsa loquitur.'

It seems unnecessary to go further with a recital of facts when the defendant Shubert, who knew Comstock was under a contract with the plaintiff, was willing to risk a lawsuit and pay $1,000 a week to secure the services of Comstock. The conclusion is therefore sustained that defendant Comstock has that personality which denotes the unusual and unique artist and enables him to pick up the attention of an audience and hold it interested, amused, or in pathos until released. Where, therefore, the services of the actor are shown to be unusual, unique, or extraordinary, and that the damage to the plaintiff will be irreparable and unascertainable, the latter may enjoin the performer from appearing elsewhere during the period of his contract, and, even though a negative covenant not to appear elsewhere may be lacking, such will be implied and enforced not only against those who are parties to the contract, but also restraining third parties from doing those acts which induce and continue the breach. This has been the law since the well-known early case of Lumley v. Wagner, 1 De G. M. & G. 604, and has been repeatedly applied in this court and elsewhere. Shubert Theatrical Co. v. Rath (C. C. A.) 271 F. 827; Shubert Theatrical Co. v. Gallagher, 206 App. Div. 514, 201 N.Y.S. 577; Pomeroy on Specific Performance (3d Ed.), § 24.

It is obvious that a court of equity is governed by principles of law impartially applied to the facts in the particular case, and that the facts, when accurately and truthfully ascertained, are alike masters of bench and bar. If the time shall ever come when a court of equity must stand helplessly by while unique and unusual theatrical performers may be induced to breach contracts with impunity, except for such damages as a jury may see fit to award at some distant date, theatrical corporations will find their business hampered by intolerable conditions. It follows that the order appealed from should be reversed with $10 costs and disbursements, and the motion granted with $10 costs.

Order reversed with $10 costs and disbursements, and motion granted with $10 costs. Settle order on notice. All concur.

Notes

1. Despite the lack of court rulings, the issue of "color-blind" casting, discussed in the piece by Chen, has generated substantial commentary. *See, e.g.,* Michael J. Frank, *Justifiable Discrimination in the News and Entertainment Industries: Does Title VII Need a Race or Color BFOQ?,* 35 U.S.F. L. Rev. 473 (2001); Martha L. Minow, *From Class Actions to Miss Saigon: The Concept of Representation in the Law,* 39 Clev. St. L. Rev. 269 (1991); Heekyung Esther Kim, Note, *Race as a Hiring/Casting Criterion: If Laurence Olivier was Rejected for the Role of Othello in Othello, Would He Have A Valid Title VII Claim?,* 20 Hastings Comm/Ent L.J. 397 (1998); Lois L. Krieger, Note, *"Miss Saigon" and Missed Opportunity: Artistic Freedom, Employment Discrimination, and Casting for Cultural Identity in the Theater,* 43 Syracuse L. Rev. 839 (1992); Mabel Ng, Note, *Miss Saigon: Casting for Equality on an Unequal Stage,* 14 Hastings Comm/Ent L.J. 451 (1992). It also has led to various initiatives, such as the Non-Traditional Casting Project (www.ntcp.org), which seek to increase theater opportunities for minority and disabled performers.

2. To ensure that George Gershwin's effort to portray the agony of the African-American experience is not compromised, his estate will not authorize productions of

his famous musical, "Porgy and Bess," unless the show is performed by an all-black cast. As a result, the piece is rarely performed and the estate has been labeled racist by some. *See* Anthony Tommasini, *All-Black Cast for 'Porgy'? That Ain't Necessarily So*, N.Y. Times, Mar. 20, 2002, at E1. If you were Gershwin's executor, would you keep or drop the requirement?

3. Was Henry Goodman too British to play Max Bialystock? Was Lynn Redgrave too controversial to be offered a part in "Heartbreak House"? Obviously, these are difficult artistic questions, and a wrong answer can result in a show losing millions of dollars. Given this fact, should courts ever be allowed to second guess a producer's decision to not hire or to fire a particular actor or actress? If so, under what circumstances and according to what standards?

The difficulty of finding just the right person to step into Nathan Lane's role in "The Producers" has generated much serious commentary (as well as much hand-wringing among those responsible for the show), but in an unusual twist it also has provided a story line for HBO's smash comedy series *Curb Your Enthusiasm*:

> For his fourth season Mr. David has introduced a new leitmotif: Larry is cast as Max Bialystock in the Broadway production of "The Producers." Mel Brooks sees him sing "Swanee" at a karaoke party in Los Angeles and is instantly convinced that Larry, who cannot sing, dance or act, is perfect for the part.
>
> Larry is easily persuaded, and his misplaced self-confidence is only one of the insufferable traits that vex his co-star, Ben Stiller, who is playing Leo Bloom. Their strained relationship in rehearsals and at social gatherings begins to mirror the tensions of the characters they portray in the musical.

Alessandra Stanley, *Sexy Women Out, Cantankerous Guy In*, N.Y. Times, Jan. 2, 2004, at E1. For a further look at how difficult casting a replacement can be, *see, e.g.*, Jesse Green, *Passing the Bra: The Search for a New Edna*, N.Y. Times, Feb. 15, 2004, § 2, at 1 (pointing out that in addition to "The Producers," a number of other recent shows have had trouble replacing their original leads, including "Hairspray" (Harvey Fierstein), "Nine" (Antonio Banderas), and "The Boy From Oz" (Hugh Jackman)).

4. Following the reinstatement of her claims, Joanna Pacitti accepted a multi-million dollar settlement from Macy's. *See* Ward Morehouse III & Bill Hoffmann, *Sacked 'Annie' a Millionaire as Macy's Settles*, N.Y. Post, May 3, 2001, at 12. In December 2003, the producers of the musical "Rent" organized a similar talent search contest using the internet. *See* Leonard Jacobs, *'Rent' Launches Web Casting Contest*, Back Stage, Dec. 12, 2003, at 6. Mindful of the *Pacitti* case, the contest's fine print "says that the sponsor of the contest 'reserves the right to cancel' the search 'and shall be under no obligation to award the prizes.'" *Id.*

5. In discussing Pacitti's dismissal from "Annie," the Third Circuit provides little detailed information. In fact, the producers had not planned to replace her. However, when the show was still in tryouts in Boston, Pacitti came down with bronchitis and lost her voice. As a result, the producers had no choice but to call on her understudy, eight-year-old Brittany Kissinger. Although Pacitti and Kissinger were both good singers, the producers felt that Kissinger's acting was better. Kissinger ended up staying with the show for its entire six-month run on Broadway. *See Happy Anniversary! It Has Been 25 Years Since Annie's Broadway Debut*, People, Apr. 29, 2002, at 114.

6. Because of past abuses, hiring an underage performer like Pacitti now requires compliance with laws designed to protect the child's health and welfare (as well as his

or her bank account). Such casting also raises the question of whether the minor really wants to act or is simply trying to please a stagestruck parent (in which case the production almost certainly will run into problems at some point). For a further discussion, *see, e.g.,* Erika D. Munro, Note, *Under Age, Under Contract, and Under Protected: An Overview of the Administration and Regulation of Contracts with Minors in the Entertainment Industry in New York and California*, 20 Colum.-VLA J.L. & Arts 553 (1996), and Erica Siegel, Note, *When Parental Interference Goes Too Far: The Need for Adequate Protection of Child Entertainers and Athletes*, 18 Cardozo Arts & Ent. L.J. 427 (2000).

7. In addition to underage performers, the show "Annie" also requires a dog to play the part of Sandy (Annie's companion). Indeed, the original production of "Annie" marked the first time a Broadway musical included an animal in a lead role and helped launch the career of William Berloni, now the leading trainer of stage animals. *See further William Berloni Theatrical Animals,* at www.theatricalanimals.com (explaining that Berloni-trained animals have appeared in such shows as "Anything Goes," "Camelot," "Dinner at Eight," "Gypsy," "Oliver!," and "The Wiz"), and David Cuthbert, *No Show's a Dog When Bill Berloni Works on It*, New Orleans Times-Picayune, Feb. 13, 2003, at 11 (Living).

Using an animal in a show raises a number of issues. First, all applicable federal, state, and local animal welfare laws must be followed. *See generally Haviland v. Butz*, 543 F.2d 169 (D.C. Cir.), *cert. denied*, 429 U.S. 832 (1976) (interpreting and applying the Animal Welfare Act of 1966, 7 U.S.C. §§ 2131-2159). Second, finding and training a suitable animal often is quite difficult—the animal must look right for the part, be able to act, and not be frightened by crowds, loud noise, music, bright lights, or sudden motions. Third, a comfort level must be established between the animal and the human members of the cast. For a further discussion, *see* Julie E. Washington, *Unleashing Doggy Drama: Canines Jumping Into Theater Careers With Parts in Productions*, Clev. Plain Dealer, Feb. 12, 2001, at 1E.

8. The court's decision in *Comstock* is an application of the well-known rule of *Lumley v. Wagner*—the famous 1852 case involving opera singer Johanna Wagner—which states that an artist with special skills cannot be made to perform but can be enjoined from working for others. Despite its venerable pedigree and universal acceptance, *Lumley* has been criticized for being both misogynistic and punitive. *See* Sharon F. Carton, *Damning with Fulsome Praise: Assessing the Uniqueness of an Artist or Performer as a Condition to Enjoin Performance of Personal Service Contracts in Entertainment Law*, 5 Vill. Sports & Ent. L.J. 197 (1998) (asserting that employers seek to have the rule applied even to mediocre talents), and Lea S. VanderVelde, *The Gendered Origins of the Lumley Doctrine: Binding Men's Consciences and Women's Fidelity*, 101 Yale L.J. 775 (1992) (showing that the rule was developed at a time when acting was one of the few professions open to women and was meant to reassert the dominance of men).

9. It often is said that actors and actresses live in their own world. Whether or not this is so, it is true that, like any profession, they have their own slang (such as calling stages "boards" and scripts "sides"), phrases (most notably, "the show must go on," "give my regards to Broadway," and "break a leg"), traditions (as in the "gypsy robe," a good luck garment that is passed from musical to musical before each opening night), watering holes (including the legendary Sardi's in New York), and trade papers (the two most important of which are "Back Stage" and "Variety"). For a further discussion, *see, e.g.,* Jeffrey Denman, *A Year with The Producers* (2002); Larry Garrison & Wallace Wang, *Breaking Into Acting for Dummies* (2002); Mari Lyn Henry & Lynne Rogers,

How to be a Working Actor: The Insider's Guide to Finding Jobs in Theater, Film, and Television (4th ed. 2000); Vincent Sardi, Jr. & Thomas Edward West, *Off the Wall at Sardi's* (1991). *See also* www.erieplayhouse.org/information/code_of_ethics.htm (code of ethics for theater performers).

Problem 11

A musical's grand finale calls for the female lead to jump from a high platform and be caught by the male lead. Halfway through the show's run, the male lead left the company. The female lead, convinced his replacement lacked the physical strength and acrobatic experience needed to catch her properly, refused to go on with the show. As a result, she was fired for insubordination. If she sues for improper termination, how should the court rule? *See Makletzova v. Diaghileff*, 116 N.E. 231 (Mass. 1917).

C. PAY AND BENEFITS

IN RE HIMES
2001 WL 34076414 (Bankr. C.D. Ill. 2001)

PERKINS, Bankruptcy Judge.

The Debtor, Franklin John Himes (DEBTOR), brings these two adversary proceedings against the Illinois Student Assistance Commission (ISAC) and the Educational Credit Management Corporation (ECMC), seeking a determination that the student loans he incurred while pursuing an undergraduate degree, a Master's degree and a Doctorate degree are dischargeable debts in his Chapter 7 bankruptcy because excepting these debts from discharge will impose an undue hardship on the DEBTOR.

The DEBTOR was born December 31, 1950, and at the time of trial was fifty (50) years of age. After graduating from high school, the DEBTOR attended the University of Illinois from 1969 through 1974, majoring in theater. He became so wrapped up in the theater that he neglected his course work and failed to obtain a degree. Anxious to begin an acting career, he headed to Los Angeles, California, in January of 1974, where he took odd jobs to support himself and worked for free in the theater in the evenings.

From 1981 to 1983, in fulfillment of his father's last wish, [the DEBTOR] attended the University of Southern California to make up the credits he needed to obtain his Bachelor of Fine Arts in theater from the University of Illinois. To finance those studies, the DEBTOR borrowed $500, which he later paid off, and also obtained a loan of $5,000 from [ECMC] in September of 1981.

Broke and discouraged, the DEBTOR filed a Chapter 7 bankruptcy in Los Angeles, California, in October, 1985. The DEBTOR'S attorney advised him that the [ECMC] loan was probably discharged by the bankruptcy and that if he did not hear anything from them he could safely assume that it was. This advice appears to have been erroneous. Under the version of Section 523(a)(8) in effect in 1985, the $5,000 [ECMC] student loan would have been nondischargeable since it was obtained within five years of the petition date unless the debt was determined to be dischargeable as imposing an undue hardship on the DEBTOR. 11 U.S.C. §523(a)(8) (1985). There is no allegation or evidence that a determination of dischargeability was made by the California Bankruptcy Court and both parties have proceeded on the assumption that the ECMC student loan was not discharged in the 1985 case.

Even after his 1985 bankruptcy, the DEBTOR experienced little success in the employment arena. During the fifteen years the DEBTOR stayed in Los Angeles, his work as an extra led to an occasional "hand modeling" assignment, but his theater jobs were scarce and never lasted more than three weeks.

In October of 1989, the DEBTOR left California, and, after living for a short time with his mother, went to Chicago to try his luck there. Unfortunately, that move did not pan out, as he was never hired for any acting jobs. After seventeen years of fruitless efforts to get into acting, the DEBTOR reluctantly redirected his career aspirations toward teaching theater at the college level. In the spring of 1991, he entered the master's program at Western Illinois University to obtain a Master of Fine Arts in theater, taking out [a] student loan [from ISAC] in the amount of $46,172.50. He did not complete that program, but transferred to the communications and broadcasting department, in hopes that his job prospects would be brighter. He received a Master of Arts degree in Communications and Broadcasting in 1994. On the advice of others in his field, the DEBTOR entered the Ph.D. program at Bowling Green State University, and earned a doctorate in theater in 1997, taking out an additional student loan [from ISAC] in the amount of $35,453. Equipped with this degree, the DEBTOR thought he could teach theater at the university level.

To the DEBTOR'S surprise and chagrin, despite a sincere and diligent job search, he remained unemployed. Lacking an agent, the DEBTOR no longer sought professional acting jobs, but he wrote many famous directors and actors, including Steven Spielberg and Tony Randall, pleading for an opportunity to demonstrate his abilities. The DEBTOR also purchased publications listing job opportunities in higher education and he pursued each plausible prospect, submitting his curriculum vitae. In addition to jobs in the theater and universities, the DEBTOR applied for factory jobs, openings in grocery stores and other unskilled positions. He was often turned down as overqualified. One of his academic advisers at Bowling Green State University cautioned him that he would not likely find work at his age (he was then in his late 40's) because the available jobs were being filled by younger persons, particularly minorities and females. During these hard times, he applied for and obtained deferments of his ISAC student loans. On Feb. 6, 1999, the loans were consolidated into a "SMART LOAN," with an "income sensitive repayment" option. The term of the note was thirty (30) years.

The DEBTOR'S one break came in the summer of 1999 when a former professor from the communications and broadcasting department at Western Illinois University retired and suggested that he fill her position for a year while the university sought a permanent replacement. The DEBTOR was offered and accepted the position, earning $30,000 during the 1999/2000 academic year. Though the DEBTOR applied for the permanent position, he was not hired because he did not have the qualifications the department was seeking. The DEBTOR learned of that rejection in the early months of 2000, at the same time his deferments of the ISAC loan ran out. The DEBTOR'S request that the payments on the student loans be postponed was denied, but the DEBTOR negotiated a reduction in payments from $600 to $133 per month. These two events triggered the DEBTOR'S Chapter 7 filing on Feb. 7, 2000, and this adversary proceeding seeking a determination that his student loans are dischargeable as an "undue hardship" under Section 523(a)(8) of the Bankruptcy Code. 11 U.S.C. §523(a)(8). As of the date the bankruptcy was filed, the balance due ISAC, with accumulated interest, was $93,075.98, and the balance due ECMC was approximately $14,364.00.

Since the filing of the bankruptcy and the termination of his position at Western Illinois University, the DEBTOR has continued his search for a suitable position. These recent efforts have also been unsuccessful. The DEBTOR'S unemployment insurance ran out in January 2001, and the DEBTOR currently has no income at all. During the final months of his job at Western Illinois University, after filing bankruptcy, the DEBTOR managed to accumulate some savings and he has been using those funds to live. He is down to his last $2,600. The DEBTOR'S current expenses are limited. In addition to paying $350 for rent, the DEBTOR'S monthly expenses include $213 for a car payment, $35 for phone bill, and $32 for car insurance. Though the DEBTOR is currently in good health, he has no health insurance. The DEBTOR testified that he has signed up for a subsistence program which will cover his utility bills.

This Court is bound by the Seventh Circuit's decision in In re Roberson, 999 F.2d 1132 (7th Cir.1993), which, like the majority of courts addressing this issue, has adopted the three-part "Brunner" test. This test was set forth by the Second Circuit in Brunner v. New York State Higher Education Services Corp., 831 F.2d 395 (2d Cir.1987). This test requires the debtor to demonstrate:

1. That the debtor cannot maintain, based on current income and expenses, a "minimal" standard of living for [himself] and [his] dependents if forced to repay the loans.

2. That additional circumstances exist indicating that this state of affairs is likely to persist for a significant portion of the repayment period of the student loans.

3. That the debtor has made good faith efforts to repay the loans.

The DEBTOR bears the burden of proving by a preponderance of the evidence that repayment would constitute an undue hardship. Roberson, supra.

To meet the first hurdle of the Brunner test, the DEBTOR must show that he cannot repay the student loans while maintaining a minimal standard of living. The focus of this inquiry is the DEBTOR'S current financial situation, as it exists at the time of trial. The DEBTOR is currently unemployed with no immediate prospects of employment, either in his field or in some other line of work. The DEBTOR'S unemployment benefits have run out. The DEBTOR cannot meet his basic expenses. An unemployed debtor with no other means of income unquestionably satisfies the first prong of the Brunner test. In re Young, 225 B.R. 312 (Bankr.E.D.Pa.1998).

Notwithstanding the DEBTOR'S present plight, ISAC argues that the first prong is not met, contending that repayment options are available which would, given those circumstances, require no payment to be made at all. ISAC referred to the "Income Contingent Repayment Plan," a deferral program devised by the Department of Education to meet the needs of debtors with minimal income. Under this program, the Department of Education reviews the debtor's income on an annual basis to determine whether the debtor has the ability to make any payments. If a debtor's income is below the federal poverty guidelines, no payment is required to be made. If the debtor's income exceeds that level, the poverty guideline is subtracted from the debtor's adjusted gross income to determine the debtor's "discretionary income" and payments are fixed at twenty percent of this amount. 34 C.F.R. §685.209(a)(2)(ii).

In this Court's view, ISAC'S suppositions with regard to the DEBTOR'S qualification for and future participation in the income contingent plan are just that and as such, they beg the issue. The first prong of the Brunner test requires simply that the DEBTOR show that he cannot, given his current circumstances, repay the student loans if forced to do so and maintain a minimal standard of living. In re Thomsen, 234 B.R. 506 (Bankr.D.Mont.1999). The focus is on the debtor's ability to pay, not the lender's willingness to grant deferments or otherwise work with the debtor.

If it were otherwise, the logical extension of ISAC'S argument would lead to the conclusion that a student loan could never constitute an undue hardship for a borrower living in poverty since borrowers with no discretionary income never have to make any payments. This Court believes that Congress did not intend for Section 523(a)(8), which expressly provides for a discharge under hardship circumstances, to be so cavalierly eviscerated by a Departmental Regulation. If nothing else, the inability to obtain a hardship discharge of a student loan because of an inexhaustible supply of deferments is contrary to the most fundamental of all bankruptcy policies: the fresh start.

Indeed, the Seventh Circuit's application of the first prong of the Brunner test focuses solely on the DEBTOR'S present ability to pay the student loans. See Roberson at 1135. Whether the DEBTOR was or was not aware of the Income Contingent Repayment Plan, or is eligible for such a program, is not relevant to the first prong of the Brunner test. As it stands now, the DEBTOR, unemployed with minimal savings, is unable to pay the student loans and still maintain a minimal standard of living. The DEBTOR has met the first prong of the Brunner test.

The more problematic issue in this case arises under the second prong of the Brunner test which requires the DEBTOR to show that his bleak financial condition is likely to exist for a significant portion of the repayment period. The term of the ISAC loan is thirty years, extending well into the DEBTOR'S golden years. No testimony or documentation was introduced by ECMC or the DEBTOR as to the repayment period of the ECMC loan. The loan was issued in 1981, nearly twenty years ago. Even if the original term of ECMC'S loan has already expired, since there is no evidence in the record of the loan's term, the Court is unable to fully evaluate Brunner's second prong with respect to the ECMC loan, and must conclude that the DEBTOR'S burden has not been met.

The DEBTOR emphasizes his futile attempts to break into stardom in California when he was armed with only an undergraduate degree in theater. This Court agrees with ISAC that the DEBTOR'S history of unemployment prior to 1991, while very unfortunate, has little bearing on the issues presently before the Court. The DEBTOR obtained his masters in 1994 and his doctorate in 1997. While the DEBTOR depicts these degrees as occasionally creating the hindrance of overqualification, this Court finds that the advanced degrees are more likely to enhance his career opportunities, perhaps significantly, in the longer run. The DEBTOR taught for a year at Western Illinois University, earning $30,000 during the academic year. Though the competition for teaching positions at the university level may be very tough, this Court believes that it would be premature to find that the DEBTOR has exhausted all reasonable possibilities of obtaining employment which would enable him to make payments on these student loans. The DEBTOR may have to lower his sights (e.g., a high school or junior college position may be more readily obtainable) and engage in a broader search. The DEBTOR is in good health and has no dependents. It is true that his age may be a detrimental factor, but the DEBTOR elected to pursue advanced degrees at that stage in his life. As the Seventh Circuit commented in Roberson:

> The government is not twisting the arms of potential students. The decision of whether or not to borrow for a college education lies with the individual; absent an expression to the contrary, the government does not guarantee the stu-

dent's future financial success. If the leveraged investment of an education does not generate the return the borrower anticipated, the student, not the taxpayers, must accept the consequences of the decision to borrow.

There is little evidence that the DEBTOR faces the kind of hurdles that render his present inability to pay near-permanent. For example, the DEBTOR suffers from no chronic, debilitating medical condition, he has no dependents, and he has a high level of education indicative of a sharp mind and a ready ability to learn and apply his knowledge. Although his age is a negative, at fifty (50) he certainly can expect to have many productive years ahead of him.

At this point, the Court cannot conclude that the DEBTOR'S current inability to obtain a position utilizing either or both of his higher degrees is likely to persist for a significant portion of the repayment period of the student loans. Because the DEBTOR failed to carry his burden as to Brunner's second prong, the student loans are not dischargeable on the basis of undue hardship at this point in time. However, the dischargeability of these student loans may be revisited in the future, if the DEBTOR'S circumstances change or, if no change for the better occurs, merely based on the passage of additional time. (The first and second prongs of the Brunner test are both time-sensitive. Even though the DEBTOR has failed to satisfy the second prong today, if his situation does not improve, that hurdle becomes easier to clear as time goes by.)

As the bankruptcy court did in Roberson, the Court has the option of ordering a deferral of the student loans. The Court finds that the following exceptional circumstances justify such a deferral:

1. The DEBTOR is presently unemployed.

2. The DEBTOR is barely maintaining a subsistence level existence.

3. The DEBTOR appears to have no non-exempt assets and is therefore "judgment-proof."

4. The consensual deferrals previously granted by ISAC have expired and ISAC has communicated an unwillingness to grant a further deferral.

5. The time which has elapsed since the DEBTOR earned his doctorate is relatively short and the degree is an advanced one in a specialized field.

6. The DEBTOR'S prior job search efforts have been limited to the university level.

7. An additional period of time during which the DEBTOR is free from collection activity, during which he may devote all of his time and energy toward finding a job, is in the best interest of both the DEBTOR and the student loan creditors.

Consistent with the Seventh Circuit's decision in Roberson, this Court will grant the DEBTOR a deferral of both student loans for a period of eighteen (18) months from the date of this Opinion, at the expiration of which the DEBTOR may reopen this proceeding to petition the Court to re-examine this issue.

Given this Court's determination that the DEBTOR failed to establish that his inability to pay the student loans without undue hardship was likely to persist for a significant portion of the repayment period of the student loans, this Court does not reach the issue of whether the DEBTOR has made a good faith effort to repay the student loans.

THIS IS ME, INC. v. TAYLOR
157 F.3d 139 (2d Cir. 1998)

JACOBS, Circuit Judge.

Actress Cicely Tyson, through her personal services corporation, plaintiff-appellant This Is Me, Inc., agreed to undertake the lead role in a Broadway production of "The Corn is Green" and in a contemplated taping of the production for television, and sues to recover unpaid fees for her services. Several contracts are arguably in issue; some are standard Actors' Equity (sometimes "Equity") form contracts, others are not; all are signed by and on behalf of various persons and entities as producers. At issue is the unpaid portion of a so-called "pay or play" guarantee of $750,000 payable if (as happened) the show closed before Tyson earned $750,000 in salary. Among the sufficiency of evidence issues are (i) whether the various contracts are sufficiently interrelated that they may be read together; (ii) whether the contractual phrase "a contract made in relation to the Play" includes a contract governing the videotaping; and (iii) who is bound in respect of the $750,000 pay or play guarantee.

Elizabeth Taylor, the actress, and Zev Bufman, the Broadway producer, formed a theater group to produce live performances of plays on the legitimate stage and video and television versions of the same plays. They chose "The Corn is Green" as their second production, and cast Cicely Tyson in the lead role. The play soon closed, and the video was never made.

This Is Me, the corporation through which Ms. Tyson provides her services, sued Taylor and Bufman (and Zev Bufman Entertainment, Inc.) under the pay or play guarantee. Plaintiff's arguments convinced the jury, which found Taylor and Bufman personally liable. The district court, however, issued judgment as a matter of law in favor of defendants on the grounds that the individual defendants were not signatories to the only contract that contained the guarantee, and that Tyson's arguments linking Taylor and Bufman to that undertaking are barred by the parol evidence rule.

We conclude that there was sufficient evidence from which the jury could find liability, and we therefore reverse. That evidence consists of the underlying and well-disclosed purpose of the enterprise to produce the play on stage as well as on videotape, the drafting history of the contracts, the contemporaneity of the undertakings, the cross-referencing between and among the contracts, and the background undertakings of the Actors' Equity rules, accepted by all the parties, that bind the individual signatories (as producers), as well as any partnership or venture controlled by them, to employment contracts.

BACKGROUND

Following a prior collaboration as producer and actor, Zev Bufman and Elizabeth Taylor decided to "put a theater group together" to produce plays on Broadway. They agreed generally that Bufman "would take care of the business end of it" and Taylor "would take care of the artistic end of it," specifically by "trying to get people to participate and become involved in the group."

Taylor and Bufman entered into a letter of intent providing that: (i) "[a]ll profits and losses will be shared equally between us;" (ii) the primary purpose of the Group was "the production of legitimate stage plays and television/film versions of such plays;" (iii) the Group would "produce three (3) plays each year;" (iv) it would be "of the essence at this time that we do not consider any play unless we are able to acquire or have an option to acquire the rights to televise such productions;" and (v) Taylor and Bufman would "be co-producers of every project" and would "each consult with the other with respect to all major decisions." Taylor testified that upon receiving the letter of intent, she scratched out the word "losses" on her copy before signing; she maintains that therefore she is not responsible for any losses. The letter of intent contemplated a more formal contract and the formation of a "new corporation" to carry out the venture, but neither eventuality came to pass.

For the Group's second project—a live production and videotape of Emlyn Williams's play, "The Corn is Green"—Bufman and Taylor decided to seek Cicely Tyson's services to star in the play. Taylor took the lead in recruiting Tyson, with whom she had worked before. In several phone calls and a lunch meeting, Taylor played a key role in reconciling creative differences between Tyson and the author of the play regarding whether use of the original screenplay would be appropriate. Throughout these discussions, Taylor referred to Bufman as her partner and noted that they were in this "50-50."

Tyson agreed to appear in the live theater production and the videotape production of "The Corn is Green," and exacted the $750,000 "pay or play" guarantee. The guarantee reflected that Tyson, who was at the height of her career, would have to turn down other opportunities in film, television, and stage, and commit nearly a year to "The Corn Is Green."

An initial contract—later superseded—addressed all the undertakings concerning the stage and videotape performances of the play. This contract (hereinafter the "superseded contract") was dated December 9, 1982, and was executed by Cicely Tyson on behalf of This Is Me and by Zev Bufman on behalf of Zev Bufman Entertainment, Inc. Ms. Tyson also signed an inducement letter to bind herself personally, which is addressed to "Zev Bufman Entertainment, Inc. d/b/a The Elizabeth Theatre Group." The obligations of the superseded contract were afterward bifurcated and expressed in two new contracts executed contemporaneously in August 1983, which provided that they were to be read together to constitute the entire agreement covering This Is Me's services in "The Corn is Green."

The first of these contracts was a standard Actors' Equity document, a run of the play contract that guaranteed Tyson's weekly salary for the Broadway run, without guaranteeing the length of the run. The producer listed on this contract was an entity called "The Corn Company" and the individual signatory was Zev Bufman.

The second of these contracts related to the video production, and contained the pay or play guarantee in the amount of the difference between $750,000 and salary paid under the run of the play contract (the "video contract"). This contract was between Zev Bufman Entertainment, Inc. and This Is Me.

Two further undertakings are potentially implicated as well, both of which arise from the efforts of Actors' Equity to protect its members from defaulting producers. [First,] it is conceded that the relationship between the actors and the producers in this production was governed by the Actors' Equity Association Agreement and Rules Governing Employment Under the Production Contract (the "Equity Agreement and Rules"). Bufman testified that "in order to put on a play in an Equity playhouse," he "had to abide by the collective bargaining agreement."

[Second,] the "Security Agreement" (also an industry standard agreement), signed by Zev Bufman, requires the producer to "promptly pay to the Actors any and all sums due," including sums due under employment agreements "made in relation to the Play," and defines "producer" broadly to "include[ ] the individual, firm, partnership or corporation or any combination thereof producing or controlling the production of said Play."

After out-of-town tryouts, "The Corn is Green" had a short run on Broadway, and its closing was unlamented by the critics. The video was never made, and Ms. Tyson received only the weekly salary payments made under the run of the play agreement.

Later, Tyson commenced an arbitration against Bufman, Taylor and Zev Bufman Entertainment, Inc. She won an award of $607,078.86 against Zev Bufman Entertainment, Inc., and at the behest of the individual defendants, agreed to permanently stay the arbitration as against Bufman and Taylor (preserving, however, the right of This Is Me to pursue claims against Bufman and Taylor in court).

The present action followed. The jury found that both Taylor and Bufman were liable to Tyson for "the unpaid balance of the $750,000 she was to receive for performing in the Corn Is Green," but the district court granted judgment as a matter of law dismissing the complaint on the grounds that (1) only the video agreement contained the pay or play guarantee; (2) that agreement unambiguously bound only Zev Bufman Entertainment, Inc.; and (3) the Security Agreement could not be "reasonably read to require anything more than the payments due under the Run-of-the Play [sic] Contract that it was designed to secure." This Is Me appealed; for the reasons that follow, we reverse.

DISCUSSION
I.

[This portion of the court's opinion is omitted.]

II.

Under New York law, all writings forming part of a single transaction are to be read together. See Gordon v. Vincent Youmans, Inc., 358 F.2d 261, 263 (2d Cir.1965); see also F.H. Krear & Co. v. Nineteen Named Trustees, 810 F.2d 1250, 1258 (2d Cir.1987); Nau v. Vulcan Rail & Constr. Co., 286 N.Y. 188, 197, 36 N.E.2d 106, 110 (1941). The district court properly instructed the jury on this principle:

> New York law requires that all writings which form part of a single transaction and are designed to effectuate the same purpose be read together, even though they were executed on different dates and were not all between the same parties. It is for you to determine whether the Actors' Equity run of the play contract, the Actors' Equity security agreement and the contractual obligation to pay This Is Me $750,000 were each intended to be binding on all the same parties, and were intended to impose the same obligations on each of the parties, even though they were set forth in different documents.

We conclude that there was sufficient evidence—the drafting history and chronology, the cross-referencing of the agreements, the integral nature of the undertakings for the stage and video performance, the relationships among the producing parties and entities, and the background assumptions furnished by the Equity rules—for the jury, as properly instructed, to find that Taylor and Bufman were personally liable on the pay or play guarantee. That conclusion requires a further look at the terms of the various contracts, and their cross-referencing of each other.

A. The Superseded Contract

The original contract for Tyson's services in the production, a letter agreement dated December 9, 1982 between This Is Me and Zev Bufman Entertainment, Inc., provided that Tyson would perform in the stage production and that a performance of that stage production would be videotaped. Zev Bufman Entertainment, Inc. undertook to pay salary for the run of the play, but not less than $750,000, installments of which would be paid at specified intervals "whether or not the Artist is actually performing":

> We guaranty [sic] to "pay or play" to [This Is Me] for the services of [Tyson], the total sum of Seven Hundred Fifty Thousand ($750,000) Dollars plus Actors Equity Minimum Rehearsal Salary during the period of rehearsals....

This document also provided that the parties would enter into a standard Actors' Equity Association run of the play contract, but that the pay or play obligation would supersede the run of the play agreement "notwithstanding any provisions therein to the contrary."

This original agreement was split into two superseding agreements, one concerned with the stage performances and undertaking to pay weekly salary for the run of the play, the other concerned with the video performance and undertaking the pay or play guarantee. Conflicting evidence was offered to explain this drafting history, but the jury was free to credit testimony that the producers wanted to keep the pay or play guarantee out of the run of the play contract that would be filed with Actors' Equity in order to reduce the bond required under the Equity rules.

B. The Run of the Play Contract

The run of the play contract was signed by Tyson on behalf of This Is Me and by Bufman on behalf of The Corn Company as "producer," a word left undefined by the contract, except that in Paragraph 9 the binding effect is said to reach the individual signatory as well as persons for whom the signatory acts:

> Individual signature required. The Producer agrees that execution of this Contract binds not only the producing company, but the individual signator to this Contract as well as any person under whose authority this Contract is executed.

The jury could find that Zev Bufman was personally bound because he affixed his signature, and that Taylor was bound because Bufman acted on her authority.

The run of the play contract incorporates by reference the Actors' Equity agreement and rules, and recites that they are the essence of the contractual relationship between the parties, that they set forth the minimum conditions under which the actor may work for the producer, and that they may not be waived or modified without Equity's written consent. It is therefore significant that Paragraph 7 of the Equity rules extends the binding effect of contracts beyond their signatories:

> All contracts of employment signed pursuant to these Rules are binding not only upon the signers on the face thereof, but upon any and all corporations, co-partnerships, enterprises and/or groups which said signers or each of them directs, controls, or is interested in, and are hereby agreed to be adopted as their contract by each of them.

By virtue of that clause, the run of the play contract is unquestionably binding upon Taylor and Bufman as producers, but that fact is of limited import, because the pay or play guarantee that this suit seeks to enforce does not appear in the run of the play contract. For reasons stated later in this opinion, however, there was sufficient evidence from which the jury could find that the video agreement, which contains the pay or play guarantee, cross-references the run of the play contract, which in turn incorporates the Equity rules. The interlocking nature of the agreements and the Equity rules is further confirmed by the fact that the Equity agreement and rules prohibit the video-taping of any production in which members of Equity are employed without the express permission of Equity and without adhering to the terms and conditions established by Equity.

C. The Video Contract

The video contract, signed on behalf of Zev Bufman Entertainment, Inc., guarantees payment to This Is Me of the difference between $750,000 and the salary paid pursuant to the run of the play contract. The contract recites that it constitutes the parties' "full and binding agreement with respect to...our proposed film and/or video recording of 'The Corn is Green,'" and that it is "intended to be executed concurrently with a 'Run of the Play' Actors Equity Association contract with respect to the Artist's services in a live stage production of the play."

D. Actors' Equity Security Agreement

The standard form Security Agreement, entered into between Actors' Equity Association and The Corn Company (Zev Bufman as signatory), provides for the posting of security and undertakes in other ways as well to ensure that actors receive payment for their services. "The subject of th[e] agreement" is the "Play," a defined term that in this instance "is the theatrical production known as 'THE CORN IS GREEN.'" The Security Agreement requires that the "producer" pay the actor all sums due under any "individual employment agreement," independent of the obligation to deposit security.

That provision is reinforced and broadened elsewhere in the agreement by language that extends the payment guarantee to other employment contracts made with the actors "in connection with said Play" or "in relation to the Play," and imposes the payment obligation on the signatory as well as the entity named as producer, and also on any partnership or other entity that is party to an individual employment agreement. Thus Paragraph 8 provides:

> All Individual Employment Contracts and collective bargaining agreements heretofore entered into, or which may hereafter be entered into, in connection with said Play are hereby made subject to all terms and conditions herein; all of which are agreed to be material and of the essence of the said Individual Employment Agreements, and as amended by these provisions, all such present and future employment contracts shall be and remain in full force and effect.

Paragraph 15 provides:

> Individual Signature Required. The Producer and Guarantor each severally agree that his signature on this agreement, if in a representative capacity, is also an individual signature binding him individually to this agreement. This provision is of the essence of this contract.

Two definitions broaden the reach of the agreement:

> "Producer" includes the individual, firm, partnership, or corporation, or any combination thereof, producing or controlling the production of said Play who has entered into an Individual Employment Agreement or who may hereafter enter into an Individual Employment Agreement with any of said Actors.

"Individual Employment Agreement" means any agreement of employment heretofore or hereafter entered into between an Actor and The Guarantor or Producer in relation to the Play.

III.

Although as finders of fact we might have read the contracts as Judge Martin did, we do not believe this reading is the only one permitted by the evidence. Considering all the circumstances, we believe that (A) the several agreements should be read together, and that (B), when they are so read in the light of all the evidence, they are capable of sustaining the jury's conclusion that Bufman and Taylor were bound by the $750,000 guarantee set forth in the video contract.

A

The various agreements in this case all relate to a single transaction: Ms. Tyson's services as an actor in the production of "The Corn is Green." The videotaped and live performances were components of a single project, as defendants Bufman and Taylor intended from the outset: the letter of intent forming the Elizabeth Theatre Group indicated that it was of the essence of the venture to obtain video and/or television rights to each play that it intended to produce. The agreements with Tyson—the run of the play contract and the video contract—were executed more or less concurrently, and the video contract expressly states that the two contracts were intended to be executed together. The lawyer for Zev Bufman Entertainment, Inc. conceded in a letter that the run of the play contract and the video contract were intended to be read together to define the parties' relationship. The jury was justified under New York law in reading the contracts together, in light of the other evidence.

B

When the contracts are read together in light of the other evidence, there are two entirely sufficient analyses that can support the jury verdict against Taylor and Bufman.

First, the video contract (which contains the $750,000 guarantee) cross-references the run of the play contract, which in turn expressly incorporates the Actors' Equity rules. And the run of the play contract, which does not say that it constitutes the parties' full and binding agreement, can be read to incorporate the video contract without contradicting its own express terms. Paragraph 9 of the run of the play contract provides that an individual who signs it in a representative capacity is also bound, and Paragraph 7 of the Equity rules extends the binding power of any employment agreement still further to any partnership or enterprise directed by the signatory. Thus the jury could have concluded that Zev Bufman's signature on the video contract on behalf of Zev Bufman Entertainment, Inc. also bound: (i) himself and (ii) the Elizabeth Theatre Group, an enterprise in which he was a partner. The jury could then further have assessed individual liability against Taylor as derivative of the Elizabeth Theatre Group's liability, because there was evidence (including Taylor's own statements to Tyson) from which the jury could conclude that Ms. Taylor was a partner in the Elizabeth Theatre Group.

Alternatively, the jury could have relied on the Security Agreement (read in conjunction with the run of the play contract and video contract). The Security Agreement provides that it applies to all "individual employment contracts," and defines such contracts as "any agreement of employment heretofore or hereafter entered into between an Actor and the Guarantor or Producer in relation to the Play." The pertinent inquiry under this theory is whether evidence was presented from which the jury reasonably could conclude: (i) that the video contract, in addition to the run of the play contract, was an agreement "in relation to the Play;" and (ii) that Taylor and Bufman fit the definition of producers.

Sufficient evidence existed to support a jury verdict on this theory: [First,] the video contract was part of what had originally been a single contract that indisputably was made "in relation to the Play." [Second,] the stage performance and the video of it were always regarded as integral components of one project; it was for this reason that Taylor and Bufman provided that an essential term of their agreement to form a production company was that the company obtain video and television rights to the plays they intended to produce. [Third,] Tyson's compensation under the video contract was related to her compensation for the live production: the longer the run, the more she collected in salary, the less she would be paid via the guarantee for the video, and of course if her salary payments reached $750,000, she would be paid nothing more for the video performance. [Fourth,] the subject of the proposed video is undoubtedly the live production of the play. [Fifth,] the Equity rules prohibit the filming of a production in which Equity members are employed without Equity's permission and provide that Equity's terms and conditions apply, from which the jury could have inferred that Equity is interested in securing payment to its members for video versions of live performances as well as the performances themselves.

The jury also heard evidence from which it reasonably might have concluded that both Elizabeth Taylor and Zev Bufman were producers of "The Corn is Green." The production ran on Broadway under a marquee that announced "Elizabeth Taylor and Zev Bufman present...." The letter of intent forming the Elizabeth Theatre Group provides that Bufman and Taylor would be co-producers of every project. And Taylor and Bufman are identified as co-producers in the advertisements for the play, the Playbill, and the letterhead used for the production.

For these reasons, the jury was free to find that Bufman and Taylor were producers, and that the video contract was an employment agreement made in relation to the play. The district court's view—that only the run of the play contract is a contract "in relation to the Play"—may be fairer, and better supported by evidence; but that is not for us to say. As long as there is some evidence based upon which the jury could have held Zev Bufman and Elizabeth Taylor individually liable, we must reinstate the verdict.

IV.

Taylor and Bufman belatedly contend that Tyson should be relegated to the Equity grievance procedures and that her failure to exhaust those procedures bars her from reliance on the Equity contracts. Defendants waited far too long to raise this as a defense; moreover, Ms. Tyson did initiate arbitration against these defendants but stipulated to a permanent stay of the arbitration (reserving to This Is Me the right to pursue claims against Ms. Taylor and Mr. Bufman) when they suggested she seek execution of the award she had already received against the corporate defendant (a company that Bufman, at least, knew lacked assets to satisfy the judgment).

CONCLUSION

The judgment of the district court is reversed, and the jury's verdict reinstated.

MILLER v. MUNICIPAL THEATRE ASSOCIATION OF ST. LOUIS
540 S.W.2d 899 (Mo. Ct. App. 1976)

KELLY, Judge.

Plaintiff-appellant, Ann Miller, appeals from a summary judgment entered in behalf of the defendants-respondents, the Municipal Theatre Association of St. Louis and the City of St. Louis by the Circuit Court of the City of St. Louis. We reverse and remand.

Appellant—hereinafter the plaintiff—brought suit against the Municipal Theatre Association of St. Louis and the City of St. Louis for injuries allegedly sustained during the performance of a play—'Anything Goes'—when she was struck by a piece of stage equipment on August 14, 1972. Both the Theatre—as Municipal Theatre Association of St. Louis shall hereinafter be identified—and the City—as the City of St. Louis shall hereinafter be identified—filed a joint Motion for Summary Judgment; the Theatre on the grounds that plaintiff was an employee as that term is defined in § 287.020(1) and that she had elected to come within the purview of § 287.090(2) both by contract and by virtue of the fact that the Theatre had obtained a Workmen's Compensation Insurance policy. The City's ground for summary judgment was that the action against it was barred by reason of the fact that it was a statutory employer by virtue of § 287.040(1).

The defendants filed affidavits in support of their motion wherein it was asserted that a Workmen's Compensation Insurance policy between the Theatre and Aetna Casualty Insurance Company was in force and effect on the date of the alleged accident and that Aetna had paid $4,161.78 to doctors, hospitals and nurses for the benefit of plaintiff and had issued seven drafts totalling $490.00 to her as indemnity payments.

Plaintiff filed her reply affidavit in opposition to the defendants' Motion for Summary Judgment averring therein that she had retained her own arranger, conductor and choreographer for purposes of creating, coordinating, refining and implementing dance routines to be performed by her in the production, etc., that she retained the exclusive right to control the manner, method and means by which she would perform her role, and that she retained and exercised, in accord with industry custom, 'creative control' over her performance. She denied that she had at any time agreed to be an employee of the defendants but rather that she occupied the status of an independent contractor. She further denied that the City was at any time engaged in the business of producing any entertainment production at the Theatre, that she had any contract with the City, and asserted that at no time did she or anyone in her behalf accept or consent to Workmen's Compensation payments by Aetna or any other person or firm.

After a hearing on the Motion, the trial court entered Findings of Fact and Conclusions of Law wherein it found that the parties elected and contracted to come under the Workmen's Compensation Act of the State of Missouri, Ch. 287 RSMo 1969, and more particularly § 287.120(1), and the Theatre and the City were thereby released from any common law liability because the plaintiff was an employee of the Theatre and a 'statutory employee' of the City. Defendants' Motion for Summary Judgment was sustained.

The only issue on appeal is the sufficiency of the evidence to support the Summary Judgment entered by the trial court on behalf of the defendants. In reviewing a Summary Judgment entered by the trial court, it is the duty of the appellate court to view the record on summary judgment in the light most favorable to the party against whom the judgment was rendered, Estate of Sample v. Travelers Indemnity Company, 492

S.W.2d 829 (Mo.1973), Allen v. St. Luke's Hosp. of Kansas City, 532 S.W.2d 505, 508 (Mo.App.1975).

Viewed from the foregoing vantage point we conclude that the critical issue in this cause is whether the plaintiff was an employee of the Theatre, and, as the trial court also determined, a 'statutory employee' of the City. The trial court decided that she was and based its finding on the Actors' Equity Association Stock Jobbing Contract of April 22, 1972, between plaintiff and the Theatre, the Agreement and Rules Governing Employment in Outdoor Musical Stock and the Managers' Stock Company Application, Questionnaire and Agreement incorporated into the Stock Jobbing Contract and the provisions of § 287.090.

Plaintiff alleged in her First Amended Petition that she was injured 'while performing on stage under a contract in a theatrical production;' and in her affidavit in opposition to defendants' Motion averred that she 'did agree' with the Theatre to perform the role of 'Reno Sweeney' in the musical production 'Anything Goes.' She then further averred those activities she engaged in to prepare for the performance, independently and at her own expense; that she provided certain enumerated 'tools of her trade,' professional persons to assist her in arranging her hair, etc., in a manner designated by herself inasmuch as she had retained the exclusive right to make such designation; that her pay was higher than other participants in the production because of her particularly unique and exceptional abilities in singing and dancing and for her acquired excellent reputation as a star performer. She further averred that it was understood between the Theatre and herself that she would retain the right to designate and control the manner, methods and means by which she would perform her role and that she exercised what is known in the entertainment trade as 'creative control,' i.e., the right of a performer with her high status to designate and control the means by which she performs her work in reaching the desired result or effect.

The Theatre argues that plaintiff was an employee and together with the Theatre elected to come under the Workmen's Compensation Act as evidenced by the contractual documents. It further argues that for members of the Actors' Equity Association to take part in performances, Equity requires the manager of a theatre to sign the Application and Agreement and agree thereby to furnish Workmen's Compensation and Disability Benefits to the 'Actor' and therefore plaintiff is bound by ratifying this agreement when she executed the Stock Jobbing Contract to accept the benefits and thereby waived her common law action. It points also to the Agreement and Rules Governing Employment in Outdoor Musical Stock incorporated into the Stock Jobbing Contract and the use of the term 'employment' throughout that document as further evidence that plaintiff was an employee and not an independent contractor as she contends.

Plaintiff's claim here is not in contract, it sounds in tort. She is not suing on the contract; rather, the contract is interposed as a defense to her common law claim. For the Act to be a bar to her claim, it must first be established that there was an employer-employee relationship existing at the time of the occurrence by which she sustained her injuries. She relies for recovery not on her contract; rather, she contends that despite what the contract may have provided, there is, and was at that time, in the entertainment trade what is known as 'creative control' reserved to a star of her standing whereby she was permitted to retain her independent contractor status.

The ordinary relationship of employer and employee exists in contract wherein, by the agreement, the employer is the one who employs another to perform service in his affairs and who controls, or has the right to control, the conduct of the other in the performance of the service and the employee is the person employed to perform services in the affairs of the employer and who, with respect to the physical conduct in the performance of the services, is subject to the employer's control. Fiedler v. Production Credit Association, 429 S.W.2d 307, 314 (Mo.App.1968). In the case where the employee seeks to enjoy the benefits of the Workmen's Compensation Act it is he who must prove the existence of the employer-employee relationship. Fiedler v. Production Credit Assn., supra, at 312. Here, however, the burden to prove this relationship is on the defendants interposing it in support of their Motion for Summary Judgment, and if there is a fact issue on that point they must fail. E. O. Dorsch Electric Co. v. Plaza Construction Company, 413 S.W.2d 167, 169 (Mo.1967).

It is apparent to us from the trial court's Findings of Fact and Conclusions of Law that it based its ruling solely on the documentary evidence filed in the cause and § 287.090(2), disregarding any pleading or averments contained in plaintiff's affidavit in opposition to defendants' Motion. In this we conclude he erred.

The Actors' Equity Association ("AEA") Stock Jobbing Contract here is one for 'Principals.' A 'Principal Actor' is defined in Rule 16(B) to include all members of AEA hired on Equity contracts other than those members engaged on Chorus contracts and/or engaged to perform chorus work. Plaintiff is identified in the Contract as 'Actor.' Rule 16(A) defines that generic term so that it refers to and includes persons who are members of AEA, including members engaged under Chorus contracts. It is apparent from this that this contract is a general form of contract.

The contract specifically provides that the Agreement and Rules Governing Employment in Outdoor Musical Stock and the Managers' Stock Company Application, Questionnaire and Agreement are a part of the Agreement. Except that it requires that plaintiff arrive and report at the theatre location on August 4, 1972, that the first rehearsal is to begin at 10 a.m., and that the opening date of the musical play is to be on August 14, 1972, the contract itself sets out no other duties of the plaintiff than that she play the part of 'Reno Sweeney' in the play 'Anything Goes.'

The Managers' Stock Company Application, Questionnaire and Agreement, so far as relevant, provides that the Manager (i.e., the Theatre) agrees that all employment agreements with members of the Actors' Equity Association, the terms of the Managers' Stock Company Application, Questionnaire and Agreement, and the Minimum Contract for Stock shall apply, and further, that 'the Actor is entitled to the benefits of all Federal and State...Workmen's Compensation and Disability Benefits;' that it will pay any and all payments required to be paid by employers under the provisions of said laws, and in the event the services of the Actor are not subject to the compulsory provisions of said laws, then it agrees that it will make application to cover the Actor under the elective provisions of said laws, or the elective provisions of the State of New York or the State of the Actor's residence.

The Agreement and Rules Governing Employment in Outdoor Musical Stock, Rule 32(A), provides that the Manager shall obtain and maintain Workmen's Compensation Insurance coverage for all Actors in his employ. Rule 24 of the Agreement sets out the duties of an Actor, and these are to be prompt at rehearsals and performances, to pay strict regard to makeup and dress, to perform his services to the best of his ability, to abide by all reasonable rules and regulations of the Manager not in conflict with Equity rules, to notify the Manager as far in advance as possible when any songs must be transposed into a different key from the key used in the score provided by the Management, and advises the Actor that repeated lateness 'may subject the Actor to disciplinary proceedings in accordance with the Constitution and By-Laws of Equity.'

From the foregoing, the trial court found that the terms of the contract are explicit in granting the Theatre 'the right to control the manner, method, mode and result of the work of plaintiff, and thus the conduct of the parties need not be analyzed.'

Having concluded from the documents in the case, other than plaintiff's affidavit, that there existed an employer-employee relationship between plaintiff and the Theatre, the trial court then further found that there was in full force and effect a Workmen's Compensation policy of insurance issued by the Aetna Casualty & Surety Company to the Theatre and that the Theatre had elected to come within the scope of § 287.090. The error in this finding is that § 287.090 has no applicability to the issues in this case in any manner whatsoever, and further, is not relied on by the Theatre in this court. The election afforded the employer under § 287.090 RSMo 1969, as amended Laws 1971, p. 84, § 2, is available in only those instances where the employer making the election to come under the provisions of the Workmen's Compensation Act, Ch. 287, is engaged in one of the three employments exempted thereby or is a minor employer not determined to be engaged in an occupation hazardous to employees. There is no evidence in this case that the Theatre is engaged in any of the exempt employments and therefore the fact that a policy of insurance was obtained by the Theatre does not constitute an election within the provisions of § 287.090.

Nor do the election provisions of § 287.120(1) have any applicability here until the employer-employee relationship has been established by unassailable proof, and any references to Workmen's Compensation Insurance in the Managers' Stock Company Application, Questionnaire and Agreement and the Agreement and Rules Governing Employment in Outdoor Musical Stock to this effect cannot bring the plaintiff under the coverage unless she is an employee and not an independent contractor.

We hold that the trial court erred in sustaining the Theatre's Motion for Summary Judgment.

We are also of the opinion that the trial court erred in finding that plaintiff was a statutory employee of the City within the meaning of that term as it is used in § 287.040(1). Before one can be held to be a statutory employee three prerequisites must be established: 1) the work was performed under a contract, 2) the injury must have occurred on or about the premises of the employer, and 3) the injury must have occurred while the employee was doing work in the usual course of the business of the employer. Dunn v. General Motors Corp., 466 S.W.2d 700, 702 (Mo.1971). The purpose of this statute is to prevent an employer from evading workmen's compensation liability by hiring independent contractors to perform the usual and ordinary work which his own employees would otherwise perform. Greiser v. Western Supplies Co., 406 S.W.2d 13, 16 (Mo.1966). While the plaintiff admits that the injuries for which she seeks damages occurred on the City's premises, she denies the other two prerequisites for the application of the statutory employee rule. The defense that the plaintiff was a statutory employee and hence cannot maintain a common law action is an affirmative defense and the burden of both pleading and proving it is on the defendant City in this case. Grieser v. Western Supplies Co., supra, at 16. The other requirements to establish the defense of 'statutory employee' in this case which plaintiff denies exist must be proved by the City for it to prevail in this defense. We therefore conclude that the City did not meet its burden by affording unassailable proof that plaintiff was a 'statutory employee' and thus barred from proceeding with her cause of action. For this defense to apply, the contract under which the work is done is one whereby the party interposing the defense has contracted either with the plaintiff or plaintiff's employer for the performance of certain duties in furtherance of the usual course of defendant's business and for the primary benefit of the statutory employer. Ferguson v. Air-Hydraulics Co., 492 S.W.2d 130, 137 (Mo.App.1973). There is no evidence here that plaintiff ever contracted with the City, and, as we held above there is a live issue whether plaintiff was an employee of the Theatre.

There is here no direct evidence of any contract between the City and the Theatre regarding the use of the Municipal Opera premises. The only evidence is a permit issued to the Theatre for the use of the premises for the purpose of producing a series of operas and to use portions of the structure for offices year-round. Nor is there any evidence that the production of shows is a part of the City's usual business. The trial court found that since the only business carried on on the premises was the performance of this and similar productions, that the premises upon which this play was performed belonged to the City, and that the City had 'contracted' with the Theatre to conduct the production of 'Anything Goes,' therefore plaintiff was a 'statutory employee' of the City. Under the evidentiary materials and other documents in this case it is impossible to determine whether the production of this play was within the usual course of the business of the City.

For the aforesaid reasons we hold that the trial court also erred in sustaining the Motion of the City for summary judgment.

Reversed and remanded.

Notes

1. As *Himes* makes clear, it is very difficult to make a living as a thespian (a famous quip attributed to Arthur Gingold goes, "Working in the theater has a lot in common with unemployment."). According to the Actors' Equity Association, in 2000 (the last year for which figures are available), fewer than 15% of its members landed parts of any sort; those who did had a median income for the year of less than $10,000. *See Actors, Producers, and Directors*, at www.bls.gov/oco/ocos093.htm. *See also* Robin Pogrebin, *Far Off Broadway, Even the Stars are Paid in Subway Fare*, N.Y. Times, June 18, 2000, § 1, at 1 (explaining that because of intense competition, even non-paying roles are fiercely sought after). Given this dismal state of affairs, should the government be doing more for people like Himes (by, for example, specifically earmarking grants, loans, subsidies, or tax credits for actors and actresses)? Or do you agree with the Seventh Circuit's conclusion in *Roberson* that because no one is forced to pursue a particular vocation, taxpayers should not have to pick up the tab when an individual makes a poor career choice?

2. In reading the Second Circuit's opinion, it is easy to lose sight of just how long Cicely Tyson was forced to chase after Elizabeth Taylor and Zev Bufman for her money.

"The Corn is Green" opened to poor reviews at the Lunt-Fontanne Theatre on August 22, 1983; on September 16, 1983, Tyson was fired for allegedly "failing to take direction" and missing a performance; on September 18, 1983, the show closed after just 32 performances (including previews). Tyson disputed the claim she was difficult to work with and blamed her missed performance on a delayed airplane flight (she had taken time off to attend a tribute in Washington, D.C., to her then-husband, jazz musician Miles Davis).

When Taylor and Bufman refused to pay, Tyson instituted arbitration proceedings against Zev Bufman Entertainment, Inc. ("ZBE") (the production company that Taylor and Bufman had jointly set up and that did business as The Elizabeth Theatre Group). In April 1985, an arbitrator found in Tyson's favor, and in September 1985 the award was confirmed by Justice David Edwards of the New York State Supreme Court. As the Second Circuit explains, Tyson then spent several years trying to collect against ZBE, but was unsuccessful because ZBE had no assets. Finally, in 1989 Tyson (through her personal services company, This is Me, Inc.) sued Taylor and Bufman personally in a New York federal court. In September 1996, following seven years of pre-trial litigation and a three-day trial, a jury found for Tyson and awarded her $1.3 million in damages (the figure had grown so large because of interest). This verdict was thrown out by District Judge John S. Martin, Jr. in January 1997, but was reinstated by the Second Circuit in September 1998—16 years after Tyson had been fired!

Tyson herself, however, was not entirely innocent. By agreeing to put the "pay or play" provision into the video contract instead of the run of the play contract, where it ordinarily would have gone, she was helping Taylor and Bufman avoid having to post what would have been a much larger security bond with Equity. Although the Second Circuit mentions this fact, it does not deem it important. Should it have, and, if so, with what effect?

3. How much an actor or actress is paid depends on how much "star power" he or she has. As has been explained elsewhere:

> The great majority of performers in the Broadway theater are covered by Actors' Equity contracts. (The situation Off-Broadway and elsewhere is otherwise.) Collective bargaining agreements do not preclude individual contracts. An employee can always try to get better terms; what he may not do is waive the minimum provisions of the collective bargaining agreement.

Alexander Lindey & Michael Landau, *Lindey on Entertainment, Publishing and the Arts: Agreements and the Law* § 5:54, at 5-265 to 5-266 (2d ed. 1980 & 2003 Supp.). Indeed, to persuade Nathan Lane and Matthew Broderick to reprise their roles in "The Producers," the producers agreed to pay them each $100,000 a week for a 14-week engagement. *See* Jesse McKinley, *Original Stars Returning to 'Producers,' at a Price*, N.Y. Times, Nov. 5, 2003, at B1. A sample actor's contract appears in Appendix E of this casebook.

4. Notice the dilemma *Miller* creates for producers and theaters. On the one hand, if they do not take out workers' compensation insurance, they leave themselves open to charges of intentionally failing to protect cast members from injuries. On the other hand, if they do arrange such coverage, they risk having to defend lawsuits like the one Ann Miller filed. Is there a solution to this problem? For other instances of an actor getting hurt and either seeking or trying to avoid workers' compensation payments, *see, e.g., Huffman v. City of Poway*, 101 Cal. Rptr. 2d 325 (Ct. App. 2000); *Jack Hammer Associates, Inc. v. Delmy Productions, Inc.*, 499 N.Y.S.2d 418 (App. Div. 1986); *Diamond Circle Corp. v. Blocher*, 691 P.2d 769 (Colo. Ct. App. 1984).

Problem 12

Recognizing that the typical performer often is unemployed and therefore unable to buy even the most basic wardrobe, a testator directs that the bulk of his considerable fortune be used after his death to establish an "actors' shoe fund." The will further provides that the fund should be administered by the Actors' Equity Association "as it sees fit." If the bequest is challenged by the decedent's heirs as too ambiguous to be enforceable, how should the court rule? *See Guaranty Trust Co. of N.Y. v. New York Community Trust*, 56 A.2d 907 (N.J. Ch.), *aff'd mem.*, 61 A.2d 239 (N.J. Err. & App. 1948).

D. REPRESENTATION

ACTORS IN ELLIS ISLAND SHOW VOTE, 7 TO 1, TO JOIN UNION

Steven Greenhouse
N.Y. Times, Aug. 15, 2002, at E1

The 10 actors who take turns in "Embracing Freedom," the play performed before visitors to Ellis Island, try their hardest to portray the oppression and poverty overseas that drove millions of immigrants to the United States.

But these actors have their own complaints about oppression and poverty, although those of a different order. With the hope of improving their working conditions and how management treats them, they decided to try to join a union, and yesterday the Actors' Equity Association announced that the Ellis Island actors had voted, 7 to 1, to unionize. Two of the 10 votes were challenged and not counted.

The actors cast their votes even though they said several managers with the Statue of Liberty-Ellis Island Foundation, which runs the museum at Ellis Island, had fought the unionization drive.

Paul Savas, who has acted on Ellis Island for more than a year, said, "It was stunning and ironic that Ellis Island, a place that stands for making people's lives better, would try to deny us an opportunity to make our lives better through union representation."

Peg Zitko, communications director for the Statue of Liberty-Ellis Island Foundation, said the foundation had never fought the unionization drive. "I don't think you can say the foundation opposed unionization," she said. "That's not fair from the get-go. The foundation never put up any resistance to the possibility of unionizing." The actors said that difficult working conditions—certainly not as trying as those faced by immigrants of old—drove them to join Actors' Equity. Many days there was no air-conditioning, which the actors said was not easy because they are dressed in wool during performances. Another problem is the lack of a dressing room near the ground-floor theater; there is one on the third floor. The actors also complained that during the half-hour breaks when they were not acting, their supervisors often ordered them to circulate among the visitors and promote the show.

"We basically wanted a union because of the way we were treated in artistic terms as well as the work environment," Mr. Savas said. "There's very little respect about what we do and how much it takes to do what we do."

The actors generally work six hours a day, with most of them performing in six half-hour shows a day. The pay is $8.75 an hour, plus $8.75 for each performance. The workers said that the pay was all right, but that they lacked health insurance and pensions.

On June 7 the actors filed a petition with the National Labor Relations Board, saying they wanted to join Actors' Equity. They asked management to grant them voluntary recognition without an election.

But, the union said, the foundation rejected voluntary recognition. Then, several actors said, one manager urged them not to join the union, saying that a negotiating process could be a negative experience and that it could drag on for months and years.

Actors' Equity enlisted help from public officials. Representative Jerrold L. Nadler, a Manhattan Democrat, wrote to the foundation, saying, "I find an unfortunate irony in the fact that the performers on Ellis Island, the Gateway to Freedom, are being discouraged from exercising their free choice to be represented by a union."

The actors and Actors' Equity say they hope to begin bargaining soon.

"These people try to create the irony of the Statue of Liberty and Ellis Island not giving liberty," Ms. Zitko said. "The foundation accepted liberty in all respects and let them choose whether or not to be in a union. Now that the union has won, the foundation is ready and willing to bargain in good faith with the union."

NATIONAL LABOR RELATIONS BOARD v. ACTORS' EQUITY ASSOCIATION
644 F.2d 939 (2d Cir. 1981)

MANSFIELD, Circuit Judge.

The National Labor Relations Board (NLRB) and Intervenor, Yul Brynner, petition this court for enforcement of the Board's order dated February 19, 1980, requiring Actors' Equity Association (Equity), a theater actors' union, to cease violating §§ 8(b)(1)(A) and 8(b)(2) of the National Labor Relations Act, 29 U.S.C. § 158(b)(1)(A) and (b)(2) (NLRA), by charging non-uniform dues that unjustifiably discriminate against aliens who belong to the union and are in this country temporarily to perform in stage productions. The order also mandates repayment of all past overcharges from April 6, 1976, to the present. We agree with the NLRB's finding that the assessment of non-uniform dues against aliens without any reasonable basis violates the Act, and find no fault in the Board's choice of remedy. We also agree that Intervenor Brynner was an employee subject to the Act's protection rather than a supervisor, and that this suit is not time-barred under § 10(b) of the Act, 29 U.S.C. § 160(b). Accordingly, we grant the Board's petition for enforcement.

Actors' Equity is an employees' association that has entered into collective bargaining agreements on behalf of stage actors with various theater organizations in New York and throughout the United States and Canada. Its bargaining agreements universally contain a "union security clause" providing that the employer will hire only union members to act in its productions.

Equity has for many years attempted to regulate participation by foreign actors in American theater performances. This regulation has taken several forms. First, since 1964 Equity has participated in an agreement with the United States Department of Labor and the Immigration and Naturalization Service to the effect that the Labor Department would seek Equity's advice on aliens' applications for visas under 8 U.S.C. § 1101(a)(15)(H), which permits resident aliens to obtain jobs in the United States only if they are rendering exceptional or temporary service in jobs which no unemployed Americans are capable of performing. Second, Equity has agreed with New York theater employers' organizations—the Council of Stock Theatres (COST), League of Resident Theatres (LORT), and the League of New York Theatres and Producers (Producers)—that members of those organizations (the primary employers of aliens in the United States) will not hire non-resident aliens without Equity's consent. (Equity's agreements with COST and LORT wholly prohibit employment of non-resident aliens without Equity's prior consent. Its agreement with Producers provides that a producer may not apply to the Immigration and Naturalization Service for admission of an alien actor unless Equity and Producers both approve the application, and that differences of opinion between Equity and Producers will be resolved by arbitration.)

Finally, Equity has imposed a separate dues schedule on non-resident aliens. Citizens of the United States and Canada who belong to Actors' Equity, as well as aliens who reside here with the intention of making this country their permanent residence, pay dues according to a sliding scale ranging from $42 per year for an actor earning no more than $2,500 per year to a maximum of $400 for an actor earning more than $30,000 per year. Once a so-called "resident member" makes more than $1,400 per year his dues will never exceed 3% of gross income, with a $400 per year limit. Non-resident aliens who are allowed to perform in the United States, on the other hand, must pay 5% of their stage income as dues, with no ceiling. Yul Brynner, the Intervenor, is a Swiss citizen and resident of France who was admitted into the United States to play the King of Siam in The King and I, a revival of a play in which he starred some years ago. If he had been a U.S. citizen or resident, his dues to Actors' Equity for the first year of the play's run would have been $400; under the separate schedule for non-resident aliens, he was required to pay $45,000.

Charges were filed with the Board on October 8, 1976, alleging that the union was violating §§ 8(b)(1)(A) and 8(b)(2) of the Act through employment of its discriminatory dues schedule. Noting that those provisions prohibit discrimination against employees except as provided by § 8(a)(3), which allows unions and employers to enter union security agreements, the charging party relied on the second proviso to § 8(a)(3), which states that employees who belong to a union having in effect a union security agreement may be required as a condition of membership only to "tender the periodic dues and the initiation fees uniformly required as a condition of acquiring or retaining membership."

The administrative law judge, and later the Board, agreed that the separate dues structure unlawfully discriminated against aliens by violating the union's duty to charge uniform dues or to demonstrate a reasonable justification for the non-uniformity. While it declined to impose a per se rule that any discrimination in dues charged to aliens was unacceptable under the Act, it nevertheless found such discrimination presumptively invalid, and declared that absent some justification for the non-uniformity it must be found illegal. It then rejected the justifications claimed by Equity that the higher dues structure was necessary (1) to limit the number of alien actors in the United States, (2) to prevent reprisals from British Equity, Britain's "friendly adversary" correlative of Actors' Equity, and (3) to counterbalance British Equity's power to exclude as many American actors as it wants simply by telling the British Labor Board whom it wants excluded. Finding no merit in Equity's claim that the suit was time-barred, the Administrative Law Judge ordered Equity to desist from imposing a discriminatory dues schedule and ordered repayment of all amounts collected after April 6, 1976 (six months before the complaint was filed in this case) in excess of what non-resident aliens would have paid if treated like residents or citizens.

DISCUSSION

Equity first contends that the Board has no jurisdiction over the rights of aliens because the NLRA is aimed at protecting American workers only and that non-resident aliens therefore have no cognizable rights under the Act. We disagree. Nothing in the terms or construction of the NLRA limits the meaning of the word "employees" to American citizens or permanent residents. The provisions in question here do not specify "American-citizen" employees as opposed to non-resident aliens. They merely proscribe discriminatory treatment of individuals or groups of employees who belong to unions, without regard to the employees' nationality or residence. For instance, Equity does not deny that Canadian citizens and resident aliens have rights as union members under the NLRA. It would be unthinkable to allow Equity to demand union membership and payment of dues by alien members performing in the United States while denying them rights associated with union membership. (Although non-resident aliens who belong to Equity are also not allowed to vote or become union officials, the Board has made no effort here to attack these restrictions as violative of the union's duty of fair representation. Instead, the Board limits its attack to Equity's alleged discriminatory failure to impose the uniform dues specifically required by the second proviso to §8(a)(3). Nor does our opinion bear on the union's power to limit the number of aliens who perform on American stages by impeding their entry into the United States or into the union.)

Having recognized that aliens possess equal rights as union members, we have no difficulty concluding that the union's two-tiered dues structure discriminates against non-residents by failing to impose uniform dues without some legitimate basis for the discrimination. See NLRB v. Kaiser Steel Corp., 506 F.2d 1057 (9th Cir. 1974); NLRB v. Electric Auto-Lite Co., 92 N.L.R.B. 1073 (1950), enf'd, 196 F.2d 500 (6th Cir. 1952). Equity attempts to justify its dues discrimination on three grounds. First, it argues that the 5% dues rate protects employment opportunities for members by limiting alien membership in American productions. Second, it suggests that the rule protects Americans from hostile or retaliatory actions on the part of British Equity, which now reciprocally charges American theater actors 5% dues. Third, and relatedly, it says that the rule (or at least the power to have the rule) provides a needed counterweight to British Equity's influence over alien admissions in England.

We find no merit in these asserted justifications. There is no substantial evidence that the 5% dues assessment, either because of parity between American and foreign pay scales or for some other reason, would inhibit foreign actors from participating in America's comparatively lucrative theater productions. On the contrary, past statements by Equity indicate that the 5% dues rate was adopted primarily as a revenue-producing measure. Moreover, Equity's power to exclude aliens derives from an entirely different source, its agreements with COST, LORT, and Producers. In the face of these agreements, which give Equity effective authority to decide which aliens to admit and which to exclude, the 5% dues rate has no significant exclusionary force.

Similarly, the asserted justification that the higher dues are necessary to protect American actors from retaliatory action on the part of British Equity, which imposes a reciprocal 5% dues rate, lacks rationality. The fairness of discriminatory acts under American labor law does not depend on what is practiced under British labor law. The 5% American dues levy seems more likely to provoke hostility than to eliminate it. Nor has it had much influence upon British Equity's decision-making, since it has been in existence for about 50 years and British Equity's retaliatory 5% dues rate has existed almost that long. Finally, on a narrower level, concerns about British Equity could hardly be relevant as a justification for charging higher dues to Brynner, who is a Swiss citizen and French resident and has never been either a citizen or a resident of Great Britain.

[The remainder of the court's opinion is omitted.]

H. A. ARTISTS & ASSOCIATES, INC. v. ACTORS' EQUITY ASSOCIATION
451 U.S. 704 (1981)

Justice STEWART delivered the opinion of the Court.

The respondent Actors' Equity Association (Equity) is a union representing the vast majority of stage actors and actresses in the United States. It enters into collective-bargaining agreements with theatrical producers that specify minimum wages and other terms and conditions of employment for those whom it represents. The petitioners are independent theatrical agents who place actors and actresses in jobs with producers. The Court of Appeals for the Second Circuit held that the respondents' system of regulation of theatrical agents is immune from antitrust liability by reason of the statutory labor exemption from the antitrust laws, 622 F.2d 647. We granted certiorari to consider the availability of that exemption in the circumstances presented by this case. 449 U.S. 991, 101 S.Ct. 526, 66 L.Ed.2d 288.

I
A

Equity is a national union that has represented stage actors and actresses since early in this century. Currently representing approximately 23,000 actors and actresses, it has collective-bargaining agreements with virtually all major theatrical producers in New York City, on and off Broadway, and with most other theatrical producers throughout the United States. The terms negotiated with producers are the minimum conditions of employment (called "scale"); an actor or actress is free to negotiate wages or terms more favorable than the collectively bargained minima. The minimum, or "scale" wage varies. In August 1977, for example, the minimum weekly salary was $335 for Broadway performances, and $175 for performances off Broadway.

Theatrical agents are independent contractors who negotiate contracts and solicit employment for their clients. The agents do not participate in the negotiation of collective-bargaining agreements between Equity and the theatrical producers. If an agent succeeds in obtaining employment for a client, he receives a commission based on a percentage of the client's earnings. Agents who operate in New York City must be licensed as employment agencies and are regulated by the New York City Department of Consumer Affairs pursuant to New York law, which provides that the maximum commission a theatrical agent may charge his client is 10% of the client's compensation.

In 1928, concerned with the high unemployment rates in the legitimate theater and the vulnerability of actors and actresses to abuses by theatrical agents, including the extraction of high commissions that tended to undermine collectively bargained rates of compensation, Equity unilaterally established a licensing system for the regulation of agents. The regulations permitted Equity members to deal only with those agents who obtained Equity licenses and thereby agreed to meet the conditions of representation prescribed by Equity. Those members who dealt with nonlicensed agents were subject to union discipline.

The system established by the Equity regulations was immediately challenged. In Edelstein v. Gillmore, 35 F.2d 723, the Court of Appeals for the Second Circuit concluded that the regulations were a lawful effort to improve the employment conditions of Equity members. In an opinion written by Judge Swan and joined by Judge Augustus N. Hand, the court said:

The evils of unregulated employment agencies (using this term broadly to include also the personal representative) are set forth in the defendants' affidavits and are corroborated by common knowledge.... Hence the requirement that, as a condition to writing new business with Equity's members, old contracts with its members must be made to conform to the new standards, does not seem to us to justify an inference that the primary purpose of the requirement is infliction of injury upon plaintiff, and other personal representatives in a similar situation, rather than the protection of the supposed interests of Equity's members. The terms they insist upon are calculated to secure from personal representatives better and more impartial service, at uniform and cheaper rates, and to improve conditions of employment of actors by theater managers. Undoubtedly the defendants intend to compel the plaintiff to give up rights under existing contracts which do not conform to the new standards set up by Equity, but, as already indicated, their motive in so doing is to benefit themselves and their fellow actors in the economic struggle. The financial loss to plaintiff is incidental to this purpose.

Id. at 726.

The essential elements of Equity's regulation of theatrical agents have remained unchanged since 1928. A member of Equity is prohibited, on pain of union discipline, from using an agent who has not, through the mechanism of obtaining an Equity license (called a "franchise"), agreed to comply with the regulations. The most important of the regulations requires that a licensed agent must renounce any right to take a commission on an employment contract under which an actor or actress receives scale wages. To the extent a contract includes provisions under which an actor or actress will sometimes receive scale pay—for rehearsals or "chorus" employment, for example—and sometimes more, the regulations deny the agent any commission on the scale portions of the contract. Licensed agents are also precluded from taking commissions on out-of-town expense money paid to their clients. Moreover, commissions are limited on wages within 10% of scale pay, and an agent must allow his client to terminate a representation contract if the agent is not successful in procuring employment within a specified period. Finally, agents are required to pay franchise fees to Equity. The fee is $200 for the initial franchise, $60 a year thereafter for each agent, and $40 for any sub-agent working in the office of another. These fees are deposited by Equity in its general treasury and are not segregated from other union funds.

The regulations have undergone revision in some details, largely as a result of negotiations between Equity and Theatrical Artists Representatives Associates (TARA), which until shortly before this litigation began was the only association voicing the concerns of agents with regard to their representation of Equity members. Until their voluntary resignation in late 1977, most of the petitioners were members of TARA. The petitioners are now members of the National Association of Talent Representatives (NATR). Unlike TARA, which functions only in the legitimate theater field, NATR also functions in the fields of motion pictures and television. In those fields, agents operate under closely analogous agent regulations maintained by the Screen Actors' Guild and the American Federation of Television and Radio Artists.

In 1977, after a dispute between Equity and TARA, a group of agents, including the petitioners, resigned from TARA because of TARA's decision to abide by Equity's regulations. These agents also informed Equity that they would not accept Equity's regulations or apply for franchises. The petitioners instituted this lawsuit in May 1978, contending that Equity's regulations of theatrical agents violated §§ 1 and 2 of the Sherman Act, 26 Stat. 209, as amended, 15 U.S.C. §§ 1 and 2.

B

The District Court found, after a bench trial, that Equity's creation and maintenance of the agency franchise system were fully protected by the statutory labor exemptions from the antitrust laws, and accordingly dismissed the petitioners' complaint. 478 F.Supp. 496 (SDNY). Among its factual conclusions, the trial court found that in the theatrical industry, agents play a critical role in securing employment for actors and actresses:

> As a matter of general industry practice, producers seek actors and actresses for their productions through agents. Testimony in this case convincingly established that an actor without an agent does not have the same access to producers or the same opportunity to be seriously considered for a part as does an actor who has an agent. Even principal interviews, in which producers are required to interview all actors who want to be considered for principal roles, do not eliminate the need for an agent, who may have a greater chance of gaining an audition for his client....
>
> Testimony confirmed that agents play an integral role in the industry; without an agent, an actor would have significantly lesser chances of gaining employment.

Id. at 497, 502.

The court also found "no evidence to suggest the existence of any conspiracy or illegal combination between Actors' Equity and TARA or between Actors' Equity and producers," and concluded that "[t]he Actors Equity franchising system was employed by Actors' Equity for the purpose of protecting the wages and working conditions of its members." Id. at 499.

The Court of Appeals unanimously affirmed the judgment of the District Court. It determined that the threshold issue was, under United States v. Hutcheson, 312 U.S. 219, 232, 61 S.Ct. 463, 466, 85 L.Ed. 788, whether Equity's franchising system involved any combination between Equity and any "non-labor groups" or persons who are not "parties to a labor dispute." 622 F.2d, at 648-649. If it did, the court reasoned, the protection of the statutory labor exemption would not apply.

First, the Court of Appeals held that the District Court had not been clearly erroneous in finding no agreement, explicit or tacit, between Equity and the producers to establish or police the franchising system. Next, the court turned to the relationship between the union and those agents who had agreed to become franchised, in order to determine whether those agreements would divest Equity's system of agency regulation of the statutory exemption. Relying on Musicians v. Carroll, 391 U.S. 99, 88 S.Ct. 1562, 20 L.Ed.2d 460, the court concluded that the agents were themselves a "labor group," because of their substantial "economic inter-relationship" with Equity, under which "the union [could] not eliminate wage competition among its members without regulation of the fees of the agents." 622 F.2d, at 650, 651. Accordingly, since the elimination of wage competition is plainly within the area of a union's legitimate self-interest, the court concluded that the exemption was applicable.

After deciding that the central feature of Equity's franchising system—the union's exaction of an agreement by agents not to charge commissions on certain types of work—was immune from antitrust challenge, the Court of Appeals turned to the petitioners' challenge of the franchise fees exacted from agents. Equity had argued that the fees were necessary to meet its expenses in administering the franchise system, but no evidence was presented at trial to show that the costs justified the fees actually levied. The Court of Appeals suggested that if the exactions exceeded the true costs, they could not legally be collected, as such exactions would be unconnected with any of the goals of national labor policy that justify the labor antitrust exemption. Despite the lack of any cost evidence at trial, however, the appellate court reasoned that the fees were sufficiently low that a remand to the District Court on this point "would not serve any useful purpose." Id. at 651.

II
A

Labor unions are lawful combinations that serve the collective interests of workers, but they also possess the power to control the character of competition in an industry. Accordingly, there is an inherent tension between national antitrust policy, which seeks to maximize competition, and national labor policy, which encourages cooperation among workers to improve the conditions of employment. In the years immediately following passage of the Sherman Act, courts enjoined strikes as unlawful restraints of trade when a union's conduct or objectives were deemed "socially or economically harmful." Duplex Printing Press Co. v. Deering, 254 U.S. 443, 485, 41 S.Ct. 172, 183, 65 L.Ed. 349 (Brandeis, J., dissenting). In response to these practices, Congress acted, first in the Clayton Act, 38 Stat. 731, and later in the Norris-LaGuardia Act, 47 Stat. 70, to immunize labor unions and labor disputes from challenge under the Sherman Act.

Section 6 of the Clayton Act, 15 U.S.C. § 17, declares that human labor "is not a commodity or article of commerce," and immunizes from antitrust liability labor organizations and their members "lawfully carrying out" their "legitimate object[ives]." Section 20 of the Act prohibits injunctions against specified employee activities, such as strikes and boycotts, that are undertaken in the employees' self-interest and that occur in the course of disputes "concerning terms or conditions of employment," and states that none of the specified acts can be "held to be [a] violatio[n] of any law of the United States." 29 U.S.C. § 52.

This protection is re-emphasized and expanded in the Norris-LaGuardia Act, which prohibits federal-court injunctions against single or organized employees engaged in enumerated activities, and specifically forbids such injunctions notwithstanding the claim of an unlawful combination or conspiracy. While the Norris-LaGuardia Act's bar of federal-court labor injunctions is not explicitly phrased as an exemption from the antitrust laws, it has been interpreted broadly as a statement of congressional policy that the courts must not use the antitrust laws as a vehicle to interfere in labor disputes.

In United States v. Hutcheson, 312 U.S. 219, 61 S.Ct. 463, 85 L.Ed. 788, the Court held that labor unions acting in their self-interest and not in combination with nonlabor groups enjoy a statutory exemption from Sherman Act liability. After describing the congressional responses to judicial interference in union activity, id. at 229-230, 61 S.Ct. at 464-465, the Court declared that

> [s]o long as a union acts in its self-interest and does not combine with nonlabor groups, the licit and the illicit under §20 [of the Clayton Act] are not to be distinguished by any judgment regarding the wisdom or unwisdom, the rightness or wrongness, the selfishness or unselfishness of the end of which the particular union activities are the means.

Id. at 232, 61 S.Ct. at 466 (footnote omitted).

The Court explained that this exemption derives not only from the Clayton Act, but also from the Norris-LaGuardia Act, particularly its definition of a "labor dispute," in which Congress "reasserted the original purpose of the Clayton Act by infusing into it the immunized trade union activities as redefined by the later Act." 312 U.S. at 236, 61 S.Ct. at 468. Thus under Hutcheson, no federal injunction may issue over a "labor dispute," and "§ 20 [of the Clayton Act] removes all such allowable conduct from the taint of being a 'violation of any law of the United States,' including the Sherman [Act]." Id.

The statutory exemption does not apply when a union combines with a "non-labor group." Hutcheson, supra, at 232, 61 S.Ct. at 466. Accordingly, antitrust immunity is forfeited when a union combines with one or more employers in an effort to restrain trade. In Allen Bradley Co. v. Electrical Workers, 325 U.S. 797, 65 S.Ct. 1533, 89 L.Ed. 1939, for example, the Court held that a union had violated the Sherman Act when it combined with manufacturers and contractors to erect a sheltered local business market in order "to bar all other business men from [the market], and to charge the public prices above a competitive level." Id. at 809, 65 S.Ct. at 1539. The Court indicated that the union efforts would, standing alone, be exempt from antitrust liability, but because the union had not acted unilaterally, the exemption was denied. Congress "intended to outlaw business monopolies. A business monopoly is no less such because a union participates, and such participation is a violation of the Act." Id. at 811, 65 S.Ct. at 1540.

B

The Court of Appeals properly recognized that the threshold issue was to determine whether or not Equity's franchising of agents involved any combination between Equity and any "non-labor groups," or persons who are not "parties to a labor dispute." 622 F.2d at 649 (quoting Hutcheson, 312 U.S. at 232, 61 S.Ct. at 466). And the court's conclusion that the trial court had not been clearly erroneous in its finding that there was no combination between Equity and the theatrical producers to create or maintain the franchise system is amply supported by the record.

The more difficult problem is whether the combination between Equity and the agents who agreed to become franchised was a combination with a "nonlabor group." The answer to this question is best understood in light of Musicians v. Carroll, 391 U.S. 99, 88 S.Ct. 1562, 20 L.Ed.2d 460. There, four orchestra leaders, members of the American Federation of Musicians, brought an action based on the Sherman Act challenging the union's unilateral system of regulating "club dates," or one-time musical engagements. These regulations, inter alia, enforced a closed shop; required orchestra leaders to engage a minimum number of "sidemen," or instrumentalists; prescribed minimum prices for local engagements; prescribed higher minimum prices for traveling orchestras; and permitted leaders to deal only with booking agents licensed by the union.

Without disturbing the finding of the Court of Appeals that the orchestra leaders were employers and independent contractors, the Court concluded that they were nonetheless a "labor group" and parties to a "labor dispute" within the meaning of the Norris-LaGuardia Act, and thus that their involvement in the union regulatory scheme was not an unlawful combination between "labor" and "nonlabor" groups. The Court agreed with the trial court that the applicable test was whether there was "job or wage competition or some other economic interrelationship affecting legitimate union interests between the union members and the independent contractors." Id. at 106, 88 S.Ct. at 1567.

The Court also upheld the restrictions on booking agents, who were not involved in job or wage competition with union members. Accordingly, these restrictions had to meet the "other economic interrelationship" branch of the disjunctive test quoted above. And the test was met because those restrictions were "'at least as intimately bound up with the subject of wages'...as the price floors." Id. at 113, 88 S.Ct. at 1570 (quoting Teamsters v. Oliver, 362 U.S. 605, 606, 80 S.Ct. 923, 926, 4 L.Ed.2d 1740). The Court noted that the booking agent restrictions had been adopted, in part, because agents had "charged exorbitant fees, and booked engagements for musicians at wages...below union scale."

C

The restrictions challenged by the petitioners in this case are very similar to the agent restrictions upheld in the Carroll case. The essential features of the regulatory scheme are identical: members are permitted to deal only with agents who have agreed (1) to honor their fiduciary obligations by avoiding conflicts of interest, (2) not to charge excessive commissions, and (3) not to book members for jobs paying less than the union minimum. And as in Carroll, Equity's regulation of agents developed in response to abuses by employment agents who occupy a critical role in the relevant labor market. The agent stands directly between union members and jobs, and is in a powerful position to evade the union's negotiated wage structure.

The petitioners argue that theatrical agents are indistinguishable from "numerous [other] groups of persons who merely supply products and services to union members" such as landlords, grocers, accountants and lawyers. But it is clear that agents differ from these groups in two critical respects: the agents control access to jobs and negotiation of the terms of employment. For the actor or actress, therefore, agent commissions are not merely a discretionary expenditure of disposable income, but a virtually inevitable concomitant of obtaining employment.

The peculiar structure of the legitimate theater industry, where work is intermittent, where it is customary if not essential for union members to secure employment through agents, and where agents' fees are calculated as a percentage of a member's wage, makes it impossible for the union to defend even the integrity of the minimum wages it has negotiated without regulation of agency fees. The regulations are "brought within the labor exemption [because they are] necessary to assure that scale wages will be paid...." Carroll, 391 U.S. at 112, 88 S.Ct. at 1570. They "embody...a direct frontal attack upon a problem thought to threaten the maintenance of the basic wage structure." Teamsters v. Oliver, 358 U.S. 283, 294, 79 S.Ct. 297, 303, 3 L.Ed.2d 312. Agents must, therefore, be considered a "labor group," and their controversy with Equity is plainly a "labor dispute" as defined in the Norris-LaGuardia Act: "representation of persons in negotiating, fixing, maintaining, changing, or seeking to arrange terms or conditions of employment, regardless of whether or not the disputants stand in the proximate relation of employer and employee." 29 U.S.C. §113(c).

Agents perform a function—the representation of union members in the sale of their labor—that in most nonentertainment industries is performed exclusively by unions. In effect, Equity's franchise system operates as a substitute for maintaining a hiring hall as the representative of its members seeking employment.

Finally, Equity's regulations are clearly designed to promote the union's legitimate self-interest. Hutcheson, 312 U.S. at 232, 61 S.Ct. at 466. In a case such as this, where there is no direct wage or job competition between the union and the group it regulates, the Carroll formulation to determine the presence of a nonlabor group—whether there is "'some...economic interrelationship affecting legitimate union interests...,'" 391 U.S. at 106, 88 S.Ct. at 1567 (quoting District Court opinion)—necessarily resolves this issue.

D

The question remains whether the fees that Equity levies upon the agents who apply for franchises are a permissible component of the exempt regulatory system. We have concluded that Equity's justification for these fees is inadequate. Conceding that Carroll did not sanction union extraction of franchise fees from agents, Equity suggests, only in the most general terms, that the fees are somehow related to the basic purposes of its regulations: elimination of wage competition, upholding of the union wage scale, and promotion of fair access to jobs. But even assuming that the fees no more than cover the costs of administering the regulatory system, this is simply another way of saying that without the fees, the union's regulatory efforts would not be subsidized—and that the dues of Equity's members would perhaps have to be increased to offset the loss of a general revenue source. If Equity did not impose these franchise fees upon the agents, there is no reason to believe that any of its legitimate interests would be affected.

III

For the reasons stated, the judgment of the Court of Appeals is affirmed in part and reversed in part, and the case is remanded for proceedings consistent with this opinion.

It is so ordered.

Justice BRENNAN, concurring in part and dissenting in part.

I join all but Part II-D of the Court's opinion. That part holds that respondents' exaction of a franchise fee is not a "permissible component of the exempt regulatory system." Rather, I agree with the Court of Appeals that the approximately $12,000 collected annually in fees is not "incommensurate with Equity's expenses in maintaining a full-time employee to administer the system," 622 F.2d 647, 651 (CA2 1980), and thus is not "unconnected with any of the goals of national labor policy which justify the antitrust exemption for labor," id.

PAWLOWSKI v. WOODRUFF
203 N.Y.S. 819 (App. Div. 1924)

PROSKAUER, Justice.

Plaintiff has recovered on a contract by which defendant engaged her as 'exclusive manager.' This imports that plaintiff was to serve as manager. The agreement further provided that plaintiff was to secure profitable engagements for defendant and to receive as compensation 10 per cent of defendant's earnings.

The judgment is challenged solely because plaintiff had not procured a license under section 171, subd. 3, of the General Business Law (as amended by Laws 1917, c. 770), which provides that every theatrical 'employment agency' must be licensed, 'but such term does not include the business of managing * * * artists * * * where such business only incidentally involves the seeking of employment therefor.' This contract provided for management, and but incidentally for seeking employment. Plaintiff's compensation was based on defendant's earnings from employment whether procured by plaintiff or not. Indeed, defendant by letter emphasized to plaintiff, 'You know you are supposed to be my personal manager,' and taxed plaintiff [with] failure to perform her duties as manager. This contract is no subterfuge to evade the General Business Law. An employment agency could not circumvent the statute by putting its contract to procure employment for an artist in the form of an agreement for management. But that is not the case at bar. The judgment should therefore be affirmed.

Judgment affirmed, with $25 costs.

GUY, Justice, dissenting.

The contract which forms the basis of plaintiff's cause of action provides, first, that defendant agrees to and does hereby engage plaintiff to be her exclusive manager; second, that plaintiff agrees to render service 'in the procuring of desirable and profitable engagements' for defendant; third, that defendant 'does hereby further agree to pay to the said Betty Payne a sum equal to 10 per cent of her earnings, such sums to be paid weekly,' the agreement to be in force for a period of two years.

The only specific duties which plaintiff undertakes to perform for defendant are to render service 'in the procuring of desirable and profitable engagements,' and the compensation provided to be paid plaintiff, equal to 10 per cent of defendant's earnings, is clearly intended to be compensation for the only duties plaintiff has contracted to perform or is obligated to perform. It is conceded that plaintiff had no license to act as a theatrical employment agent.

Section 171, subd. 3, of the General Business Law (as amended by Laws 1917, c. 770) provides:

> The term 'theatrical employment agency' means and includes the business of conducting an agency, bureau, office or any other place for the purpose of procuring or offering, promising or attempting to provide engagements for circus, vaudeville, theatrical and other entertainments or exhibitions or performances, or of giving information as to where such engagements may be procured or provided, whether such business is conducted in a building, on the street or elsewhere, but such term does not include the business of managing such entertainments, exhibitions or performances, or the artists or attractions constituting the same, where such business only incidentally involves the seeking of employment therefor.

Section 172 of said laws (as amended by Laws 1910, c. 700) provides:

> A person shall not open, keep, maintain or carry on any employment agency, as defined in the preceding section, unless he shall have first procured a license

—and that any one so doing without a license shall be guilty of a misdemeanor. As the contract runs for two years, during which period plaintiff is to endeavor to obtain engagements of the character described in the statute, and to receive a percentage of plaintiff's professional earnings during said entire period, the service which by said contract plaintiff undertook to perform, and defendant undertook to compensate plaintiff for performing, constituted a carrying on of the business of an employment agency as prohibited by the statute, and clearly the contract does not come within the exception provided by section 171, for the reason that by said contract the obtaining of employment is not incidental, but is the main purpose of the contract, and the management is incidental. Sirkin v. Fourteenth Street Store, 124 App. Div. 384, 389, 108 N.Y. Supp. 830; Johnston v. Dahlgren, 166 N.Y. 354, 59 N.E. 987; Meyers v. Walton, 76 Misc. Rep. 510, 135 N.Y. Supp. 574.

The judgment should therefore be reversed, with $30 costs, and the complaint dismissed, with costs.

PERSONAL MANAGEMENT
Gerald A. Margolis et al.
598 PLI/Pat 1149 (Mar. 2000)

There is considerable confusion surrounding the role a personal manager plays in the career of a performing artist. Whether the artist's focus is recording, musical performance, television, motion pictures, literary property or legitimate theater, the role of personal manager can be a central and, in many instances, critically necessary element in the development and exploitation of an artist's career. The manager's professional guidance and economic support can provide the struggling artist with the very ability to survive until anticipated opportunities arise.

One of the reasons for the uncertainty of the role of the personal manager is related to the lack of formal requirements—both statutory and administrative—and the absence of any licensing procedures before an individual can become a personal manager. It is, essentially, a self-ordained role. This lack of formal prerequisite is a double-edged sword: While it invites a wide variety of individuals to contribute their time, effort and money to the development of artists' careers, it also allows the occasional unscrupulous person to prey on the unsuspecting and often overly eager aspiring artist without any built-in mechanism for screening or supervision. The unions associated with performing artists have procedures for franchising and regulating booking agents, but no such procedures exist for personal managers. (The American Federation of Musicians supplies suggested personal management contract forms, but their use is essentially voluntary, and even when utilized, they are often substantially amended.)

Another reason for the ambiguity surrounding the personal manager's role has to do with the wide range of other individuals who perform related services for the professionally active artist. Accordingly, a discussion of some of these other related services and individuals may help to define the role of the personal manager and to clear up some of the confusion. If it thus cannot be made clear all that a personal manager is, at least one can begin to see what he [or she] is not.

A. Related Business and Management Personnel

1. Accountant

While the personal manager often handles money and gives advice on financial matters, he does not normally provide the tax planning, bookkeeping and payroll functions, which are the accountant's domain. Tour accountants specialize in managing finances while an artist is on the road.

2. Business Manager

A term born and bred in California (but now in general use on both coasts), the business manager is most usually an accountant, but occasionally a tax attorney performs this function. It is difficult to distinguish between the functions of the accountant and the business manager, although some believe that the grander role, suggested by the business manager's somewhat meatier title, involves particularly complex and substantial arrangements or more long-range economic and tax planning. As a matter of day-to-day practice, there is no real difference, and the accountant (or tax attorney) and business manager are definitionally interchangeable (transforming, if at all, only as the result of bicoastal travel and the prevailing jargon).

3. Attorneys

While the distinctions may seem obvious, many personal managers are, in fact, also attorneys; and some practicing attorneys double as personal managers. There are difficult questions involving conflict of interest and the extent of fiduciary duty where the attorney-manager performs both functions for the artist-client, but such questions are beyond the scope of this chapter. Because of the pervasive role many entertainment attorneys play in the careers of their artist-clients, the personal manager and the attorney often work closely together in counseling the artist with respect to business and contractual matters.

4. Booking Agents

Confusing the personal manager with the booking agent is perhaps the biggest factor contributing to the ambiguity surrounding the personal manager's function. It must be remembered that in both New York and California, an employment agency license is required before one can engage in the business of seeking or procuring employment for others, and there are civil (and in New York, criminal) penalties for "booking" (procuring employment) without a proper license. In addition to statutory sanctions, the courts have dealt harshly with unlicensed personal managers who, as a part of their regular duties, engage in booking activities on behalf of their artists. These managers not only may forfeit their entitlement to commissions (and the right to continue any ongoing contractual relationship with the artist), but they also may be unable even to secure repayment of costs and loans they advanced to the artist in the course of the personal management relationship. The personal manager should be cautioned specifically against any conduct that could open him up to an accusation (which accusation, not surprisingly, might come from a disgruntled artist-client) of performing a booking agent's (an employment agency's) function without a license.

As noted, unlicensed booking constitutes a crime (a misdemeanor) in New York; by contrast, in California, unlicensed employment activities are specifically excluded from the criminal statutes, although the civil penalties in California for such activities can be harsh. The New York employment agency statute, however, contains an exception to the licensing requirement for persons engaged in "the business of managing such entertainments...[and] artists...where such business only incidentally involves the seeking of employment therefor." This fairly nonspecific notion of "incidental booking" has, as one might imagine, given rise to numerous litigations, and it is still far from clear what the phrase means. However, adhering to the plain import of this phrase, using common sense, avoiding any prolonged or regular course of conduct involving the seeking or securing of employment, and relying on the "California exception" seem to be the best available guidelines. The "California exception" is contained in the California employment agency Talent Agencies Act, which provides that no employment agency license is required where a representative is involved in securing a recording contract for his clients.

Having considered what the personal manager is not, and what personal management does not ordinarily encompass, a discussion of the personal manager's typical functions seems appropriate.

B. Job Functions of the Personal Manager—Guidance, Counsel and Advice

While phrased in various ways, "guidance, counsel and advice" is the key language most often associated with the personal manager's primary job function. The personal manager is expected to advise the artist in all facets of the artist's career, including the following areas:

1. Selection of Material: This can include the proper script, the right song or the appropriate staging, scenery and lighting.

2. Selection of Costumes: Appearances mean image, and image can mean everything. Makeup, wardrobe, styling and accessories are all important particulars about which the personal manager's guidance will be sought.

3. Selection of Personnel: The choice of the individuals to render support services to the artist is either made by, or at least recommended by, the personal manager. Included in this nearly endless list might be the booking agent, publicist, accountant, attorney, record producer, backup musicians, stage or road manager, promoter, technical crew and other creative and business individuals whose services will be required. Keep in mind that it is the artist and not the personal manager who will actually employ and pay these people, but normally their hiring will be on the authority or recommendation of the personal manager.

4. Selection of the Proper Vehicle: This can involve selection of the most suitable record label; selection of the right television series; the best theater; the most appropriate stadium, venue or city for a particular act; an acceptable stage engagement; and the decision whether to do (and how to do) a video project. Here again, the list can be as long as the situations and opportunities encountered in the development of an artist's career.

5. Personal Management: No misprint—it really is a personal relationship. Not infrequently, the personal manager will play confidant, psychiatrist, nursemaid, father-figure (or mother-figure), or any other such personally oriented role that might be called for. The entertainment industry spawns its own special kind of tensions, and artists often find themselves the focus of conflicting pressures and influences. The personal manager must be able to sense these difficulties and respond thoughtfully.

6. Representation with Third Parties: Since often it is neither appropriate nor wise for the artist to conduct business affairs directly with third parties, the personal manager (together with the attorney, booking agent, accountant and so on, where called for) will serve as the artist's alter ego in negotiations with third parties. Some common examples follow....

c. Legitimate stage: Live stage entails negotiation with theater managers ("professional managers"), investors and the entire panoply of creative and administrative people whose efforts go into putting together a live stage production.

7. The Personal Manager as a Source of Funds: Although no longer as common as it once was, it is still not at all unusual for a personal manager to provide an artist-client with money while they both await that big break. Providing an artist with clothing, food and shelter is sometimes a necessary personal management function if an impecunious client is to have any chance of developing. Purchasing costumes and equipment, paying for voice or acting lessons, arranging, at the personal manager's cost, for rehearsal halls or showcase clubs, can all be financial burdens shouldered by the personal manager. Again, such risks and sacrifices are not necessarily expected of each personal manager, and the extent of this type of financial commitment should be thoroughly discussed at the earliest possible time.

8. Self-Imposed Limitations on the Management Job Function: It is sometimes appropriate to limit the scope of the personal manager's role. Not all artists require, or desire, worldwide services; some have a personal manager in the United States and an-

other for the U.K. and Europe. Other artists require representation only in particular fields, such as phonograph records and music performance. While this is perfectly acceptable, note that the personal manager would ordinarily want to avoid eliminating any field of entertainment from the scope of the agreement. This is another subject requiring early discussion.

THE ECONOMIC RELATIONSHIP

The basic economic structure of all personal manager agreements is the payment of a commission to the manager based upon some percentage of the artist's gross earnings. This percentage is ordinarily in the area of 10 to 25 percent. The commission can and often does vary, depending upon the amount of gross earnings (with the commission escalating as the gross earnings escalate); the percentage can also increase in subsequent years of the term, or with respect to particular areas of endeavor, or in the event of certain significant agreements being consummated.

Nearly all personal manager commissions are computed on gross income (it is the same with booking agents). Thus, an artist receiving $10,000 for a television role would pay $2,000 to the personal manager under a 20 percent commission clause. That $2,000 would not decrease even though the artist might also have to pay $500 (5 percent) to a business manager, $1,000 (10 percent) to a booking agency and $1,000 in staff, wardrobe, travel, lodging and related personal expenses. When one factors in the Internal Revenue Service's share (assuming the artist is in the 36 percent tax bracket), one can see that, out of the $10,000 gross payment, the artist's net is only $2,000 before any applicable tax deductions are considered.

Notes

1. Two months after unionizing, the Ellis Island actors had a new contract giving them increased wages, health insurance, a pension, paid sick days, and a promise from management that it would do its best to provide two dressing rooms near the theater. *See further* Steven Greenhouse, *Pact for Actors at Ellis Island*, N.Y. Times, Oct. 18, 2002, at B8.

2. The *N.L.R.B.* and *H. A. Artists* cases recognize an important fact: unions often are sued when they use their leverage against "outsiders." Yet the chief reason to belong to a union is to harness the power that comes from concerted action, as the Ellis Island actors did. Can this dichotomy be reconciled? *See* Emily C. Chi, *Star Quality and Job Security: The Role of the Performers' Unions in Controlling Access to the Acting Profession*, 18 Cardozo Arts & Ent. L.J. 1 (2000), and Mark D. Meredith, Note, *From Dancing Halls to Hiring Halls: Actors' Equity and the Closed Shop Dilemma*, 96 Colum. L. Rev. 178 (1996).

3. As Justice Stewart pointed out, Actors' Equity Association (www.actorsequity.org) traditionally has represented the vast majority of American stage actors (it currently has about 45,000 members). Although Equity's principal mission always has been to negotiate better working conditions and help performers in financial need, it also was an early supporter of the civil rights movement (helping to integrate the National Theatre in Washington, D.C.), led the effort to create the National Endowment for the Arts, and participates in a number of philanthropic efforts, including "Broadway Cares/Equity Fights AIDS" (www.bcefa.org), which recognizes the impact that HIV has had on the theater world, and "Broadway Barks!" (www.officialbroadwaybarks.org), an annual pet adopt-a-thon and animal shelter fundraiser. *See further About Equity: A Handbook,*

available at www.actorsequity.org/library/Misc/aboutequity_booklet.PDF. *See also* Renee Antoinette Simmons, *Frederick Douglas O'Neal: Pioneer of the Actors' Equity Association* (1996) (a biography of Equity's first African-American president, who was elected in 1964).

4. Does New York's "incidental booking exception," which proved decisive in *Pawlowski*, make sense? Conversely, is the lack of official oversight of personal managers troubling? *See further Cheng v. Dispeker*, 1995 WL 86353 (S.D.N.Y. 1995) (obligations of booking agents); Paul K. Lukacs, *How New York and Tennessee Regulate Talent Agencies*, 14 Ent. & Sports Law. 15 (Fall 1996); Heath B. Zarin, Note, *The California Controversy Over Procuring Employment: A Case for the Personal Managers Act*, 7 Fordham Intell. Prop. Media & Ent. L.J. 927 (1997).

5. As Margolis explains, a given actor or actress may be simultaneously represented by a number of different professionals. If the artist is to be well served, these individuals must work together as a team:

> Picture a wagon wheel. At the very center is the axle. The axle is the performing artist around which everything revolves. The hub protects and supports the axle. That is the personal manager. The rim of the wheel is the artist's career which travels on what can often be a bumpy, long, winding road. Connecting the hub with the rim are many spokes which give the wheel support in different directions. These are the agents, publicists, attorneys, business managers, and other industry professionals which support an artist on the road to success. When the wheel is well constructed, the artist's journey can be smooth, speedy and successful.

What is a Personal Manager?, at www.ncopm.com.

6. One of the recurring characters on the long-running NBC sitcom *Friends* was Estelle Leonard (played by June Gable), Joey's flighty, chain-smoking agent. In Episode 125, entitled "The One Where Joey Loses His Insurance," the writers had particular fun with their relationship:

Joey: (entering) Hey Estelle, listen...

Estelle: Well! Well! Well! Joey Tribbiani! So you came back huh? They think they can do better but they all come crawling back to Estelle!

Joey: What are you talkin' about? I never left you! You've always been my agent!

Estelle: Really?!

Joey: Yeah!

Estelle: Oh well, no harm, no foul.

Problem 13

An actor has hired one agent to represent him and another to represent his personal service corporation. The two contracts are identical except for their arbitration clauses. Should the actor be worried? *See William Morris Agency, Inc. v. Cambridge*, 328 N.Y.S.2d 62 (Sup. Ct. 1971).

Chapter 7

Designers, Musicians, and Crew

A. OVERVIEW

It takes a bevy of men and women working diligently behind the scenes for a production to be successful. These are the technical folks, who toil in the "back of the house," and it is their job to build and operate the sets, light the stage, provide the sound, music, and special effects, and see to the costumes, props, and makeup needed by the performers.

B. BEHIND THE SCENES

LION'S DEN: BACKSTAGE AT BROADWAY'S HOTTEST NEW MUSICAL
Michael Riedel
N.Y. Daily News, Nov. 16, 1997, at 1 (Sunday Extra)

An eerie silence hangs over the vast, empty stage of the New Amsterdam Theater. Then...

Whoosh! An 8-foot column of smoke blasts from the floor.

Whoosh! A second column erupts at the opposite end of the stage.

Now, the entire playing area is a minefield of smoke.

"Okay, the geysers are working!" says a voice from the wings.

Suddenly, the stage is swarming with stagehands and technicians, dressers and dancers. Large pieces of scenery are flying overhead. Spotlights are blinking on and off. And in a dark corner of the stage, a young woman, dressed as a lioness, is practicing her roar.

Welcome to the behind-the-scenes jungle that is "The Lion King."

A $20 million musical extravaganza from the Walt Disney Company, "The Lion King" opened on Broadway last week to spectacular reviews. Not since the chandelier descended on the first-night audience at "The Phantom of the Opera" has a show so captivated the Great White Way.

Recently, Sunday Extra was given an exclusive backstage look at this lavish stage spectacular, which seems destined to reign over Broadway for years to come.

It takes a small army of cast and craftsmen to make this "Lion" roar. The show employs more than 40 actors, 50 stagehands and 24 musicians. It features hundreds of puppets, props and costumes, plus thousands of pounds of scenery all crammed into an area no wider than your average suburban living room.

Standing backstage during a performance, a careless visitor could easily get squashed by a life-size elephant puppet, gored by an actor wearing a warthog costume or run over by a herd of dancers dressed as wildebeests.

But what at first glance appears to be chaos is actually a painstakingly choreographed behind-the-scenes routine designed to keep everyone involved with "The Lion King" out of harm's way.

For the actors, memorizing the backstage choreography is just as crucial as learning the dance routines they do in front of the audience.

"Back here, you've got to know where you're supposed to be at all times," says stage manager Steve (Doc) Zorthian. "Because if you're an inch out of place, you're going to be in trouble."

Preparations for every performance of "The Lion King" begin an hour-and-a-half before the curtain goes up. During the "pre-set," a platoon of stagehands runs a safety check of the musical's numerous special effects. Cast members begin applying complicated makeup to transform themselves into lions, baboons and hyenas. Dancers, dressed as various jungle animals, limber up in the wings.

Zorthian oversees all this backstage activity. If a piece of the set is malfunctioning, he sees that it gets fixed. If an actor is suffering from a pulled muscle, he makes sure the performer visits one of three physical therapists employed by the production.

A half-hour before curtain, cast and crew begin to take their places. In a booth high above the stage at the back of the balcony sits Jeff Lee, the production stage manager. Lee runs "The Lion King," calling out, via radio, every light, sound and set cue. Five television monitors above his desk give him different views of the stage. He is in constant radio contact with the people who operate the backstage computer systems that make the sets move.

During the show, he says things like "up to the half and stand by to drop the knife. And...drop the knife." The result: A big piece of the set comes down from the wings, the lighting shifts and a new scene begins.

The set for "The Lion King" is extremely complicated and dangerous. Its main feature is a turntable set atop an elevator that rises up from beneath the stage. In the wings, hanging perilously above the cast and crew's heads, are two 3,000-pound hydraulic units used in the wildebeest stampede, one of the show's many pulse-racing scenes.

Because there is always the possibility of a malfunction, bright red emergency buttons are scattered throughout the backstage area. Press one, and the entire show comes to a standstill.

We are now just moments away from the start of the show. At the back of the theater, curtained off from the audience, is "the corral." It is stocked with life-size animal puppets including an elephant, a rhinoceros, birds and gazelles that are operated by the performers. As the music swells, the actors, now inside their puppets, march down the aisles to the stage. It's a show-stopping moment. "Think of it as the African nativity," a stagehand whispers.

"Kids go absolutely crazy," says Sam McKelton, one of two actors who operate the rhino puppet. "They try to reach out and touch us."

Of course, some of the younger kids in the audience can be a bit spooked by the parade of animals that opens the show. In fact, even adults are startled by the sight of a giant elephant, ears flapping, walking down the aisle of a Broadway theater. But young and old recover quickly, and are soon staring in wonderment at the mythical jungle kingdom created by the show's director, Julie Taymor.

A blackout ends the opening number. As the actors rush backstage, they are set upon by dressers. Holding tiny flashlights in their mouths, the dressers rip off old costumes and slap on new ones. Costume changes take no more than 15 seconds; the disgarded clothes are stored in a long, narrow room beneath the stage called "the bunker." Here there are rows and rows of wildebeest masks, hyena skins and lion heads. The bunker sometimes feels like a lockerroom, with sweaty performers of both sexes in various states of dress.

The next scene is one of Taymor's most inventive. In it, the vast African savanna is suggested by a row of actors wearing long, flat headboards out of which sprout stalks of grass. There are over 20 "grassheads," as the company calls them. When the scene ends, the actors file off stage and hand their grass heads to a dresser, who places each board in a large hat rack. When the rack is full, it is hoisted high above the stage for storage.

By now, "The Lion King" is up and running, purring along like a finely tuned engine. There's no goofing off backstage, although the company is relaxed enough to crack jokes and exchange the latest gossip. Rosie O'Donnell is in the audience, and a couple of dancers are debating who's the bigger diva: O'Donnell or Patti LuPone. An actor dressed as a hyena reads the sports pages of the Daily News. A stagehand pulling a rope that supports two dancers suspended in midair during the song "Can You Feel the Love Tonight?" groans and jokes: "They must have had pasta for lunch."

"The Lion King" ends with a reprise of "The Circle of Life." As it has done every night since the show played its first preview performance a month ago, the audience leaps to its feet, cheering.

Standing in the wings, propman Victor Amerling smiles and says: "I worked on 'The Phantom of the Opera' after it first opened. And even with Michael Crawford in the lead, that show never got the kind of reaction 'The Lion King' does. It is just amazing."

FARCE OF NATURE
David Johnson
Ent. Design, Mar. 1, 2002, at TCI

Twenty years after its West End premiere, Noises Off continues to be one of the most popular farces staged by regional and community theatres alike, a significant accomplishment considering the amount of pain inevitably inflicted upon those involved in bringing the show to life.

Michael Frayn's classic comedy is one of those productions that seems, on paper, deceptively simple. But once you get knee-deep into the mechanics of the piece—the bruised and battered cast hurtling down stairs and passing through slamming doors, the harried director losing her voice after the umpteenth plea of "Faster!," the frazzled backstage crew nervously waiting for a door to get stuck or one of the many props to turn up missing—it soon becomes apparent that, if not done right, the complete breakdown of order that occurs in the play could easily come true in the real world as well, turning the whole enterprise into something smelling vaguely of sardines.

This also holds true of the set design. Though it consists essentially of one simple, two-level household set—okay, two, if you count Act II's backstage set, though most designers simply opt for a revolve—designers who sign on for Noises Off inevitably find themselves faced with a variety of problems they had never expected. Three recent productions—the current Broadway revival, designed by Robert Jones and based on a production originally done by the Royal National Theatre, a version done at the Trinity Rep and designed by David Jenkins, and a third mounted by a tiny community theatre troupe in the wilds of Canada by David Antscherl—all underscore these challenges.

A quick recap for those unfamiliar with the play, or perhaps more accurately, the play within the play: We see the first act of a creaky English farce called Nothing On three times. Act I takes place on the set just before opening night, as the cast of middling British actors fumble their way through a dress rehearsal, missing cues, losing props, all while the increasingly exasperated director looks on. The mostly wordless second act takes place backstage one month later, as cast and crew, most of whom already hate each other, try desperately to keep things moving onstage without killing or maiming a fellow cast member behind the scenes. Act III takes place, once again, on closing night; we see what's left of the first act of Nothing On after months of broken relationships, in-fighting, drunkenness, and general pettiness have taken their toll, and it's not a pretty sight.

O, Canada

David Antscherl designed the set for the Curtain Call production of Noises Off by proxy; Curtain Call is a small community theatre based in the tiny hamlet of Timmins, Ontario. Antscherl, a British-born and trained designer who does a lot of work around Ontario and is a member of both the Associated Designers of Canada and Theatre Ontario's Talent Bank, was hired by the company but wasn't able to get up to Timmins before the production. "They built it all locally, and I sent fairly extensive painting instructions, since it was an amateur production," he says.

Initial meetings with the Curtain Call group involved the space itself. "We had discussed different ways of doing it," Antscherl recalls. "The thing was, the space it was going into had quite wide sightlines horizontally, which wasn't particularly helpful. Also, it was basically a school theatre auditorium, a multi-use/no-use space, so that threw some extra difficulties in the pot." In the end, the designer opted for placing the main part of the set on a 28' revolve, stacking the two stories and the staircase on it, and setting up the backstage area as the backstage area. "We had some ancillary pieces of scenery stage left and right of the revolve that we used to frame and mask off in the first and third act, and in the second act we had a couple of supplementary pieces with backstage exit signs," Antscherl notes.

The set was built almost completely of wood. The front walls were sponge-painted, the front stairs done in dark walnut; the door frames and floorboards were made of Styrofoam and painted walnut. The backstage area was painted black and beige. The various doors (the script calls for nine in all, plus a large downstairs window) were made of wood and sported actual frames, hinges, and doorknobs. The revolve was built of solid wood. It consisted of 18 easily removable sections, which were configurable, so that sections could be added or removed if needed. The revolve moves via four to six heavy-duty construction casters per section.

The biggest challenge with the revolve was the theatre space itself. The floor of the theatre consisted of a stage and a strikable forestage, which were in sections and thus not entirely level. "The differences was something like 5/8" between the stage level and the forestage level," Antscherl recalls. "It was crazy. So the way I designed the revolve was with independent, floating, pie-shaped segments that were sort of like gravity cleats put together, in order to accommodate the vertical movement as it revolved. And then I provided little mini-ramps along the lines of casters, so that it ramped up between the two different levels. Pretty Mickey-Mouse, but it worked."

One thing Antscherl did not want to be Mickey Mouse was the actual look and feel of the set. "The thing has to be reasonably sturdy," he explains. "I don't think the show needs to have a set become a comedy on its own. To me, the set is the supporting cast, it's not a character in its own right, and in this particular case there's too much going on anyway, and there's no need to throw in visual aids."

A Moving Experience

Most productions of Noises Off move the set around to show the goings-on backstage for Act II; David Jenkins, designer of the recent Trinity Rep production, moved the audience. Director Amanda Dehnert and he frequently toy with the Trinity Rep footprint; in a recent production of Othello, they reconfigured the entire space and flooded the stage, filling water underneath the scenery and holding everything up with I-beams.

"Trinity Rep is a terrific theatre in which to work because they don't say, 'Oh my God, you want to move the seats?' That's not their first question. They're very helpful, and they've gotten used to Amanda and me coming up with these crazy ideas to re-orient the relationship between the audience and the stage. What happened with Noises Off is that she said in the first sentence, 'Let's move the audience.' And I thought, what a great idea."

But not necessarily an easy one to pull off. Because Trinity is subscription-based, the immediate concern was getting the necessary seats backstage for the subscription audience to be viable. There was also the issue of what the audience would actually be sitting on, since nice comfy seats installed backstage were not an option. In the end, Jenkins and the Trinity production staff were able to fit 458 seats into the backstage area, all made up of 2' x 12' wooden benches ("just like in school gyms," notes Jenkins). The audience watched Act I, then, after a normal 15- to 20-minute intermission, moved to their seats at the Act II set behind the stage, helped by Trinity Rep acting school students sporting British accents and usherette costumes. Then, with a short break between Acts II and III, the audience returned to their Act I seats.

"Most of the work in designing the show was getting the same amount of seats on both sides," Jenkins explains. "Because every time you joggled six seats, then you had to joggle six in the back as well. We had to make sure everyone was accommodated; wheelchair accessibility became a big factor, and what kind of seating it was going to be became a big factor, because we didn't just want to replicate what was out front. We wanted to keep the backstage look so we went with raw, wooden bleachers."

Compared to the design of the seating, Jenkins says, the set design was a breeze. "The set's not a hard set, frankly. You have to have the prerequisite number of doors and they all have to be in relative position to one another. The minute you try changing something and being inventive you get into trouble. The temptation is to make it more than it should be. My favorite remark was when the cast came in for the first time and said it was like the summer stock they remembered here or a regional thing they remembered there.

"But how do you design tacky?" Jenkins continues. "It's not an easy challenge. For instance, all the scenery was painted. We had some stone wall in the set, reflecting some of the mill idea in the play, which was all painted stone. It would normally be my tendency to make it dimensional stone. We didn't worry about making sure it all masked properly. The main thing was making it all safe. It could look a little shabby, but because it gets such a workout, we had to make sure it was secure for the actors running around on the stairs and the balcony."

The set (and seating) was built in place onstage by the Trinity rep staff. "Like a lot of regional theatres, they build in place and add about a week to 10 days, depending on the show," Jenkins explains. "They have an extended period of time between shows, because the nature of the shop is not large enough to build the whole show and then load it in."

The sturdy set still took its fair share of abuse, a given for this play. "The doors required constant repair," Jenkins says. "We had a carpenter on the show who just wore out his toolbelt. He'd arrive half an hour before the house opened and repair the doors and latches. He was exactly like the character in the play. I heard reports that during the show, when a door would start to fall off, he'd just walk out and fix it."

Farce of Steel

Robert Jones' sets for the Broadway production of Noises Off didn't have that problem: every single door, and in fact the central core of the set, was built out of steel. Protecting the set from all that physical abuse was only part of the reason for opting for something so strong.

"The doors really clang when they close," Jones explains. "It was done for both the noise and the strength; we really wanted that thunderclap noise. When you see the back of the set, the doorframes are all steel, but they're painted to look like timber, as is all the structure at the back of the set."

The Broadway revival, now playing at the Brooks Atkinson, contains some slight modifications from most productions of the play: Frayn tinkered with Act III, shortening it a bit, and there is no intermission between the second and third act. Jones tried tinkering with the set as well, and that's where he got into trouble.

"The original concept was based on a flat wall with all the doors on the same plane," Jones explains, "and I said to Jeremy [Sams, the director], and to Michael, 'I think we need to set the set on an angle to give it a different dynamic.' So we put it on an angle, just to make it look more interesting, which of course set up all sorts of problems. We had to work out, for instance, if someone was standing, say, in a door downstage right, could they be seen by a person on the upper level upstage left?"

"It was all those little things," he continues. "Every little decision that was made influenced another decision. We would do something, and then it wouldn't make sense when we turned the set around, and vice versa. I remember sitting with Jeremy, and having little colored dots for each character, saying, can the blue dot be seen by the red dot in that position, and how long did it take that dot to get from door A to door B while someone else is doing it from door C to door D. You set out to design this play and it turns into this huge can of worms."

In designing the set, Jones was keen to not make it a joke in itself. "It was very important to me that it wasn't a comedy set, that it wasn't cutouts, or cartoony, because the play is funny, it's rooted in reality, and it's out of that reality that comes the sheer comedy of the evening. When the curtain goes up, if you have a set that makes the audience smile, or if it's a joke in itself, then it doesn't really have anywhere to go. We have to believe that we're watching a fairly good production of Nothing On. It's not very good farce, but they've spent money on it and done it to the best of their ability. If there's wobbly walls and door handles coming off and everything at weird angles, then it wouldn't be right."

From a pure aesthetic standpoint, Jones' real innovation for this production was to add a double-height window, allowing the audience to see through all the way up to the top of the set. "It was originally written with one window on the lower level (through which one of the characters, playing a burglar, breaks into), and I think there was a door above it, which doesn't quite make sense in terms of the logic of a real house. So we added this window, which works in that we can see what's happening on both levels when the set is turned around."

In its original incarnation, Noises Off was performed in rep for the Royal National at the Lyttelton, where it would be on for several performances and then off again; as a result, the set needed to have elements that would come apart easily. In that initial production, because the Lyttelton has a wide proscenium, Jones had designed the set with a false proscenium with scrim walls allowing the audience to see backstage; in Act I, you could see the stage manager and a nearby stage door. For the subsequent UK tour and West End production, that surrounding area dropped, putting the set about 9m or 10m across (or approximately 32'). All versions have included a turntable, including the Broadway production, though the latter is smaller and completely motorized. In fact, the show's New York incarnation required quite a lot of re-thinking.

"The New York production cosmetically looks very similar to the London production, but technically it's completely different," Jones says. "We were very concerned about fitting the production into the Brooks Atkinson; it's half the depth of West End theatres, but we have the same width we had at the Royal National. So it went into Cinemascope. What we tried to do was focus it all in so that the actual playing space of the center didn't differ too much in terms of the distances it had taken the actors so long to work out. What we didn't want to do was reconceive the piece, because we knew what we got worked, and it had taken us weeks and weeks to get everything fitted. To reconceive would not give us the production we'd gotten."

But perhaps the biggest change in the New York production comes in the second act; a major portion of what the audience sees in Act II is actually not the back of what they've seen in the first act but a duplicate. The center section, which includes the majority of the doors and the gallery, is spun around, but the side pieces are brought out on a series of small wagons, and upper pieces are dropped in; these are completely new prefab versions of the back, with the angle cheated slightly. Technical supervision for the New York production was by Unitech; the computer motion control and the automation of the scenery and rigging was by Feller Precision.

In the end, Jones agrees with his fellow set designers about the deceptiveness of this enduring farce. "It's one of those things that people look at, and think is quite simple, but once we actually started designing it, it took us quite a while to work out the logic of it all, because it can be very complicated. I actually think it was one of the most difficult things I've designed in many years, just in terms of sheer logistics. If anyone dismisses farce as being easy, they're very much mistaken."

STATE EX REL. O'BRIEN v. PETRY
397 S.W.2d 1 (Mo. Ct. App. 1965)

GREENE, Special Judge.

This case is an action in quo warranto, and for a declaratory judgment, which was filed on September 10, 1962, in the Circuit Court of St. Louis County, in which action Tillman Hardy was the informant, and William Petry, Jack Scatcherd, Carmen Rand,

Ritchey Calahan, Richard Coates, William Cohen, Joseph Rosel, Warren Burgess, and Charles Cromwell, were respondents.

The relevant facts are as follows: Informant had been a member of The Theatre Guild of Webster Groves, Missouri, for ten years. The Guild is a corporation organized under Chapter 352, V.A.M.S., and its function is to promote interest in the dramatic arts, and to produce dramatic and theatrical performances for the benefit and enjoyment of the general public in Webster Groves and the surrounding area.

The record does not reveal the criteria for becoming a member of this civic group, but does show that Section 8 of Article II of the By-Laws of the Guild provides that expulsion of members for reasons other than nonpayment of dues shall be a matter of discretion of the Board of Directors. Sec. 8, Art. II further provides that the Board may not act in any such case without notification, in writing, to the member, of the charges against him, and such notice is to inform him of a date for a closed session hearing. Only after such a hearing and a vote of at least two-thirds of the whole Board assembled therefor, in favor of expulsion, shall the member be dropped.

Article IV of the Articles of Association provides that the Board shall consist of nine members, who are elected by the membership, from their own number. Article III of the By-Laws provides that Board members are elected at the annual meeting of the membership prior to March 15th, but their term of office does not begin until the following June 1st. Article IV of the By-Laws provides that no member shall be eligible for election or appointment to the Board who has not been a member in good standing for one full year next preceding his election or appointment.

On May 12, 1960, informant was working on the construction of a set for a play called 'The Rainmaker.' Without obtaining permission from the technical director, or production manager, of the play, informant made changes in the design, by painting portions of the set, the wall of the building, and part of the stage a different color than had been prescribed. To accomplish his purpose, he left the outside door unlocked, as he had no key to the building, and then returned to the building after the other workers had left. He also drilled holes in the ceiling tile in violation of orders from the Director and Production Manager. Informant was served with written notice directing him to appear before the Board of Directors on June 8, 1960, to answer charges preferred against informant by the Board, the substance of which charges are set out above. Informant appeared at the hearing and represented himself. He objected to the Board being his judges; asked for a jury trial; objected to the hearing not being public; and objected to the By-Laws providing for the hearing.

The president, in each instance, stated that the Board was complying with the By-Laws, specifically Article II, Section 8. Informant admitted the charges, and admitted he was wrong in re-entering the building, after leaving the door open the night before, and painting the set without authority. He was asked to conform to the wishes of the group, and was told that his actions, which were done without authority, caused inconvenience and unhappiness to the Guild. He assured the Board that if he was allowed to remain a member, he would not do anything in the future without consulting the person in charge. Informant was advised by the president that if there was any repetition of his individual actions without authority of the Guild, or its officers, there would be no question of his expulsion. A vote was taken and the vote was 7 to 1 against expulsion. Informant was told, and he considered he was on probation.

On March 11, 1962, informant was elected to the Board for a two-year term. His term of office was to begin June 1, 1962.

Some time after March 11th, but before April 4, 1962, informant was in charge of set construction for a play called 'Autumn Garden.' Gwen Springett was production manager, and Mr. William Petry was technical director. The production manager is responsible for set design, and the technical director is responsible for all technical production aspects of the play, including lighting, and is responsible for all equipment, including the equipment in the sound and light booth. The equipment kept there was valuable.

Without authority from Mr. Petry, informant had keys to the light and sound booth made for his own use. Also, without authority from Gwen Springett, he completely changed one side of the set, and enlarged the other side. He did not consult with Gwen Springett before he did this. After he changed the set, he found that he had closed off access from one side of the stage to the other for the actors back stage, so he cut a hole through a main innerwall of the building that opened out onto a narrow nine or ten inch ledge over which the actors had to move to get to the other side of the stage. He also changed the lighting of the set by putting some lights behind the set. Mr. Petry had not given him authority to do this.

On April 4, 1962, Mr. Hardy was served with written notice to appear before the Board on that same evening at 8 P.M. to answer to the charge that he had altered the innerwall at the rear of the stage without proper authority.

The notice called attention to Section 8, Article II of the By-Laws, and set out the pertinent portions of said article, as previously stated. April 4th was evidently a regular meeting night, as Mr. Hardy was at the meeting. Although his term as a board member did not start until June 1st, he had authority to attend board meetings, but could not vote. He received the notice a few minutes before the meeting started. Informant was called before the board. He did not request a continuance, and presented his case. Informant admitted cutting the hole in the wall, and gave his reasons for doing so. The minutes of the meeting (Respondents' Exhibit A) indicate considerable discussion between the board and informant on the issue. After the discussion a ballot was taken and the board voted 6 to 1 to expel informant, the president abstaining. Informant was called in, and told of the board's decision. He remarked 'This is not the end of it,' which was a most prophetic statement.

Informant continued to appear at Board meetings. He appeared on May 2, 1962, at which time he was given written notice of his expulsion. He was asked to pick up his personal possessions, and he left. He appeared at a general meeting of the membership in May, and at another board meeting June 8th. He was asked to explain his presence. He said he had come to take his rightful place on the new board. He was advised again that he was not a member of the Guild or the Board. They refused to seat him on the Board, and after a heated discussion, informant left, saying they would hear from him again. To avoid further incidents and contacts with informant, the Board went underground, and met at times and places unknown to informant. He thereafter filed suit, on September 10, 1962, against respondents, asking that they be ousted from their offices for unlawfully using their offices as Board members (meeting without him), and asking for a declaratory judgment to construe the franchise, by-laws, and articles of association of the Theatre Guild of Webster Groves, and to declare whether or not informant was validly expelled from membership in the Guild. Informant, on January 10, 1964, requested the court to prepare a statement of the grounds for its decision, and to make findings of fact on any and all principal controverted fact issues.

On February 10, 1964, the cause was heard in the Circuit Court of St. Louis County, and on April 1, 1964, a decree was entered which found the issues for defendants, and against the informant. The decree further recited that informant was afforded such due process as he requested, wanted, and was entitled to under all the circumstances; that informant was given notice of the meeting at which he was expelled, and that if the notice was inadequate the informant waived his right to object to this by his attendance at and participation in the meeting. The decree further found that the informant had been validly expelled, and was not legally a member of the Guild, nor a member of its Board of Directors, and that nothing in the franchise, By-Laws, nor Articles of Association of said Guild could be construed to the contrary. All costs were taxed against informant. No separate findings of fact and conclusions of law were filed by the trial court.

Informant timely filed his motion for new trial alleging sixteen major errors on the part of the trial court. The trial court overruled said motion, and informant appealed to this court.

The issues raised by informant on appeal are many and diffuse. The case is not as complicated, however, as he would have us believe. While the courts will protect a member of an association against illegal expulsion, the field of judicial interference with the actions of voluntary associations as to controversies between their members over the method and manner in which the rights of membership may be maintained and terminated is and should be a very narrow one, and its boundary should be maintained with the utmost care, so that only upon the clearest kind of showing, that the constitution and rules are violated by the decisions of the tribunals set up by them should the courts permit their jurisdiction to be invoked. Junkins v. Local Union No. 6313, Communication Workers of America et al., 241 Mo.App. 1029, 271 S.W.2d 71, l. c. 76.

There is no showing here that the Board's decision to expel informant violated such rules, or that informant was not granted a fair hearing, either before the Board, or the court below.

The judgment is affirmed.

Notes

1. There are numerous books and web sites dedicated to the technical aspects of theater production. As to the former, *see, e.g.*, Drew Campbell, *Technical Theater for Nontechnical People* (1999); Warren C. Lounsbury & Norman C. Boulanger, *Theatre Backstage from A to Z* (4th ed. 2000); Thomas A. Kelly, *The Back Stage Guide to Stage Management* (1999). As to the latter, *see, e.g.*, www.backstagejobs.com and www.theatrecrafts.com. A sample scenery rental agreement appears in Appendix F of this casebook.

2. The plaintiff's actions in *O'Brien*, although inexplicable, are a good illustration of the chaos that can reign when a crew member becomes a rogue. For other cases involving theatrical equipment, *see Production Resource Group, L.L.C. v. Stonebridge Partners Equity Fund, L.P.*, 6 F. Supp. 2d 236 (S.D.N.Y. 1998); *Jones Beach Theatre Corp. v. Commissioner*, 25 T.C.M. (CCH) 527 (T.C. 1966); *Allied Sound, Inc. v. Neely*, 58 S.W.3d 119 (Tenn. Ct. App. 2001); *Merrick v. Four Star Stage Lighting, Inc.*, 378 N.Y.S.2d 65 (App. Div. 1975). *See also* Rebecca Ishaq Foster, Comment, *Protect the Bastard Child of the Arts: Copyright Protection for Theatrical Costumes*, 22 Sw. U. L. Rev. 431 (1993), and Rebeca Sanchez-Roig, Note, *Putting the Show Together and Taking It On the Road: Copyright, the Appropriate Protection for Theatrical Scenic and Costume Designs*, 40 Syracuse L. Rev. 1089 (1989).

3. Computers have revolutionized the way scenes can be written and executed, and audiences now expect to see special effects when they go to a play. This innovation has not been universally hailed, however, for some observers believe the increasing use of special effects is cheapening the theater-going experience. In addition, computers have drastically reduced the number of stagehands needed to run a play. *See further* Jesse McKinley, *Act II: Enter the Computers*, N.Y. Times, Oct. 17, 2002, at E1.

4. In March 2003, Broadway musicians went on strike after producers announced plans to begin using computer-generated music to cut costs. The job action shut down 18 musicals and caused losses estimated at $7 million a day. At issue was the union's contract, which required the employment of between three and 26 musicians, depending on the size of the theater, at salaries starting at $1,350 per week. Over the years, these minimums had resulted in the hiring of scores of unneeded musicians (known as "walkers"), resulting in higher costs and lower profits for producers. *See* Christopher Milazzo, *A Swan Song for Live Music?: Problems Facing the American Federation of Musicians in the Technological Age*, 13 Hofstra Lab. L.J. 557 (1996); Mindy Schwartz, Comment, *The American Federation of Musicians: An Unearned Encore for Featherbedding*, 47 Wayne L. Rev. 1339 (2001-2002); Anthony Tommasini, *A Long, Loud Journey Toward 'Virtual' Broadway Music Began Years Ago*, N.Y. Times, Mar. 11, 2003, at A27.

Surprised by the decision of actors and stagehands to honor the musicians' picket lines (Harvey Fierstein, the star of "Hairspray," was widely quoted as saying, "We're professionals, we're artists—a machine is a dead thing"), and pushed by both Mayor Michael Bloomberg and theatergoers to resolve the dispute, the producers quickly abandoned their plans and agreed to a more modest 25% reduction in the minimums. *See* Robin Pogrebin & Steven Greenhouse, *Broadway's Lights Go Back On as Musicians Reach an Accord*, N.Y. Times, Mar. 12, 2003, at A1 (noting that the new contract will still result in annual savings of at least $600,000 for the very largest Broadway musicals).

Problem 14

To ensure that a fight in a play appears authentic, it has been decided that a real knife will be used instead of a rubber one. As the production's lawyer, what steps should you take to minimize any potential liability? *See Bishop v. Texas A & M University*, 35 S.W.3d 605 (Tex. 2000).

C. EMPLOYMENT DISPUTES

OSTERTAG v. THE HISTORIC THEATER GROUP, LTD.
221 F.3d 1343 (8th Cir. 2000)

PER CURIAM.

After he was passed-over in favor of younger job candidates, Donald E. Ostertag ("Ostertag") sued The Historic Theater Group, Ltd. ("HTG") and alleged a violation of the Age Discrimination in Employment Act of 1967, 29 U.S.C. §621 et seq. ("ADEA"). On summary judgment, the district court dismissed Ostertag's complaint because HTG offered nondiscriminatory reasons for discharging Ostertag, and he, in turn, failed to show that those reasons were pretextual. Ostertag appeals. We affirm.

Ostertag is a sixty-one-year-old man. Since 1966, he has worked in numerous theatrical productions as a stagehand and department head supervising carpenters, electricians, and props. HTG manages the Historic State and Orpheum Theaters ("Theaters") in Minneapolis, Minnesota.

Ostertag applied for positions as an operations assistant for various shows to be produced at the Theaters. Although HTG selected six applicants, it rejected Ostertag. Of the six individuals hired by HTG to fill the operations assistant positions, only one was over forty years of age at the time of hiring. In addition, Ostertag had more stage and theatrical work experience than any of the individuals hired by HTG. Thus, Ostertag brought suit contending HTG discriminated against him because of his age, in violation of the provisions of the ADEA.

In granting summary judgment for HTG, however, the district court, among other evidence, quoted, and credited, the affidavit testimony of HTG's president, Herbert Frederick Krohn, Jr. as follows:

> Based on these incidents and complaints, as well as my own observations that Mr. Ostertag was often argumentative, temperamental and disruptive, and had problems working with his fellow stagehands and clients, I decided that Mr. Ostertag did not fulfill the criteria for the Operations Assistant positions. In particular, I did not believe that Mr. Ostertag had the ability to interface with theater clients in a professional and problem-solving way, nor work with the current operations managers and operations assistants as a member of an effective and cohesive team.

Dist. Ct. Op. at 7. On this affidavit and other corroborating evidence, the district court concluded HTG had articulated a legitimate, nondiscriminatory reason for selecting others instead of Ostertag.

Further, the district court determined that Ostertag provided no evidence to establish pretext in the employer's decision. The district court observed: Plaintiff does not present evidence sufficient to challenge directly the basis for or the validity of Defendant's proffered reason for the adverse employment action. To the contrary, Plaintiff does not deny engaging in the "argumentative, temperamental and disruptive" behavior upon which Defendant bases its conclusion that he lacks "ability to interface with theater clients in a professional and problem-solving way" and the ability to work "as a member of an effective and cohesive team." Rather than presenting evidence to refute the foundation for HTG's proffered reason for failing to hire Plaintiff, Plaintiff attempts to minimize the altercations and "inappropriate" behavior that comprise such foundation. Dist. Ct. Op. at 14.

Ostertag asserts that he has rendered excellent services for theatrical productions and that his occasional temperamental episodes should not disqualify him from serving as the operations assistant for HTG. Ostertag's assertion relates to a business judgment—which is the prerogative of the employer to make—and is not a matter for the courts to overturn. See Slathar v. Sather Trucking Corp., 78 F.3d 415 (8th Cir.1996); Walker v. AT & T Techs., 995 F.2d 846 (8th Cir.1993).

Our review reveals no error of fact or law. Accordingly, we affirm for the reasons set forth by United States District Judge Michael J. Davis in his well-reasoned and well-documented opinion.

ANDERSON v. LONG
56 Pa. Super. 183 (1914)

ORLADY, Judge.

The plaintiff is a designer of theatrical costumes, resident of London, England, and the defendant a playwright of Philadelphia. The parties were well known to each other in their respective occupations. The defendant was engaged in the creation of a play, and secured the services of the plaintiff to make the designs for the costumes necessary for its production. A number of letters were exchanged in regard to its general and special nature, its locale, characters, and description of costumes, etc.

On May 5, 1908, Mr. Anderson wrote, "When I know the date I can finish the drawings I will write, and on receipt of the cheque for the work the designs will be dispatched to you immediately." Mr. Anderson declined to forward the plates until he received the draft covering their value. On April 18, 1910, Mr. Anderson assigned his claim against Long to David R. Perkinpine of Philadelphia, and this action was begun. The title of the case was amended during the trial to read "Percy Anderson to the use of David R. Perkinpine" by leave of court. A trial before the court and a jury was had, and after four days resulted in a verdict in favor of the plaintiff for $1,051.95.

The appellant states the prominent defense to be that Percy Anderson had not performed his contract and the designs were not in compliance with the directions of the defendant, and that an inspection of the plates disclosed this failure to comply with the instructions given. The conditions of the contract are to be gathered from the letters passing between the parties, but on the trial an entirely new feature was added. The written instructions given by Long to Anderson were quite meager and indefinite, and much was left to the designer, to present the thought of the play. This view is apparent from the letters. Anderson writes "I think I grasp your ideas sufficiently to make the drawings as you wish them to be." He never saw the manuscript of the play. He received a general description of the costumes of five participants and these—as testified to by defendant's expert witnesses—were of the type suggested by the description given, but entirely different from the national peculiarities of the characters presented. Long wrote, "Use your own inventions. Yes, the play is poetical and a bit fanciful. I do not think the designs will be hurt a bit if this feeling does creep into them. I here add some details of each, more in the way of suggestion than anything else, preferring to leave you to be original. The play calls for seven or eight smart Viennese men and women in hunting things and so on. I am running this off merely to get you into the spirit of the thing.—There are a number of other smart women in the play who I suppose should wear modern clothes. The wanton should be somewhat overdressed, yet in an artistic fashion. She should be a big woman, suggesting a bit the gipsy. The beggar-student is a very picturesque youth—there will be priests, acolytes, nuns, officers, a crowd—two brides, with thirty differently colored petticoats apiece on them. The locale of the play will be modern Hungary—but there will be about it all a remoteness, such for instance, as is found in the less accessible parts of the kingdom. The story begins and ends in an ancient convent of a peculiar foundation."

The above excerpts are taken from the letters of the parties, showing the indefinite description given of the characters and their costumes, and the wide scope given to the designer. An exact, literal compliance with such an order would be impossible as the mind of the author seems to be in as much doubt as to the mounting of this play as his written description of its materials.

On the other hand, there was no promise by Mr. Anderson that his work should meet the criticism of Mr. Long or his friend. He accepted the employment upon specific terms. "I may charge you as little as one hundred and fifty pounds—in any case not more than two hundred pounds," and, as before quoted, "When I know the date I can finish the drawings I will write and on receipt of the cheque for the work the designs will be shipped to you immediately." In response to this Mr. Long wrote, "Your terms are satisfactory and I will see that a bill of exchange is sent to you as soon as you let me know that the plates are ready, and then I will tell you how to ship them." On May 22, 1908, Mr. Anderson wrote, "The designs for your play will be completed the first day of June, and the price for them will be one hundred and sixty guineas (equal to 168 pounds), on hearing from you I will at once forward the designs." To this Mr. Long answered, "All right, dear Mr. Anderson, and thank you for the work in advance. I am sending your letter on to Mrs. Carter, who is on tour, who will send you your draft and direct you how to ship the designs."

On the trial, Mr. Long admitted that he had never demanded an inspection of the plates prior to bringing this suit, or of a delivery of them to him. He made no offer of payment or explanation, further than that he had an understanding of some undisclosed character with Mrs. Leslie Carter, who, he stated, "Was mad to send you your draft and have the plates." Nowhere in the contract is found any suggestions that they were to be paid for on approval of Mrs. Carter, or on delivery to Mr. Long. The price was due and payable when they were completed by Mr. Anderson, and on the trial there was a mass of evidence received under objection from the plaintiff that was irrelevant—of this the plaintiff does not complain, because, despite its admission, he recovered his verdict and the defendant had the advantage of it with the jury.

There was nothing in the writings to suggest that Mr. Long was acting for an undisclosed principal. No name is mentioned other than his own. He writes, "The contents of your letter are satisfactory to me. I will see that a bill of exchange is sent to you—then I will tell you how to ship them." It was his play, the designs were to be sent to him, he negotiated on his own responsibility. Having entered into the contract in his own name, without disclosing the identity of any principal, he rendered himself personally liable.

The case was carefully conducted by able and zealous counsel, and while the defendant was given much wider range than he was entitled to, the verdict is fully warranted by the plaintiff's proofs, which were rightfully received. The charge of the court was adequate, and clearly presented the conflicting evidence in a way that the jury understood the facts. We discover no reversible error in the record and all the assignments are overruled and the judgment is affirmed.

CARELL v. THE SHUBERT ORGANIZATION, INC.
104 F. Supp. 2d 236 (S.D.N.Y. 2000)

SCHWARTZ, District Judge.

FACTUAL BACKGROUND

This action arises out of a dispute concerning the copyright in certain makeup designs (the "Makeup Designs" or "Designs") created for the cast of the Broadway musical Cats ("Cats" or "the musical"). Plaintiff Candace Anne Carell ("plaintiff") filed this action on July 12, 1999, asserting claims for copyright infringement, false designation of origin, antitrust violations, and an accounting for profits, arising out of defendants' use and publication of the Makeup Designs. Plaintiff also seeks a declaration of sole ownership of the copyright in the Designs. Currently before the Court is defendants' motion to dismiss pursuant to Fed.R.Civ.P. 12(b)(6) ("Rule 12(b)(6)") and as to certain defendants pursuant to Fed.R.Civ.P. 12(b)(2) ("Rule 12(b)(2)"). For the reasons set forth below, the motion is granted in part and denied in part.

The Parties and Subject Matter

Plaintiff, a makeup designer and artist, was the makeup designer for the New York production of Cats. (Complaint ("Compl.") ¶¶ 1, 162.) [W]hile plaintiff was the makeup artist for the first Cats company (the "National I" company), she was not chosen as the makeup artist for the National II Company, which began performances in 1985. (Compl. ¶¶ 69-71.) The Complaint notes that, in 1991, plaintiff worked on the Cats production in Mexico, purportedly because producers in Mexico requested the musical's "original makeup designer." (Id. ¶ 74.)

The 18 defendants include entities and individuals engaged in producing or in licensing the rights to Cats, or who own an interest in corporations that have been and are so engaged. Defendants are: (1) The Shubert Organization, Inc. ("Shubert"), a New York corporation that is a producer of Cats and a licensee of defendant The Really Useful Group, Ltd. (Id. ¶ 163); (2) John Napier ("Napier"), the set and costume designer for the musical (Id. ¶ 3); (3) The Really Useful Group, Ltd. (formerly Really Useful Company, Ltd.) ("RUG"), a British corporation that is among the producers or licensors of Cats productions in New York and overseas (Id. ¶ 165); (4) The Really Useful Theatre Co., Ltd. ("RUT"), a British corporation that is among the producers or licensors of Cats (Id. ¶ 166); Really Useful Films, Ltd. ("RUF"), a British corporation that is among the producers or licensors of Cats (Id. ¶ 167); (6) Really Useful Holdings, Ltd. ("RUH"), a British corporation that is among the producers or licensors of Cats (Id. ¶ 168); (7) The Cats Company, an organization that is among the producers of Cats and is controlled by defendant Shubert (Id. ¶¶ 10 n. 1, 169); (8) Polygram NV, a Netherlands corporation that owned approximately 30 percent of defendants RUG and/or RUT from 1991 to December 1998 (Id. ¶ 170); (9) Universal Music Group, Inc., a California corporation that acquired defendant Polygram NV and owned 30 percent of defendants RUG and/or RUT from December 1998 to mid-April 1999 (Id. ¶ 171); (10) Cameron Mackintosh, Inc., a Delaware corporation owned by individual defendant Cameron Mackintosh that is among the producers of Cats productions in London and New York (Id. ¶ 172, 180); (11) Flummery Corporation, a New York corporation that is the official licensing agent for Cats (Id. ¶ 173); (12) Nina Lannan Associates, Inc. (formerly The Nina Lannan Management Company, a division of defendant RUG from 1993 to 1997), a New York corporation that is one of the managers of defendant The Cats Company (Id. ¶¶ 10 n. 1, 174); (13) Polygram Video, a division of defendant Polygram Records, Inc. that manufactured and marketed the video version of Cats (Id. ¶ 175); (14) Polygram Records, Inc., a Delaware corporation of which Polygram Video is a division (Id. ¶ 176); (15) Gerald Schoenfeld ("Schoenfeld"), chairman of defendant Shubert (Id. ¶ 177); (16) Andrew Lloyd Webber ("Webber"), producer of the video version of Cats and sole or majority owner of defendant Really Useful businesses (Id. ¶¶ 163, 178); (17) David Geffen ("Geffen"), a producer of the New York productions of Cats (Id. ¶ 179); and (18) Cameron Mackintosh ("Mackintosh"), a producer and/or licensor of Cats productions and sole or part owner of defendant Cameron Mackintosh, Inc. (Id. ¶ 180.)

Plaintiff's Contract and Creation of the Makeup Designs

Cats is reportedly "the longest running, most financially successful property" in the history of American theater. (Id. ¶ 9.) There have been over 40 productions of the musical in 27 countries, and within the last three years there has been a United States tour, European tour, and productions in Budapest, Hamburg and Tokyo. (Id. ¶¶ 66-67.)

The musical opened in London, England in May 1981, and is still running there. (Id. ¶ 34.) Early in 1982, plaintiff heard that Cats was coming to New York City and contacted the musical's executive producer and manager, R. Tyler Gatchell, about designing the cast's makeup. (Id. ¶ 31.) Communications between plaintiff, Gatchell and Napier followed, and in March 1982, The Cats Company commissioned plaintiff to create the Makeup Designs for the musical's New York productions. (Id. ¶¶ 31-32, 58.)

Napier allegedly told plaintiff that he wanted her "pure imagination" for the creation of the Designs, and plaintiff "promised to create something beautiful." (Id. ¶¶ 5, 32.) Plaintiff was cautioned not to read the poems on which the musical is based, nor to see the London production. (Id. ¶ 32.) In August 1982, approximately two months before Cats opened at the Winter Garden Theatre (the "Theatre") in New York City, plaintiff and Napier began what plaintiff terms a "collaboration" on the Designs. (Id. ¶ 37.)

Napier provided ideas for the makeup for at least two of the Cats characters. In particular, one of plaintiff's first creations was the "White Cat," which Napier suggested should be "soft, white, and sensual." (Id. ¶ 41.) Grizabella was to be "full of aging beauty and despair, confronting her mortality." (Id.) Plaintiff contends that, for these characters, she gave Napier's ideas full expression in her Design. (Id. ¶ 42.) Each Design contains a number of elements that "hel[p] turn human faces catlike." (Id. ¶ 44.) Moreover, their application involves "extensive layering." (Id. ¶ 45.) Plaintiff notes that some were created with six or seven layers and originally took as long as an hour and a half to apply. (Id.)

In certain cases, plaintiff and Napier "both did hands work on a design." (Id. ¶ 43.) In most of these cases, plaintiff created the Design and Napier made adjustments and suggestions. On "rare occasions," Napier created the Design and plaintiff made alterations and suggestions. (Id.) During these design sessions, Napier did not show plaintiff Napier's costume sketches from the London production of Cats. (Id. ¶¶ 5, 38.)

While the Makeup Designs were completed by the end of September 1982, plaintiff's contract was made final on or about July 7, 1983. (Id. ¶¶ 54, 58, 59.) The contract provided for a flat fee to plaintiff of $2,000 for "executing makeup designs," a weekly payment of $750 beginning September 20, 1982 (after the Designs had been created) and ending shortly after opening night, and a weekly stipend of $200 for the run of the show in return for plaintiff's "ongoing supervisory services." (Id. ¶¶ 56, 59.) Plaintiff therefore receives annual compensation of more than $10,000 and, in total, has received over $170,000. (Defendants' Memorandum of Law in Support of Motion to Dismiss ("Def.'s Mem. Law") at 4.)

Plaintiff has received wide recognition for the creation of the Makeup Designs. While she is not listed as one of Napier's assistants in the playbill for the musical's New York production, she is credited in a "stand-alone" playbill credit that reads: "Makeup by Candace Carell." (Id. ¶ 4.) Plaintiff asserts that she has regularly conducted interviews as the musical's makeup designer (Id. ¶¶ 63-64), participated in photo shoots with Cats characters (Id. ¶¶ 46-49), and was credited as the musical's makeup designer by the New York Times. (Id. ¶¶ 7, 65.)

Competing Registrations and Ownership Claims

Plaintiff's contract makes no reference to copyrights in the Makeup Designs. (Id. ¶¶ 20, 56, 60.) According to plaintiff, Napier's contract for the New York production of Cats, executed in early August 1982, did address copyrights by providing for Napier to assign his own unspecified copyrights to RUG. (Id. ¶ 61.) In 1983 and 1984, plaintiff consulted two lawyers concerning the copyrightability of the Makeup Designs, neither of whom opined that the Designs were copyrightable. (Id. ¶¶ 68, 83.) A third, Marc Jacobsen, whom plaintiff consulted in 1986 or 1987, opined that the Designs were copyrightable. (Id. ¶ 84.)

Plaintiff also retained an agent and drafted a proposal for three books related to the Makeup Designs, and allegedly received authorization from Nina Lannan, an agent for The Cats Company and RUG, to proceed with the books. (Id. ¶¶ 77-78.) Lannan indicated that plaintiff's books would be considered for sale in the Theatre lobby. (Id. ¶ 79.) Plaintiff's attorney also contacted Flummery Corporation, the official licensing agent for Cats. (Id. ¶ 78.) In 1990, plaintiff "often discussed" certain projects, including the books and a makeup kit, with the president of Flummery Corporation and his wife over dinner, and the couple was allegedly enthusiastic about these projects. (Id. ¶ 81.)

In October 1990, Jacobsen filed plaintiff's application for copyright registration. (Id. ¶ 85.) Plaintiff's Certificate of Registration has an effective date of October 11, 1990, and the certificate was granted on April 8, 1991. (Id. ¶¶ 85, 90.) Jacobsen registered the copyright in plaintiff's Designs as a group, and, over plaintiff's objections that Napier be given credit as joint author of certain of the Designs, filed the registration solely in plaintiff's name. (Id. ¶ 86; Plaintiff's Memorandum of Law in Opposition to Defendants' Motion to Dismiss (Pl.'s Mem. Law) at 10.) Jacobsen allegedly had concluded that all of Napier's contributions were "either de minimis or merely uncopyrightable ideas." (Id. ¶ 87.) Plaintiff has never "licensed, assigned, or otherwise transferred any of her copyrights" in the Makeup Designs. (Id. ¶ 8.)

By letter dated January 10, 1992, Jacobsen informed the managers of The Cats Company of plaintiff's registration, and sought to negotiate a license for the company's use of the Makeup Designs. (Id. ¶ 91.) On June 30, 1992, the company's attorney sent plaintiff a letter by certified mail, stating that:

> The Cats Company and The Really Useful Company have heard that...you are preparing a coloring book or other such book on the Cats facial designs and makeup....The drawings and designs of the Cats faces have been duly registered for copyright in the United States Copyright Office by The Really Useful Company and are protected by copyright in many other countries throughout the world. If you infringe upon said copyright or trademark, it will constitute a willful infringement thereof, and The Cats Company and/or The Really Useful Company will take such legal action against you as is appropriate.

(Id. ¶¶ 92-93; Letter from Edward E. Colton to plaintiff dated June 30, 1992, Ex. D to Affirmation of Judith Jobin in Opposition to Defendants' Motion to Dismiss ("Jobin Aff.").) Copies of the letter were sent, inter alia, to Jacobsen, Lannan, and Schoenfeld. (Ex. D to Jobin Aff.) Plaintiff alleges that the letter asserted false information, because defendants had not filed a registration for the Makeup Designs. (Transcript of oral argument held on January 10, 2000 ("Tr.") at 37:16-20.) Plaintiff claims that the letter instead referred to certain of Napier's costume sketches that had been registered incidentally to the registration of the 1983 publication, Cats, The Book of the Musical. (Compl. ¶ 97.) Jacobsen's request for a copy of The Cats Company's registration of the "designs of Cats faces" went unanswered. (Id. ¶ 96.) Because of the threat of litigation, plaintiff subsequently was unable to find a publisher for her proposed books related to the Makeup Designs. (Id. ¶ 98.)

In August 1992, The Cats Company's attorney informed Jacobsen that the attorney would seek to cancel plaintiff's copyright registration. (Id. ¶ 104.) In March 1993, Napier, Shubert, and RUG petitioned the Copyright Office requesting cancellation of plaintiff's copyright registration in the Makeup Designs. (Id. ¶ 105.) Napier asserted in his petition that "the designs of the facial appearances...were my creation and not those of Candace Carell." (Id. ¶ 108.) A letter sent to plaintiff from the Copyright Office on March 31, 1993 stated that Napier had alleged that the registration made with "[plaintiff's] name given as author of the designs and copyright claimant of the designs" states incorrect facts and that Napier "[was] the author and copyright owner of the designs." (Letter from Copyright Office to plaintiff dated March 31, 1993, Ex. A to Jobin Aff.)

Also in 1993, Jacobsen unsuccessfully sought to amend plaintiff's copyright certificate to include Napier as sole author of three Designs and co-author of 15 others, leaving 10 with plaintiff as sole author. (Compl. ¶ 87; Jobin Aff. ¶ 4; Ex. B to Jobin Aff.) Plaintiff contends that Napier and RUG "repudiated co-authorship and co-ownership." (Compl. ¶ 87, 120; Tr. at 34:8-9.)

On July 13, 1993, Napier and RUG registered Napier's costume sketches as "Designs for the Costumes and Facial Expressions of the Characters in the Musical Play Cats." (Compl. ¶ 129.) While plaintiff asserts that these "facial expressions" are not the Makeup Designs, (Tr. at 34:1-5, 35:3-5.), the Copyright Office viewed Napier's and RUG's registration and plaintiff's 1990 registration as asserting adverse claims. On June 30, 1994, the Copyright Office informed the parties that the Office had decided not to cancel plaintiff's registration. (Compl. ¶ 125; Letter from Copyright Office to Edward A. Colton, Esq., Ex. B. to Affidavit of David Rabinowitz ("Rabinowitz Aff.").) The notice stated inter alia that the "Copyright Office is an office of record, and is not an adjudicator of disputed claims...it is Copyright Office policy to register both claims...[and] to leave this matter to the courts to decide the factual issues." (Ex. B. to Rabinowitz Aff.) In addition, the Copyright Office declined to amend plaintiff's certificate to reflect joint authorship with Napier for some of the Designs, citing defendants' explicit rejection of co-authorship of any of the Designs. (Compl. ¶ 126; Pl.'s Mem. Law at 11.)

In 1995, the managers of The Cats Company again allegedly warned plaintiff "not to claim authorship." (Compl. ¶¶ 10 n. 1, 94.) Also in that year, RUG started a toy and game division. (Id. ¶ 99.) Through that division, in or about 1997, one of more of the defendants authorized the "creation, production, and distribution" of the "Official Cats Coloring and Activity Book." (Id. ¶ 101.) The video version of Cats, which was taped in England, was thereafter aired on the Public Broadcasting Service (PBS) television network, and was released for international sale in the fall of 1998. (Id. ¶¶ 17, 67, 165.) The video gives credit, inter alia, to RUT, RUF, and Schoenfeld, and the makeup design credit to another designer affiliated with defendants. (Jobin Aff. ¶ 7; Compl. ¶ 176.) Also in the fall of 1998, a Cats makeup kit entitled the "Face Painting Set" was released, featuring the faces of four Cats cast members. (Compl. ¶ 102.) Plaintiff states that the "Face Painting Set" omits the name of any author; playbills or similar programs have omitted plaintiff's name and/or credited others for the Makeup Designs; and defendants have published press releases giving credit to Napier for the Designs and omitting credit to plaintiff. (Id. ¶ 196.) PBS has also broadcast a video about the making of Cats that allegedly excluded plaintiff and featured another designer. (Id. ¶ 67.) The Cats

Company has acquired an Internet web-site for merchandising these and other products. (Id.)

Plaintiff commenced this action on July 12, 1999, seeking monetary damages, and declaratory and injunctive relief, as well as costs and attorneys fees. The Complaint asserts claims under: (i) the Copyright Act of 1976 ("Copyright Act"), 17 U.S.C. §§ 502, 504, 505, and several foreign copyright statutes, alleging copyright infringement; (ii) the Declaratory Judgment Act, 28 U.S.C. §§ 2201, for a declaration of sole copyright ownership; (iii) the Lanham Act, section 43(a), 15 U.S.C. § 1125(a), alleging false designation of origin; (iv) the Sherman Act, 15 U.S.C. § 1, and the Clayton Act, 15 U.S.C. § 15, alleging anti-trust violations; and (v) the Copyright Act and New York common law for an accounting of profits by a co-owner, in the event that plaintiff is precluded from asserting independent copyright ownership.

On December 1, 1999, the instant motion to dismiss was filed by defendants Shubert, RUG, RUT, RUF, RUH, The Cats Company, Flummery Corporation, Schoenfeld, and Webber. They move to dismiss the action in its entirety pursuant to Rule 12(b)(6) and as against RUT, RUF and RUH pursuant to Rule 12(b)(2). Defendants also specifically allege that plaintiff's claims against Schoenfeld and Webber should be dismissed under Rule 12(b)(6), because plaintiffs have failed to identify any actionable conduct by these defendants. (Def.'s Mem. Law at 37-39.) On January 10, 2000, the Court heard oral argument on the motion. Pursuant to a stipulation of the parties dated February 28, 2000, the following defendants joined the pending motion: Napier; Mackintosh; Cameron Mackintosh, Inc.; Nina Lannan Associates, Inc.; Polygram NV; Polygram Records, Inc.; and Universal Music Group, Inc. (Stipulation dated February 28, 2000.) Defendant Geffen joined the pending motion by stipulation of the parties dated May 2, 2000. (Stipulation dated May 2, 2000.)

DISCUSSION
Copyright Claims

Plaintiff's first, second, and fifth causes of action are copyright claims. The first cause of action, brought pursuant to the Copyright Act, 17 U.S.C. §§ 502, 504, 505, alleges that defendants infringed plaintiff's copyright in the Makeup Designs during the three-year period prior to the filing of the instant action. (Compl. ¶ 185.) The second cause of action, brought pursuant to the Declaratory Judgment Act, 28 U.S.C. §§ 2201, 2202, seeks a declaration that plaintiff is the sole owner of the copyright in the Makeup Designs, and "has the unfettered right to exploit them commercially or otherwise in any medium, as well as the right to receive damages and injunctive relief." (Id. ¶ 192.) Plaintiff's fifth cause of action alternatively seeks an accounting for profits as a co-owner, pursuant to the Copyright Act, and New York common law. Moreover, in addition to her claims brought under the U.S. Copyright Act, plaintiff brings infringement claims under several foreign copyright statutes. (Id. ¶¶ 25, 181.)

There is no disagreement between the parties that the Makeup Designs are copyrightable, or that the creator of such Designs is entitled to protection even if he or she does not apply the makeup to the show's performers. The Designs contain the requisite degree of originality, and are fixed in tangible form on the faces of the Cats actors.

While the parties appear to agree on the facts surrounding the creation of the Makeup Designs, they disagree on the specifics of authorship and, consequently, the ownership of the Designs. Each side has made seemingly inconsistent claims. While plaintiff acknowledges that she worked "[i]n collaboration with [defendant] Napier," she maintains that she created certain "design elements and entire designs." (Pl.'s Mem. Law at 9.) She states that in her 1990 copyright registration, she claimed ownership to all 28 of the Designs at issue, and that this was not erroneous. But in 1993, her attorney, Jacobsen, "revised his legal opinion as to some of the designs." (Id. at 10, 23; Compl. ¶ 87.) In particular, Jacobsen claimed that plaintiff was the sole author of 10 of the Designs, that 15 were co-authored with Napier, and 3 were authored solely by Napier. (Pl.'s Mem. Law at 11; Compl. ¶ 87). Plaintiff asserts that she is not bound by Jacobsen's opinions. (Pl.'s Mem. Law at 23). While plaintiff's allegations are far from a model of clarity, it is clear that she claims sole authorship, and thereby sole ownership, of some or all of the Makeup Designs. She has consistently maintained that at least 10 of the Makeup Designs are solely hers. (Id. at 11, 24; Compl. ¶¶ 86-87; Jobin Aff. ¶ 4.)

Defendants acknowledge that plaintiff created a certain number of the Designs, and specifically refer to Jacobsen's findings as to the respective authorship of plaintiff and Napier. (Def.'s Mem. Law at 16-17.) However, they assert that they have "consistently and unequivocally treated all 'Cats' copyrights as their own." (Id. at 5.) In this motion, they challenge both of plaintiff's ownership claims as time-barred, and her sole ownership claim on the basis that the Makeup Designs are a "joint work" authored by plaintiff and Napier. (Id. at 7-11, 15-18.) Because the Court finds that plaintiff's ownership claims are barred by the statute of limitations, it need not consider the joint work argument here.

Pursuant to section 507(b) of the Copyright Act, a plaintiff seeking a declaration of copyright co-ownership must commence an action within three years of the accrual of the claim. See Merchant v. Levy, 92 F.3d 51, 56 (2d Cir.1996). Courts in this district have extended this rule to parties seeking a declaration of sole ownership. See, e.g., Minder Music Ltd. v. Mellow Smoke Music Co., No. 98 Civ. 4496 (AGS), 1999 WL 82075, at *2 (S.D.N.Y. Oct. 14, 1999) (applying the three-year limitations period to plaintiff's assertion of sole ownership); Aday v. Sony Music Entertainment, Inc., No. 96 Civ. 0991, 1997 WL 598410, at *3-5 (S.D.N.Y. Sept. 25, 1997) (same); Fort Knox Music, Inc. v. Baptiste, 47 F.Supp.2d 481, 483-84 (S.D.N.Y.1999), remanded on other grounds (applying the three-year limitations period in declaratory judgment action to bar defendant songwriter from asserting sole ownership). Copyright claims begin to accrue when the plaintiff "knows or should have known of the injury on which the claim is premised." Merchant, supra, 92 F.3d at 56.

In this case, it is clear from the facts alleged in the Complaint that plaintiff's sole ownership and accounting claims, which both involve a declaration of ownership rights, accrued more than three years prior to the commencement of the action. Although plaintiff contends that defendants appeared to recognize her "proprietary interest" in the Makeup Designs before 1992, (Compl. ¶¶ 11-12), she has never received royalty payments from defendants for use of her copyrights. (Id. ¶ 49; Def.'s Mem. Law at 5.) Thus, although defendants did not directly acknowledge their repudiation of plaintiff's rights during the 1980s, their non-payment of royalties should have put her on notice of this fact. (Def.'s Mem. Law at 5.); cf. Dewan v. Blue Man Group Ltd. Partnership, 73 F.Supp.2d 382, 386-87 (S.D.N.Y.1999) (finding that non-payment of royalties was one element triggering accrual of claim in a suit for a declaration of co-ownership).

Even if the non-payment of royalties were not sufficient to put plaintiff on notice as to her ownership claims, the claims accrued in 1992 based on defendants' clear assertion of ownership and their repudiation of plaintiff's claims to both sole and co-ownership. In January 1992, plaintiff sent a letter to defendants asserting copyright ownership of the Makeup Designs and demanding that defendants seek a license from plaintiff in order to continue their theretofore illegal use of the Designs. (Compl. ¶ 91); see Fort Knox, supra, 47 F.Supp.2d at 483-84 (holding that sole ownership claim accrued when putative sole owner first attempted to assert sole ownership); Dewan, supra, 73 F.Supp.2d at 386-87 (holding that co-ownership claim accrued when plaintiff first attempted to have defendants recognize his ownership interest). Instead of complying with plaintiff's request, defendants asserted ownership of the copyrights in the Designs in their July 30, 1992 letter, in which they warned plaintiff that her use of the Designs to produce, inter alia, a Cats coloring book would constitute a "willful infringement." (Compl. ¶¶ 92-93.) In March 1993, Napier refused to allow plaintiff to add his name to plaintiff's copyright registration, and Napier, Shubert and RUG petitioned the Copyright Office to cancel plaintiff's registration of the Designs. In the petition, Napier asserted inter alia that "the designs of the facial appearances...were my creation and not those of [plaintiff]". (Id. ¶ 108.) Further, in July 1993, Napier and RUG themselves registered a copyright adverse to that of the plaintiff. (Id. ¶ 129.); cf. Aday, supra, 1997 WL 598410 at *4-5 (holding that sole ownership claim accrued when defendants first asserted ownership by entering into contract with plaintiff in which a work-for-hire clause granted sole ownership of the copyrights to defendants). Plaintiff subsequently engaged in significant correspondence with the Copyright Office concerning defendants' cancellation proceedings. (Compl. ¶¶ 114-116, 122).

Accordingly, at the latest, plaintiff was afforded notice of the facts giving rise to her ownership claims by July 1993. Because these claims accrued approximately six years prior to the commencement of the action, plaintiff's ownership claims are barred by the statute of limitations. (Tr. at 38:21-25.)

The Court notes that plaintiff's claim for accounting is asserted under state as well as federal law. Section 301 of the Copyright Act expressly preempts state law claims that are equivalent to claims "falling within the scope" of the Copyright Act, including a state law claim for an accounting. See Richard Feiner & Co., Inc. v. H.R. Indus., Inc., 10 F.Supp.2d 310, 316 (S.D.N.Y.1998). The Court therefore dismisses plaintiff's claim for accounting, insofar as it is asserted under New York law, as pre-empted.

[Despite the foregoing, the] Court finds that plaintiff's Complaint sufficiently pleads a cause of action for copyright infringement. The gravamen of plaintiff's copyright claims is infringement, not ownership; it is her principal cause of action and the Complaint focuses primarily on instances of infringement. (Compl. ¶¶ 1, 181-85; Pl.'s Mem. Law at 4, 14 n. 14.) In this respect, the instant case is clearly distinguishable from Minder Music. Because the plaintiff in Minder Music was an acknowledged co-owner, his infringement action depended on a successful declaration of sole ownership. The ownership claim was therefore the critical element of the case, and the Court reasoned that because that claim was barred, the infringement claim was also barred. Id. at *2. Here, on the other hand, plaintiff's infringement claim is separate and distinct from the adjudication of her ownership claims. Plaintiff's ownership claims were brought as separate mechanisms for declaratory relief: her sole ownership claim was brought in response to threats of litigation by defendants to reserve the possibility of an expedited hearing under Rule 57 (Pl.'s Mem. Law at 17-18); her claim for an accounting, the co-ownership claim, was brought in the alternative to the infringement and sole ownership claims, in order to safeguard plaintiff's right to royalty payments if defendants succeeded on their joint authorship defense. (Id. at 17; Compl. ¶¶ 205-07.) Plaintiff's infringement claim is not dependent upon either of these claims. Barring plaintiff's claims requesting a declaration of copyright ownership cannot preclude her from suing for infringement.

The instant case is more similar to Maurizio v. Goldsmith, 84 F.Supp.2d 455 (S.D.N.Y.2000). In that case, the plaintiff filed copyright infringement, co-authorship and accounting claims, arising out of the plaintiff's individual contributions to the novel The First Wives Club, which later served as the basis for a motion picture of the same title. As in this case, the dispute centered on the rights of two individuals who contributed to a project (i.e. the composition of a novel) that one party had seen to fruition and, eventually, reaped considerable profits. See id. at 458-60. Ruling on the defendant's motion for summary judgment, the court applied Merchant in finding that the plaintiff's ownership claims were time-barred. See id. at 463-64. However, the Court refused to recast the plaintiff's infringement claims as one for ownership, and found that the plaintiff, by sufficiently alleging her individual authorship of draft chapters of the book, and copying by the defendant, had stated a prima facie case of infringement. See id. at 468. Citing Merchant, the court declined to dismiss plaintiff's infringement claims for acts of infringement occurring within three years of the filing of the action. See id. at 463, 467-68.

The Court denies the motion to dismiss plaintiff's copyright infringement claims for alleged acts of infringement occurring after July 12, 1996, three years before the filing of the present suit. As in Maurizio, and unlike the infringement claimants in Minder Music and Fort Knox, plaintiff has alleged an infringement claim sufficient to defeat defendants' motion. Plaintiff's alleged ownership interest may therefore serve as the basis for plaintiff's infringement claims even if plaintiff is barred from seeking a formal declaration of ownership rights.

Defendants assert that plaintiff's infringement claim should be barred on the ground that plaintiff and Napier were co-authors, and the Makeup Designs constitute a single joint work. (Def.'s Mem. Law at 15-18.) In particular, defendants contend that because "the facts pleaded...show that defendant John Napier [from whom all defendants' derive their rights] was at least the co-author of [and, therefore, co-owner of the copyright in] the Makeup Designs," plaintiff's infringement claims must be dismissed. (Id. at 15.) However, while it is true that an infringement action will not lie between co-owners because an individual may not infringe his own copyright, the record does not support the conclusion that plaintiff and Napier were co-authors of the Makeup Designs as a group.

A "joint work" under the Copyright Act is one "prepared by two or more authors with the intention that their contributions be merged into inseparable or interdependent parts of a unitary whole." 17 U.S.C. § 101. The authors of a joint work are "co-authors" or "joint authors," and if no assignments have been made, "co-owners." The Second Circuit has established a two-part test for joint authorship, whereby each putative co-author must have (1) fully intended, at the time of creation, to be a co-author, and (2) made independently copyrightable contributions to the work. See Thomson v. Larson, 147 F.3d 195, 200 (2d Cir.1998) (citing Childress v. Taylor, 945 F.2d 500, 507-508 (2d Cir.1991)).

Viewing the Complaint in the light most favorable to plaintiff, the Court finds that defendants' claim to joint authorship cannot preclude plaintiff's assertions of her infringement claim. We first note that defendants' reference to the Makeup Designs as a single work is misguided. The mere fact that the 28 Designs were incorporated into a single registration does not automatically make them a single work for copyright purposes. (Def.'s Mem. Law at 16; Def.'s Rep. at 8.) In the absence of a joint work, the fact that one party contributes to certain designs, but not to others, does not mean that the party is a co-author of the entire set of designs. Thus, even if plaintiff acknowledged

Napier's co-authorship of some of the Designs, this does not preclude her from bringing an infringement action to enforce her rights to those Designs that she claims she individually owns.

With regard to the intent prong of the analysis, "[a]n important indicator of authorship is a contributor's decisionmaking authority over what changes are made and what is included in a work." Thomson, supra, 147 F.3d at 202-03 (citing Erickson v. Trinity Theatre, Inc., 13 F.3d 1061, 1071-72 (7th Cir.1994) (holding that an actor's suggestions of text did not support a claim of co-authorship where the sole author determined whether and where such suggestions were included in the work)). There is no indication in the Complaint that either plaintiff or Napier intended their "collaboration," (Compl. ¶¶ 37, 116), to be inseparable parts of a unitary whole. Rather, plaintiff's allegations support her control over the production of at least some of the Designs, with Napier contributing certain ideas and concepts to those Designs. (Id. ¶¶ 40-45, 65.) Defendants point to Jacobsen's unsuccessful effort in 1993 to amend plaintiff's copyright registration as a reflection of co-authorship by Napier of the Designs. (Id. ¶ 87; Def.'s Mem. Law at 16-17.) However, the actions of plaintiff's attorney more than a decade after creation indicate nothing about plaintiff's intent at the time of creation. Moreover, even if Jacobsen's actions were indicative of plaintiff's intent, at most they support joint authorship of 15 of the Designs. (Compl. ¶ 87; Jobin Aff. ¶ 4.) A finding of joint authorship to such Designs does not invalidate plaintiff's copyright infringement claim. Because defendants cannot satisfy the intent prong required to establish a joint work, the Court need not consider the copyrightability prong.

Plaintiff asserts her copyright infringement claims not only pursuant to U.S. law but also pursuant to several foreign copyright statutes, specifically those of Australia, Canada, Japan, and the United Kingdom, and pursuant to the Berne Convention for the Protection of Literary and Artistic Works ("Berne Convention"), Sept. 9, 1886, 25 U.S.T. 1341, and the Universal Copyright Convention ("UCC"), Sept. 6, 1952, 6 U.S.T. 2732. (Compl. ¶¶ 25, 181; Pl.'s Mem. Law at 25 & n. 22.)

Plaintiff's Complaint and motion papers are unclear as to whether plaintiff premises her claims upon violations of copyrights she claims to possess in other countries, or whether her claims are premised upon the infringement, under the laws of other nations, of her alleged U.S. copyright. However, the Court finds that, regardless of this ambiguity, to the extent that plaintiff alleges that some or all of the defendants in this action committed violations of foreign copyright laws, dismissal is not appropriate at this time.

Lanham Act Claim

Plaintiff's third claim is asserted pursuant to section 43(a) of the Lanham Act, 15 U.S.C. § 1125(a), which prohibits, inter alia, misrepresentation likely to cause confusion about the source of a product. In particular, plaintiff alleges that certain defendants' misrepresentations concerning authorship of the Makeup Designs and their concomitant failure to credit plaintiff with authorship was a "false designation of origin" in violation of section 43(a). (Compl. ¶ 196.)

In the Complaint, plaintiff alleges that she is the owner of the copyrights in the Makeup Designs, and that: (i) the copyright registration of Napier and RUG falsely implies that Napier is the creator of the Designs; (ii) the makeup credit on the allegedly infringing Cats video omits plaintiff's name and instead gives credit to another makeup designer, "Karen Dawson-Harding"; (iii) the "Face Painting Set" fails to credit plaintiff for the Designs; (iv) playbills for certain infringing productions have either omitted plaintiff's name and/or credited others for the Designs; and (v) after the Copyright Office's referral of the dispute to the courts, The Cats Company circulated press releases claiming that Napier designed the makeup and omitting mention of plaintiff. (Compl. ¶ 196.) Plaintiff also alleges that these violations are likely to cause consumer confusion, and that she has been harmed by defendants' activities. (Id. ¶¶ 198-200.)

Defendants assert that plaintiff's claim is barred by the statute of limitations and by the doctrine of laches. Defendants argue that plaintiff's claim is time-barred for two reasons. First, defendants assert that the six-year statute of limitations applicable to New York Lanham Act claims expired prior to the commencement of the instant suit. (Def.'s Mem. Law at 20.) Defendants argue that the alleged violations "first occurred some time in 1985, when... a different makeup artist was engaged for the National II production of Cats." (Id. at 21.) Defendants therefore contend that since plaintiff discovered, or should have discovered, her claim in 1985, her claim is now time-barred. (Id.) Second, defendants contend that a Lanham Act claim premised on a time-barred claim of copyright ownership must be dismissed. (Def.'s Rep. at 11.) The Court disagrees with both contentions.

In arguing that the six-year statute of limitations is dispositive here, defendants refer to [cases] where the plaintiffs alleged false attribution [claim arose] out of the defendants' failure to provide co-authorship credit. In each case, the alleged misrepresentation was the publication of a single work [that] predated the commencement of the suit by several years, which was enough to remove the respective suits from the statute of limitations. In this case, however, plaintiff alleges several affirmative acts of misrepresentation beyond mere publication of the Makeup Designs, occurring at various points in time. Unlike the ongoing broadcast or performance of a piece of music or successive publications of a comic book character in a series of comic books, each act alleged by plaintiff is a distinct offense, and may be separately considered as a Lanham Act violation.

Defendants also argue that dismissal of plaintiff's copyright ownership claims as time-barred bars plaintiff's assertion of a Lanham Act claim. (Def.'s Mem. Law at 22; Def.'s Rep. at 10-11.) In particular, defendants argue (as they did with regard to plaintiff's copyright infringement claim), drawing on Merchant, supra, 92 F.3d 51, that the "Lanham Act remedy is clearly a remedy that would flow from a declaration of authorship." (Def.'s Mem. Law at 22.)

However, where, as here, the plaintiff has sufficiently alleged an infringement cause of action, a Lanham Act claim cannot be barred on the ground that her ownership claim is time-barred. See Maurizio, supra, 84 F.Supp.2d at 468 (holding that the mere dismissal of an ownership claim as time-barred does not mean that the court cannot consider the issue of ownership as part of plaintiff's Lanham Act claim). Defendants themselves acknowledge this possibility, asserting that "because plaintiff cannot cite an underlying copyright claim, her Lanham Act claim is time-barred." (Def.'s Rep. at 11.) However, underlying copyright claims, namely plaintiff's infringement claims, are present here. The Court therefore declines to bar plaintiff's Lanham Act claim simply because plaintiff's copyright ownership claims are time-barred.

[T]he Court also refuses to find that plaintiff's Lanham Act claim is barred by the doctrine of laches. Laches is an equitable affirmative defense employed instead of the statutory time bar. In order to prevail, a defendant must prove that it has been prejudiced by the plaintiff's unreasonable delay in bringing the action. See Tri-Star Pictures Inc. v. Leisure Time Prods., BV, 17 F.3d 38, 44 (2d Cir.1994). A defendant has been prejudiced when the assertion of a claim available some time ago would be "inequitable" in light of the delay in bringing that claim.

Plaintiff alleges that defendants have committed certain acts beginning in 1993 that have resulted in a misattribution of the copyrights in the Makeup Designs. Because plaintiff did not file suit to assert her rights with regard to any acts until 1999, there is a possibility of prejudice to defendants. However, it is not clear from the face of the Complaint that prejudice resulted from the delay, and, as plaintiff points out, defendants have not argued for, or demonstrated, prejudice. Defendants' assertion of laches in their motion to dismiss is based solely on their incorrect conclusion that because the statute of limitations has run, the presumption of laches inures to defendants. (Def.'s Mem. Law at 23.) Defendants have not asserted prejudice in the alternative, and they point to no specific facts in the Complaint that would support such a finding. Moreover, plaintiff alleges that the defense of laches is unavailing because defendants' acts were wilful and intentional, and because of defendants' unclean hands. (Pl.'s Mem. Law at 28-29.) The Court declines to dismiss plaintiff's Lanham Act claim on laches grounds, because "the factual allegations in the pleadings do not afford the Court sufficient basis for weighing the reasons for [plaintiff's] delay against the prejudice to [defendants] caused by that delay." Fort Knox, supra, 47 F.Supp.2d at 484 n. 1.

Thus, the Court finds that plaintiff's Lanham Act claim is barred neither by the statute of limitations nor by laches. Nor is plaintiff's Lanham Act claim barred as duplicative of her copyright claims. Courts of this district have barred Lanham Act claims where the plaintiffs' trademark allegations merely restate the allegations of their copyright claims, and in particular, fail to show the "requisite affirmative action of falsely claiming originality beyond that implicit in any allegedly false copyright." In order for a Lanham Act claim to survive in addition to a copyright claim, "an aggrieved author must show more than a violation of the author's protected right to credit and profit from a creation". The author must make a greater showing that the designation of origin was false, was harmful, and stemmed from "some affirmative act whereby [the defendant] affirmatively represented itself as the owner."

In this case, plaintiff pleads facts that are adequate to meet this burden. She does not allege merely that Napier's copyright registration is a false designation of origin, or merely a failure to credit plaintiff for her Designs, although each constitutes an element of her claim. Rather, she also alleges affirmative misrepresentation of ownership in, inter alia, the video version of Cats and press releases concerning the musical. This is enough, on a motion to dismiss, to make the greater showing necessary to assert a Lanham Act claim.

Antitrust Claim

Plaintiff's fourth cause of action alleges that defendants' prevented plaintiff from exploiting her copyright in the Makeup Designs, which constitutes a conspiracy in restraint of interstate trade in violation of section 1 of the Sherman Act and section 15 of the Clayton Act. (Compl. ¶ 201; Pl.'s Mem. Law at 31-32.) Defendants contend, inter alia, that this claim should be dismissed because plaintiff has not adequately pleaded either a relevant product market or an antitrust injury. The Court agrees.

In this case, plaintiff defines the relevant product market as the market for licensing the Makeup Designs and other Cats-related intellectual property "for uses that range from merchandise and promotion to theatrical productions and filmed versions." (Compl. ¶ 204.) Plaintiff asserts that the "Cats products" at issue here are "sui generis," and are therefore not interchangeable "with any other available product." (Pl.'s Mem. Law at 34; Complaint ¶ 144.) However, courts in this district have rejected the proposition that allegedly unique products, by virtue of customer preference for that product, are "markets unto themselves."

Plaintiff [therefore] contends [in the alternative] that one brand or product may constitute a relevant product market. However, [p]laintiff's analysis of Eastman Kodak Co. v. Image Technical Servs., Inc., 504 U.S. 451, 482, 112 S.Ct. 2072, 119 L.Ed.2d 265 (1992), which plaintiff cites for support, is flawed.

In Kodak, service and spare parts for Kodak equipment were not interchangeable with those of any other manufacturer and had to be purchased from Kodak. The Supreme Court found Kodak equipment to constitute a relevant product market because owning the equipment compelled customers to continue to by Kodak parts. See id. Here there is nothing to indicate compulsion. Customers can freely choose to purchase or not to purchase Cats products as opposed to those of, for example, other shows, based on their individual preference. Moreover, it is customer preference, not any sort of compulsion, that leads to licensing of the Makeup Designs. It is simply not true that licensees and consumers are "locked in." (Pl.'s Mem. Law at 35.) Kodak's narrow exception for a one brand market is inapposite.

Moreover, there are readily available substitutes for licensing the Makeup Designs and other Cats-related intellectual property. Nothing in the Complaint explains why products associated with other Broadway shows or other forms of entertainment are not reasonably interchangeable with products associated with Cats. The Court concludes that there is little reason to believe that the market for the Makeup Designs is so wholly segmented from the available substitutes that a rise in the price for the Makeup Designs would not shift demand to some of the alternatives. Accordingly, plaintiff's claim is dismissed for failure to adequately plead a relevant product market.

The second element required to assert a cognizable Sherman Act claim is antitrust injury. Even were the Court to find that plaintiff has adequately alleged a relevant product market, plaintiff's failure to allege a cognizable antitrust injury warrants dismissal.

To satisfy the antitrust injury requirement, a plaintiff must show that "the challenged action has had an actual adverse effect on competition as a whole in the relevant market; to prove it has been harmed as an individual competitor will not suffice." Capital Imaging Assocs. P.C. v. Mohawk Valley Medical Assocs., Inc., 996 F.2d 537, 543 (2d Cir.1993); see also Atlantic Richfield Co. v. USA Petroleum Co., 495 U.S. 328, 343-44, 110 S.Ct. 1884, 109 L.Ed.2d 333 (1990) ("The antitrust injury requirement ensures that a plaintiff can recover only if the loss stems from a competition-reducing aspect or effect of the defendant's behavior.").

Here, plaintiff alleges "manifest" antitrust injury because plaintiff's inability to license or market the Makeup Designs has caused a "reduction in output" of products using the Makeup Designs. (Compl. ¶ 145.) Plaintiff also asserts that defendants' products are of poor quality. (Pl.'s Mem. Law at 33.) These are conclusory allegations with no support in the Complaint, and do not adequately plead antitrust injury. In particular, plaintiff's statement that output was reduced is not supported by any statement or indication that there were fewer Cats products licensed or sold. Plaintiff's elimination from the market simply does not equate to reduced output.

Further, plaintiff's own allegations of infringement contradict her assertions that there has been a reduction in output that would harm the public. The Complaint is replete with statements that the Makeup Designs have been made widely available to the public through Cats productions around the world and through merchandise marketed by defendants, including a coloring book, a video, and a makeup kit. (Compl. ¶¶ 17, 67, 101, 102, 185.) Plaintiff's allegations therefore support the conclusion that her alleged exclusion from the market for licensing the Makeup Designs has had negligible effect on output and has chiefly prevented plaintiff from generating revenue. The Court finds that plaintiff has only alleged harm to plaintiff, not the market, and that plaintiff sets forth no facts upon which a court could find competition-reducing antitrust injury.

Plaintiff's antitrust claim also alleges "per se violations" of section 1 of the Sherman Act. (Compl. ¶¶ 142, 202). In most cases, in determining whether conduct restrains competition in violation of the antitrust laws, a rule-of-reason analysis is applied which requires a showing of antitrust injury. However, in limited circumstances the "challenged action falls into the category of 'agreements or practices which because of their pernicious effect on competition and lack of any redeeming virtue are conclusively presumed to be unreasonable and therefore illegal without elaborate inquiry as to the precise harm they have caused.'" Northwest Wholesale Stationers, Inc. v. Pacific Stationery and Printing Co., 472 U.S. 284, 289, 105 S.Ct. 2613, 86 L.Ed.2d 202 (1985) (citation omitted).

As defendants point out, (Def.'s Rep. at 13-14), the application of the per se rule is limited to very few forms of illegal conduct. In particular, the per se rule has been limited to situations where one entity attempts to disadvantage a competitor by coercing necessary suppliers or customers to cut off their relationship with the competitor. Plaintiff has not alleged similar conduct on the part of defendants in this case, as her only allegation is that defendants' "control over all other Cats intellectual property... gives them access to all potential licensees of the Designs" and excludes plaintiff from the market. (Pl.'s Mem. Law at 32.) Accordingly, plaintiff must allege specific antitrust injury in order to maintain her antitrust claims. Since, as discussed supra, plaintiff has not done that here, her allegations of a per se antitrust violation must fail.

[The remainder of the court's opinion is omitted.]

ST. LOUIS THEATRICAL COMPANY v. ST. LOUIS THEATRICAL BROTHERHOOD LOCAL 6, IATSE
715 F.2d 405 (8th Cir. 1983)

BRIGHT, Circuit Judge.

The St. Louis Theatrical Brotherhood, Local 6 (Union) appeals from the district court's judgment granting the St. Louis Theatrical Company's (Company) motion for summary judgment. The district court partially set aside an arbitrator's award reinstating with partial backpay a former Company employee. We affirm.

I. Background

This dispute arises out of a brief series of events that culminated in the Company's discharging Richard McCarthy, its head electrician and the Union's shop steward. The Company engages in the booking and presentation of touring Broadway shows at the American Theater in St. Louis, Missouri. The Union represents the Company's stagehands and has entered into a collective bargaining agreement with the Company. Each of the Company's four permanent employees is designated as a department head. The Company employs additional stagehands as needed. All of these employees are members of the Union's bargaining unit.

During the last week of February, 1981, many of the Company's temporary and permanent employees worked substantial overtime hours preparing for the Company's performance of a world premiere musical, "Copperfield." On March 4, at 4:00 p.m., Jack Beckman, the Union's business agent, picked up his members' paychecks for the ten day period ending on March 1. Beckman soon realized that many of the checks were inaccurate; some were $1,000 less than he calculated they should be.

Beckman immediately began looking for the Company's president, Frank Pierson. Unable to locate Pierson, Beckman walked approximately five feet onto the stage during rehearsal and directed McCarthy to turn up the house lights. McCarthy did so and the three actors on stage stopped rehearsing. Beckman, still on the stage, asked his membership to assemble to discuss the paychecks.

Soon thereafter, Pierson appeared and suggested that he, Beckman, and the four department heads discuss the paycheck problem in his office. Everyone agreed; once in Pierson's office, they also agreed that the rehearsal could continue. The rehearsal resumed and matters began to return to normal. The work stoppage lasted a total of ten to fifteen minutes.

The following day, Pierson terminated McCarthy for his participation in the work stoppage. Pierson told McCarthy that he regretted discharging him. He also referred to a prior incident in which McCarthy had gone to a nearby bar during a show's intermission. The Company took no disciplinary action against any of the other employees involved in the work stoppage. The Union filed a grievance on McCarthy's behalf and the matter proceeded to arbitration.

The arbitrator held that the March 4 incident constituted an unauthorized work stoppage in violation of the collective bargaining agreement. He also held that McCarthy participated in the work stoppage and was therefore subject to discipline under the collective bargaining agreement. The arbitrator, however, set aside McCarthy's discharge and reduced his discipline to a 30-day suspension without pay.

The Company refused to comply and filed suit in the district court to vacate the award, except for that part of it which found McCarthy guilty of participating in the work stoppage. The Union counterclaimed for enforcement of the arbitrator's award. Thereafter the parties filed cross motions for summary judgment.

The district court determined that the arbitrator had exceeded his authority under the collective bargaining agreement and granted the Company's motion. The district court held that the arbitrator exceeded his authority under the collective bargaining agreement in awarding reinstatement and backpay. Specifically, the court held that the collective bargaining agreement bound the arbitrator to consider only "the fact, vel non, of [McCarthy's] participation in the work stoppage," and that the nature and extent of the punishment imposed upon McCarthy was not an arbitrable issue once his participation had been established. Only the Union has appealed this district court judgment.

II. Discussion

If an arbitrator's award does not draw its essence from the collective bargaining agreement, the reviewing court must vacate it or modify it accordingly. Vulcan-Hart Corp. v. Stove, Furnace & Allied Appliance Workers International Union, Local No. 110, 671 F.2d 1182, 1184 (8th Cir.1982). Although a reviewing court must give great deference to arbitration awards, this deference is not unlimited. Thus, "[w]hen the arbitrator's words manifest an infidelity to his obligation, courts have no choice but to refuse enforcement of the award." United Steelworkers of America v. Enterprise Wheel & Car Corp., 363 U.S. 593, 597, 80 S.Ct. 1358, 1361, 4 L.Ed.2d 1424 (1960).

The pertinent provisions of the collective bargaining agreement are as follows:

(30) * * *

(c) The Arbitrator may consider and decide only the particular issue or issues presented by the grievance or by the parties submitted to him in writing and only issues relating to the interpretation and/or application of the Agreement. The Arbitrator shall not have jurisdiction over the rights of management not expressly and specifically restricted by this Agreement and shall have no right to alter, amend, modify or change the terms or provisions of this Agreement. The decision of the Arbitrator shall be final and binding.

(31) No Strikes—No Lock Outs.

There shall be no slow-downs, picketing, boycotts, cessation of work, strikes, interference with the business of the Company or other disruptive activities by either employees or the Union for any reason whatsoever during the term of this Agreement. The Company shall not lock out its employees. Any employee violating this provision may be disciplined or discharged and shall have no recourse to any other provisions of this Agreement except as to the fact of participation. In the event of any unauthorized action of this character, the Union, upon receiving notice thereof, shall use every reasonable means to obtain an end to the violation of the article and a return to work of its members. In addition to the above, the Company may pursue any other remedies it may have in law or in equity.

Under this agreement, the arbitrator's authority is narrow. The arbitrator must determine whether the grievant did, in fact, participate in a prohibited activity. In the case at bar, the arbitrator found that "[McCarthy] participated in [the] work stoppage by the overt act of turning on the house lights and * * * must, therefore, be subject to discipline." Having found discipline justified, the arbitrator went further and concluded that discharge was an excessive penalty for the misconduct. In so doing, he exceeded his authority.

This court construed a similar arbitration clause in Truck Drivers and Helpers Union, Local 784 v. Ulry-Talbert Company, 330 F.2d 562 (8th Cir.1964). In that case the court stated:

The arbitration clause in the agreement between the parties is narrowly drawn. It appears to be the clear intendment of the agreement that in the event of the discharge of an employee by the employer the arbitrator is forbidden to substitute his judgment for that of the employer. He had the right, however, to reverse the employer's decision but only upon making specific findings; that is, that the charge was "not supported by the facts, and that the management has acted arbitrarily and in bad faith or in violation of the express terms of this Agreement."

Id. at 562. Here the collective bargaining agreement provides that the only arbitrable issue be the fact of an employee's participation in a prohibited activity.

The Union contends the arbitrator's authority properly extended to interpreting the phrase "fact of participation" in the agreement. We disagree. As the Supreme Court has stated, "An arbitrator is confined to interpretation and application of the collective bargaining agreement; he does not sit to dispense his own brand of industrial justice." United Steelworkers of America v. Enterprise Wheel & Car Corp., supra, 363 U.S. at 597, 80 S.Ct. at 1361. The agreement clearly and specifically states that an employee disciplined under Article 31 has no recourse, except "as to the fact of participation." Under the agreement, therefore, the arbitrator has no authority to evaluate the propriety of the Company's discipline.

In the instant case, the arbitrator's award is not the result of his interpretation of the agreement within the context of a specific set of facts. Nowhere does the agreement give the arbitrator the authority to determine the fairness or equity of the company's discipline of employees who engage in work stoppages or other prohibitive activities. Moreover, there are no tensions between sections inherent in the agreement and no ambiguities within the sections. The agreement is not susceptible to any construction beyond its plain meaning.

Although "[t]here is a significant distinction to be recognized between the opinion of an arbitrator and the award he actually renders," Resilient Floor and Decorative Covering Workers, Local Union 1179 v. Welco Manufacturing Co., 542 F.2d 1029, 1031 (8th Cir.1976), we observe that the arbitrator's opinion reflected the arbitrator's efforts to balance the equities of the situation, rather than to interpret and apply the agreement. Thus, in his opinion, the arbitrator stated:

> Where an employee is guilty of wrongdoing but management is also at fault in some respects in connection with the employee's conduct, the Arbitrator may be persuaded to reduce or set aside the penalty assessed by management. It is felt that the President of the Company contributed to this situation by his actions relative to the distribution of the payroll and by not having previously taken steps to make certain that the checks would be accurate. His actions are not excused because his accountant was in Kansas City and the computer at the bank which prepared the checks on his behalf was not programmed to issue checks where there was so much as one thousand * * * dollars overtime on six checks. Pierson, an experienced producer, knew or should have anticipated this problem.

While the Company's form of discipline may have been severe, this fact is neither the arbitrator's nor our concern. The arbitrator does not point to, nor can we find, any provision of the agreement that grants the arbitrator the authority to balance the equities of the company's discipline for an employee who engaged in a work stoppage. An employee disciplined under Article 31 has "no recourse to any other provisions of this Agreement, except as to the fact of participation."

III. Conclusion

Under the contract, the arbitrator's authority extended only to finding whether McCarthy engaged in a work stoppage. The district court correctly determined that the arbitrator decided issues not properly before him and, therefore, that the arbitrator's award failed to draw its essence from the collective bargaining agreement. Accordingly, we affirm the judgment of the district court in partially setting aside the arbitrator's award.

Notes

1. In *Ostertag*, the job of "Operations Assistant" was open to all interested persons. This is rather unusual, for most backstage theater jobs must be filled by a union member. *See generally* www.iatse-intl.org (web site of the International Alliance of Theatrical Stage Employes). Although attempts have been made from time to time to change this state of affairs, such efforts have been largely unsuccessful. *See further* Carolyn Casselman, *Staffing the 21st Century Theater: Technological Evolution and Collective Bargain-*

ing, 25 Colum. J.L. & Arts 401 (2003). *See also Charlotte Ampitheater Corp. v. NLRB*, 82 F.3d 1074 (D.C. Cir. 1996); *Phalen v. Theatrical Protective Union No. 1, IATSE*, 238 N.E.2d 295 (N.Y.), *cert. denied*, 393 U.S. 1000 (1968); *New Orleans Opera Guild, Inc. v. Local 174, Musicians Mutual Protective Union*, 134 So. 2d 901 (La. 1961); *Opera on Tour v. Weber*, 34 N.E.2d 349 (N.Y.), *cert. denied*, 314 U.S. 615 (1941); *Gateway Theatrical of Bellport, Inc. v. Associated Musicians of Greater New York*, 658 N.Y.S.2d 692 (App. Div. 1997); *Saginaw Stage Employees, Local 35, IATSE v. City of Saginaw*, 387 N.W.2d 859 (Mich. Ct. App. 1986); *Lafayette Dramatic Productions v. Ferentz*, 9 N.W.2d 57 (Mich. Ct. App. 1943).

2. As *Anderson* demonstrates, once the finished product is delivered, a craftsperson has relatively few options if payment is not forthcoming. For a more recent case that makes this same point, *see Corto v. National Scenery Studios, Inc.*, 705 A.2d 615 (D.C. 1997) (designer that built custom deck for unsuccessful production of "West Side Story" was forced to spend years suing producer while value of the scenery fell to zero).

3. The *Carell* decision caused quite a stir when it was first released. For a useful analysis of the opinion, *see* Jeffrey M. Dine, *Are the Cats Out of the Bag? Lessons from the Makeup Designer's Case*, 19 Sports & Ent. Law. 1 (Fall 2001) (observing that the parties "might have avoided their dispute had they fully understood the copyright issues and addressed them at the beginning of their relationship.").

4. Collective bargaining agreements, like the one at issue in *St. Louis Theatrical Company*, normally are strictly construed. Of course, where a patent ambiguity exists, courts will use their common sense to interpret the contract. *See, e.g., Tulsa Theatrical Stage Employees Union, Local 354 v. Broadway Theatre League of Tulsa, Inc.*, 550 P.2d 922 (Okla. 1976) (defining the phrase "George Washington's Birthday" in a collective bargaining agreement that required stagehands to be paid overtime for work done on holidays).

5. For a further look at crew employment disputes, *see, e.g., Lawrence v. Legitimate Theatre Employees Local No. B-183*, 1996 WL 107297 (S.D.N.Y. 1996) (usher), and *Kentucky Center for the Arts v. Handley*, 827 S.W.2d 697 (Ky Ct. App. 1992) (ticket taker).

Problem 15

As a class assignment, a theater professor had his students design and build several elaborate sets. After they were finished, the school decided to lease them to a third party for use in an upcoming play. Does the professor have any claim against the third party? *See Condell v. New School for Social Research*, 48 N.Y.S.2d 733 (Sup. Ct. App. T. 1944).

D. HAZARDS

EAVES BROOKS COSTUME COMPANY, INC. v. Y.B.H. REALTY CORP.
540 N.Y.S.2d 464 (App. Div. 1989),
aff'd, 556 N.E.2d 1093 (N.Y. 1990)

MEMORANDUM BY THE COURT.

In an action to recover damages for injury to property, the defendants Aprill and Wells Fargo Alarm Services separately appeal, as limited by their briefs, from so much of an order of the Supreme Court, Queens County (Joy, J.), dated August 15, 1988, as denied, in part, their respective motions for summary judgment dismissing the complaint insofar as it is asserted against them.

ORDERED that the order is reversed insofar as appealed from, on the law, with one bill of costs, the appellants' respective motions are granted in their entireties, and the complaint is dismissed insofar as it is asserted against the appellants.

The plaintiff, which is in the business of renting and selling theatrical costumes, alleged that it suffered property damage in excess of $1,000,000, when, as a result of a faulty sprinkler system, a large amount of water was released which destroyed numerous costumes which it had stored in a warehouse. An alarm system which was supposed to issue a warning when the sprinkler was activated, proved defective and contributed to the extent of the loss. The defendants Aprill and Wells Fargo Alarm Services (hereinafter Wells Fargo) had entered into contracts with their codefendants, but not with the plaintiff, to inspect the sprinkler and alarm systems for defects.

The Supreme Court erred in denying the appellants' respective motions for summary judgment dismissing the complaint insofar as it is asserted against them.

A review of the record indicates that Aprill's actions consisted, at most, of a failure to properly inspect the sprinkler heads for age. It is also alleged that Wells Fargo similarly failed to inspect its alarm system on a timely basis and also improperly positioned a water paddle device which was to transmit a signal when leakage occurred.

The appellants' alleged failure to properly and timely inspect the sprinkler and alarm systems were examples of nonfeasance, not of misfeasance. A plaintiff cannot recover in the absence of privity where an affirmative act of negligence has not been committed (see Melodee Lane Lingerie Co. v. American Dist. Tel. Co., 18 N.Y.2d 57, 271 N.Y.S.2d 937, 218 N.E.2d 661). Furthermore, the alleged improper placement of the water paddle by Wells Fargo was not a proximate cause of the failure of the alarm system.

ARTISTS' EMBASSY v. HUNT
320 P.2d 924 (Cal. Ct. App. 1958)

DORAN, Justice.

The present appeal is from that part of a judgment which awarded plaintiff $4,607.54 as damages resulting from the defendants' negligent delay in transporting theatrical scenery, equipment, costumes, etc., from Los Angeles to San Francisco. There is no appeal from that part of the judgment which awarded the defendants $976.49 on a counterclaim.

It appears that from May 21, through June 23, 1956, the plaintiff had presented the play 'Will Success Spoil Rock Hunter' at the Carthay Circle Theatre in Los Angeles, and on May 9th, had contracted to present the same play at the Curran Theatre in San Francisco for three weeks commencing June 25, 1956. Plaintiff closed the show in Los Angeles on the night of June 23rd and delivered the scenery, etc. to the defendant common carriers for delivery at the Curran Theatre at 8:00 a.m. Monday morning, June 25, 1956, so that the play could open at 8:30 p.m. that evening. Defendants were familiar with the necessity of delivering theatrical properties in sufficient time for the show to open.

The defendants, appellants herein, failed to deliver the properties at San Francisco until 9:55 Monday evening, for which reason the first night's performance was not given. The trip could normally be made in 12 hours in place of the 33 hours consumed on this occasion. It was appellants' claim that the delay was due to unforeseeable mechanical breakdowns necessitating the rental of other equipment. Appellants, however, 'concede the fact that the record will support a finding of negligence'.

The trial court found that as a result of defendants' failure to make the delivery, 'and despite the fact that plaintiff received no income from said lost performance, plaintiff was compelled to pay salaries and compensation to actors, press agents, pro rata cost of insurance, its share of advertising, waiting time of stage hands on Monday, June 25, 1956, * * * contractual amount to Curran Theatre for rental for lost performance and contractual penalty to Curran Theatre because of weekly gross falling below contractual minimum, the total amount paid for aforesaid being $2,607.54; that the press notices for the performance given on June 26, 1956 were unfavorable to the management, caused in part by the fact that the cast and company had not been afforded the usual opportunity to rehearse prior to the giving of said performance, and because of the disorganized condition resulting from defendants' failure to deliver the scenery * * * as agreed upon. That as a result of the unfavorable reception of the play in San Francisco, California, the plaintiff was compelled to cancel the third week of the contract period with the Curran Theatre * * * and as a result thereof is liable for the cancelled rental period under the terms of said contract in the sum of $2,000.00'.

The contract with the Curran Theatre provided that the theatre will pay plaintiff '70% of the gross receipts, or 65% * * * if the weekly gross receipts are less than $12,000.' It also provides that in the event the play is closed, the plaintiff will pay the rent of the theatre for the time it is closed.

Appellants contend that there is no competent evidence of damage to support the judgment; 'that the award of theatre rental and house costs and one-eighth of plaintiff's weekly operating costs was prejudicially erroneous'. It is also argued that 'there is no competent evidence that the gross receipts for the first week' would have been greater than '$12,000, and therefore the award of $600.00 for the additional 5% rental was prejudicially erroneous'; likewise that 'there was no competent evidence that the failure to present the first night's performance caused the show to be closed one week early, and therefore the award of $2,000.00 for the theatre rent for the third week was prejudicially erroneous.' Appellants also complain that the admission in evidence of newspaper clippings of critics' reviews was erroneous.

One of appellants' foremost contentions is that the measure of damages is fixed by Civil Code section 3317, which provides that 'The detriment caused by a carrier's delay in the delivery of freight, is deemed to be the depreciation in the intrinsic value of the freight during the delay, and also the depreciation, if any, in the market value thereof, otherwise than by reason of a depreciation in its intrinsic value, at the place where it ought to have been delivered, and between the day at which it ought to have been delivered, and the day of its actual delivery'. Appellants then argue that 'The evidence does not disclose any such depreciation and therefore does not support the findings on damages or the judgment'.

This argument must be deemed specious and untenable as applied to the circumstances of the instant case. As respondent points out, section 3317 of the Civil Code 'applies only where the criterion for measuring damages is appropriate—where the goods are perishable, and/or they have a market for the use intended, by which their value can be determined'. In the present litigation plaintiff does not claim that the scenery and properties were reduced in market value by reason of defendants' delay.

The properties were not purchased by plaintiff for resale, but to be used in the giving of the performance, and the measure of damages would be the loss sustained, arising from the defendants' negligent action, rather than any difference in value of the properties.

More applicable to the present situation is section 3355 of the Civil Code which provides that 'Where certain property has a peculiar value to a person recovering damages for deprivation thereof, or injury thereto, that may be deemed to be its value as against one who had notice thereof, * * * or against a willful wrongdoer'.

The trial court properly allowed such items of damage as were found to proximately flow from the defendants' delay. Such damages included rental of the theatre for the missed performance, house costs and one-eighth of the weekly operating costs. So likewise, the award of $600 for additional rental and $2,000 for the last week's rental cannot be deemed erroneous since they were expenditures made and obligations incurred in the preparation of performance, and within the contemplation of the parties. Defendants were admittedly familiar with the necessity of delivering theatrical properties in sufficient time for the performance; costs and theatre rental were matters reasonably to be anticipated.

Appellants' contention that these items of damage were 'speculative in nature and not supported by any competent evidence' cannot be sustained. The record discloses evidence to the effect that a delayed opening can cause hostility in the critics; that hostile critics can cause poor business, and that the show was prematurely closed because of poor business—causal links from appellants' breach to the loss sustained. The critics' reviews of the show were not admitted in evidence for the purpose of proving the truth of the matter contained therein, but merely to show adverse criticism; the admission thereof did not constitute prejudicial error. No merit is found in any of the appellants' contentions.

The judgment is affirmed.

DONALDSON v. SELECT THEATRE CORPORATION
227 N.Y.S.2d 501 (App. Div. 1962)

MEMORANDUM DECISION.

Appeal from decision and award of the Workmen's Compensation Board.

Appellant, Select Theatre Corporation, owned the Broadway Theatre in New York City. By written instrument it leased the premises to one Lesser for the production therein of a theatrical performance known as 'Ballet de Paris'. The term demised commenced on April 7, 1958; the rent reserved was based on a percentage of the box-office receipts.

On April 1, 1958 and before the show had opened claimant, a stagehand, was injured in the theatre when struck by a falling crate containing stage accessories. The Referee, applying the doctrine of general and special employment to claimant's status, found the theatre owner and the producer equally liable for the award of compensation which he made. Upon review the board ruled that Select was the employer and modified his decision by imposing sole liability for its payment upon appellants.

It is conceded that claimant sustained an accidental injury arising out of and in the course of his employment. Appellants principally contend that the board's decision is not supported by substantial evidence.

The owner had made the theatre available to the producer before the opening date of the show in order to permit him to install the necessary stage settings to be used in connection with its presentation. The producer had brought with him a corps of hands in his permanent employ who were familiar with the intricacies of the process. Pursuant to a collective bargaining agreement with the Union, the owner hired claimant on a 'shape-up' basis to assist in the operation; he had been employed by the same theatre corporation on prior occasions. It would seem that only it had the right to discharge him. For the period between the arrival of the show at the theatre and its public advent the owner carried claimant on its payroll, deducted his withholding and Social Security contributions, paid him his wages and protected him with a compensation insurance policy. In accordance with prevailing theatrical custom the producer reimbursed the owner for all expenditures incurred by it in connection with claimant's preshow employ. Directions in connection with the work were given by the chief stagehand of the producer to the house carpenter of the theatre who in turn relayed them to claimant. The claim alleged that the theatre corporation was claimant's employer when he was injured; its report of injury filed with the Workmen's Compensation Board confirmed this relationship.

In this employment milieu peculiar to the theatre we think that the board could have reasonably found the owner to have been the employer.

Appellants also argue that on the facts the board in any event should have found joint employment and assessed liability for the award against both the owner and producer. Our limited power of review does not permit the substitution of our judgment for that of the board. We look to see whether there is substantial evidence to support its finding. (Miller v. Trebuhs Realty Co., 4 A.D.2d 724, 163 N.Y.S.2d 816.) On this record we are of the opinion that there is. The decision of the board was not defective because of its failure to make an explicit converse finding that the producer was not an employer.

Decision and award unanimously affirmed, with costs to the respondent carrier.

MINTIKS v. METROPOLITAN OPERA ASSOCIATION, INC.
550 N.Y.S.2d 143 (App. Div. 1990)

LEVINE, Justice.

On July 23, 1980, decedent, an accomplished violinist, performed at the Metropolitan Opera House (hereinafter Met) in New York City as a member of an orchestra engaged to accompany the Berlin Opera Ballet. At 9:30 P.M., during an intermission in the performance, decedent left the orchestra pit and never returned. It was later discovered that decedent had been brutally murdered on the roof of the Met. Craig Crimmins, a stage hand employed by the Met, was subsequently convicted of killing decedent (People v. Crimmins, 99 A.D.2d 439, 470 N.Y.S.2d 617, affd 64 N.Y.2d 1072, 489 N.Y.S.2d 879, 479 N.E.2d 224).

The events leading to decedent's death were pieced together by evidence obtained from claimant (decedent's husband), other performers who saw decedent prior to her disappearance, the investigation by the police and Crimmins' written confession. Based on this evidence, it was determined that during the intermission decedent was looking for Valery Panov, one of the principal dancers and choreographers for the Berlin Opera Ballet. Decedent wanted to arrange a meeting between Panov and her husband, who is a sculptor, to discuss various scene and set designs.

In her attempt to locate Panov, decedent boarded an elevator backstage. Riding the elevator with decedent was Crimmins. While on the elevator, Crimmins said something to decedent which prompted her to slap him. When the elevator stopped on the second floor, both decedent and Crimmins exited and Crimmins ordered decedent to walk with him to a rear stairwell where they descended approximately five flights to a sub-basement level. There, Crimmins produced a hammer and, after decedent removed her clothes, attempted to rape her. Crimmins then directed decedent to get dressed and to begin walking upstairs to the roof. On the roof, Crimmins tied decedent up with a rope. Crimmins had started to leave when he noticed that decedent had freed her legs and was running away. He caught her and brought her back to the same spot and retied her feet. Crimmins then carried decedent to a ledge near an air conditioning fan, removed her shoes, cut off her clothing, gagged her, and laid her flat on her stomach on the ledge. Crimmins threw decedent's clothing and pocketbook down the side of the air conditioning shaft. As he was leaving, decedent again began to struggle to free herself, at which point Crimmins returned to where decedent was and kicked her off the ledge. Decedent died as a result of the injuries sustained in the fall.

In August 1980, the Met filed a C-2 "Employer's Report of Injury" form with the Workers' Compensation Board and the Board indexed a death claim in the matter. Thereafter, claimant entered a special appearance challenging the jurisdiction of the Board on the grounds that decedent was an independent contractor and not an employee of the Met, and that her assault and murder did not arise out of or occur in the course of any employment.

Claimant also commenced a wrongful death action against the Met in Supreme Court, New York County. This action was stayed pending a final determination of the workers' compensation case.

A hearing was held before a Workers' Compensation Law Judge which resulted in an award of death benefits based upon a finding that decedent was an employee of the Met and that the accident and death arose out of and in the course of her employment. Claimant appealed this decision to the Board. On appeal, the Board affirmed the award, based on its determination that an employment relationship existed and that the assault occurred in the course of decedent's employment and, therefore, is presumed to have arisen out of her employment (see Workers' Compensation Law § 21). This appeal by claimant ensued.

Claimant contends that the Board's determination that an employer-employee relationship existed is not supported by substantial evidence. We disagree. There was evidence adduced that decedent was on the Met's payroll and that the usual withholding taxes were deducted from her earnings. The Met had also obligated itself to provide workers' compensation insurance for the orchestra members. Moreover, the evidence indicates that the Met exercised significant control over decedent's hours and the manner in which she was to perform. Although conflicting inferences could be drawn from the evidence, this court's review is limited to determining whether the record contains substantial evidence to support the Board's finding (see Matter of Davison v. Holder, 137 A.D.2d 899, 900, 524 N.Y.S.2d 871), and we conclude that it does.

Claimant also contends that the Board erred in determining that decedent's death arose out of and occurred in the course of her employment. As to whether the assault occurred in the course of decedent's employment, the Board determined that decedent was on a break between performances at the time of the incident and that her activity in leaving the orchestra pit to locate Panov was reasonable and did not constitute a deviation from her employment. We are not persuaded that the Board's conclusion on this point was in any way improper (see Matter of Richardson v. Fiedler Roofing, 112 A.D.2d 551, 491 N.Y.S.2d 489, affd 67 N.Y.2d 246, 502 N.Y.S.2d 125, 493 N.E.2d 228).

Having determined that the assault occurred "in the course of" decedent's employment, the Board relied on the presumption in favor of compensability (see Workers' Compensation Law § 21) as the basis for its decision that the assault also "arose out of" the employment. The Board also stated in its decision that "[w]ere it not for the employment, she [decedent] would not have been in a position which became not only dangerous, but which ultimately became fatal". Claimant contends that this statement evidences that the Board utilized an erroneous "but for" standard in determining whether the assault arose out of the employment. In support of this contention, claimant relies on Matter of McCarter v. La Rock, 240 N.Y. 282, 284-285, 148 N.E. 523 and Matter of Scholtzhauer v. C & L Lunch Co., 233 N.Y. 12, 134 N.E. 701, which rejected such a broad view of workers' compensation coverage and required that a rational causal nexus exist between the employment and the injury. Recent decisions of the Court of Appeals demonstrate that this remains the operative standard in New York (see, e.g., Matter of Lemon v. New York City Tr. Auth., 72 N.Y.2d 324, 532 N.Y.S.2d 732, 528 N.E.2d 1205; Matter of Malacarne v. City of Yonkers Parking Auth., 41 N.Y.2d 189, 391 N.Y.S.2d 402, 359 N.E.2d 992).

In the context of assaults upon an employee, the causal link may be supplied by a work environment which increased the risk of attack (see 1 Larson, Workmen's Compensation § 11.11[b]) or a work-related motivation for the assault (see id., at § 11.12; see also Matter of Seymour v. Rivera Appliances Corp., 28 N.Y.2d 406, 409, 322 N.Y.S.2d 243, 271 N.E.2d 224). In the instant case it is not argued, nor does there appear to be any basis in the record for concluding, that the Met, at 9:30 P.M. in the midst of a performance, constituted a dangerous work environment. Thus, the issue to be determined is whether, based on the uncontroverted circumstances of decedent's attempted rape and murder, the Board could properly find, in reliance on the statutory presumption, that the assault was motivated by some factor related to decedent's employment. In our view, the circumstances of the attempted rape and murder, as well as the facts that decedent had never met Crimmins prior to encountering him in the elevator and that whatever he initially said to her provoked decedent to slap him across the face, strongly support an inference that the motivation for the attack was unrelated to either Crimmins' or decedent's employment. Moreover, as one authority has observed, "there is no clearer example of non-industrial motive than rape" (1 Larson, Workmen's Compensation § 11.11[b]).

Most troublesome, however, is the Board's failure to give any indication in its decision that it considered this uncontroverted evidence for its potential to rebut the statutory presumption of compensability. This is particularly significant in light of the fact that the evidence of the circumstances surrounding the homicide was provided by the testimony of an apparently impartial police officer who investigated the crime. In addition, Crimmins' written confession, which was also admitted into evidence and supports the inference that he chose his victim arbitrarily and that there was no employment-related animus between himself and decedent, is not self-serving and therefore should not be summarily discredited simply to preserve the presumption (see Matter of Kaylor v. 133 East 80th Street Corp., 43 A.D.2d 999, 1000, 352 N.Y.S.2d 62; see also Matter of Magna v. Hegeman Harris Co., 258 N.Y. 82, 84-85, 179 N.E. 266). Nor was the Board free to ignore this evidence in making its determination (cf. Matter of Oehley v. Syracuse Boys Club, 151 A.D.2d 825, 542 N.Y.S.2d 799, 801). Because it is not clear from the Board's decision whether an improper "but for" standard was applied, or whether the Board in fact weighed the available evidence and properly determined that the statutory presumption was not rebutted, the matter should be remitted for clarification (see Matter of Seidel v. Crown Indus., 132 A.D.2d 729, 731, 517 N.Y.S.2d 310).

KANE, Justice, dissenting.

We are not persuaded that this matter should be remitted to the Board for further proceedings.

The majority accepts the Board's findings that decedent's attempted rape and murder by her coemployee occurred in the course of her employment, but concludes that the circumstances "strongly support an inference that the motivation for the attack was unrelated to either Crimmins' or decedent's employment". They then criticize the Board for failing to consider "this uncontroverted evidence for its potential to rebut the statutory presumption of compensability". After making other factual determinations, they find that the Board may have applied an improper standard or improperly weighed the available evidence in determining whether the statutory presumption had been overcome.

In our view, this reasoning is unacceptable. It is well established that in a claim for death benefits, when the death has occurred in the course of employment and is unwitnessed or unexplained, it is presumed, first, to have arisen out of the employment, and, second, to be the result of an accident (Workers' Compensation Law §21[1], [3]). It is equally well established that the Board's decisions on questions of fact, if supported by substantial evidence, are conclusive and the inferences to be drawn from that evidence are for the Board to determine (Matter of Masek v. St. Vincent's Med. Center, 97 A.D.2d 580, 467 N.Y.S.2d 925). Moreover, it is in the exclusive province of the Board to decide what evidence it will accept or reject and, in so deciding, it may cull from the record that which it finds to be substantial and reject any other part thereof. In order to overcome the presumption that an accident arose out of the employment, the burden is upon the party seeking to overcome that presumption by the production of the requisite substantial evidence (Matter of Wiktorowicz v. Kimberly-Clark Corp., 99 A.D.2d 903, 472 N.Y.S.2d 505, lv. denied 62 N.Y.2d 605, 479 N.Y.S.2d 1026, 467 N.E.2d 895). Here, the only evidence available to shed any light upon what occurred when decedent was confronted by Crimmins are the statements made by Crimmins to the police and the Assistant District Attorney. Under the circumstances, the Board had the absolute right to reject this evidence (see Matter of Kaylor v. 113 East 80th St. Corp., 43 A.D.2d 999, 352 N.Y.S.2d 62).

Thus, in this case, involving an assault by one employee against a coemployee, controlling case law instructs us that an award may be sustained "so long as there is any nexus, however slender, between the motivation for the assault and the employment" (Matter of Seymour v. Rivera Appliances Corp., 28 N.Y.2d 406, 409, 322 N.Y.S.2d 243, 271 N.E.2d 224). In this case, that nexus is provided by the relationship between Crimmins and decedent as coemployees. Significantly, and unlike cases relied upon by the majority, there is no showing of any personal animosity, or even a prior relationship, between decedent and Crimmins. Absent such a showing, personal animosity cannot be inferred without substantial evidence to support it (see id.). The decision of the majority is founded either upon its factual determinations after weighing the evidence or upon pure speculation. In our view, Matter of Seymour v. Rivera Appliances Corp. (supra) is the controlling authority and mandates an affirmance of the Board's decision.

Notes

1. Why did the defendants get off in *Eaves Brooks* but not in *Artists' Embassy*? Likewise, why was an award of workers' compensation held to be due in *Donaldson* but not necessarily in *Mintiks*?

2. The death of Helen Hagnes Mintiks at the hands of Craig Crimmins remains one of New York City's most celebrated murders. Dubbed the "Phantom of the Opera" case, its details are recounted at length in David Black, *Murder at the Met* (1984).

3. In *Tillander v. Latin Quarter Cafe, Inc.*, 189 N.Y.S.2d 39 (App. Div. 1959), the plaintiff suffered a debilitating stroke while sewing a zipper on a costume. She had been the show's wardrobe mistress for 13 years, but claimed that on the night of her injury she had been particularly tense due to a performer's insistence that the zipper be sewn on quickly. Although the Worker's Compensation Board awarded benefits, the appellate court reversed after concluding the plaintiff's injury was not caused by her employment. How would you have ruled?

Problem 16

A stagehand was injured when he fell on a ladder that had been supplied by a fellow employee. Can he sue his co-worker? *See Oakes v. Gaines*, 437 N.E.2d 738 (Ill. App. Ct. 1982).

Chapter 8

Houses

A. OVERVIEW

In most respects, theaters are just like other buildings: they must be paid for, managed, repaired, insured, and kept current on their taxes. But because they are intended to be used in a specific way for a specific purpose, theaters also raise their own unique issues.

B. BUILDING CODES

NEMER v. MICHIGAN STATE BOARD OF REGISTRATION FOR ARCHITECTS, PROFESSIONAL ENGINEERS AND LAND SURVEYORS
146 N.W.2d 704 (Mich. Ct. App. 1966)

FITZGERALD, Judge.

Plaintiff in this action for mandamus or superintending control, Basil Bernard Nemer, graduated from the University of Michigan School of Architecture and Design in June, 1956, and applied to defendant board for permission to take appropriate examinations required as a prerequisite to certification as an architect in the State of Michigan. Plaintiff took part 1, the structural design section of the examination and, following a four-year apprenticeship, made application for permission to take the remaining six parts of the written architectural examination in June, 1963.

In November, 1963, plaintiff was advised that he had passed portions of the examination involving mechanical equipment; composition; specifications; supervision; counseling and administration; and history; but that he had not passed the design problem. Passing grade on all parts of the examination was 75% and plaintiff received 51% on the design problem.

Following conferences with defendant board, plaintiff was advised that the examination was scored by persons other than members of the board and that the board members were unable to advise in what manner and for what reason the design problem submitted by plaintiff was unsatisfactory.

That it was unsatisfactory to the scorers is indicated by the following advisory scores submitted by each individual member of the scoring panel, as furnished by defendant:

Bruno Leon: 45; James W. Conn: 66; Paul B. Moffett: 54; Thomas H. Hewlett: 48; William E. Kapp: 15; A. Arnold Agree: 60; Philip Brezner: 68.

Plaintiff claims that the design problem is not capable of objective scoring and as such is not a proper or reasonable test for purposes of certification. He maintains that if the design problem were scored according to the same objective standards as used in other parts of the examination, he would have received a passing grade.

This Court, lacking the training of an architect or engineer, finds itself in the position that a review here of plaintiff's examination papers would be of no avail. The allegations that defendant has acted arbitrarily and improperly are not borne out by the individual scores cited, supra. Indeed, there was no member of the scoring panel who considered plaintiff's answer satisfactory.

The legislature has vested defendants with the duty of prescribing the scope of the examinations for the profession under consideration. For a fuller understanding of the problem before this Court, we reproduce in full the examination question which proved to be plaintiff's nemesis.

MICHIGAN STATE BOARD OF REGISTRATION FOR ARCHITECTS, PROFESSIONAL ENGINEERS, LAND SURVEYORS

ARCHITECTURAL EXAMINATION

PART III DESIGN PROBLEM

Wednesday—June 12, 1963

All day—8:00 A.M.—(12 Hours)

Candidates will put title block in lower right hand corner with the following information: (a) Identification number; (b) June 12, 1963; (c) 'A University Theater'; (d) Location.

NO BOOKS OF REFERENCE PERMITTED

The objective of this examination is to test the candidate's understanding of the principles of architectural design in the widest meaning of that term and his skill in applying them to a specified problem, such as he might meet in practice.

SUBJECT: A University Theater

GENERAL: At a University located in central Michigan, it is planned to erect a theater for the educational program in Speech and the Dramatic Arts. The theater will serve the University community, and the actors, staff, and audience will be comprised of faculty and students. An open-stage type theater, in which the audience faces the performing area from three adjacent sides, has been selected as the most versatile type for teaching purposes. Plays planned for prosecenium or theater-in-the-round productions will be adjusted to suit the open-stage. No grid or overhead facilities for hanging are planned, and all seats will be fixed.

SITE: The building site, generally level and rectangular, measures 300 feet along the south side of a main campus drive, and 200 feet along campus walks bordering it on the east and west. To the south of the site are various other academic buildings three storeys in height, for the most part. North of the main campus drive are dormitories and recreational facilities, plus parking accommodations adequate for the theater-goers.

BUILDING: Facilities are to be provided for as follows, with deviations limited to 10%, plus or minus, for the areas noted.

1. Production facilities
   a. Work Shop (2-storeys high): 2,000 sq. ft.
   b. Costume and Scene Design: 750 sq. ft.
   c. Storage for materials and properties: 750 sq. ft.
   d. Loading dock: 250 sq. ft.
   e. Lighting Gallery (in truss plenum): 800 sq. ft.

2. Performers' Facilities
   a. Open-stage: 1,000 sq. ft.
   b. Back stage (2-storeys high): 3,000 sq. ft.
   c. Rehearsal room: 2,000 sq. ft.
   d. Dressing rooms and toilets, men and women: 1,000 sq. ft. each
   e. Costume storage: 800 sq. ft.

3. Viewers' Facilities
   a. Foyer, with ticket counter: 1,500 sq. ft.
   b. Lobby: 2,500 sq. ft.
   c. Coat and Toilet Rooms, total: 600 sq. ft.
   d. Auditorium for 600 seats: 6,000 sq. ft.

4. Teaching Facilities
   a. Classrooms, four (4) at 500 sq. ft. each: 2,000 sq. ft.
   b. Offices, eight (8) at 200 sq. ft. each: 1,600 sq. ft.
   c. Library and office: 1,600 sq. ft.

5. Service Facilities
   a. Mechanical equipment (space as required, may be in basement)
   b. Custodial (as required, may be in basement)
   c. On-site parking: six cars

DRAWINGS REQUIRED: All drawings are to be done on a single sheet of heavy white tracing paper 24" x 30", to be presented horizontally. Some furnishings and equipment may be shown to indicate the use of spaces, but all spaces shall be identified as per the building requirements. In orienting the plan drawings on the sheet, north should be at the top.

1. Site plan, indicating general development and landscaping, at the scale of 1"=32'-0";

2. Floor plans (basement may be omitted if providing for service facilities only) at the scale of 1"=16'-0";

3. Rendered perspective, showing one of the major elevations of the building, measuring approximately 10" x 20";

4. Cross-section at the scale of 1"=16'-0";

5. Detail of typical wall section, indicating materials and framing system, at the scale of 3/4"=1'-0".

It is impossible for this Court to say that such a question is incapable of proper interpretation or of proper grading. Further, we cannot hold that the board has arbitrarily exceeded its powers in requiring a passing answer to such a question.

While an objective examination in any of the arts, sciences or professions might be easier to grade, and provide a more black-and-white delineation between passing and failing, many areas are not susceptible to such procedures and it is not in the province of this Court to order an examinee certified when in the judgment of the certifying board his performance does not meet the standard of the profession. Nor can any court sit as a super-examining board.

Plaintiff's complaint for a writ of mandamus or superintending control is dismissed.

[The concurring opinion of Judge Gillis is omitted.]

HART v. CITY THEATRES CO.
128 N.Y.S. 678 (Sup. Ct. 1911)

SEABURY, Justice.

The defendant is the owner of the City Theater. The plaintiff is the lessee of the adjoining premises on the west and south. The present action is upon an agreement, the purpose of which is to permit the defendant in the use of its theater to cut a door through the plaintiff's westerly wall and use the stairway of plaintiff's building as one of the exits from the theater for the use of the audience. For this privilege the defendant agreed to pay $1,200 per annum in monthly installments, and this action is brought to recover installments for six months. The answer of the defendant alleges the illegality of the contract sued upon as a defense.

The demurrer admits the facts alleged in the defense. For the purposes of this appeal, therefore, it is conceded that the defendant's theater is fireproof, and that plaintiff's building is entirely nonfireproof; that written plans and specifications for the work were prepared by defendant and submitted to plaintiff, and application duly made to the building department of the city of New York for a certificate approving the same and approving the work called for, and that the building department refused to issue a certificate and expressly disapproved the plans submitted, declined to approve any plans or permit any work for the cutting of a doorway as provided for in said agreement, and expressly disapproved the use of plaintiff's premises as called for in said agreement; that this refusal is based upon the ground that no part of plaintiff's premises "was made or constituted fireproof." It is further alleged that the Building Code provides that all stairways, openings, structures, and all parts of any such structures used for any theatrical purpose, or as a theater, or for the use of any audience or portions of an audience, shall be completely fireproof.

Taking the facts admitted by the demurrer in connection with the provisions of the agreement which is annexed to the complaint, the following propositions appear to be established: (1) That plaintiff agreed to allow the defendant to cut a door through the wall of his building, which was not fireproof, and to use the stairway as one of the exits from defendant's fireproof theater. (2) That the plaintiff's building, or a part thereof, if used as contemplated by the contract, would be used as a theater, or for the use of an audience or portions of an audience. (3) That the Building Code provides that all stairways, openings, structures, and all parts of any such structures used for any theatrical purpose, or as a theater, or for the use of any audience or portions of an audience, shall be completely fireproof.

Assuming, as we must, that these propositions are correct, it necessarily follows either (1) that the defendant must rebuild the whole of the plaintiff's building, so that it should be a fireproof structure, which the contract does not contemplate it should do; or (2) that the contract, if carried out, would involve an illegal and unlawful use of the plaintiff's building. The Building Code of the city of New York has the force of law, and any contract made in violation of its provisions is void. Burger v. Koelsch, 77 Hun. 44, 28 N.Y. Supp. 460. Under the contract the defendant was required to do a thing which cannot be done without a violation of the law, and it follows that such an obligation is void.

Nor does the fact that at the time the contract was made the parties knew the law alter the situation in any respect. For the purpose of this appeal we must assume that the answer correctly sets forth the provisions of the Building Code. If these provisions are not as comprehensive as they appear to be from the allegations of the answer, that fact will appear upon the trial of the action. In determining the issue raised by the demurrer, we must assume that the allegations of the defense are true.

We think that the learned court below was right in holding the defense alleged to be sufficient in law and in overruling the demurrer interposed thereto.

The judgment appealed from should be affirmed, with costs.

All concur.

THEATRE MANAGEMENT GROUP, INC. v. DALGLIESH
765 A.2d 986 (D.C. 2001)

FARRELL, Associate Judge.

Plaintiff-appellee Dalgliesh, a partially disabled person, was injured when he fell as he began walking down an aisle ramp leading to his seat in the Warner Theatre. In his ensuing action for negligence against appellants Theatre Management Group, Inc. and LRW Theatre Group (both doing business as Warner Theatre Operating Group, J.V.), the jury awarded him $983,177.00 in damages. On appeal, the primary issue is whether the trial judge erred in allowing the jury to consider, as evidence of the standard of care, the fact that under the Americans With Disabilities Act (ADA), 42 U.S.C. §§ 12101 et seq., and related regulations an interior ramp may not have a slope exceeding a ratio of 1:12, or one unit of rise for every twelve units of distance. Appellants contend that the decisional law of this jurisdiction prohibits use of such statutes and regulations to prove negligence unless they are laws designed to protect "public safety," and that the ADA, as an anti-discrimination law, does not meet that description. We conclude both that our decisional law is not so inflexible in this regard as appellants make it out to be and that, in any event, the ADA has an obvious safety component to the ends it is designed to serve. We therefore sustain the trial judge's admission of the ADA standard as evidence of the care required in the circumstances.

I.

Dalgliesh suffers from Charcot Marie Tooth Syndrome (CMT), a rare neurological disorder that causes the myelin—the coating of the nerves—in the arms and legs to deteriorate over time. As the myelin is lost, electric conduction through the nerves to the attached muscles slows down, generally resulting in progressive neurological impairment. Dalgliesh was diagnosed with CMT at the age of twenty, and at the age of thirty-five was fitted with MAFO braces for both legs. The braces supported his feet and legs but prevented all movement in his ankles. By the time he was age forty-three, he was using a cane in addition to the braces. The immobility of his feet, combined with sensory problems in the feet, the MAFO braces, and the cane all made it difficult for him to negotiate uneven surfaces.

Viewing the evidence in the light most favorable to Dalgliesh, on March 18, 1994, he came to the Warner Theatre with four friends to attend a show. Entering the theatre some forty-five minutes before showtime, he and a companion, Bill Tucci, were directed to the far end of the lobby where they were met by a female usher named Heidi. Dalgliesh told her that he had a muscular disorder and would need assistance getting to his seat because he walked with a cane and wore MAFO braces. After Heidi left briefly and returned, he again told her it was important that he get help to his seat "because when I'm in crowds and...there are surfaces...I'm unsure of, I really like to have assistance." Heidi replied, "No problem. I'll take care of that."

Dalgliesh, Tucci, and Heidi waited in the lobby for Dalgliesh's other friends to park the car and join them. They talked about Dalgliesh's CMT, and at one point he showed Heidi the MAFO braces. When she asked what kind of help he wanted he replied, "I could have [Tucci] on one arm and you or someone else on the other arm as long as I have support on each side. Or, if you have a wheelchair of some sort...." Heidi said "No problem." By this time, according to Dalgliesh's testimony, he had asked Heidi for assistance three or four times and was confident she would provide it.

When the others arrived Dalgliesh beckoned to Heidi, who told the group to follow her into the auditorium, which by now was very crowded. As they entered the theatre Heidi turned and took the tickets from Tucci, then went down the center aisle and, after finding the seats, summoned the group to follow her. Since the house lights had begun to blink, Dalgliesh was anxious: "people were all around me. I didn't see any help. And I was concerned....I had asked for help. I had been told I was going to get it." He took a step forward on the aisle ramp and fell, landing on his right leg. He could feel the bone in his leg snap, experiencing pain more excruciating than he had ever felt. As he was carried out of the auditorium by paramedics, Heidi apologized to him saying, "I'm so sorry I didn't get you the help....I should have done more. I should have gotten you a wheelchair or something." Dalgliesh suffered a leg fracture from the fall that was very slow to heal and, in combination with the underlying CMT, resulted in his being permanently confined to a wheelchair.

II.
A.

The Warner Theatre was built in 1924. A historic renovation, including restoration and modernization of the interior theatre space, was begun in 1988-89 and completed in 1992.

At trial Dalgliesh presented expert testimony by an architect, Robert D. Lynch, that the slope at the top of the aisle ramp (where Dalgliesh fell) was 13.5 percent or a ratio of one unit of rise (or "vertical distance") to 4 units of "run" or level distance. Lynch testified that uniform architectural standards for ramps going back to 1961 ("probably the oldest unchanged...accessibility standards" [Tr. 195]) establish "a run of 12 units [a ratio of one to twelve] as [the] maximum slope for a ramp." [Id.] Most recently, he stated, the Accessibility Guidelines for Buildings and Facilities promulgated under the ADA specify a "one in 12 slope" as the "maximum allowable [ratio]" for ramps [Tr. 196, 199]. In Lynch's opinion, the ramp at the point where Dalgliesh fell "significantly" exceeded "maximum ramp slopes...contained within the [ADA] and/or the architectural guidelines which supplement and apply to [it]." [Tr. 236]

Although Lynch recognized that "the basic nature of the geometry of the theatre" meant that the ramp slope could not be altered [due to the age and design of the theater] [Tr. 238], he testified to specific steps—installation of handrails, warning signs, or an alternative entry route into the auditorium—that in his view appellants could reasonably have taken to provide safe access for someone with Dalgliesh's condition.

B.

Appellants objected to any evidence about the ADA and its accessibility standards on the ground that the ADA is not a "public safety" statute and thus its specifications could not provide evidence of the standard of care in what they term this "garden variety" negligence action. The trial judge disagreed. Besides instructing the jury on a landowner's common law duty of care in the circumstances to keep premises safe and warn invitees of hazardous conditions, he instructed it that the ADA and its accompanying regulations "set [ ] forth a standard of conduct" which it could consider in deciding whether appellants were negligent. On appeal, appellants renew the argument that in this jurisdiction only public safety laws can furnish proof of the standard of care in a negligence suit, and that the ADA does not fit that description.

Ultimately, however, this case does not compel us to resolve the issue of evidentiary use of statutes having no public safety objective, because it is evident to us that the ADA—and specifically the physical accessibility guidelines promulgated under it—possess such an aim. Title III of the ADA provides that "no individual shall be discriminated against on the basis of disability in the full and equal enjoyment of the goods, services, facilities, privileges, advantages, or accommodations of any place of public accommodation." 42 U.S.C. § 12182(a). Discrimination includes the "failure to remove architectural barriers...that are structural in nature...where such removal is readily achievable." 42 U.S.C. § 12182(b)(2)(A)(iv); see also 28 C.F.R. § 36.304. If removal of a barrier is not readily achievable, discrimination may yet be shown by the "failure to make such goods, services, facilities, privileges, advantages, or accommodations available through alternative methods if such methods are readily achievable." 42 U.S.C. § 12182(b)(2)(A)(v); see also 28 C.F.R. § 36.305.

As mentioned earlier, Department of Justice (DOJ) standards issued under the ADA include the ADA Accessibility Guidelines for Buildings and Facilities (see 28 C.F.R. Part 36, App. A), which are "legally binding regulation." Independent Living Resources v. Oregon Arena Corp., 1 F.Supp.2d 1124, 1130 n.2 (D.Or.1998). The DOJ considers any element of a facility that does not meet or exceed the Guidelines to be a barrier to access. See Parr v. L & L Drive Inn-Restaurant, 96 F.Supp.2d 1065, 1086 (D.Hawai'i 2000). And, as the jury learned in this case, under the Guidelines the maximum slope of an interior ramp in an existing facility shall generally be a ratio of 1:12, or one unit of rise for every twelve units of run. See 36 C.F.R. Pt. 1191, App. A, § 4.82 (1999).

Appellants contend, alternatively, that the evidence was unrebutted that they complied with the ADA's requirement of barrier removal by providing alternative means of access to seating, i.e., a wheelchair available on request and a special seating area in the rear of tdingtheatre. It needs reminding, however, that the issue before the jury was not whether appellants in fact violated the ADA or any other statute (that would have been so if the case were tried on a theory of negligence per se), but whether they breached their duty to the plaintiff in the circumstances, and whether that breach caused his injuries. The ADA standard constituted evidence of the standard of care, no more. The jury had ample evidence before it from which to find that appellants had been negligent. Besides the deviation from the norm in the slope ratio of the ramp, the jury had the opinion of the plaintiff's expert that a warning sign could have been posted or hand railings installed at the uppermost point of the ramp, or an alternative entrance to the auditorium constructed for disabled persons at relatively modest cost. Moreover, Dalgliesh and his lay witnesses testified that the usher (who appellants concede was their employee-agent) disregarded his repeated requests for a wheelchair or other assistance in light of his condition, leaving him essentially to fend for himself as the theater lights began to dim. We find no basis on which to disturb the trial court's submission of liability to the jury.

Affirmed.

Notes

1. The most famous theater in the world is the Globe Theater in London. Built in 1599, destroyed by fire in 1613, and then quickly rebuilt, it was closed by Oliver Cromwell and the Puritans in 1642 and torn down in 1644. In 1970, American film maker and actor Sam Wanamaker began a decades-long drive to erect a working replica. Although Wanamaker died in 1993, in 1997 the new Globe opened to rave reviews. *See* Alan Riding, *After Four Centuries, Shakespeare Comes to Life in His Natural Habitat*, N.Y. Times, June 12, 1997, at C13.

Much of the credit for the restoration's success belongs to a Canadian historian named John Orrell:

> The details—from size to seating—of what may be the world's most famous theater ha[d] long eluded historians, but Dr. Orrell brought new techniques, including mathematics, to the search.
>
> Dr. Orrell's breakthrough was to use a famous 17th-century etching, "The Long View of London," by the Bohemian artist Wenceslaus Hollar, and overlay it on a present-day map showing which 17th-century buildings survive.
>
> He then did trigonometric analyses of building proportions to determine the size of the Globe.
>
> Dr. Orrell added [to his discovery the] small amount of archaeological evidence [that had survived, such as] Shakespeare's own stage directions, a building contract for a similar theater, the writings of Italian theater architects and several other contemporaneous images, and came up with a description of the size and nature of the theater.
>
> The importance of the Globe in theatrical history is hard to overstate. Shakespeare made a personal cash contribution to the theater and helped plan it. Some of his greatest works—among them "Julius Caesar," "Hamlet" and "Macbeth"—were written for it.
>
> The reproduction, several hundred yards from the original site, is a 20-sided polygon that is 99 feet across. [It] has become a working theater and a major tourist attraction.

Douglas Martin, *John Orrell, 68, Historian on New Globe Theater, Dies*, N.Y. Times, Sept. 28, 2003, §1, at 39. For a further look at the restoration, *see Shakespeare's Globe Research Database*, at www.rdg.ac.uk/globe/home.htm.

2. As *Nemer* makes clear, designing a theater is a complex undertaking, so much so that the subject has generated an extensive (and fascinating) literature. *See, e.g.*, Martin

Bloom, *Accommodating the Lively Arts: An Architect's View* (1997); Terri Hardin, *Theatres & Opera Houses: Masterpieces of Architectures* (2000); Iain Mackintosh, *Architecture, Actor & Audience* (1994); William Morrison, *Broadway Theatres: History and Architecture* (1999); Hardy Holzman Pfeiffer Associates, *Theaters* (2000).

3. Although separated by 90 years, *Hart* and *Dalgliesh* are really two sides of the same coin: not only must a theater protect against natural perils, it also must keep occupants safe from man-made dangers. For further discussions of theater safety, *see, e.g.*, the web sites of Arts, Crafts, and Theater Safety (www.caseweb.com/acts/) and the International Secondary Education Theater Safety Association (www.isetsa.org). *See also* Elaine Marie Tomko, *Products Liability: Theatrical Equipment and Props,* 42 A.L.R.5th 699 (1996).

4. Fires pose special risks to theaters—recall Justice Holmes's famous observation in *Schenck v. United States,* 249 U.S. 247, 249 (1919): "The most stringent protection of free speech would not protect a man in falsely shouting fire in a theatre and causing a panic."

History's two most deadly theater fires occurred, respectively, in Guangzhou, China, in 1845 (1,670 killed), and in Vienna, Austria, in 1881 (800 killed). In the United States, the worst theater fire occurred in 1903 at the Iroquois Theatre in Chicago:

> The Iroquois Theatre was a mere five weeks old that day in 1903. Located on Randolph between State and Dearborn, it was a magnificent palace of marble and mahogany, a "virtual temple of beauty", and had been advertised as "absolutely fireproof". On the afternoon of December 30th, an audience of 1,900 was present to see Eddie Foy and Annabelle Whitford in the musical comedy "Mr. Blue Beard". The crowd consisted of mostly women and children.
>
> As the orchestra played "Let Us Swear by the Pale Moonlight" during the second act, a malfunctioning arc light ignited the muslin drapes. The fire quickly spread to the backdrops hanging above the stage, pieces of which then fell toward the performers. The actors fled; Eddie Foy soon returned and urged the audience to remain calm and in their seats.
>
> The crew tried to lower the asbestos curtain between the stage and the audience. Midway down, it stuck—the cheap wooden tracks had caused it to jam. As the stage collapsed, the audience panicked and ran for the twenty-seven exits, only to find most of them locked. Those in front were trampled and crushed against the doors, which opened inwards.
>
> By the time firefighters arrived, the auditorium was silent. Five hundred and seventy five were dead; at least 25 more would die from their injuries.
>
> The Iroquois fire prompted new safety standards nationwide. Under the new laws, exits had to be clearly marked; be openable from the inside at all times; and open outwards.

Graveyards of Chicago: Montrose Cemetery, at www.graveyards.com/montrose/iroquois.html. For further accounts, *see* Nat Brandt et al., *Chicago Death Trap: The Iroquois Theatre Fire of 1903* (2003), and Anthony P. Hatch, *Tinder Box: The Iroquois Theatre Disaster 1903* (2003).

5. The passage of the Americans with Disabilities Act of 1990, 42 U.S.C. §§ 12101-12213, has accelerated the efforts of theaters to accommodate patrons with special needs. *See, e.g.,* Mervyn Rothstein, *Making Theater Accessible to People with Trouble Hearing,* N.Y. Times, July 18, 2002, at B5. Nevertheless, bringing older theaters into compliance often has proven costly and difficult. It took five years, for example, for the

federal government and the Shubert Organization just to reach agreement on an accessibility plan for the latter's Broadway theaters. *See* Neil Graves, *Shubert in Deal for Disabled*, N.Y. Post, Sept. 26, 2003, at 2 (reporting that the pact will result in $5 million worth of remodeled seating areas, restrooms, entrances, exits, ticket windows, concession areas, and drinking fountains).

Problem 17

Because of the local topography, a theater was built high on a hill. This design was felt to be particularly beneficial because it would facilitate run-off. During a recent storm, however, the theater sustained extensive damage. A subsequent inspection revealed that a sewer pipe had been clogged at the time of the downpour, thereby causing water to enter the building. If the theater's insurance policy excludes coverage for floods but covers damage "caused by sewer water back-up," does the insurer have any duty to pay? *See Front Row Theatre, Inc. v. American Manufacturers Mutual Ins. Cos.*, 18 F.3d 1343 (6th Cir. 1994).

C. NAMING RIGHTS

BOOTH v. JARRETT & PALMER
52 How. Pr. 169 (N.Y. C.P. 1876)

VAN BRUNT, Judge.

In or about the year 1868 the plaintiff, at the corner of Twenty-third street and Sixth avenue, in the city of New York, built a theater, which he called "Booth's theater." From February, 1869, to the 30th of January, 1873, the plaintiff managed the said theater and obtained a great reputation for the said theater under the name of "Booth's theater."

On this last mentioned date the plaintiff executed a lease to [his brother] Junius B. Booth, of the theater in question, under the following designation: "All those certain premises situate on the southerly side of Twenty-third street, between Fifth and Sixth avenues, and known as Booth's theater, in the city of New York." On the 7th day of April, 1874, the said Junius B. Booth assigned this lease to the defendants.

In the month of November [1874] Edwin Booth executed a mortgage to Oakes Ames upon the theater, in which mortgage the premises are described by metes and bounds, to which description is added the words, "being the premises known as Booth's theater, in the city of New York." A mortgage was also given to Simon Wormser on the said premises, which was foreclosed, and the premises conveyed to Oliver Ames, in February, 1876, by the same description.

Mr. William M. Pritchard, having been duly appointed receiver of said premises in the action to foreclose the Wormser mortgage, by direction of the court executed an agreement by which the defendants were accepted as tenants of the property known as Booth's theater, upon the terms and conditions set forth in the said lease to Junius B. Booth, excepting certain modifications contained in said agreement, and since the execution of this agreement up to the present time the defendants have been carrying on the theatrical business at said theater, designating the same on their hand-bills and billboards as "Booth's theater," but representing themselves as the lessees and managers.

The plaintiff, claiming that by the use of the name of "Booth's theater" the public will be misled into believing that he is still the manager of this theater, and that they will be deceived into going to the theater, supposing that plaintiff still acts there, and that he will be injured thereby, brings this action to restrain the defendants from the use of the name of "Booth's theater."

I am unable to see how the injunction asked can be granted. The plaintiff has built a public building and christened it "Booth's theater." He has acquired under that name a reputation as a place of public amusement. Having thus increased the value of the premises by that reputation, he has mortgaged and leased them under the name he had given them, and there is no doubt from the manner in which the premises are described in the lease to Junius B. Booth that one of the inducements to the lease was the public reputation which Booth's theater had acquired as a place of public amusement. The defendants have succeeded to all these rights, and one of them seems to me is the name by which the plaintiff has conveyed these premises. It is to be borne in mind that there is no attempt upon the part of the defendants to conceal the fact that they are the lessees and managers of this theater.

What, under these circumstances, does the use of the name "Booth's theater" indicate to the public? Nothing more, I imagine, than that this theater was built by the plaintiff; that this is the theater which he named upon its construction "Booth's theater," and the place of amusement which had become known to the public under that name.

The facts developed in this case are far from bringing it within the principles laid down in the case of Howe v. Searing (19 How. Pr. R. 14), relied upon by the plaintiff as an authority to support his claim in this action. In that case the assignees of Howe conducted the whole business in his name, and the court upheld the injunction on the ground "that it was against public policy to allow a business to be conducted under any other name than that of the actual parties doing it." It seems to me that the plaintiff, by his acts, has affixed his name to the theater, so that his grantees and their successors have the right to call this building "Booth's theater," the name which he has given it.

The motion for an injunction must be denied, with ten dollars costs.

SOUTHEAST BANK, N.A. v. LAWRENCE
489 N.E.2d 744 (N.Y. 1985),
reargument denied, 490 N.E.2d 558 (N.Y. 1986)

MEMORANDUM.

The order of the Appellate Division, 104 A.D.2d 213, 483 N.Y.S.2d 218, should be reversed, without costs, complaint dismissed, preliminary injunction vacated, and question certified answered in the negative.

Plaintiff, a Florida-based bank acting as personal representative of the estate of the late playwright Tennessee Williams, a Florida domiciliary at the time of his death, commenced this action to enjoin defendants, the owners of a theatre located on West 48th Street in Manhattan, from renaming the theatre the "Tennessee Williams." In its complaint, plaintiff alleges, among other things, that the renaming of the theatre without its consent violates the decedent's descendible right of publicity.

Special Term granted plaintiff's motion for a preliminary injunction and denied defendants' cross motion to dismiss the complaint. That order has been affirmed by the

Appellate Division, First Department, which granted leave to appeal on a certified question. We now reverse.

The parties have assumed that the substantive law of New York is dispositive of the appeal and have addressed Florida law only tangentially. Both Special Term and the Appellate Division decided the case under what they believed to be New York law. In doing so, all have overlooked the applicable choice of law principle (cf. James v. Powell, 19 N.Y.2d 249, 256, 279 N.Y.S.2d 10, 225 N.E.2d 741), followed by both New York and Florida, that questions concerning personal property rights are to be determined by reference to the substantive law of the decedent's domicile (EPTL 3-5.1[b] [2]; [e]; Matter of Fabbri, 2 N.Y.2d 236, 239, 159 N.Y.S.2d 18 to 40 N.E.2d 269; Quintana v. Ordono, 195 So.2d 577 [Fla.App.], cert. discharged 202 So.2d 178 [Fla]; In re Tim's Estate, 161 So.2d 40 [Fla.App.], decree quashed on other grounds 180 So.2d 161 [Fla.], judgment conformed to 180 So.2d 502 [Fla.App.], cert. denied sub nom. Rudawski v. Florida, 384 U.S. 952, 86 S.Ct. 1569, 16 L.Ed.2d 549; see also Restatement [Second] of Conflict of Laws § 263; Weintraub, Conflict of Laws §§ 2.13, 8.25 [2d ed.]). For choice of law purposes, at least, rights of publicity constitute personalty (see Acme Circus Operating Co. v. Kuperstock, 711 F.2d 1538, 1541; Groucho Marx Prods. v. Day & Night Co., 689 F.2d 317; Factors Etc. v. Pro Arts, 652 F.2d 278, cert. denied 456 U.S. 927, 102 S.Ct. 1973, 72 L.Ed.2d 442).

Under Florida law (Fla.Stats.Ann. § 540.08), only one to whom a license has been issued during decedent's lifetime and the decedent's surviving spouse and children possess a descendible right of publicity, which is extremely limited and which Florida courts have refused to extend beyond the contours of the statute (see Loft v. Fuller, 408 So.2d 619 [Fla.App.], review denied 419 So.2d 1198 [Fla.]). Since Tennessee Williams did not have a surviving spouse or child and did not issue a license during his lifetime, plaintiff possesses no enforceable property right. In light of this holding, we do not pass upon the question of whether a common-law descendible right of publicity exists in this State.

We do not reach the merits of the remaining causes of action asserted in the complaint because plaintiff has no standing to assert them.

Order reversed, etc.

CADILLAC ON MARQUEE AT WINTER GARDEN

Jesse McKinley
N.Y. Times, May 7, 2002, at E3

In the latest indication of a growing corporate presence on Broadway, the Shubert Organization announced yesterday that it had struck a deal with General Motors to rename its historic Winter Garden Theater the Cadillac Winter Garden.

The announcement, made by the Shubert president, Philip J. Smith, culminates two years of on-and-off negotiation between the theater company and the automaker. It marks the first time that one of the three major Broadway theater chains—the Shuberts, Jujamcyn and the Nederlanders—has sold the rights to a Broadway theater's name.

While the practice of affixing a corporate logo to a marquee is common in the sporting world, it is still rare on Broadway. In 1998 the Livent theater company, now defunct, opened the Ford Center for the Performing Arts, complete with a Ford emblem atop the theater's marquee. Two years later the nonprofit Roundabout Theater Company sold the naming rights to the refurbished Selwyn Theater to American Airlines for $8.5 million over 10 years.

The terms of the Shubert deal were not disclosed, but it is believed to be worth more than $1 million a year over several years. As to the financial details, Mr. Smith would only say it is a "multiyear, multimillion-dollar deal." While purists might chafe at the thought of a car company's name on an artistic landmark, Mr. Smith said his company had no such qualms.

"We welcome the idea that a major corporation is interested in spending some money on Broadway," Mr. Smith said. "This is not done in any cheap, shoddy way. We held out for a most tasteful and aesthetic look," adding that the words "Winter Garden" would still be prominent on the marquee.

The Winter Garden, at 50th Street and Broadway, was the longtime home of the musical "Cats" and now houses "Mamma Mia!," the hit musical based on the songs of Abba. Opened in 1911, the theater has been home to landmark productions like "Mame," "Funny Girl," "West Side Story," "Pacific Overtures," "42nd Street" and "Follies."

Notes

1. As the court explains, the plaintiff in *Booth* was Edwin T. Booth (1833-93), considered by many to be America's greatest Shakespearean actor and a member of one of the country's most notable theatrical families. Today, however, most people are more familiar with his brother John Wilkes Booth, who in April 1865 killed President Abraham Lincoln while the latter was attending a performance of "Our American Cousin" at the Ford Theater in Washington, D.C. For a further look at the Booth family, *see The Booths of Hartford County* at www.hartfordhistory.net/Booths.htm.

2. Despite his victory at the New York State Court of Appeals, songwriter Jack Lawrence did not resume using Tennessee Williams's name. Instead, in November 1987 he sold his building to a commercial developer, who tore it down. *See Jack Lawrence Theater is Sold to a Developer*, N.Y. Times, Nov. 25, 1987, at C26.

Originally a Presbyterian church, in 1968 the property was converted into the Playhouse Theater by producer Arthur Cantor. Lawrence purchased the structure for $2 million in 1983 and then spent $2 million on improvements. Nevertheless, its small size, location on the extreme western fringe of the theater district, and unfavorable union contracts made failure all but inevitable.

During the renovations, Lawrence toyed with the idea of re-naming the building for Ethel Merman or Henry Fonda but finally settled on Tennessee Williams; he then renamed the building's smaller second stage the "Audrey Wood Theater," in honor of Williams's longtime literary agent. Because Wood was still alive but in a coma, Lawrence obtained permission from her attorney, but was advised by his lawyers that similar authorization was not needed for the main stage because Williams was dead.

Today, there is no theater named for Williams on Broadway; one does exist, however, on the campus of a community college in Key West, Florida. *See* www.tennesseewilliamstheater.com.

3. As the article by McKinley explains, the tradition of naming Broadway houses after famous theatrical figures is beginning to give way to corporate monikers. In your opinion, does it make a difference what a theater is called? Obviously, Edwin Booth thought it did; so did Charles V. Carroll, Jr., Williams's administrator:

> Carroll, Luis Sanjorjo, Williams's last agent, and John L. Eastman, Williams's lawyer and now a trustee of the trust the playwright left for the care

of his invalid sister Rose, have argued that the Playhouse Theater was not sufficiently "first-class" to bear [Williams's] name. In court testimony and public statements, they have referred to it as an "Off Broadway theater" because of its "small" size. They have also contended that by naming the theater for Williams, Mr. Lawrence will do better business there. "If it were thought by the theatergoing public that Tennessee Williams's estate or Tennessee Williams during his lifetime were involved in the theater," Mr. Eastman testified, "they might well buy tickets for productions of unknown plays."

Mr. Lawrence disputes all this. "How is there going to be commercial gain for me?" he said in a recent interview. "As Shakespeare said, 'The play's the thing.' Do people go to see a play because it's in the Eugene O'Neill Theater?"

Samuel G. Freedman, *Producer Seeks a Theater Named Williams*, N.Y. Times, Mar. 24, 1984, § 1, at 1.

Problem 18

Last year, a high-profile business entered into a long-term, multi-million dollar naming rights agreement with a theater. A few months ago, however, the company was forced to declare bankruptcy. When the theater tried to take back the name and sell it to a new buyer, the bankruptcy trustee objected, arguing that it was an asset of the estate. Given these facts, how should the court rule? *See In re Flying Squirrel Sports, LLC*, 2002 WL 31947152 (N.D. Cal. Bankr. 2002).

D. LEASES

THEATRE PARTY ASSOCIATES, INC. v. SHUBERT ORGANIZATION, INC.
695 F. Supp. 150 (S.D.N.Y. 1988)

LEISURE, District Judge.

This is an antitrust action concerning an alleged market for "choice" theatre party group tickets to the "hits" of each Broadway theatre season in New York. Plaintiff alleges, in essence, that defendant, the Shubert Organization, was aware that the show "The Phantom of the Opera" was destined to become the only Broadway "hit" for the 1987-88 theatre season, that Shubert bid competitively to book that show in one of its theatres, and that Shubert then used its control of tickets to "Phantom" to pursue a scheme to dominate the relevant market.

Defendant has moved, pursuant to Fed.R.Civ.P. 12(b)(6), to dismiss the complaint. For the reasons below, defendant's motion is granted.

I.

Plaintiff Theatre Party Associates, Inc. ("Associates") is a New York corporation with its principal place of business in New York. Associates is licensed by the New York City Department of Consumer Affairs as a "theatre party agent." According to Associates, "theatre party" agents sell large blocks of advance tickets to charitable organizations or other similar groups, which in turn resell those tickets to individual theatre patrons at a substantial premium. That premium normally serves as a charitable contribution to the charitable organization. Such "theatre party" sales differ from what plaintiff labels "group sales," in that group sales are normally made after the opening date of a show has been announced, are generally not intended for resale at a premium, and are made in smaller quantities.

According to plaintiff, theatre party sales have historically been the most important source of advance ticket sales, normally accounting for fifty percent of pre-opening receipts. According to plaintiff, those pre-opening receipts typically determine the financial success or failure of a show in a New York Broadway theatre. Plaintiff claims that a given theatre will normally pay theatre party agents a commission equal to ten percent of the face value of the tickets sold.

According to plaintiff, a number of months before the public announcement of the opening date of a show—that is, the time at which groups and the general public are allowed to buy tickets—theatre party agents have historically been given allocations of seats, for particular dates, by the theatre or other entity controlling the ticket distribution. However, according to plaintiff, only one or two shows during each Broadway season will be perceived by theatre party agents and their clients as appealing to theatre party patrons. Such perception is, according to plaintiff, based upon such factors as pre-opening publicity, the presence of "stars" in the show, or success of the show in another city.

Shows for which [the foregoing] factors are present are known as "theatre party hits," and theatre party agents will normally, according to plaintiff, not accept tickets to any other shows. Moreover, plaintiff alleges that theatre party agents will only accept choice seats on choice dates of performances of those shows. Choice seats are understood to be seats with unobstructed views in the forward sections of the center of the theatre. Choice dates are understood to be dates early enough in the run of a show to enable a patron to feel that he or she enjoys a significant advantage over the general ticket buying public, typically the first six weeks of a show's engagement.

Plaintiff claims that purchasers of theatre party tickets have normally and historically relied on theatre party agents' experience and expertise to help select a show and date combination that best suits the purchasers' needs. Normally, a given theatre party agent has a number of regular clients whose needs are filled from the allocation of dates given to that agent. According to plaintiff, the organizations purchasing theatre party tickets from the agents compete among themselves for sales of tickets to patrons. Thus, a given agent's clients will only be willing to continue to rely on that agent for so long as the clients perceive that the agent is capable of providing "choice" tickets to theatre party hits.

Defendant, The Shubert Organization, Inc., is a New York corporation doing business principally in New York. Of the thirty-eight theatres in New York which are considered "Broadway theatres" Shubert is alleged to own sixteen, and is alleged to be an equal partner in a seventeenth theater. Plaintiff alleges that in the three Broadway seasons preceeding the 1987-88 season, Shubert theatres booked seventy percent of all plays considered "theatre party hits."

Plaintiff's amended complaint discusses a 1950 antitrust lawsuit in which the federal government challenged the means through which the Shubert theatres acquired a dominant position in the Broadway theatre market. [See United v. Shubert, 348 U.S. 222 (1955).] In 1956, that lawsuit was settled through the entry of a consent decree which placed numerous restrictions upon Shubert's activities. [See United States v. Shubert,

1956 Trade Cas. (CCH) ¶ 68,272 (S.D.N.Y. 1956).] That consent decree forbade Shubert, inter alia, from "entering into any contract by which a producer is required to leave the disposition of theatre tickets...to the sole discretion of [Shubert]" and from "owning, controlling or having any financial interest in any theatre ticket agency doing business in...any city...[in which Shubert]...operates a theatre." Amended Complaint ¶ 21.

According to the Amended Complaint, the consent decree was modified in 1981 to eliminate the prohibition on Shubert's operating a theatre ticket agency. At about that time, Shubert organized a "group sales" division, which sells tickets to shows appearing in Shubert theatres and in theatres operated by Shubert's competitors.

Plaintiff alleges that, prior to the fall of 1987, Shubert did not compete with plaintiff or other theatre party agents in the sale to theatre party clients of choice tickets to the theatre party hits of each Broadway season. Indeed, prior to the fall of 1987, Shubert apparently allowed theatre party agents to handle all such sales.

Plaintiff claims, however, that when the 1987-88 Broadway season began, Shubert determined to engage, and did engage, upon a course of conduct intended to monopolize the Theatre Party Ticket market through interference with plaintiff's relationships with its clients. Plaintiff alleges that for the 1987-88 Broadway season, only one show qualified as a theatre party "hit"—namely, "Phantom of the Opera." Plaintiff claims that the show's "hit" status was determined because the play's author, Andrew Lloyd Webber, is internationally famous as the author of numerous hits; the play's producer, Cameron Mackintosh, is internationally famous as the producer of numerous hits; its director, Hal Prince, is internationally famous as a director and producer; Phantom was a hit in London; and Phantom received considerable publicity in New York because of, among other reasons, the opposition of the Actors Equity Association to Andrew Lloyd Webber's wife, Sarah Brightman, playing the starring role in the New York production.

Plaintiff claims that Shubert received the right to present Phantom only after it took the unprecedented step of offering to make almost $1,000,000 worth of structural modifications to the Majestic Theatre and offering a $500,000 investment in a less successful production. There are theatres owned by competitors of Shubert which would have been satisfactory without modification, and it was reported that Mackintosh had already decided to stage the play at the Martin Beck Theatre, owned by a Shubert competitor, when Shubert made its unmatchable offer. Amended Complaint at ¶ 33.

Plaintiff alleges that a number of events have made the 1987-88 Broadway season "propitious" for Shubert's scheme. Amended Complaint ¶ 41. First, in January 1987, the United States District Court for the Southern District of New York relieved itself of all remaining jurisdiction over compliance with the consent decree of 1956. Second, because Phantom was anticipated to be the largest theatre party hit of all time, Shubert could be confident both that it would not require plaintiff's services, or any other agent's services, in order to sell tickets to the show, and that plaintiff's clients could easily be persuaded to abandon plaintiff and buy tickets from Shubert. Third, because no other hits were anticipated to open during the 1987-88 season, plaintiff was left without an alternate access to the market.

According to plaintiff, demand for Phantom was so great that advance sales totaled approximately $15 million, the largest advance sale in the history of Broadway theatre. Moreover, plaintiff alleges that while "choice" dates for theatre party sales normally exist only for the first six weeks of a show's run, theatre party demand for tickets to Phantom continued long beyond the choice date period.

II.
The Monopolization Claim

The essential elements of a monopolization claim under Section 2 of the Sherman Act are: "(1) the possession of monopoly power in the relevant market and (2) the willful acquisition or maintenance of that power as distinguished from growth or development as a consequence of a superior product, business acumen or historic accident." United States v. Grinnell Corp., 384 U.S. 563, 570-71, 86 S.Ct. 1698, 1704, 16 L.Ed.2d 778 (1966). To state a claim properly under Section 2 a complaint must allege a definition of the relevant product market. Nifty Foods Corp. v. Great Atlantic & Pacific Tea Co., Inc., 614 F.2d 832, 840 (2d Cir.1980). This relevant product market must include all products that are reasonably interchangeable, and this alleged product market must be plausible.

Plaintiff's proposed market—advance sales of selected tickets to the early run of Phantom—does not comprise a viable antitrust market. Artful pleading can not disguise that plaintiff is merely alleging that defendants had a monopoly in the distribution of tickets to Phantom of the Opera. Plaintiff seeks to include the 1985-87 seasons as relevant to its monopolization claim, yet plaintiff also alleges that defendant only entered the proposed market in the 1987-88 season. Defendant cannot have monopoly power in a market in which they were not present.

Furthermore Associates claim to freedom from competition for its clients is barred by controlling precedents which establish that Shubert had the right to refuse to deal with plaintiff completely, or alternatively, to compete with plaintiff. Because a manufacturer or seller is free to control the distribution of its own product, it can unilaterally terminate or replace independent distributors and vertically integrate without violating the antitrust laws. Vertical integration without more, even by a monopolist, does not offend Section 2. Belfiore v. New York Times Co., 826 F.2d 177 (2d Cir.1987).

Here defendant concededly had a monopoly over the distribution of the tickets to Phantom of the Opera which ran at its theatre. Defendant decided to change its distribution system and enter the market itself as a theatre party agent. In so doing it delayed date allocations and offered fewer tickets to plaintiff. Even if defendant changed its distribution system, this would constitute no violation of the antitrust laws. Such vertical integration increases competition. [Indeed,] Plaintiff's complaint [recognizes] that there is now more competition among "theatre party agents".

Plaintiff's claim also fails to meet the second element of a valid Section 2 claim of monopolization—that there was a wilful acquisition or maintenance of monopoly power by Shubert through unlawful conduct. Plaintiff has alleged no illegal act by Shubert. Shubert could have decided to be the sole distributor of Phantom tickets without running afoul of the antitrust laws. Plaintiff's only possible objection is that defendant's acts took business away from plaintiff. This is not cognizable under the antitrust laws, which were designed to protect competition and not competitors. Brown Shoe Co. v. United States, 370 U.S. 294, 82 S.Ct. 1502, 8 L.Ed.2d 510 (1962); Kelco Disposal, Inc v. Browning-Ferris Industries, 845 F.2d 404 (2d Cir.1988).

Attempt to Monopolize

The elements of the offense of attempt to monopolize are: (1) anticompetitive or exclusionary conduct, (2) specific intent to monopolize and (3) a "dangerous probability" that the attempt will succeed. American Tobacco Co v. United States, 328 U.S. 781, 785, 66 S.Ct. 1125, 1127, 90 L.Ed. 1575 (1946); International Distribution Centers, Inc. v.

Walsh Trucking Co., Inc., 812 F.2d 786 (2d Cir.1987), cert. denied, — U.S. —, 107 S.Ct. 3188, 96 L.Ed.2d 676 (1987).

The "dangerous probability" element of an attempt to monopolize claim requires proof of "significant market power" in a relevant product market. Since plaintiff has failed to define a relevant market it is unable to show that Shubert possesses a significant market share. Additionally, as Phantom is a unique show, Amended Complaint ¶ 29, proving to be the largest Broadway hit of all time, Amended Complaint ¶ 41(b), there is no dangerous probability that any alleged power Shubert may have will extend to other seasons. Plaintiff has failed to state a necessary element of the claim of attempted monopolization.

CONCLUSION

Defendant's motion to dismiss pursuant to Rule 12(b)(6) is granted.

LIZA CO. v. MARK HELLINGER THEATRE, INC.
240 N.Y.S.2d 1000 (App. Div. 1963),
aff'd mem., 200 N.E.2d 775 (N.Y. 1964)

EAGER, Justice.

The action was brought by plaintiff, a limited partnership, engaged in the production of the musical 'My Fair Lady', against the defendants, as the owners of the Mark Hellinger Theatre, for certain declaratory judgment and injunctive relief with respect to plaintiff's alleged rights and obligations under an agreement for the use of the theatre for its said production.

Following a trial at Special Term, the court directed judgment denying plaintiff the declaratory and injunctive relief demanded, dismissing plaintiff's complaint, and directing judgment for defendants declaring that the plaintiff had breached the theatre agreement, that the run of 'My Fair Lady' at defendants' theatre had been validly and lawfully terminated and that the plaintiff vacate and remove itself from the theatre.

Under the agreement for the use of the theatre by the show (hereinafter referred to as the 'theatre agreement'), the theatre owner was to receive 25% of the first $50,000 and 15% of the excess of gross receipts of the show in each week, after the deduction of certain expenses. The theatre agreement contained the following provisions particularly relevant to the issues, to wit: (a) That '[i]n the event that for any two (2) consecutive weeks the gross box office receipts shall be less than the sum of Thirty-five thousand dollars ($35,000.) per week then either party hereto shall have the right to terminate the run of the attraction by serving upon the other a written notice of its election to exercise such rights'; (b) That the attraction 'shall advertise only in such papers as are approved by the Manager of this Theatre, it being especially agreed that no billing, distributing or advertising of any kind whatsoever in the newspapers or in any other shape or manner shall be done by the party of the second part without the written consent of the party of the first part or its duly authorized representative, and a violation of this clause shall be considered a violation of the whole contract'; and (c) That the sale of all tickets was to be under the jurisdiction of the theatre and that the prices of tickets 'shall be subject to mutual understanding.'

'My Fair Lady' opened at the Mark Hellinger Theatre on March 15, 1956 and, concededly, it was one of the most successful productions in theatre history. In the latter part of 1960, however, the receipts for the show began falling off, and plaintiff suggested to defendants that the 'stop clause' in the theatre agreement be raised from $35,000 to $42,000 to the end that either party would have the right to terminate the contract if weekly gross receipts fell below $42,000 for two consecutive weeks. The defendants, however, rejected the suggestion to so raise the 'stop clause' believing that it was not advantageous to them at that time. Then, in January, 1961, the parties, in order to increase receipts, agreed that plaintiff should distribute 'twofers'. These are cards which are on occasion distributed by a show and which provide that a holder turning one in at the box office during certain specified performances is entitled to obtain two tickets for approximately the regular price of one.

Ultimately there was a dispute between the parties as to whether or not their agreement provided for a time limit for the distribution of 'twofers'. In any event, the defendants claim that, in July, 1961, in a conversation between Adler, the general manager of the show, and the defendant Stahl, there was some talk about terminating the distribution of the 'twofers' or raising the 'stop clause' figure from $35,000 to $42,000. There is a dispute here as to what was said and whether or not the parties did come to any agreement. On August 7, 1961, the defendant corporation entered into an agreement with Richard Rodgers for a letting of the theatre to him for use of his play 'No Strings' commencing during the week ending February 22, 1962 or within two weeks subsequent thereto. Thereafter, on September 27, 1961, the defendants by their attorneys wrote to the plaintiff demanding 'that the practice of issuing 'twofers' be stopped immediately' and that they expected 'a reply * * * indicating compliance with the Owner's demands not later than October 2, 1961.' Thereupon, on October 2, this action was brought by plaintiff, alleging the dispute between the parties with respect to the right of the show to issue 'twofers', and the plaintiff demanded declaratory judgment and injunctive relief with respect to its rights in this connection.

The decision of the trial court that the defendants were entitled to a decree terminating the theatre agreement was based upon the following grounds, viz., first, that the 'timely decision and notice of the theatre to terminate 'twofers', plus its change of position following Adler's [plaintiff's representative] permission to use his name with the Rodgers orgainzation, acts in equity to estop the plaintiff from remaining in the Hellinger Theatre', and, second, that the theatre agreement was subject to termination and terminated by the defendants by reason of plaintiff's breach of the provisions of the theatre agreement in its use of 'spot' TV advertisements in January, 1962, without defendants' consent.

The estoppel on the part of plaintiff to claim continuance of the theatre agreement rested upon defendants' claim of the alleged agreement or representations by Adler, that the plaintiff would raise the 'stop clause' figure from $35,000 to $42,000 weekly or discontinue, at the end of the 1961 summer season, the issuance of 'twofers'. The defendants claim that they 'relied on the fact that one or the other would take place' (quote from defendants' brief), and, by reason thereof, committed the use of the theatre effective February 22, 1962 for the production 'No Strings'. Specifically, the defendants' position is that the refusal of plaintiff to discontinue the use of the 'twofers' resulted in keeping the gross receipts of the show barely above the original 'stop clause' figure of $35,000 and that such refusal, or, in the alternative, plaintiff's failure to raise the 'stop clause' figure operated to prevent defendants from terminating the theatre agreement under the 'stop clause'.

An agreement between the parties to increase the 'stop clause' figure from $35,000 to $42,000 was not, however, established. Significantly, the trial court did not find that such an agreement was actually made and effective. There was some discussion between

Adler and defendants looking toward such an agreement, the trial court merely finding, however, that 'Adler indicated that he thought Levin [plaintiff's general partner] would approve the suggestion upon his return from Europe. Upon his return, however, Levin did not approve any change in the 'stop clause' provision.' But, clearly, the defendants were not entitled to rely upon the mere proposal for the change where it was never approved and did not ripen into a binding agreement.

During the conversation in July, 1961, concerning the raising of the 'stop clause' figure, the parties did discuss the possibility of the gross weekly receipts falling below the level of the proposed figure of $42,000 and the consequent vacating of the theatre by the plaintiffs; and in this conversation, there was also a talk about a new musical 'No Strings' which Richard Rodgers was producing. Adler said he was acquainted with Rodgers' general manager Jacobs, gave Stahl his name and stated that Stahl could use Adler's name as a reference in calling this manager. Assuming, as found by the trial court, that Adler was then envisaging a demise of 'My Fair Lady' on the raising of the 'stop clause' figure and that Stahl was then talking about the possibility of interesting Rodgers in the use of the theatre for 'No Strings' for the next season, nevertheless, the defendants have not shown the basis for an estoppel to support Stahl's contract on August 7, 1961 for use by Richard Rodgers of the theatre. Stahl then well knew that Levin, the general partner, was to have the final say as to whether or not the 'stop clause' figure was to be raised. It is clear that defendants' commitment to 'No Strings' was nothing more than a calculated risk voluntarily assumed by defendants with full awareness of the uncertainty of the situation. Adler's permission to Stahl to use his name to get in touch with Rodgers' manager was certainly not intended to and would not operate by way of an estoppel or otherwise to terminate the written theatre agreement.

Furthermore, there is no basis for defendants' claim of estoppel or material breach arising out of plaintiff's alleged refusal to stop issuing 'twofers' following the 1961 summer season. We find that there was no agreement between the parties fixing a time limit for the distribution and sale of 'twofers'. Also, assuming arguendo as found by the trial court that the agreement was 'temporary in nature and not intended by either party to be for an indefinite period,' the defendants nevertheless failed to establish any breach by the plaintiff of such an agreement. The defendants, when they wrote plaintiff on September 27, 1961 giving it notice that they demanded that the practice of issuing 'twofers' be stopped and demanding a reply by October 2, 1961, were not claiming a breach of or a right to terminate the theatre agreement. Then, on October 2, 1961, the plaintiff started this action alleging the dispute between the parties with respect to the right to distribute 'twofers'. Thereupon, most significantly, on October 10, 1961, the parties expressly entered into a stipulation in writing whereby, pending trial of the action and decision rendered thereon, the defendants were to continue to honor the 'twofers'. So, the continuance of the distribution of 'twofers' by the plaintiff following the notice by the defendants was consented to by the defendants subject to a determination of the rights of the parties by the court.

The defendants' letter of September 27, 1961, constitutes most cogent evidence refuting their claim of estoppel. They had contracted on August 7, 1961, to lease the Hellinger Theatre to Rodgers. Yet, as late as September 27, 1961, they were recognizing the theatre agreement with plaintiff as fully effective and binding. They made no claim in their letter of said date that they had a right to terminate the agreement. Nor did they therein make any claim that the 'stop clause' figure should be raised to $42,000. They were merely then demanding 'that the practice of issuing 'twofers' be stopped immediately' and that they expected 'a reply * * * indicating compliance with the Owner's demands not later than October 2, 1961.' So, it is clear that their claim of estoppel was merely an afterthought.

Finally, there is no proper support for the second ground of the trial judge's determination for the defendants, namely, his conclusion that the defendants had the right to terminate and did duly terminate the theatre agreement because of plaintiff's alleged violation of the advertising clause. In this connection, the allegations of defendants' amended answer were that the plaintiff, without consent, had caused certain 'spot' advertisements of the show to be run on TV during 10 days or more in or about January, 1962. The fact is, however, that theretofore, from the day the show opened and for nearly six years, the plaintiff had continually used many forms of advertising, including TV advertising, without consent or protest from the defendants. It is true that, as aforesaid, the advertising clause provided that 'a violation of this clause shall be considered a violation of the whole contract', and that the defendants could have insisted upon full compliance by the plaintiff with the advertising clause, but they never did so. The letter of September 27 was not a notification by defendants that they were insisting upon compliance with such clause as respects advertising generally. Such letter was directed solely to the demand for discontinuance of the use of 'twofers' insofar as it constituted advertising. The defendants must be deemed to have waived the right to claim, without notice, an abrogation of the contract by ordinary advertising.

Moreover, on the record here, it appears that, prior to the time the defendants were claiming a breach by the plaintiff of the advertising clause in the theatre agreement, the defendants themselves had broken and were repudiating the contract. They were in charge of the sale of tickets at the box office and were bound by their agreement to continue the sale in the usual course as long as the show remained in the theatre. But they admit (by their answer) that they had issued instructions to their box office personnel not to sell tickets for performances scheduled after February 24, 1962. As early as December, 1961 they had stopped the sale of tickets for all such performances and, in any event, on January 11, 1962, plaintiff's attorneys wrote to defendants complaining of their violation of the theatre agreement in this connection and stating that the defendants would be held responsible for such violation. Significantly, it was not until the receipt of said letter that the defendants, by their letter of January 15th, formally notified plaintiff of their alleged election to terminate the theatre agreement for the advertising breach. This made it necessary for the defendants to take the position that their determination to stop the sale of the tickets for performances beyond February 24, 1962 was made, not because of any alleged breaches by the plaintiff of the advertising clause, but because of their commitment already made to allow 'No Strings' to use the theatre as of February 22, 1962. This had been defendants' position right along and the last-minute adopting by them of the alleged advertising clause breach as a ground for termination of the theatre agreement does not appear to have been in good faith. They had already determined to end the theatre agreement, and the claim of the advertising breach was also a mere afterthought seized upon by them in an effort to justify a position which they had already assumed.

In any event, if as demonstrated aforesaid, there was no material breach of the theatre agreement or estoppel on plaintiff's part prior to the defendants' commitment in August, 1961, to 'No Strings', then the defendants' said material breach in connection with ticket sales should preclude it from claiming a forfeiture of the agreement for plaintiff's alleged later breach of the advertising clause. Moreover, the breach by plaintiff of the advertising clause, if any, was of such a minor and technical nature that, under the circumstances, it should not have been given the effect of abrogating the agreement.

Clearly, in view of the foregoing, the judgment for the defendants is not supported. The plaintiff, in compliance with the judgment herein, did vacate and remove its show from the defendants' theatre, but, inasmuch as there remains undetermined the rights of the parties with respect to alleged damages on account of alleged breaches of the theatre agreement and certain issues having a bearing thereon were fully litigated, the issues are not academic and there should be a declaration in connection therewith. Under the circumstances, the plaintiff is entitled to judgment declaring that the plaintiff's continuance in the sale of 'twofers' up to and including the time of the trial was not in breach of any agreement of the parties; declaring that the written 'stop clause' provision was not modified by any agreement of the parties to increase the 'stop clause' figure to $42,000; declaring that the defendants were not entitled to terminate the theatre agreement because of the alleged television advertising in January, 1962; declaring that the defendants were not entitled to terminate the theatre agreement or to a removal of the plaintiff's show from the premises; and dismissing defendants' counterclaims.

Findings of fact contained in the decision at Special Term which may be inconsistent herewith should be reversed, and new findings of fact made as indicated herein. Thereupon, the judgment of the trial court should be reversed, with judgment for plaintiff as herein directed, with costs.

A THEATER CLOSING, A HIT SHOW IN THE COLD
Bruce Weber
N.Y. Times, Oct. 29, 2003, at E1

"Urinetown," the unlikely musical hit that has been occupying Henry Miller's Theater on West 43rd Street for more than two years under the threat of eviction, has finally gotten the bad news. The producers were told on Monday that the show would have to leave the theater by Feb. 15 because a 57-story skyscraper was about to be built on the Avenue of the Americas between 42nd and 43rd Streets, a site that includes the theater.

The show's future is unclear. Two of its producers, Michael Rego, of the Araca Group, and Michael David, of Dodger Stage Holding, said "Urinetown" could possibly move to another theater but that there were complications, among them that no other Broadway houses were currently available.

A move to Off Broadway is not out of the question, but economic factors, including union contracts, make this possibility "a long shot," Mr. David said.

Mr. Rego added: "We always knew this would be happening. We knew that the building would be coming down. And now it's coming down for real."

The news adds just one more peculiar chapter to an anomalous theater story. A faux-Brechtian comedy and political satire about a futuristic world in which certain bodily functions are taxed, "Urinetown" was written by two relatively unknown Chicagoans, Greg Kotis and Mark Hollman.

It began life at the New York International Fringe Festival in 1999 and climbed the theatrical food chain to Off Broadway and, finally, Broadway, where its opening was delayed by the 9/11 attacks. More than two years later, it is still going strong. In fact, the producers, who said they were expecting "Urinetown" to last perhaps another year, were about to announce that the show had recouped its $3.7 million capital investment when they learned that it would have to leave the theater.

"The little show that could actually did," Mr. Rego said, adding that a full American tour was now traveling and that the musical, which has already been produced twice in South Korea, was expected to open new productions next year in London, Toronto, Tokyo and Melbourne.

The producers emphasized that their relations with the Durst Organization—the developer of the site and the owner of the theater—and in particular with Douglas Durst, its president, were amicable, and that they had received the news without rancor. When they first took over the theater, they said, they were promised only six months, which seemed like plenty, given the nature of the show and the crapshoot of producing musicals on Broadway.

"Who knew it was going to last two years?" Mr. David said. "Douglas Durst was kind enough to let us make his life miserable for this long. The organization has been unbelievably supportive and generous, and we couldn't be more grateful. It's just that we got to like it there."

For his part, Mr. Durst, interviewed by phone yesterday, expressed admiration for the producers and their show.

Henry Miller's Theater, now a roomy, suggestively squalid auditorium, was named for an English-born actor and producer who had it built for his own performances and productions. It opened in 1918, and has had a motley history since. Major productions that have had their premieres there include Thornton Wilder's "Our Town" (1938); T.S. Eliot's "Cocktail Party" (1950); and Agatha Christie's "Witness for the Prosecution" (1954).

In 1997 the theater was the first home of the current Broadway revival of "Cabaret." In the 1970's and 80's, it was, among other things, a pornographic movie house and a nightclub. Some 55 performances from now, "Urinetown" will become the theater's longest-running tenant, surpassing "The Moon Is Blue," which ran for 924 performances in the early 50's.

The facade has landmark status, and Mr. Durst said the theater itself would be rebuilt as part of the new building, which is scheduled to open in 2008. The original theater, he said, had 950 seats in 12,000 square feet. When it is rebuilt, he added, its original seating capacity will be restored. (It currently holds 631.) To accommodate an audience of that size today, he said, will require 35,000 square feet.

"The theater we intend to build will be the finest playhouse on Broadway," Mr. Durst said.

One reason "Urinetown" had been allowed to remain in the theater so long was that construction of the new skyscraper, which is to be the New York headquarters of Bank of America, had been delayed by the refusal of two property owners on the block to sell their space. Now, Mr. Durst said, he is confident that the state will condemn those properties, allowing the developers to buy or lease them for a nominal sum. Mr. Durst said he expected demolition to begin in March.

"This building is being held together with Scotch tape and rubber bands," he said. "We've really been pushing it by letting them stay in as long as they have."

Notes

1. As the foregoing readings make clear, to be successful theater owners must continually do three things: book hits (*Theatre Party Associates*), replace shows when profits

begin to tumble (*Liza Co.*), and keep a sharp lookout for more lucrative uses for their property (*Urinetown*). At the same time, however, they must make sure their theaters do not sit empty ("go dark"), for having some show paying some rent is (almost always) better than having no show.

2. Upon receiving their eviction notice, the producers of "Urinetown" undertook a search for another theater. Their efforts quickly came to naught, however, because an onslaught of new productions had gobbled up all of the available Broadway theaters. *See Real Estate Ricochet*, Back Stage, Nov. 7, 2003, at 1 (reporting that 22 shows opened in the fall of 2003). Although many of these quickly folded, by the time they did a firm closing date already had been announced for "Urinetown." *See further* Jason Zinoman, *On Stage and Off*, N.Y. Times, Nov. 28, 2003, at E1.

Having a house to call one's own, however, is not always a good thing. In November 2003, the Manhattan Theater Club, a not-for-profit company with 22,000 annual subscribers, moved into the remodeled Biltmore Theater (restored at a cost of $35 million), marking the first time in the Club's 33-year history that it had been housed in a Broadway venue. Yet this triumph was soon overshadowed by an unprecedented string of on-stage flops: the inaugural play (Terrence McNally's "Dedication") was scrubbed because it needed more work, and the next three shows—Richard Greenberg's "Violet Hour," Neil Simon's "Rose's Dilemma," and Regina Taylor's "Drowning Crow"—all bombed badly. *See further* Jesse McKinley, *Manhattan Theater Club Opens a New Home and Finds Trouble*, N.Y. Times, Feb. 25, 2004, at B1.

3. An agreement to lease a theater, often called a "license," may be based on rent only, rent-and-profit sharing, or profit sharing only. Regardless of which method is chosen, the contract should cover all issues likely to arise during the engagement, including maintenance, repairs, insurance, security, advertising, staffing, taxes, and concessions. A sample lease agreement appears in Appendix G of this casebook.

4. For other cases involving theater leases, *see, e.g., C.R. Theatricals, Inc. v. Concert Ass'n of Florida, Inc.*, 802 So. 2d 1159 (Fla. Dist. Ct. App. 2001) (sprinklers); *MTIS Ltd. v. Corporacion Interamericana de Entretenemiento S.A. de C.V.*, 64 S.W.3d 62 (Tex. Ct. App. 2001) (operating rights); *Belasco Theatre Corp. v. Jelin Productions*, 59 N.Y.S.2d 42 (App. Div. 1945), *appeal denied*, 59 N.Y.S.2d 924 (App. Div. 1946) (sublease); *Liveright v. Waldorf Theaters Corp.*, 221 N.Y.S. 194 (App. Div. 1927) (morals); *Tootle Theater Co. v. Shubert Theatrical Co.*, 162 N.Y.S. 111 (App. Div. 1916) (abandonment); *Hughes v. Robinson*, 60 Mo. App. 194 (1895) (non-performance); *Today's Theatre, Inc. v. Ernest Co.*, 204 N.Y.S.2d 448 (Sup. Ct. 1960) (air conditioning); *Century Paramount Hotel v. Rock Land Corp.*, 327 N.Y.S.2d 695 (N.Y.C. Civ. Ct. 1971) (holdover); *Mawson v. Leavitt*, 37 N.Y.S. 1138 (N.Y.C. Ct. 1896) (liquidated damages).

Problem 19

A concessionaire and a theater owner signed a 15-year lease under which the former was granted the exclusive right to sell refreshments to the latter's patrons. So that it could conduct business, the concessionaire installed various appliances in the theater, such as refrigerators, soda dispensers, and ovens. The relationship proved to be a troubled one, however, and when the lease expired the parties decided to go their separate ways. Having reached the end of their useful lives, and having only minimal scrap value, the concessionaire decided to leave behind the appliances. Assuming the contract is silent on the issue, which party is responsible for getting them out of the theater? *See Boston Concessions Group, Inc. v. Criterion Center Corp.*, 673 N.Y.S.2d 111 (App. Div. 1998).

E. HISTORIC PRESERVATION

FRIENDS OF THE ASTOR, INC. v. CITY OF READING
1998 WL 684374 (E.D. Pa. 1998)

GAWTHROP, Distict Judge.

Before the court is plaintiff's motion for a preliminary injunction, requesting that this court enjoin defendants from demolishing or otherwise adversely acting against the Astor Theater (the "Astor"). Plaintiff's complaint alleges that the attempted demolition of the Astor violates the National Environmental Protection Act of 1969 ("NEPA"), the National Historic Preservation Act of 1966 ("NHPA"), and the Community Development Grant Act of 1974. Defendants counter that they have complied with all applicable statutes and regulations and should thus be allowed to demolish the Astor. On August 19, 1998, the Honorable William H. Yohn, Jr., Emergency Judge, granted a temporary restraining order prohibiting the demolition of the Astor. An initial scheduling hearing was held on this matter on August 25, 1998, at which time the TRO was extended with the consent of defendants pending a ruling on plaintiff's motion. After a two-day hearing, argument, and careful review of the numerous briefs filed by the parties, I find that plaintiff has not demonstrated a likelihood of success on the merits and thus shall deny the motion for a preliminary injunction.

I. Background

A. The Astor Theater

The Astor was built in 1928, on the 700 block of Penn Street in Reading, Pennsylvania, and is an example of the early Twentieth Century Art Deco movement. At the Dedication Program of 1928, it was stated that the Astor was

> [d]esigned and created by expert craftsmen, whose one paramount thought was to build into it beauty, comfort and convenience, rivaled by no other theater in the State. No trouble has been spared to make the Astor Theater worthy of the town and its patrons.

Pl.'s Ex. 17. For many years, the Astor operated as a movie house and a theater for performing arts. In the early 1970s, it operated for a few years as an X-rated movie theater. In 1976, the Astor was purchased by the Reading Redevelopment Authority ("RRA"), which nominated it for inclusion in the National Register of Historic Places. In the nomination application, the RRA stated, "[w]ith the demolition of the area's other 'palaces' the Astor stands as unique in this community architecturally and as a monument to the theatrical tradition of Reading." Pl.'s Ex. 15. The Astor was placed on the National Register in 1978 and has since been recognized, by the Program Chief of the State Historic Preservation Office, as "an important (and increasingly rare) community asset which should be able to contribute to Reading's economic base and the quality of life." Pl.'s Ex. 1. It has, however, stood unused since the late 1970s, and although structurally sound, is in substandard condition.

B. The Reading Downtown East Renewal Project

In the early 1970s, the City of Reading (the "City") commenced revitalization efforts for the "Downtown East" section of Reading, in which the Astor is located. This effort, termed the "Reading Downtown East Urban Renewal Project," received financial assistance from the U.S. Department of Housing and Urban Development ("HUD"). Although HUD's 1975 environmental impact statement for the Reading Downtown East Urban Renewal Project proposed the preservation of the Astor, no improvements to the building were ever actually made. In May 1980, the City and HUD entered into a Downtown Urban Renewal Development Close Out Agreement. Although the Close Out Agreement provides for the preservation of the Astor, it also allows the City "to change the status of the Astor Theater by following the procedures set forth in Title 36, Ch. VIII, Part 800 of the Consolidated Federal Register." Pl.'s Ex. 22.

C. Attempted Rehabilitation of the Astor

In the last twenty years, as part of the effort to revitalize downtown Reading, the restoration of the Astor has occasionally been discussed. For example, from 1977-79, the RRA funded a feasibility study that recommended the restoration of the Astor. In 1985, another proposal for the development of the Astor was outlined, but never implemented. In 1987, a grant from the Pennsylvania Historical and Museum Commission was awarded to conduct a conceptual design and cost estimate for the Astor's restoration. And, in 1989, a recommendation for the renovation of the Astor was prepared but never came to fruition. The costs for these various proposals ranged from a few million dollars to $17.5 million. However, in 1997, the Pennsylvania Historical and Museum Commission noted that "no effort has been made within the last 8 years to market or preserve the Astor Theater or Harold Furniture Building." Pl.'s Ex. 3.

D. The Convention Center

In 1994, the City obtained funding from the State of Pennsylvania. The State funds match the Community Development Block Grant ("CDBG") funds HUD agreed to provide the City to assist it and the RRA in other aspects of the planned rejuvenation of Reading's downtown business area, [such as] the rehabilitation of the Rajah Theater, an operational performing arts venue. The Rajah is itself eligible for listing in the National Register of Historic Places, as both a building of historic significance and as a contributing structure in the Thomas Penn Historic District.

With the State funding commitment in hand, the City began to implement its plan for the construction of a convention center in downtown Reading. The preferred site for the convention center was the block of Penn Street where the Astor is situated. In 1996, plaintiff Friends of the Astor ("FOTA"), a non-profit corporation, brought suit in federal court to prevent the demolition of the Astor, which is required for the construction of the proposed convention center. The case was settled upon the City's representations that it had taken no action toward the demolition of the Astor at that time. The City further stated that, prior to initiating the demolition of the Astor, it would comply with all statutory and regulatory requirements.

The property upon which the Astor is located is currently under an agreement of sale to the Berks County Convention Center Authority ("BCCCA") for approximately $500,000. The BCCCA proposes to demolish the Astor and use the site to construct the Berks County Convention Center, which will serve as a multipurpose facility, including hosting a minor league ice hockey franchise. In addition to the State's grant funds, the

Astor demolition/Convention Center construction project (the "Project"), is to be funded by a 5% hotel room tax and a commitment by First Union Capital Markets Group to purchase $9.5 million of tax exempt Fixed Rate Hotel Room Rental Tax Revenue Bonds.

E. The Memorandum of Agreement

On April 8, 1998, after more than a year of negotiations, a Memorandum of Agreement ("MOA") was executed between the City, the Advisory Council on Historic Preservation (the "Advisory Council"), and the Pennsylvania State Historic Preservation Officer for the Pennsylvania Historical and Museum Commission ("PASHPO"). The MOA was intended to satisfy Section 106 of the National Historic Preservation Act. The MOA detailed the actions the City and BCCCA must take before demolishing the Astor and constructing the convention center. FOTA participated in the MOA negotiations as a consulting party.

The MOA notes that "all marketing attempts [of the Astor] have proved unsuccessful [and]... that further marketing would be unproductive based on the facts that the availability of the Astor Theater has been general knowledge for nearly 20 years and no feasible reuse plan has been offered in those years." Pl.'s Ex. 6. The MOA identifies two alternative sites for construction of the Project, explaining that "both...were deemed inadequate." The MOA further acknowledges that "the demolition of the [Astor] will be a significant historical and architectural loss for the City," and thus requires that the City comply with three conditions prior to demolishing the Astor. Under the MOA, the City must (1) obtain "confirmations of the financing commitments...with copies being forwarded to the PASHPO," (2) "utilize the appropriate guidelines for Level II Documentation of the Historic Building Survey/Historic American Engineering Record (HABS/HAER) Division of the National Parks Service," and (3) "ensure that the salvageable items selected...are removed in a manner that minimizes damage."

F. BCCCA, HUD and NEPA

In the spring of 1998, a HUD representative recommended that, despite the fact that no federal funds are being used to finance the Project, the City should prepare an environmental assessment under NEPA for the proposed Project because of public perception that it was tied to the rehabilitation of the Rajah Theater, which is receiving federal funds. In May, 1998, the City hired an outside community development consulting firm, Mullin & Lonergan Associates, Inc. ("Mullin"), to assist Pamela Shupp-Straub, then Reading's Director of Community Development, in the preparation of the environmental assessment. Ms. Straub and Mullin utilized HUD-approved forms, which provided a checklist of all environmental factors to be considered in a NEPA environmental assessment.

Based on the environmental assessment, the City issued a finding of no significant impact, which, as required, it published in the Reading Eagle/Reading Times. Under HUD regulations, the City maintained and made publicly available an environmental review record ("ERR"). FOTA submitted objections to the City's finding of no significant impact during the thirty-day review period for pubic comment on the ERR. Mullin responded to the objections on behalf of the City.

After the thirty-day review period expired, the City transmitted its certification and Request for Release of Funds to HUD. All objections to the certification and Request were required to be received by HUD within fifteen days. FOTA submitted objections to HUD, objecting to the City's spending funds on the project prior to approval and also stating that the PASHPO has lodged objections to the commencement of the Astor's demolition. FOTA's objections were originally rejected as untimely. They were later considered timely, but rejected on the basis that they did not state any permissible objection under HUD regulations. HUD issued a Notice of Removal of Grant Conditions and released the funds to the City.

II. Preliminary Injunction Standard

In deciding whether to grant a preliminary injunction, a court weighs the following factors: (1) has the movant shown a reasonable probability of eventual success on the merits?, (2) will the movant be irreparably injured by denial of injunctive relief?, (3) will the grant of preliminary relief result in even greater harm to the non-movant?, and (4) will granting preliminary relief be in the public interest? SI Handling Sys., Inc. v. Heisley, 753 F.2d 1244, 1254 (3d Cir. 1985).

III. Discussion

NEPA

NEPA requires federal agencies to prepare an environmental impact statement relating to "proposals for...major Federal actions significantly affecting the quality of the human environment." 42 U.S.C. §4332(2)(C). The Council on Environmental Quality regulations implement NEPA and provide that an agency should prepare an environmental assessment for an action if the agency decides it is not categorically excluded from the impact statement requirement. The environmental assessment functions as a preliminary environmental inquiry. See 40 C.F.R. §1501.4(b).

Once an agency has prepared an assessment, it determines whether to prepare an environmental impact statement. The regulations state, in part, that this impact statement:

> shall provide full and fair discussion of significant environmental impact and shall inform decisionmakers and the public of the reasonable alternatives which would avoid or minimize adverse impacts or enhance the quality of the human environment.

40 C.F.R. §1502.1. In contrast, if the agency determines on the basis of the environmental assessment not to prepare an impact statement, it must prepare a finding of no significant impact.

The parties disagree as to the appropriate standard by which the City's decision not to prepare an environmental impact statement should be reviewed by this court. FOTA argues that the court should employ a reasonableness standard. Defendants contend that the appropriate inquiry is whether the agency's decision was arbitrary or capricious.

Although the most recent and persuasive case law suggests that the arbitrary-and-capricious standard is appropriate for a court's review of an agency's decision not to prepare an environmental impact statement, I need not decide this issue here. I find that under either standard, plaintiff has not met its burden.

Plaintiff argues that the environmental assessment performed by the City was inadequate and that the City erred in finding no significant impact and not preparing an environmental impact statement. Thus, the primary issue here is whether the adverse affect of the demolition of the Astor has a sufficiently significant impact on the environment to warrant the preparation of an environmental impact statement.

An environmental assessment is to "[b]riefly provide sufficient evidence and analysis for determining" whether to prepare an impact statement. 40 C.F.R. § 1508.9(a)(1). Demonstrating that the environmental assessment was obviously inadequate or prepared in bad faith, with a pre-ordained analysis of the anticipated environmental impact, warrants the grant of a preliminary injunction, see Public Serv. Co. of Colo. v. Andrus, 825 F. Supp. 1483 (D. Idaho 1993). Here however, other than issues concerning the Astor, plaintiff did not present any evidence raising substantial questions as to the inadequacy or conclusory nature of the City's environmental analysis. FOTA has not presented any substantive evidence relating to any specific area of land development, noise, air quality, environmental design, historic value, socioeconomic factors, or community facilities and services—other than the demolition of the Astor—that tends to demonstrate that the environmental assessment on these points was superficial or manipulated. Instead, FOTA makes broad, general allegations of inadequacy. These allegations do not suffice to show that FOTA is likely to succeed on the merits of its NEPA violation claim.

I must then address FOTA's specific allegation that the environmental assessment is inadequate because it allegedly fails to address the significant impact the demolition of the Astor will have on the quality of the human environment. Specifically, FOTA argues that the environmental assessment neglects the Astor's historical importance, incorrectly concludes that there is no economically feasible use for the Astor, and fails to meaningfully address possible alternative sites for the project. FOTA argues that the conclusory nature of the environmental assessment results from the City's "failure to market or otherwise actively attempt to preserve the Astor and indeed has allowed it to deteriorate and remain unsecured." Pl.'s Proposed Findings of Fact, ¶ 10.

The environmental assessment states that the Astor is a "historic resource," makes numerous references to the MOA, which itself speaks directly to the historical importance of the Astor, and states that its demolition is in accord with 36 C.F.R. § 800—a regulation addressing the "Protection of Historic and Cultural Properties." Then Director of Community Development Straub participated extensively in both the negotiations of the MOA and the preparation of the environmental assessment. It is thus difficult to conclude that the City was either uninformed of or unaware of the Astor's historic value, or that its importance was neglected. Notably, at the preliminary injunction hearing, FOTA introduced little evidence tending to establish the Astor's historic significance beyond its inclusion on the National Register. I thus find it hard to determine what additional evidence the City could have included in the ERR.

As to FOTA's claim that the City unreasonably concluded that rehabilitation of the Astor was not economically feasible, the record shows that various proposals for the Astor's restoration have been entertained over the past 20 years, yet none have culminated in its actual rehabilitation. The MOA, which is incorporated in the ERR, outlines these proposals. Further, the MOA evidences that both the PASHPO and the Advisory Council agreed with the City that it was not economically feasible to redevelop the Astor.

Finally, contrary to plaintiff's assertion, the ERR includes a discussion of a "Do Not Undertake Project" alternative, alternative sites, and alternative construction, namely, incorporation of the Astor into the Convention Center design. The City, however, rejected each of these proposals and provided its reasoning for doing so. The City concluded that the alternatives did not support the City's long-term planning for redevelopment of downtown Reading. Paramount to the decision to construct the convention center on the site currently occupied by the Astor is the planned construction of an intermodal transportation center on the site immediately south of the Astor property. The proposed design includes a pedestrian walkway connecting the convention center and the transportation center. The City briefly discusses this factor, in addition to other reasonable factors, as a reason for eliminating the alternatives.

I thus find that the City both performed an adequate analysis of the environmental effects of the Project and correctly found that the preparation of an environmental impact statement was not necessary. Thus, plaintiff has not shown a likelihood of success on its NEPA claim.

NHPA

FOTA argues that the City has failed to comply with the requirements of the National Historic Preservation Act ("NHPA"), 16 U.S.C. § 470f, et seq. Specifically, FOTA contends that, contrary to the provisions of the MOA, defendants have not properly "taken into account" the effect the Project will have on the Astor by not ensuring the necessary funding for the convention center's construction following the Astor's demolition.

FOTA contends that much of the funding for the Project is "conditional" rather than "firm." Among other things, FOTA points out that the proposed hotel room tax has been challenged in State Court, and a finding of illegality would jeopardize the bond purchase commitment. Accordingly, FOTA argues that:

> The significance of the MOA, and its implicit determination that demolition is warranted if and only if the Convention Center is constructed, therefore depends on the meaning of the requirement of commitment for funding in the MOA, and whether it is enforceable.
>
> It was not the intention of the parties that the MOA create a meaningless condition to demolition; the parties intended to create a meaningful condition, and a condition is not meaningful if it is unenforceable or if it is interpreted in a way inconsistent for its purpose.

Pl.'s Proposed Findings of Fact, ¶¶ 53-54.

In addition to questioning FOTA's ability to represent the intent of the parties to the agreement and its standing to challenge the City's compliance with the MOA, I find plaintiff's argument to be without merit. The City conducted a consultation process as required under Section 106 of the NHPA, which took in excess of a year, and included participation by FOTA as a consulting party. Although not apparently challenging the consultation process, FOTA argues that the City failed to fulfill its obligations as set forth in the MOA. I disagree. Both Ms. Straub and [Brenda Barrett, Esq., Pennsylvania's Deputy State Historic Preservation Officer] agree that the City has provided the required documentation regarding the financing commitments for the Project and that "unconditional" commitments are not required. The City's obligations cannot be read to extend any further than what is expressly stated in the MOA.

HUD Statute

The City presently proposes to spend $4.5 million of CDBG funds, granted under the Housing and Community Development Act ("HCDA"), 42 U.S.C. § 5304, to rehabilitate the Rajah, which has not been historically certified, but is eligible for listing in the National Register. FOTA argues that this use of the CDBG funds violates the HCDA in that "eligibilty for Block Grant funds entails that a project either benefit primarily low and moderate income persons, or be part of a thirty percent exemption from that restriction in each year." Pl.'s Proposed Findings of Fact, ¶ 59. FOTA concludes that "[i]t appears likely that HUD acted inappropriately in releasing the Block Grant funds for the Rajah, contrary to 24 C.F.R. § 570.202."

Section 570.202 specifically states that "CDBG funds may be used for the rehabilitation, preservation, or restoration of historic properties, whether publicly or privately owned. Historic properties are those sites or structures that are either listed in or eligible to be listed in the National Register of Historic Places." 24 C.F.R. § 570.202(d). Thus, rehabilitation of the Rajah falls into this category. As to the question of the percentage of CDBG funds the City will expend on persons of low to moderate income, neither party has submitted sufficient evidence to be able to determine whether FOTA has a viable claim. I find however that I need not reach the merits on this point because FOTA lacks standing to bring this claim.

IV. Conclusion

Clearly, denying the motion for preliminary injunction will result in irreparable harm to the Astor. However, because I find that FOTA has not shown its probability of success on the merits of any of the asserted claims, I am constrained to deny its motion.

SHUBERT ORGANIZATION, INC. v. LANDMARKS PRESERVATION COMMISSION OF THE CITY OF NEW YORK

570 N.Y.S.2d 504 (App. Div.),
appeal denied, 587 N.E.2d 289 (N.Y. 1991),
cert. denied, 504 U.S. 946 (1992)

ASCH, Justice.

Petitioners, several theatre owners as well as trade organizations, had sought, inter alia, in this declaratory relief and CPLR Article 78 proceeding, to annul the designation of twenty-two Broadway theatres as landmarks, and to declare null and void the underlying Landmarks Legislation and the anti-demolition provision of the City Zoning Resolution.

Petitioners claim that the designation process in this case manifested an improper exercise in spot zoning, rather than a detailed analysis leading to the designation of a specific building or buildings as historic landmarks. The municipal respondents counter that the different, respective decisions of the Landmarks Preservation Commission and the Board of Estimate were based on exhaustive studies and reports, as well as public discussion on notice, and that the final vote of the Board of Estimate, although accomplished expeditiously, was not simply expediently arrived at and was supported by a rational basis.

The present challenge is both for a declaratory judgment, invoking the constitutional challenge, and on Article 78 grounds. The Landmarks Law seeks to protect those buildings, structures and landscape features which have a special character or have special historic or aesthetic interest or value. The statutory vehicle for protection is either a designation as landmarks or their inclusion within historic districts. There is a distinction between the criteria for designation of an individual landmark or an interior landmark, on the one hand, and the criteria for designation of an historic district, on the other hand.

In December of 1967, the Board of Estimate approved the City Planning Commission's proposal to create a special theatre district to protect the district from the expansion of midtown construction. The Special District roughly approximated the Times Square area. The City Planning Commission sought to encourage the construction of new theatre space in newly constructed buildings by giving a bonus with respect to the utilization of space. The City, as well as the State Office of Parks, Recreation and Historic Preservation, entered a memorandum of agreement with the federal government which required the City to begin consideration of landmark status for theatre buildings within the Broadway theatre district. The Landmarks Preservation Commission selected thirty-five theatres for potential designation, which included the twenty-two theatres relevant to this appeal. The municipal authorities took heed of the public outcry following the demolition of the Helen Hayes and Morosco Theatres in 1982 and subsequently the midtown zoning amendments to the Zoning Resolution targeted Broadway theatres to enhance their preservation. The Zoning Amendment continued the space use bonuses for construction of new theatres, and gave bonuses for the rehabilitation of specified theatres. Special permits for demolition were required as to forty-four listed theatres.

The Landmarks Preservation Commission calendared public hearings to consider the designation of forty-five Broadway theatres. These were scheduled in June of 1982, to allow preparation of reports on the historical, cultural, and architectural significance of the individual theatres. Respondents contend that the petitioners received individual notice and offered testimony. While not required as part of the process, Community Board 5 eventually voted in favor of landmark designation for all of the listed theatres. The record was kept open for additional comments and petitioners' architect submitted a report analyzing the listed theatres. From April 21, 1984 through January 5, 1988, the Landmarks Preservation Commission held twenty-nine public executive sessions for consideration of the subject designations. On August 6, 1985, the Commission designated exteriors and/or interiors of three theatres as landmarks.

In December of 1985 and March of 1987, respectively, the Landmarks Preservation Commission compiled two reports on preservation of the Broadway theatres and guidelines therefor. The record shows that the Landmarks Preservation Commission consistently received copious materials from numerous sources emphasizing the unique qualities, as set forth by the statutory criteria, relevant to each theatre. There is also evidence that at many of the executive sessions, a staff member would present the cultural, historical, architectural, and/or aesthetic value of each of the listed theatres. Further, a thirty-five to forty page designation report was prepared for each building. Each theatre was then addressed, in alphabetical order, at public executive sessions commencing November 4, 1987. Respondents note that again petitioners were given notice and attended the meetings.

Between November 4, 1987 and January 5, 1988, the Landmarks Preservation Commission designated the interior and exterior of nineteen of the listed theatres, the interior of seven theatres, and the exterior of two more theatres. Thirteen theatres were not designated during this process. Of the twenty-eight designated theatres, petitioners own twenty-two; of the thirteen non-designated theatres, petitioners own ten.

Within five business days of each designation, the Landmarks Preservation Commission filed the designation reports with the Board of Estimate. After a public hearing, the

Board of Estimate ratified the designations of all of the listed theatres in a single vote. Respondents note that this practice of a single vote on related matters has been the usual procedure of the Board of Estimate since 1950, and is the norm for approving or disapproving landmark designations.

After the Board of Estimate approved these matters, the Landmarks Preservation Commission issued forty-seven landmark designations for twenty-eight theatres, in alphabetical order, which gave rise to the present action.

Petitioners assert that the landmark designations, both interior and exterior, have had detrimental effects on the owners' ability to adapt theatres to changing productions and changing times. They also submit there is a cost factor borne by the owners, in keeping up the theatres, and by producers who use the landmarked theatres.

Further, petitioners attack the voting procedure of the Board of Estimate when, in approving these designations, it exercised a single roll-call vote. Petitioners argue that these are separate structures with no common architectural style and thus the single roll-call vote underscores their contention that the purpose was to preserve the theatre industry by means of sham designations. Petitioners note the boilerplate introduction to the description and analysis in each report for each theatre as bearing untoward uniformity. Petitioners also emphasize their contention that this was protection of an industry, rather than of individual buildings, by noting that those theatres within the Theatre Subdistrict which were not landmarked were not currently in use as legitimate theatres, or otherwise were protected from demolition. Further, petitioners argue that the aesthetic, cultural, and architectural attributes of the landmarked and the non-landmarked theatres are essentially indistinguishable.

This Court is circumscribed by the scope of judicial review of administrative determinations. It is well established that the court may not substitute its judgment for that of the administrative body. Considering the wealth of analyses and reports, as well as anecdotal testimony, provided to the Landmarks Preservation Commission prior to the subject designations, it appears to be beyond serious challenge that a reasonable basis existed for the designations as to each theatre upon a consideration of the statutory criteria.

There is no basis to argue that the proposals were "railroaded" through the Landmarks Preservation Commission; the preliminary analyses and reports were exhaustive [and] the decision making occurred over the course of several years. Three days of public hearings simply concluded the input into the decision making, and the final decisions do not appear to have been arrived at with any great dispatch. While petitioners complain of the limited time allowed to them for comments before the Board of Estimate, there is no indication that they were deprived of a meaningful opportunity to submit their own reports or comments prior to the Board of Estimate hearing, particularly at the Landmarks Preservation Commission phase of proceedings.

Further, there is criticism by petitioners of the single roll-call vote by the Board of Estimate. But, the Board had received individual reports, as well as the Planning Commission reports, prior to the Board of Estimate hearing. Finally, in this regard, we note, as mentioned above, that since the 1950s the Board had routinely entertained a single vote on similar matters, particularly those involving zoning and landmark designations.

Manipulation of the Landmarks Law by the Landmarks Preservation Commission only for the purpose of preserving the Broadway theatre industry, rather than individual theatres, would have been improper. Such a practice would misconstrue zoning matters for landmark matters. However, notwithstanding the district within which the theatres stand, the designation proceedings addressed the exteriors and/or interiors of the specific buildings in terms of the criteria of the Landmarks Law. Municipal respondents point out that the Landmarks Preservation Commission has designated theatres which are located outside of the Broadway District, such as the Apollo, the Beacon, City Center, Carnegie Hall, and Town Hall, on the basis of the same statutory criteria. This is further evidence that the Landmarks Preservation Commission was not seeking to protect the Broadway theatre industry by sham designations.

Accordingly, we agree with the nisi prius court that the administration determination was based on substantial evidence, was not arbitrary and capricious and did not violate the law.

With respect to the constitutional challenge, Penn Central Transportation Co. v. City of New York, 438 U.S. 104, established the constitutionality of the Landmarks Law. Petitioner's challenge, that Penn Central is not controlling since it did not address the method of designation, is without merit. Penn Central involved the alteration of a landmark, a restriction which arises out of the designation. Since the Supreme Court in Penn Central clearly ruled that the application of the Landmarks Law does not affect a taking of the property, the constitutional challenge thereby is resolved. Further, under the standards set forth in Spears v. Berle, 422 N.Y.S.2d 636, and Honore de St. Aubin v. Flacke, 505 N.Y.S.2d 859, the petitioners have not carried their burden of demonstrating that the Landmarks Law as applied to these particular theatres denies them essential use of their property.

Finally, with respect to the constitutional argument, the scheme of law embodied in the Landmarks Law serves a legitimate purpose of saving historical landmarks. With respect to any claim that petitioners are deprived of any economic use of their property, in the absence of final agency action on applications by petitioners for renovations or alterations, the matter is not ripe for review. In the meantime, there is no prohibition against petitioners receiving economic benefit from continuing the use of the buildings as theatres.

Petitioners also challenge the provision of the Zoning Resolution which requires listed theatres to obtain a special permit from the City Planning Commission for demolition. This, of course, is a zoning matter, rather than a landmark matter. Petitioner bears the heavy burden of demonstrating the unconstitutionality of the zoning ordinance and discriminatory effects of a statute will not render the statute invalid if there exists a reasonable basis. There is no evidence that this provision is not based on a comprehensive plan and, as municipal defendants point out, similar demolition permits are required by the Zoning Resolution in several other special districts.

Accordingly, the order and judgment of the Supreme Court, New York County entered February 6, 1990, which denied petitioners' motion for summary judgment, granted summary judgment to municipal respondents, and dismissed the petition and complaint, should be affirmed, without costs or disbursements.

FISHER v. GIULIANI
720 N.Y.S.2d 50 (App. Div. 2001)

FRIEDMAN, Justice.

This appeal involves a challenge to recent zoning amendments affecting the Manhattan Theater District. Specifically, petitioners allege that the City was required to prepare an Environmental Impact Statement before implementing the changes to the New York City Zoning Resolution (ZR). For the reasons that follow, we conclude that, insofar as the amendments created a mechanism permitting the transfer, as-of-right, of a theater's development rights and implemented design controls, no Environmental Impact Statement was required. However, because the City failed to analyze the potential environmental impact of the amendments providing for special permits and discretionary authorizations, such amendments should be severed and annulled.

For more than 30 years, New York City has recognized the importance of the Manhattan Theater District—a district that, by some estimates, generates $2 billion in economic activity annually and employs, in the aggregate, 250,000 people. A crucial lynchpin in the success of the district is, of course, Broadway theaters.

The City's commitment to its theaters dates back at least to 1967, when it established the Special Theater District. Thereafter, in 1982, the City amended the Zoning Resolution in response to the destruction of several theaters. These amendments created a new "Theater Subdistrict" that restricted the demolition of designated theaters and attempted to make them more viable by permitting the transfer of development rights to nearby parcels. Over time, however, it became evident that the 1982 measures were insufficient to achieve the stated goal of theater preservation. Thus, in 1998, further amendments to the Zoning Resolution were adopted in an effort to assure the vitality of this irreplaceable asset.

Unlike the earlier provisions of the Zoning Resolution, the 1998 amendments authorize the transfer of development rights from designated theaters to receiving sites anywhere within the Theater Subdistrict. Under the proposed amendments, the transfer is limited to a 20% increase in the base Floor-to-Area ratio (FAR) of the receiving site, inclusive of, or in combination with, all other as-of-right zoning incentives. The transfer must be accompanied by the execution of a covenant ensuring the continued operational soundness of the transferring theater and its continued use as a legitimate theater, as well as a contribution to a Theater Subdistrict Fund that, among other things, will be used to monitor transferring theaters. As part of this plan, the Zoning Map was also amended to extend the western boundary of the Theater Subdistrict to include the west side of Eighth Avenue between 42nd Street and 45th Street, which is the westernmost fringe of the Special Clinton District, a neighboring residential area.

In addition to the as-of-right transfer mechanism, an additional discretionary mechanism was also established in the Theater Subdistrict. Thus, at certain sites in the district, including sites on Eighth Avenue, a developer may obtain an additional 20% of the base FAR via special permit or discretionary authorization (see ZR §§ 81-744[b] & [c]).

In crafting the amendments, the City Planning Commission (CPC), which is responsible for overall city development (N.Y.C. Charter § 192[f]), was cognizant that the Special Clinton District consists, to a large extent, of smaller residential buildings. Because of this, the Theater Subdistrict amendments establish urban design controls such as street wall, height, and setback requirements. These design controls, which require the building base to be at least 50 feet high with setbacks above the base, would constrain tower-type construction that had been permissible under prior zoning provisions.

Before submitting the proposed amendments for public review, the CPC, through the Environmental Assessment and Review Division of the Department of City Planning (DCP), conducted an environmental assessment as required by the State Environmental Quality Review Act (SEQRA) and our local regulations, the City Environmental Quality Review (CEQR). Under the statutory scheme, an Environmental Assessment Statement is prepared that sets forth the environmental analysis. If it is determined that the proposed action may have a significant effect on the environment, the agency (here CPC) must then issue a positive declaration and an Environmental Impact Statement must be prepared before the proposed zoning may be adopted. If, on the other hand, it is determined that the action will have no significant impact, the agency issues a negative declaration and no environmental impact statement need be prepared.

To assess the potential environmental impact of the proposed zoning changes, the DCP examined the reasonable worst case scenario that could result under the as-of-right amendments and compared it with the development that would otherwise have occurred without the amendments. To do this, the DCP first identified those sites in the Theater Subdistrict where, because of location, market trends, and physical conditions, development was most likely to occur, with or without a change in zoning. It found that there were 23 such "soft sites," which currently had the capacity for 10.9 million square feet of residential and commercial floor area (assuming that each site was built to the maximum density permitted as-of-right). The DCP then considered the potential demand for additional development in the study area within the foreseeable future, that is, over the next ten years.

To make these future projections, DCP examined development trends in the larger midtown area during the 10-year period between 1983 through 1993. The 10-year period was chosen because it reflected a business cycle for midtown development, including periods of both significant and limited growth. Assuming that there would be a similar demand over the next 10 years, the DCP found that the existing zoning capacity could accommodate, more than twice over, the projected demand.

With regard to development under the proposed zoning, the DCP determined that the amendments did modestly increase the density of particular sites via the transfer of development rights from theaters. This, it was indicated, would likely induce builders to construct taller buildings to achieve the greatest economy of scale (i.e., by distributing the cost of the land over the largest possible building volume). However, this would not affect overall market conditions and would not induce development beyond what was already likely to occur.

In this regard, while an individual developer might build to the maximum density on a particular site by purchasing development rights from a theater, collectively, developers would build only enough floor area to satisfy an overall unchanged market demand. Viewed otherwise, the higher density of specific sites would accommodate the projected demand for space—it would not change the overall demand.

Next, the DCP analyzed the potential impact that any development might have on traffic, transit, and air quality. Since it could not be predicted with certainty which of the sites would eventually contain the expected development, the DCP selected the reasonable worst case scenario. For modeling purposes, the DCP chose those sites located in areas where commercial and residential development were most likely to occur, and that were in close proximity to each other, thus giving rise to a concentrated effect.

Using this worst case scenario, the DCP concluded that any potential development would give rise to less than 50 peak-hour vehicle trips at any given intersection in the area. According to the CEQR Technical Manual, this was below the threshold requiring further analysis because it would not have a significant effect upon traffic and transit. Further analysis also determined that any additional traffic would have no significant impact on air quality.

As to the socioeconomic conditions of the area, the DCP analyzed whether the proposed amendments would lead to the displacement of area residents or businesses. Because the amendments would not induce development different in kind or magnitude from that which was already expected to take place, the DCP concluded that the change in zoning would not result in any significant displacement.

The findings and conclusions reached by the DCP resulted in a negative declaration, which was supported by an Environmental Assessment Statement that included a 75-page single-spaced report. Thereafter, the Environmental Assessment Statement and negative declaration were filed with a revised Land Use Review Application on January 8, 1998, and, in accordance with public review requirements, referred for review to Community Boards Four and Five, the Manhattan Borough Board, and the Manhattan Borough President. After public hearings at which approximately 80 people testified both for and against the proposal, and consideration of written submissions, the CPC adopted the proposed amendments on June 3, 1998.

The matter was then referred to the New York City Council pursuant to City Charter §§ 197-d and 200(a)(2). By resolutions dated August 6, 1998, the Council, after a further round of public hearings involving the testimony of approximately 100 people, found that no significant environmental impact would result from the proposed action and approved the amendments and map change (subject to certain modifications). This litigation ensued.

Petitioners, among whom are residents of the neighboring Special Clinton District, commenced this CPLR article 78 proceeding seeking to challenge the adequacy of the environmental review and consequent negative declaration. According to petitioners, the underlying analysis supporting the negative declaration was deficient and preparation of an Environmental Impact Statement was warranted. Petitioners also alleged that the proposed amendments were not within the scope of the City's zoning power.

Supreme Court, without reaching this latter argument, annulled the Theater Subdistrict Amendments and the Zoning Map Change and directed the DCP to prepare an Environmental Impact Statement. In so doing, the court concluded that the amendments would stimulate development, relying, in large part, upon a newspaper article about the current state of the midtown real estate market.

Stripped to its essentials, the purported flaws identified by petitioners are threefold: first, that the DCP (which, as noted, prepared the environmental assessment) underestimated the projected market demand for development in the Theater Subdistrict; second, that the DCP erroneously determined that the amendments would not stimulate development beyond that which would already have occurred; and, third, that the DCP improperly limited its analysis to 10 years into the future and failed to consider that every single square inch of buildable space might, in fact, be developed. None of these claims has merit.

In analyzing a SEQRA determination, a court is required to sustain an agency's negative declaration unless the court concludes that it "was affected by an error of law or was arbitrary and capricious or an abuse of discretion" (Chinese Staff & Workers Assn. v. City of New York, 509 N.Y.S.2d 499, quoting CPLR 7803[3]). Under this standard, it is not the role of the court to weigh the desirability of the proposed action, choose among alternatives, resolve disagreements among experts, or substitute its judgment for that of the agency. Rather, the limited issue for the court's review is whether the agency identified "the relevant areas of environmental concern," took a "hard look" at them, and made a "reasoned elaboration of the basis for its determination" (Matter of Merson v. McNally, 665 N.Y.S.2d 605).

Viewed against this analytical backdrop, we first address petitioners' claim that the DCP underestimated future demand in the Theater Subdistrict. This charge flows from petitioners' belief that historical development trends in the Theater Subdistrict are no longer meaningful. In this connection, it is asserted that the recent reduction in the number of adult establishments has made the Theater Subdistrict more attractive to developers. This argument, however, ignores the forecasting method used by the DCP.

In developing its projections, the DCP examined the larger midtown area, not just the Theater Subdistrict. Thus, in applying the historic trends of the midtown area to the much smaller Theater Subdistrict, it is uncontroverted that the DCP projected future growth in excess of historic levels. Hence, this conservative forecasting method necessarily took into account relatively recent changes in the Theater Subdistrict.

With regard to the claim that the as-of-right amendments will stimulate development, it is true that certain soft sites might enjoy greater profitability (because taller buildings may be permitted). It is also true that theaters will have a wider geographic area in which to sell their development rights. But these observations, without more, do not undermine the rationality of the DCP's determination that market demand and consequent development will remain relatively constant.

As the CPC convincingly notes, potential zoning capacity will not induce development beyond that which would otherwise have occurred unless the demand for additional space exceeds current zoning capacity. Since current zoning capacity already far exceeds demand, the CPC's central conclusion is rational. Moreover, petitioners failed to provide any meaningful evidence that the monetary savings realized from developing taller buildings would be significant enough to spur development beyond that which would in any event take place. This is especially so since the modest increases in floor area permitted by the proposed amendments would apparently result in only a few additional stories to new buildings.

Contrary to petitioners' claim, the CPC also properly considered the long-term impact of the proposed as-of-right amendments. At its core, petitioners' argument is that the CPC was required to look beyond 10 years from the enactment of the zoning amendments and assume that every single square foot of buildable area will eventually be developed, regardless of the likelihood that it will occur. This argument is without merit since the DCP was only obligated to examine environmental consequences into the foreseeable future, not to examine theoretical possibilities that were steeped in nothing more than unsupported speculation. To adopt a ten-year time frame was hardly an irrational examination of the long-term foreseeable future.

Petitioners' reliance upon Neville v. Koch, 583 N.Y.S.2d 802, in support of a contrary conclusion is misplaced. In Neville, which involved the rezoning of a full city block, the City considered the environmental impact that could result from a full build-out of the allowable floor area. Petitioners, pointing to this aspect of Neville, read the case as establishing a requirement that a full build-out be examined in every instance. This interpretation of Neville is erroneous.

The necessity to assume a full build-out in Neville was premised on the observation that developers will generally seek to build to the maximum capacity allowable. Thus, where the rezoning involves a discrete parcel of property, the necessity of assuming a full build-out is apparent. Where, however, the rezoning involves a larger geographic area, the underlying assumptions at play in Neville are no longer applicable. As previously noted, while any single developer will seek to develop its property to capacity should it choose to build, that does not mean, when dealing with the rezoning of a wider geographic area, that the entire area will be developed to full capacity. Development to full capacity will obviously not occur, because market forces act as a constraint. This being so, it was rational for the City to conclude that a full build-out of the Theater Subdistrict was constrained by economic forces.

What the foregoing reveals is that the DCP's detailed analysis, as reflected in the Environmental Assessment Statement, was entirely rational insofar as the as-of-right amendments were concerned. Hence, an Environmental Impact Statement was not required. This, however, does not conclude the matter.

As previously noted, in addition to the as-of-right transfer mechanism established by the zoning amendments, a discretionary mechanism was also established in the Theater Subdistrict. The DCP was of the view that no environmental review of these amendments was required because when an owner applied for a special permit, an assessment would be made at that time. Hence, the DCP believed that it could defer its analysis. This was error.

It is well settled that "SEQRA's goal [is] to incorporate environmental considerations into the decisionmaking process at the earliest opportunity" (Matter of Neville v. Koch, 583 N.Y.S.2d 802). Thus, the mere fact that environmental review may be required at the time an applicant seeks a special permit does not, by itself, obviate the CPC's obligation to consider possible environmental impact at the time it enacts the zoning changes, at least on a conceptual basis.

In reaching this conclusion, we do not suggest that the grant of additional FAR beyond that permitted as-of-right would have a significant environmental impact. It may very well be that a grant of additional FAR will have no impact. But, whatever the case may be, the DCP was obligated to consider the matter now, not just in the future. In view of this, we turn to the remedy for this isolated error.

Zoning Resolution §11-50(a) provides that "[i]f a court...finds any provisions of this Resolution to be invalid...all other provisions of this Resolution shall continue to be separately and fully effective." Here, even though the DCP failed to examine the possible impact from future discretionary grants of FAR, this aspect of the Zoning Resolution was entirely discrete from the other provisions of the Resolution, i.e., those dealing with as-of-right transfers and those dealing with design controls. The discrete provisions relating to discretionary grants of FAR, therefore, should be annulled. The balance of the Resolution should, however, remain effective.

Finally, we address petitioners' claim that the zoning amendments were not within the scope of the City's legitimate zoning power. Preservation of the Theater Subdistrict through zoning has long been recognized as an appropriate exercise of the City's zoning power. The 1998 amendments to the Zoning Resolution merely represent the City's latest attempt to continue its 30 year tradition of protecting the character of one of New York's most valuable resources, the Broadway Theater Subdistrict. Since these amendments are directly related to this legitimate goal, petitioners' claim is without merit.

We have examined the remaining contentions for affirmative relief and find them to be without merit.

Notes

1. Although efforts to save a historic theater do not always succeed (as the *Reading* case demonstrates), support from both government officials and private developers clearly is on the upswing. As a result, more than 200 theaters now are listed on the National Register of Historic Places (www.cr.nps.gov/nr/). Much of the credit, of course, belongs to public advocacy groups like the League of Historic American Theatres (www.lhat.org) and the Theatre Historical Society of America (www.historictheatres.org).

2. New York City's innovative use of historic preservation laws to save the Broadway theaters, described in the *Shubert* and *Fisher* cases, has been widely hailed. Nevertheless, some commentators have expressed concern that the poor are being left behind:

> From its inception, the Times Square plan was promoted as an effort to restore the decrepit theaters along Forty-second Street, which had become venues for pornography and cheaply priced action movies, to their former glory as Broadway stages. By any objective measure the theaters represented a tiny component of the redevelopment project, but in public discourse they represented much more. The image of the Great White Way, a reference to the historic Broadway theater district of the early twentieth century, provided an alluring contrast to the images of XXX's, and of black and Latino youth gangs, that defined Forty-second Street in the 1970s. The cultural agenda was therefore the key to the project's economic and political success.
>
> The strategy of using cultural resources to drive economic development is appealing to cities precisely because it promises to address the negative images of cities and neighborhoods that deter investment. Cities can utilize a vast array of programs and policies that have evolved to serve arts- and preservation-based development projects, including Community Development Block Grants (and earlier Urban Development Action Grants), historic tax credits, transferable development rights, zoning bonuses, and contextual zoning laws.
>
> Although historic districts and cultural hubs have sparked the revitalization of many inner city areas, there are concerns about the effects of such development. Frequently these cultural resources are designed to appeal to the tastes of middle- and upper-income residents and tourists in order to create marketable city places. As a result, such developments can contribute to gentrification and the displacement of lower-income residents, thereby furthering the polarization of city life.

Alexander Reichl et al., *From Subsidies to Tax Credits: Entrepreneurial Efforts at Affordable Housing in New York's Times Square*, 12 J. Affordable Housing & Community Dev. L. 282, 288-89 (2003). As a policymaker, how would you address this concern? *See further* Matthew P. Garvey, *When Political Muscle is Enough: The Case for Limited Judicial Review of Long Distance Transfers of Development Rights*, 11 N.Y.U. Envtl. L.J. 798 (2003) (arguing that the problem is more illusory than real).

3. Outside New York, no city has done more to save its historic theaters than Minneapolis:

> [T]he City of Minneapolis has not only actively supported the arts but also recognized the architectural and cultural importance of protecting those theaters worth renovating. In 1988, the Minneapolis Community Development

Agency, on behalf of the City of Minneapolis, purchased, financed and renovated (and continues to own) two significant Hennepin Avenue theaters, the Orpheum and the State. By 1993, renovations on both theaters were completed, giving the community two Broadway quality facilities that enhanced its musical and theatrical tradition.

In the same decade, the City of Minneapolis also took on another major project: moving the 5.8 million pound Schubert Theater one and one-half blocks to make room for the Block E development project. Artspace Projects Inc. is currently working to raise the $34 million needed to transform the 1910 vaudeville house into a vital component of the new Minnesota Schubert Center, an intriguing three-building complex for showcasing the performing arts. Plans are for the Schubert Center to serve as an anchor at the north end of the revived Theater District by 2005.

In 1998, the city protected another piece of its history by purchasing the Pantages Theatre, now known as the Mann Theatre, from its owner, Ted Mann, who had intended to demolish it and the adjoining Stimson Building. The plans to restore the Pantages Theatre to its former glory (and its original name) will bring the third of the [city's] four historic theaters back to life.

Along with theater renovations, the city is also undertaking major streetscape upgrades that will turn Hennepin Avenue into a tree-lined promenade offering a variety of quality entertainment options.

Hammel, Green and Abrahamson, Inc., *Historic Theatre Adds to Revitalized Minneapolis Theatre Community This Holiday Season*, Oct. 9, 2002, at www.hga.com/news_and_accolades/news/Pantages_Revitalized.html.

4. For a further look at the subject of theater preservation, *see, e.g.*, John W. Frick & Carlton Ward, *Directory of Historic American Theatres* (1987); Mary Henderson, *The New Amsterdam: The Biography of a Broadway Theatre* (1997); Nicholas Van Hoogstraten, *Lost Broadway Theatres* (1996).

Problem 20

After sitting unused for years, a theater on Fourth Avenue was purchased by an investment group, which restored the building to its former glory and, in the process, sparked a neighborhood renaissance. When tourists started streaming into the area, a local entrepreneur began a sightseeing service which he dubbed "Fourth Avenue Theater Trolley Tours." If the investment group objects, claiming the phrase infringes its trademark "Fourth Avenue Theater," how should the court rule? *See Alderman v. Iditarod Properties, Inc.*, 32 P.3d 373 (Alaska 2001).

Chapter 9

Audiences

A. OVERVIEW

Although they are part of a show for just a few hours, theatergoers have a host of legal rights, as well as a few obligations. As will be seen, these flow primarily from the patron's ticket and his or her status as a business invitee of the theater.

B. TICKETS

LUXENBERG v. KEITH & PROCTOR AMUSEMENT CO.
117 N.Y.S. 979 (App. Term 1909)

SEABURY, Justice.

This action was brought to recover damages for breach of contract, and the only question presented for our determination is the measure of the damages to be awarded the plaintiff. The plaintiff purchased four tickets at the box office of the defendant's theater. When these tickets were presented, the plaintiff and her three friends were denied admittance. The statement that the plaintiff was expelled and ejected from the theater conveys a wrong idea of what took place. The fact disclosed by the evidence is that the defendant's agent refused to accept the tickets when they were tendered and told the plaintiff and her friends to "get out." Special damage was neither alleged nor proved, and the court below directed judgment for the plaintiff for $2, the amount of the purchase price of the tickets.

Many of the authorities upon which the appellant relies are cases of common carriers, and seem to me to be inapplicable to the case now under consideration. In Purcell v. Daly, 19 Abb. N.C. 301, the court very clearly stated what I understand to be the correct rule applicable to this case. The court there said:

> The theater is owned by the defendant, is private property, and is governed, so far as the public is concerned, by such rules and regulations as the defendant may see fit to make. It is in no sense a public enterprise, and is consequently not governed by the same rules which relate to common carriers or other public institutions of a like character. This being so, the proprietor of a theater has a perfect right to say whom he will or will not admit to his theater, and should any one apply at the box office of a theater, and desire to purchase tickets of

admission, and be refused, there can be no question that he would have no cause of action against the proprietor of the theater for such refusal. And in the same way, if tickets are sold to a person, the proprietor may still refuse admission, in which case the proprietor would be compelled to refund only the price paid for the tickets of admission together with such other expense as the party might have been put to, but which expense must be directly connected with the issuing of the ticket of admission; for he could not accept money for the right of admission to his theater, and then, upon refusing that admission, seek to retain possession of the price of the privilege. A theater ticket is simply a license to the party presenting the same to witness a performance to be given at a certain time, and, being a license personal in its character, can be revoked.

In Collister v. Hayman, 183 N.Y. 250, 76 N.E. 20, 1 L.R.A. (N.S.) 1188, 111 Am. St. Rep. 740, the court, through Judge Vann, noted the legal difference between the position of a proprietor of a theater and that of a common carrier. "A theater," said Judge Vann, "may be licensed, like a circus; but the license is not a franchise, and does not place the proprietors under any duty to the public, or under any obligation to keep the theater open." Again, in the same opinion, he points out that:

> Unlike a carrier of passengers, for instance, with a franchise from the state, and hence under obligation to transport any one who applies, and to continue the business year in and year out, the proprietors of a theater can open and close their place at will, and no one can make lawful complaint.

These rules were recognized in People ex rel. Burnham v. Flynn, 189 N.Y. 180, 82 N.E. 169, and in that case the court stated the rule of damages to be applied to a case where the purchaser of a theater ticket is denied admission in the following language:

> The holder of a ticket which entitled him to a seat at a given time in a place of amusement, being refused admission, is entitled to recover the amount paid for the ticket, and, undoubtedly, such necessary expenses as were incurred in order to attend the performance.

There is no suggestion in this statement that the holder of a ticket may recover damages to compensate him for the disappointment or humiliation which he may have suffered by reason of his being wrongfully denied admission to the theater. The statement quoted above from Purcell v. Daly, supra, not only does not contain such a suggestion, but in positive language expressly negatives such an inference. The ruling of the court below was correct, and the judgment should be affirmed, with costs.

Judgment affirmed, with costs, with leave to appeal to the Appellate Division.

DAYTON, Justice, dissenting.

Action for damages. Verified complaint, alleging that on January 13, 1909, plaintiff purchased at the box office of defendant's theater four tickets for a matinee performance January 16, 1909, for herself and guests, and paid therefor $2, whereby she was entitled to admission to said theater; that on January 16, 1909, she with her friends presented said tickets at said place, but defendant's agents and servants without just cause refused admission and insolently ordered plaintiff and her friends to leave the theater, all in the presence and within the hearing of divers persons, by reason of which she has suffered indignity, humiliation, disgrace, and injury to her feelings, to her damage $500. The answer was practically a general denial. The cause was tried before a judge and jury. The latter, by direction of the court, found a verdict against the defendant for $2, the price of the tickets. From the judgment entered upon that verdict, plaintiff appeals.

The record shows that on January 16th plaintiff, with a woman guest from out of this city, another woman, and plaintiff's son, went to defendant's theater and presented the tickets, bought and paid for at defendant's box office January 13th. Admission was refused by the doorkeeper on the sole ground that the tickets had been purchased from a ticket speculator. Plaintiff was told by defendant's employee to "get out." She proceeded to the box office, and was there met with the response: "Don't bother me. I am busy. Get out." She left with her party, retaining the tickets so refused. Many people were present during this happening. Defendant offered no testimony. The question presented is whether plaintiff is limited in her recovery to the price paid for the tickets and her necessary expenses in attempting to attend the performance, or whether she may also have compensatory damages for the contumely to which she was subjected, to her public humiliation in the company of her friends and her child. The Court of Appeals in People ex rel. Burnham v. Flynn, 189 N.Y. 180, 82 N.E. 169, said:

> The holder of a ticket which entitled him to a seat at a given time in a place of amusement, being refused admission, is entitled to recover the amount paid for the ticket, and undoubtedly such necessary expenses as were incurred in order to attend the performance.

But that case arose upon habeas corpus, and discussed the right of the managers of certain theaters to exclude the relator therefrom, thereby to protect themselves from public articles (written or to be written by him) reflecting upon their personal integrity and upon the patrons. The court further said:

> A dramatic critic, indulging in such intemperate language, may reasonably expect to arouse unpleasant antagonisms.

In Collister v. Hayman, 183 N.Y. 250, 76 N.E. 20, 1 L.R.A. (N.S.) 1188, 111 Am. St. Rep. 740, a ticket speculator sought to enjoin the proprietors of a theater from interfering with his business of selling tickets on the sidewalk, and the court wrote:

> Neither the license to the owner of the theater, nor the license to the ticket speculator, adds to or takes from the rights of the parties to the contract made when the proprietor sells a ticket. The rights of the purchaser and the duties of the proprietor are measured by the terms of the contract as in fact made. The ticket is not the contract, although to some extent it is evidence thereof. The contract is implied from the circumstances, and is an agreement on the part of the proprietor, for the consideration mentioned, to admit the holder of the ticket upon presentation thereof to his theater at the date named, with the right to occupy the seat specified and to there witness the performance. The main question presented for decision is whether the defendant had the right to make a contract with purchasers upon the conditions printed in the ticket.

The court then proceeded to discuss conditions which may appear on the face of the ticket as to speculators, and holds that defendant should not be enjoined. In the case at bar, however, plaintiff purchased her unconditioned tickets at defendant's box office, and she was not personally obnoxious to the defendant or its patrons. Unless reasonable ground or legal cause is shown, defendant might not revoke the tickets. Collister v. Hayman, supra, does not contravene this proposition; for in that case Judge Vann writes:

> The case would be very different if, after the sale of a ticket containing no evidence of the restriction, an attempt were made to enforce it against a purchaser without notice.

So far as the authorities supra are applicable to the facts here, they tend in plaintiff's favor (though cited by respondent) as establishing her rights under an agreement or contract with defendant. To expel plaintiff [by] actual force was unnecessary. To be boisterously told to "get out" after refusing to accept her tickets was sufficient for plaintiff to realize that, if she did not comply and leave, physical force was imminent, and she was thereby doubtless placed in bodily fear. With the conceded premise that plaintiff possessed an unconditional agreement, right, or privilege to attend defendant's theater at a specified time and location therein, but nevertheless and without just cause was denied admittance, harshly treated, insulted, and noisily driven away by defendant's employees, in the presence of other people, may justice be done if her only remedy is restoration of the cost of her tickets and necessary expenses in attending a performance she was in the manner charged prohibited by defendant from witnessing? She brought no such action, but, on the contrary, in her complaint seeks further damages for injuries, recoverable if her complaint be true.

Wood v. Leadbitter, 13 Meeson & Welsby 837 (1843), has long been cited as a leading case on this subject. Wood purchased a ticket for the inclosure attached to and surrounding the great stand on the Doncaster race course, of which Lord Eglintoun was steward. Being ordered to leave the inclosure, and refusing, plaintiff was removed therefrom. The court discussed with erudition whether Wood by his ticket or license derived an interest in land, whether a license under seal or by parol was revocable, whether the ticket gave Wood an easement, and sustained the trial court in its direction to the jury, to wit:

> Even assuming the ticket to have been sold to plaintiff under the sanction of Lord Eglintoun, still it was lawful for Lord Eglintoun, without returning the guinea, and without assigning any reason for what he did, to order the plaintiff to quit the inclosure, and that if the jury were satisfied that notice was given by Lord Eglintoun to plaintiff, requiring him to quit the ground, and that, before he was forcibly removed by defendant, a reasonable time had elapsed, during which he might conveniently have gone away, then plaintiff was not at the time of the removal on the place in question by the leave and license of Lord Eglintoun.

In Horney v. Nixon, 213 Pa. 20, 61 Atl. 1088, 1 L.R.A. (N.S.) 1184, 110 Am. St. Rep. 520, one Somers purchased eight reserved seats for a theatrical performance, one of which he sold to plaintiff. After this purchase the fire commissioner of Philadelphia directed the aisles of the theater to be widened. Owing to the carrying out of this direction, before the night of the performance a resale of tickets was had. When the eight tickets bought by Somers were presented, the holders thereof were courteously informed that other seats would be substituted. "The party, however, refused every proposition, and became noisy, to the annoyance of those witnessing the performance, which had commenced. They were told that they could not continue discussing the matter inside of the theater, and were directed to go outside, when, according to the testimony of the treasurer of the appellants, they were tendered back the money they had paid for their tickets. After having so declined every offer to give them other seats to witness the performance, they left the theater; and the plaintiff afterwards brought this action to recover the price of the tickets purchased by him and for the inconvenience and annoyance and mortification and indignity and humiliation suffered by him." The court held that on the complaint there could be no recovery in trespass, and then discussed many authorities reaching the following conclusion:

In the light of these and other authorities, a theater ticket is to be regarded as a mere license, for the revocation of which, before the holder has actually been given his seat and has taken it, the only remedy is in assumpsit for the breach of the contract.

The facts in that case differ widely from the facts in the case at bar in many essential particulars. There the seats were obliged to be changed for the safety of the theater, whose proprietor was not at fault. He endeavored to satisfy the ticket holders who became obstreperous. In the light of more modern adjudications, this arbitrary theory that a purchased ticket for an entertainment is a mere license, revocable at the whim or caprice of the proprietor of a place of public amusement, is no longer tenable. An unobjectionable holder of such a contract or agreement may not, without cause, be subjected to disgrace and contumely by the other party, and then left to recover only the price paid. If this be so, a great wrong would be without a civil remedy for the injury inflicted. I therefore do not assent to that proposition and believe I am sustained by reason and authority. "Where the holder of a ticket of admission to a place of public amusement is wrongfully ejected, the wrongdoer is liable for all consequential damages resulting from the unlawful ejection." Am. & Eng. Ency. of Law, vol. 28, p. 124.

In Smith v. Leo, 92 Hun. 242, 36 N.Y. Supp. 949, plaintiff sued for $2,500 damages because of his expulsion from a dancing school to which he had been admitted on payment of the entrance fee. He claimed to have been greatly injured in his good name, fame, and credit, and brought into public scandal, infamy, and disgrace with and among his associates and others. On an appeal, affirming a judgment in plaintiff's favor, the court, Merwin, J., writing, said:

> In substance it was alleged that defendant had willfully deprived the plaintiff of the enjoyment of a right that he had purchased of the defendant. The method of expulsion is not stated, but the word 'expel' ordinarily means to drive or force out or eject. So that defendant impliedly not only deprived the plaintiff of his right, but with indignity and disgrace put him out of the hall, where by his contract with defendant he had a right to be. The action is quite analogous to that of a passenger for illegal removal from a railroad train, and is, we think, maintainable under the allegations of the complaint. The court in effect charged that the plaintiff might be compensated for the indignity and disgrace—citing cases where persons were improperly ejected from railroad cars.

This authority, not reversed or distinguished, so far as I am aware, has been approved in Ray v. Cortland & Homer Traction Co., 19 App. Div. 530, 46 N.Y. Supp. 521, and Rhodes v. Sperry & Hutchinson Co., 120 App. Div. 469, 104 N.Y. Supp. 1102. See also Gillespie v. Brooklyn Heights R.R. Co., 178 N.Y. 347, 70 N.E. 857, 66 L.R.A. 618, 102 Am. St. Rep. 503, where it is held that damages resulting from insulting behavior of an employee are compensatory, not punitive or exemplary. The principles decided in Smith v. Leo, supra, it seems to me are in harmony with People ex rel. Burnham v. Flynn and Collister v. Hayman, supra, so far as plaintiff's rights are concerned, and therefore Purcell v. Daly, 19 Abb. N.C. 301, and Wood v. Leadbitter and Horney v. Nixon, supra, do not apply. The refusal to admit this plaintiff, as proved, was in substance and effect as much an ejection or removal from defendant's theater as though, after being seated in her place therein, she had been told to "get out" and had complied, pursuant to that hostile command. In the latter instance the situation might have been intensified, leading possibly to an aggravation of damages; but otherwise the grievance complained of is identical. The rule of damages applying alike to railroad corporations and to the proprietors of public places of amusement, whose employees violate the rights of their patrons, it follows that the trial court erred in not permitting the jury to find what, if any, money compensation plaintiff was entitled to by reason of defendant's conduct in addition to the price paid for her tickets.

The judgment should be reversed, and a new trial ordered, with costs to appellant to abide the event.

EX PARTE QUARG
84 P. 766 (Cal. 1906)

SHAW, Justice.

The act of March 18, 1905, added a new section to the Penal Code, numbered 526, which reads as follows: "Every person who sells or offers for sale any ticket or tickets to any theater or other public place of amusement at a price in excess of that charged originally by the management of such theater or public place of amusement is guilty of a misdemeanor." (Stats. 1905, p. 140, c. 140.) The petitioner is in custody upon conviction of a violation of this section, and seeks a discharge on the ground that the provisions of the section are unconstitutional, and consequently that the judgment of conviction is void.

The constitutional guaranty securing to every person the right of "acquiring, possessing, and protecting property," refers to the right to acquire and possess the absolute and unqualified title to every species of property recognized by law, with all the rights incidental thereto, and, in connection with the right of personal liberty, it includes the right to dispose of such property in such innocent manner as he pleases, and to sell it for such price as he can obtain in fair barter. Any statute which interferes with this right, except in cases where the public health, morals, or safety, or the general welfare authorizes such restriction as an exercise of the police power, is, to the extent of such interference, unconstitutional and void. (8 Cyc. 886.) These rights are in fact inherent in every natural person, and do not depend on constitutional grant or guaranty. Under our form of government by constitution, the individual, in becoming a member of organized society, unless the constitution states otherwise, surrenders only so much of these personal rights as may be considered essential to the just and reasonable exercise of the police power in furtherance of the objects for which it exists. (Cooley on Statutory Limitations, pp. 68, 244; 1 Barbour on Rights, pp. 122, 284.)

It is, perhaps, not important in this case to consider and define the precise nature of a theater ticket. It may be either a mere license, revocable at the will of the proprietor of the theater, or it may be evidence of a contract whereby, for a valuable consideration, the purchaser has acquired the right to enter the theater and observe the performance, on condition that he behaves properly. These are matters which concern only the proprietor and the purchaser. No third person can question the right of the purchaser. However, by the act of 1893 (Stats. 1893, p. 220, c. 185), a ticket of admission to a public place of amusement, when sold, is made at least an irrevocable license to the purchaser of the ticket to occupy a place therein during the performance. (Greenberg v. Western Turf Assn., 140 Cal. 360, [73 Pac. 1050].) Such a ticket, therefore, represents a right, positive or conditional, as the case may be, according to the terms of the original contract of sale. This right is clearly a right of property. The ticket which represents that right is also necessarily a species of property. As such, the owner thereof, in the absence of any condition to the contrary in the contract by which he obtained it, has the clear right to dispose of it; to sell it to whom he pleases and at such price as he can obtain. The statute in question forbids any sale for a price higher than that at which it was sold by the proprietor of the theater, and, to that extent, it infringes upon the right of property guaranteed by the constitution and existing in the individual. It is therefore a void enactment, unless it can be upheld as an exercise of the police power.

The police power is broad in its scope, but it is subject to the just limitation that it extends only to such measures as are reasonable in their application and which tend in some appreciable degree to promote, protect, or preserve the public health, morals, or safety, or the general welfare. The prohibition of an act which the court can clearly see has no tendency to affect, injure, or endanger the public in any of these particulars, and which is entirely innocent in character, is an act beyond the pale of this limitation, and it is therefore not a legitimate exercise of police power.

The sale of a theater ticket at an advance upon the original purchase price, or the business of reselling such tickets at a profit, is no more immoral, or injurious to public welfare or convenience, than is the sale of any ordinary article of merchandise at a profit. It does not injure the proprietor of the theater; he must necessarily have parted with the ticket at his own price and upon his own terms before such resale can be made. It does not injure the second buyer; he must have had the same opportunity as the first buyer to purchase a similar ticket, and no greater right thereto, and having neglected that opportunity, or being unwilling to undergo the necessary inconvenience, and willing to pay a higher price rather than forego the privilege which the other by his greater diligence and effort has obtained, the transaction is just, so far as he is concerned. The fact that such tickets are obtained and resold at an advance does not compel the manager of the theater to put the tickets upon the same plane as ordinary articles of merchandise. He can make them non-transferable and place in the contract of sale any conditions necessary for the protection of himself or his patrons, and by printing such conditions on the tickets he can prevent their resale to innocent buyers. He can restrict or limit the number of tickets sold to one person, and, in general, manage his own business according to his own will, except that, by the act of 1893, he cannot refuse admission to a well-behaved and proper person, holding a ticket which he has sold without conditions affecting such holder. There is nothing in that act, nor in the decision in Greenberg v. Western Turf Assn., 140 Cal. 360, [73 Pac. 1050], which would operate to prevent the imposition of such conditions. The act of 1893 does not purport to regulate or control the original sales of tickets, nor to make them assignable at all events, contrary to the terms of such sale.

Section 526 of the Penal Code, above quoted, does not purport to forbid the resale of tickets which by the original contract of sale have been made non-transferable, nor a resale for a price equal to or less than that of the original sale. It only forbids sales at an advanced price, and as to such sales, it forbids them all. It is plainly not enacted for the purpose of preventing such frauds as the sale of tickets to innocent purchasers, contrary to the conditions of the original sale forbidding a transfer. The act must be considered as intended to be operative without regard to the willingness or unwillingness of the manager to allow the transfer, to be directed to the transfer of all tickets, assignable or non-assignable, and to have been intended to interfere with the purchaser who for any reason wishes to engage in the unhurtful transaction or business of reselling at a profit a property right which he has lawfully acquired.

It is perhaps unnecessary to add that the right to attend a theater is not so sacred or important in character as to require or justify legislation regulating the price of admission. Viewed in any aspect, we think the legislation in question is an unwarrantable interference with the inherent and constitutional rights of individuals, and for that reason is void.

Let the petitioner be discharged.

GOLD v. DICARLO
235 F. Supp. 817 (S.D.N.Y. 1964),
aff'd per curiam, 380 U.S. 520 (1965)

KAUFMAN, Circuit Judge.

Plaintiffs squarely challenge the constitutionality of a New York statute regulating the price at which licensed brokers may re-sell tickets to theatres and other places of public amusement. General Business Law, Art. X-B, Section 169-c. In the face of recent widely-publicized investigations in this area and a long history of legislative concern, Joey Gold, a licensed ticket broker, and New York Ticket Brokers, Inc., a membership corporation of licensed brokers, have brought this class action against the New York City Commissioner of Licenses, Joseph C. DiCarlo, and the State Attorney-General, Louis J. Lefkowitz. They seek to enjoin the defendants from enforcing or attempting to enforce Section 169-c against ticket brokers and also a declaratory judgment that the statute is unconstitutional under the Fourteenth Amendment of the Federal Constitution.

Section 169-c of the New York General Business Law makes it unlawful to re-sell a ticket to a public amusement event at a price more than $1.50, plus lawful taxes, in excess of the maximum price printed on the ticket. The legislative purpose, expressed in Section 167, declares that the admission price for public amusements is 'a matter affected with a public interest' and subject to supervision to safeguard the public against fraud, extortion, exorbitant rates and similar abuses.

This three-judge District Court was convened pursuant to 28 U.S.C. 2284 because the complaint raised a 'substantial federal question,' under 28 U.S.C. 2281, particularly since the predecessor of Section 169-c was declared unconstitutional in 1927 by a closely divided United States Supreme Court in Tyson & Brother v. Banton, 273 U.S. 418, 47 S.Ct. 426, 71 L.Ed. 718, which has never been explicitly overruled.

We hold that the purpose of Section 169-c is within the power of the New York legislature and that the means chosen to effect that purpose—the regulation of ticket brokers' re-sale prices—are reasonable and constitutional. Accordingly, the request for equitable relief against the state and city enforcement machinery must be denied.

We note, at the outset, that the complaint presents a justiciable controversy. On May 18, 1964, Gold was arraigned in New York City Criminal Court on a 39-count information charging violations of Section 169-c. Previously, he had been summoned by the Commissioner of Licenses to show cause why his license should not be suspended or revoked, in part because of alleged violations of Section 169-c. And the Commissioner admits that he is investigating the activities of ticket brokers generally, whom plaintiffs represent in this class action. Because the brokers are under the cloud of imminent investigation and perhaps prosecution, this case is riper for adjudication than the controversy presented by Idlewild Bon Voyage Corp. v. Epstein, 370 U.S. 713, 82 S.Ct. 1294, 8 L.Ed.2d 794 (1962). There jurisdiction was taken although the plaintiff had simply been informed by the State Liquor Authority that its business was illegal under state law.

Turning then to the merits, Tyson & Brother v. Banton is only an illusory barrier. The Supreme Court there held that the state lacked power to regulate re-sale prices of theatre and sports tickets because they were not deemed by the Court to be matters 'affected with a public interest.' But Justice Stone, dissenting, recognized that this approach only begged the question for it simply meant that only those businesses, regulation of which was countenanced by the Court, would be deemed to be affected with a public interest. 273 U.S. at 451, 47 S.Ct. 426. Justice Holmes also dissented and proposed the much sounder standard that, subject to constitutionally required compensation, a state legislature may regulate any business when it has sufficient force of public opinion behind it. 273 U.S. at 446, 47 S.Ct. 426.

Tyson's fictional test was soon thereafter rejected in Nebbia v. New York, 291 U.S. 502, 54 S.Ct. 505, 78 L.Ed. 940 (1934), where the Supreme Court upheld against constitutional challenge a state statute fixing the minimum and maximum retail prices of milk. The Court declared that 'the guaranty of due process * * * demands only that the law shall not be unreasonable, arbitrary, or capricious, and that the means selected shall have a real and substantial relation to the object sought to be attained.' 291 U.S. at 525, 54 S.Ct. at 510-511. In truth, the Tyson test was obsolescent even when pronounced in 1927. The Nebbia standard portended increased deference by the Court to the growing need for governmental regulation in America's burgeoning industrial society.

Nebbia's approach was reaffirmed in Olsen v. Nebraska, 313 U.S. 236, 61 S.Ct. 862, 85 L.Ed. 1305 (1944), which upheld a statute regulating the fees charged by employment agencies. The Court there stated, in effect, that Tyson's standard had been discarded. 313 U.S. at 244, 61 S.Ct. 862. And, most recently, in Ferguson v. Skrupa, 372 U.S. 726, 83 S.Ct. 1028, 10 L.Ed.2d 93 (1963), Justice Black not only declared that Tyson's philosophy had been abandoned, but quoted the rationale of Justice Holmes' dissent in that case with approval. We would be abdicating our judicial responsibility if we waited for the Supreme Court to use the express words 'We hereby overrule Tyson,' as the plaintiffs contend we should, before recognizing that the case is no longer binding precedent but simply a relic for the constitutional historians. Judges do not have such mechanical or wooden attitudes nor are they devoid of all powers of interpretation, analogy and application of constitutional principles; they and the law must keep pace with our vibrant and dynamic society and the changes in the law which the courts have pronounced.

The ticket brokers contend, however, that the merits of the Tyson decision may not be challenged here since, under principles of res judicata, the Attorney-General is bound by Tyson's holding that New York may not regulate the re-sale price of tickets to public amusements. Quite apart from questions whether res judicata is applicable to successor Attorneys-General and whether it is properly invoked by a third party affirmatively rather than defensively, the res judicata argument must fall because the philosophy of Tyson has been so completely repudiated. At least in the constitutional area, the considerations of finality that stand behind the res judicata doctrine must be balanced against and ofttimes give way to government's need to regulate abuses that change with the passage of time. See Kelly-Sullivan, Inc. v. Moss, 174 Misc. 1098, 1107, 22 N.Y.S.2d 491, aff'd, 260 App.Div. 921, 24 N.Y.S.2d 984 (1940); cf. Commissioner v. Sunnen, 333 U.S. 591, 599-601, 68 S.Ct. 715, 92 L.Ed. 898 (1948); 39 Ops.Atty.Gen. 22 (U.S.1937). It would surely be anomalous to hold that forty-nine states have constitutional power to curb grave abuses in the entertainment industry, but that New York—the entertainment capital of the nation—must stand by idly because of the force of an antiquated, legally unsound decision.

So we come to the ultimate question—is the re-sale price limitation of 169-c unconstitutional under the Fourteenth Amendment? The test of constitutionality is whether the method of regulation embodied in the statute bears a rational relation to a constitutionally permissible objective. Ferguson v. Skrupa, 372 U.S. 726, 733, 83 S.Ct. 1028, 10

L.Ed.2d 93 (1963) (Harlan, J., concurring). In applying the Fourteenth Amendment we must simply determine whether circumstances vindicate the challenged statute as a reasonable exertion of governmental authority or condemn it as arbitrary or discriminatory. The courts no longer resort to the due process clause as a weapon 'to strike down state laws, regulatory of business * * * conditions, because they may be unwise, improvident, or out of harmony with a particular school of thought.' Williamson v. Lee Optical Co., 348 U.S. 483, 488, 75 S.Ct. 461, 464, 99 L.Ed. 563 (1955).

The ticket brokers urge upon us that Section 169-c is not reasonably related to the legislative purpose expressed in Section 167. They claim that effective price control clearly is not and cannot be expected to be achieved solely by a limitation of their fees, without any restriction on the promoter's or producer's principal charge. But we read the declaration of Section 167 that the admission prices for public amusements are a matter of public interest as an expression of the legislature's concern with the price the public must ultimately pay, absent fraudulent manipulations, which of course permits regulation of broker's re-sale prices. If the legislature thought that such regulation was sufficient to accomplish its objective, it is not for us to say that the prices charged by theatre owners and sports promoters also required regulation; the legislature need not cover the whole field of possible abuses in order to render constitutional a more limited form of regulation. Farmers & Merchants Bank v. Federal Reserve Bank, 262 U.S. 649, 661, 43 S.Ct. 651, 67 L.Ed. 1157 (1923).

That there have been and still exist abuses nobody doubts. Although Eugene O'Neill's 'The Iceman Cometh' has passed from Broadway and off-Broadway, the 'iceman' still is a familiar behind-the-scenes figure on the Great White Way. The 'ice' he carries, we are told, has not thawed and still represents the tribute paid by some brokers to box-office treasurers in return for allocations of a substantial portion of the choice seats for each performance. The brokers pass on the cost of such 'ice' to their customers, in most instances businessmen accommodating out-of-town clients, and charge prices much higher than the box offices. The legislature and those knowledgeable in the circumstances believed the resultant effects of this situation, not only on those who must pay exorbitant rates to the brokers, but also on the typical theatre-goer and show business in general, cried out for legislative remedy. On the other hand, we are informed that the brokers play a vital role in the entertainment industry, for they sustain the second and third years of the run of a hit show and thereby bring to the industry the bulk of its profits. See J. Keating, 'Theater Tickets: Is There a Basis for Hope?,' New York Times, November 15, 1964, sec. 2, pg. 1. But the legislative solution in Section 169-c, while it may not entirely eliminate the grave abuses and may not be the perfect remedy, cannot be faulted as unreasonable. See Kelly-Sullivan, Inc. v. Moss, 180 Misc. 3 (1943), 39 N.Y.S.2d 797; Kelly-Sullivan, Inc. v. Moss, 174 Misc. 1098, 22 N.Y.S.2d 491, aff'd, 260 App.Div. 921, 24 N.Y.S.2d 984 (1940).

Finally, there is no basis for claiming that the statute violates the equal protection clause because it is unfairly discriminatory. It is hornbook law that a person seeking to establish discrimination must show that he belongs to the same class as those allegedly receiving preferential treatment. Steward Machine Co. v. Davis, 301 U.S. 548, 57 S.Ct. 883, 81 L.Ed. 1279 (1937). Here the plaintiffs cannot meet that requirement. Section 169-c operates alike upon all ticket brokers, who certainly fall within a reasonably distinguishable class from theatre owners and boxing promoters for purposes of state regulation. The ticket broker, for example, does not face the competitive hazards of running a theatre, producing shows, and making large capital investments.

We therefore hold that there is no basis for a permanent injunction or a declaration that Section 169-c is unconstitutional. The complaint is dismissed.

Notes

1. During the 1990-91 season, Broadway shows sold 7.32 million tickets; by 2000-01, the number had increased to 11.89 million tickets. Although sales slumped following the September 11th terrorist attacks, by 2003 they had largely bounced back. *See* Elysa Gardner, *Theaters Say Tourists Cruising Back to Broadway*, USA Today, Nov. 20, 2003, at D6 (reporting that 11.4 million tickets were sold during the 2002-03 Broadway season).

National figures are harder to come by, although a 1992 study by the National Endowment for the Arts, entitled "American Participation in Theater" (arts.endow.gov/pub/Researcharts/Summary35.html), found that 25 million adults annually attend live theater in the United States. Cities with high rates of theater attendance include Atlanta (45% of all residents), Chicago (45%), Minneapolis (82%), Philadelphia (25%), Seattle (56%), and St. Louis (24%).

Despite outreach and diversity programs, race, gender, age, and socio-economic status remain important factors in determining who goes to the theater. Broadway audiences, for example, are overwhelming white (80%), female (64%), middle-aged (43), college-educated (76%), and wealthy (average annual income of $107,400). *See* League of American Theatres and Producers, Inc., *Who Goes to Broadway? 2002-2003* (2003), at www.livebroadway.com/audience.html.

2. A night at the theater has become an ever-more expensive proposition: the cost of attending a Broadway show increased 29% between 1999 and 2002. The average ticket to a Broadway play now sells for $49; for a Broadway musical, the figure is $62. For a prime seat at a hit Broadway show, the cost can easily reach (and at times surpass) $100. Even Off-Broadway productions, long considered bargains, have become pricey, with tickets ranging from $25 to $55 and some seats going for as much as $75. In contrast, the most expensive ticket in London's West End is $60, with the average ticket just $35.

3. As the court in *Luxenberg* explains, the purchase of a ticket creates a contractual relationship terminable at will by the theater owner. Of course, this common law rule has been substantially cut back by the passage of federal, state, and local civil rights laws, which prohibit theater owners from discriminating against patrons on the basis of race, sex, physical disability, and other immutable characteristics. In addition, many jurisdictions now have legislation that expressly limits a theater owner's revocation rights. Connecticut's statute, for example, reads as follows:

> §§ 53-330. Admission to public performances
>
> As used in this section, "places of public entertainment and amusement" means legitimate theaters, burlesque theaters, music halls, opera houses, concert halls, circuses and motion picture theaters. No person, agency, bureau, corporation or association, being the owner, lessee, proprietor, manager, superintendent, agent or employee of any place of public entertainment and amusement shall refuse to admit to any public performance held at such place any person over the age of eighteen years who presents a ticket of admission to the performance or shall eject or demand the departure of any such person from such place during the course of the performance, whether or not an offer is made to refund the purchase price or value of the

ticket of admission presented by such person; but no provision of this section shall be construed to prevent the refusal of admission to or the ejectment of any person whose conduct or speech in such place is abusive or offensive or any person engaged in any activity which may tend to a breach of the peace.

4. What recourse exists if a performance is cancelled? Normally, a ticket holder only has a claim for breach of contract and a right to a refund of the ticket price. Some states, however, have enacted statutes requiring any service fees to also be returned. Tennessee's law is typical:

§§ 47-50-118. Cancelled performance; refund of ticket cost

(a) Upon cancellation of any performance or event for which a ticket for admission is sold, the ticketing service company that contracts to sell tickets for such event or performance at retail ticket outlets shall refund to all ticket purchasers the purchase price of the ticket plus any service fees or charges paid by the purchaser for such ticket.

(b) It is deemed to be an unfair business practice under the Consumer Protection Act, chapter 18 of this title, if a ticketing service company fails to refund the purchase price in accordance with subsection (a).

5. In his opinion in *Gold*, Judge Kaufman makes a reference to "ice." This term has been defined elsewhere as "money paid, in the form of a gratuity, premium, or bribe, in excess of the printed box office price of a ticket to an operator of any 'place of entertainment' or their agent, representative, or employee." See Andrew Kandel & Elizabeth Block, *The "De-icing" of Ticket Prices: A Proposal Addressing the Problem of Commercial Bribery in the New York Ticket Industry*, 5 J.L. & Pol'y 489, 490 (1997).

6. The *Gold* court was concerned with ticket brokering, as opposed to ticket scalping. While the former is legal (but highly regulated), the latter is illegal. This represents a significant shift from the previous view, expressed in *Quarg*, that one who holds a ticket "has the clear right to dispose of it; to sell it to whom he pleases and at such price as he can obtain." What accounts for the change?

7. The difference between ticket brokers and ticket scalpers may not be readily apparent. One commentator has distinguished them as follows:

> Ticket scalping is the resale of tickets, usually to an entertainment or sports event, above face value. By contrast, ticket brokers such as Ticketron, who have the authorization of the event sponsor to charge a one to two dollar service charge, have been declared extensions of the box office and thus exempt from most ticket scalping legislation.

Sheree Rabe, Note, *Ticket Scalping: Free Market Mirage*, 19 Am. J. Crim. L. 57, 57 (1991). It should be pointed out that ticket brokers now routinely charge much more than one or two dollars for their services. See, e.g., Jesse McKinley, *These Choice Tickets Cost a Mere $240*, N.Y. Times, Feb. 1, 2002, at B2 (discussing the $40 commission charged by Broadway Inner Circle for prime seats to "The Producers").

Problem 21

A couple who had purchased tickets far in advance were disappointed when, after entering the theater, they learned that the play's star was sick and the show would go on with her understudy, a relatively unknown actress. Given these facts, does the couple have a right to a refund? *See Seko Air Freight, Inc. v. Transworld Systems, Inc.*, 22 F.3d 773 (7th Cir. 1994).

C. SAFETY AND COMFORT

ROBBINS v. MEMPHIS LITTLE THEATRE PLAYERS ASSOCIATION
1997 WL 585743 (Tenn. Ct. App. 1997)

LILLARD, Judge.

This is a slip-and-fall case. At the end of the plaintiffs' proof, the trial court granted the defendant a directed verdict, based on a lack of evidence of causation and of the defendant's creation or knowledge of the dangerous condition. We affirm.

On June 22, 1991, at approximately 7:45 p.m., Appellants Melba Robbins ("Mrs. Robbins") and Dewey Robbins ("Mr. Robbins") arrived to see a play at a theater run by Appellee Memphis Little Theatre Players Association ("the Theatre"). The Robbins went to the entrance to the theater's upper seating area, where they were met by an usher. The usher was holding some theater programs in her hands and was cradling a large number of programs between her left arm and her body. The usher took Mr. and Mrs. Robbins' tickets but did not give them a program. She led them single file down into the seating area, with Mrs. Robbins directly behind her and Mr. Robbins following.

The aisle to the theater had alternating wide steps and narrow steps. Mrs. Robbins stepped down onto the first narrow step. She was following closely behind the usher, who effectively blocked her view of the steps. There were no hand rails. Her right foot slipped on something "slick," and she fell down three or four steps, sustaining a compound fracture in her right leg.

A paramedic in the audience rushed to her aid, as did Mr. Robbins. A Theatre employee subsequently appeared and asked Mr. and Mrs. Robbins to fill out an accident form. As all this was going on, Mrs. Robbins saw a crumpled program lying on the step immediately behind her. She had not seen it before the fall. Several people helped carry her out into the foyer, and the paramedic handed Mr. Robbins her purse, a shoe, and the crumpled program.

Mr. and Mrs. Robbins subsequently filed a premises liability lawsuit against the Theatre. At the jury trial, Mr. and Mrs. Robbins testified. At one point during Mrs. Robbins' testimony, when asked to describe how the program was crumpled, she responded:

> A. I don't know whether it was the front or the back of the program. I don't know how it happened, but it was crumpled up—and I don't want to do this one—as if someone had actually stepped on it and crumpled it. This is a very firm, slick paper, and it just doesn't happen if you just dropped it, it doesn't just happen that it would crumple like that.

After a bench conference, the court sustained the Theatre's objection and instructed the jury to disregard Mrs. Robbins' last response. During Mr. Robbins' testimony, he also said that the program "looked like someone had stepped on it." The Theatre objected. The trial court replied, "We already spoke about that," apparently sustaining the objection.

In addition, the paramedic from the theater's audience testified, and the Robbins read into evidence the deposition testimony of the treating physician and of the Theatre's general manager. At the close of the plaintiffs' proof, the Theatre moved for a directed verdict, pointing out that no one had seen the program on the steps prior to the fall, no one knew who had dropped it, and no one could testify that Mrs. Robbins actually slipped on the program. In addition, the crumpled program, which had been given to Mr. Robbins, had not been introduced into evidence, and no one knew what had happened to it. The trial court, stating that "it would be pure speculation to allow this jury to get this case for consideration," granted the directed verdict. Mr. and Mrs. Robbins' subsequent motion to reconsider or grant a new trial was denied. They now appeal to this Court.

On appeal, Mr. and Mrs. Robbins raise several issues, which can be narrowed down to two. They assert that the trial court improperly sustained the Theatre's objection to the testimony that the program looked like it had been stepped on. In addition, they argue that there was sufficient evidence from which the jury could find the Theatre liable, and that the trial court erred in granting a directed verdict.

Mr. and Mrs. Robbins argue on appeal that the trial court erred in not allowing testimony to the effect that the crumpled program looked like it had been stepped on. They concede that testimony that the program could not have been crumpled any other way was properly excluded, but they argue that the testimony that the program looked like it had been stepped on was proper lay opinion under Tennessee Rules of Evidence 701.

The trial court has great discretion in the admission or rejection of evidence, and the court's action will be overturned on appeal only when there is a showing of abuse of discretion. Otis v. Cambridge Mut. Fire Ins. Co., 850 S.W.2d 439, 442 (Tenn.1992). At the time of the trial, Rule 701 provided, in pertinent part:

> (a) Generally. If the witness is not testifying as an expert, the witness's testimony in the form of opinions or inferences is limited to those opinions or inferences where:
>
> (1) The opinions and inferences do not require a special knowledge, skill, experience, or training;
>
> (2) The witness cannot readily and with equal accuracy and adequacy communicate what the witness has perceived to the trier of fact without testifying in terms of opinions or inferences; and
>
> (3) The opinions or inferences will not mislead the trier of fact to the prejudice of the objecting party.

Tenn. R. Evid. 701(a). In this case, the crumpled condition of the program could have been described without opining that it looked "stepped on." The trial court did not abuse its discretion in disallowing this testimony.

Second, the Robbins argue that they presented sufficient evidence for the jury to find the Theatre liable. Therefore, they maintain that the trial court erred in granting the Theatre's motion for directed verdict.

In reviewing a trial court's grant of a motion for directed verdict, the appellate court must examine all the evidence, take the strongest legitimate view of that evidence in favor of the party opposing the motion, draw any reasonable inferences from the evidence in favor of that party, discard all countervailing evidence, and reverse the trial court if there remains any material fact dispute or doubt as to the proper conclusions to be drawn from all the evidence. Hurley v. Tennessee Farmers Mut. Ins. Co., 922 S.W.2d

887, 891 (Tenn.App.1995). If the record contains any material evidence in support of a verdict for the non-moving party under any of his theories, then this Court must reverse. Id.

In order to prevail in a negligence action, a plaintiff must prove each of the following elements: a duty of care owed him by the defendant, a breach of that duty, an injury, causation in fact, and proximate cause. McCall v. Wilder, 913 S.W.2d 150, 153 (Tenn.1995). In a premises liability action where the plaintiff has been injured by a dangerous condition, he must prove either that the defendant had actual or constructive knowledge of the condition or that the defendant caused the condition. Keene v. Cracker Barrel Old Country Store, 853 S.W.2d 501, 503 (Tenn.App.1992).

To determine whether the trial court erred in granting the Theatre's motion for directed verdict, we must examine the Robbins' proof that (1) slipping on the crumpled theater program was the cause of her injury, and (2) the Theatre had actual or constructive knowledge that the program was on the theater's steps or that an employee of the Theatre caused the program to be on the step.

In this case, the evidence was that Mrs. Robbins slipped because she stepped on something "slick," that the paper on which the theater programs were printed had a "slick" surface, and that a crumpled program was found near Mrs. Robbins after she fell. The Robbins argue that a jury could permissibly infer from this evidence that the crumpled theater program caused Mrs. Robbins' fall. The Theatre argues that the proof that the crumpled theater program was the cause of Mrs. Robbins' fall is too speculative, where no one saw the program on the steps prior to Mrs. Robbins' fall, the program was not introduced into evidence, and no one knew what happened to it.

While a jury is not permitted to speculate regarding two equally probable inferences, a plaintiff, to bring his case before the jury, need not produce evidence that excludes every other reasonable conclusion. Benson v. H.G. Hill Stores, Inc., 699 S.W.2d 560, 563 (Tenn.App.1985). The plaintiff need only present proof which, if found credible, makes the plaintiff's theory more probable than that of the defendant. Id. Although the plaintiff's evidence is far from strong, it is sufficient for a jury to conclude that the crumpled theater program was the cause of Mrs. Robbins' fall.

However, the Robbins presented no evidence that an employee of the Theatre either caused the dangerous condition by dropping the program or had actual or constructive notice of its presence. No one saw the program before the fall. It could have been dropped by an employee or a patron and could even have been dropped immediately after the fall. Under these circumstances, the Theatre argues that it is too speculative to permit a jury to infer that the usher dropped it or that it had been on the steps sufficiently long enough for an employee to have knowledge of it.

The Theatre cites Jones v. Zayre, Inc., 600 S.W.2d 730 (Tenn.App.1980), in which this Court upheld a directed verdict. The plaintiff in Jones slipped on a plastic clothes clip at the defendant store. There was no evidence of how the clip got on the floor, how long it had been there, or that the defendant or any of his employees knew it was there. This Court held that there was no evidence that the store either caused the dangerous condition or had actual or constructive knowledge of it. Id. at 731-32; see also Neff v. Southeastern Salvage Co., 694 S.W.2d 311, 313 (Tenn.App.1985).

Mr. and Mrs. Robbins argue that, if the jury can infer from the evidence that the crumpled program caused the fall, it is also reasonable to infer that the program was dropped by the usher or should have been seen on the steps by the usher prior to the fall. It is well settled in Tennessee that an inference cannot be drawn from another inference. Benton v. Snyder, 825 S.W.2d 409, 415 (Tenn.1992). However, a fact may be inferred from circumstantial evidence. If "the evidence supporting the first inference [is of] such a character and so strong that it justifies a conclusion or a finding of fact," then a second fact "may be inferred without contravening the rule that an inference cannot be based upon an inference." Id. In the instant case, however, the inference that the program caused Mrs. Robbins to slip and fall is too weak to support a second inference.

To support their argument, the Robbins cite Keene v. Cracker Barrel Old Country Store, Inc., 853 S.W.2d 501 (Tenn.App.1992). In Keene, a customer in a restaurant slipped and fell while following a waitress to her table. Afterwards, her sister discovered two grease spots on the slacks which the plaintiff had been wearing at the time of the accident. Id. at 502. The Court determined that there was enough evidence to support a prima facie case of negligence and that summary judgment had thus been improperly granted to the restaurant. Id. at 504. The evidence indicated that the grease was the type found in that restaurant, and that only employees carried food to and from the tables. There was no other explanation for the grease stains on the plaintiff's slacks. The Court found that it was reasonable to infer that any grease on the floor must have been spilled by an employee. The Court also found that it was reasonable to infer from the stains on the plaintiff's slacks that negligently spilled grease caused her to fall. Id.

The facts in this case, however, are distinguishable from Keene. In Keene, the evidence showed that the grease could have come from no source other than an employee. In the instant case, either a patron or an employee could have dropped the program. Thus, unlike Keene, there is no evidence that it was more likely than not that the dangerous condition was caused by the defendant.

Mr. and Mrs. Robbins also cite Simmons v. Sears, Roebuck & Co., 713 S.W.2d 640 (Tenn.1986). In Simmons, the plaintiff's foot slipped on something while he was descending some stairs at a department store. He fell and sustained injuries. Id. at 640-41. After the fall, someone discovered a pencil at about the same spot where the plaintiff fell. Nothing in the record showed who dropped the pencil or how long it had been on the stairs. The trial court granted the defendant a directed verdict, concluding that the plaintiff had failed to demonstrate actual or constructive knowledge on the part of the store for a period of time long enough to rectify the problem. The Court of Appeals affirmed. Id. at 641.

The Tennessee Supreme Court reversed. Id. at 642. The Court cited testimony that the stairs were littered with debris and that store employees had been using the stairs, in their littered condition, for at least fifteen minutes prior to the accident. Id. at 640-41. Under these circumstances, the Court found that it did not matter whether the pencil had caused the fall. There was so much litter on the steps that it was evident that some of this litter, whether the pencil or not, had caused the plaintiff to slip. In addition, the evidence indicated that the litter had been on the steps long enough that the employees using the stairs should have noticed the debris and taken action to clean it up or warn customers. Thus, the store had at least constructive knowledge of the dangerous condition. Id. at 641-42.

In this case, unlike Simmons, the Theatre's stairs were not littered with debris. Consequently, it is not evident that, if the program did not cause the slip, the slip must have been caused by some other condition for which the Theatre was responsible. Moreover, there was no evidence of how long the crumpled program had been on the floor and whether or not the Theatre should have known of it. Therefore, unlike Simmons, there is no evidence that the Theatre had actual or constructive knowledge of the alleged dangerous condition.

Accordingly, we must conclude that the evidence was insufficient to permit the jury to find that the Theatre caused the alleged dangerous condition or had actual or constructive knowledge of it.

The Robbins also assert on appeal that the trial court's disallowance of their testimony that the program looked "stepped on" caused confusion to the jury. This issue is pretermitted by our affirmance of the trial court's grant of the Theatre's motion for directed verdict.

In sum, we affirm the trial court's decision to disallow the Robbins' testimony that the theater program looked as though it had been "stepped on." The evidence was barely sufficient for the jury to find that the crumpled program caused Mrs. Robbins' fall. However, the Robbins presented no evidence that the Theatre caused the alleged dangerous condition or had actual or constructive knowledge of it. Any other issues raised on appeal are pretermitted by this holding.

The trial court is affirmed. Costs are assessed against Appellants, for which execution may issue if necessary.

LUDWIG v. JEFFERSON PERFORMING ARTS SOCIETY
737 So. 2d 1267 (La. 1999)

PER CURIAM.

We granted certiorari in this case to determine whether the trial court's finding that an obstruction on defendant's premises did not constitute an unreasonable risk of harm to plaintiff is manifestly erroneous or clearly wrong.

FACTS AND PROCEDURAL HISTORY

On November 4, 1994, Sandra Ludwig accompanied her daughter's middle school class to the Jefferson Performing Arts Center to see a performance of Peter Pan. During the second act of the play, Mrs. Ludwig went into the lobby to use the restroom. As she returned to her seat in the darkened auditorium, Mrs. Ludwig struck her leg on the protruding metal base of an "acoustical shell" which was being stored near the rear aisle of the theater during the performance in question. These shells, which are used to enhance the sound properties of a choir or symphonic production, are approximately six feet high, six feet wide, and two-and-a-half to three feet deep, and sit on a four-wheeled metal base that is about one foot high and which protrudes outward approximately one foot.

Mrs. Ludwig developed a hematoma at the injury site which became badly infected. She was given antibiotics and instructed to see an infectious disease specialist if the infection did not clear up within two days. When it did not, she was ultimately referred to a surgeon to have the abscess opened and drained. After the wound healed, Mrs. Ludwig continued to seek treatment for more than one year for pain in her leg. Mrs. Ludwig testified that she has a permanent scar on her left shin and that she still experiences shooting pains in her leg "every now and then" as a result of the accident.

Several months [after the accident], Mrs. Ludwig and her husband, Walter, filed suit against the Jefferson Performing Arts Society ("JPAS"), the non-profit organization that presented the play. The case was tried as a bench trial in February 1997. Plaintiffs also filed suit against the Jefferson Parish School Board, in its capacity as owner of the auditorium, but later dismissed this claim.

At the close of the evidence, the trial court rendered judgment in favor of defendant and dismissed plaintiffs' suit with prejudice, finding that Mrs. Ludwig's own negligence was the sole cause of her injuries. Plaintiffs appealed. The court of appeal affirmed the trial court's judgment, with one dissent. Ludwig v. Jefferson Performing Arts Soc'y, 98-48 (La.App. 5th Cir.6/30/98), 714 So.2d 1268.

Upon the application of plaintiffs, we granted certiorari to consider the correctness of this ruling. Ludwig v. Jefferson Performing Arts Soc'y, 98-2431 (La.11/25/98), 729 So.2d 580. The sole issue presented for our review is whether the trial court's determination that Mrs. Ludwig's negligence was the sole cause of the accident is supported by the record.

DISCUSSION

It is well settled that the operator of a darkened theater is not an insurer of the safety of its patrons and is not required to eliminate every conceivable source of danger on its premises. However, the operator owes a heightened duty to its patrons to keep the premises safe. Cassanova v. Paramount-Richards Theatres, Inc., 204 La. 813, 16 So.2d 444 (1943).

The record reveals that Mrs. Ludwig's injury resulted when she struck the protruding metal base of a piece of stage equipment which was being stored near the rear aisle of the theater during the performance in question. Dennis Assaf, the Executive Artistic Director of the JPAS, testified that there was nothing on or around this equipment to warn patrons of its presence, and that no announcements are made during the performance cautioning patrons to be careful walking along the back wall of the auditorium. The evidence further shows that during the performance, it was particularly dark in the rear of the auditorium, with the only light in that area coming from the red "exit" signs over the doors. Based on all these factors, we conclude the record clearly demonstrates JPAS was negligent in storing this equipment in a darkened theater in such a way such that it protruded into an aisle used by patrons and in failing to warn patrons of the presence of these devices.

Nonetheless, the record also reveals some negligence on the part of Mrs. Ludwig. Mrs. Ludwig testified that when she re-entered the auditorium from the lobby, she did not allow her eyes to adjust to the darkness, but immediately proceeded along the rear aisle, the same way she had left to go to the restroom. While Mrs. Ludwig denied that she was distracted by the events on stage as she walked to and from the restroom during the second act of the play, the darkened condition of the theater during the performance created a heightened duty on her part to proceed with caution as she returned to her seat.

The trial court made a factual finding that Mrs. Ludwig was distracted by the play as she returned to her seat. However, the only evidence in the record on this point is Mrs. Ludwig's testimony, in which she denies she was distracted. Accordingly, we conclude there is no basis for the trial court's finding in this regard.

Thus, while we find Mrs. Ludwig bears some fault for the accident, we find the trial court was clearly wrong in not assigning any fault to JPAS. We must now determine the percentage of fault to be assigned to each party.

In Clement v. Frey, 95-1119 (La.1/16/96), 666 So.2d 607, we held that when a trial court's allocation of fault is manifestly erroneous or clearly wrong, the reviewing court must lower (or raise) the allocation of fault to the highest (or lowest) point which is reasonably within the trial court's discretion. Applying this rule to the instant record, we find Mrs. Ludwig's fault is relatively slight in comparison to JPAS's fault. JPAS chose to store the equipment in an area of the theater where it knew patrons would walk, and in such a way that a portion of the part of the equipment jutted into the aisle. JPAS did not place barricades around the equipment, nor did it mark the equipment in such a way as to warn patrons of the danger it presented. While Mrs. Ludwig did not use the requisite degree of caution while walking in the darkened theater, we find the highest degree of fault the trial court could have assigned to her based on the record is twenty percent. The remaining eighty percent of the fault must be allocated to JPAS.

Given the disposition of this case in the trial court, there was no award of damages made to plaintiffs. Therefore, we must remand the case to the court of appeal to make an appropriate award of damages based on the record, after briefing and argument by the parties on that issue.

For the reasons assigned, the judgment of the court of appeal is reversed.

KNOLL, Justice, dissenting in part.

In my view the defendant is 100% at fault.

TANTILLO v. GOLDSTEIN BROS. AMUSEMENT CO.
162 N.E. 82 (N.Y. 1928)

O'BRIEN, Judge.

This case was tried upon the theory of negligence. In it is involved a principle important to proprietors and operators of theaters to which the general public is invited.

Plaintiff, 14 years of age, accompanied by two other boys, visited defendant's theater at Utica and bought tickets for admission. Before entering the auditorium, they were accosted by a man unidentified either as an employee of the theater or of the troupe then performing. At his suggestion the three boys returned their tickets, had their money refunded, passed the ticket taker without paying, and entered the auditorium with the unknown man. He provided them with seats and later induced them to go upon the stage and to participate in a vaudeville act then in progress. This act was played by a troupe known as George Brown & Co., who had been secured by the theater management through a booking agency and paid by appellant. The act was intended to be amusing. Plaintiff and his two young companions, as well as others among the spectators, were each encircled by a leather belt to which a rope was attached, and then they mounted a machine similar to a treadmill. They trotted on the machine and caused it to move like a treadmill. The faster they trotted, the more rapidly it revolved. While so engaged, someone, either a member of the troupe or an employee of the theater, would jerk the rope, pull the performer from the machine, and cause him to fall upon a mat. This operation was supposed to furnish the comedy and to raise a laugh among the spectators. Brown's part consisted in catching the performer as he was catapulted from the treadmill. While in the act of attempting to catch plaintiff, Brown slipped and, falling, broke plaintiff's arm. He has recovered judgment which has been affirmed against the theater. Brown also was made a defendant but was never served and did not appear as a party or as a witness.

We think that plaintiff's right to the theater's protection ought not to be distinguished from that of an ordinary patron. Concededly he did not pay admission, but the circumstances under which payment was waived by the theater invest him with a status different from that of a guest. The evidence makes clear that he was given free entrance for no purpose other than to promote the interests of the theater and those of Brown. Both shared in the success added by plaintiff's presence on the stage and his propulsion, intended to be ludicrous, from the treadmill. If the spectators' amusement at this treadmill act were heightened by plaintiff's performance, the theater's monetary receipts on occasions when the act was to be repeated might be enhanced. The man who procured admission for plaintiff and, for such a consideration, induced him to perform for the theater's benefit, is unidentified. From the evidence, no inference can be drawn that he was employed by the theater rather than by Brown. It was the theater, however, and not Brown, who admitted him. No free admissions were allowed by the ticket taker except upon orders by the theater's manager.

The relation between Brown and the theater does not distinctly appear. The evidence does not warrant the conclusion that he was an independent contractor. Even if he were proved to be such, the evidence is of a nature to justify submission to the jury of the issue of fact relating to negligence by the theater. If its responsible agent allowed the performance on its stage of an act which was inherently dangerous and passively consented to participation in it by its invitees, it is liable. While plaintiff was on the stage, the manager of the theater stood in the rear of the hall and witnessed this act. The jury could find that the act was inherently dangerous, that the operation of the machine in such a manner as violently to propel a human being from it required intense activity and caution by Brown to prevent himself from slipping and falling upon the invitee. Brown's services in catching the performer after propulsion from the machine seem to have been regarded as necessary. Otherwise he would have allowed the performer to fall without assistance. One of defendant's witnesses described the act in these words:

> 'The idea was at the end of the act, Brown would grab the boy and as he took hold of the boy's arm, take him clear of the treadmill, and that was the laugh, because the boy would fall and fall on the mattress or pad.'

The act must be viewed as the joint product of Brown and the theater. One could not have produced it without co-operation by the other. The jury could and did find that it was inherently dangerous.

Patrons of theaters are frequently invited upon the stage to be used as foils for the actors. Sleight of hand performers and acrobats avail themselves of the services of spectators as accessory to their tricks and feats. The management is bound to know whether the character of the act is dangerous. Patrons are entitled to protection against acts which by their nature might cause a menace to safety. One who collects a large number of people for gain or profit must be vigilant to protect them. Arnold v. State, 163 App. Div. 253, 148 N.Y.S. 479; Platt v. Erie County Agricultural Society, 164 App. Div. 99, 149 N.Y.S. 520. Plaintiff, having responded to the theater's advertisement to witness the performance, having originally paid for his admission and having secured the return of his admission fee for the purpose of participating in an entertainment which was gainful to defendant, and having been admitted to the theater by order of the manager, cannot fairly be regarded as possessing rights lesser in degree than those of a patron. Defendant was bound to protect its patrons from dangers inherent in George Brown's act and it was bound likewise to protect plaintiff.

The judgment should be affirmed, with costs.

THIELMIER v. LOUISIANA RIVERBOAT GAMING PARTNERSHIP
732 So. 2d 620 (La. Ct. App. 1999)

WILLIAMS, Judge.

On September 14, 1996, Mary Thielmier was injured when she fell while walking off of a stage at the Isle of Capri Casino ("Isle") in Bossier City, Louisiana. As a result of this accident, she filed the present personal injury suit against the Isle. Since some of the allegations of the Isle's negligence were based upon the conduct of Christopher Nolan, the celebrity impersonator that Thielmier was watching, the Isle named Four Star Entertainment, Nolan's employer, as a third party defendant.

After discovery was completed, the Isle filed a motion for summary judgment. At the conclusion of the hearing on the motion, the trial court granted the motion, dismissing all of Thielmier's claims with prejudice. Thielmier now appeals contending that material issues of fact exist regarding Nolan's alleged negligence. For the reasons that follow, we affirm.

FACTS

On the day of her accident, Thielmier, a sixty-nine-year-old woman, went to the Isle to see an Elvis impersonator who was performing there. One of the opening acts was a Nat King Cole impersonator, Christopher Nolan. During his act, Nolan came out into the crowd to select an audience member to come on stage with him, and he chose Thielmier. When the two were on stage, Nolan sang a song to her, and they danced.

Thielmier had to go down three steps as she left the stage. The steps extended across the entire front of the stage, and as such, there were no handrails. In an attempt to assist Thielmier, Nolan held her hand and went down the steps before her. Despite his assistance, Thielmier either slipped or missed the second step completely, and she fell to the floor. As a result of the fall, she incurred several injuries, including one to her knee which subsequently required surgery.

For the purposes of the summary judgment hearing, the Isle admitted Nolan was its employee so that it would be vicariously liable for his actions. At the hearing, the Isle submitted an affidavit from Nolan and portions of Thielmier's deposition. Thielmier also submitted portions of her deposition and an affidavit that she had executed subsequent to her deposition. In his affidavit, Nolan stated that Thielmier volunteered to come on stage with him, and she appeared to have the ability to walk up and down the steps. She fell when she misstepped while walking down the steps. He further stated the stage was well lit, but the lights were not blinding. The steps were clean when Thielmier used them, and none of the other people using the steps that night had any problems.

In her deposition, Thielmier stated she was reluctant to go on stage because of embarrassment, but she agreed to go. Nolan helped her up the steps, and she did not have any problems going up. He sang a song to her, and they danced. He held her hand as he led her down the steps. She stated that she could not see the audience as she came to the steps because she was blinded by the lights. She saw the first step when she looked down and was able to step on it. Her testimony conflicted as to whether she saw the second step. At one point, she stated she did not remember seeing the second step, but she later said that she did see it. She further stated that she did not know how the fall occurred, i.e., whether she slipped or just missed the step.

In her affidavit, Thielmier stated that before taking the first step, she was temporarily blinded by the stage lights. While she saw the first step, she did not see it clearly. She did not see the second step, and she fell when attempting to step down. She had been receiving medical treatment for her knee prior to the accident, and she had surgery on a toe on her right foot five weeks before the accident.

After hearing the arguments of the parties, the trial court ruled in favor of the Isle. The court found that no genuine issues of material fact existed regarding the alleged negligence of the Isle, either in its own capacity, or under the theory of vicarious liability.

ANALYSIS

Appellate courts review summary judgments de novo under the same criteria that govern the district court's consideration of whether summary judgment is appropriate. Schroeder v. Board of Supervisors of L.S.U., 591 So.2d 342 (La.1991).

Because this is a tort case, the summary judgment analysis must be employed in the context of a negligence analysis. The standard negligence analysis under La. C.C. art. 2315 is the duty risk analysis. For liability to attach, the plaintiff must establish that: 1. The conduct in question was a substantial factor in bringing about the harm to the plaintiff, i.e., it was a cause-in-fact of the resultant harm; 2. The defendant owed a duty to the plaintiff; 3. The duty owed was breached; and, 4. The risk or harm caused was within the scope of protection afforded by the duty breached. See Mathieu v. Imperial Toy Corporation, 94-0952 (La.11/30/94), 646 So.2d 318; Mart v. Hill, 505 So.2d 1120 (La.1987).

On appeal, the only finding questioned by Thielmier is the trial court's determination that Nolan was not negligent. In her attempt to show that Nolan was negligent, Thielmier alleges he should be held to a heightened duty of care because: (1) she provided an economic benefit to him; (2) he induced her to go on stage; (3) she is elderly; and (4) he is an experienced stage performer while she is not. Thielmier further alleges genuine issues of material fact exist regarding whether Nolan breached his duty.

Assuming, for the sake of argument, that Nolan's actions were a cause-in-fact of Thielmier's injuries, we will address the duty question. Duty is a question of law. Harris v. Pizza Hut of Louisiana, Inc., 455 So.2d 1364 (La.1984). Whether a legal duty is owed by one party to another depends on the facts and circumstances of the case and the relationship of the parties. Seals v. Morris, 410 So.2d 715 (La.1981). In all cases, duty can be stated generally as the obligation to conform to the standard of conduct of a reasonable man under the circumstances. Id.

Even if Thielmier provided an economic benefit to Nolan by joining him on stage, this did not heighten the duty he owed to her. As the law only requires the owner or operator of a business to act with reasonable care toward his or her customers, there is no justification for having any economic benefit Nolan received extend his duty.

Thielmier also argues that a heightened duty of care should be imposed when a plaintiff has little effective choice about entering a relationship with the defendant. However, Thielmier voluntarily went on the stage. While she may have felt some pressure to go on stage because of the other audience members, this pressure did not leave her without a choice in the matter. Also, her statements in her deposition and her affidavit do not indicate that she was in any way forced or coerced to go on stage.

Even though Thielmier is elderly, Nolan was not under a higher duty of care. The mere fact that a plaintiff is elderly does not mean that he or she is entitled to greater care and assistance. Walden v. Pat Goins Benton Road Beauty School, Inc., 501 So.2d 1014 (La.App. 2d Cir.1987). The deciding factors are whether there are any signs of feebleness, impairment of vision or hearing, disorientation of mind or body, or any other infirmities that may sometimes accompany old age. Id. While Thielmier had problems with her knee and her right foot prior to the accident, the evidence presented indicates that she went on the stage without any problems and that she even danced while there. These actions do not indicate that she had visible infirmities which would heighten Nolan's duty of care.

The fact that Nolan was an experienced stage performer while Thielmier was not does not heighten his duty of care. Thielmier argues that a person who has superior knowledge or experience should be judged in light of that knowledge. However, despite his experience on stage, Nolan's duty toward Thielmier was not heightened because his experience would not put him on notice that he needed to exercise more than reasonable care while assisting someone who is walking off a stage.

Because Nolan assumed the obligation of helping Thielmier walk down the steps, he had a duty to exercise reasonable care in doing so. See Harris v. Pizza Hut of Louisiana, Inc., supra. However, despite Thielmier's contentions, Nolan's duty was not higher than one of reasonable care. We must now determine whether any genuine issues of material fact exist regarding whether he breached this duty.

The breach of a duty is a question of fact. Mundy v. Department of Health and Human Resources, 620 So.2d 811 (La.1993). Even though breach is a question for the trier of fact, summary judgment was proper in this case as no genuine issues of material fact exist regarding whether Nolan exercised reasonable care in assisting Thielmier from the stage. She argues that an issue of fact exists regarding whether she saw the second step, but even if she could not see the step, summary judgment was proper because no evidence has been offered to show that Nolan had any way to perceive that she was blinded. If she could not see the step, she should have informed him of this. Without such knowledge, Nolan was not required to do more to prevent the accident. There has been no suggestion that Nolan did anything to cause Thielmier to fall, only that he did not do enough to prevent such an accident. Under the circumstances, his taking her hand and going down the steps in front of her in an effort to guide her is all the law required.

In its supporting documents, the defendant set forth facts which established that Nolan did not breach his duty of care while assisting Thielmier. She then failed to produce factual support which would prove a breach of his duty of care. Therefore, summary judgment was proper.

CONCLUSION

For the foregoing reasons, the judgment of the trial court is affirmed at the appellant's costs.

AFFIRMED.

BLOOMBERG DISCONNECTS CELL BAN
Curtis L. Taylor
Newsday, Jan. 15, 2003, at A7

Mayor Michael Bloomberg yesterday hung up on City Council legislation that would have banned cell phone use in theaters, movie houses and all public performance stadiums, saying the law would be impossible to enforce.

"We can agree that the use of a mobile telephone during a public performance is, in most cases, rude and disrespectful behavior," Bloomberg said in his veto message to City Clerk Victor Robles. He added, though, that such a law "would be virtually impossible to enforce with the limited resources available."

The bill, introduced in August, sparked loud public debate and was criticized as an attempt to legislate behavior. Nonetheless, the bill passed the council 40-9 in December.

The bill's sponsor, Councilman Phil Reed (D-Harlem), admitted in December that enforcement might be difficult but said the law would arm those who operate public performance stadiums with a way to deter potential violators.

"There is nothing more discourteous and jarring than when a cell phone rings during a concert," Reed said when the bill passed.

Reed couldn't be reached for comment late yesterday. A City Council spokesman said the mayor's veto of the legislation was under review. It could not be determined late yesterday whether the council has enough votes to override the veto.

Notes

1. Theater programs like the one that may have caused Ms. Robbins to fall are invariably referred to as "playbills," due to the famous magazine that has been used in Broadway theaters since 1884:

> Playbill is published every month and each edition contains news items and articles on the general topic of theatre. Each theatre has a customized edition, which shows the current production on the cover and an insert in the middle giving the cast of characters, all other aspects of the publication being the same for all theatres that month.

American Theatre Press, Inc. v. Tax Commission of State of New York, 446 N.Y.S.2d 300, 301 (App. Div.) (Kupferman, J.P., dissenting), *aff'd*, 441 N.E.2d 1105 (N.Y. 1982). See further www.playbill.com.

2. As the facts in *Robbins, Ludwig, Tantillo*, and *Thielmier* make clear, patrons can be injured in a variety of ways. Of course, these cases do not exhaust the range of possibilities.

In Edward Albee's play, "The Goat or Who is Sylvia?," the character Stevie begins smashing things when she learns her husband is having an affair with a goat. Early in the show's 2002 run at Broadway's Golden Theatre, actress Mercedes Ruehl, as Stevie, accidentally threw a glass vase so hard that a shard flew into the audience and struck an elderly woman sitting in the third row (she was taken to the hospital and needed four stitches to close her wound). *See* Justin Glanville, *Actress Has Fun in 'Smashing' Role*, Newark Star-Ledger, Aug. 22, 2002, at 29. For an earlier case in which a theatergoer was attacked by a monkey, who had unexpectedly come off the stage during a performance, *see Abrevaya v. Palace Theatre & Realty Co.*, 197 N.Y.S.2d 27 (Sup. Ct. 1960).

3. What do you think of Councilman Reed's idea to make it illegal to use a cell phone in a theater? Was it as impractical as Mayor Bloomberg stated in his veto message? The New York City Council did not think so and, with strong support from the theater industry, overrode the mayor's veto by a vote of 38-5. *See further* Leonard Jacobs, *Council Overrides Mayoral Veto: Cell Phone Ban at Public Performances Becomes Law April 13*, Back Stage, Feb. 21, 2003, at 4 (explaining that lawbreakers are subject to a $50 fine, but the penalty does not apply if the phone was used in an "emergency"). Of course, cell phones are not the only interruptions that theatergoers must sometimes put up with: crying infants, unruly children, talkers, fidgeters, latecomers, and patrons who constantly leave their seats also can be quite trying. For an interesting discussion of what constitutes proper theater etiquette, *see* Anthony Tommasini, *Bravos at Opera Are Expected, But Booing?*, N.Y. Times, Feb. 1, 2003, at B9. *See also* Jesse McKinley, *The Tyranny of the Standing Ovation: How the Highest Compliment Became the Standard Response*, N.Y. Times, Dec. 21, 2003, §2, at 1 (complaining that theater audiences are cheapening the standing ovation through overuse).

4. The traditional starting time for an evening show on Broadway is 8:00 p.m. (although during the 1970s, when the area was at its physical worst, many houses began

shows at 7:30 p.m.). Recently, however, some theaters have begun experimenting with a 7:00 p.m. start time to accommodate those patrons who need to get home earlier. *See* James Barron, *Broadway Stars, Out a Little Early*, N.Y. Times, Feb. 18, 2003, at A23.

5. As the house lights go down, it is common for patrons to be informed that they may not photograph or tape the performance. Although this is done primarily to protect the show's intellectual property rights, it also helps the audience by reducing extraneous noise and light. *See generally* Elias A. Alcabes, Note, *Unauthorized Photographs of Theatrical Works: Do They Infringe the Copyright?*, 87 Colum. L. Rev. 1032 (1987).

Individuals who engage in unauthorized recording are subject to both civil and criminal penalties. The New York Arts and Cultural Affairs Law, for example, provides as follows:

§ 31.01. Unauthorized photographs and sound recordings of performances

1. Definitions. The following words as used in this section shall have the following meanings:

(a) "Performance" shall mean any presentation consisting in whole or in part of a musical, dramatic, dance or other stage rendition by living persons who appear in the immediate presence of their audience.

(b) "Theatre" shall mean a concert hall, recital hall, theatre or other auditorium in which a performance is rendered and admission to which is limited by its management to persons holding admission tickets or other written evidence of permission to enter.

(c) "Management" shall mean: (i) the operator of a theatre; and (ii) with respect to a particular performance, the person hiring the theatre to present such performance unless such person shall have agreed in writing with such operator not to photograph or make sound recordings of such performance.

2. No person shall take any photograph or make any sound recording of any performance presented in a theatre without having first obtained the written consent of the management to do so. The management of any theatre may maintain an action for an injunction, an accounting, or for damages resulting from or in respect of any photographs or sound recordings of any performance made without the consent required by this section having been obtained, or resulting from or in respect of any distribution or attempted distribution of any such photographs or sound recordings or reproductions thereof.

3. If any person admitted or seeking admission to a theatre in which a performance is to be or is being presented, attempts to bring into, or brings into such theatre any photographic or sound recording device without having first obtained the written consent of the management to do so, such management shall have the right to request and obtain possession of such photographic or sound recording device until the conclusion of such performance. The management shall give a receipt for such device, and shall be liable for any damage to such device or loss or theft of such device while in their care.

4. If any person admitted or seeking admission to a theatre in which a performance is to be or is being presented, refuses or fails to give or surrender possession of any photographic or sound recording device which such person has brought into or attempts to bring into such theatre without having first obtained the written consent of the management to do so, then the management

shall have the right to remove such person therefrom or refuse admission thereto to such person, and shall thereupon offer to refund and, unless such offer is refused, refund to such person the price paid by such person for admission to such theatre. If such person refuses to leave such theatre after having been informed by the management thereof that possession of any photographic or sound recording device in such theatre without the written consent of the management is prohibited, then such person shall be deemed to be remaining in the theatre unlawfully within the meaning of subdivision five of section 140.00 and section 140.05 of the penal law, and in addition, the management shall have the right to maintain an action in trespass and for punitive damages against such person.

5. The criminal penalties and civil remedies provided by this section shall be without force or effect unless the management of the theatre shall have posted signs at the box office and at or near the audience entrance to the portion of the theatre wherein the performance is to be presented and printed in any program which may be furnished to the audience for such performance, stating in substance as follows:

WARNING

The photographing or sound recording of any performance or the possession of any device for such photographing or sound recording inside this theatre, without the written permission of the management is prohibited by law. Offenders may be ejected and liable for damages and other lawful remedies.

6. Sadly, even the best contingency plans cannot fully protect a theater audience from harm. In October 2002, a heavily-armed guerrilla group seized control of the Palace of Culture Theatre in Moscow during a performance of "Nord-Ost," a hit Broadway-style musical based on Veniamin Kaverin's novel *Two Captains*. *See* www.thenordost.com. The rebels quickly released 150 hostages (out of 800), but then threatened to blow up the five-story building unless the government agreed to end all military action against the break-away province of Chechnya. After three days of fruitless talks, authorities gassed the theater with Fentanyl, a powerful opiate-based anaesthetic. *See* Michael Wines & Sabrina Tavernise, *Russia Recaptures Theater After Chechen Rebel Group Begins to Execute Hostages*, N.Y. Times, Oct. 26, 2002, at A1. While this succeeded in bringing the crisis to an end, it resulted in 169 deaths and international criticism for using such a dangerous drug (and initially refusing to reveal its identity). *See* Michael Wines, *Russia Names Drug in Raid, Defending Use*, N.Y. Times, Oct. 31, 2002, at A1. When city officials later announced they would provide $1.5 million in compensation to the hostages and their families, a number of the injured, believing the amount was too low, filed lawsuits. *See* Steven Lee Myers, *Russians Become Litigious: Survivors of Theater Siege Sue*, N.Y. Times, Dec. 6, 2002, at A3.

Problem 22

While standing in a theater lobby, a patron noticed a suspicious-looking man near the coat check room and reported the matter to an usher. Thirty minutes later, another patron was robbed in front of the coat check room by the man. What liability, if any, does the theater have for the attack? *See Antonelli v. Majestic Theater*, 373 N.Y.S.2d 375 (App. Div. 1975).

Chapter 10

Critics

A. OVERVIEW

Theater critics wield enormous power: favorable reviews can make a show a hit, while bad ones can force it to fold. As a result, a critic is expected to be objective, fair, and impartial, yet at the same time not flinch from providing his or her honest opinion, regardless of the consequences.

B. QUALIFICATIONS

WANTED: THEATER CRITIC
Juneau (Alaska) Empire Online, Sept. 9, 1999

The Juneau Empire is looking for someone with insight, attitude and excellent writing skills to review plays for the upcoming theater season.

Tickets will be provided to the shows and the reviewer will be paid $50 for each review.

Reviews should be about 500 to 600 words. Ideally, the reviewer would have a strong background in theater. The writer would judge Perseverance Theatre by the standards of a professional company and other local theatres by the standards of a community company. The reviewer should not have any present ties to the theater group he or she would review.

Reviews must be written after the opening-night show, with a deadline the following day. The reviewer may wish to see a preview in advance of the opening night.

Submit writing samples to Riley Woodford, 3100 Channel Drive, or fax them to 586-3028. Call 586-3740 for more information.

REPUBLICAN PUBLISHING CO. v. AMERICAN NEWSPAPER GUILD
172 F.2d 943 (1st Cir. 1949)

PER CURIAM.

Two complaints were filed on March 6, 1946, in the court below by numerous employees of the Republican Publishing Company seeking to recover from their employer unpaid overtime compensation, liquidated damages, attorneys' fees and costs, pursuant to Sec. 16(b) of the Fair Labor Standards Act of 1938, 52 Stat. 1060, 29 U.S.C.A. §216(b). The defendant—appellant herein—is the publisher of several newspapers in Springfield, Massachusetts. The complaints were consolidated in the district court and referred to a master. The master's report, one of exceptional thoroughness and clarity, was in all respects confirmed by the district judge, who filed only a brief memorandum. Judgments were entered for plaintiffs on June 22, 1948, in accordance with the master's report. Republican Publishing Company appealed from these judgments, and this court ordered that the two appeals be docketed as a single case upon a consolidated transcript of record.

The district judge pointed out that by agreement of the parties the testimony had not been stenographically reported. "Therefore," he said, "I am largely confined to considering whether the report is internally consistent and whether there are errors of law. It is not open to me to determine whether the evidence supports the findings." On appeal, the scope of review in this court is similarly restricted. We have examined the master's report, and have satisfied ourselves that his findings of fact fully support his conclusion of law respecting the points pressed by appellant on this appeal. In the proceedings below, reference was made to the Portal-to-Portal Act of 1947, 61 Stat. 84, 29 U.S.C.A. §251 et seq. However, at the oral argument before us, appellant's counsel expressly disclaimed any reliance upon the provisions of this Act, and we have accordingly not taken it into consideration.

We think this appeal is lacking in substance. One point, relating to plaintiff Annette Doyle, is perhaps worthy of brief comment.

Miss Doyle was originally hired as a proofreader. In September, 1941, she was promoted to the editorial staff as a reporter, covering social agencies and general assignments. Later, in April, 1942, "she took over the labor and industry beat, and on February 22, 1944 was assigned the job of theater editor in addition to her other duties." Originally she worked a basic 45-hour week, and after October 15, 1945, she went on a six-day 40-hour week. During all this period she was paid a flat weekly salary, which was $20 at the start and was gradually increased to $50 per week beginning August 8, 1946. The master found: "There is no doubt from the testimony of the defendant that she was considered one of the ablest and most conscientious reporters on the staff and that she could always be depended on to finish her job."

The responsibility of Miss Doyle as theater editor extended to seeing that new moving pictures and plays were covered by someone, not necessarily by her. In computing her hours worked, for the purpose of determining the amount of overtime pay due under the statute, the master included, in addition to her basic regular workweek, the hours spent by her in the theaters, seeing the pictures or plays which were personally reviewed by her for the newspaper. Appellant objects to the inclusion of these extra hours in the computation of hours actually worked by Miss Doyle, because it was the policy of the paper not to pay for this work, well understood by Miss Doyle when she took the extra assignment of theater editor.

On this point the master made the following findings:

> With reference to this aspect of Miss Doyle's overtime claim it should be added that the defendant had never compensated members of its staff for reviewing movies or legitimate stage productions. Indeed a specific proposal sometime during this period to pay $1 for each review was vetoed [because] the incidental benefits of free passes, parties, Christmas gifts from the theatres,

etc., made the position of theatre editor so attractive that at least up until the war years there was active bidding for it among the staff. The evidence is strong that Miss Doyle's assignment to the job in 1944 was at her own request, although she was well aware of the practice of the paper with regard to compensation for it.

There is no doubt that the defendant considered the job as a plum to be handed out to deserving reporters rather than as an assignment to work. There is also no doubt that Miss Doyle was aware of this attitude. The defendant contends therefore that her assumption of the duties was a purely voluntary act and that there is no obligation on its part to pay her anything let alone time and a half.

Section No. 203 of the Act defines "to employ" as including to suffer or permit to work. Hence the crucial question is not whether the work was voluntary, but rather whether the plaintiff was in fact performing services for the benefit of the employer with the knowledge and approval of the employer. Under the circumstances here, to pose the question is to answer it. And a contract to pay nothing for work stands in no better light under the Act than a contract to pay below the minimum wage. I conclude that the time she spent in the role of critic is working time under the Act.

We think that the master ruled correctly in this matter. The theater editor could not very well write a review of a picture or play without seeing it; and therefore her attendance at the theater for this purpose must be deemed physical or mental exertion (whether burdensome or not) controlled or required by the employer, and "pursued necessarily and primarily for the benefit of the employer and his business." See Jewell Ridge Coal Corp. v. Local No. 6167, 1945, 325 U.S. 161, 164-165, 65 S.Ct. 1063, 1066, 89 L.Ed. 1534. Consequently, these hours must be included in the workweek, and compensated at the statutory rate, despite any custom or understanding to the contrary. Tennessee Coal, Iron & R. Co. v. Muscoda Local, 1944, 321 U.S. 590, 602, 64 S.Ct. 698, 88 L.Ed. 949, 152 A.L.R. 1014. See also Anderson v. Mt. Clemens Pottery Co., 1946, 328 U.S. 680, 66 S.Ct. 1187, 90 L.Ed. 1515.

Walling v. Portland Terminal Co., 1947, 330 U.S. 148, 67 S.Ct. 639, 91 L.Ed. 809, and Rogers v. Schenkel, 2 Cir., 1947, 162 F.2d 596, are in no way contrary to our conclusion in the case at bar. The Portland Terminal case involved the question whether certain "trainees" were "employees" of the railroad within the meaning of §§ 6 and 7 of the Fair Labor Standards Act, 29 U.S.C.A. §§ 206, 207, and the court held they were not. In Rogers v. Schenkel, the plaintiff and defendant had been friends, and after the plaintiff had received a 4-F Selective Service classification he took a job as helper in defendant's plant so as to assist in some way in the war effort. He had independent means and intended to render his services without compensation. On several occasions when the defendant asked him to turn in a weekly report of time worked, the plaintiff stated that his services were voluntary and that he would not accept wages in any form. Plaintiff refused to be placed upon the defendant's payroll because he did not wish to be listed as an employee. Notwithstanding this, the plaintiff had a change of heart and eventually brought suit under the Fair Labor Standards Act for the statutory minimum wages and liquidated damages. He recovered judgment in the district court on the ground that he was an employee within the meaning of the Act, since the defendant had suffered or permitted him to work in defendant's business. The court of appeals reversed upon the authority of Walling v. Portland Terminal Co.

By way of contrast with the cases just cited, Annette Doyle was undoubtedly an employee of appellant "whose employment contemplated compensation." Under Sec. 7(a) of the Act, she was entitled to be compensated at one and one-half times her regular rate of pay for the hours worked in each workweek in excess of 40 hours. Miss Doyle's attendance at the theaters for the purpose stated fulfilled "all three of the essential elements of work" as set forth in the Tennessee Coal, Iron & R. Co. and Jewell Ridge cases, supra, and the time so spent must be included in the computation of hours worked. The statute overrides any custom or understanding to the contrary.

The judgment of the District Court is affirmed, with the addition of $400 for attorneys' fees in this court.

BLANCHARD v. NORTHWEST PUBLICATIONS, INC.
2000 WL 54354 (Minn. Ct. App. 2000)

SHORT, Judge.

For five years, Jayne Blanchard was employed as a theatre critic by Northwest Publications, Inc. (hereinafter "Pioneer Press"). After her termination for "proven dishonesty," Blanchard sued Pioneer Press for sex discrimination, retaliation and reprisal, and wrongful termination in violation of public policy. On appeal, Blanchard argues the trial court erred by: (1) directing a verdict on her discrimination claim; and (2) summarily dismissing her reprisal and public policy claims. We affirm.

I.

A directed verdict motion presents a question of law regarding the sufficiency of the evidence to present a fact question for the jury. Minn.R.Civ.P. 50.01; see Wall v. Fairview Hosp. & Healthcare Servs., 584 N.W.2d 395, 405, 408 (Minn.1998) (reinstating trial court's directed verdict because evidence presented was insufficient to create question of fact for jury); M.W. Ettinger Transfer & Leasing Co. v. Schaper Mfg., Inc., 494 N.W.2d 29, 34 (Minn.1992) (finding trial court properly granted directed verdict where insufficient evidence existed to submit negligence claim to jury). In a bench trial, the defense motion made at the close of the plaintiff's case is not a directed verdict, but a rule 41 motion to dismiss. Compare Minn.R.Civ.P. 41.02(b) (involuntary dismissal) with Minn.R.Civ.P. 50.01 (directed verdict); see Fidelity Bank & Trust Co. v. Fitzimons, 261 N.W.2d 586, 587 n.1 (Minn.1977) (noting proper motion at end of plaintiff's case would have been dismissal under rule 41.02, not directed verdict). On appeal from an involuntary dismissal under rule 41.02(b), we reverse only where the trial court abused its discretion. See Bonhiver v. Fugelso, Porter, Simich & Whiteman, Inc., 355 N.W.2d 138, 144 (Minn.1984) (applying abuse of discretion standard to involuntary dismissal).

At the close of Blanchard's case, the trial court found: (1) no disciplinary action was taken against Blanchard because of her gender; (2) Pioneer Press's reasons for firing Blanchard were nondiscriminatory and credible; (3) Pioneer Press's treatment of a male reporter for his soliciting behavior did not demonstrate that Pioneer Press's reasons for terminating Blanchard were pretextual; (4) Blanchard lied to her editor during the investigation and made or adopted by acquiescence untrue statements on the Barbara Carlson radio show; (5) no evidence was presented that another employee committed a similar offense and was treated more favorably by Pioneer Press; and (6) Pioneer Press, as a rule, terminates employees upon discovery of dishonesty. After a careful review of the record, we conclude the trial court's findings are supported by the evidence. See State by Burnquist v. Bollenbach, 241 Minn. 103, 109, 63 N.W.2d 278, 282-83 (1954) (deferring to trial court's determination of witness credibility and refusing to set aside findings supporting dismissal unless clearly erroneous). Under these circumstances, the trial court did not abuse its discretion in dismissing Blanchard's discrimination claim.

II.

In response to a motion for summary judgment, the nonmoving party must present "specific facts" demonstrating a material issue of fact exists. Minn.R.Civ.P. 56.05; Patton v. Newmar Corp., 538 N.W.2d 116, 119 (Minn.1995). We view the evidence in the light most favorable to the nonmoving party to determine whether genuine issues of material fact exist and whether the trial court correctly applied the law. Fahrendorff by Fahrendorff v. North Homes, Inc., 597 N.W.2d 905, 909-10 (Minn.1999); Ciardelli v. Rindal, 582 N.W.2d 910, 912 (Minn.1998); Fabio v. Bellomo, 504 N.W.2d 758, 761 (Minn.1993).

Blanchard argues the trial court improperly granted summary judgment on her reprisal claim. See McGrath v. TCF Bank Savings, 509 N.W.2d 365, 366 (Minn.1993) (holding plaintiff may prevail on reprisal claim despite employer's legitimate reason for discharge if illegitimate reason "more likely than not" motivated termination) (citing Anderson v. Hunter, Keith, Marshall & Co., 417 N.W.2d 619, 627 (Minn.1988)). To establish a prima facie case of reprisal, Blanchard must show statutorily-protected conduct, adverse employment action, and a casual connection between her conduct and Pioneer Press's action. Cross v. Cleaver, 142 F.3d 1059, 1071 (8th Cir.1998); Hubbard v. United Press Int'l, Inc., 330 N.W.2d 428, 444 (Minn.1983).

The record demonstrates: (1) Blanchard worked as a theatre critic for Pioneer Press from 1992 until her termination in 1997; (2) during her employment, Blanchard complained about alleged disparate treatment of women and an editor's reference to her marital status; (3) in April 1997, Blanchard was suspended for one week without pay because her financial involvement with a local theater company created a conflict of interest with her employment; (4) in May 1997, Blanchard again was suspended for one week without pay because she wrote, and Pioneer Press published, a theatre story quoting as its chief source an actress with whom Blanchard had a financial relationship; (5) on May 8, 1997, Blanchard appeared on the Barbara Carlson radio show and engaged in [off-air] banter about the circumstances of her suspension, her employer's treatment of other employees, and personal matters relating to a co-worker and his wife; (6) on May 13, Blanchard repeatedly denied that she was or knew the source for the radio host's misinformation about the co-worker, but the host confirmed Blanchard was the source of all the information; (7) Blanchard later admitted she provided the host with the information about her employment and her co-worker; (8) in May 1997, Blanchard provided false information regarding her employment status to two news organizations; and (9) on May 16, 1997, Pioneer Press terminated Blanchard for "proven dishonesty."

Blanchard's complaints about the alleged disparate treatment do not immunize her unprofessional conduct. See Jackson v. St. Joseph State Hosp., 840 F.2d 1387, 1391 (8th Cir.1988) (holding Title VII's protection from retaliation does not protect unsatisfactory performance). The proximity of Blanchard's protected acts with Pioneer Press's adverse action is insufficient to prove a causal connection without a demonstration that "but for" the protected activity, Blanchard would not have suffered the adverse employment action. Fields v. Phillips Sch. of Bus. & Tech., 870 F.Supp. 149, 153 (W.D.Tex.1994), aff'd mem., 59 F.3d 1242 (5th Cir.1995); see Rath v. Selection Research, Inc., 978 F.2d 1087, 1090 (8th Cir.1992) (holding termination six months after protected activity was insufficient to establish casual connection).

Blanchard failed to offer any evidence establishing pretext for Pioneer Press's proffered nondiscriminatory reasons for her termination. See Kennedy v. GN Danavox, 928 F.Supp. 866, 872 (D.Minn.1996) (assigning plaintiff burden of proving adverse employment action motivated by intentional discrimination); Hermeling v. Montgomery Ward & Co., 851 F.Supp. 1369, 1378 (D.Minn.1994) (holding actions and comments by nondecisionmaking employee cannot provide basis for charging other employees with discriminatory intent); Rademacher v. FMC Corp., 431 N.W.2d 879, 882 (Minn.App.1988) (recognizing summary judgment is appropriately granted when employee fails to set forth evidence establishing pretext for employer's proffered nondiscriminatory reasons). Under these circumstances, the trial court properly granted summary judgment on her retaliation and reprisal claims.

Blanchard also argues the trial court improperly granted summary judgment on her common law public policy claim. See Novosel v. Nationswide Ins. Co., 721 F.2d 894, 898-99 (3d Cir.1983) (recognizing common law cause of action exists where no statute governs terminations in violation of public policy). But common law claims for retaliatory discharge have been displaced by the state Whistleblower Act. See Minn.Stat. § 181.932 (1998) (protecting employees from adverse employment action resulting from reporting employer's violation of law); Thompson v. Campbell, 845 F.Supp. 665, 676 (D.Minn.1994) (noting Minnesota courts have not recognized a common law wrongful discharge claim) (citing Piekarski v. Home Owners Sav. Bank, 956 F.2d 1484, 1493 (8th Cir.1992); Steinbeck v. Northwestern Nat'l Life Ins. Co., 728 F.Supp. 1389, 1394 (D.Minn.1989)); Bolton v. Dept. of Human Servs., 527 N.W.2d 149, 154 (Minn.App.1995) (recognizing common law retaliatory discharge claims displaced by Whistleblower Act), rev'd on other grounds, 540 N.W.2d 523 (Minn.1995). Thus, Blanchard has no common law claim for discharge in violation of public policy independent of Minn.Stat. § 181.932. Under these circumstances, the trial court properly granted summary judgment on her common law public policy claim.

Affirmed.

CODE OF CONDUCT
American Theatre Critics Association
Adopted July 19, 1997, at Cedar City, Utah

Our love of theater has brought us together from a variety of backgrounds, careers and levels of experience. It is important for us to remember that our actions reflect on the organization, its members and the professions.

Membership in ATCA is a privilege.

As a condition of my ATCA membership, I agree to the following:

I will respect the intent of complimentary items (tickets, merchandise) given to me in the course of my job and not use them for financial gain.

I will respect the graciousness of our hosts at ATCA functions and the right of my fellow members to share equally in the hospitality they provide. I will not take more than my share or assume remaining items are free for the taking.

I will respect the reputation of the organization and not invoke ATCA's name or my membership in it to threaten or intimidate.

Within the association, I shall treat all my colleagues with professional respect, courtesy and integrity.

I recognize that failure to abide by this agreement may jeopardize ATCA's relationship with press agents, event hosts, the theater community and others who offer us hospitality. It also compromises our professional reputation.

I have read and understood the above and agree to abide by this code of conduct.

Notes

1. As the *Juneau Empire's* "help wanted" ad makes clear, just about any one can become a theater critic. Although good writing skills are helpful, no special education is required, and unlike other professions, there is no accrediting body or national test for theater critics. Is this how it should be? What are the consequences of not requiring theater critics to have academic training and practical experience in the theater, particularly if (as is usually the case) their readers lack such credentials?

2. In recent years, university drama departments have begun to focus more attention on training would-be critics. As a result, a growing number of schools now offer master or doctoral degrees in theater theory, history, and criticism. In addition, the International Association of Theatre Critics (www.aict-iatc.org) has begun hosting "young critics" training seminars. For a list of the things aspiring critics are taught to look for, *see* artswork.asu.edu/arts/teachers/standards/theatre.htm.

3. Annette Doyle, the theater critic in the *Republican Printing* case, worked her way up from proof reader to theater critic. Her career is not atypical—critics normally still start as beat reporters and then slowly move into theater criticism. Ben Brantley, currently the chief theater critic of *The New York Times*, began his career as a staff writer for *The New Yorker*. *See* Jennifer Baker, *So What Do You Do, Ben Brantley?*, June 17, 2003, at www.mediabistro.com/articles/cache/a410.asp.

4. As the court in *Republican Printing* points out, it long has been common for theater critics to receive gratuities (both small and large) from the people they write about. In recent years, however, many publications have promulgated tough "no gift" rules that prohibit their employees from accepting such items. For an example of such a policy, *see Los Angeles Times Code of Ethics (Adopted 1999)* at www.asne.org/ideas/codes/losangelestimes.htm.

5. Even where no gift is involved, a theater critic's integrity can be compromised in other ways. Recall that in *Blanchard* the plaintiff was fired (in part) because she had financial relationships with a local actress and theater company that undermined her independence and objectivity.

6. The Code of Ethics of the American Theatre Critics Association (www.americantheatrecritics.org), reproduced in the readings above, cautions members about re-selling complimentary tickets and abusing their power, but is otherwise silent regarding the ethical obligations of critics. Are you surprised by the Code's brevity? What accounts for its lack of specificity? If it was up to you, what additional provisions, if any, would be included in the Code?

7. The charge that theater critics have too much power and are prone to abuse it is an old and oft-made one. *See, e.g., The Man Who Came to Dinner* (1939) (a play by Moss Hart and George S. Kaufman that lampoons real-life theater critic Alexander Woollcott, who was roundly despised because of his imperious behavior); *Theatre of*

Blood (1973) (a film in which Vincent Price, as Shakespearean actor Edward Lionheart, exacts deadly revenge on the members of the Critics' Circle after they snub him); and "Bobby and the Critic" (1981) (an episode of the ABC sitcom *Taxi* in which John Harkins plays John Bowman, an influential theater critic who taunts cabbie Bobby Wheeler by writing—but not publishing—a favorable review of his performance as naturalist Charles Darwin).

Notwithstanding these unflattering portraits, there are theater critics who are loved and admired. One particularly notable example is Walter Kerr (1913-96), who despite his power to make and break shows (*Newsweek* once referred to him as America's "supercritic") was unfailingly modest and generous throughout his long life.

Kerr was the theater critic for the *New York Herald Tribune* (1951-66) and *The New York Times* (1966-83); in 1978, he was awarded a Pulitzer Prize for his insightful commentaries. Prior to becoming a critic, Kerr had been both a Broadway playwright and director; his wife Jean, who also was a playwright, based her famous novel *Please Don't Eat the Daisies* (1957) on her life with Kerr (the book later was turned into a movie starring Doris Day and then a short-lived NBC sitcom). Even in death, Kerr remains a fixture on Broadway—literally: in 1990, the owners of the Ritz Theatre renamed their venue in his honor.

8. Given the importance attached to reviews, it has been a theater tradition to anxiously wait up on opening night for the early morning papers. Recent advances in technology, however, are changing this ritual:

> By the time Momma Rose had had her turn, they knew they had a hit.
>
> At about 9:30 p.m. on Thursday, a good 10 minutes before the opening-night curtain fell on "Gyspy" at the Shubert Theater, the producers of this $8.5 million revival had already read several major reviews—on a hand-held BlackBerry—confirming that the critics loved their show, and that they loved Bernadette Peters's performance as Momma Rose even more.
>
> [T]he advent of [the] BlackBerry may have killed the romantic notion of Broadway investors nervously awaiting the morning papers....

Jesse McKinley, *New 'Gypsy' Struts, Silencing Naysayers*, N.Y. Times, May 5, 2003, at B1.

9. For all their power, critics do not always have the last word. When the Off-Broadway musical "The Fantasticks" debuted in May 1960, the critics were not impressed and, as a result, ticket sales were slow. Indeed, had it not been for the unwavering faith of the producers, the show likely would have folded during its first week. In the end, however, it outlasted all of its critics, finally closing in January 2002 after a record 17,162 performances—and then only because a new landlord took over the theater and bought out the show's lease. *See further* Peter Marks, *For Little Musical That Could, a 42-Year Run*, N.Y. Times, Jan. 9, 2002, at A1.

10. For a further look at theater critics, *see, e.g.*, Lehman Engel, *The Critics* (1976); Tice L. Miller, *Bohemians and Critics: The Development of American Theatre Criticism in the Nineteenth Century: The Early Victorians* (1981); Montroes Moses & John Mason Brown, *American Theater as Seen by Its Critics, 1752-1934* (1934); Benedict Nightingale, *Fifth Row Center: A Critic's Year On and Off Broadway* (1986); Richard H. Palmer, *The Critics' Cannon: Standards of Theatrical Reviewing in America* (1997); Frank Rich, *Hot Seat: Theater Criticism for The New York Times, 1980-1993* (1998); Wesley Monroe Shrum, Jr., *Fringe and Fortune: The Role of Critics in High and Popular Culture* (1996); Kalina Stefanova-Peteva, *Who Calls the Shots on the New York Stage?: The New York Drama Critics* (1993); Yael Zarhy-Levo, *The Theatrical Critic as*

Cultural Agent: Constructing Pinter, Orton and Stoppard as Absurdist Playwrights (2001). *See also* Jesse McKinley, *This Crop of Broadway Shows is Finding Dog Days in the Fall*, N.Y. Times, Nov. 20, 2003, at A1 (suggesting that the early closure of numerous shows during the 2003-04 Broadway season was due, at least in part, to overly-harsh reviews).

Problem 23

As a lark, a theater patron began including musings on her weblog about the plays she was seeing. Eventually, she became quite serious about her endeavor, and now regularly posts lengthy and detailed analyses. Given these developments, may she deduct the cost of her tickets as a business expense by claiming she has become a "bona fide theater critic with a worldwide readership"? *See Downs v. Commissioner*, 307 F.3d 423 (6th Cir. 2002).

C. IMMUNITIES

MERIVALE v. CARSON
(1888) L.R. 20 Q.B.D. 275 (C.A.)

[Appeal by the defendant against the refusal of a Divisional Court (Mathew and Grantham, JJ.) to allow a new trial of the action, or to enter judgment for the defendant.

The action was brought to recover damages in respect of an alleged libel. At the trial before Field, J., it appeared that the plaintiff and his wife were the joint authors of a play called "The Whip Hand." The defendant was the editor of a theatrical newspaper called The Stage. Early in May, 1886, the play was performed at a theatre in Liverpool. On May 7 a criticism of the play was published in the defendant's newspaper. The part of the article charged in the statement of claim as libellous was as follows:—
"'The Whip Hand,' the joint production of Mr. and Mrs. Herman Merivale, gives us nothing but a hash-up of ingredients which have been used ad nauseam, until one rises in protestation against the loving, confiding, fatuous husband with the naughty wife and her double existence, the good male genius, the limp aristocrat, and the villainous foreigner. And why dramatic authors will insist that in modern society comedies the villain must be a foreigner, and the foreigner must be a villain, is only explicable on the ground, we suppose, that there is more or less of romance about such gentry. It is more in consonance with accepted notions that your Continental croupier would make a much better fictitious prince, marquis, or count than would, say, an English billiard-marker or stable-lout. And so the Marquis Colonna in 'The Whip Hand' is offered up by the authors upon the altar of tradition and sacrificed in the usual manner when he gets too troublesome to permit of the reconciliation of husband and wife, and lover and maiden, and is proved, also much as usual, to be nothing more than a kicked-out croupier." The innuendo suggested was that the article implied that the play was of an immoral tendency. It was admitted that there was no adulterous wife in the play.

Field, J., in the course of his summing-up to the jury said: "The question is, first, whether this criticism bears the meaning which the plaintiffs put upon it. If it is a fair temperate criticism, and does not bear that meaning, or is not fairly to be read as having that meaning, then your verdict will be for the defendants. It is not for a moment suggested by any one that the defendant is animated by the smallest possible malice towards the plaintiffs. There is no ground for saying so, and no one has said so. The malice which is necessary in this action is one which, if it existed at all, will be because the defendant has exceeded his right of criticism upon the play. You have the play before you, you must judge for yourselves. If it is no more than fair, honest, independent, bold, even exaggerated, criticism, then your verdict will be for the defendant. It is for the plaintiffs to make out their case. They have to satisfy you that it is more than that, otherwise they cannot complain. If you are satisfied upon the evidence that it is more than that, then you will give your verdict for the plaintiffs."

The jury found a verdict for the plaintiffs with one shilling damages, and the judge entered judgment for the plaintiffs accordingly, and declined to deprive them of costs.

The defendant appealed.]

LORD ESHER, Master of the Rolls.

This action is brought in respect of an alleged libel contained in a criticism by the defendant upon a play written by the plaintiffs. The first thing to be considered is, what are the questions which in such a case ought to be left to the jury. The first question to be left to them is, what is the meaning of the alleged libel? The jury must look at the criticism, and say what in their opinion any reasonable man would understand by it. I am not prepared to say that in coming to their conclusion they would not also have to look at the work criticised. That, however, is not very material for us to consider now. The proper question was put to the jury in the present case. Two interpretations of the defendant's article were placed before them. One was that it meant that the play is founded upon adultery, without containing any stigma on the fact that it is so founded. The defendant's article is alleged to be libellous in that it attributed to the plaintiffs that they had written a play founded upon adultery, without any objection to it on their part, in other words, that they had written an immoral play. On behalf of the defendant it was said that the article had no such meaning, that the expression "naughty wife" does not mean "adulterous wife." It would not have that meaning in every case, but the question is whether, looking at the context of the article, it has that meaning. If the Court should come to the conclusion that the expression could not by any reasonable man be thought to have that meaning, they could overrule the verdict of the jury; otherwise the question is for the jury.

What is the next question to be put to the jury? Are they to be told that the criticism of a play is a privileged occasion, within the well-settled meaning of the word "privilege," and that their verdict must go for the defendant, unless the plaintiff can prove malice in fact, that is, that the writer of the article was actuated by an indirect or malicious motive? I think it is clear that that is not the law, and that it was so decided in Campbell v. Spottiswoode, 3 B. & S. 769, which has never been overruled. All the judges, both before and ever since that case, have acted upon the view there expressed, that a criticism upon a written published work is not a privileged occasion. Blackburn, J., in his judgment, shews why it is not a privileged occasion. A privileged occasion is one on which the privileged person is entitled to do something which no one who is not within the privilege is entitled to do on that occasion. A person in such a position may say or write about another person things which no other person in the kingdom can be allowed to say or write. But, in the case of a criticism upon a published work, every person in the kingdom is entitled to do, and is forbidden to do exactly the same things, and therefore the occasion is not privileged. Therefore the second question to be put to the jury is, whether the alleged libel is or is not a libel.

The form in which that question should be put is, I think, best expressed by Crompton, J., in Campbell v. Spottiswoode, 3 B. & S. at p. 778. He says: "Nothing is more important than that fair and full latitude of discussion should be allowed to writers upon any public matter, whether it be the conduct of public men, or the proceedings in Courts of Justice, or in Parliament, or the publication of a scheme, or a literary work. But it is always to be left to a jury to say whether the publication has gone beyond the limits of a fair comment on the subject-matter discussed. A writer is not entitled to overstep those limits, and impute base and sordid motives which are not warranted by the facts, and I cannot for a moment think, because he has a bona fide belief that he is publishing what is true, that is any answer to an action for libel." He says that upon the answer to the question there stated it depends whether the article upon which the action is brought is or is not a libel. The question is not whether the article is privileged, but whether it is a libel.

What is the meaning of a "fair comment"? I think the meaning is this: is the article in the opinion of the jury beyond that which any fair man, however prejudiced or however strong his opinion may be, would say of the work in question? Every latitude must be given to opinion and to prejudice, and then an ordinary set of men with ordinary judgment must say whether any fair man would have made such a comment on the work. It is very easy to say what would be clearly beyond that limit; if, for instance, the writer attacked the private character of the author. But it is much more difficult to say what is within the limit. That must depend upon the circumstances of the particular case. I think the right question was really left by Field, J., to the jury in the present case. No doubt you can find in the course of his summing-up some phrases which, if taken alone, may seem to limit too much the question put to the jury. But, when you look at the summing-up as a whole, I think it comes in substance to the final question which was put by the judge to the jury: "If it is no more than fair, honest, independent, bold, even exaggerated, criticism, then your verdict will be for the defendants." He gives a very wide limit, and, I think, rightly. Mere exaggeration, or even gross exaggeration, would not make the comment unfair. However wrong the opinion expressed may be in point of truth, or however prejudiced the writer, it may still be within the prescribed limit. The question which the jury must consider is this—would any fair man, however prejudiced he may be, however exaggerated or obstinate his views, have said that which this criticism has said of the work which is criticised? If it goes beyond that, then you must find for the plaintiff; if you are not satisfied that it does, then it falls within the allowed limit, and there is no libel at all.

I cannot doubt that the jury were justified in coming to the conclusion to which they did come, when once they had made up their minds as to the meaning of the words used in the article, viz. that the plaintiffs had written an obscene play, and no fair man could have said that. There was therefore a complete misdescription of the plaintiffs' work, and the inevitable conclusion was that an imputation was cast upon the characters of the authors. Even if I had thought that the right direction had not been given to the jury, I should have declined to grant a new trial, for the same verdict must inevitably have been found if the jury had been rightly directed.

Another point which has been discussed is this. It is said that if in some other case the alleged libel would not be beyond the limits of fair criticism, and it could be shewn that the defendant was not really criticising the work, but was writing with an indirect and dishonest intention to injure the plaintiffs, still the motive would not make the criticism a libel. I am inclined to think that it would, and for this reason, that the comment would not then really be a criticism of the work. The mind of the writer would not be that of a critic, but he would be actuated by an intention to injure the author.

In my opinion this appeal must be dismissed.

[The concurring opinion of Lord Justice Bowen is omitted.]

ADOLF PHILIPP CO. v. NEW YORKER STAATS-ZEITUNG
150 N.Y.S. 1044 (App. Div. 1914)

LAUGHLIN, Justice.

Appeal by the defendant, New Yorker Staats-Zeitung, from an order of the Supreme Court, made at the New York Special Term and entered in the office of the clerk of the county of New York on the 23d day of October, 1914, overruling its demurrer to the amended complaint and granting plaintiff's motion for judgment on the pleadings.

This is an action for libel. The plaintiff pleaded nine separate causes of action. The defendant demurred to each on the ground that it fails to state facts sufficient to constitute a cause of action.

It is alleged in each count of the complaint that the plaintiff is a domestic corporation, and the lessee of a theatre at 205-207 East Fifty-seventh street in the borough of Manhattan, New York, known as the "Adolf Philipp 57th Street Theatre," and that its business consists in maintaining and conducting that theatre as a German theatre, and in producing therein plays exclusively in the German language for profit, and that it depends for its patrons and income entirely upon the German-speaking people; that Adolf Philipp is a well-known author of German plays and a composer of music and a German actor and singer, and for upwards of twenty years last past has been connected with and has acted in German plays in the city of New York and elsewhere, and has achieved a great reputation and high esteem among the German people and German theatregoers in particular, for which reason the plaintiff was incorporated under his name and he was elected its president, treasurer and manager, and the plaintiff has secured his services as an author, producer and composer, actor and singer, and procured said theatre to be erected and took possession thereof under a binding lease for twenty-one years from October 1, 1912, and named the theatre with a view to obtaining the benefits and advantages of the good name of Philipp, and has made large expenditures in the establishment of its business; that it opened the theatre for the purpose of rendering performances therein in the German language on or about the 24th day of November, 1912, and successfully produced therein in the German language several plays adapted and staged by said Adolf Philipp, and that thereby said theatre became widely known and highly reputed and esteemed by the public at large and German theatregoers as a German theatre of high class and wholesome entertainment and amusement in the German language; that the theatre was successful and became a source of large income, revenue and profit to the plaintiff; that owing to these facts the managers of English productions became accustomed to visit said theatre whenever a new production was presented and to buy the English rights therefor on the basis of a royalty to plaintiff, and that royalties received from such source afforded plaintiff additional income and profit, all of which was known to the defendant; that prior to the month of January, 1914, the plaintiff, at a great expenditure of money, procured a certain play in the German language based upon the controversy shortly theretofore reported in the defendant's and other newspapers between several of the officers of the German army and some of the civilian residents of Zabern, in one of the provinces of the German Empire, which play was revised and adapted for the plaintiff by said Philipp and was produced by the plaintiff at said theatre under the title of "Zabern" on the 28th of January, 1914, at an outlay of over $5,000, and proved to be a great success and was attended by many Germans residing in the city of Greater New York and vicinity, all of whom expressed their appreciation of the play and of the production and performance thereof, and that by reason thereof the production of the play at the plaintiff's theatre became widely known, well liked and frequently visited by many of the German theatregoers until shortly after the first publication of which the plaintiff complains; that after several performances of the play a well-known manager and producer of English plays negotiated with plaintiff and offered to buy the rights for the English production of the play, "which the plaintiff was about to sell to him upon terms and conditions greatly advantageous and remunerative to this plaintiff"; that by reason of the publication by defendant of the article, of which complaint is made, and the impression it was calculated and intended to make upon the German theatregoers and the public at large known as "German-Americans," the offer theretofore made to the plaintiff by the prospective purchaser of the English rights of the production was withdrawn specifically on the ground that the prospective purchaser feared to undertake the production of the play in English lest he incur the enmity and hatred of the public who had been enraged against the play by said publication, and that thereby "this plaintiff was deprived of the benefits of the English rights of production of the said play 'Zabern,' to the damage of this plaintiff in royalties and compensation to the extent of many thousands of dollars"; that the defendant is a domestic corporation and owns and publishes in the city of New York three newspapers in the German language, namely, a morning edition known as the New Yorker Staats-Zeitung, an evening edition known as the Abendblatt der New Yorker Staats-Zeitung, and a Sunday edition known as the Sonntagsblatt der New Yorker Staats-Zeitung, which have a very large circulation and were and are issued in several editions daily, and are daily read by several thousand German speaking people throughout the United States, and particularly and mainly within the city of New York.

It is then alleged in each count that the alleged libel of which complaint is therein made was falsely, wickedly and maliciously composed, printed and published in the German language and circulated [and] broadcast "of, and concerning the plaintiff, its theatre, its officers, its business and its property," and that the defendant at the time of the publication was well aware of the facts hereinbefore stated, and composed and published the articles with malicious and wicked intent to injure the plaintiff "in its business" and "in the good name and reputation of" its said theatre and of said play, and "to bring the plaintiff's theatre and its business and the said play 'Zabern' into public scandal, infamy and disgrace, and to hold this plaintiff, its officers, its business and" said play, which it owned, "up as an object of hatred, ridicule, contempt and obloquy."

Following the quotation of the alleged libelous article, it is alleged in each count, in substance, that the publication was widely circulated in the city of New York and in other cities and States of the Union, and was read and understood by hundreds of thousands of German speaking people, which caused "the plaintiff, its theatre and the said play 'Zabern' to be condemned, shunned and boycotted by all German theatregoers, including those who, prior to the said publication, visited, appreciated and lauded the plaintiff's theatre and its productions, and, as a result thereof, the German public ceased to patronize the plaintiff's theatre and the said performance of 'Zabern,' causing this plaintiff great damage and injury in its good name and reputation with the German theatregoers and great financial loss in its said business"; that the publication caused and provoked the "German theatregoers in the city of New York and vicinity to shun and avoid the plaintiff's theatre and to withhold their patronage from the plaintiff and its said business," and caused and incited several German societies and associations "to adopt and promulgate among its members, resolutions censuring the plaintiff and its production of said play 'Zabern,' and calling upon its members and other German societies to boycott and withhold their patronage and support from the plaintiff's said theatre," to its great damage.

The first article is alleged to have been published in the New Yorker Staats-Zeitung on the 29th day of January, 1914, and the English translation thereof, with the innuendoes in brackets, is as follows:

> Well, last night there was given by Adolf Philipp [meaning the President and Treasurer of the plaintiff], in the 57th Street Theatre [meaning the said plaintiff's theatre], Zabern, a military drama, in three acts, by F. Schumacher, the great bait, still more, German baiting [meaning and charging that the said play Zabern has for its object baiting or harassing or annoying the Germans].
>
> After the second act [meaning the second act of the play Zabern] the first night claque had hardly begun [meaning and intending to convey that the public applause was not genuine, but persons were hired to applaud], there was Manager Philipp [meaning the President and Treasurer of the plaintiff] already on the stage. He declared it to be a true pleasure to prove how unpartisan the play was maintained. This downright insult [meaning that the statement attributed to Mr. Philipp was an insult to the intelligence of the audience] was superfluous. Whoever of those present yesterday [meaning the audience who witnessed the performance] had the German feeling—and that is, indeed, thank God, the strong point of the German-American—had it clearly before him already that Zabern [meaning the play produced by the plaintiff] is a point-blank malevolent biased play [meaning that the play was maliciously biased against Germans] not as Mr. Philipp [meaning the plaintiff's President and Treasurer] expressed it, "a free word in a free land." To characterize that thing in short [meaning the play Zabern] one can, indeed, say, an anti-German play [meaning that the play Zabern is principally anti-German] which ostensibly plays in Alsace in front of a scenic design that comes from "Auction Pinochle," and depicts Russian conditions [meaning thereby to ridicule the said play by referring to it as a "thing" and the production thereof, by imputing to the plaintiff an intent to make the audience believe that a scene from an old play, "Auction Pinochle," represents a scene in Alsace, and to incite ill-feeling and hatred on the part of the German-American population against the plaintiff and its said business, by asserting and conveying the belief that cruel and barbaric methods, usually attributed to the Russian Government, are depicted in the play Zabern, as being practiced by the German Government].
>
> Only that at the end [meaning at the end of the play Zabern] the one recruit, the grandson of an Alsace-French veteran of war, is especially shot to death before his grandfather and his sweetheart, is backstairs romance fiction—and affects, even without mentioning that in this act [meaning the last act of Zabern] the tricolor [meaning the French flag] is glorified and the black-white-red flag [meaning the German flag] is figuratively trampled under foot, like the typical stir-mush [meaning and intending thereby to ridicule the said play Zabern as a composition of fiction called the back-stairs romance variety which appeals to the lower classes and that the whole play is a senseless and un-

interesting conglomeration referred to as a "stir-mush," and meaning and intending to incite hatred in the hearts and minds of the patriotic German population in this country against the plaintiff and its business, by asserting that in the play Zabern the German flag is being insulted and derided to an extent equal to that of trampling under foot].

The second article is alleged to have been published in the Sonntagsblatt der New Yorker Staats-Zeitung on the 1st day of February, 1914, and the English translation, with the innuendoes, is as follows:

If after my thorough utterance on Thursday [meaning and referring to the utterance hereinbefore quoted] concerning Zabern, the so-called military play by F. Schumacher, for which [meaning the play Zabern] Mr. Ad. Philipp [meaning the President and Treasurer of the plaintiff] has taken out an American copyright and which [meaning the play Zabern] he [meaning the said President and Treasurer of the plaintiff] has presented to the German theatregoers, I still find space here for a supplemental remark, it is this:

We leave as undecided what a German theatre manager [meaning and referring to the plaintiff] actually has in view by the production of Zabern [meaning the play Zabern] whether he too [meaning the plaintiff's President as producer of the said play Zabern] has only an eye for mammon or if he [meaning plaintiff's President and Treasurer] even gazed toward Paris with button-hole ache—[meaning a craving for honors from France], he has at least earned the red ribbon, if not, indeed, the rosette [meaning and intending to ridicule the plaintiff and its officers, and provoke and excite the German population in this country against the plaintiff and its President, Adolf Philipp, who produced the play Zabern, by charging and intending to convey that the plaintiff and its said officer in producing the said play Zabern followed two selfish motives: greed for money and desire for honors from Paris, France, for ridiculing and abusing Germany by the production of the play Zabern]. No French, German-hating "shoemaker" could have so quickly cobbled together so biased a play [meaning the play Zabern] in which [meaning the play Zabern] a still quivering bleeding wound of Germany is made a show of [meaning and intending to convey that the play Zabern produced by the plaintiff is worse and more biased against Germany than any such as might have been composed by any "shoemaker" who hates Germany, the word "shoemaker" in quotation marks being used to impute to a person roughness and ignorance]. And in New York [meaning in the adaptation of the play Zabern by the plaintiff] there was then evidently stirred into the thick, sticky mush of the play [meaning the play Zabern] all sorts of so-called "spice," all sorts of worn-out burlesque, which already served in various Philipp-kind popular plays [meaning that indecent, commonly known as spicy, matter from other plays formerly produced by Adolf Philipp was used in the play Zabern]. This [meaning the matter alleged to have been stirred into the play Zabern] is worse than the Schumacher-kind caricature [meaning the original play Zabern] of the evil Zabern chapter [meaning the occurrences at Zabern on which the play was founded].

Zabern [meaning the play Zabern], as one sees it in 57th Street [meaning the plaintiff's theatre], with the scenery of an upper Italian mountain lake, with its North German, Bavarian and Austrian "Alsatians," its caricatures in uniform [meaning and intending to ridicule and incite hostile feeling of the German-Americans against the plaintiff's production of the play Zabern by asserting that caricatures in uniforms are therein represented as German Army officers] is no play, it is a lampoon. One could crack as miserable jokes about it [meaning the play Zabern] as those which come from the stage [meaning in the play Zabern] were not the whole matter, and even more, the production of this play [meaning the play Zabern] in New York [meaning at the plaintiff's theatre] so lamentable a matter to the perceptive German-Americans [meaning the German residents in America who uphold the dignity of their nationality].

The third article is alleged to have been published in the New Yorker Staats-Zeitung on the 3d day of February, 1914, and the English translation, with the innuendoes, is as follows:

The German Kriegerbund protests against "insults to German officers" [meaning that the production of the play "Zabern" by the plaintiff was an insult to German officers].

That the Zabern affair [meaning the occurrence at Zabern] is also playing over here to us, was noticed last week when the comedy Zabern attained its first American production at Philipp's Theatre [meaning the plaintiff's theatre]. The Board of Managers of the German Kriegerbund [a certain German society entitled Kriegerbund, which means in English "Warriors' League"] presided over by Pres. Chr. Rebhan, yesterday unanimously adopted the following resolution, after the gentlemen had rendered their report of their visit to the theatre [meaning the plaintiff's theatre] and the things which they have there seen and heard [meaning at the performance of the plaintiff's production of Zabern]:

"Whereas the military play entitled 'Zabern,' which is being produced every evening in the German theatre managed by Adolf Philipp [meaning and referring to the President and Treasurer of the plaintiff corporation], at 57th Street, near Third Avenue [meaning and referring to the plaintiff's theatre], which [meaning the plaintiff's play Zabern], because of the frivolous, shameless and impure representations of the German military scandal, must excite public vexation in all well-thinking German-Americans [meaning the German population in this country and intending to excite and provoke hostile sentiment among such German-Americans against the plaintiff's business for its alleged unpatriotic tendency, and to incite and create hatred of the German public against the plaintiff and its officers, the adapter of the play Zabern, by asserting and seeking to create an impression that the play Zabern produced by the plaintiff, intentionally and brazenly, by impure and immoral motives, so misrepresents and derides the German military to its discredit, disparagement and detriment, as to hurt the feelings of every well-thinking German living in America]; and

"Whereas in this play [meaning the play Zabern produced by the plaintiff] the German army, and especially the position of its officers, is being derided, ridiculed and slandered in the unworthiest manner; the German flag having been trampled under foot in the mud [meaning to provoke the German public against the plaintiff's production by charging that, in the play Zabern the German flag is being publicly and intentionally abused], that even the German Imperial Family [Kaiserhaus] was, through a falsely composed telegram of the Kronprinz [meaning the Crown Prince of the Empire of Germany] drawn into this scandalous performance [meaning the performance of the play Zabern and intending to create ill-feeling and hostility against the plaintiff's theatre and the performance rendered therein, by intimating and giving the impression that in said play Zabern, the Crown Prince of the Empire of Germany is falsely represented as having sent a certain telegram, the contents of which were falsely composed, for the purpose of casting reflection upon and discrediting the German Crown Prince and the German Imperial family on a public stage before an audience of German people]; and

"Whereas on account of this nightly repeated play, our entire population [meaning the German population] is damaged in its esteem of other nations in this country [meaning the United States of America, and charging that the play Zabern produced by the plaintiff, depicts and represents the Germans in such an offensive and disparaging light as to incite and cause disrespect and hatred of the German population in this country by people of other nationalities]; so

"Be it Resolved that the German 'Kriegerbund' [Soldiers' or Warriors' League] quite energetically rise in protest against further performance of this scandalous play [meaning the play Zabern produced by the plaintiff], and all German Societies be requested to adopt similar energetic resolutions and that every German, who still has some national pride in him, must stay away from such scandalous play [meaning and intending to convey to the public that the play Zabern produced by the plaintiff herein, is so scandalous and so abusive to the Germans and is intended to so hurt the feelings and the national pride of every German as to make said play unfit to be seen by any German, and meaning to urge and urging all German societies to adopt resolutions, whereby their members will be pledged not to visit the performance of the said play Zabern at the plaintiff's theatre, and meaning to intimidate, and intimidating every German that if he visited the said play Zabern at the plaintiff's theatre, he would be deemed by his countrymen to be devoid of national pride]."

The fourth article is alleged to have been published in the Abendblatt der New Yorker Staats-Zeitung on the same day, and it is precisely the same as the third article.

The fifth article is alleged to have been published in the Abendblatt der New Yorker Staats-Zeitung on the 6th day of February, 1914, and the English translation, with the innuendoes, is as follows:

At the meeting of the New York German Druggists' Society held on February 5th, 1914, ex-Pres. Schleussner proposed the following resolution, which was unanimously adopted:

"With indignation the members of the New York German Druggists' Society have taken cognizance of the fact that a local German theatre manager [meaning the plaintiff] has made use of the Zabern occurrence [meaning the occurrence at Zabern reported in the newspapers as aforesaid] in the most disgusting manner as an object of sensation, solely for the sake of the beloved dollar, to make profit out of the same. It is this lamentable occurrence [meaning the production of the play Zabern at the plaintiff's theatre], a direct blow in the face to all those who have guarded their pride in their German parentage [meaning and intending to provoke ill-feeling of the German-Americans against the plaintiff and its said theatre and its production, by charging that the production of the play Zabern by the plaintiff was intended as a gross insult to the pride of the German population here]. Our Society, which has always upheld its German spirit, cannot refrain from condemning, in the severest manner, this conduct devoid of every feeling of decency [meaning the plaintiff's act in producing the said play Zabern].

"The Druggists' Association hopes that other German societies also will join in this protest and that the Germans of New York will teach the gentleman in question [meaning the plaintiff and producer of the play Zabern] a lesson by not visiting the theatre [meaning the theatre conducted by this plaintiff].

"The German Press of New York is most courteously requested to take notice of this resolution and to publish the same in its columns."

The sixth article is alleged to have been published in the New Yorker Staats-Zeitung on the 7th day of February, 1914, and is the same as the fifth, excepting that the last paragraph was not repeated therein.

The seventh article is alleged to have been published in the New Yorker Staats-Zeitung on the 17th day of February, 1914, and the English translation, with innuendoes, is as follows:

"The German National Merchants also protest against the performance of the play [meaning plaintiff's production of the play Zabern].

"Also the local group of the 'Deutschnationale Handlungsgehilfen Verbandes' [German National Commercial Clerks' Association] (Headquarters, Hamburg) District North America, which, with its 150,000 members, the largest mercantile society, which maintains ten local groups in the [United States], Canada and Mexico, and is spread over the entire world with a total of 1400 local groups, takes a position against the production of the bungling piece 'Zabern' [meaning the said play 'Zabern'] in the Adolf Philipp Theatre here [meaning the plaintiff's said theatre]. The writing of the Society to the Manager of the theatre [meaning the plaintiff] reads:

"To the Management of the Adolf Philipp Theatre, 57th St. and 3rd Av., New York.

"True to our German National principles and in the spirit of the aims of our largest mercantile association, numbering 150,000 members, we hereby also protest against the production of that miserable, bungling piece of work 'Zabern' [meaning the play Zabern produced by the plaintiff]. Although we do not expect a practical success, as the Management [meaning the plaintiff] apparently cares more for a box office success than for the reputation of German stage art in a foreign country, we regret nevertheless that this practice should be made use of to injure the esteem, honor and reputation of the Germans. Our pity is for the German actors [meaning the actors in the employ of the plaintiff connected with the performance of Zabern] who, perhaps, 'obeying compulsion not their own liking' must offer nightly that spurious (or basest) art [meaning the performance of Zabern] to a sensation-seeking audience [meaning and intending to injure the plaintiff in its business and destroy the value of its property by inciting and provoking the German public to hatred of and prejudice against the plaintiff and its business and property, by charging and asserting that the production of Zabern in the plaintiff's theatre is not only inartistic and deserving of no practical success, but that said production was made use of by the plaintiff to injure the Germans in their esteem, honor and reputation]. A manager would never dare to bring before an Irish, French or Jewish audience a villification of its country or of its national characteristics, such as is offered to the German element in New York in 'Zabern' [meaning the plaintiff's production].

"Calling herewith also upon the other mercantile associations to join in our protest [meaning in the protest against the plaintiff's production of Zabern] we would like, at the same time, to express our recognition to the management of Christians of the Irving Place Theatre [meaning the competitors of the plaintiff in New York] for its earnest endeavors to again bring esteem and honor to the German stage in New York [meaning and intending thereby to urge the public generally to condemn the plaintiff's theatre and to urge the German theatregoers to prefer the plaintiff's competitor for alleged efforts to restore the honor of the Germans which, it alleges, the plaintiff has offended]."

The eighth article is alleged to have been published in the Abendblatt der New Yorker Staats-Zeitung on the 17th of February, 1914, and is precisely the same as the seventh.

The ninth article is alleged to have been published in the Sonntagsblatt der New Yorker Staats-Zeitung on the 22d day of February, 1914, and the English translation, with the innuendoes, is as follows:

Later in the course of the evening [referring to an alleged meeting held by a certain German society] a resolution of protest in the form of an open letter against the production in the Adolf Philipp Theatre [meaning the plaintiff's theatre] of the scandalous play "Zabern" which villifies German patriotism, was passed by the meeting.

The first point to be decided is whether there is a sufficient allegation of special damages, for, if so, all counts of the complaint are good, and the demurrer was properly overruled. There is no allegation with respect to the amount that plaintiff was offered for the English rights for the production of the play, or with respect to the damages sustained by the withdrawal thereof. There is no allegation that any particular patron or patrons of the theatre, who otherwise would have attended, remained away on account of the publication; nor is there any allegation of any particular loss of box-office receipts on account of any of the publications. The allegations with respect to the withdrawal of the offer for the English rights, and instigating a boycott against the plaintiff's theatre, are the only ones which it is or could be claimed constitute allegations of special damage. The general rule applicable to actions for libel and slander is, that if special damages are claimed they must be expressly alleged, and with such particularity as to enable defendant to meet the charge, and in this respect such actions are unlike those in which the defendant's remedy is for a bill of particulars if the damages are not alleged with sufficient definiteness. Reporters' Assn. v. Sun Printing & Pub. Assn., 186 N.Y. 437. I am, therefore, of [the] opinion that such special damages are not alleged, and that the sufficiency of each cause of action depends upon whether the article therein quoted was published of and concerning the plaintiff and was libelous per se with respect to the plaintiff.

It is to be borne in mind that the articles were all published in German. They are alleged in the complaint as published in the German language, and this is followed by the English translation thereof, with the innuendoes in brackets. Each of the articles relates to the production of this play at the plaintiff's theatre; but neither the corporate name of the plaintiff nor that of the theatre is given, and it is charged that the production was given by Adolf Philipp at the Philipp Theatre, or the Fifty-seventh Street Theatre. The plaintiff claims that each of the articles libeled it in its business. The defendant claims that it is not shown and cannot be made to appear by innuendo that the articles were in any respect published of or concerning the plaintiff, for the reason that they relate principally to the authorship of the play and to Philipp individually as an actor, playwright and theatrical manager. I am of opinion that there is no force in this contention. We are not now concerned with those parts of the articles relating to Philipp individually or with the motive of the author of the play; but in so far as they reflect upon the management of the theatre, and the character of the play it was producing, and the motive underlying its production by the plaintiff, they are sufficiently shown to have been published of and concerning the plaintiff by the mere allegation that the plaintiff is the lessee of the theatre and producing the play threat, and no innuendoes were necessary and, being superfluous, they are harmless. Soper v. Associated Press, 115 App. Div. 815, affd., 188 N.Y. 550; Nunnally v. New-Yorker Staats-Zeitung, 111 App. Div. 482; Weston v. Commercial Advertiser Assn., 184 N.Y. 479. See also Parker v. Bennett, 68 App. Div. 148.

If the articles merely constitute a libel or slander on the theatre or the play, as distinguished from the plaintiff and its business and the nature and management thereof, then they would fall within the rule that an action for libeling a "place or thing" will not lie without allegation and proof of special damages. See Marlin Fire Arms Co. v. Shields, 171 N.Y. 384, 390; Maglio v. New York Herald Co., 83 App. Div. 44, 93 id. 546; Kennedy v. Press Pub. Co., 41 Hun. 422; Le Massena v. Storm, 62 App. Div. 150; Bosi v. New York Herald Co., 33 Misc. Rep. 622, affd., 58 App. Div. 619; Felt v. Germania Life Ins. Co., 149 id. 14. I am of opinion that the articles relate to the theatrical business conducted by the plaintiff and to the plaintiff's production of the play "Zabern," and, therefore, they relate to the plaintiff's business. It is now well settled that an article may be libelous per se against a corporation. There is, however, a marked difference between an action by an individual for libel and one by a corporation, inasmuch as the basis of an action by an individual is usually the injury to his private character and reputation, whereas those elements are necessarily eliminated in an action by a corporation, which can only be damaged by an attack upon its business methods of a nature calculated and tending to injuriously affect it pecuniarily in its business reputation and credit; but when it may fairly be inferred from a malicious and false publication that it will injuriously affect the corporation in its business and credit, then the article is libelous per se and damages are presumed. Reporters' Assn. v. Sun Printing & Pub. Assn., 186 N.Y. 437; Arrow Steamship Co. v. Bennett, 73 Hun. 81; Town Topics Pub. Co. v. Collier, 114 App. Div. 191; Kemble & Mills v. Kaighn, 131 id. 63; Mutual Reserve Fund Life Assn. v. Spectator Co., 50 N.Y. Super. Ct. [18 J. & S.] 460; Union Associated Press v. Heath, 49 App. Div. 247; New York Bureau of Information v. Ridgway-Thayer Co., dissenting opinion of Ingraham, J., 119 id. 339, on which the judgment was reversed, 193 N.Y. 666. See also Moore v. Francis, 121 N.Y. 199; Davey v. Davey, 22 Misc. Rep. 668. The demurrer admits the facts alleged, including the application of the words published as charged in the innuendoes, in so far as they are susceptible of the meaning ascribed to them by the innuendoes; but an innuendo can neither extend nor enlarge the publication, and where the article is not libelous on its face with appropriate innuendoes showing its application, and becomes so only by reference to extrinsic facts, such facts must be alleged in traversable form, for they relate to the substance and not to the application of the charge, and if the article be libelous per se or may be on the facts as found by the jury, it is immaterial whether or not it is susceptible of another meaning ascribed in the innuendo. Van Heusen v. Argenteau, 194 N.Y. 309; Parker v. Bennett, supra; Morrison v. Smith, 177 N.Y. 366; Fleischmann v. Bennett, 87 id. 231; Hoey v. N.Y. Times Co., 138 App. Div. 149.

The press is accorded, for the public interests, a qualified privilege to discuss and criticise the management of and productions at a theatre to which the public are invited, and this privilege in the absence of actual malice extends even to ridicule and is without limitation; but since it is accorded for the benefit of the public only and the guidance of public opinion and taste, when the discussion or criticism exceeds the bounds of fair and honest criticism, and becomes an intemperate, aspersive attack upon the motive of the management of the theatre, or the character of the production thereat, an evil and malicious motive for the publication may be inferred; and if found to exist, the publication is not protected by the qualified privilege, but may, of course, be justified by absence of malice or by pleading and proving that it was true. Triggs v. Sun Printing & Pub. Assn., 179 N.Y. 144; Hamilton v. Eno, 81 id. 116; Hoey v. N.Y. Times Co., supra. See also Klinck v. Colby, 46 N.Y. 427; Ashcroft v. Hammond, 197 id. 488; Laughton v. Bishop of Sodor and Man, L. R. [1871-1873] 4 P.C. 495, 505.

It only remains to apply these general principles to the alleged libelous articles and to decide whether, in the light thereof, they are libelous per se. I do not deem it necessary, and it would unduly lengthen this opinion, to separately analyze and discuss the different articles. It is evident to me, on reading them in the light of these rules of law, that some of them do not exceed the bounds of fair and honest criticism, and do not necessarily tend to injure the plaintiff in its business and credit, and although the line of demarcation is not so well defined that the task is easy, I am of opinion that the alleged libelous articles set forth in the first, second and ninth counts fall in this category. On the other hand, it is quite clear that the articles which are the bases of the other causes of action alleged are not protected by the qualified privilege, for they are not confined to criticism of the play and to informing the public with respect to the nature thereof, or of defendant's views concerning it, but constitute aspersive attacks in violent and intemperate language upon the plaintiff's business and upon its motive in producing the play by what are conceded by the demurrer to be false charges with respect to the character of the play that are calculated and expressly stated to be intended to induce the German-speaking public to refrain from patronizing the theatre, and thereby to inflict damages upon the plaintiff.

It follows, therefore, that the order, in so far as it overrules the demurrer to the first, second and ninth causes of action should be reversed, with ten dollars costs and disbursements, and in all other respects affirmed, without costs, but with leave to defendant to withdraw its demurrer to the other causes of action and to answer.

DOWLING, Justice, dissenting.

Where the proprietor of a theatre, for the sake of profit, deliberately places upon the stage a production which is bound to arouse controversy by the nature of its subject, or the manner of its treatment, and particularly where he offers for popular patronage a play which is offensive to the racial or religious sentiments of such public, or any considerable portion thereof, he must accept not only criticism of his offering but of his motives in voluntarily challenging the open hostility of the community at large, or of such section of it as he has chosen to attack. Instances are not wanting where such attack has been deliberately made with the hope of consequent profit from the section of the community holding different views from the one attacked. In so far as the articles complained of referred to the business conducted by the plaintiff, they were criticisms directed against an enterprise which, while posing as a German theatre, and appealing for support solely to the German element in New York city, for reasons of its own chose to present a play which was repugnant to the ideas of Germans who still entertained an affection for the country of their birth. The feeling of hostility which might reasonably be supposed to be aroused by such a course of conduct was aggravated by the presentation of this play, having to do with the German military system, at a time when Germany's relations with at least one other nation referred to were strained. For the proprietors of a German theatre to present a play involving issues vital to Germany and lying at the very root of the controversial issues then being vigorously debated, it seems to me was an open invitation to a discussion by Germans of its methods and motives which was bound to be severe and perhaps could not escape being abusive. So far as the English translation of these articles discloses, they contain such criticism as might be expected to be called for in response to the plaintiff's production of the play, and having in view all the conditions under which the play was produced and the articles published, I do not think that they are libelous, or that they go further than might naturally be expected under such circumstances. There being no appropriate allegation of special damage, and the articles in my opinion not being libelous per se, I believe the demurrers to all the causes of action should have been sustained.

PHANTOM TOURING, INC. v. AFFILIATED PUBLICATIONS
953 F.2d 724 (1st Cir.), cert. denied, 504 U.S. 974 (1992)

COFFIN, Senior Circuit Judge.

Appellant Phantom Touring Company produces a musical-comedy version of "The Phantom of the Opera" that is not the hugely successful, widely acclaimed Broadway show later created by Andrew Lloyd Webber. In a series of articles published in late 1989, the Boston Globe queried, in a disparaging tone, whether appellant's advertising made the distinction between the two "Phantoms" clear to the ticket-buying public. Appellant sued for defamation, claiming that the newspaper falsely accused it of a deliberate effort to pass off its show—dubbed the "Fake Phantom"—as "the real thing." The district court dismissed the complaint on the ground that the articles contained only statements of opinion protected by the First Amendment. We agree that none of the articles is actionable and, therefore, affirm. (The complaint also contained causes of action for interference with contractual rights and interference with prospective business advantage. Appellant does not press these claims on appeal.)

I
Background

The original "Phantom of the Opera" is a 1911 novel by Gaston Leroux, which is now in the public domain and therefore available for adaptation by anyone who chooses to make use of it. Appellant's version, a musical comedy show featuring the music of several classical composers, was created by British playwright Ken Hill and performed publicly for the first time in 1977 at the Duke's Playhouse in England. In 1984, the Hill production again was staged in England, where Andrew Lloyd Webber saw it. Webber and Hill began negotiations to bring the show to London's West End, but nothing ever came of the collaboration. Instead, Webber wrote and, in October 1986, opened his own "Phantom" in London. The Webber production, a drama with an original musical score, became what the Globe termed a "megahit." In January 1988, Webber's "Phantom" opened in New York. Meanwhile, in July 1986, Hill's "Phantom" was revived for a short run in St. Louis. It attracted the attention of Jonathon Reinis, a theatre producer, who brought the show to San Francisco for a nine-month run beginning in September 1988. Buoyed by the show's success in San Franciso, Reinis and others formed the appellant Phantom Touring Company to take the show on a national tour that included a visit to the Wang Center in Boston.

In September 1989, about a week before tickets for Hill's "Phantom" at the Wang were to go on sale, the Globe published the first of a number of articles suggesting that ticket buyers should be wary of Hill's "Fake Phantom." According to the article, headlined "The Phantom of 'The Phantom,'" Hill had been "thriving off the confusion created by the two productions." The article quoted a drama critic for The Washington Post who said Hill's version "'bears as much resemblance to its celebrated counterpart as Jell-O does to Baked Alaska,'" and who further described the show as "'a rip-off, a fraud, a scandal, a snake-oil job.'" This story and at least one other that followed not only pointed out that Hill was benefitting from mistaken identity, but also suggested that the confusion was intentional. The newspaper observed that the show was being advertised in bold type as "The Original London Stage Musical." While technically accurate, since Hill's production in fact predated Webber's, the notice appeared to the Globe to be drawing heavily on the reputation of the Webber show.

Appellant filed suit in November 1989 [against the owners of the Boston Globe and two individual writers, Kevin Kelly and Patti Hartigan], alleging that the Globe articles contained false and defamatory statements and innuendo concerning Phantom Touring. The complaint referred to numerous specific phrases and words in the articles as well as to an alleged underlying message that the plaintiff was dishonest and intentionally misleading or cheating the public.

Defendants moved for judgment on the pleadings pursuant to Fed. R. Civ. P. 12(c) and, in a brief order written on the face of the motion, the district court ruled for the Globe. It explained its decision as follows:

> I have carefully examined the publications and conclude that in context they contain only protected expression of opinion and do not imply criminal conduct on the part of the plaintiffs.

Appellant unsuccessfully moved for reconsideration and, following the Supreme Court's decision in Milkovich v. Lorain Journal Co., 110 S. Ct. 2695, 111 L. Ed. 2d 1 (1990), which clarified the principles governing the First Amendment's protection of statements of opinion, urged the district judge to vacate its ruling. The district court denied appellant's motion, holding, without discussion, that "the judgment should stand even in the light of Milkovich."

In this appeal, Phantom Touring contends that the district court's decision reflects the erroneous view that all of the disputed statements in the Globe articles were privileged under the First Amendment simply because they could be classified as opinion. Appellant argues that a careful analysis of the articles, in light of the principles set out in Milkovich, demonstrates that it is entitled to jury consideration of its libel claim. In the next section, we describe briefly how Milkovich affected defamation law and why application of the principles expressed in that opinion require us to affirm the district court's judgment.

II
Discussion

A. Legal Framework

In Milkovich, the Supreme Court dismissed the notion that there is a "wholesale defamation exemption for anything that might be labeled 'opinion.'" 110 S. Ct. at 2705. It concluded that the relevant question is not whether challenged language may be described as an opinion, but whether it reasonably would be understood to declare or imply provable assertions of fact. See id. at 2707.

Notwithstanding its rejection of a specific "opinion" privilege, the Court assured that opinions about matters of public concern would continue to receive substantial constitutional protection under various extant First Amendment principles. It reaffirmed three propositions which are relevant to our consideration of this case in its present posture. The first, of "foremost" importance, is the principle established in Philadelphia Newspapers, Inc. v. Hepps, 475 U.S. 767, 106 S. Ct. 1558, 89 L. Ed. 2d 783 (1986), that statements made by a media defendant "must be provable as false" before there can be defamation liability. 110 S. Ct. at 2706. The Court reaffirmed that "Hepps ensures that a statement of opinion relating to matters of public concern which does not contain a provably false factual connotation will receive full constitutional protection." Id. (footnote omitted). Thus, a statement such as, "That's the worst play I've ever seen," would be protected not because it is labeled an opinion but because it is so subjective that it is not "susceptible of being proved true or false," id. at 2707.

Secondly, Milkovich emphasized a line of cases establishing protection for statements that "cannot 'reasonably [be] interpreted as stating actual facts' about an individual," 110 S. Ct. at 2706 (quoting Hustler Magazine, Inc. v. Falwell, 485 U.S. 46, 50, 108 S. Ct. 876, 99 L. Ed. 2d 41 (1988) (involving ad parody)). See also Letter Carriers v. Austin, 418 U.S. 264, 284-86, 94 S. Ct. 2770, 2781-82, 41 L. Ed. 2d 745 (1974) (use of the word "traitor" not basis for defamation action since used "in a loose, figurative sense"); Greenbelt Cooperative Publishing Ass'n, Inc. v. Bresler, 398 U.S. 6, 14, 90 S. Ct. 1537, 26 L. Ed. 2d 6 (1970) (the word "blackmail" not actionable in context). These cases explicitly protect "rhetorical hyperbole" and other types of "imaginative expression" that writers use to enliven their prose. 110 S. Ct. at 2706. For example, a theater critic who wrote that, "The producer who decided to charge admission for that show is committing highway robbery," would be immune from liability because no reasonable listener would understand the speaker to be accusing the producer of the actual crime of robbery.

In addition to considering whether the challenged speech contained "loose, figurative, or hyperbolic language which would negate the impression" that a factual statement was being made, id. at 2707, the Court also indicated that the context in which language appears must be evaluated to see whether "the general tenor of the article negates this impression," id. Thus, while eschewing the fact/opinion terminology, Milkovich did not depart from the multi-factored analysis that had been employed for some time by lower courts seeking to distinguish between actionable fact and nonactionable opinion. See, e.g., McCabe v. Rattiner, 814 F.2d 839, 842 (1st Cir. 1987) (adopting totality of the circumstances analysis); Ollman v. Evans, 750 F.2d 970, 974-75 (D.C. Cir. 1984) (en banc) (same).

Finally, the Court referred to what we would characterize as a safety valve determination, in which we are obliged to "'make an independent examination of the whole record,'" Milkovich, 110 S. Ct. at 2705 (quoting Bose Corp. v. Consumers Union of United States, Inc., 466 U.S. 485, 499, 104 S. Ct. 1949, 80 L. Ed. 2d 502 (1984) (quotation omitted)), to "assure that the foregoing determinations will be made in a manner so as not to 'constitute a forbidden intrusion on the field of free expression,'" id. at 2707 (quoting Bose, 466 U.S. at 499 (quotation omitted)).

B. Application of the Legal Principles

In its complaint, appellant referred to six articles that appeared in the Globe between September 22 and October 7, 1989. One of those articles is not discussed in the brief on appeal, and we therefore assume that appellant does not seek review of the district court's decision with respect to that article. Appellant does argue in its appellate brief, however, that another article, one not cited in the complaint, was defamatory. The story, "'Phantom' Confusion Still Flaring," was published on October 13, 1989, before appellant filed its complaint. We believe this article is not properly before us, and therefore decline to consider it. Accordingly, we turn to our consideration of the remaining five articles.

In our view, most of the challenged language is easily identified as non-actionable under the principles outlined in Milkovich. Many of the statements cited in the complaint and appellate brief either constitute obviously protected hyperbole or are not susceptible of being proved true or false. Such, for example, is the language in "The Phantom of the 'Phantom'" quoting a critic who described the Hill production as "a rip-off, a fraud, a scandal, a snake-oil job." Not only is this commentary figurative and hyperbolic, but we also can imagine no objective evidence to disprove it. Whether appellant's "Phantom" is "fake" or "phony" is similarly unprovable, since those adjectives admit of numerous interpretations. See McCabe v. Rattiner, 814 F.2d at 842 ("The lack of precision [in the meaning of the word 'scam'] makes the assertion 'X is a scam' incapable of being proven true or false.").

Appellant's claim of defamation is patently deficient with respect to one news story, "Ticket Buyers are Still Hot for 'Phantom,'" because the article lacks any even arguably defamatory assertions.

In our view, appellant's claim of defamation is colorable in only one respect. Two of the contested articles, both columns written by theater critic Kevin Kelly, contain language insinuating that Phantom Touring was marketing its production dishonestly—that it deliberately was confusing the public. The first such statement appears in "The Phantom of the 'Phantom'" [hereafter "The Phantom 'Phantom'"], [while the] second reference appears in "Canny, Confusing Marketing for This 'Phantom'" [hereafter "Canny Marketing"].

Arguably, the connotation of deliberate deception is sufficiently factual to be proved true or false, and therefore is vulnerable under Milkovich. To rebut the implied assertion, appellant might be able to present objective evidence demonstrating longstanding plans to take its "Phantom" on a nationwide tour of the United States, or evidence showing that the "Original London production" language in its advertising was developed before Webber's "Phantom" rose to prominence, and thus was not designed to deceive consumers.

Whether or not the allegation of intentional deception meets the "provable as true or false" criterion, however, we think the context of each article rendered the language not reasonably interpreted as stating "actual facts" about appellant's honesty. The sum effect of the format, tone and entire content of the articles is to make it unmistakably clear that Kelly was expressing a point of view only. As such, the challenged language is immune from liability.

The nonfactual nature of Kelly's articles is indicated at first glance by the format. Both appeared as a regularly run theater column, a type of article generally known to contain more opinionated writing than the typical news report. The structure and tone of the language reinforced this subjective design. In "The Phantom 'Phantom,'" for example, the question of appellant's dishonesty was posed rhetorically and then immediately defused by Reinis' lengthy response:

> So the question comes down to, is Hill & Company trying to score off the success of Andrew Lloyd Webber's "Phantom"?
>
> "Whatever confusion there is between the two," Reinis said, "it's about time Ken Hill got his just desserts," a statement implying that Hill has been ill used

by Webber and [his producer] Mackintosh. "They've wished us luck. Our attitude is: we're not Andrew Lloyd Webber's 'Phantom.' We say that clearly in the ads. We're not a melodrama. We're musical comedy in the old-fashioned sense. We're nothing near the scope and size of Webber's 'Phantom.' We're an evening's event for entertainment. Our attitude is, you can enjoy both for completely different reasons."

In "Canny Marketing," the issue again was raised as a question posed to the Wang Center's manager, and Kelly's snide, exasperated language indicated that his comments represented his personal appraisal of the factual information contained in the article:

> When it was suggested to Josiah Spaulding, who heads the Wang (and wags it), that, surely, he must be aware the incoming "Phantom"—a musical comedy by Ken Hill—is deliberately confusing people; that, in fact, it wouldn't be on tour at all if the Webber "Phantom" had not become the megahit it has, he said to me, "We're not in the business of denying any genre to come here and rent the hall."

Of greatest importance, however, is the breadth of Kelly's articles, which not only discussed all the facts underlying his views but also gave information from which readers might draw contrary conclusions. In effect, the articles offered a self-contained give-and-take, a kind of verbal debate between Kelly and those persons responsible for booking and marketing appellant's "Phantom." Because all sides of the issue, as well as the rationale for Kelly's view, were exposed, the assertion of deceit reasonably could be understood only as Kelly's personal conclusion about the information presented, not as a statement of fact.

Kelly explained, for example, that he considered appellant's advertising to be misleading—despite Hill's accurate claim to be the "original" London production—because

> it is the Webber "Phantom" that is currently the big hit in London, and has been since it opened in 1986. It is the Webber "Phantom" that has broken box office records wherever it has played. It is the Webber "Phantom" that's original. Hill uses music from Verdi, Gounod, Offenbach, Mozart and Donizetti. Webber wrote his own. Hill's is a self-styled "melodramatic spoof." Webber's has a serious book written by himself and Richard Stilgoe.

Kelly also made clear that he doubted appellant's marketing sincerity because—while distinguishing between the two "Phantoms" in its advertising—it did so discreetly, reserving "the big type...for the show's resonant title with a banner head reading 'The Original London Stage Musical.'" The articles additionally reveal that Kelly's judgment about the advertising was based at least in part on his subjective view that Hill's show lacked artistic merit; it must be the result of deceptive marketing, he implied, if "a spoof without stars or anyone of theatrical name value" could produce $400,000 in ticket sales in a few days. Cf. United States Medical Corp. v. M.D. Buyline, Inc., 753 F. Supp. 676, 677, 679 (S.D. Ohio 1990) (no background facts offered to readers to explain statement that plaintiff "consistently gouges customers on price and service").

On the other hand, Kelly forthrightly reported that not everyone shared his artistic judgment, and that the Hill production had encountered its fair share of success. In "The Phantom 'Phantom,'" he quoted producer Reinis' report that 200,000 people saw the production during a lengthy run in San Francisco, as well as Reinis' claim that "critics may not like us, but audiences do." This competing information about the merit of Hill's "Phantom" underscored the personal and nonfactual nature of Kelly's views about the production and its attendant publicity.

Kelly's full disclosure of the facts underlying his judgment—none of which have been challenged as false—makes this case fundamentally different from Milkovich. The column found actionable there focused on a court decision reversing an administrative ruling that had suspended a high school wrestling team from a tournament because of a brawl at an earlier meet. The column was headlined, "Maple [Heights High School] Beat the Law with the 'Big Lie,'" and the writer's theory was that school officials had lied at the court hearing in order to persuade the judge to overrule the athletic association's decision. See 110 S. Ct. at 2698 n.2.

The reporter had not been at the judicial proceeding. The column noted, however, that he had been the only non-involved person at both the controversial meet and the administrative hearing, a fact that could have suggested to readers that he was uniquely situated to draw the inference of lying. The column contained no response from the targets of the criticism.

Thus, the article in Milkovich, unlike Kelly's "Phantom" columns, was not based on facts accessible to everyone. Indeed, a reader reasonably could have understood the reporter in Milkovich to be suggesting that he was singularly capable of evaluating the plaintiffs' conduct. In contrast, neither of Kelly's columns indicated that he, or anyone else, had more information about Phantom Touring's marketing practices than was reported in the articles. While Kelly's readers implicitly were invited to draw their own conclusions from the mixed information provided, the Milkovich readers implicitly were told that only one conclusion was possible. This is a crucial distinction, and it makes it clear why the result reached in Milkovich is inappropriate here.

In this case, the comprehensive nature of the information provided in the articles, aided by the column format and the style and tenor of the writing, lead inevitably to the conclusion that no reasonable reader could interpret Kelly's statements as factual assertions of dishonesty. Accordingly, under Milkovich, they are not actionable.

III
Conclusion

The Supreme Court in Milkovich reasserted its commitment to ensuring that debate on public issues remain "'uninhibited, robust, and wide-open,'" 110 S. Ct. at 2706 (quoting New York Times Co. v. Sullivan, 376 U.S. 254, 270, 84 S. Ct. 710, 11 L. Ed. 2d 686 (1964)), while acknowledging the countervailing concern that due weight be given to society's "'pervasive and strong interest in preventing and redressing attacks upon reputation,'" id. at 2707 (quoting Rosenblatt v. Baer, 383 U.S. 75, 86, 86 S. Ct. 669, 15 L. Ed. 2d 597 (1966)). For the reasons we have explained, the Globe articles tread a permissible path.

The judgment of the district court is therefore affirmed.

SOUL v. WRIGHT
1998-S-No. 1477 (Q.B. 2001)

STATEMENT IN OPEN COURT BEFORE MISTER JUSTICE GRAY

Graham Atkins, Claimant's Solicitor: Your Lordship, in this claim for libel I appear for the Claimant, and Mark Bateman appears for the Defendant. The Claimant is a well-known actor and performer, who over the course of a 35-year career has worked as an actor, singer, director and producer. He is perhaps best remembered for his role as Detective Ken Hutchinson in the long running international hit television series

"Starsky and Hutch" and a series of hit records in the 1970s. The Defendant was at all relevant times the "showbiz" correspondent of the Mirror with his own daily column called "Matthew Wright." He currently works as a television presenter.

This action arises from an article headed "Soul Destroying—Just 45 Turn Up for David's Show" which was published as the lead item in the Defendant's column in the Mirror on 13 October 1998. The article concerned a play named The Dead Monkey, a black comedy, which at the time of the article was showing at the Whitehall Theatre. The play was produced by the Claimant and his partner, Alexa Hamilton, both of whom played the leading roles. It was financed by a group of independent investors.

The article alleged that the production and the performance of the Claimant were so poor that members of the audience were laughing derisively at him and that he had pitifully instructed the ushers to beg anyone who wanted to walk out to return to their seats. It was stated that only 45 people turned up for Monday's night's show and that it would have made more sense to use the theatre to shelter the homeless. The attempt to sell a souvenir compact disc was also characterised as pitiful, the suggestion being that there were only two purchases on the night. It was also stated that the Claimant had ploughed his fortune into the play. The Defendant concluded that it was without doubt the worst West End show that he had ever seen. On the same day the Defendant repeated elements from the article on the GMTV breakfast show.

In fact, the Defendant had not seen the show but had sent a freelance journalist, Henrietta Knight, on his behalf. Contrary to what was stated in the article, the attendance for the performance in question (which was on a Thursday, there being no performance on Mondays) was around 130, which was well over half the capacity. The audience reaction was very positive and there had been no instructions from the Claimant or the Whitehall theatre to ushers to prevent any person from leaving. The souvenir compact disc sold out over the course of the run and there was nothing pitiful or inappropriate about the way in which it was sold. Furthermore, the Claimant had not financed the production.

The Claimant accepts that a reviewer is entitled to express his honest views about a play in forceful terms. However, he took legitimate objection to the fact that the Defendant had characterised the play as the worst that he had ever seen, without him actually having seen it, as well as the attacks on the Claimant in the article. He was not prepared to allow them to remain unchallenged and therefore brought these proceedings.

I am pleased to tell your Lordship that the Defendant is here today, through Mr. Bateman, to apologise to the Claimant for the inaccuracies in the article. He has also agreed to pay the Claimant a significant sum in damages together with his legal costs. Furthermore, a summary of this statement will be published in the Mirror newspaper. While the Claimant would have preferred that the article had not been published, he accepts that he has achieved all that he can by bringing these proceedings and feels suitably vindicated. He is prepared now to let the matter rest.

Mark Bateman, Defendant's Solicitor: I agree with what Mr. Atkins has said and offer the Defendant's apologies to the Claimant for the inaccuracies in the article. The article was written in the Defendant's column and it was his practice to write in the first person even when relying on information supplied by a third party. He maintains that he is entitled to express an opinion on the subject matter of a play, without himself having seen it.

Graham Atkins, Claimant's Solcitor: In the circumstances, I simply ask your Lordship for permission to withdraw the record.

Notes

1. As *Merivale* and *Adolf Philipp Co.* make clear, both English and American courts permit "fair criticism" of a play, but draw the line when it comes to matters that go beyond the work itself. This rule is felt to balance the needs of a free press with the privacy rights of individuals. However, where, as in *Phantom Touring*, the critic gives the person being written about an opportunity to respond, much greater leeway is permitted, particularly if the story is obviously being offered as "opinion," "commentary," or "gossip" rather than "hard news."

2. To get David Soul to drop his lawsuit against Matthew Wright, its former theater critic, the *Mirror* agree to pay £20,000 in damages and £150,000 in attorneys' fees. As a result of the settlement, Wright's claim that a critic need not see a play before expressing an opinion about it was not judicially tested. Soul, however, made it clear he disagreed with Wright's position: "I think it's a cornerstone of the theatre but you have to see the play, you have to be there, you have to have the facts." See Paul Kelso, *Monkey Business: Critic Costs Mirror £170,000 for Review of the Worst Play He'd Never Seen*, Guardian, Dec. 12, 2001, at P2. With whom do you agree?

3. For other instances in which a critic was sued for libel, see, e.g., *Cleveland Leader Printing Co. v. Nethersole*, 95 N.E. 735 (Ohio 1911); *Cherry v. Des Moines Leader*, 86 N.W. 323 (Iowa 1901); *Lawrence v. Sun Printing & Publishing Ass'n*, 120 N.Y.S. 384 (App. Div. 1909). For two interesting cases in which a critic sued *his* critics, see *Metcalfe v. Bill Board Publishing Co.*, 163 N.Y.S. 757 (App. Div. 1917), and *Barry v. The Players*, 132 N.Y.S. 59 (App. Div. 1911), aff'd mem., 97 N.E. 1102 (N.Y. 1912).

4. Rather than sue for libel, some theater owners have denied access to critics they feel are unfair. In two early cases, reviewers who had been banned went to court but were rebuffed because the theaters, being private establishments, were under no obligation to admit them. See *Woollcott v. Shubert*, 111 N.E. 829 (N.Y. 1916), and *Metcalfe v. Klaw*, 114 N.Y.S. 955 (App. Div. 1909).

Banning still sometimes occurs today. In 1995, for example, actor Steven Berkoff publicly criticized *Sunday Times of London* drama critic John Peter and "prohibited" him from attending his performances; in 1996 and again in 1999, Gail Wiltshire, the owner of the Twelfth Night Theatre in Brisbane, Australia, banned several critics for writing unfavorable reviews; and in 1997 Mary Brennan, a Glasgow critic, was banned from a local theater because the manager objected to her review of a tap-dancing show, which Brennan had described as "a gather-up of superannuated, souvenir tea-towel kitsch masquerading as heritage." See further David Bray, *Theatre Owner Ejects Courier Critic from Play*, Queensland Courier-Mail, Sept. 20, 1996; Rebecca Fowler, *Luvvies Declare War on Hostile Theatre Critics*, Sunday Times (London), June 11, 1995; Sandra McLean, *Art Space*, Queensland Courier-Mail, Oct. 9, 1999, at W15; Ken Smith, *Critic Bowled Over by Pavilion Ban*, Glasgow Herald, Oct. 15, 1997, at 9.

Problem 24

Although he greatly enjoyed opening night, a theater critic wrote a scathing review of a new play because the producer is his hated brother-in-law. Perhaps not surprisingly, this tidbit was left out of the column. Given these facts, can the critic be sued for libel? See *Fisher v. Washington Post Co.*, 212 A.2d 335 (D.C. Ct. App. 1965).

Chapter 11

Touring Companies

A. OVERVIEW

If a show turns out to be a hit on Broadway (or even just a modest success), it normally will be put on tour to maximize its profits. Successfully sending a play out on the road, however, requires a great deal of planning and coordination.

B. ECONOMICS

FOR TOURING SHOWS, RULES OF THE ROAD CHANGING
Maureen Dezell
Boston Globe, Apr. 27, 2003, at N1

By most accounts, the production of "The Music Man" that opens Thursday at the Colonial Theatre looks, sounds, and feels like a bona fide Broadway musical.

Based on Susan Stroman's celebrated 2000 Broadway revival, the show is a 36-actor, 21-musician rendering of Meredith Willson's beloved tale of big dreams in a small town. The story of how huckster Harold Hill changes and is changed in River City features such familiar songs as "Till There Was You" and "76 Trombones."

The show's national tour, which has been on the road since October 2001, is the springtime headliner in a 2002-03 Broadway in Boston season lineup that includes "Medea," "Mamma Mia!," and "The Producers."

But unlike those certified hits—and the vast majority of plays and musicals that load in and out of Boston's Theater District each season—this version of the all-American Broadway musical has never basked in the glow of the Great White Way.

That's because "The Music Man" is a non-Equity production. None of its actors are members of the Broadway actors union; like most non-Equity actors, they tend to be young or semiprofessional performers. Nor do the players in the orchestra belong to the American Federation of Musicians.

In the words of another famed "Music Man" song, that spells trouble with a capital "T"—certainly according to the Actors' Equity Association and its supporters.

"Consumers are getting [cheated]," charges Flora Stamatiades, director of organizing for the national union. Producers pay nonunion actors less than half the industry standard, says Stamatiades. The union has sought to make these points clear to theatergoers through public protests around the country.

The AFL-CIO and Actors' Equity announced a boycott when the show first hit the road, in Des Moines. Since then, actors union representatives have organized small public protests, garnering media attention at most stops.

The only problem: the protests haven't dissuaded many ticket buyers from seeing the show.

In Boston, the union won't raise a public fuss. But union representatives say productions like this "Music Man" take work away from their members and give theater lovers less than they deserve for the price of their tickets.

According to the show's presenters, however, ticket prices are lower than usual because the show isn't an Equity production.

For both sides, the stakes are high.

Tours of Broadway shows across North America account for more than half the industry's total ticket receipts, according to the League of American Theatres and Producers.

In fact, non-Equity shows have made stops at downtown Boston theaters for a long time, points out Wang Center for the Performing Arts president Josiah Spaulding, citing recent runs of "Cats" and the 2000 "Annie."

"I've gotten good reviews for non-Equity shows and bad reviews for Equity shows," he says.

But in the past, a road show would come first in a union tour and return in a non-Equity version. For example, "Miss Saigon," scheduled for next season at the Wang, is coming in a "newly conceived" nonunion version, but it played Boston earlier in a union tour.

Produced by a company called Big League Theatricals, "The Music Man" is the first successful national non-Equity tour of a recent Broadway hit to play multiple nights in top-tier theater towns such as Chicago, Los Angeles, Seattle, and now Boston.

The minimum weekly salary for actors in the show is between $400 and $450 a week, according to union figures and information provided by Big League executive director Dan Sher.

If housing, travel, a percentage of health-insurance coverage, and bonuses are added in, the "carrying costs" of a nonunion actor are approximately $1,000 per week, says Sher.

An Equity actor in a comparable role costs his or her producer nearly $3,000 per week: $1,302 in salary, plus health benefits and per diem payments, among other add-ons, according to Sher and the actors union.

With nonunion pay scales, "producers are saving 66 percent on actor costs, and those savings are not reflected by theater presenters' ticket prices," says Stamatiades. "They are not that different. That isn't fair to the consumer, or to actors who are doing the same level of work for eight shows."

To see "The Music Man" will cost less than to see another Broadway in Boston show—the Equity "Mamma Mia!," which closed yesterday at the Colonial. Orchestra seats for that musical are $87. And for "The Producers," coming later this spring, they'll be $97.

With road productions continuing to generate huge sums, the struggle over who performs in them is likely to get even more entrenched.

For one thing, producers such as Big League are moving into the big leagues with their shows.

The old rules of the road held that a city like Boston hosted a national tour that was a near-replica of the Broadway production and usually featured a star. A second-city tour of towns such as Providence, Cincinnati, or Buffalo might boast a smaller cast and scaled-down set, but it was still typically an Equity show.

Non-Equity producers like Big League got their start doing "bus and truck tours" of one-night stops in small towns such as Edmond, Oklahoma, and Tyler, Texas, says Sher.

Equity executive director Alan Eisenberg told his membership last year that nearly half of the road bookings across the country were nonunion productions.

Producers and promoters of road shows say that's because Equity has trained its attention on New York theater and paid little heed to working rules and conditions on the road.

When it tried, with "The Music Man" as a test case, the results didn't go as the union had hoped.

Having failed to persuade audiences to stay away when the show played in Cleveland, Chicago, and Seattle, Equity abandoned its demonstrations and attempted to organize the cast instead, according to Stamatiades. But the cast voted, 28-8, against Equity last fall. "The vote was devastating," acknowledges Stamatiades, adding that the union questioned the fairness and legality of some of Big League's tactics in discouraging unionization.

It wasn't that the cast members are antiunion, says Pam Feicht, who plays Mrs. Paroo, Marian the Librarian's mother, in "The Music Man." "All of us eventually plan to be in the union. Nonunion touring is a stepping stone for actors, a way to cut their teeth."

At the start of the tour, "the union's tactic was to denigrate the actors to try to build support for [an Equity] boycott," Feicht says. "They called us part-time actors and nonprofessionals and said this [show] was not of Broadway quality because none of us had ever been on Broadway. Well, there are a lot of Equity actors who've never been on Broadway." When the union began to try to organize the cast, "suddenly they saw us as talented enough to be in their union. I felt manipulated."

ON WITH THE $HOW: UNION DEAL TO WORK FOR LOWER PAY LETS '42ND STREET' GET ON THE ROAD
Tony Brown
Clev. Plain Dealer, Feb. 17, 2003, at C1

The musical "42nd Street" harks back to a long-gone era of glitz on Broadway, when chorus girls' legs were the starring attractions and the average businessman knew whether he liked a show before the curtain was halfway up.

But the national tour of the current Tony Award-winning New York revival of "42nd Street," which opens a two-week run at Cleveland's Palace Theatre tomorrow, also might represent the future of Broadway road shows.

The producers of "42nd Street" on Broadway struck a deal with the Actors' Equity Association union that sent the show out to the hinterlands with the cast making $575 week, less than half the standard weekly rate of $1,302.

And instead of paying the actors an additional $763 per week to cover hotels and meals, the producers are providing the accommodations and $161 to $231 a week (depending on whether the actors agree to single or double rooms) to cover meals.

The producers say the special contract allowed them to send the show out with a cast of 52, only a few shy of the 55 performing on Broadway. Many of the performers are young and just earned their union cards. But, the producers said, if they had to pay the full contract rate, the tour would have been much smaller.

The union got to say the tour went out as an Equity show, albeit at a reduced rate.

But now, some of the 43,000 members of Equity wonder if their union went too far in its concessions to Dodger Theatricals Inc., the producer of "42nd Street" in New York and on tour.

At the center of attention is what is known as Equity's "production contract," the highest-paying contract for stage actors and stage managers.

"The cost of shows has become absurd," said Richard Martini, a New York-based producer of Broadway touring shows such as "Fame," which played Cleveland two years ago.

"When you have 55 to 80 people on the road, and one body costs you $3,000 a week, including transportation, for a full Equity show, that gets to be expensive."

For some producers, the answer has been to send out nonunion tours. There are now more of them than union tours, Martini said, many of them older shows such as "Cats" and "Miss Saigon" that already have had numerous union tours.

The certifiable big hits on Broadway are almost always full union tours.

The current big sellers on the road are "Mamma Mia!," "The Producers" and "The Lion King."

And all are under a full production contract with Equity, as will be the tour of the current Broadway hit "Hairspray" that is expected to stop in Cleveland next season.

Musicals with smaller casts that have been successful in New York, such as "Urinetown" (expected in Cleveland next season), also tour under a full production contract.

"With the blockbusters, they can command whatever fee they want on the road," said Ed Strong, a partner with Dodger, which has headquarters in New York.

"But it's a shame that shows that have a good life on Broadway but aren't huge hits, there's often no way to replicate that on the road under a production contract."

Strong pointed to the tours of "Kiss Me, Kate" and "The Full Monty." Both operate under a full production contract, and both are struggling. "They've had a tough time of it," he said.

The concessions made a "42nd Street" tour a reality, Strong said.

"To their credit, Equity helped us put on the big version that you'll get to see in the Cleveland market, with the original creative team," Strong said. "When we first produced it on Broadway, we didn't imagine we could have a tour of this show, at least not a union tour."

Many members of the union, however, are not happy with the outcome of the talks.

"Because of the position we were in after 'The Music Man' went out without a contract, a lot of our members were writing us, saying, 'Make a deal, make a deal,'" said Flora Stamatiades, the national director of organizing for Equity in New York.

"Now a lot of those same members are writing to say, 'No, you made the wrong deal.'"

The union members fear that concessionary bargaining on long-running musicals on Broadway will mean the end of the production contract for road shows.

Variety reported that the producers of planned tours of "Thoroughly Modern Millie" and "Oklahoma!" both of which have had only moderate success on Broadway, as well as tours of "Oliver" and "Sweet Charity," were seeking concessions from the union.

The union, under attack from its members for the concessions on "42nd Street," appeared likely to fight some if not all of these requests from producers.

If shows such as "The Music Man" and "42nd Street" go out non-Equity or with low-paying union jobs, the caliber of the performers theoretically might not be as good because seasoned performers don't want to work for a pittance.

If the producers could have their way, tours would operate under a different contractual arrangement with Equity. The production contract came to cover both Broadway and road shows decades ago when tours often used the original New York actors.

"The [Broadway and road] contracts have been historically together, but they now need to be separated," Martini said. "I don't know if the union will come around to that, but that's what needs to happen."

Stamatiades agreed, up to a point. "Equity is going to have to figure out how to move forward."

If the union does agree to a separate road contract, it probably will be the result of producers offering incentives to actors. One such incentive could be profit-sharing, which is getting a trial run with the "42nd Street" tour.

With some tweaks, "42nd Street's" profit-sharing might be a model for future tour contracts. But so far, the kids in the chorus line are not exactly singing "We're in the Money."

IT'S BROADWAY. WELL, VIRTUALLY: SLIMMED-DOWN SHOWS THRIVE ON THE ROAD

Bruce Weber
N.Y. Times, Mar. 18, 2003, at E1

It was a Wednesday evening at the Thousand Oaks Civic Arts Plaza in this suburb north of Los Angeles, and the recent labor dispute that darkened Broadway was not on anybody's mind. Well, maybe one man, Louis B. Crocco, was thinking about it. But with the opening bars of "Miss Saigon" minutes away, the atmosphere in the orchestra pit was relaxed, business as usual. Eleven of the 12 musicians—two string players, five brass players, two reed players, a keyboard player and a percussionist—were warming up.

There was plenty of space down there; the pit could easily accommodate twice as many musicians. But the orchestra would not lack for fullness or volume. That is because its 12th member, Mr. Crocco, would be playing the equivalent of up to 19 instruments at a time on the Sinfonia, the music-making computer that has come to be known as the virtual orchestra, or V.O. in insider parlance.

The likes of Louis Crocco and the Sinfonia are now in orchestra pits all over the place, New York included, and have been for several years. The function is supplemental, usually to supply additional body in the strings and reeds and the occasional eccentric instrument, like the Asian percussion in "Miss Saigon."

To see musical theater almost anywhere other than New York City—where about half of America's musical theatergoers see their musical theater—is to get a different, and valuable, perspective on these matters. Touring shows are necessarily streamlined, and it is hard to know how much streamlining turns a Broadway show into something less than a Broadway show.

The Thousand Oaks Civic Arts Plaza here, which includes a rather unattractive 1,800-seat auditorium with a high school ambience, is a typical stop on the current "Miss Saigon" tour, which began last fall and will run for three years.

This is a non-Equity tour, which means that the performers are not necessarily union members and that the cost of running the show is therefore lower.

The "Miss Saigon" orchestra on Broadway had 26 musicians; a previous Equity tour had 19 as opposed to the current 12. This sounds chintzy, perhaps, but it isn't. It is not just that the amount of sheer stuff that is transported every week to a new theater—including 65 speakers, 385 lighting instruments and a 30,000-watt sound system, not to mention 687 costumes, 57 hats and 46 M-16's and AK-47's—defies the idea of chintzy. It takes six 53-foot trucks to get it all there.

But in addition, the way the business works is that the presenting theaters guarantee the tour producer a minimum—in the case of "Miss Saigon," the figure is $235,000 per week—that ostensibly becomes the maximum budget for the show. (For the sake of comparison, the guarantee for the current Equity tour of "Les Miserables" is $425,000 per week.)

The "Miss Saigon" company—including the orchestra, the cast, 15 stagehands and a handful of other crew and staff members—travels every Monday by bus or airplane and gives eight performances in a new city every Tuesday through Sunday. The rigors of such a schedule cause wear and tear on a show, particularly on the performers who have to cope with abrupt changes in temperature and altitude.

The size of the house also makes a difference to cast and crew. Even the distance between the stage and the first row of seats, different in each theater, can pose a challenge. In Thousand Oaks the orchestra pit, the stage, the wing space and the fly space are commodious, a luxury for everyone, particularly the stagehands who are responsible for moving scenery in and out, up and down, onstage and off. The "footprint" for the show—that is, the distance it needs from front to back—is 36 feet, easily accommodated here.

To witness the nightly preparation of "Miss Saigon" is to be impressed by the care, professionalism and pride of the people involved; it's a team working to the limits of its resources and to the height of its integrity. And as several cast members pointed out, every Tuesday night is an opening night, giving the production a fresh weekly jolt of adrenaline.

In the pit, Mr. Crocco was no different, defending the Sinfonia, both its sound and its function.

"It is a musical instrument," he said. "People call it canned music, but I have to play along. It's about timekeeping, listening to the other players and watching the conductor. It's not just plugging it in and turning it on."

Mr. Crocco is a friendly, voluble man, a drummer by training and also the company's associate conductor, and he doesn't much like it that he is viewed, in his role as Sinfonist, as the unwanted wave of the future. The machine looks musical—it has a keyboard that resembles a piano's—but it is just a computer. The keyboard is fundamentally for show; it functions more like a computer keyboard. Mr. Crocco controls the tempo of the digitized musical lines by tapping on a single key, following the conductor on a video screen in front of him and listening through headphones to the sound of the orchestra as a whole. The common term for him and his counterparts in other shows is "tapper." He does not really need to be in the pit.

"People don't understand that I'm not replacing anybody," Mr. Crocco said. "If I wasn't here, it's not like there would be 19 other people down here."

It is evident that a road show is about accommodation, giving an audience as much for its money as possible. And the argument goes that as time goes on and technology improves, more becomes possible.

Notes

1. As a result of his appearing as the irascible Captain Von Trapp in a non-Equity production of "The Sound of Music" in 2000, the union slapped Barry Williams (better known as Greg on the 1970s television sitcom "The Brady Bunch") with a $30,000 fine. Although Williams had resigned from Equity prior to starting the play, the union contended he had begun negotiating for the role while he was still a member. Williams responded by filing an unfair labor practice charge, but the National Labor Relations Board upheld the fine. *See further* Roger Armbrust & Leonard Jacobs, *NLRB Hears "Music," Makes Barry Fine Final*, Back Stage, May 10, 2002, at 4.

2. The first bus-and-truck tours occurred in 1949, when buses carried the casts, and trucks hauled the sets, for the tours of "Mister Roberts" and "Death of a Salesman." *See* Chris Jones, *Clark Fetes 50 Years of Happy Trails*, Variety, June 28, 1999, at 75. Previously, theatrical productions were transported by railway. *See, e.g., Auditorium Theatre Co. v. Oregon-Washington R. & Nav. Co.*, 137 P. 489 (Wash. 1914); *Weston v. Boston & M. R. R.*, 76 N.E. 1050 (Mass. 1906); *Western Union Telegraph Co. v. Austlet*, 115 S.W. 624 (Tex. Civ. App. 1909).

Although trucks remain vital to tour companies, the term "bus-and-truck tour" is becoming increasingly outdated. Today, tours normally are referred to as "first class" and "second class" or "Equity" and "non-union." Generally speaking, first class tours play only big cities, feature lavish production values, employ union actors, remain in a given location for weeks at a time, and use airplanes rather than buses to transport the cast. In contrast, second class tours visit smaller markets, tend to move frequently, have limited sets, and hire non-union casts.

3. The economics of theatrical tours are discussed further in Charles Grippo, *The Stage Producer's Business and Legal Guide* (2002); Amelia David, *Taking a Look at Bus & Truck Touring*, Back Stage, Apr. 23, 1999, at 28; Robert J. Hughes, *The New Music Man*, Wall St. J., Feb. 21, 2003, at W9; Jesse McKinley, *Bombing on Broadway, Thriving on the Road: With a Few Tweaks, Musicals Play in Peoria*, N.Y. Times, Feb. 10, 2003, at E1; Jason Zinoman, *Actors Rally to Protest Non-Equity Road Shows*, N.Y. Times, Oct. 30, 2003, at B1.

Problem 25

Although it charged Broadway prices and billed itself "As originally performed on Broadway," a play on tour used non-Equity actors and a virtual orchestra. These facts were not disclosed in the show's advertising or playbill. As a result, have any laws been broken? *See Metropolitan Opera Ass'n v. Wagner-Nichols Recorder Corp.*, 107 N.Y.S.2d 795 (App. Div. 1951).

C. ARRANGEMENTS

INGE v. TWENTIETH CENTURY-FOX FILM CORPORATION
143 F. Supp. 294 (S.D.N.Y. 1956)

LEVET, District Judge.

This is a motion by plaintiffs for a preliminary injunction to restrain the defendant during the pendency of this action and until December 1, 1956, from exhibiting in the United States or Canada any motion picture version of the work entitled 'Bus Stop,' and for other collateral relief. The action was begun in the Supreme Court, New York County, and later removed to this Court.

The plaintiff William Inge was the author and The W-S Bus Stop Company, a Limited Partnership, hereinafter referred to as plaintiff company, was the Broadway producer of the play 'Bus Stop.' The defendant is a Delaware corporation engaged in the production of moving pictures.

Prior to May 19, 1954, plaintiff Inge wrote the original dramatic work entitled 'Bus Stop.' The plaintiff company is the assignee of Whitehead-Stevens Productions, Inc. under a contract with the plaintiff Inge, dated November 15, 1954, and has the sole and exclusive right to produce and present the play on the stage of the United States and Canada, subject, however, to the contract between plaintiff Inge and the defendant, hereinafter mentioned.

On March 23, 1955, an agreement was made between plaintiff Inge and the defendant, whereby Inge granted to the defendant certain motion picture and other rights in the play. The plaintiff company consented to the agreement. The provision which is involved here is Paragraph Fifteenth of this contract, which is as follows:

(a) With respect to release of the first motion picture version of the Play, Purchaser agrees as follows:

1. With respect to United States and Canada, Purchaser agrees not to release said motion picture anywhere therein until all first-class stage presentations of the Play therein have closed (as herein defined), or June 1, 1956, whichever is earlier. All first-class stage presentations of the Play in the United States and Canada shall be deemed to have 'closed' if (i) the first-class stage presentation of the Play on Broadway, New York shall have closed and (ii) after September 15, 1955 there shall have elapsed a period of thirty (30) days during which period no first-class road company of the Play shall have been presented in the United States or Canada and during which period there has not been executed a contract for a first-class road booking of the Play in the United States or Canada thereafter and contracts with the two leads in the Play to appear therein. Seller agrees that, after the close of the first-class presentation of the Play on Broadway, New York, Seller will in good faith notify Purchaser of plans concerning a road tour of the Play in the United States or Canada.

2. With respect to England, Scotland and Wales (herein called England) if prior to January 1, 1956 a contract has been executed for a first-class presenta-

tion of the Play in England and pursuant to said contract said presentation is scheduled to open on or before March 1, 1956, then and in that event Purchaser agrees not to release said motion picture in England until the said first-class presentation of the Play shall have closed or June 1, 1956, whichever is earlier.

3. With respect to Australia and New Zealand, if prior to January 1, 1956 a contract has been executed for a first-class presentation of the Play in Australia or New Zealand and pursuant to said contract said presentation is scheduled to open on or before March 1, 1956, then and in that event Purchaser agrees not to release said motion picture in Australia or New Zealand until the said first-class presentation of the Play shall have closed or June 1, 1956, whichever is earlier.

(b) With respect to United States and Canada, England and Australia, Purchaser agrees that until four (4) weeks prior to the earliest date on which the first motion picture produced hereunder may be released in each of said countries, Purchaser will not cause any theatre in such territory under the control of Purchaser, to advertise the date of the opening in said theatre of the said motion picture. Nothing herein contained shall prevent Purchaser at any time from advertising or publicizing the said motion picture in such manner as Purchaser may determine.

By a letter agreement or modification bearing the same date, the date 'June 1, 1956' was changed to 'December 1, 1956.'

The play had a successful run of well over a year on Broadway, closing on April 21, 1956. A road company was able to earn profits for the producer of $86,139.13. The then current road company closed in New Haven, Connecticut, on May 5, 1956. Under the terms of the agreement between the parties, the defendant was to become entitled to release its film 'Bus Stop,' unless within thirty days, or by June 4, 1956, contracts were signed for a further first-class road company.

On May 8, 1956, Audrey Wood as attorney-in-fact for plaintiff Inge, wrote Joseph Moskowitz, vice president of the defendant, to the effect that the last road company of the play closed on May 5, 1956, in New Haven, and notified the defendant that the plaintiffs intended to take the play on tour in the Fall of the year, enclosing a projected road company tour schedule commencing on August 13 at Chicago and running through the months of October and November 1956 and continuing through December 1956 and January and February 1957.

At some time before May 19, 1956, apparently the defendant determined to release the picture 'Bus Stop' in August 1956. Notice of this intention appears in an inconspicuous line of a copy of the Motion Picture Herald of May 19, 1956. The same announcement was contained in the same publication of May 26, 1956. Whatever defendant's reasons were for this proposed action, it appears that its vice president in his affidavit said: 'This company has no picture of the quality and box office appeal of 'Bus Stop' to substitute for it.' Defendant may have been confronted with the problem arising from its error in schedule production.

Plaintiffs contend that they were unaware of the defendant's decision to release prematurely the film and, therefore, went ahead with their plans for a further road company.

On May 28, 1956, plaintiff company and one Jules Pfeiffer entered into a sub-licensing agreement, whereby Pfeiffer secured first-class stage rights in 'Bus Stop' for a first-class company on tour. Plaintiff Inge concurred in this agreement in a rider accompanying the same. This contract with Pfeiffer obligated him to present the play in a first-class theatre, with a first-class cast, and with a first-class director. Pfeiffer is reputed to be an experienced producer. On May 31, 1956, it appears that Pfeiffer entered into a contract for a theatre in Chicago. Miss Helen Gallagher, star of 'Hazel Flagg' and 'Pajama Game' and featured in other plays, and Rip Torn, who is reputedly playing the lead on Broadway in 'Cat On A Hot Tin Roof,' were engaged to play the two leads.

The defendant opposes this application upon the following grounds: (1) The restrictions on the release date of the motion picture 'Bus Stop' are illegal, immoral and unenforceable; (2) That the conditions of Paragraph Fifteenth have not been met; and (3) That there is no basis for equitable relief presented by plaintiffs' application for a preliminary injunction.

It is elementary that under the terms of the present copyright statute, 17 U.S.C.A. § 1 et seq., the unauthorized public performance of a dramatic work by means of a moving picture is unquestionably an infringement. Metro-Goldwyn-Mayer Distributing Corporation v. Bijou Theatre Co., 1 Cir., 1932, 59 F.2d 70; Stodart v. Mutual Film Corp., D.C.S.D.N.Y.1917, 249 F. 507, affirmed 2 Cir., 1949, 249 F. 513; Stonesifer v. Twentieth Century-Fox Film Corp., D.C.S.D.Cal.1942, 48 F.Supp. 196, affirmed 9 Cir., 1944, 140 F.2d 579.

The plaintiff Inge, of course, had a right to license his copyright for moving picture and other purposes. In Fox Film Corp. v. Doyal, 286 U.S. 123, 127, 52 S.Ct. 546, 547, 76 L.Ed. 1010, Chief Justice Hughes said:

> * * * The owner of the copyright, if he pleases, may refrain from vending or licensing and content himself with simply exercising the right to exclude others from using his property. Compare Continental Paper Bag Co. v. Eastern Paper Bag Co., 210 U.S. 405, 422, 424, 28 S.Ct. 748, 52 L.Ed. 1122.

Any limitations or conditions which the parties see fit to insert will be binding and may be enforced except where they are contrary to public policy or in violation of law. Buck v. Hillsgrove Country Club, Inc., D.C.R.I., 1937, 17 F.Supp. 643; Manners v. Morosco, 252 U.S. 317, 40 S.Ct. 335, 64 L.Ed. 590; Underhill v. Schenck, 238 N.Y. 7, 143 N.E. 773, 33 A.L.R. 303.

There appears to be nothing in the agreement nor its background which sustains the defendant's contention in reference to the alleged invalidity of the restrictions in reference to the release date. The defendant asserts that the Dramatist Guild, to which plaintiff Inge belonged, required:

> (1) That the so-called 'pre-production deal,' that is, a sale of the motion picture rights in a play which has not yet opened on the stage, be completed before the opening of the play on the stage; and

> (2) That the Dramatist Guild made it mandatory in transactions for purchasing the rights to make motion pictures from proposed or active Broadway stage plays, that there be a restriction on the time before which the motion picture may be released.

The fact that this feature may have influenced plaintiff Inge in refusing to execute a contract without such a restrictive date is not necessarily indicative of any improper restriction in the agreement itself nor any indication of so-called restraint of trade or other invalidity. The fact is that the copyright belonged to Inge, that he is a party who made the contract, that there was no necessity for the purchase of this particular film by the defendant since it appears that as a matter of fact film companies draw only a portion of their stories from the members of the Guild. According to the affidavit of Edward E. Colton, the negotiator appointed by the Dramatist Guild, in 1953, 1954 and 1955, fewer than sixteen plays per year were sold in negotiations in which the Guild participated, whereas according to the affidavit of Rae Fixel, in 1955, American film companies made a total of 392 films. Since there are so many other sources of supply in existence and the relevant market is so broad, it does not appear that there is an illegal monopoly under Section 2 of the Sherman Act, 15 U.S.C.A. 2. See United States v. E.I. du Pont de Nemours and Company, 76 S.Ct. 994.

The antitrust defense of defendant, Twentieth Century-Fox Film Corporation, does not appear to be sustained by the facts, and this defense, I believe, does not constitute a bar to injunctive relief. See Alfred Bell & Co. v. Catalda Fine Arts, 2 Cir., 1951, 191 F.2d 99; Mytinger & Casselberry, Inc. v. Numanna Laboratories Corp., 7 Cir., 1954, 215 F.2d 382. In the Bell case, supra, Judge Frank expressed the principles involved as follows:

> * * * We have here a conflict of policies: (a) that of preventing piracy of copyrighted matter and (b) that of enforcing the anti-trust laws. We must balance the two, taking into account the comparative innocence or guilt of the parties, the moral character of their respective acts, the extent of the harm to the public interest, the penalty inflicted on the plaintiff if we deny it relief. As the defendants' piracy is unmistakably clear, while the plaintiffs' infraction of the antitrust laws is doubtful and at most marginal, we think the enforcement of the first policy should outweigh enforcement of the second.

191 F.2d at page 106.

In contending that the conditions of Paragraph Fifteenth of the contract have not been met by the plaintiff, the defendant alleges, among other things, as follows: (1) That the language of the agreement has no application to successive road companies; (2) That the language relates to so-called W-S Productions; (3) That the contemplated tour by Pfeiffer is not that of a first-class company; (4) That the contracts with the two actors for the two leading roles were not entered into within thirty days from May 5, 1956, and that the sub-license to Pfeiffer by its terms has expired.

An examination of the contract and the facts alleged by the plaintiff, which are not substantially controverted by the defendant, shows due compliance with the contract sufficient to preclude the release of the film. The net effect of the contract, Paragraph Fifteenth, was that the defendant was forbidden to release its film in the United States and Canada until December 1, 1956, (i) if any first-class road company were appearing or (ii) if within thirty days following the closing of any current first-class company contracts were signed for a new first-class company.

In this connection the plaintiff notified the defendant by letter of a projected stage company, the plaintiff signed the contract for a first-class company, the defendant asked for and received copies of these contracts, and the plaintiff sought to induce the defendant to withdraw its threatened release of the film set for August 1956.

Equity will not open its doors to one who seeks its aid for the purpose of violating a contract. 30 C.J.S., Equity, § 99, p. 497. The Court will not be zealous to seek a defense to this action upon behalf of the defendant to enable it to avoid what appears to be a plain obligation of a contractual character.

I believe that the plaintiffs have shown, for the purpose of this motion, that they have duly complied with the conditions necessary to require the defendant to defer release of the picture.

The defendant asserts that there is no basis for equitable relief by way of a preliminary injunction. The gist of defendant's contentions appear to be: (1) That plaintiffs' losses will be small or that in fact the release of the film before December 1, 1956 will promote, rather than diminish, stage profits; (2) That a preliminary injunction would alter the status quo rather than retain it; (3) That the 'balance of convenience' between plaintiff and defendant favors the defendant; (4) That no irreparable injury will result to plaintiff.

It may be noted at the outset that in cases of infringement of copyright, an injunction has always been recognized as a proper remedy because of the inadequacy of the legal remedy; that the remedy exists both by statute and independently thereof. American Code Co. v. Bensinger, 2 Cir., 1922, 282 F. 829.

The present defendant was enjoined pendente lite after appeal to the Second Circuit in a somewhat similar action in L. C. Page & Co. v. Fox Film Corporation (now Twentieth Century-Fox Film Corporation), 1936, 83 F.2d 196. Here, as there, the defendant apparently was in effect a wilful infringer. (In the case at bar, at least to the extent of the threatened prematurity of release.) There, likewise, Twentieth Century-Fox raised the defense of substantial investment and its own solvency. Judge Swan, however, stated:

> The defendants acted with their eyes open; they were expressly warned before they began production of the picture that the plaintiff would seek equitable as well as legal relief; and there was no laches in starting the suit. * * * They urge that an injunction should be denied because they are solvent, recovery on the accounting will amply compensate the plaintiff, and their own losses, if enjoined from releasing the picture for exhibition, will be great. We recognize, of course, that, where damages will adequately compensate a complainant and where granting an injunction might work injury to the defendant out of proportion to that resulting to the complainant from its refusal, a preliminary injunction may be denied. New York Grape Sugar Co. v. American Grape Sugar Co., C.C.N.D.N.Y., 10 F. 835; Overweight Counterbalance Elevator Co v. Cahill & Hall Elevator Co., C.C.N.D.Cal., 86 F. 338; Gillette Safety Razor Co. v. Durham Duplex Razor Co., D.C.N.J., 197 F. 574. But we do not see that the principle is applicable. An accounting—usually a protracted proceeding at the best—will be particularly complex here because the infringement relates only to 'talking' motion picture rights. The apportionment of profits between 'talking' and 'silent' rights is sure to raise difficult and controverted questions. Under such circumstances we do not think the remedy of an accounting is an adequate substitute for an injunction. Any inconvenience or loss which an injunction may cause the defendants should not appeal strongly to the chancellor's conscience, for it made its investment with full knowledge of the plaintiff's rights. A willful infringer should not by the extent of his investment be allowed to gain immunity from the injunctive remedy.

83 F.2d at 200. See also Houghton Mifflin Co. v. Noram Pub. Co., D.C.S.D.N.Y.1939, 28 F.Supp. 676.

Under the circumstances, if a preliminary injunction is not granted the computation or determination of plaintiffs' damages would be a difficult and complex task, although the damages may be real and in all likelihood substantial. There is no easy way of measuring a comparison of return to the stage production under a condition without film competition and that with film competition. The plaintiff is entitled to that for which he bargained, and it appears that he will sustain an irreparable loss if he is subjected to

[the] uncertainty of film rivalry, especially in the short period remaining before December 1, 1956.

Any extra expense to which the defendant may have committed itself in seeking to release the film before December 1, 1956, was wilfully incurred with wide-open eyes and in face of the notice given to it by plaintiffs. There is no substantial proof here upon this motion that the defendant has subjected itself to irretrievable expenses in addition to those it normally would have had in order to market this film for the December 1, 1956 (or earlier) release. There is no proof that defendant will lose anything by deferral. It may, in fact, be argued that the prolongation of the stage production will increase the public desire to attend the moving picture production. The fact that the defendant may gain by an earlier release than anticipated, that the defendant now seeks an outstanding film for its market, or that the leading actress in the film 'Bus Stop' has recently secured certain publicity is not germane to the more tangible issues of this motion.

The prospective losses to the plaintiffs from the threatened violation of the agreement are as follows:

First, plaintiff's revenues from their contract with Mr. Pfeiffer would be prejudiced. Under that contract, plaintiffs are entitled to three types of payment. Plaintiff Inge is entitled to 10% of the gross weekly box office receipts; plaintiff company is to receive 3% of the same receipts, or $300 per week, whichever is greater, plus 5% of the net profits of the production. The gross receipts and the profits would both be affected by competition from the motion picture. Present calculation of the extent of this harm is impractical; measurement afterwards would be impossible.

Second, plaintiffs are entitled under their agreement with defendant to continuing weekly payments for the motion picture rights, if a first-class road company is touring profitably. These payments are set at 10% of the gross weekly receipts of any touring companies, up to a maximum of $1,250 per company per week, and provided further that plaintiffs shall not receive, in total payment for the motion picture rights, more than $250,000. Under the agreement between plaintiffs and defendant, $226,807.16 has now been paid or is payable, leaving an additional $23,192.84 which may still be earned by plaintiffs as a result of profitable weeks of first-class road companies. If defendant's picture were allowed to compete with Mr. Pfeiffer's road company, such company would not be likely to earn profits. Although plaintiffs concede that defendant could damage them in this field by no more than $23,192.84, there is no method of measuring how close to that sum the damage actually would be.

Third, defendant's wrongful competition would adversely affect plaintiffs by hurting the 'stock' companies which plaintiffs have licensed. Mr. Moskowitz states that 'Bus Stop' is being done in 'stock' in at least thirty-three summer theatres this summer, pursuant, of course, to licenses from plaintiffs. These 'stock' companies would surely be hurt by competition from defendant's film (and so the royalties received by plaintiffs would be reduced), but measuring the loss would be impossible.

If defendant's picture is released in advance of the contractual date, this harm cannot be measured, now or later, but it will certainly be substantial.

Consequently, I conclude that the plaintiffs are entitled to an injunction enjoining and restraining the defendant, its agents, servants and employees and all persons acting in concert with them, during the pendency of this action and until December 1, 1956, from in any way causing or permitting to be publicly exhibited in the United States or Canada any motion picture version of the work entitled 'Bus Stop' and from causing or permitting any theatre in the United States or Canada to advertise the date of opening in the said theatre of any motion picture version entitled 'Bus Stop' until four weeks prior to December 1, 1956.

The preliminary injunction, however, is made without prejudice to the right of the defendant to vacate such preliminary injunction in the event that plaintiffs, in the subsequent opinion of this Court, shall have no longer complied or shall have ceased to comply with the essential prerequisites to defer the issuance or release of the film 'Bus Stop' as stated in the agreement.

The granting of the preliminary injunction herein is also conditioned upon the plaintiffs supplying a good and sufficient bond approved by this Court in the sum of $50,000 to indemnify the defendant against any loss in the event said defendant shall ultimately succeed in the final disposition of this matter.

The defendant, by counter-motion, moved this Court for an order vacating the temporary restraining order issued on July 17, 1956 by the Hon. Henry Epstein, Justice of the Supreme Court, New York County. This stay was deemed by the parties to be transferred to the jurisdiction of this Court at the time of removal from the State Court. Since the plaintiffs will be protected by the preliminary injunction to be made herein, this motion will be granted, to take effect however only upon the signing, entry and service upon the defendant of a copy of the order hereon.

The above constitutes the findings of fact and conclusions of law upon which this preliminary injunction is granted.

Settle order on notice.

UNITED STATES v. SHUBERT
348 U.S. 222 (1955)

Chief Justice WARREN delivered the opinion of the Court.

This is a civil antitrust action brought by the Government in the United States District Court for the Southern District of New York. Named as defendants are Lee Shubert, Jacob J. Shubert, Marcus Heiman, and three corporations controlled by them.

The defendants are principally engaged in the business of producing legitimate theatrical attractions and operating approximately 40 theatres in eight states for the presentation of legitimate attractions. The defendants, according to the complaint, operate or control all the theatres in virtually all key "try-out" cities (including Boston, Philadelphia, and Baltimore), all the theatres in several important "road-show" cities (including Baltimore, Boston, Cincinnati, Los Angeles, and Philadelphia), almost all the theatres in other important "road-show" cities (Chicago and Detroit), and approximately half of the theatres in New York City. The Government's complaint charges that the defendants, in the course of this business, have violated §§ 1 and 2 of the Sherman Act. These sections provide:

> § 1. Every contract, combination in the form of trust or otherwise, or conspiracy, in restraint of trade or commerce among the several States, or with foreign nations, is declared to be illegal.... Every person who shall make any contract or engage in any combination or conspiracy declared by sections 1-7 of this title to be illegal shall be deemed guilty of a misdemeanor....

> § 2. Every person who shall monopolize, or attempt to monopolize, or combine or conspire with any other person or persons, to monopolize any part of the trade or commerce among the several States, or with foreign nations, shall be deemed guilty of a misdemeanor....

On the defendants' motion, after this Court's decision in Toolson v. New York Yankees, 346 U.S. 356, the District Court dismissed the Government's complaint on the authority of the Toolson decision and Federal Baseball Club of Baltimore v. National League of Professional Baseball Clubs, 259 U.S. 200. The case is here on direct appeal under the Expediting Act, 15 U.S.C. §29.

The Government's complaint describes the interstate phases of the defendants' theatrical business in considerable detail. It concludes that the business of producing, booking, and presenting legitimate attractions requires

> a constant, continuous stream of trade and commerce between the States of the United States, consisting of the assemblage of personnel and property for rehearsals, the transportation of said personnel and property to various cities throughout the United States, the making and performing of contracts under which attractions are routed and presented in various States of the United States, and the transmission of applications, letters, memoranda, communications, commitments, contracts, money, checks, drafts and other media of exchange across State lines.

The complaint alleges that the defendants have restrained this trade and commerce, and have monopolized certain phases of it, through a conspiracy (a) to compel other producers to book their legitimate attractions exclusively through the defendants, (b) to exclude others from booking legitimate attractions, (c) to prevent competition in the presentation of legitimate attractions, (d) to discriminate in favor of their own productions with respect to booking and presentation, and (e) to combine their power in booking and presentation in order to maintain and strengthen their domination in each of these fields. The main relief sought by the Government is the divorcement of the booking and presentation branches of the business.

The allegations of the complaint, on a motion to dismiss, must of course be taken as true. And the defendants do not deny that the allegations state a cause of action if their business is subject to the Sherman Act. The question presented is thus a narrow one: whether the business of producing, booking, and presenting legitimate attractions on a multistate basis constitutes "trade or commerce" that is "among the several States" within the meaning of those terms in the Sherman Act.

Both terms have been interpreted broadly in the decisions of this Court. "Trade or commerce" has been held to include the production, distribution, and exhibition of motion pictures (United States v. Paramount Pictures, 334 U.S. 131; Schine Theatres v. United States, 334 U.S. 110; United States v. Griffith, 334 U.S. 100; United States v. Crescent Amusement Co., 323 U.S. 173; Interstate Circuit v. United States, 306 U.S. 208; Binderup v. Pathe Exchange, 263 U.S. 291); real estate brokerage (United States v. National Association of Real Estate Boards, 339 U.S. 485); the gathering and distribution of news (Associated Press v. United States, 326 U.S. 1); medical services to members of a health cooperative (American Medical Association v. United States, 317 U.S. 519); and insurance underwriting (United States v. South-Eastern Underwriters Association, 322 U.S. 533).

A similarly liberal construction has been given the requirement of §§ 1 and 2 that the "trade or commerce" be "among the several States." Thus, in the South-Eastern Underwriters case, the requirement was satisfied by a "continuous and indivisible stream of intercourse among the states" involving the transmission of large sums of money and communications by mail, telephone, and telegraph. In the Associated Press case, the requirement was satisfied by the interstate dissemination of news. And in the motion picture cases, the requirement was satisfied by the interstate transportation of films, Binderup v. Pathe Exchange, supra, even though the actual "showing of motion pictures is of course a local affair." United States v. Crescent Amusement Co., supra, at 183. See also Hart v. B. F. Keith Vaudeville Exchange, 262 U.S. 271.

These decisions, apart from Federal Baseball and Toolson, make it clear beyond question that the allegations of the Government's complaint bring the defendants within the scope of the Sherman Act, even though the actual performance of a legitimate stage attraction "is of course a local affair." The defendants contend, however, that Federal Baseball and Toolson have already established their immunity under the Act. While conceding, as they must, that the motion picture industry is subject to the antitrust laws, they insist that all other businesses built around the performance of local exhibitions are exempt. We believe that Federal Baseball and Toolson afford no basis for such a conclusion.

The defendants seek to distinguish the motion picture cases on the ground that the product of the motion picture industry is "an article of trade...an inanimate thing—a reel of photographic film in a metal box—which moves into interstate commerce like any other manufactured product"; on the other hand, according to this argument, a legitimate theatrical attraction is "intangible and evanescent, unique and individual...an experience of living people." Compare United States v. South-Eastern Underwriters Association, 322 U.S. 533, 546: "Congress can regulate traffic though it consist of intangibles." And see Hart v. B. F. Keith Vaudeville Exchange, 262 U.S. 271. That other segments of the entertainment business, besides the motion picture industry, may constitute interstate commerce is well established. See, e.g., Federal Radio Commission v. Nelson Bros. Co., 289 U.S. 266, 279 (radio).

In Federal Baseball, the Court, speaking through Mr. Justice Holmes, was dealing with the business of baseball and nothing else. The Court considered the nature of the game, its history and league organization, the necessity of arranging games between cities in different states, and the resulting travel across state lines. The travel, the Court concluded, was "a mere incident, not the essential thing." On that basis, the Court held that "the restrictions by contract that prevented the plaintiff from getting players to break their bargains and the other conduct charged against the defendants were not an interference with commerce among the States." 259 U.S. at 209.

At the very next Term, in Hart v. B. F. Keith Vaudeville Exchange, 262 U.S. 271, the Court was directly concerned with the effect of the Federal Baseball decision on the status of the theatrical business under the Sherman Act. The complaint in the Hart case, much like the complaint here under review, alleged a conspiracy to control the booking and presentation of vaudeville acts in theatres throughout the country. The district court, like the district court in the instant case, dismissed the complaint on the authority of Federal Baseball. This Court, again speaking through Mr. Justice Holmes, unanimously reversed. The Court took note of the plaintiff's argument "that in the transportation of vaudeville acts the apparatus sometimes is more important than the performers" and concluded that the complaint, at least to that extent, sufficiently alleged a violation of the Act to permit the case to go to trial. The Court distinguished Federal Baseball on the ground that "what in general is incidental, in some instances may rise to a magnitude that requires it to be considered independently." The Court thus established, contrary to the defendants' argument here, that Federal Baseball did not automatically immunize the theatrical business from the antitrust laws.

In Toolson, where the issue was the same as in Federal Baseball, the Court was confronted with a unique combination of circumstances. For over 30 years there had stood a decision of this Court specifically fixing the status of the baseball business under the antitrust laws and more particularly the validity of the so-called "reserve clause." During this period, in reliance on the Federal Baseball precedent, the baseball business had grown and developed. Compare Helvering v. Hallock, 309 U.S. 106, 110. And Congress, although it had actively considered the ruling, had not seen fit to reject it by amendatory legislation. Against this background, the Court in Toolson was asked to overrule Federal Baseball on the ground that it was out of step with subsequent decisions reflecting present-day concepts of interstate commerce. The Court, in view of the circumstances of the case, declined to do so. But neither did the Court necessarily reaffirm all that was said in Federal Baseball. Instead, "without re-examination of the underlying issues," the Court adhered to Federal Baseball "so far as that decision determines that Congress had no intention of including the business of baseball within the scope of the federal antitrust laws." 346 U.S., at 357. In short, Toolson was a narrow application of the rule of stare decisis.

The defendants would have us convert this narrow application of the rule into a sweeping grant of immunity to every business based on the live presentation of local exhibitions, regardless of how extensive its interstate phases may be. We cannot do so. If the Toolson holding is to be expanded—or contracted—the appropriate remedy lies with Congress. See United States v. South-Eastern Underwriters Association, 322 U.S. 533, 561. Moreover, none of the considerations which led to the decision in Toolson are present here. This Court has never held that the theatrical business is not subject to the Sherman Act. On the contrary, less than a year after the Federal Baseball decision, the Court in the Hart case put the theatrical business on notice that Federal Baseball could not be relied upon as a basis for exemption from the antitrust laws. The rule of stare decisis undoubtedly embodies a policy of basic importance, but the rule cannot help the defendants here. If it is to be applied, Hart and the motion picture cases—not Federal Baseball and Toolson—are the controlling decisions.

We are not yet called upon to determine whether the defendants have in fact violated the Sherman Act or if they have what relief would be appropriate. We hold only that the allegations of the complaint state a cause of action and that the Government is entitled to an opportunity to prove those allegations. The judgment of the court below is reversed.

RAPAGNANI v. JUDAS COMPANY
736 A.2d 666 (Pa. Super. Ct. 1999)

ELLIOTT, Judge.

In this appeal, we are asked to decide whether the trial court erred when it granted summary judgment to all defendants/appellees. Finding no error, we affirm. The factual and procedural history, taken from the trial court's opinion and supported by the record, follows:

> [Appellant] Michael Rapagnani was hired to be a musical director for a non-first class touring production of the Andrew Lloyd Webber musical 'Jesus Christ Superstar.' He worked for eight months before being terminated with three weeks notice. [Appellant] alleged two claims of improper termination and a claim of defamation against eight Defendants. [Appellant] sued his employer the Judas Company and the three joint venturers who made up Judas: Landmark Entertainment, Magic Productions and Tap Productions. He also

sued Niko Associates, Inc., the entity who provided general management services for the tour, and Allen Spivak and Larry Magid, individually and trading as Electric Factory Concerts, Inc., who were listed as producers in the Playbills in various cities.

Following the close of discovery, appellees moved for summary judgment. The motion was granted July 9, 1998, and this timely appeal followed.

The gravamen of appellant's argument is that there exists a genuine issue of fact as to whether he was an at-will employee whose employment could be terminated before the tour ended without a showing of cause. With the factual and procedural posture of the case in mind, we turn to the law relevant to summary judgment.

In this case, appellant bore the burden of overcoming the firmly entrenched presumption that he was an at-will employee who could be discharged for any reason or no reason at all. Luteran v. Loral Fairchild Corp., 455 Pa. Super. 364, 688 A.2d 211, 214 (1997), appeal denied, 549 Pa. 717, 701 A.2d 578 (1997). The trial court concluded that appellant presented insufficient evidence to overcome the presumption that he was an at-will employee; therefore, he could not make out a prima facie cause of action for breach of contract based on a claim that he could only be terminated for cause.

"As a general rule, there is no common law cause of action against an employer for termination of an at-will employment relationship." Luteran, 688 A.2d at 214. "'The sine qua non of the presumption is that except in rare instances, discharge will not be reviewed in a judicial forum.'" Id., quoting Scott v. Extracorporeal, Inc., 376 Pa. Super. 90, 545 A.2d 334, 336 (1988).

> In order to rebut the presumption of at-will employment, a party must establish one of the following: (1) an agreement for a definite duration; (2) an agreement specifying that the employee will be discharged for just cause only; (3) sufficient additional consideration; or (4) an applicable recognized public policy exception.

Luteran, 688 A.2d at 214. In this case, appellant attempted to rebut the presumption of at-will employment by showing that the agreement provided for employment for a definite duration and specified that he would be discharged for just cause only, and also by showing that he provided appellees with sufficient additional consideration. We address these arguments in turn.

The parties' agreement consisted of an express written contract in three parts: 1) the "Musician's Individual Employment Contract" ("the contract"); 2) a rider to this contract ("the rider"); and 3) "Pamphlet B," containing the collective bargaining agreement between the American Federation of Musicians of the United States and Canada and the League of American Theaters and Producers ("Pamphlet B"). (S.R.R. at 8b-55b.) Appellant's complaint alleged a breach of paragraphs 4(a), 4(b), 4(d), 4(e), and 4(f) of the rider. Those paragraphs provide:

> 4. The musician's duties shall include the following:
>
> a. Conducting and playing for all cast rehearsals during pre-production and the run of the tour, including all put in and understudy rehearsals.
>
> b. Conducting and playing for all orchestra rehearsals during pre-production and the run of the tour, including all put in and local orchestra rehearsals. Local orchestra rehearsals after pre-production shall be four hours in length....

d. Conducting and playing all promotional and advertising events for all mediums, as well as the creation, implementation and any adjustments of all click tracks used for the performance throughout the tour.

e. To create new orchestra parts as needed and to maintain all orchestra parts throughout the tour.

f. To create and maintain all midi designs and synthesizer programs and to adjust if needed during the run of the tour.

S.R.R. at 9b. Appellant argues that the [foregoing] supports his claim that the contract provided for employment for a definite term, the run of the tour, and therefore he could only be terminated for just cause.

"Where an employment arrangement does not contain a definite term, it will be presumed that the employment at-will rule applies." Marsh v. Boyle, 366 Pa. Super. 1, 530 A.2d 491, 493 (1987). "'[G]enerally an employment contract for a broad, unspecified duration does not overcome the presumption of at will employment.... Definiteness is required....'" Id., quoting Murphy v. Publicker Industries, Inc., 357 Pa. Super. 409, 516 A.2d 47, 51-52 (1986). The Marsh court found that an employer's assurance that Marsh would be working as publisher for at least two years was not sufficiently definite to rebut the at-will employment presumption. Marsh, 530 A.2d at 494. See also Darlington v. General Electric, 350 Pa. Super. 183, 504 A.2d 306, 312 (1986) (a contract for "permanent employment" or to work on a long-term project is insufficient to overcome the presumption of at-will employment), disapproved on other grounds as stated in Krajsa v. Keypunch, Inc., 424 Pa. Super. 230, 622 A.2d 355, 360 (1993).

Appellant argues, however, that the entertainment industry is different from most industries because of the inherent uncertainty in the duration of any theatrical undertaking. While this may be true, it does not negate the fact that none of the three documents that form the basis of the parties' agreement in this case explicitly discusses the anticipated duration of appellant's employment; the sub-paragraphs cited by appellant occur in a paragraph delineating appellant's duties. We agree with appellees that references to "the run of the tour" in a paragraph describing an employee's duties are far too vague and indefinite to form a contract for a definite duration, thus overcoming the presumption of at-will employment. See DiBonaventura v. Consolidated Rail Corp., 372 Pa. Super. 420, 539 A.2d 865, 867 (1988) ("[M]odification of an 'at will' relationship to one that can never be severed without 'just cause' is such a substantial modification that a very clear statement of an intention to so modify is required[.]"), quoting Veno v. Meredith, 357 Pa. Super. 85, 515 A.2d 571, 578 (1986), appeal denied, 532 Pa. 665, 616 A.2d 986 (1992). "Courts are highly reluctant to make definite that which the parties themselves failed to do." Darlington, 504 A.2d at 312.

Furthermore, the only paragraph in the parties' agreement addressing termination of the employment relationship is silent as to the basis for termination: it indicates neither that termination may only be for cause nor that employment is guaranteed for the duration of the tour absent cause. Rather, Pamphlet B provides only that a musician may be terminated at any time during his first twenty-one days of employment provided he is given one week's wages plus transportation costs; and that after the twenty-one-day period, either the company or the musician may terminate employment on three weeks' notice. (Pamphlet B, ¶ 14A, S.R.R. at 27b.) This paragraph supports rather than rebuts the presumption that appellant was an at-will employee.

Appellant also claims, however, that the parties' intention to create an employment contract that could only be terminated for cause can be gleaned from the surrounding circumstances. In particular, appellant claims that he gave additional consideration in the form of giving up his studio in California to go "on the road" with the touring company.

> [A] court will find "additional consideration" when an employee affords his employer a substantial benefit other than the services which the employee is hired to perform, or when the employee undergoes a substantial hardship other than the services which he is hired to perform. "If the circumstances are such that a termination of the relation by one party will result in great hardship or loss to the other, as they must have known it would when they made the contract, this is a factor of great weight in inducing a holding that the parties agreed upon a specific period." 3 A. Corbin, Corbin on Contracts § 684 (1960).

Darlington, 504 A.2d at 315. In Darlington, the court found that Darlington did not render additional consideration sufficient to overcome the at-will presumption by foregoing an opportunity for advancement with his former employer to take a position with General Electric, which he held for fifteen years. Id. Likewise, the court found that neither the heavy travel schedule nor the additional teaching duties constituted additional consideration for a professional engineer such as Darlington. Id. As a result, the court affirmed the trial court's entry of j.n.o.v. in favor of G.E.

While we recognize that Darlington retained his employment with G.E. for fifteen years while appellant retained his employment for only eight months, we cannot conclude that appellant gave additional consideration to accept the music director's job. By its very nature, that job required appellant to go on the road, thus leaving behind his home and his former employment. As appellant candidly admits in his brief, "anyone who goes on a road tour clearly has to leave their [sic] residence." Furthermore, as appellant also candidly admits, "In this case there was no guarantee that the show, 'Jesus Christ Superstar', would even open in Baltimore[,]" much less run for any definite period of time. Thus, appellant knew that by allegedly closing his studio to join the tour, he was merely taking the sort of risk associated with being employed by a touring company in the entertainment industry, a risk for which appellant was compensated.

Nevertheless, appellant argues that the question whether he offered sufficient additional consideration to rebut the presumption of at-will employment is a question of fact for the jury, not a question of law for the judge. While in the usual case, "[t]he court must allow the jury to consider [the employee's] alleged 'additional consideration' as well as all the circumstances surrounding the agreement[,]" Marsh, 530 A.2d at 494-495, quoting Greene v. Oliver Realty, Inc., 363 Pa. Super. 534, 526 A.2d 1192, 1202 (1987), appeal denied, 517 Pa. 607, 536 A.2d 1331 (1987), in this case, we disagree. "It is elementary that [before a case should proceed to trial,] the employee must first present averments which would raise a legally sufficient factual dispute." Scott, 545 A.2d at 340. As the Scott court continued, "Recent decisions have held it proper in similar instances for the court to examine the factual averments and decide that the surrounding circumstances and additional consideration do not sufficiently manifest an intent to overcome the at-will presumption." Id., citing, inter alia, Darlington, supra, and Veno, supra.

In this case, "[t]he burden of overcoming the presumption and proving that one is not employed at-will 'rest[ed] squarely' with" appellant. Luteran, 688 A.2d at 214. Furthermore, as we have already observed, one opposing a motion for summary judgment may not rest on the pleadings, but must identify evidence in the record establishing the facts essential to the cause of action which the motion cites as not having been produced. Pa. R. Civ. P. 1035.3(a)(2). Appellant, however, has failed to identify any evidence supporting his claim that he sold his studio, much less that he did so in order to take the music director's job or that he has suffered harm as a result. In response to appellees' motion for summary judgment, appellant filed a response to which he attached a letter supporting his defamation claim, his notice of dismissal letter, and a Playbill for the show, indicating the members of the staff. None of this evidence indicates that appellant provided additional consideration.

We therefore find this case distinguishable from Marsh, supra, in which Marsh resigned his position with a newspaper, moved from one city to another, and placed his house on the market in order to accept a publisher's job, only to be terminated three months after he began employment. Marsh relied on assurances that he would be working as a publisher for at least two years. He was also returning to his hometown, to a stable job in a stable community. As a result, the Marsh court found that Marsh presented a question for the jury as to whether he had proffered sufficient additional consideration to rebut the at-will employment presumption. Marsh, 530 A.2d at 494-495. Unlike the situation in Marsh, appellant has presented no evidence, nor could he, that he was assured his employment would continue beyond eight months: by his own admission, the show might never have opened. The harm he suffered, if any, was therefore intrinsic to the nature of the job he took, and thus cannot be considered additional consideration. As a result, the trial court properly found as a matter of law that appellant failed to sustain his burden of rebutting the presumption of at-will employment.

Order granting summary judgment affirmed.

CUCCIOLI v. JEKYLL & HYDE NEUE METROPOL BREMEN THEATER PRODUKTION GMBH & CO.

150 F. Supp. 2d 566 (S.D.N.Y. 2001)

KAPLAN, District Judge.

Plaintiff, the star of the New York production of the musical Jekyll & Hyde, here sues the producer of the German production for violation of Sections 50 and 51 of the New York Civil Rights Law. He contends that the German producer is using his likeness on merchandise and other materials in violation of the statute. The matter is before the Court on cross motions for summary judgment. The two main issues at this stage are whether there is any genuine issue of material fact regarding the exercise of personal jurisdiction over the defendant and whether the New York Civil Rights Law has extraterritorial effect.

I.

The following facts are undisputed. The plaintiff appeared in the eponymous role(s) in the Houston, off-Broadway, and Broadway productions of the musical Jekyll & Hyde from 1995 to 1999. The defendant, a German company, is in the business of theatrical productions and related endeavors. Its principal place of business is Bremen, Germany. Following negotiations in New York, Music Theatre International ("MTI"), Wildhorn Productions, Inc. ("WPI"), and Stage and Screen Music, Inc. ("SSMI"), licensed the defendant to produce Jekyll & Hyde in Germany, Austria, and Switzerland.

This dispute dates back at least to 1998. On March 20, 1998, the defendant received a fax from MTI stating that "[p]er my voice mail message, PACE [one of various affiliates or successors that produced Jekyll & Hyde in New York] has signed off on the use of the title treatment for Jekyll & Hyde." The parties disagree concerning whether this approved defendant's title treatment only or the logo as a whole. In any case, defendant's musical and art director wrote to the plaintiff in August 1998, enclosing samples of merchandise and stating that "our logo is a combination of the tour logo (red and black) and the Broadway logo. If you have a closer look at it, you will see that the face is yours! So I thought it a nice idea to get you some samples of it...." So much for good intentions.

During the following month, plaintiff's management firm demanded that defendant cease and desist from this use of plaintiff's image. The parties agree that the defendant never obtained written consent from the plaintiff to use his likeness.

The German production of Jekyll & Hyde premiered on February 19, 1999, a month after plaintiff's final appearance in the Broadway production. In March 1999, defendant signed an agreement with Polydor Records, GmbH, to release a compact disc of its German-language cast recording of Jekyll & Hyde. The logo containing plaintiff's image appears on the CD itself, on the back of the package liner, and on pages of the liner that offer other merchandise featuring the disputed image. The parties agree that this CD made its way to New York consumers through at least one sale off defendant's web site, <www.jekyll-hyde.de>, and several sales through local record stores, although there is no evidence that defendant was responsible for the CD reaching the local stores.

Plaintiff brought this action in March 2000, premising subject matter jurisdiction on diversity or, more properly, alienage. The amended complaint alleges use of the plaintiff's image in violation of New York Civil Rights Law Sections 50 and 51 and requests compensatory and exemplary damages as well as injunctive relief. Defendant has interposed five affirmative defenses: lack of personal jurisdiction, the statute of limitations, lack of subject matter jurisdiction based on the alleged insufficiency of the minimum amount in controversy, failure to state a claim upon which relief may be granted, and forum non conveniens.

On September 21, 2000, following discovery, plaintiff moved for summary judgment and to dismiss defendant's affirmative defenses. Defendant cross-moved for summary judgment dismissing the complaint on the ground that it fails to state a claim upon which relief may be granted. It argues that its use of plaintiff's likeness outside New York is not reached by the New York Civil Rights Law, that plaintiff cannot establish any injury from any use of his likeness in New York, and that the Court lacks jurisdiction over defendant's person. It seeks dismissal of plaintiff's prayer for an injunction on the ground of mootness.

II.

A. Personal Jurisdiction

Plaintiff moves for summary judgment dismissing the affirmative defenses, one of which is that the Court lacks personal jurisdiction over the defendant. Ultimately, of course, the burden of pleading and proving facts justifying the exercise of personal jurisdiction over the defendant lies with the plaintiff. In order to prevail on the motion to dismiss the defense at this stage of the proceeding, moreover, plaintiff must show that there is "no genuine issue as to any material fact on the jurisdictional question." In looking to the affidavits and other materials, courts "'must resolve all ambiguities and draw all reasonable inferences in favor of the party against whom summary judgment is sought.'" In other words, resolution of the personal jurisdiction defense must await trial unless plaintiff has established on this motion that jurisdiction over defendant exists even if any factual disputes were resolved in defendant's favor.

Plaintiff argues that he has satisfied three alternative bases for the exercise of personal jurisdiction in this case under New York's long-arm statute, Section 302 of New York's Civil Practice Law and Rules ("CPLR"). He asserts that defendant has transacted business in New York and that there is a direct relationship between that conduct and his cause of action. He contends that his claim arises out of defendant's commission of a tortious act within the state. In any case, he argues that defendant committed a tortious act outside the state that caused injury to the plaintiff within the state and that defendant either "regularly does or solicits business, or engages in any other persistent course of conduct, or derives substantial revenue from goods used or consumed or services rendered, in the state," or "expects or should reasonably expect the act to have consequences in the state and derives substantial revenue from interstate or international commerce." As the Court concludes that this action arises out of defendant's transaction of business in New York, however, it is unnecessary to address plaintiff's other jurisdictional arguments.

1. "Transacts Business"

The Second Circuit not long ago summarized the criteria relevant to determining whether a defendant has transacted business in New York within the meaning of CPLR §302(a), subd. 1:

> The question of whether an out-of-state defendant transacts business in New York is determined by considering a variety of factors, including: (i) whether the defendant has an on-going contractual relationship with a New York corporation...; (ii) whether the contract was negotiated or executed in New York...and whether, after executing a contract with a New York business, the defendant has visited New York for the purpose of meeting with parties to the contract regarding the relationship...; (iii) what the choice-of-law clause is in any such contract...; and (iv) whether the contract requires franchisees to send notices and payments into the forum state or subjects them to supervision by the corporation in the forum state....Although all are relevant, no one factor is dispositive. Other factors may also be considered, and the ultimate determination is based on the totality of the circumstances.

Agency Rent A Car Sys., Inc. v. Grand Rent A Car Corp., 98 F.3d 25, 29 (2d Cir. 1996).

Here, defendant negotiated licensing and supplemental production agreements for foreign productions of Jekyll & Hyde in New York with MTI, WPI and SSMI (collectively the "Licensors"). It pays royalties to these New York parties. It is subject to the Licensors' supervision in that the supplemental production contract appointed an artistic consultant to exercise all of the Licensors' approvals and to travel to Bremen as necessary. Although the original contract called for the application of California law, the supplemental production agreement elected New York law and stated that the parties submitted to the jurisdiction of the State of New York. Moreover, the location of contract negotiations in New York was not fortuitous. As a practical matter, the musical's successful Broadway performance certainly affected the desirability to defendant of the license as well as the fact that it obtained the license in New York. In all the circumstances, there is little doubt that defendant transacted business in New York.

2. "Arising out of" Business Transacted in New York

The fact that defendant transacted business in New York is not the end of the inquiry, as the statute permits the exercise of personal jurisdiction here on the basis of such activity only if the claim arose out of that transaction of business. Thus, the question remains whether plaintiff's claim is sufficiently related to defendant's transaction of business with the Licensors to warrant the exercise of specific jurisdiction over this claim.

As many courts have pointed out, determining whether a claim stands in sufficient proximity to the transaction of business in the forum state to permit the forum to exercise jurisdiction over the defendant with respect to the claim is not an exact science. It involves a judgment as to whether the cause of action is "'sufficiently related to the business transacted that it would not be unfair to deem it to arise out of the transacted business.'" "To determine whether a sufficient nexus exists, a court must evaluate the 'totality of the circumstances surrounding defendants' activities in New York in connection with the matter giving rise to the lawsuit."

There unquestionably is a connection between the production and license agreements and plaintiff's claim. The gravamen of the claim is plaintiff's contention that defendant used his likeness without consent. But the defendant rejoins that its use was appropriate because plaintiff's contracts with the New York producers permitted use of his likeness, and defendant acquired that right by virtue of its license to produce the German version of the show. Thus, while this case is unusual in that the plaintiff was not a party to the licensing and production agreements that defendant negotiated in New York—in other words, defendant did not transact business in New York with plaintiff—the statute does not so require. Consideration of the totality of the circumstances leads to the conclusion that there is a sufficient relationship between plaintiff's claim and the business defendant transacted in New York so that there is no unfairness to subjecting defendant to suit here on this claim.

For the reasons set forth above, plaintiff has shown that there is no genuine issue as to any material fact and that it is entitled to judgment as a matter of law on the jurisdictional issue. Accordingly, insofar as plaintiff seeks summary judgment dismissing the defense of lack of personal jurisdiction, the motion is granted.

B. Statute of Limitations

Plaintiff moves also for summary judgment dismissing the statute of limitations defense. As the statute of limitations is an affirmative defense on which the defendant bears the burden of proof at trial, the allocation of the burden of going forward on a motion for summary judgment is different than on the issue of personal jurisdiction. The plaintiff, as he has done here, "may satisfy its Rule 56 burden by showing 'that there is an absence of evidence to support [an essential element of] the [non-moving party's] case.'" At that point the burden shifts to the defendant to establish either that the claim is untimely as a matter of law or that there is a genuine issue of fact material to the limitations defense in order to preserve the defense for trial.

Plaintiff concedes that the statute of limitations on Section 51 claims is one year and that this action was commenced two years after defendant began to produce merchandise bearing the allegedly offending logo. He nevertheless argues that defendant's actions have been of a continuing nature and that the statute first began to run from the most recent abuse, thus saving the entirety of his claim. The argument is without merit.

Under New York law, a statute of limitations begins to run when a claim accrues. A tort claim accrues upon the occurrence of the last event necessary to give rise to a claim, generally at the time of injury. In defamation and invasion of privacy cases, this almost invariably occurs at first publication—generally interpreted as when the publication first goes on sale to the public. And the New York Court of Appeals, in adopting the single publication rule, long ago rejected the proposition advanced by plaintiff, viz. that each subsequent publication or distribution of challenged material sets the statute running anew. Indeed, any other view could produce a "vast multiplicity of suits which could arise from mass publications…and the attendant problem[ ] of…endless tolling of the statute of limitations."

In view of these principles, plaintiff's concession that it did not sue until more than one year after the defendant's first use of the logo would appear to be fatal to his claim. But the matter is not quite so simple for two reasons.

First, each new edition of a work—such as a paperback edition of a work previously published only in hard cover—ordinarily is viewed as "a new publication upon which a separate cause of action may be based and for which the statute of limitations begins to run again." The same principle applies to merchandise bearing names or images allegedly violative of Section 51. [T]he statute of limitations runs separately as to each new product distributed with a name or image, the use of which contravenes the statute. Hence, the statute began to run as to the CD of the German cast recording on the date that it first was placed on sale in violation of Section 51, and it began to run as to each other item of merchandise on the analogous date for each.

The second difficulty is implicit in what has been said already and is intertwined with defendant's principal argument—that plaintiff has no claim for the allegedly unconsented to use of his likeness outside the State of New York. As the statute of limitations begins to run upon the occurrence of the last event necessary to give rise to a claim, the date of first publication or distribution of a given article of merchandise triggers the statute only if that publication or distribution is actionable. Hence, if Section 51 gives rise to a claim only for use of plaintiff's likeness in the State of New York, then the last event necessary to give rise to a claim occurs—and the statute begins to run—only upon first publication or distribution in New York. Accordingly, the Court turns to that question.

C. Effect of Section 51 With Respect to Out-of-State Uses

Defendant seeks dismissal of so much of plaintiff's claim as relates to out-of-state uses of his likeness on the ground that Section 51 of the Civil Rights Law creates a cause of action in favor only of "[a]ny person whose name, portrait, picture, or voice is used within this state for advertising purposes or for the purposes of trade" without written consent as required by Section 50. Plaintiff disputes this conclusion, contending that the single publication rule permits a plaintiff injured in the manner claimed here to bring a single action and to recover therein damages for all injuries sustained, wherever the publication occurred. But plaintiff misses the point.

To be sure, the single publication rule usually is summarized as standing for the propositions that a plaintiff, as to any single publication, may bring only one action and may recover in that action "all damages suffered in all jurisdictions." But this summary does not do away with choice of law analysis. Plaintiff brought this action in a federal court in New York, thereby submitting himself to application of New York choice of law rules. New York applies its own substantive law to claims for violation of the right of publicity brought by New York domiciliaries such as plaintiff.

The inquiry does not end there. For application of New York law to comport with due process New York must have "a significant contact or significant aggregation of contacts" with the parties and transaction "creating state interests, such that choice of its law is neither arbitrary nor fundamentally unfair." Choice of New York law meets this standard. Plaintiff is a New York domiciliary, and the dispute arises from contracts that both plaintiff and defendant negotiated in New York. At least one of those contracts contains a New York choice-of-law provision. Defendant's agreements provide for ongoing contacts between the defendant and New York. Moreover, just as New York, in its role as "financial capital of the world, serving as an international clearinghouse and market place for a plethora of international transactions," has an interest in resolving financial disputes related to it, New York has an interest in resolving disputes involving subsidiary rights to Broadway theater productions.

Having concluded that New York substantive law controls this dispute, the Court proceeds to its determination. In Roberson v. Rochester Folding Box Co., 171 N.Y. 538, 64 N.E. 442 (1902), the New York Court of Appeals broadly declared that there is no common law right of privacy in the State of New York and denied recovery to an infant plaintiff whose photograph had been distributed widely by the defendant in order to advertise its baking flour. The Legislature promptly adopted the statute here in question to overturn the holding of Roberson, albeit not its broad dictum, by creating a cause of action for the commercial or trade use of one's name or picture without one's consent. In doing so, however, it created a claim in favor only of one whose likeness had been used for prohibited purposes "within this state." In consequence, as New York courts uniformly have held, the substantive law of New York is that one may recover for trade or commercial use of one's likeness only to the extent that the use occurs in New York.

This conclusion has two implications here. The first is that out-of-state uses of plaintiff's likeness for trade or advertising purposes are not actionable under New York law. To the extent that plaintiff seeks damages based on such uses, his claim must be dismissed. Second, as the out-of-state uses are not actionable, they cannot trigger the running of the statute of limitations. Accordingly, the statute of limitations as to each type of merchandise on which plaintiff's likeness has appeared runs from the date on which it first was offered for sale in New York.

The merchandise that indisputably was sold by defendant in New York was the one CD purchased in July 1999 from defendant's web site. As that sale occurred less than one year before the commencement of this action, the claim with respect to that sale is timely unless the offering of the German language cast recordings via the Internet web site accessible from New York (a) began more than one year before the commencement of this action, and (b) was sufficient to trigger the running of the statute of limitations—in other words, was a use "within this state."

New York courts do not seem to have addressed the question whether items on a web site that can be viewed in New York are published or offered for sale to the public in New York. Perhaps the most useful analogy is to jurisdictional analysis of commercial torts such as trademark infringement because such a tort is committed within New York if infringing goods have been offered for sale in New York. There is consensus in the developing case law that whether a defendant has committed a tort in the state through its web site depends on how interactive the web site is.

In Bensusan Restaurant Corp. v. King, 126 F.3d 25, 29 (2d Cir.1997), a New York club sued a Missouri jazz club of the same name, basing jurisdiction on defendant's web site, which contained the infringing name and a hyperlink to the New York club. The

Second Circuit affirmed the district court's holding that defendant committed a tort where the web site was created rather than where it was viewed.

Courts have reached different conclusions when faced with more interactive web sites that offer chatting, ordering, or downloading of forms or when e-mail that contains the disputed image is sent into the state.

These cases suggest the appropriate result here. Defendant's web site was created and maintained in Germany in connection with the Bremen production of the show. The CD in question was of a German language cast recording, certainly an item of limited appeal in the United States. The web site itself was in German. The only suggestion that the merchandise, the web site, or the Bremen production was promoted in New York or, for that matter, elsewhere in the United States is plaintiff's unsupported assertion that there was a hyperlink from the New York production's web site to defendant's web site. Although such a hyperlink might be a factor suggesting an offer for sale in New York, plaintiff here alleges only that defendant's web site was "accessible" through that hyperlink, not that defendant was responsible for the connection. In these circumstances, the Court holds that the offering of merchandise containing the plaintiff's image on the German web site did not constitute a use of the image "within this state." Accordingly, it neither began the running of the statute of limitations nor gave rise to a broader cause of action.

III.

For the foregoing reasons, plaintiff's motion for summary judgment dismissing the affirmative defenses is granted to the extent that the defense of lack of personal jurisdiction is dismissed. The defenses of lack of subject matter jurisdiction and forum non conveniens, which lack substantial basis, also are dismissed. Plaintiff's motion is denied in all other respects. Defendant's cross-motion for summary judgment dismissing the complaint is granted to the extent that the action, insofar as it seeks damages for allegedly unconsented to uses of plaintiff's likeness outside the State of New York, is granted. It is denied in all other respects.

Notes

1. A sample road show booking agreement appears in Appendix H of this casebook.

2. In his opinion, which was issued at the end of July 1956, District Judge Levet cryptically mentions "that the leading actress in the film 'Bus Stop' has recently secured certain publicity[.]" He was referring to the fact that one month earlier, Marilyn Monroe had stunned the world by marrying playwright Arthur Miller, who in 1949 had rocketed to stardom with "Death of a Salesman." Like her earlier union with baseball legend Joe DiMaggio, Monroe's marriage to Miller ended in divorce in 1961; many people believe that Maggie, the self-destructive central character of Miller's 1964 play, *After the Fall*, is based on Monroe (a claim repeatedly denied by Miller).

3. At one time, the Shuberts controlled 60% of the nation's first-class theaters and typically booked more than 1,000 shows per year. After the United Supreme Court ruled they were subject to the anti-trust laws, however, the Shuberts were forced to sell most of their holdings. *See further* Maryann Chach et al., *The Shuberts Present: 100 Years of American Theater* (2001); Foster Hirsch, *The Boys from Syracuse: The Shuberts' Theatrical Empire* (1998); Brooks McNamara, *The Shuberts of Broadway: A History Drawn from the Collection of the Shubert Archive* (1990). *See also* www.shubertarchive.org.

4. Did the plaintiffs in *Rapagnani* and *Cuccioli* get a fair shake? Assuming they did, is there anything they could have done differently that would have led to a more favorable result (or avoided the need to sue altogether)?

Problem 26

While performing in a year-long tour, an actress received (per her contract) a daily allowance of $100 to cover the cost of food and lodging. Living on the road proved expensive, however, and she wound up having to pay an additional $15,000 out of her own pocket. Is this amount tax deductible? *See Boyer v. Commissioner*, 1977 WL 3158 (T.C. 1977).

Chapter 12

Not-For-Profit Productions

A. OVERVIEW

In prior chapters, we have focused chiefly on for-profit theatrical companies. But many not-for-profit entities (such as schools, fraternal societies, religious groups, and community organizations) also put on plays. When they do, distinct questions arise regarding funding and artistic freedom.

B. FUNDING

PLUMSTEAD THEATRE SOCIETY, INC. v. COMMISSIONER OF INTERNAL REVENUE
74 T.C. 1324 (1980),
aff'd, 675 F.2d 244 (9th Cir. 1982)

WILBUR, Judge.

Respondent determined that petitioner does not qualify for exemption from Federal income tax as a charitable or educational organization under section 501(c)(3) [of the Internal Revenue Code]. Petitioner challenges respondent's determination and has invoked the jurisdiction of this Court under section 7428 for a declaratory judgment. All of the prerequisites for declaratory judgment have been satisfied. The issue for our decision is whether petitioner is operated exclusively for charitable or educational purposes within the meaning of section 501(c)(3).

This case was submitted on a stipulated administrative record under Rule 122, Tax Court Rules of Practice and Procedure. The stipulated record is incorporated herein by this reference. The evidentiary facts and representations contained in the administrative record are assumed to be true for the purposes of this proceeding.

Petitioner Plumstead Theatre Society was incorporated on January 18, 1977, as a nonprofit corporation under the laws of the State of California. Its principal place of business is in Los Angeles, Calif. It filed its application for recognition of exemption under section 501(c)(3) on June 17, 1977, with the Internal Revenue Service. On July 31, 1978, respondent issued to petitioner a final adverse ruling denying petitioner exempt status under section 501(c)(3). The reasons stated in the letter for denial are:

You are not operated exclusively for charitable or educational purposes within the meaning of section 501(c)(3) of the Code. A substantial purpose of your organization is a commercial purpose which is not an exempt purpose. Additionally, part of your net earnings will inure to the benefit of a private individual or shareholder. Furthermore, you are operated for private interests rather than public interests.

As stated in its articles of incorporation, petitioner was formed as a nonprofit corporation for the following specific and primary purposes:

To cultivate, promote, foster, sponsor, develop, and encourage understanding of and public interest in the fields of theatre, dance, music, motion pictures, and the arts, all of the classic nature, whether ancient or contemporary;

To promote and encourage talent and ability in composition and creation of, as well as performance of, works in each of the said fields, through commissions for new and original works, awards and scholarships and grants to existing organizations and individuals active in these fields; to provide a training ground and workshop to develop dancers, choreographers, playwrights, writers, artists, composers, performers, designers, directors, musicians, technicians, and administrative personnel and the like in each of these fields;

To institute, organize and conduct workshops where the foregoing can meet, study, discuss, exchange and develop techniques in each of these fields;

To give recognition to experiments and achievements in each of these fields through citations, awards, scholarships and grants to individual writers, performers, organizations and the like and to give public performances in each of the above fields;

To receive contributions and to make donations to, dispense contributions to, and otherwise aid and support those organizations qualified for exemption from federal income tax under the Internal Revenue Code of 1954, as now in effect or subsequently amended, that are organized and operated exclusively for the above mentioned purposes.

In addition, the articles of incorporation provide that petitioner is not organized and shall not be operated for pecuniary gain; that no part of its net earnings shall inure to the benefit of any private member or individual; that upon dissolution, any remaining assets shall be distributed to a nonprofit organization organized for the same purpose as petitioner and qualifying as tax exempt under section 501(c)(3).

The members of the board of directors of petitioner are a diversified group of individuals interested in the performing arts. No officer or director is salaried in his or her capacity as an officer or director of petitioner. Several members of the board of directors advanced non-interest-bearing loans ranging from $100 to $250 to petitioner to cover [the] initial costs of incorporation.

Initially, petitioner proposes to fulfill its purposes by presenting professional dramatic theatre productions of the classical nature, ancient and contemporary; by forming a workshop in the Los Angeles area for new American playwrights; and by establishing a fund to assist new and established playwrights in writing new plays for petitioner to produce. During 1977, petitioner engaged in extensive negotiations with Ambassador International Cultural Foundation (the Ambassador Foundation), a nonprofit, cultural foundation, for joint sponsorship by petitioner and Ambassador College of a season of three family-oriented plays to be shown in the Ambassador Auditorium in

Pasadena, Calif. Petitioner chose Ambassador Auditorium as the site for its resident theatre with the hope of rebuilding the theatre audiences from Glendale, San Gabriel, Orange County, and San Bernardino County after the demise of the Pasadena Playhouse. An agreement between petitioner and the Ambassador Foundation setting forth the respective rights and duties of each entity with regard to the production of the season of plays in Pasadena was executed on July 27, 1977.

Petitioner intends to use accomplished performers, directors, and technicians in its productions. Because petitioner is organized as a nonprofit corporation, it is able to operate under an Equity League of Resident Theatres Contract (LORT contract) which provides for lower compensation for the professionals used in its productions than that which is normally demanded of commercial theatre. As of December 1977, approximately 60 theatre companies in the United States, all tax-exempt, nonprofit corporations, used the LORT contract.

Petitioner plans to present its productions in Pasadena, Calif., and Washington, D.C., and in any other city where subscription prices and/or theatre guarantees will help defray the costs of production. Petitioner contemplates that contributions, donations, and low-cost loans will cover production costs and that ticket sales and/or theatre guarantees will cover the running costs. Any profits that may accrue to petitioner from specific performances will be used to fund future production projects, a playwriting commission for American playwrights, and an experimental workshop for actors and playwrights.

On August 15, 1977, petitioner entered into an agreement with the John F. Kennedy Center for the Performing Arts (Kennedy Center), a nonprofit tax-exempt organization, to co-produce the play, "First Monday in October" (First Monday). Under the agreement, petitioner and the Kennedy Center were each to provide one-half of the capitalization required for the production, and to share equally any profits or losses derived from the presentation of the play in Washington. Petitioner's president, Henry Fonda, starred in the play and agreed to accept a lesser salary than he would normally demand of commercial theatre, and to waive a royalty interest in the gross receipts. The play premiered at the Kennedy Center on December 26, 1977. The Washington, D.C., production of First Monday was petitioner's only theatrical production prior to the issuance of the final adverse letter ruling by respondent. Upon completion of the run of First Monday at the Kennedy Center, there remained over $90,000 in unrealized production costs with respect to the presentation of the play.

Prior to the premiere of First Monday at the Kennedy Center, petitioner encountered difficulties in raising its share of capitalization costs required for the production. In order to meet its obligations under the agreement with the Kennedy Center, petitioner sold a portion of its rights in First Monday to outside investors through a limited partnership entitled the First Monday in October Co. (the partnership). Petitioner is the general partner, and two individuals and Pantheon Pictures, Inc., a for-profit corporation, are the limited partners. The purpose of the partnership was to co-produce First Monday in Washington, D.C., and to individually produce or co-produce the play in New York or elsewhere. Under the partnership agreement, the limited partners were required to contribute capital to the partnership totaling $100,000. In return, they collectively received a 63.5 percent share in any profits or losses resulting from the production of First Monday. Petitioner was not required to make a capital contribution to the partnership. Petitioner closed First Monday on February 24, 1978, at a loss.

The issue for our decision is whether petitioner qualifies as a tax-exempt organization under section 501(c)(3). Respondent does not dispute that petitioner is organized for charitable and educational purposes, the first test an organization must pass in order to qualify for exemption. Rather, it argues that petitioner is not operated exclusively for charitable purposes within the meaning of section 501(c)(3), because petitioner has a substantial commercial purpose and is operated for the benefit of private, rather than public, interests. Petitioner maintains that it is operated in a manner harmonious with the requirements of section 501(c)(3). We agree with petitioner that it is operated exclusively for charitable and educational purposes under section 501(c)(3).

Section 501(a) exempts from Federal income tax any organization which meets the criteria set forth in section 501(c). Section 501(c)(3) provides that a corporation which is organized and operated exclusively for charitable or educational purposes, among others, is an organization referred to in section 501(a), if no part of its net earnings inures to the benefit of any private individual or shareholder, and if it does not engage in other prohibited activity. It has long been recognized that the promotion and encouragement of the arts can be both charitable and educational. Broadway Theatre League of Lynchburg, Va. v. United States, 293 F. Supp. 346 (W.D. Va. 1968); 6 J. Mertens, Law of Federal Income Taxation, sec. 34.09, p. 45 (1975 rev.); B. Hopkins, Law of Tax Exempt Organizations, sec. 6.9, pp. 84-86 (3d ed. 1979). Cultural organizations such as museums, symphony orchestras, ballet, opera, repertory, modern dance, theatre, and other similar organizations may clearly qualify for tax-exempt status as educational and/or charitable organizations under section 501(c)(3), so long as the activities of the organization are in furtherance of its exempt purpose. See sec. 1.501(c)(3)-1(d)(3)(ii), example (4), Income Tax Regs. These organizations are viewed as charitable and educational because they promote public appreciation of the arts, considered useful to the individual and beneficial to the community, as well as provide instruction and training to individuals for the purposes of improving or developing their capabilities. See secs. 1.501(c)(3)-1(d)(2) and 1.501(c)(3)-1(d)(3), Income Tax Regs.

Indeed, respondent has recognized in his revenue rulings that organizations devoted to the promotion of the arts may qualify for tax exemption. In Rev. Rul. 64-175, 1964-1 C.B. (Part 1) 185, respondent ruled that a nonprofit corporation, organized and operated primarily for the purpose of developing the interest of the American public in the dramatic arts, qualified for exemption under section 501(c)(3). The main activity of the organization described in the ruling was that of producing plays and making classical works of the theatre available in cities throughout the United States by means of a permanent touring repertory theatre company of the highest professional standards. In ruling that the theatre company qualified for tax exemption, respondent stated that the repertory company is educational, much in the same way a symphony orchestra is educational, for purposes of section 501(c)(3). Similarly, in Rev. Rul. 73-45, 1973-1 C.B. 220, respondent ruled that a nonprofit organization created to foster the development of an appreciation for drama in a particular community by sponsoring professional theatrical productions qualified for tax exemption under section 501(c)(3). The organization was not deemed to be operated for private rather than public benefit, even though it procured the theatre productions through a renewable contract with a commercial booking agency that had also played a major role in its creation.

In spite of public acknowledgment that nonprofit corporations which produce and present dramatic plays to the American public in furtherance of an exempt purpose of promoting cultural arts may qualify for tax exemption, respondent ruled adversely for petitioner in the instant case. First, respondent argues that petitioner has a substantial commercial purpose which defeats tax-exempt status under section 501(c)(3). See Better Business Bureau v. United States, 326 U.S. 279 (1945). Rephrased, respondent argues that despite the stated purposes in its articles of incorporation, petitioner is operating in a manner indistinguishable from a commercial enterprise involved in the business of producing plays, because its only activity thus far is co-producing (with the Kennedy Center) a play that has a commercial hue.

We do not believe the administrative record supports such a contention. It is clear from the record that petitioner's main focus is to organize a regional theatre in Pasadena, Calif., to produce and present plays for an area that lacks a community theatre. Toward this goal, members of the board of petitioner have spent countless uncompensated hours negotiating a contract with Ambassador College for the use of its auditorium to house a season of three dramatic productions. An arrangement was worked out with the Ambassador International Cultural Foundation to jointly sponsor the plays. A committee was formed to review and select appropriate dramatic plays in accordance with the highest literary and artistic standards.

We do not agree with respondent that because these productions, as well as the planned community workshops for actors and playwrights and the fund for American playwrights, have yet to materialize they do not count as activities. Respondent took a still shot of what is an ongoing motion picture of many dimensions. It is quite clear that petitioner is anxious to effectuate its projects as soon as it can obtain funding. Especially in the formative years, a nonprofit community theatre needs a great deal of financial support in the form of contributions and donations before it can function. See Rockefeller Panel Report, "The Performing Arts: Problems and Prospects," p. 62 (1965). Until it is declared tax exempt, solicitation for foundation support and individual contributions is useless.

Nor do we agree with respondent that the activity of co-producing the play, "First Monday in October," with the Kennedy Center is indicative of a substantial commercial purpose. In fulfilling its goals of promoting and fostering the American dramatic arts, petitioner plans not only to resurrect past literary works, but to encourage and develop new and original theatre productions. Indeed, developing new works of artistic quality is considered one of the obligations of a nonprofit performing arts organization. See Rockefeller Panel Report, supra at 55.

Respondent has not alleged that petitioner should not be allowed to produce and present original plays. Rather, it points to the manner in which First Monday was presented—that it was advertised in newspapers, that tickets were sold, that professionals were used in the productions—to argue that petitioner has a substantial commercial purpose.

We feel that respondent is completely misdirected in his objections. The Kennedy Center is a tax-exempt organization chartered by Congress and built partially with federal funds. For major theatrical performances, it generally advertises in the newspaper, charges the public for tickets, and uses paid professionals. Symphony orchestras are considered per se educational under section 501(c)(3). See sec. 1.501(c) (3)-1(d)(3)(ii), example (4), Income Tax Regs. Yet they too advertise performances, sell tickets, and pay their musicians, and such activity does not render them "substantially commercial." Indeed, all nonprofit performing arts organizations, from opera to ballet to theatre to symphony orchestras, depend upon ticket sales to cover a portion of their operating budgets. See 1 Ford Foundation, Finances of the Performing Arts 64-67 (1974); Rockefeller Panel Report, supra at 53-56. The purpose of presenting dramatic productions is for the public to see, to appreciate, to reflect, and to be educated. Nothing in section 501(c)(3) dictates that the public find out about petitioner's performances through word of mouth, that they be forced to watch amateurs act, or that they be seated totally free of charge. The kind of activity respondent deems objectionable in the instant case is no different from that which he has sanctioned on public record. See Rev. Rul. 73-45, 1973-1 C.B. 220; Rev. Rul. 64-175, 1964-1 C.B. (Part 1) 185.

Admittedly, the line between commercial enterprises which produce and present theatrical performances and nonprofit, tax-exempt organizations that do the same is not always easy to draw. Indeed, the theatre is the most prominent area of the performing arts in which commercial enterprises coexist, often in the same city, with nonprofit, tax-exempt charitable organizations that also sponsor professional presentations. See B. Hopkins, Law of Tax Exempt Organizations, sec. 6.9, p. 38 (3d ed. 1979).

However, there are differences. Commercial theatres are operated to make a profit. Thus, they choose plays having the greatest mass audience appeal. Generally, they run the plays so long as they can attract a crowd. They set ticket prices to pay the total costs of production and to return a profit. Since their focus is perennially on the box office, they do not generally organize other activities to educate the public and they do not encourage and instruct relatively unknown playwrights and actors.

Tax-exempt organizations are not operated to make a profit. They fulfill their artistic and community obligations by focusing on the highest possible standards of performance; by serving the community broadly; by developing new and original works; and by providing educational programs and opportunities for new talent. Thus, they keep the great classics of the theatre alive and are willing to experiment with new forms of dramatic writing, acting, and staging. Usually, nonprofit theatrical organizations present a number of plays during a season for a relatively short specified time period. Because of a desired quality in acoustics and intimacy with the audience, many present their performances in halls of limited capacity. The combination of the shortness of the season, the limited seating capacity, the enormous costs of producing quality performances of new or experimental works, coupled with the desire to keep ticket prices at a level which is affordable to most of the community, means that, except in rare cases, box office receipts will never cover the cost of producing plays for nonprofit performing arts organizations. See Rockefeller Panel Report, supra at 53-62. We feel that petitioner has shown that it is organized and operated similar to other nonprofit theatre organizations, rather than as a commercial theatre.

Respondent's last argument is that because of the partnership petitioner entered into with two private individuals and a corporation, whereby the limited partners provided capital in exchange for an interest in the profits and losses of First Monday, petitioner is operated for private, rather than public interests. We do not agree. After entering into an agreement with the Kennedy Center, petitioner discovered it was in need of funds for its share of the capitalization costs of First Monday. The record shows that in an arm's-length transaction, it obtained those funds by selling a portion of its interest in the play itself, for a reasonable price. Petitioner is not obligated for the return of any capital contribution made by the limited partners from its own funds, and the partnership has no interest in petitioner or in any other plays it is planning to produce. The limited partners have no control over the way petitioner operates or manages its affairs, and none of the limited partners nor any officer or director of Pantheon Pictures, Inc., is an officer or director of petitioner. We find this arrangement, limited to one play produced by petitioner, is no more intrusive or indicative of private interests than the contractual, percentage arrangement approved of in Broadway Theatre League of Lynchburg, Va. v. United States, 293 F. Supp. 346 (W.D. Va. 1968).

Therefore, we find that petitioner is organized and operated exclusively for charitable and educational purposes under section 501(c)(3).

An appropriate order will be entered.

EYCHANER v. GROSS
779 N.E.2d 1115 (Ill. 2002)

FREEMAN, Justice.

Plaintiffs, Fred Eychaner and Betty Lou Weiss, were directors of the Auditorium Theatre Council (Council). Plaintiffs brought an action against defendants, Roosevelt University and its president, Theodore Gross (collectively Roosevelt), in the circuit court of Cook County. In the claims and counterclaims that developed in this case, the Auditorium Theatre Council, Inc. (ATC Inc.) and Roosevelt, respectively, asserted their authority to control and operate the Auditorium Theatre (Theatre). Specifically, plaintiffs and ATC Inc. claimed that Roosevelt placed the right to control and operate the Theatre into a charitable trust with ATC Inc. as trustee.

At the close of a bench trial, the trial court found in favor of Roosevelt and rejected all theories supporting ATC Inc.'s control of the Theatre. The trial court, inter alia, declared Roosevelt the sole and exclusive owner of the Theatre. The court also ordered an accounting of ATC Inc.'s funds to separate public donations from operating revenues.

The appellate court, with one justice dissenting, reversed these orders and remanded the cause for further proceedings. 321 Ill.App.3d 759, 254 Ill.Dec. 557, 747 N.E.2d 969. We allowed defendants' petition for leave to appeal. 177 Ill.2d R. 315(a). We now reverse the judgment of the appellate court, affirm the order of the trial court, and remand the cause to the trial court for further proceedings.

BACKGROUND

During the 10-week bench trial, the court received approximately 400 documents and heard testimony from 37 witnesses, all of which generated 98 record volumes. The bench trial adduced the following facts.

Setting

The Auditorium Building is located in downtown Chicago, bordered by Michigan Avenue on the east, Congress Parkway on the south, and Wabash Avenue on the west. The building was designed and built in the late nineteenth century by the renowned architects Louis Sullivan and Dankmar Adler. The building originally contained a hotel, commercial office space, and the Theatre, which comprises approximately 40% of the entire building. The Auditorium Building, including the Theatre with its near-perfect acoustics, was recognized as an architectural masterpiece. However, by the end of World War II, the building, including the Theatre, was abandoned and in a state of disrepair.

Cast

In 1945, Roosevelt was incorporated as an Illinois not-for-profit corporation. In 1946, it became possible for Roosevelt to purchase the Auditorium Building and, to that end, the University solicited and received donations. In 1947, Roosevelt purchased the building, protected the Theatre from further deterioration, and converted the remaining space for use as Roosevelt's campus.

In the mid-1950s, Roosevelt began exploring ways to restore the Theatre. On September 11, 1958, a committee of Roosevelt's board of trustees recommended to the full board that a separate not-for-profit corporation be created to restore and operate the Theatre under that corporation's "trusteeship." On September 25, the full board rejected the proposal amid concerns of giving away rights to the University's property. The board recommended that "[t]he University should remain the 'trustee' of the Auditorium Theatre."

At a December 4, 1958 board meeting, trustee Beatrice Spachner submitted "a plan for the restoration of the Auditorium Theater and its operation under the auspices of Roosevelt University." On February 17, 1959, Roosevelt's board of trustees established the Auditorium Restoration and Development Committee (ARDC), composed of Roosevelt Board members and faculty and community representatives. The ARDC was directed to examine Spachner's Theatre restoration plan.

On October 29, 1959, the ARDC reported to Roosevelt's board of trustees. At that meeting, the board passed a motion tentatively approving a fund drive to restore the Theatre, subject to the following conditions: that the committee's fund-raising efforts not impair Roosevelt's financial resources or credit; that Roosevelt's legal counsel recommend to the board "the legal entity and manner of contract" that would enable Roosevelt to obtain its objectives; and "[t]hat the University not lose ownership or control of the Auditorium Theatre."

The ARDC oversaw the drafting of a resolution to implement the fund drive. Attorney Elmer Gertz was the principal drafter of the resolution. In a letter dated January 21, 1960, Gertz asked Kenneth Montgomery, Roosevelt's attorney, to review the draft resolution. Gertz stated:

> [A] draft of the resolution has been agreed upon. I am sending a copy of it herewith. It is the consensus of all involved in this situation that it is best not to form any separate corporation, foundation, trust or other legal entity, but to proceed in the manner set forth in the resolution.

Gertz asked for Montgomery's ideas on the resolution, specifically on the subject of tax exemption.

The ARDC presented the draft resolution to Roosevelt's trustees at their February 11, 1960 board meeting. The proposed resolution renamed the ARDC the Auditorium Theatre Council (Council) and authorized it to raise funds for and to restore the Theatre. Several trustees continued to express concerns that the proposed resolution was not sufficiently explicit in its description of Roosevelt's control over the ARDC. They questioned whether the resolution complied with the board's October 29, 1959 motion that Roosevelt "not lose ownership or control of the Auditorium Theatre." Criticizing the proposed resolution, trustee Lerner stated that the "Theater would be given away in perpetuum, under this proposal. No [Roosevelt] trustee who understands the word 'trust' should vote for it."

As reflected in the minutes of the board meeting, Gertz responded to these concerns:

> [Gertz] was not attempting to make policy for the Board, he said, but had simply tried to realize its intent as derived from the Board's own earlier resolutions and statements of policy. He went on to say that no separate corporation had been proposed because this arrangement would be even more subject to the objection that the University would be prevented from exercising control over the Auditorium. He asserted that any action taken by the proposed Auditorium Council could be changed or rescinded by the Board of Trustees.

The resolution was tabled to allow the ARDC to address the concerns that had been raised.

On February 18, 1960, the ARDC presented a revised resolution to Roosevelt's board of trustees. The revision renamed the ARDC the Auditorium Theater Council. The revision made Roosevelt's control more explicit and further limited the authority of the Council. Language stating that the Council would "fully control" the fund-raising, restoration, maintenance, management, and programming for the Theatre was deleted, leaving the Council only "responsible" for fund-raising and restoration and "charged with the responsibility of carrying out the details of" the fund-raising campaign and the management, programming, and operation of the Theatre. Language that would have allowed the Council to "adopt such procedures…as it may deem necessary" was dropped. Language was added to ensure Roosevelt board approval, on an annual basis, of all new members to the Council's executive committee. Language was added to ensure the board's involvement in establishing a development reserve amount for the Theatre, with all Theatre revenues above that amount being transferred to Roosevelt's unrestricted funds. Language was added requiring the Council to make periodic progress reports regarding the restoration to the board, to provide information requested by the board, to make annual reports of operations to the board, and to submit to an annual audit by accountants. Finally, language was added requiring that the actions and programming of the Council "be in harmony with the aims of the University in serving the educational and cultural aspirations of the community."

Some trustees proposed additional amendments based on their concerns that the revised resolution did not sufficiently describe the control that the University would have over the Council. Kenneth Montgomery, Roosevelt's attorney, opposed any additional amendments as unnecessary. He described the Council as an "agency" of the University and assured the board that nothing would "prevent the Board of Trustees from 'deactivating' the Auditorium Council and Committee [ARDC], who would owe their origin and authority to the Board." [Ultimately], the Roosevelt University board of trustees rejected the proposed amendments. The board adopted the revised resolution by a vote of 18 to 7.

Subsequent to the February 18, 1960 board meeting, Montgomery wrote a letter to the United States Internal Revenue Service (IRS) in which he sought a determination on behalf of Roosevelt that contributions to the Council would be tax deductible. Montgomery asked the IRS to grant Roosevelt's request because contributions to the Council were "in fact contributions to [Roosevelt] because the Council is its agent." The IRS ruled that contributions to the Council would be tax-deductible to the donor, stating: "Since it appears that contributions to the Council will inure entirely to your [Roosevelt's] benefit such contributions will be considered contributions to you."

The Council employed architects, engineers, construction experts and others to determine a plan to restore the Theatre. The cost of restoration was estimated at a minimum of $2.75 million. Roosevelt would often advance funds for the restoration of the Theatre. On October 31, 1967, the Theatre was reopened to the public.

The Council operated the Theatre under the supervision and control of Roosevelt. At the March 4, 1971 meeting of Roosevelt's board of trustees, Chairperson Jerome Stone reported that Standing Policies and Operating Procedures (SOPs) had been developed for the Theatre. According to the minutes, Stone reported: "This statement reaffirms and supplements the Board's resolution of February 18, 1960 establishing the Council." At its April 22, 1971 meeting, the board approved the SOPs. They mandated procedures the Council was to follow for the day-to-day operation of the Theatre and further secured the University's control over Theatre operations. For example, the SOPs mandated that all Theatre employees be paid by the University and be subject to University regulations.

In the late 1970s, some Council members posited that fund-raising for the Theatre would improve if the Council could obtain its own tax-exempt status from the IRS. According to the minutes of the December 20, 1977 meeting of the Council's executive committee, the Council and Roosevelt were discussing "the establishment of a 'Shell Corporation' for the purpose of separate tax-exempt status of the [Council]."

Robert Gorman, the University's attorney, revised a draft of the articles of incorporation and bylaws of the proposed corporation. In a letter dated October 22, 1979, Gorman opined:

> In review, the Articles of incorporation and By-laws establish a separate Illinois not-for-profit corporation named the Auditorium Theatre Council. It is explicitly set forth in the Articles of Incorporation and in the By-laws that this new corporation is for fund raising purposes only and has no duties, rights, or operating responsibilities in connection with the Auditorium Theatre....
>
> If the Board of Trustees approves the establishment of a new corporation, the Auditorium Theatre Council will exist in two legal capacities. In one capacity it will continue to exist as it has in the past as an unincorporated agency of Roosevelt University operating under, and subject to, the direction and control of the Board of Trustees of Roosevelt University. The books and accounts of the Auditorium Theatre Council will also continue to be subject to inspection by[,] and among the fiscal responsibilities and duties of[,] the Roosevelt Controller. The use, maintenance, operation and restoration of the Auditorium Theatre will continue in the identical fashion it has always done pursuant to the Resolution of the Board of Trustees of Roosevelt University dated February 18, 1960 and the [1971 SOPs].
>
> In its other legal capacity the Auditorium Theatre Council will exist as an Illinois not-for-profit corporation in accordance with the Articles of Incorporation and By-laws submitted. It will use the name 'Auditorium Theatre Council.' However, the corporation will exist and be used for the solicitation of funds only. It will not affect in any way whatsoever the operations of the...Council and the...Theatre which will continue in the same manner as in the past.

Gorman concluded that the articles of incorporation and bylaws of the proposed corporation, Auditorium Theatre Council, Inc. (ATC Inc.), "are satisfactory and not in conflict with the interests of Roosevelt University."

Beatrice Spachner, University trustee and chairperson of the Council, reported on the Council's fund-raising efforts at the October 25, 1979 meeting of Roosevelt's board of trustees. She stated that potential donors hesitated to contribute to the Council because it was not separately identified as a not-for-profit corporation organized for tax-exemption purposes. According to Spachner: "To overcome this concern of contributors, it was concluded that an affiliate of the Council should be incorporated only for the purpose of raising funds...for the restoration, operation and maintenance of the Auditorium Theatre....[T]his will be the only function of the Corporation."

Both the Council and ATC Inc. would share similar names and would have largely the same membership. However, the resolution authorizing the incorporation of ATC Inc. expressly stated:

> This corporation is authorized for fund raising purposes only. The corporation will have no rights whatsoever for the use, operation, maintenance, or restoration of the Auditorium Theatre. The use, operation, maintenance and

restoration of the Auditorium Theatre will continue, without change, to be the responsibility of the Auditorium Theatre Council in its separate legal capacity as an unincorporated agency of Roosevelt University subject to the control of the Roosevelt University Board of Trustees as set forth in the [1971 SOPs].... In the event that at any time in the future [ATC Inc.] should exceed any of the duties, rights, or powers granted it by this resolution, the Board of Trustees hereby reserves the right to terminate any uses, duties or rights of [ATC Inc.] in connection with the...Theatre.

Roosevelt's board of trustees adopted the resolution.

On September 8, 1981, ATC Inc. filed its articles of incorporation with the State of Illinois and was incorporated under the General Not For Profit Corporation Act (see 805 ILCS 105/101.01 et seq. (West 2000)). According to its articles of incorporation, ATC Inc.'s corporate purpose was, in pertinent part:

To raise funds and gifts from individuals and organizations for the restoration, operation and maintenance of the Auditorium Theatre...and the presentation of educational, civic and cultural programs therein, with due regard for safeguarding the right, title and interest of Roosevelt University in and to the Theatre, so that it will serve as a cultural center for the people of Chicagoland.

ATC Inc. subsequently obtained an IRS ruling that ATC Inc. was a tax-exempt organization and that donations to it would be tax-deductible by the donor.

Subsequent to the incorporation of ATC Inc., the University updated the 1971 SOPs. The 1983 SOPs stated in pertinent part:

The purpose of the...Council is to maintain, operate and continue the restoration of the internationally famed Auditorium Theatre of Roosevelt University. The Council will operate the Theatre for the benefit of the faculty and students of Roosevelt University and also, subject to the academic priorities of the University, to make artistic, cultural and educational contributions to the people of Greater Chicago through the sponsorship of events in the performing arts.

The 1983 SOPs are substantially similar to those of 1971. Significantly, the 1983 SOPs distinguish the identity and the function of the Council from those of ATC Inc. The 1983 SOPs recount that the University created the Council through the 1960 resolution of Roosevelt's board of trustees and that the University created ATC Inc. through the board's October 25, 1979 resolution. The 1983 SOPs state that the "sole purpose" of ATC Inc. "is to solicit funds for the Auditorium Theatre."

Dialogue

The University paid the Theatre's operating costs, such as insurance and employee payroll, from the University's general account. Roosevelt was supposed to be repaid from the Theatre revenue account. However, by the late 1980s, the Theatre's operating expenses exceeded its revenues. The Theatre lost more money than fund raising could offset. The general funds that Roosevelt expended were not reimbursed. Theatre losses and the operating deficit increased. Roosevelt paid this deficit by transferring money from its endowment fund to Theatre accounts.

On July 1, 1986, Roosevelt trustee Robert Mednick met with Council chairperson Jack Whitney to discuss this problem. According to a July 7, 1986 letter from Mednick to Whitney, they agreed that if the Theatre's cumulative operating deficit increased over approximately $250,000, the Theatre would be discontinued due to a lack of community support.

An April 29, 1987 letter by a Council officer reflected the understanding that if the cumulative deficit exceeded this amount "at any time, Roosevelt may close down the Council."

The Theatre's cumulative operating deficit eventually totaled over $400,000. However, despite the above-stated understanding, the University kept the Theatre open and continued to support the Theatre. Eventually, during the 1990s, the Theatre attracted large Broadway productions such as "Miss Saigon," "Les Miserables," "Phantom of the Opera," and "Show Boat." These productions and other popular programs enabled the Council to increase its revenues from ticket sales and to repay the funds transferred to the Theatre accounts from the University's other accounts.

Strife

Beginning in the late 1980s, the Council and Roosevelt disputed their respective rights over the Theatre. As reflected in a November 15, 1988 letter from Council chairperson Edward Weil to University President Gross, the Council recognized signs of success. "Things are coming together nicely in the operation of the Theatre and at the same time the Council is starting to get the favorable recognition it deserves, and is beginning to tap into major funding sources." However, a June 26, 1989 memo from Gross to a committee of University trustees reflected the University's view: "The distinction that must continually be made is between authority and responsibility: the RU Board of Trustees has authority over the Theatre; the [Council] has the responsibility to manage the Theatre."

A rift grew between the parties. In 1989, Roosevelt informed the Council that a Council fund-raising campaign, initiated without the approval of Roosevelt's board of trustees, possibly violated the 1983 SOPs. At the April 14, 1989 meeting of the Roosevelt board, Gross reported this and other violations. He suggested options including "[d]rawing up a new agreement that retains our ownership of the theatre but that establishes the [Council] as a no[t]-for-profit, separate corporation which pays $1 a year rent to the university and is responsible for its own operating budget and its own fund-raising."

On July 10, 1989, the Council's executive board agreed with Gross' recommendations. The group also concluded that the Council should continue to manage the day-to-day operations of the Theatre.

At its July 20, 1989 meeting, the Roosevelt board of trustees approved a resolution concerning "the organizational structure between Roosevelt University and the Auditorium Theatre." The resolution stated that the Council "has responsibility for the artistic direction of the Theatre and the executive director of the Theatre reports directly to the president of the University with regard to budgetary and general operating matters."

The Council viewed this resolution essentially as Roosevelt transferring authority for managing the Theatre from the Council to Roosevelt. The Council's executive board rejected Roosevelt's resolution.

On August 1, 1989, the Council's executive board presented to Roosevelt a proposal to change the relationship between the University and the Council. The proposal acknowledged that Roosevelt owned the Theatre. Under the proposal, subject to conditions such as repayment of funds to Roosevelt, the Council would be disbanded and all operating authority would be transferred to ATC Inc., which would conduct fund raising independently of the University. Roosevelt rejected this proposal.

On August 24, 1989, the Council's executive board resigned. The Council assumed "no further responsibility" for Theatre operations and advised University trustees to prepare to do so.

As a result of this discord, Roosevelt and the Council reached a disharmonious decision. The Council would continue its day-to-day operations of the Theatre; members of the Council's executive board rescinded their resignations; and Gross was elected chairperson of the Council. At its October 10, 1989 meeting, Roosevelt's board of trustees approved the following resolution:

> The Auditorium Theatre is an aesthetic and financial asset of Roosevelt University, an integral unit led by an Executive Director who reports to the President of the University. The President serves as Chairman of the Auditorium Theatre Council. The Executive Director is assisted by the Auditorium Theatre Council in programming, fund-raising, special events, and other activities directly related to the Theatre.
>
> Although Roosevelt University retains final authority over all matters pertaining to the Auditorium Theatre, the Board of Trustees recognizes that the Auditorium Theatre Council must remain as autonomous as possible, contingent upon sound fiscal management. The University endorses the concept that Roosevelt University and the Auditorium Theatre are one entity. Roosevelt University wishes to assist the Auditorium Theatre in all of its efforts and supports the principle that, as a matter of first priority, all revenues raised in its behalf be placed in the account of the Auditorium Theatre for its continuing advancement.
>
> The Auditorium Theatre should now be presented as the Auditorium Theatre of Roosevelt University.

Whatever understanding the parties may have reached faltered from the beginning. Roosevelt and the Council constantly disputed their respective powers over the Theatre and the ownership of the Theatre's operating revenues.

Throughout the early 1990s, the parties conducted continuous negotiations regarding various forms of agreements to change their relationship to each other and to the Theatre. For example, in 1991, John Blew, Council and ATC Inc. secretary, presented another proposal for transfer of Theatre operations from the Council to ATC Inc. His proposal included several justifications. First, pointing to the Council's board, Blew stated that the Council had an opportunity to move the board's composition "into a higher tier by attracting a group of more influential and higher profile members who both have more money themselves and, perhaps more important, have greater access to other sources of major funding." Blew posited that it was "essential for such broad development that there be a separate legal entity and organization with its own identity and mission in place. The 'heavy hitters' we are talking about will simply not lend their names and prestige to an 'advisory committee' or anything of the sort." Blew suggested that operating the Council through ATC Inc. was a necessary condition to strengthening the Council's board.

Blew also recommended that the relationship between the Council and ATC Inc. be clarified. According to Blew: "The minutes of meetings of the two 'mirror' organizations which now exist—the unincorporated association and the corporation—are not in acceptable shape. Most of our own board members don't really know or understand the organizational structure." Blew continued that "if producers, artists and vendors were aware of the structure or lack thereof, they might be reluctant to enter into contracts with respect to the Theatre. It is not a healthy situation, and it is one which should not be permitted to continue."

In the course of his proposal, Blew acknowledged: "There is no question but that the University owns the Theatre and controls the Council—period." Roosevelt rejected the proposal.

Through 1993 and 1994, Roosevelt and ATC Inc. discussed a license or lease agreement under which Roosevelt would transfer Theatre operations to a reorganized ATC Inc. On June 22, 1993, ATC Inc. sent a letter to the IRS inquiring into the corporation's tax-exempt status if it took over Theatre operations. In the letter, ATC Inc. represented to the IRS, under penalty of perjury, that the Council operated the Theatre as a "part" of, or "unit within," the University since 1960 and that a "proposal" had been made to transfer Theatre operations to ATC Inc. prospectively. The IRS determined that the proposed reorganization would not affect the tax-exempt status of ATC Inc. By December 1994, the parties had agreed on neither the terms of a license nor the makeup of the proposed reconstituted ATC Inc.

During this time, ATC Inc. made additional proposals to Roosevelt regarding the Theatre. In mid-1994, ATC Inc. offered to purchase the Theatre from Roosevelt for $1 million, but the University rejected the offer. In November 1994, ATC Inc. offered to purchase the Theatre for $3 million, which offer the University rejected.

At a December 15, 1994 meeting of the Council's executive committee, Gross requested that the committee recommend the transfer of $1.5 million out of the $3 million then contained in the Theatre's operating accounts into Roosevelt's general accounts. Roosevelt wanted to use the $1.5 million to finance its new Schaumburg campus. The money would be transferred from the Theatre's operating revenues and not from contributions. The Theatre's executive director stated at this meeting that the transfer would not impair Theatre operations. ATC Inc. members objected to the transfer. It was agreed that no action would be taken on the request pending receipt of an opinion from Roosevelt's counsel regarding the legality of the proposed transfer.

Adversaries

The next day, plaintiffs brought this lawsuit. In July and November 1995, the Roosevelt University board of trustees approved resolutions that: (1) dissolved the Council; (2) withdrew any and all powers given to ATC Inc.; and (3) authorized a new not-for-profit corporation to manage and operate the Theatre, known as the Auditorium Theatre of Roosevelt University (AT of RU).

In their complaint, plaintiffs sought an injunction prohibiting defendants and ATC Inc. from directing the transfer of any money from ATC Inc. to Roosevelt for non-Theatre purposes. Also, plaintiffs sought a declaration that Roosevelt had placed the Theatre "in the public domain for the benefit of the people of Chicagoland," with the Council and its successor, ATC Inc., as trustee. Plaintiffs also sought a declaration that, inter alia: ATC Inc. had legal title to all funds donated and all revenue generated from its operations; any transfer of money from ATC Inc. to Roosevelt for non-Theatre purposes would violate the articles of incorporation and bylaws of ATC Inc.; and such transfer would violate the General Not For Profit Corporation Act of 1986 (805 ILCS 105/101.01 et seq. (West 2000)).

Roosevelt filed an answer in which the University raised defenses. Roosevelt claimed that ATC Inc.'s sole corporate purpose was to raise funds for the Theatre and that the board of trustees of the University, the owner of the building, had never granted ATC Inc. authority or power to restore, maintain, or operate the Theatre. Roosevelt also claimed that ATC Inc. did not succeed the Council created in 1960.

Roosevelt also filed a counterclaim against plaintiffs and ATC Inc. for declaratory and injunctive relief. Roosevelt sought a declaration that the University own[ed] all right, title, and interest in the Theatre. Roosevelt sought a further declaration that: the

University has the sole power and authority to restore, maintain, and operate the Theatre; that the University granted a revocable license to the Council to perform those tasks; and that ATC Inc. has no right to perform those tasks, but was created solely for fund-raising purposes. Roosevelt also sought, inter alia, an accounting of ATC Inc.'s funds and an injunction to prevent ATC Inc. from operating the Theatre.

ATC Inc. filed its own counterclaim against Roosevelt. The corporation asserted a number of alternative legal theories in support of its claimed control of the Theatre.

The trial court granted Gross' motion to dismiss all claims against him as legally insufficient (see 735 ILCS 5/2-615(a) (West 2000)). Also, granting Roosevelt's motion for partial judgment on the pleadings (see 735 ILCS 5/2-615(e) (West 2000)), the trial court held that: (1) Roosevelt had the authority and right to restore, maintain, and operate the Theatre; (2) ATC Inc.'s sole right is to raise money for the Theatre; and (3) the positive net operating revenues from Theatre performances are the property of the University.

In a Rule 23 order, the appellate court reversed the orders of the circuit court and remanded the cause for a trial. Eychaner v. Gross, Nos. 1-95-3614, 1-96-1412 cons., 286 Ill.App.3d 1110, 237 Ill.Dec. 536, 709 N.E.2d 1005 (1997) (unpublished order under Supreme Court Rule 23). The appellate court determined that disputed questions of material fact existed regarding the parties' relationship. The appellate court also held that plaintiffs' claims were legally sufficient.

On remand, plaintiffs and ATC Inc. (hereafter referred to as plaintiffs) amended their pleadings. They, inter alia, altered their trust theory to assert an "express trust" of the right to restore, maintain, and operate the Theatre, which they referred to as the "Auditorium Theatre Trust." Plaintiffs maintained their allegations that the Council was the trustee and ATC Inc., as legal successor to the Council, became, and remains, the trustee. In its counterclaim against Roosevelt and Gross, ATC Inc. alleged, inter alia: (1) an express charitable public trust; (2) constructive trust; (3) breach of contract based on the 1960 resolution and SOPs; (4) equitable estoppel; and (5) promissory estoppel.

At the close of a bench trial on September 28, 1998, the court entered judgment in favor of Roosevelt on its counterclaim and denied plaintiffs' theories of relief. The trial court declared the University to be the sole and exclusive owner of the Theatre. The trial court ordered plaintiffs to turn over control of the Theatre to the newly formed AT of RU; barred the Council and ATC Inc. from operating and controlling the Theatre; and ordered an immediate accounting of Theatre operations. On September 29, the trial court made an express written finding making these orders immediately enforceable (see 155 Ill.2d R. 304(a)).

A divided appellate court reversed these orders and remanded the cause for further proceedings. 321 Ill.App.3d 759, 254 Ill.Dec. 557, 747 N.E.2d 969. The appellate court held that the trial court's conclusion that there was no express trust was clearly erroneous. 321 Ill.App.3d at 779, 254 Ill.Dec. 557, 747 N.E.2d 969. Based on that holding, the court declined to address plaintiffs' alternative claims. 321 Ill.App.3d at 780-81, 254 Ill.Dec. 557, 747 N.E.2d 969. A concurring justice wrote separately to disagree with the dissent. The dissenting justice concluded: "Because there is enough admissible evidence to support the trial judge's view that this was a takeover attempt by an instrumentality of Roosevelt University, I would affirm his conclusion that there is no trust." 321 Ill.App.3d at 788, 254 Ill.Dec. 557, 747 N.E.2d 969 (Wolfson, J., dissenting). We allowed defendants' petition for leave to appeal.

ANALYSIS

Express Charitable Trust

Plaintiffs claim that the 1960 resolution of Roosevelt's board of trustees, together with the surrounding circumstances, created an express charitable trust with the Council and its successor, ATC Inc., as trustee in charge of restoring and operating the Theatre. The trial court rejected plaintiffs' claim, and concluded that Roosevelt created the Council as its agent for restoring and operating the Theatre. The appellate court reversed and remanded for further proceedings, finding "legal and factual errors in the trial court's resolution of the charitable trust issue." 321 Ill.App.3d at 771, 254 Ill.Dec. 557, 747 N.E.2d 969.

Before this court, plaintiffs, as appellees, not only defend the appellate court's judgment, but also request, as cross-relief, that we declare the existence of the alleged trust. We decline plaintiffs' request. The record contains ample evidence that supports the trial court's findings of fact.

The controlling legal principles are quite settled. A trust "is a fiduciary relationship with respect to property, subjecting the person by whom the title to the property is held to equitable duties to deal with the property for the benefit of another person, which arises as a result of a manifestation of an intention to create it." Restatement (Second) of Trusts §2 (1959). In Illinois, creation of an express trust requires: (1) intent of the parties to create a trust, which may be shown by a declaration of trust by the settlor or by circumstances which show that the settlor intended to create a trust; (2) a definite subject matter or trust property; (3) ascertainable beneficiaries; (4) a trustee; (5) specifications of a trust purpose and how the trust is to be performed; and (6) delivery of the trust property to the trustee. Each of the requisite elements of an express trust must be established. If any one of the necessary elements is not described with certainty, no trust is created.

A. Trust Element of Intent

The trial court found that Roosevelt did not intend to create an express charitable trust through the 1960 resolution, but rather intended to create the Council as its agent. As earlier emphasized, an express charitable trust arises, by definition, "as a result of a manifestation of an intention to create it." Restatement (Second) of Trusts §§2, 348 (1959). "The intention of the settlor to presently create a declaration of trust is essential." Kavanaugh v. Estate of Dobrowolski, 86 Ill.App.3d 33, 39, 41 Ill.Dec. 358, 407 N.E.2d 856 (1980). Indeed, "the primary focus in determining the existence of a trust must be on the intent of the settlor to establish a trust at the time of the creation of the alleged trust...." 76 Am.Jur.2d Trusts §64, at 92 (1992).

1. The Resolution Standing Alone

Plaintiffs claim that the 1960 resolution "comprehensively defined the relationship between Roosevelt and the Council." Plaintiffs contend that the 1960 resolution of the Roosevelt University board of trustees, by itself, manifests the University's intent to create a charitable trust, in which the Council acts as trustee over the right to restore and operate the Theatre for the benefit of the public. When a document makes clear the existence of a trust, no particular form of words is necessary. A court will support an intention to create a trust wherever such intention can be fairly collected from the language of the instrument.

Assuming, without deciding, that restoration and operation of the Theatre constitute possessory interests in real property that can be held in trust, it is clear that the 1960 resolution, standing alone, did not manifest an intent on the part of Roosevelt to create a charitable trust. On its face, the resolution lacks many indicia that are consistent with charitable trusts.

Initially, the resolution does not contain any words of alienation or conveyance, i.e., there are no words of transfer of an interest in the property from a "settlor" to someone or something that might be a "trustee." Plaintiffs point to certain "rights" that the resolution transferred to the Council. The resolution "authorized and directed" the Council to raise funds for the Theatre restoration. The resolution made the Council "responsible" for supervising the restoration. The resolution also "empowered" the Council to hire a fund-raiser and staff and gave the Council "authority to supervise" the reconstruction while reporting to the Roosevelt University board of trustees. According to plaintiffs: "Virtually every paragraph of the Resolution grants broad discretion to the Council as trustee."

Plaintiffs specifically discuss paragraph 12 of the 1960 resolution, which authorized the Council to retain any Theatre operating surplus in a development reserve. Plaintiffs describe paragraph 12 as expressing "Roosevelt's intent that the Theatre would be operated by the autonomous independent Council, using Theatre revenues to defray all expenses." According to plaintiffs, paragraph 12 gave the Council the "widest discretion to determine the adequacy of the development reserve, not only to assure the future of the Theatre for the public, but also to provide Roosevelt with additional protection from liability. Once an adequate reserve was established, Roosevelt would share in surpluses to support its academic mission." Indeed, plaintiffs go so far as to argue that Roosevelt, by paragraph 12 of the 1960 resolution, gave away its fundamental right of ownership of the Theatre.

It is clear that plaintiffs fail to distinguish the concepts of agency and trust. It must be remembered that "[t]here are a number of widely varying relationships which more or less clearly resemble trusts, but which are not trusts, although the term 'trust' is sometimes used loosely to cover such relationships." Restatement (Second) of Trusts, ch. 1, topic 2, at 15 (1959). "An agency is not a trust." Restatement (Second) of Trusts § 8 (1959). An agent is one who undertakes to manage the affairs of another, on the authority and for the account of the latter, who is called the principal, and to render an account to the principal.

In this case, the resolution never uses the word "rights" in connection with the restoration and operation of the Theatre. Rather, the resolution delegated duties to the Council. The only time the resolution uses the word "rights" is when Roosevelt preserved and safeguarded its own property rights in the Theatre.

The intent to grant authority to take action with respect to real property is not the same as the intent to permanently alienate or transfer an ownership interest. See Olson v. Etheridge, 177 Ill.2d 396, 406, 226 Ill.Dec. 780, 686 N.E.2d 563 (1997) (distinguishing an assignment of rights from a delegation of duties). Although the resolution makes the Council responsible for performing these duties, nothing in the resolution indicates an intent to alienate any alleged "rights" from Roosevelt. Rather, the delegation of duties to the Council created an agency relationship.

The 1960 resolution lacks other indicia that are consistent with charitable trusts. The resolution contains no words of delivery or any provision directing a delivery of property or an interest in property. The resolution states no "charitable" or "public" purpose, or any purpose to benefit anyone else. Also, the resolution does not state any purpose to confer benefits through the medium of a trust.

Further, the 1960 resolution contains a number of provisions that are inconsistent with the creation of a trust. The resolution states that the legal title to and all rights in the Theatre are to remain in Roosevelt, which precludes an alienation or transfer of such rights to a "trustee" as would be necessary for a trust. The resolution affirmatively states that it is intended to benefit its author, Roosevelt.

Also, the 1960 resolution contains many restrictions on the Council. Pursuant to the resolution, the Council was required to report periodically to the board regarding the restoration of the Theatre and to provide the board with requested information. The Council had to deposit all funds raised into a special, segregated University account. The Council could not enter into any contracts, purchases, or obligations unless certain criteria were met, including having the money on hand to pay for the obligation. The Council's programming for the Theatre was required to be in harmony with the University's aims. The Council had to prepare an annual report for Roosevelt's board of trustees and submit to an annual audit. Also, all nominees for the Council's executive committee required approval of Roosevelt's board of trustees. These controls on the Council indicate an agency relationship.

2. Parol Evidence

Plaintiffs additionally rely on parol evidence, i.e., evidence outside of the resolution itself, to prove their claim of an express charitable trust. It is settled that an express trust may be established by parol evidence. However, one seeking to establish an express trust by parol evidence bears the burden of proving the trust by clear and convincing evidence. The acts or words relied upon must be so unequivocal and unmistakable as to lead to only one conclusion.

Plaintiffs contend that the trial court erroneously excluded certain parol evidence offered at trial and ignored other parol evidence admitted at trial. Plaintiffs presented parol evidence from several sources: (a) the official actions of Roosevelt, the purported settlor, through its board of trustees; (b) statements by individual trustees and executives of Roosevelt and by others; and (c) statements made to the public. The evidence consisted of both exhibits and witness testimony.

Plaintiffs posit that the official actions of Roosevelt show that the University intended to establish a charitable trust to protect the University's real estate tax exemption. We recounted at length the history that gave rise to and the debate that surrounded the resolution's adoption on February 18, 1960. The record includes: the rejection of the suggestion that a separate entity run the Theatre under its own "trusteeship"; the October 29, 1959 motion passed by Roosevelt's board of trustees requiring that under the ultimate arrangement Roosevelt not lose "ownership or control" of the Theatre; and the Trustees' direction on February 11, 1960 that the resolution be revised to comply with the conditions of the October 29, 1959 motion. Also surrounding the February 18, 1960 resolution was the "agreed understanding" that Roosevelt would exercise unlimited control over the Council and could change the terms of the resolution, including paragraph 12, at any time. These official actions of the Roosevelt University board of trustees clearly show that the University never intended to relinquish its ownership and control over the Theatre.

Also, subsequent official actions of Roosevelt demonstrated its intent to create an agency relationship through the 1960 resolution. The 1971 SOPs expressly "reaffirm[ed] and supplement[ed]" the 1960 resolution. The 1983 SOPs, expressly recounting the 1960 resolution, mandated that the Council operate the Theatre for the benefit of Roosevelt. The 1983 SOPs also recounted that the "sole purpose" of ATC Inc. was "to solicit funds" for the Theatre. Notably, in July 1995, Roosevelt's board of trustees dissolved the Council.

However, plaintiffs contend that Roosevelt expressed its intent to create a charitable trust in two documents approved by Roosevelt. The Council's 1962 bylaws and ATC Inc.'s 1981 bylaws each state that Roosevelt would "take no unilateral action to terminate the availability" of the Theatre as long as the property was used for purposes consistent with the objectives set forth in the bylaws. In the Council's 1962 bylaws, Roosevelt additionally stated that it would not "sell the building without undertaking to provide for the continued functioning of the Council program."

This evidence is not clear and convincing. The above statements can be viewed consistently with an agency relationship. Accordingly, they are insufficient to establish an express charitable trust.

Plaintiffs next point to statements of individual Roosevelt officials made subsequently to the resolution's adoption on February 18, 1960 to prove that the University intended by that resolution to create an express charitable trust. However, these statements are outweighed by ample evidence. Statements from officials of Roosevelt, the Council, and ATC Inc. establish that, through the resolution, Roosevelt did not intend to create an express charitable trust but, rather, intended to create an agency relationship with the Council.

The IRS ruled in 1960 that contributions to the Council would be tax deductible because the Council was not a separate entity from Roosevelt. In 1993, ATC Inc. represented to the IRS, under penalty of perjury, that the Council had operated the Theatre as a "part" of or "unit within the University" since 1960 and that a "proposal" had been made to transfer Theatre operations to ATC Inc. prospectively. Thus, ATC Inc. admits that the Council never was an entity separate from Roosevelt.

In addition to the evidence already discussed, the record contains additional evidence against plaintiffs' claim of an express charitable trust. The trial court heard the testimony of Roosevelt University trustees Gidwitz, Stone, Mednick, Newman, Anixter, and Gross. The court summarized their testimony as follows:

> Six Roosevelt trustees testified in the case at bar. All agreed that during each's tenure on the Roosevelt Board, the University never placed the Theatre in trust nor did it take any action to divest itself of any control over the Theatre. These same individuals all testified that they never heard of a purported public trust until the onset of this litigation.

The trial court heard the testimony of these witnesses, observed their demeanor, and assessed their credibility. The court's findings based thereon are entitled to deference.

Also, members of ATC Inc.'s executive committee testified at trial. They conceded that ATC Inc.'s offers to lease or buy the Theatre from Roosevelt were attempts by the corporation to gain the control over the Theatre that it lacked. They testified that such actions would have been "unnecessary and superfluous" if ATC Inc. actually had control of the Theatre. As John Blew, secretary of the Council and of ATC Inc., stated to University President Gross: "There is no question but that the University owns the Theatre and controls the Council—period."

Plaintiffs point to the following as evidence of trust intent. On April 5, 1960, Harland Allen, chairperson of Roosevelt's board of trustees, and Beatrice Spachner, University trustee and Council chairperson, jointly issued a statement "for the purpose of clarifying any misunderstandings which may exist regarding plans for restoration and operation of the Auditorium Theatre." [This so-called] "Seven-Point Statement" was printed in several Chicago newspapers the next day. It explained that the Council would "have full authority and responsibility for the restoration campaign and the operation of the theater" and would have "full authority and responsibility for the programs that go into the theater and for supervision of theater operations."

Plaintiffs point to additional statements by individual Roosevelt trustees and executives. For example, on March 4, 1960, Allen announced in a press release:

> The University's trustees have been impressed by and are fully cognizant of the public trust which the ownership of the Theater has imposed upon them.... By creating the Auditorium Theater Council...the Board hopes to establish the reconstruction and operation of the Theater as a project from which the entire community will benefit and of which every citizen of the community can justly be proud.

In the April 1960 edition of "Progress," a Roosevelt publication, Dr. Edward Sparling, University president, reported in his column in pertinent part:

> Ever since Roosevelt University purchased the Auditorium building as its home in 1946 we have held the theater itself in trust for the people of Chicago....
>
> The recent action of the Board of Trustees, in granting permission to an independent civic group—the Auditorium Theater Council—to restore and operate the Auditorium Theater, frees Roosevelt University of the financial burden carried these years, and also frees it from any financial liability in regard to the restoration and operation of the theater. It makes available to the people of Chicago this added cultural and educational facility.
>
> The Auditorium Theater Council is taking a large burden from the University's shoulders, leaving all those dedicated to the academic program free to develop and expand the educational service to the community for which the University was founded and for which it lives.

Also, President Sparling wrote a letter to the Chicago Tribune which was printed on April 6, 1960. He stated that the University "has held the theater in trust for the community."

Additionally, Spachner spoke at a 1961 fundraiser. There, Spachner described to potential donors the goals of the Council and referred to the Theatre as a community treasure "held in trust." In a January 2, 1962 letter, Elmer Gertz, principal drafter of the resolution, referred to a "trust imposed upon the property."

These statements do not constitute unequivocal evidence that Roosevelt intended to create an express charitable trust though the 1960 resolution. None of these statements refer to the resolution creating a trust. To the contrary, most of these statements declare that Roosevelt held the Theatre "in trust" or was cognizant of the "public trust" that ownership of the Theatre involved. Terms such as "held in trust" or "public trust" can be loosely made and could broadly refer to other relationships. See Restatement (Second) of Trusts, ch. 1, topic 2, at 15 (1959).

It is true that the record contains some evidence that supports plaintiffs' claim. However, the record contains ample evidence to support the trial court's findings. Given the entire record on appeal, we cannot say that the trial court's factual findings were against the manifest weight of the evidence.

In this appeal, the controlling issue is whether Roosevelt intended to create an express charitable trust. The trial court's finding, supported by ample evidence, that Roosevelt did not so intend controls the disposition of the remaining issues.

CONCLUSION

For the foregoing reasons, the judgment of the appellate court, which reversed the order of the circuit court of Cook County, is reversed, and the cause is remanded to the trial court for further proceedings consistent with this opinion.

Notes

1. The issue of whether a particular theater company is entitled to not-for-profit status, discussed in *Plumstead*, is frequently litigated, particularly at the state and local level. *See, e.g., Theatre West of Lincoln City, Ltd. v. Department of Revenue,* 873 P.2d 1083 (Or. 1994); *City of Fayetteville v. Phillips,* 811 S.W.2d 308 (Ark. 1991); *Paper Mill Playhouse v. Millburn Township,* 472 A.2d 517 (N.J. 1984); *Washington Theatre Club, Inc. v. District of Columbia,* 311 A.2d 492 (D.C. 1973); *Stockton Civic Theatre v. Board of Supervisors of San Joaquin County,* 423 P.2d 810 (Cal. 1967); *Community Drama Ass'n of Des Moines v. Iowa State Tax Comm'n,* 109 N.W.2d 23 (Iowa 1961); *Memphis Development Foundation v. State Board of Equalization,* 653 S.W.2d 266 (Tenn. Ct. App. 1983); *Department of Revenue v. Louisville Children's Theater, Inc.,* 565 S.W.2d 643 (Ky. App. 1978); *Greek Theatre Ass'n v. County of Los Angeles,* 142 Cal. Rptr. 919 (Ct. App. 1978); *Little Theatre of Dallas v. City of Dallas,* 124 S.W. 863 (Tex. Civ. App. 1939). *See also* John H. Derrick, *Exemption of Nonprofit Theatre or Concert Hall from Local Property Taxation,* 42 A.L.R.4th 614 (1995).

2. Entities that qualify for §501(c)(3) status are prohibited from donating money to candidates, influencing legislation, and holding political fundraisers. In addition, any revenue they earn that "is not substantially related...to the exercise or performance" of their charitable functions is taxable as unrelated business income. *See* 26 U.S.C. §513(a).

Nevertheless, the benefits of being a §501(c)(3) organization are substantial. Not only do the tax breaks reduce operating costs, they make it easier to solicit money (because the donor can claim a deduction on his or her tax return). In addition, §501(c)(3) status allows a group to qualify for reduced bulk mail rates, is often a pre-requisite for applying for government and foundation grants, and permits the use of cheaper labor agreements.

3. Should the government give tax breaks to theater groups? If so, why? Put another way, what does society receive in return for its generosity? Likewise, to what extent does being a not-for-profit affect a theater company's artistic direction and vision (by, for example, making it hesitant to put on certain types of plays)?

4. Broadway has begun paying "enhancement fees" to some not-for-profits to induce them to develop and test out new plays (thereby saving the cost of the more traditional, and expensive, method of holding out-of-town tryouts). As a result, some observers believe the terms "for-profit" and "not-for-profit" have become obsolete and should be replaced by "taxable" and "non-taxable" or "subsidized" and "non-subsidized." Is the law in need of a similar change?

5. In January 2003, Roosevelt University President Ted Gross delivered a lengthy speech to the Chicago Literary Club regarding the *Eychaner* case. Although the full text can be found at www.chilit.org/GROSS1.HTM, the following excerpt is instructive:

> Who were the members of this Auditorium Theatre Council? The leader for many years was Edward Weil, whose great grandfather was Dankmar Adler [the theater's architect] and who was so enamored with the theater that he had his second wedding on its stage; Stanley Warshauer, the long-time owner of the Auditorium Theatre Garage who depended financially on a thriving theater season for his parking revenues; Gordon Newman, who was the chief counsel at Sara Lee and wanted the Auditorium Theatre to be the popular counterpart to the Lyric Opera and the Chicago Symphony Orchestra and who withdrew when the ATC made the conflict personal and bitter; David Smerling, who had once owned concessions for the theater [which was the reason] we called him popcorn man—and at one meeting found himself unwittingly elected chairman of the Council and then its spokesman; Thomas Kallen, who had inherited his wife's cookie company, Bakeline, and when he sold it for a fortune spent much of his time micromanaging the theater; others who had a sentimental attachment to the theater, its preservation and restoration and architecture. And then Fred Eychaner, wealthy entrepreneur, owner of Channel 50 and Newsweb, which printed neighborhood newspapers, and real estate across town; Fred Eychaner, a man who was the ninth largest contributor to the Democratic party and entertained President Clinton when he came to Chicago; Fred Eychaner, a man of silences, a nondescript loner who was intent on controlling that theater regardless of what it would cost in legal fees. I never fully understood his obsession, I never understood him. But he would not yield nor compromise and he had reserves of money that seemed endless....
>
> Soon, ATC sought legal separation from the University....My own view was that the Auditorium Theater should be operated independently but be a subsidiary of Roosevelt University. Its successful programming of mega-hits had to continue. The university would become its home and provide long-range fiscal stability. The tax-free status of the theater, so vulnerable now that it was enjoying huge profits from commercial shows, would be protected by this relationship and an extraordinary cultural and educational and commercial symbiosis would be forged. Was there any more noble use of the theater's net proceeds from ticket sales than scholarships for music and theater students who would be our future artists or for programs that would promote their development or for distinguished faculty who would teach them? But between the conception and the reality does fall the shadow, and I knew that it did not matter what grandiose notions I might have about the arts and society or how surpluses could be nobly used. Distrust had grown to the point where the Council and the University were fated to do battle on the fundamental question of who controlled the Auditorium Theatre.
>
> My public statements, I must confess, had private passions. I was convinced that the real reason ATC members wanted independence was not only to have a theater of their own but to separate themselves from the image of the university—from the scruffy working class, the upwardly mobile, struggling and straining, multi-ethnic student body, many of whom

were black and brown and yellow, most of whom were poor or had memories of recent poverty, almost all of whom could not afford the price of admission to Phantom of the Opera or Show Boat, future Ellingtons and Perlmans and Midoris among them. At one point, I imagined inner-city youngsters watching these shows from our balconies—I suggested that we make a request of the producers for free or discounted tickets—and was told that the kids would make the theater dirty. Would there be, I asked in a heated moment of provocation, this desire for independence if the Auditorium Theatre were on the campus of the University of Chicago or Northwestern? They vehemently denied the suggestion—class and race and ethnicity were not the question, they protested—but I did not believe them. I did not trust them. I did believe that underlying the public reasons for autonomy was the search for an image of high status and class and snobbery, and the discordant music in my mind was buried deeper than the words I dared to speak, and I found it repugnant....

The rhetoric grew intense as the lines between us rigidified. I tried to reassure them [the ATC]—but they would not be reassured. I sought their trust, but there was no trust. They were sitting in the board room of the university that owned the theater, but they saw the two as entirely separate—most importantly they did not trust the university and they did not trust me.

In the middle of the meeting, Eychaner marched toward me in a dramatic, defiant flourish, his eyes so hostile I thought they would burn through me, I even feared that he might pull a knife, and submitted his letter of resignation from the Roosevelt University Board of Trustees—he was, he said, in an impossible conflict of interest.... Toward the end of the meeting, Gordon Newman, who was more moderate than his two colleagues, sympathized with my dilemma and wondered whether transfer of the funds was legal. He asked our attorney to secure an opinion. He needed an opinion before he could act.

The Greeks had it right, after all: character is finally fate. All of us left that board room with the agreement that we would wait for a ruling of whether it was legal to transfer theater revenues to Roosevelt accounts. But Eychaner had already instructed his lawyers to prepare a lawsuit and was ready to strike—he had no intention of waiting for any legal opinion....

By that afternoon, December 16, Fred Eychaner had filed an injunction together with another Council member, Betty Lou Weiss. She was married to the nephew of Bea Spachner and was a new member of the ATC. She did not know Eychaner and was totally unfamiliar with the origins and history of the case—she simply wanted to "protect" the theater for her Aunt Bea....

ATC now filed a lawsuit. Eyachner had his own suit. The attorney general entered the case. We hired Sidley & Austin to counter Winston Strawn, and I found myself lost in a blizzard of documents and depositions, while I was admonished not to say a word lest it be used against the university or me in court....

For Roosevelt University, the dispute with the Auditorium Theatre resulted in huge legal fees, amounting finally to $3.3 million from our own budgets and $1.8 million from the Theatre, which of course was our money as well. In addition, Eychaner had his own legal fees and whatever he was spending on public relations. It was conviction that bordered on zealotry and, I often thought, a kind of madness.

These accumulating expenses as well as adverse publicity for the university were the primary reasons for our seeking compromise and avoiding litigation. Enough, we often told ourselves: we have a university to run, this is distracting and out of proportion to the university's purposes, wasteful and destructive to our image and troubling to trustees who do not want controversy. Enough, we often thought, but then we reconsidered—the case is too important, the theater is 40 percent of our physical space, this is a decision that will affect the university for years to come. Enough, I thought, this is all ego and will and personalized pettiness. Eychaner and the ATC, which seemed to follow him blindly so long as he was willing to pay part of the bills, were truly irrational not to have settled, for they would have controlled the theater and simply shared profits with the University. They would have had almost all they wished; but if there is any truth to the cliche that pride goeth before a fall, it was embodied in their egoistical, uncompromising behavior. They wanted all or nothing, and they got—nothing....

6. As the *Eychaner* case makes clear, a not-for-profit theater company can run into all sorts of legal problems while engaged in fundraising. In one particularly notorious case, *Rochester Civic Theatre, Inc. v. Ramsay*, 368 F.2d 748 (8th Cir. 1966), the plaintiff made false statements while seeking donations for the construction of a new theater. As a result, the defendant was permitted to back out on her promise to donate $40,000. *See also ZZYZX Studios v. Volvo Cars of North America, Inc.*, 2001 WL 958996 (S.D.N.Y. 2001) (theater company took word of unauthorized employee that corporate grant had been approved), and *Board of Trustees of University of North Carolina v. Unknown and Unascertained Heirs of Prince*, 319 S.E.2d 239 (N.C. 1984) (school could not take money donated for theater construction and unilaterally reallocate it to drama department's general fund).

7. Even when they have a paid staff, not-for-profit theater companies rely primarily on volunteers—the American Association of Community Theatre (www.aact.org) puts the number of theater volunteers at nearly one million. Collectively, they are responsible for a staggering number of shows:

> Accurate figures are not available, but it is estimated that there are about 40,000 high school, college and university drama groups, community theatres, drama clubs, and miscellaneous amateur producing entities (church, labor and Armed Forces groups) scattered over this country. Amateurs present about 50,000 productions a year, and draw audiences in excess of forty million. Thornton Wilder's hardy perennial "Our Town" was produced by 985 different non-professional groups in one year.

Alexander Lindey & Michael Landau, *Lindey on Entertainment, Publishing and the Arts: Agreements and the Law* § 5:31, at 5-215 (2d ed. 1980 & 2003 Supp.).

Because the experience and ability of volunteers varies greatly, it is common to take out a blanket liability insurance policy to pay for mistakes. *See, e.g., State ex rel. Fisher v. Warren Star Theater*, 616 N.E.2d 1192 (Ohio Ct. App. 1992), *appeal dismissed*, 612 N.E.2d 1244 (Ohio 1993) (claims for improper ticket-selling).

Since 1997, volunteers also have been protected by a federal law known as the Volunteer Protection Act, 42 U.S.C. §§ 14501-14505. However, as even a casual reading of the statute makes clear, it contains a number of significant caveats:

> The federal Volunteer Protection Act of 1997 (the "Act") provides liability protection for volunteers of nonprofit organizations and governmental entities

"for harm caused by an act or omission of the volunteer on behalf of the organization or entity." This includes economic and non-economic losses. Nevertheless, volunteers may still be liable for certain non-economic losses, such as physical and emotional pain and suffering, loss of society, injury to reputation, etc., based on the "percentage of responsibility" of each volunteer.

The Act excludes liability protection in several situations. First, a volunteer is still liable in an action brought by the nonprofit organization or governmental entity, because the purpose of the Act is to protect the volunteer from liability to third persons, not from liability to the organization for breach of fiduciary duties. Second, the Act does not affect the liability of the organization or entity itself. In addition, liability protection under the Act does not apply to some types of crimes.

The Act preempts any state law inconsistent with the Act unless the state law provides additional liability protection. Nevertheless, any state may pass specific legislation to opt out of the Act.

Dean Papademetriou, *Legal Issues for Nonprofit Cultural Organizations: A Primer for Lawyers and Board Members*, 44 Boston B.J. 12, 27-28 (Sept./Oct. 2000) (footnote omitted).

8. One of the reasons why not-for-profits must raise money is to be able to purchase the rights to the plays and musicals they are interested in staging. A sample licensing agreement appears in Appendix I of this casebook. Sadly, many amateur groups are under the mistaken impression that they do not have to pay royalties:

> Here is the most dangerous myth of all concerning copyright: "They'll never know what I do in my little high school in the middle of nowhere and, besides, even if the publisher/licensing agency finds out, they never go after high school and community theatres anyway." It is more accurate to say that you rarely hear about licensing agencies or music publishers going after high school theatres. It is not good public relations for either the publisher or the high school to advertise the fact that it has happened, but the licensing agencies and the music publishers have a fiduciary responsibility to the authors and composers they represent to not allow the rights of those authors and composers to be infringed by anyone at any level of production. If they find out about an infringement, they are bound to pursue it....
>
> This is why most of these cases never come to court. A private, confidential settlement is made, to the advantage of [the publisher/licensing agency]. No one not directly involved in the case ever hears about it, preserving the reputation of both the school and the publisher/licensing agency. The school district somehow swallows paying for a drama director's costly mistake (and remembers it well when budget time rolls round), and the myth [of non-prosecution] continue[s] to live.

Kevin N. Scott, *Who Owns the Rights? Copyright, the Law, and Licensing the Show*, 10 Teaching Theater 1, 12-13 (Summer 1999).

Problem 27

During the past few years, an amateur theater ensemble has been extremely active. Although it charges admission and sells t-shirts, programs, and refreshments at every performance, it has consistently lost money. Last week, the American Society of Composers, Authors and Publishers sued the group in federal court, claiming that many of its productions included copyrighted musical compositions for which the required licensing fees were not paid. Will the fact that the defendant is an impecunious not-for-profit have any bearing on the case? See *Bourne Co. v. Speeks*, 670 F. Supp. 777 (E.D. Tenn. 1987).

C. ARTISTIC FREEDOM

BORING v. BUNCOMBE COUNTY BOARD OF EDUCATION
136 F.3d 364 (4th Cir.) (en banc),
cert. denied, 525 U.S. 813 (1998)

WIDENER, Circuit Judge.

The only issue in this case is whether a public high school teacher has a First Amendment right to participate in the makeup of the school curriculum through the selection and production of a play. We hold that she does not, and affirm the judgment of the district court dismissing the complaint.

I.

Margaret Boring was a teacher in the Charles D. Owen High School in Buncombe County, North Carolina. In the fall of 1991, she chose the play Independence for four students in her advanced acting class to perform in an annual statewide competition. She stated in her amended complaint that the play "powerfully depicts the dynamics within a dysfunctional, single-parent family—a divorced mother and three daughters; one a lesbian, another pregnant with an illegitimate child." She alleged that after selecting the play, she notified the school principal, as she did every year, that she had chosen Independence as the play for the competition. She does not allege that she gave the principal any information about the play other than the name.

The play was performed in a regional competition and won 17 of 21 awards. Prior to the state finals, a scene from the play was performed for an English class in the school. Plaintiff informed the teacher of that class that the play contained mature subject matter and suggested to the teacher that the students bring in parental permission slips to see the play. Following that performance, a parent of one of the students in the English class complained to the school principal, Fred Ivey, who then asked plaintiff for a copy of the script. After reading the play, Ivey informed plaintiff that she and the students would not be permitted to perform the play in the state competition.

Plaintiff and the parents of the actresses performing the play met with Ivey urging him not to cancel the production. Ivey then agreed to the production of the play in the state competition, but with certain portions deleted. The complaint states that the students performed the play in the state competition and won second place. The complaint does not state, but we assume, that the play was performed in accordance with Ivey's instructions.

In June 1992, Ivey requested the transfer of Margaret Boring from Owen High School, citing "personal conflicts resulting from actions she initiated during the course of this school year." Superintendent Yeager approved the transfer stating that she had failed to follow the school system's controversial materials policy in producing the play.

Plaintiff states that the purpose of the controversial materials policy is to give the parents some control over the materials to which their children are exposed in school. She alleges that at the time of the production, the controversial materials policy did not cover dramatic presentations, and that the school's policy was amended subsequently to include dramatic presentations.

Plaintiff appealed the transfer to the Board of Education. A hearing was held on September 2, 1992, following which the Board upheld the transfer. Plaintiff alleges that prior to the hearing there was considerable public discussion of the transfer, including that the play was obscene and that she was immoral. She alleges that members of the school board asked questions at the hearing that demonstrated their consideration of matters outside the evidence presented at the hearing.

Plaintiff filed the present action on January 10, 1994. Her amended complaint claims that her transfer was in retaliation for expression of unpopular views through the production of the play and thus in violation of her right to freedom of speech under the First and Fourteenth Amendments and Article I, § 14 of the North Carolina Constitution. She also claimed a violation of due process under the Fourteenth Amendment and Article I, § 19 of the North Carolina Constitution based on the allegation that members of the school board considered information that was not presented at the hearing; and a violation of a liberty interest under Article I, §§ 1 and 19 of the North Carolina Constitution.

The district court construed the complaint broadly. Not only did it address plaintiff's federal First Amendment claim, it considered claims plaintiff may have made under the federal due process clause of the Fourteenth Amendment; a federal liberty interest claim under the Fourteenth Amendment; a state claim for violation of free speech; a state claim for deprivation of due process; and a state claim for deprivation of liberty. It decided against the plaintiff on each of these claims.

Plaintiff appeals only the dismissal of her federal First Amendment claim. A divided panel of this court reversed the district court's dismissal of that claim which decision was vacated by the order of the en banc court which granted rehearing. Boring v. Buncombe County Bd. of Educ., 98 F.3d 1474 (4th Cir. 1996), vacated by order of December 3, 1996. We now affirm the judgment of the district court holding that the plaintiff's selection and production of the play Independence as part of the school's curriculum was not protected speech under the First Amendment.

II.

The district court held that the play was a part of the school curriculum and:

> Since plaintiff has not engaged in protected speech, her transfer in retaliation for the play's production did not violate Constitutional standards.

With this holding, the plaintiff takes issue on appeal as follows:

> Whether the district court erred in holding that plaintiff's act of selecting, producing and directing a play did not constitute "speech" within the meaning of the First Amendment.

We begin our discussion with the definition of curriculum:

> all planned school activities including besides courses of study, organized play, athletics, dramatics, clubs, and home-room program.

Webster's Third New International Dictionary, 1971, p. 557.

Not only does Webster include dramatics within the definition of curriculum, the Supreme Court does the same. In Hazelwood School District v. Kuhlmeier, 484 U.S. 260 (1988), a case involving student speech in a school newspaper which was edited by the principal of a high school, the Court distinguished cases which require a school to tolerate student speech from those cases in which the school must affirmatively promote student speech. Although in [a] different context, the reasoning of the Court as to what constitutes the school curriculum is equally applicable here:

> The latter question concerns educators' authority over school-sponsored publications, theatrical productions, and other expressive activities that students, parents, and members of the public might reasonably perceive to bear the imprimatur of the school. These activities may fairly be characterized as part of the school curriculum, whether or not they occur in a traditional classroom setting, so long as they are supervised by faculty members and designed to impart particular knowledge or skills to student participants and audiences.

Hazelwood, 484 U.S. at 271.

It is plain that the play was curricular from the fact that it was supervised by a faculty member, Mrs. Boring; it was performed in interscholastic drama competitions; and the theater program at the high school was obviously intended to impart particular skills, such as acting, to student participants. These factors demonstrate beyond doubt that "students, parents, and members of the public might reasonably perceive [the production of the play Independence] to bear the imprimatur of the school." Hazelwood, 484 U.S. at 271.

III.

With these thoughts in mind, we are of opinion that the judgment of the district court is demonstrably correct.

A.

Plaintiff's selection of the play Independence, and the editing of the play by the principal, who was upheld by the superintendent of schools, does not present a matter of public concern and is nothing more than an ordinary employment dispute. That being so, plaintiff has no First Amendment rights derived from her selection of the play Independence.

This principle was illustrated in Connick v. Myers, 461 U.S. 138 (1983), in which the Court upheld the firing of an assistant district attorney who had circulated a questionnaire questioning the manner in which the district attorney operated that office. The Court held that "if Myers' questionnaire cannot be fairly characterized as constituting speech on a matter of public concern, it is unnecessary for us to scrutinize the reasons for her discharge." Connick at 146. Because the questionnaire almost wholly concerned internal office affairs rather than matters of public concern, the court held that, to that extent, it would not upset the decision of the district attorney in discharging Myers. It stated:

> We hold only that when a public employee speaks not as a citizen upon matters of public concern, but instead as an employee upon matters of personal interest, absent the most unusual circumstances, a federal court is not the appropriate forum in which to review the wisdom of a personnel decision taken by a public agency allegedly in reaction to the employee's behavior.

Connick at 147.

We followed Connick in DiMeglio v. Haines, 45 F.3d 790 (1995), in which we upheld the transfer of a public employee who had insisted on advising some affected citizens as to the merits of a zoning dispute contrary to the instructions of his employer. We stated "a government employer, no less than a private employer, is entitled to insist upon the legitimate, day-to-day decisions of the office without fear of reprisals in the form of lawsuits from disgruntled subordinates who believe that they know better than their superiors how to manage office affairs." DiMeglio at 806.

In a case on facts so near to those in the case at hand as to be indistinguishable, the Fifth Circuit came to the conclusion we have just recited in Kirkland v. Northside Independent School District, 890 F.2d 794 (5th Cir. 1989), cert. denied, 490 U.S. 926 (1990). Kirkland was a case in which the employment contract of a high school history teacher was not renewed. He alleged the non-renewal was a consequence of, and in retaliation for, his use of an unapproved reading list in his world history class. The high school had provided the teacher with a supplemental reading list for his history class along with a copy of the guidelines used to develop and amend that list. He was aware of the guidelines and understood that if he was dissatisfied, a separate body of reading material could be used in his class if he obtained administrative approval. The teacher, however, used his own substitute list and declined to procure the approval of the school authorities for his substitute list. The authorities at his high school then recommended that his contract not be renewed at the end of the next academic year, which was affirmed by the board of trustees, much like Margaret Boring's transfer was affirmed by the school board in this case after a recommendation by the administrative authorities. The court held that to establish his constitutional claim, Kirkland must have shown that his supplemental reading list was constitutionally protected speech; not different from Mrs. Boring's selection of the play Independence in this case. It went on to hold that under Connick v. Myers, 461 U.S. 138 (1983), the question of whether a public employee's speech is constitutionally protected depends upon the public or private nature of such speech. It decided that the selection of the reading list by the teacher was not a matter of public concern and stated that:

> Although the concept of academic freedom has been recognized in our jurisprudence, the doctrine has never conferred upon teachers the control of public school curricula.

Kirkland at 800.

Since plaintiff's dispute with the principal, superintendent of schools and the school board is nothing more than an ordinary employment dispute, it does not constitute protected speech and has no First Amendment protection. Her case is indistinguishable from Kirkland's.

B.

The plaintiff also contends that the district court erred in holding that the defendants had a legitimate pedagogical interest in punishing plaintiff for her speech. Of course, by speech she means her selection and production of the play Independence.

As we have previously set out, the play was a part of the curriculum of Charles D. Owen High School, where plaintiff taught. So this contention of the plaintiff is in reality not different from her first contention, that is, she had a First Amendment right to participate in the makeup of the high school curriculum, which could be regulated by the school administration only if it had a legitimate pedagogical interest in the curriculum. While we are of [the] opinion that plaintiff had no First Amendment right to insist on the makeup of the curriculum, even assuming that she did, we are of opinion that the school administration did have such a legitimate pedagogical interest and that the holding of the district court was correct.

Pedagogical is defined as "of or relating to teaching or pedagogy. Educational." Webster's Third New International Dictionary, 1971, p. 1663. There is no doubt at all that the selection of the play Independence was a part of the curriculum of Owen High School.

The makeup of the curriculum of Owen High School is by definition a legitimate pedagogical concern. Not only does logic dictate this conclusion, in only [a] slightly different context the Eleventh Circuit has so held as a matter of law: "[T]he purpose of a curricular program is by definition 'pedagogical'...." Searcey v. Harris, 888 F.2d 1314, 1319 (11th Cir. 1989). Kirkland, 890 F.2d at 795, held the same in the same context present here.

If the performance of a play under the auspices of a school and which is a part of the curriculum of the school is not by definition a legitimate pedagogical concern, we do not know what could be. In our opinion, the school administrative authorities had a legitimate pedagogical interest in the makeup of the curriculum of the school, including the inclusion of the play Independence. The holding of the district court was correct and the plaintiff's claim is without merit.

IV.

The question before us is not new. From Plato to Burke, the greatest minds of Western civilization have acknowledged the importance of the very subject at hand and have agreed on how it should be treated:

> For a young person cannot judge what is allegorical and what is literal; anything that he receives into his mind at that age is likely to become indelible and unalterable; and therefore it is most important that the tales which the young first hear should be models of virtuous thoughts.

Plato's Republic: Book II, Jowett Translation, Walter J. Black, Inc., 1942, p. 281.

> The magistrate, who in favor of freedom thinks himself obliged to suffer all sorts of publications, is under a stricter duty than any other well to consider what sort of writers he shall authorize, and shall recommend by the strongest of all sanctions, that is, by public honors and rewards. He ought to be cautious how he recommends authors of mixed or ambiguous morality. He ought to be fearful of putting into the hands of youth writers indulgent to the peculiarities of their own complexion, lest they should teach the humors of the professor, rather than the principles of the science.

Letter to a Member of the National Assembly (1791) IV, 23-34, found in The Philosophy of Edmund Burke, University of Michigan Press, 1960, p. 247.

And Justice Frankfurter, in concurrence, related the four essential freedoms of a university, which should no less obtain in public schools unless quite impracticable or contrary to law:

> It is an atmosphere in which there prevail "the four essential freedoms" of a university—to determine for itself on academic grounds who may teach, what may be taught, how it shall be taught, and who may be admitted to study.

Sweezy v. New Hampshire, 354 U.S. 234, 255, 263-264 (1957) (quoting from a statement of a conference of senior scholars from the University of Cape Town and the University of the Witwatersrand).

We agree with Plato and Burke and Justice Frankfurter that the school, not the teacher, has the right to fix the curriculum. Owen being a public school does not give the plaintiff any First Amendment right to fix the curriculum she would not have had if the school were private. Connick, 461 U.S. at 147.

Someone must fix the curriculum of any school, public or private. In the case of a public school, in our opinion, it is far better public policy, absent a valid statutory directive on the subject, that the makeup of the curriculum be entrusted to the local school authorities who are in some sense responsible, rather than to the teachers, who would be responsible only to the judges, had they a First Amendment right to participate in the makeup of the curriculum.

The judgment of the district court is accordingly AFFIRMED.

MOTZ, Circuit Judge, dissenting.

School administrators must and do have final authority over curriculum decisions. But that authority is not wholly unfettered. Like all other state officials, they must obey the Constitution. The Supreme Court has long recognized that the Constitution, specifically the First Amendment, "does not tolerate laws that cast a pall of orthodoxy over the classroom." Keyishian v. Board of Regents, 385 U.S. 589, 603 (1967). See also Tinker v. Des Moines Indep. Sch. Dist., 393 U.S. 503, 506 (1969) ("teachers" no less than "students" do not "shed their constitutional rights to freedom of speech or expression at the schoolhouse gate"). Thus, teachers' in-class speech retains some, albeit limited, First Amendment protection.

Examination of Margaret Boring's complaint is instructive. Boring alleges that she is a "tenured teacher" in the Buncombe County public schools, that she has "built a national reputation for excellence in teaching drama and directing and producing theater," and that "[h]er plays have won numerous awards and, each year, many of her students have gone on to college on theater-related scholarships." She further alleges that in the fall of 1991—twelve years after her initial employment by the Board, after her plays had been "regularly" entered in competition and won "numerous awards"—she notified her principal "as she did every year" of the name of the play she had chosen for the annual competition, and the principal "did not comment or react."

True, as the majority observes, Boring "does not allege that she gave the principal any information about the play other than the name." But a fair reading of the above allegations, let alone a reading that gives Boring "all reasonable inferences" from them, reveals that Boring provided her principal with precisely the same advance notice of the chosen play that she had in every previous year—notice that, until 1991, had been sufficient. According to Boring, the principal did not question her choice, ask for further information, or in any way "comment or react" to her choice. It may be that Boring pulled a fast one on the principal, choosing a more controversial play than in previous years and giving him just its name to preclude negative reaction from him. Nothing in the complaint supports this inference, however, and the School Board has not so asserted.

Boring further alleges that no violation of the "controversial materials policy" provided a basis for her transfer and that the play was performed in the state competition only after the principal insisted that she delete certain portions of the play. Taking all of these allegations together, a fair reading of them is that Boring complied with the school administration's requirements and policies in every respect, but was nonetheless disciplined "to punish and retaliate against her for expressing an unpopular point of view through the production of the play" in violation of her First Amendment rights. Thus, as the district court recognized, Boring "does not ask the Court to find that a unilateral selection and production of the play 'Independence,' without prior approval, would have been protected First Amendment speech"; rather, she "argues that having passed on the play prior to its production and performance, the school does not have a right to discipline [her] in retaliation for its use in the curriculum." It is this complaint that Boring presents to us, and this complaint that we must assess to determine whether it states a claim upon which relief can be granted.

In Kirkland v. Northside Indep. Sch. Dist., 890 F.2d 794 (5th Cir. 1989), cert. denied, 490 U.S. 926 (1990), Timothy Kirkland, unlike Boring, admitted that he refused to follow the school's well-established rules. For example, he admitted using a "non-apprnlik reading list." Kirkland, 890 F.2d at 795. Boring, by contrast, alleges that her principal initially acquiesced in her choice and production of Independence. Moreover, Kirkland did not concede, as Boring does, that the school authorities were entitled to the broad discretion vested in them under the Hazelwood standard. Rather, Kirkland contended that "his control of the world history class curriculum [was] unlimited." Kirkland, 890 F.2d at 801. The Kirkland court properly rejected this argument. Id. But the Fifth Circuit's reasoning in Kirkland does not foreclose Boring's quite different and far more modest contention that although administrators may discipline a teacher even when the teacher does follow the school's rules, they may do so only "so long as [administrators'] actions are reasonably related to legitimate pedagogical concerns." Hazelwood, 484 U.S. at 273.

The Buncombe County Board of Education may possess legitimate pedagogical concerns reasonably related to its discipline of Boring. But to date, the Board has not even attempted to state those concerns, lencerone offered a scintilla of evidence establishing them. On this record, I do not see how a court can conclude, as the majority does, that "the school administrative authorities had a legitimate pedagogical interest" justifying discipline of Boring and dismissal of her complaint.

The only other possible basis that I can see for the majority's holding is a mistake as to the nature of Boring's claim. The speech for which Boring seeks First Amendment protection does not constitute a private personnel grievance. Boring does not allege that she selected and produced Independence after being instructed not to choose that play, nor does she allege that school administrators disciplined her because she publicized her dissatisfaction with their treatment of her. Such a claim, much like Kirkland's insistence on using a disapproved reading list, would constitute an "ordinary employment dispute" rather than speech relating to a matter of public concern. Boring instead alleges that the school administration disciplined her for the selection and production of the play itself. This is not an employment dispute. Rather, it is a challenge to a restriction on classroom speech, which involves matters of public concern.

By holding that public school administrators can constitutionally discipline a teacher for in-class speech without demonstrating, or even articulating, some legitimate pedagogical concern related to that discipline, the majority extinguishes First Amendment rights in an arena where the Supreme Court has directed they should be brought "vividly into operation." For these reasons, I must respectfully dissent.

[The concurring opinions of Chief Judge Wilkinson and Circuit Judge Luttig, as well as the dissenting opinion of Circuit Judge Hamilton, are omitted.]

DIBONA v. MATTHEWS
269 Cal. Rptr. 882 (Ct. App.),
cert. denied, 498 U.S. 998 (1990)

WIENER, Acting Presiding Justice.

Plaintiffs Alan DiBona and J. Scott Gundlach, a college teacher and student respectively, appeal following the entry of summary judgment in favor of defendants Robert

L. Matthews and James Hardison, administrators with the San Diego Community College District. Plaintiffs claim there are issues of fact which remain to be litigated in their claim that defendants violated their constitutional rights by canceling a drama class because of the subject matter of the play DiBona had selected for the students to perform. We agree and reverse the summary judgment.

Factual and Procedural Background

Viewed in the light most favorable to the plaintiffs, the record before the court on the motion for summary judgment reveals the following story. The Educational Cultural Complex (ECC) is a branch of the San Diego Community College District located in Southeast San Diego. ECC offers college and adult education courses. Alan DiBona began teaching at ECC on a part-time basis in the fall of 1985. He taught the Drama 250 course during the fall and spring semesters and was asked to again teach the same course for the summer session. The curriculum for Drama 250 requires that the students produce and perform a play.

Although his formal teaching contract for the summer was not signed until April 1986, DiBona began to prepare for the class in March. He selected a play written by Dennis McIntyre entitled "Split Second." The play concerns a Black New York City police officer who, in the course of a routine arrest of a White suspect, is subjected to a flurry of racial slurs and epithets. In a split-second loss of control, the officer shoots and kills the suspect. He then places a knife in the hand of the victim and fabricates a story that the shooting was in self-defense. According to DiBona, "[t]he play centers around the morality of [the officer's] actions, exploring one man's rationalization of why he should not tell the truth and the repercussions of his decision."

ECC does not require that teachers obtain the approval of the college administration for plays to be performed in drama classes. DiBona nonetheless gave a copy of the script to Sylvia M'Lafi Thompson, the ECC cultural affairs adviser, and discussed the content of the play with defendant Robert Matthews, the ECC president. In late May, DiBona made copies of the play available to students interested in taking the class.

Summer session classes were scheduled to begin at ECC on Monday, June 16. DiBona made special arrangements for the class to begin meeting on Monday, June 9. Over the course of the week auditions were held. By Friday, June 13, DiBona and plaintiff Scott Gundlach—an ECC student and the play's assistant director—had selected and notified the cast. Other students were assigned technical functions such as lighting and costumes.

Approximately 14 students met on Saturday to do an initial read-through of the play. Only two or three were formally enrolled in Drama 250 at that point. The remainder, including Gundlach, signed "add" cards on Saturday. Defendant James Hardison, the dean of arts and sciences at ECC, conceded it was generally understood that students did not pre-enroll for drama classes because most preferred to wait for the results of the auditions before deciding whether to take the class. DiBona collected the "add" cards and instructed the students to bring any necessary additional fees [required to take the course] to class on Monday. He indicated he would submit everything to the registrar's office on Monday evening.

On Monday morning June 16, Matthews received a call from the past president of ECC informing him that certain church leaders in the community were upset about the "Split Second" play and asking him to look into it. Matthews spoke with DiBona at about 2:30 that afternoon. He explained he had received some phone calls which included "negative remarks about the proposed production" and indicated "there might be some unrest" as a result of the play. Matthews told DiBona he "was not prepared or had no desire to take on our religious community." At Matthews's request, DiBona provided him with a copy of the play. Matthews quickly skimmed the script, focusing on the first two scenes. He concluded the plot "was weak, and that the language was inappropriate in an educational setting." Meeting with DiBona a few minutes later, Matthews expressed his opinion that "this play would not be produced publicly at [ECC]." He refrained from further comment because he wanted to consult with Dean Hardison.

At about 5 p.m. Matthews met with DiBona, Gundlach, and two other students interested in working on the play. Although he had still not read the bulk of the script, Matthews reiterated his concerns with the "community opposition" to the play. According to DiBona, "He told me...that he didn't want organized opposition from the ministers of the community and that he was responsible to the community...and that he felt that the language was unacceptable for [ECC]." DiBona and the students attempted to explain that while the language in the first scene was strong, it was appropriate given the theme of the entire play. Matthews agreed to read the complete script that night.

The class met as scheduled Monday evening. DiBona and Gundlach briefed the class on their meeting with Matthews, explaining that for the time being, the play was "on hold." DiBona suggested it was pointless to submit the "add" cards and additional fees to the registrar pending resolution of the controversy. The students discussed potential alternatives open to them and whether the administration reaction had been influenced by the Sagon Penn case currently being tried in San Diego County Superior Court.

Sagon Penn, a young Black man living in Southeast San Diego, was charged with murder and attempted murder in the shootings of two police officers and a civilian ride-along. Penn was stopped by one of the officers for an alleged traffic violation. He admitted shooting the victims using a gun belonging to the officer who originally stopped him. He claimed, however, that the officer used the traffic stop as a pretext to verbally abuse and physically assault him because he was Black. After a hung jury in his first trial, a second jury acquitted Penn of all major charges. Following the second trial, the remaining charges were dismissed.

Sometime on Monday or Tuesday, Matthews asked Hardison to read the play. When they discussed the issue again, they agreed the play was inappropriate for presentation at ECC. Hardison termed the characters "a little weak," the plot "anticlimactic," and concluded "it's not very uplifting." He thought "Split Second" "would [not] fit into the category of...Tennessee Williams or any of the [sic] George Bernard Shaw's works, in my opinion. Just is not of that caliber." Matthews suggested that Hardison talk to DiBona.

DiBona spoke with Hardison on Tuesday evening. According to DiBona, "Hardison...told me the decision to cancel the class was due to the sensitivity of the community to the subject matter. [He] said perhaps the play would do well in La Jolla [a wealthy white community located to the north], but not in Southeast San Diego. Hardison said the community needed to be uplifted, and suggested the class put on [the successful all-black musical] 'The Wiz.'" DiBona declined Hardison's suggestion to use another play, pointing out that he had been preparing "Split Second" for months. He then asked whether it would be possible to conduct the class and perform the play privately so that the students could receive credit. Hardison said he would check with Matthews. The next evening, Hardison told DiBona he and Matthews had decided there would be no class with "Split Second" as the subject matter.

At about this same time, Hardison e anived a list of classes at ECC with insufficient enrollment. The Drama 250 class was included on this list because only three students were officially registered. As noted previously, due to the controversy over "Split Second" DiBona had never submitted the "add" cards for 11 of the 14 students to the registrar's office. Hardison testified it was the "general practice" at ECC to drop classes with less than 10 students. ECC records reflect that Drama 250 was canceled on Tuesday, June 17. DiBona stated and Hardison confirmed, however, that Hardison never mentioned class enrollment during their discussions. In fact, DiBona never heard the class had been canceled due to low enrollment until after this litigation began.

After the administration's decision was communicated to the students, they decided to rehearse and perform the play off campus. None of the students, including Gundlach, received course credit, and DiBona was not paid pursuant to his contract for teaching a summer session course.

DiBona and Gundlach filed this action alleging violation of their constitutional rights and seeking declaratory and injunctive relief. At that time, DiBona was no longer a teacher and Gundlach no longer a student at ECC. DiBona, however, was employed as a teacher at the City College campus of the San Diego Community College District. Gundlach was enrolled as a student at the District's Mesa College campus.

Matthews and Hardison moved for summary judgment, arguing that the case was moot, that DiBona and Gundlach lacked standing, and that there was no violation of plaintiffs' constitutional rights. The trial court agreed with defendants, reasoning as follows:

> [A]fter going through it very carefully, I just feel that the defense position, with regard to the fact that there is no justiciable issue, is appropriate under these circumstances, that to...render an opinion would be contrary to the law's admonition that we not engage in moot acts or advisory opinions.
>
> I further agree with the position which is espoused in the moving papers... that there is no standing with regard to the remaining parties....
>
> And then, finally, I found the argument persuasive that this really didn't involve a violation or an improper...impact on the First Amendment rights of the parties who brought the action.

Commenting on the language in the play, the court added:

> And I read the play, by the way. And maybe somebody would have been offended, but having sat nine months in a criminal department—that was everyday testimony.

The court later expanded on its view that the plaintiffs' First Amendment rights had not been affected:

> I don't think that there was censorship herande don't think that there was an improper denial or cancellation of that class. And I do think that what did occur, under thesd norcumstances, most assuredly was reasonable.
>
> And I think I'm capable of taking a little bit of judicial notice as to what the political atmosphere in Southeast San Diego and in the City of San Diego was at about the time that this arose, with regard to a certain well known and well publicized criminal action that was proceeding through our courts.
>
> And I think that what happened was that the administration weighed the potential of the harm that could have been caused by that play, the fact that obviously, justifiable or not, there were segments of the society that was going

to be exposed to it that had evidenced the fact that they were not very happy with it, that the Saigon [sic] Penn situation was a very volatile and potentially violent situation.

I think all of these things were properly in consideration. I don't view it at all as being a First Amendment matter at all. And, even if it were, I think it's the same situation about the ability to yell "Fire" in a crowd of a theater. I think, under those circumstances, calmness and awareness of the problem justified the action that was taken.

DISCUSSION

County Counsel on behalf of the defendant college administrators seeks to defend the court's grant of summary judgment on the same three theories raised and relied on below. We address these arguments seriatim.

Constitutional Issues

[The court's discussion of the standing and mootness arguments is omitted.]

Having disposed of the alleged procedural barriers, we now confront the fundamental question whether the evidence before the court on defendants' motion for summary judgment establishes as a matter of law that plaintiffs' constitutional rights were not violated. Defendants first argue the evidence establishes the class was canceled for reasons unrelated to First Amendment concerns. They assert it is uncontested Hardison authorized and Matthews approved the cancellation on June 17 because of low enrollment. This argument misconstrues the central issue. The record reflects that beginning on June 16, Matthews and Hardison expressed their opinions that "Split Second" would not be performed at ECC. While it is true only three students were formally enrolled on June 17, it is equally clear that eleven other students wanted to enroll and would have enrolled had defendants not acted to prohibit performance of the play. Under these circumstances, it cannot be said that the cancellation of the class was unrelated to the content of the play and plaintiffs' attempted exercise of their constitutional rights in performing it.

Of course, the mere fact that defendants considered the content of the play in deciding to cancel the class does not in itself establish a violation of plaintiffs' constitutional rights. Under the guise of free speech, the First Amendment does not transfer control of a public school's curriculum from school administrators to individual teachers and students. Equally important, however, "[n]either teachers [n]or students shed their constitutional rights to freedom of speech or expression at the schoolhouse gate." Tinker v. Des Moines School Dist. (1969) 393 U.S. 503, 506, 89 S.Ct. 733, 21 L.Ed.2d 731. As with so many First Amendment issues, the question is one of identifying permissible governmental purposes and balancing the competing interests. To paraphrase the Supreme Court in Tinker, our problem lies in the area where the exercise of First Amendment rights by students and teachers collides with the discretion of school administrators in deciding what is appropriate instructional material. Id. at p. 507.

The facts before the court on the motion for summary judgment suggest three principal reasons for the cancellation of the class articulated by Matthews and Hardison at various points in time: (1) there was opposition to the play from the religious community; (2) the subject matter of the play was sensitive given the community unrest in the wake of the Sagon Penn trial; and (3) the language of the play was "inappropriate."

A.

Plaintiffs contend the first and second justifications were the "real" reasons for cancellation of the class. The sequence of events would certainly support such a conclusion since Matthews admitted it was a phone call regarding opposition from religious groups which triggered his initial inquiries of DiBona. Moreover, the trial judge specifically accepted the pending Penn criminal case as a valid reason justifying ECC's caution in producing a play raising similar issues.

Both the United States and California Supreme Courts have spoken to the question of whether government may regulate the content of speech because of concern that it may provoke dissension, dispute or disturbance. More than 40 years ago in Terminiello v. Chicago (1949) 337 U.S. 1, 69 S.Ct. 894, 93 L.Ed. 1131, Justice Douglas wrote:

> [A] function of free speech under our system of government is to invite dispute. It may indeed best serve its high purpose when it induces a condition of unrest, creates dissatisfaction with conditions as they are, or even stirs people to anger. Speech is often provocative and challenging. It may strike at prejudices and preconceptions and have profound and unsettling effects as it presses for acceptance of an idea. That is why freedom of speech, though not absolute, is nevertheless protected against censorship or punishment, unless shown likely to produce a clear and present danger of a serious substantive evil that rises far above public inconvenience, annoyance, or unrest.

Twenty years later in Tinker v. Des Moines School Dist., supra, 393 U.S. 503, Justice Fortas repeated Terminiello's rationale in rejecting a school district's argument that the wearing of black armbands by some students might provoke a disturbance.

Because it concerned conduct on a state college campus, the California Supreme Court's opinion in Braxton v. Municipal Court (1973) 10 Cal.3d 138, 109 Cal.Rptr. 897, 514 P.2d 697, is of particular interest. Writing for the court, Justice Tobriner echoed themes similar to those articulated in Terminiello and Tinker:

> [N]either the "content" of speech nor freedom of association can be restricted merely because such expression or association disrupts the tranquility of a campus or offends the tastes of school administrators or the public. Protest may disrupt the placidity of the vacant mind just as a stone dropped in a still pool may disturb the tranquility of the surface waters, but the courts have never held such "disruption" falls outside the boundaries of the First Amendment.

Id. at p. 146.

The facts of this case present a classic illustration of "undifferentiated fear" of disturbance on the part of school administrators. DiBona was given the authority to select curriculum materials. The administration became interested in the subject matter of the class only after "community" opposition was first manifest. When they reacted to this pressure by canceling the class, there were no facts known to either Matthews or Hardison indicating a "clear and present danger" of any evil, let alone a "serious substantive" one. Nor was there any suggestion that the production of the play would "'materially and substantially interfere with the requirements of appropriate discipline in the operation of the school.'" Tinker, supra, 393 U.S. at p. 509 (quoting Burnside v. Byers (5th Cir. 1966) 363 F.2d 744, 749.) Rather, school officials were merely concerned with "avoid[ing] the discomfort and unpleasantness that always accompany" an unpopular or unorthodox point of view. Tinker, supra, 393 U.S. at p. 509.

Similar issues were similarly resolved in Brown v. Board of Regents of University of Nebraska (D.Neb. 1986) 640 F.Supp. 674. There, the University of Nebraska canceled the scheduled showing of a controversial film, "Hail Mary," after several members of the public and a state senator complained that the film blasphemed certain religious beliefs. The director of the campus art gallery (within which the theatre showing the film was housed) ordered cancellation of the film because it was "'offensive to a segment of society and did not merit the efforts it would take to defend it.'" Id. at p. 677. The director was also concerned that the negative publicity concerning the film would adversely affect the university's and the gallery's ongoing budgetary battles in the Legislature. Id. In a suit for declaratory relief, the district court relied on Tinker in holding that the decision to cancel the film violated the constitutional rights of persons wishing to view it.

Here, Matthews's expressed desire to avoid "taking on" the religious community is clearly an insufficient basis for cancellation of the class. As to the "politically sensitive" nature of the play's subject matter, not only is it a constitutionally inappropriate reason for censorship, ultimately it may also be counterproductive for the community. A central premise of the constitutional guaranty of free speech is that difficult and sensitive political issues generally benefit from constructive dialogue of the sort which might have been generated by "Split Second."

B.

Defendants suggest their decision may be upheld and the summary judgment affirmed based on the independent ground that the language used in "Split Second" was "inappropriate" for a school play. While it is clear the trial court did not rely on this ground, our obligation is equally clear to affirm the judgment if there is an adequate independent basis which establishes as a matter of law that defendants must prevail.

We have previously alluded to the fact that school administrators possess considerable discretion in deciding on the content of school curriculum. See, e.g., Hazelwood School District v. Kuhlmeier (1988) 484 U.S. 260, 273, 108 S.Ct. 562, 98 L.Ed.2d 592; Epperson v. Arkansas (1968) 393 U.S. 97, 104, 89 S.Ct. 266, 21 L.Ed.2d 228. The appropriateness of language used in a play has—at least in certain contexts—traditionally been viewed as the sort of factor which may legitimately be considered in making curriculum decisions. For varying reasons, however, we conclude it cannot support defendants' decision to cancel the Drama 250 class and prohibit the performance of "Split Second."

Numerous cases have considered the question under what circumstances school officials may regulate the performance of dramatic productions or the availability of written materials on grounds of inappropriate language or content. Nearly all these cases, however, have involved minors rather than adult college students.

Defendants contend as college administrators they should be afforded the same broad discretion in controlling their curriculum as school administrators at the elementary and secondary level. As a general proposition, however, where children are concerned the legitimate role of the government in regulating speech is substantially broader. In contrast, as the Supreme Court explained in Healy v. James (1972) 408 U.S. 169, 92 S.Ct. 2338, 33 L.Ed.2d 266, "[T]he precedents of this Court leave no room for the view that...First Amendment protections should apply with less force on college campuses than in the community at large." Id. at p. 180. In Papish v. University of Missouri Curators (1973) 410 U.S. 667, 93 S.Ct. 1197, 35 L.Ed.2d 618, the court considered the question whether a student could be disciplined for distributing a newspaper on campus containing "indecent" language and material. In a per curiam opinion, the court invalidated the student's expulsion explaining, "We think Healy makes it clear that the mere dissemination of ideas—no matter how offensive to good taste—on a state university campus may not be shut off in the name alone of 'conventions of decency.'" Id. at p. 670.

Relying principally on Hazelwood School District v. Kuhlmeier, supra, 484 U.S. 260, defendants suggest that the broad pronouncements of Healy and Papish have been undercut by more recent decisions recognizing an enhanced governmental interest in regulating school-sponsored expressive activities such as the play in this case. They suggest this more deferential standard is equally applicable in the college and adult education context.

We question whether the rationale underlying the "school sponsorship" rule would allow its wholesale extension to educational settings involving adults. The general public is likely to view school-sponsored student speech as bearing the "imprimatur of the school," Hazelwood, supra, 484 U.S. at p. 271, largely because of the greater control elementary and secondary schools exercise over the conduct of minor students. Defendants have cited no authority—and we are aware of none—which would allow a college or university to censor instructor-selected curriculum materials because they contain "indecent" language or deal with "offensive" topics.

Moreover, there was no danger anyone likely to be offended would be forced to participate in or view the play. DiBona made the script available to students several weeks before the first class so they could decide whether they wished to audition. Assuming the play was performed publicly, no one would have been required to attend.

In any event, we may assume school sponsorship is a factor which under some circumstances can be considered at the college level. We nonetheless cannot validate defendants' decision here to cancel the Drama 250 class. Although Hazelwood mentions a school's production of a play as the type of expressive activity which may be viewed as "sponsored," 484 U.S. at p. 271, one can produce a play without advocating or subscribing to every idea the author of the play intends to communicate. No one could reasonably argue that a school which presented a play by Shakespeare was thereby advocating the social and sexual mores of 17th century England which are implicit and often explicit in Shakespeare's works. Moreover, defendants' objection here was based on the indecency of the language used in "Split Second," particularly its first scene. But in contrast to a school paper—which if it allowed students to express themselves using profanity would implicitly condone its use—"Split Second" does not advocate the use of vulgar speech. If anything, the play suggests that the use of profanity and racial slurs may cause people to react emotionally rather than rationally. As the trial court in this case recognized, profane speech is unfortunately the accepted vocabulary of some segments of our society. "Split Second" simply recognizes this reality and uses it to create the emotional tension necessary to develop the moral and philosophical issues which are central to the play.

Our conclusions do not leave college administrators powerless to control college curriculum. Although the "legitimate pedagogical concerns" at the college and university level may be more limited than in elementary and secondary schools, they are not nonexistent. Certainly college officials may limit the drama curriculum to works of an acceptable literary quality and they undoubtedly are entitled to broad deference where such determinations are made in advance rather than, as here, some time after the class had already begun to meet.

At least where adults are concerned, however, literary quality cannot be measured simply by counting the number of "indecent" words in a book or play. As Justice Harlan recognized in Cohen v. California (1971) 403 U.S. 15, 91 S.Ct. 1780, 29 L.Ed.2d 284, taking a page from McLuhan, no bright line can be drawn between the manner of communication and the content of the ideas communicated:

> [W]e cannot indulge the facile assumption that one can forbid particular words without also running a substantial risk of suppressing ideas in the process. Indeed, governments might soon seize upon the censorship of particular words as a convenient guise for banning the expression of unpopular views. We have been able...to discern little social benefit that might result from running the risk of opening the door to such grave results.

Id. at p. 26.

Judgment reversed.

HUFFMAN, Associate Justice, dissenting.

This case presents the question of who should control the curriculum of an educational institution—the administration, the faculty, or the students. Unfortunately, although it disclaims such result, the majority answers the question by permitting the faculty and students to determine curriculum content. To the extent any administration control will remain, it will have to be pursuant to "objective standards" which will lead to court supervision. To reach this unhappy result, the majority opinion has struggled to attempt to overcome the lack of standing of appellant Scott Gundlach and the mootness of the declaratory relief claim of appellant Alan DiBona.

I believe the majority opinion, although scholarly and well written, is truly "advisory" because neither injunctive nor declaratory relief is appropriate to these parties whose relationship with the defendants was severed four years ago. Moreover, the advice it renders is at odds with recent United States Supreme Court authority regarding the power of school administrators to control curriculum content.

Constitutional Issues

Recognizing as I do the dissenter's lot of crying out against the inevitable, I turn then to a discussion of the First Amendment issues.

The majority's analysis of the actions by the ECC administration in this case includes a characterization of the reasons its officials offered to support their conduct in canceling the class: "(1) there was opposition to the play from the religious community; (2) the subject matter of the play was sensitive given the community unrest in the wake of the Sagon Penn trial; and (3) the language of the play was 'inappropriate.'" Thus, the majority's focus rests largely on the concerns of ECC administrators for the effects of the play "Split Second" on the community in which ECC is located and on ECC's relationship with the people it seeks to serve. Those concerns are dismissed, however, with the statement the school administrators had only an "'undifferentiated fear' of disturbance" because they knew no facts "indicating a 'clear and present danger' of any evil, let alone a 'serious substantive' one."

I respectfully disagree with this somewhat cavalier dismissal of what the trial court found, and I believe to be, legitimate concerns of a community college branch. Further, I believe the majority implies that any curriculum content regulation based upon the impact on the school and the community in such a circumstance must rise to the level of "clear and present danger." In other words, according to the majority only concerns amounting to a cry of "Fire" in a crowded theatre permit action by school administrators.

The majority's analysis is at distinct odds with the United States Supreme Court holding in Hazelwood School District v. Kuhlmeier (1988) 484 U.S. 260, 108 S.Ct. 562, 98 L.Ed.2d 592. [I]n my view, Hazelwood clearly authorizes the kind of action taken by school administrators in this case.

The majority opinion seeks to distinguish Hazelwood principally because it dealt with high school students and, after all, ECC is a community college branch. I submit the majority's attempt to distinguish a clear analysis of the relationship between administrators and students is overly facile. A reading of Hazelwood shows the court was concerned with returning discretion to school administrators when dealing with curriculum, particularly where, as here, the school would have to sponsor, promote, advertise, and financially support the [play].

The Supreme Court made clear in Hazelwood that the concern of the "imprimatur of the school" is a legitimate one that needs to be addressed by those persons who must make the daily decisions for the school and who are held accountable for them. To substitute the judgment of an appellate court made after lengthy contemplation and reflection for that of school administrators in a community already wracked by racial tension between the police and the members of that community is, in my opinion, simply inappropriate.

Having examined the actions of the ECC officials in light of Hazelwood, I find they set no censorship policy and did not discipline either teacher or students. It was the teacher who brought the play to the attention of the school officials and, in light of its content, its vulgarity, and its impact on the relationship of a community-based educational facility and the community it serves, the school officials made the decision not to produce it. To the extent their concerns regarding the play formed a part of the basis to cancel a class (along with 23 other classes) which had only three enrolled students, this was, in my view, a valid exercise of the discretion vested in them. There was, therefore, no violation of the First Amendment rights of either DiBona or Gundlach.

Finally, the majority opinion recognizes some authority in college officials to limit drama curriculum in light of school sponsorship and "literary" concerns, and that judgments made by those officials are entitled to broad deference if made in advance of the class rather than "as here, sometime after the class has already begun to meet."

The class in this case had not officially commenced, as witness the enrollment of only three students. The issues concerning the play were not known to the administration before the unofficial meetings of the class and the administrators acted immediately upon becoming aware of those issues. Respectfully, the majority's attempt to distinguish the facts of this case from those which recognize the authority of school administrators over curriculum content is a recognition of the weakness of its position. The majority's creation of a "post-commencement" limitation on curriculum control is not authorized by law and it is an unwarranted judicial intrusion upon the legitimate authority of a school to deal with the content of its curriculum. I would not impose such a rule.

LINNEMEIER v. INDIANA UNIVERSITY-PURDUE UNIVERSITY FORT WAYNE

155 F. Supp. 2d 1034 (N.D. Ind. 2001)

LEE, Chief Judge.

This cause is before the court upon the Plaintiffs' Complaint and Motion for Preliminary Injunction filed on July 5, 2001. On July 17, 2001, the court heard evidence and argument on the Plaintiffs' request for a preliminary injunction. After considering this evidence in addition to reviewing the briefs and arguments of counsel, the court now enters its ruling on the Plaintiffs' request for a preliminary injunction. Entered simultaneously herewith are the court's rulings on the Defendants' motions to dismiss. For the following reasons, the Plaintiffs' request for a preliminary injunction will be DENIED.

GENERAL BACKGROUND

A group of Plaintiffs, originally including eleven residents and taxpayers of the state of Indiana and twenty-one members of the Indiana General Assembly (hereafter, "the Plaintiffs"), filed suit against the Defendants, Indiana University-Purdue University Fort Wayne ("IPFW") and ten members of the Board of Trustees of Purdue University ("the Board") (collectively, "the Defendants") pursuant to 42 U.S.C. § 1983 alleging that the Defendants will violate the Establishment Clause of the United States Constitution if they are not enjoined from presenting playwright Terrence McNally's play Corpus Christi (hereafter "the Play") on August 10, 2001 at the Studio Theater located in Kettler Hall on IPFW's campus. In an Order entered contemporaneously with this one, the undersigned dismissed the members of the Indiana General Assembly and various individual plaintiffs because they lacked standing to assert an Establishment Clause violation. In addition, the court dismissed IPFW because it was not a corporate entity subject to be sued under Indiana law. Finally, the court declined to exercise supplemental jurisdiction over the Plaintiffs' claim of an Indiana constitutional violation. There remain three plaintiffs of the original thirty-two and a single legal claim asserting an Establishment Clause violation. It is to this claim the court turns its attention in the instant order.

FACTUAL BACKGROUND

The Plaintiffs seek to enjoin the Play from going forward because they believe the Play is an "undisguised attack on Christianity and the Founder of Christianity, Jesus Christ," and thus, the performance of the Play in a publicly funded, taxpayer owned, educational facility such as IPFW violates the separation between church and state as required by the Establishment Clause. The Complaint sets forth four and a half pages of alleged hostile references to Christianity and affidavits from several of the Plaintiffs in which they articulate their religious objections to the Play and their belief that the Play attacks basic tenets of Christian belief.

The Play's protagonist is a Christ-like figure named Joshua. Joshua is a young gay man from South Texas, who is surrounded by his disciples, a group of twelve gay men. Each disciple takes the name of one of the historical disciples of Christ in the New Testament of the Bible. The Play includes scenes where Joshua engages in homosexual relations with the disciples and portrays the Last Supper as a food fight.

It is a fair characterization of this Play that it is patently and grossly offensive to many traditional Christian beliefs and that this is the intent of the Play. The Playwright states as much in the Preface and the actor tells the audience this at the end of the Play when he says "[i]f we have offended, so be it."

Jonathan Gilbert ("Gilbert") is a senior at IPFW majoring in theater with an emphasis in directing. As part of his course work, he is enrolled in a course numbered THTR 499 bearing the description "Senior Performance Project." According to IPFW's catalog description "all theatre majors will register for this course, which serves as the curricular capstone, during their final semester. Students will develop, with their advisor, a public performance or presentation appropriate to their area of emphasis." For his senior project, Gilbert selected the Play with permission from IPFW faculty and plans (unless enjoined from doing so) to direct its performance at the IPFW Studio Theater.

Larry Life ("Life") is employed by IPFW as a full professor of theater and Chair/Artistic Director of the Department of Theater. In his capacity as Chair/Artistic Director, Life is responsible for supervising all activities in the Department. Life testified that a student enrolled in THTR 499 must complete a "Senior Project Proposal Cover Sheet" which inquires of the student the reasons for selecting a particular project and how that student is prepared to undertake the project. This form is then submitted to a board of five Theater Department faculty members, which includes Life, for their review. According to Life, in approving a work proposed by students enrolled in THTR 499, the Theater Department relies on the neutral criteria provided by the student on the form and does not evaluate the viewpoint of the proposed work. Life further testified that the Department has never evaluated the viewpoint of a work proposed by a student as part of the THTR 499 course requirement and the Department remains "viewpoint neutral" as to all theater productions.

Life has worked actively with Gilbert in the production of the Play, consulting with him after a rehearsal and, at other times, regarding the technical and dramatic aspects of the direction of the play. Life testified that this aid is essentially "volunteer work" in that he is not required under his contract with IPFW to advise students in the summer months. Life intends to attend each rehearsal of the Play and "make suggestions" to Gilbert as to the presentation of the Play and the technical and dramatic aspects of the direction of the Play.

Eleven of the thirteen actors in Corpus Christi are students who voluntarily auditioned for the Play. The remaining two actors are volunteers from the Fort Wayne community. Other students have volunteered to serve as lighting, set and costume designers, stage hands and ushers. In addition, Gilbert has raised $3,000 to pay for certain costs of the Play including scripts, royalties, costumes, and props. Private donors have also provided money for two County Police officers to provide security during the six performances of the Play. The remainder of the security will be provided by IPFW through its operating budget. IPFW has invited the public to purchase tickets and attend the Play by way of a season brochure authorized and distributed by IPFW. This brochure was funded by non-taxpayer university funds.

Corpus Christi is one of nine plays that IPFW plans to stage during the 2001-2002 theater season. The others include: Bye Bye Birdie, by Michael Stewart, Charles Strouse and Lee Adams; The Rivals, by Richard Sheridan; Atlas's Cigar, by Betsy Breitenbach; Protest, by Vaclav Havel; Harvey, by Mary Chase; Picasso at the Lapine Agile, by Steve Martin; The Vagina Monologues, by Eve Ensler; On the Town, by Leonard Bernstein; and Tennessee Williams: The Foolish Dreamer, devised by Larry Life. All of these plays were chosen without regard to their viewpoint. Aside from its general theater season, IPFW also permits outside groups to utilize the Studio Theater so long as their use complies with the educational mission of the school. To date, only one outside group has utilized the Studio Theater, a group of high school students from the drama department at North Side High School in Fort Wayne. Life testified that the students were permitted to utilize Studio Theater without regard to the viewpoint of their drama presentation. He further testified that any group that desires to use Studio Theater would be permitted to do so without regard to the viewpoint of the group's presentation. IPFW Chancellor Michael Wartell ("Wartell") likewise testified that the Studio Theater was open to outside groups without regard to the content of the speech which would occur there.

The plays presented at IPFW are chosen without the intervention of Wartell. Wartell did not read the script of the Play and did not interfere with the decision of the Theater Department to stage the Play as an academic offering. Wartell testified that if a play "is brought up through the theater department in standard form" he would not stop it, no matter its content, unless the content was illegal. According to Wartell, this is because there is "a general university policy, universities around the world actually, of academic freedom where administrators do not interfere with either how or what subject matter is taught in the classroom."

As a result of the controversy surrounding the Play, IPFW has taken affirmative steps to convey to the community the lack of university sponsorship of the Play. The playbill for the production will contain the following disclaimer: "This play was selected for its artistic and academic value. The selection and performance of the play do not constitute an endorsement by Indiana University Purdue University Fort Wayne or Purdue University of the viewpoints conveyed by the play." IPFW has also taken steps to permit organizations objecting to the viewpoint of the Play to make that objection known by passing out informational letters to those attending the Play.

Finally, IPFW has agreed to sponsor a public forum permitting open discussion of all viewpoints occasioned by the Play in the middle of the scheduled performance week.

DISCUSSION

The Establishment Clause of the First Amendment provides that "Congress shall make no law respecting an establishment of religion...." The Fourteenth Amendment imposes this substantive limitation on the legislative power of the States, [for it] is the Establishment Clause which "prevents the government from promoting or affiliating with any religious doctrine or organization." The Plaintiffs contend that the performance of the Play on IPFW's campus violates this general prohibition in that the state (acting through IPFW) is improperly endorsing an attack on their religion. This court's sole role is to determine, as a legal matter, whether a preliminary injunction should issue.

1. Plaintiffs' Likelihood of Success on the Merits

This case implicates two fundamental principles of our Constitution. The First Amendment requires caution from the government to "abstain from regulating speech when the specific motivating ideology or the opinion or perspective of the speaker is the rationale for the restriction," Rosenberger v. Rector and Visitors of University of Virginia, 515 U.S. 819, 827 (1995). At the same time, the First Amendment prohibits the government, through its speech, from "coerc[ing] anyone to support or participate in religion or its exercise, or otherwise act in a way which 'establishes a [state] religion or religious faith or tends to do so.'" Lee v. Weisman, 505 U.S. 577, 587 (1992) (quoting Lynch v. Donnelly, 465 U.S. 668, 678 (1984)). The Plaintiffs claim the latter has occurred in this case; the Defendants assert the former is at work. It is this court's task to reconcile the two views.

The hallmark of the Establishment Clause inquiry is whether the government convey[s] or attempt[s] to convey a message that religion or a particular religious belief is favored or preferred. There is a crucial difference between government speech endorsing religion, which the Establishment Clause forbids, and private speech endorsing religion, which the Free Speech and Free Exercise Clauses protect. This distinction leads the court to the fundamental question presented by the parties in their arguments and briefs, that is, who is the speaker in this instance? This determination is critical for when the government speaks, either directly or through private intermediaries, it is constitutionally entitled to make "content based choices" and to engage in "viewpoint based funding decisions." In contrast, when the speech is private speech, the government may not regulate it in the same way it regulates its own speech, particularly where the government has evinced either "'by policy or by practice' any intent to open [school facilities] to 'indiscriminate use.'" Hazelwood School Dist. v. Kuhlmeier, 484 U.S. 260, 270 (1988).

The Plaintiffs assert that the speech at issue here, i.e., performance of the Play, is government sponsored speech or, at the very least, speech which conveys a message of endorsement or disapproval of religion regardless of its actual purpose. Plaintiffs rely primarily on the fact that the speech will occur on government property and be aided by utilities paid for from a taxpayer funded university account to support this assertion. However, not every message delivered [on government property at government-sponsored school-related events] is the government's own. Indeed, the Supreme Court has upheld private religious speech on government property in numerous cases. See Good News Club v. Milford Central School, 121 S.Ct. 2093 (2001) (private Christian club permitted to meet on school property); Rosenberger, 515 U.S. 819 (university student organization which published Christian newspaper entitled to university funding the same as other student organizations); Lamb's Chapel v. Center Moriches Union Free School District., 508 U.S. 384 (1993) (church permitted to use school facilities for religious oriented film series on family values and child-rearing); Widmar v. Vincent, 454 U.S. 263 (1981) (members of registered religious group at state university permitted to use university facilities).

Plaintiffs distinguish these cases by claiming that the particular facts of this case demonstrate that the Studio Theater in Kettler Hall is a non-public forum. If they are correct, the test becomes that articulated in Lemon v. Kurtzman, 403 U.S. 602 (1971), which requires this court to examine (1) whether the government activity in question has a secular purpose; (2) whether the activity's primary effect advances or inhibits religion; and (3) whether the government activity fosters an excessive entanglement with religion. If they are wrong, the aforementioned cases (Good News Club, Rosenberger, Widmar, and Lamb's Chapel) are controlling and foreclose their contention that the speech in this case gives the appearance of government endorsement of a religious (or anti-religious) viewpoint.

Having reviewed the evidence presented at the preliminary injunction hearing, the court concludes that the teachings of Good News Club, Rosenberger, Widmar, and Lamb's Chapel must inform the court's decision in this case and, when the evidence is considered in light of those cases, it conclusively demonstrates that the plaintiffs have little chance of prevailing on the merits.

The evidence shows that IPFW has evinced, by both policy and practice, an intent to open the Studio Theater to both the student body and the public at large. As part of its theater department curriculum, IPFW permits students to utilize Studio Theater to stage a "public performance," thereby creating a limited forum for its students. In addition to making its theater open to its students, two university administrators testified that any group who desires to utilize Studio Theater would be permitted to do so on a viewpoint neutral basis so long as the group's activities comport with the educational mission of the university. At least one outside group, North Side High School's drama organization, has done so. These facts, the court believes, clearly establishes that IPFW has created, at the very least, a limited public forum in the Studio Theater.

Having created a public forum, IPFW may not discriminate against the viewpoint of those speaking within the very forum they created without violating the First Amendment's free speech guarantee. The Supreme Court teaches that "a significant factor in upholding governmental [action] in the face of Establishment Clause attack is their neutrality towards religion." Good News Club, 121 S.Ct. at 2104 (quoting Rosenberger, 515 U.S. at 839). [T]he guarantee of neutrality is respected, not offended, when the government, following neutral criteria and evenhanded policies, extends benefits to recipients whose ideologies and viewpoints, including religious ones, are broad and diverse. Viewpoint neutrality by the university is precisely what the evidence shows in this case. Life testified that viewpoint is never considered in determining theater productions nor is it a factor in approving particular student projects, such as the one in this case, or outside performances to be performed in the theater by other groups. Thus, the university has done all that the Constitution requires of it and it cannot be said to have violated the Establishment Clause.

Plaintiffs emphasize, however, that the question in this case is whether there is a "perception or message of endorsement" occasioned by the Play's performance on a public university campus. In support of this proposition, the Plaintiffs analogize the instant case to cases where courts have found religious statues or monuments to violate the Establishment Clause when they are situated on government property. In each of these cases, the courts concluded that because the religious statue or monument was situated in a building that was the heart of the city or county's government, such as a municipal building or county courthouse, its placement created the perception of endorsement by the government itself.

What these cases firmly hold is that the court must look to the unique facts and circumstances presented to determine whether a reasonable person would perceive the performance of the Play to be a government endorsement or attack on religion or a particular religious belief. In each of the monument cases, there was no question that the facts and circumstances in those cases, particularly the location of the monument itself, created a perception of government endorsement. Taking into account the unique facts and circumstances of this case, however, the court concludes that the performance of this Play on a public university campus is not, as Plaintiffs' contend, akin to a monument's placement "at the seat of the government." Indeed, the fact that the Play will be performed on a state university campus greatly distinguishes it from the cases cited above and would not create the perception of government endorsement in a reasonable observer.

Having observed the Plaintiffs' testimony at the preliminary injunction hearing it is clear that they sincerely and validly perceive the performance of the Play to be a message attacking their religious beliefs. However, the endorsement inquiry is "not about the perceptions of particular individuals or saving isolated nonadherents from...discomfort." Good News Club, 121 S.Ct. at 2106. The law requires the court to go beyond the particularized perceptions of individuals and inquire into the mind of a reasonable observer "deemed aware of the history and context of the community and forum in which the religious [speech takes place]." Id.

A university setting is a place where "the State acts against a background and tradition of thought and experiment that is at the center of our intellectual and philosophic tradition." Rosenberger, 515 U.S. at 834. It is a "hub of ideas" and a place citizens traditionally identify with creative inquiry, provocative discourse, and intellectual growth. When considered in this context, the Play falls squarely within this general notion of subjects accepted by the public for a university.

In sum, the open nature of the forum in this case in tandem with the history and context of the university setting in which the performance will occur highlighted by the steps the university has taken to disassociate itself from the speech in question leads to the conclusion that the Plaintiffs have failed to sustain their burden of demonstrating a substantial likelihood of success on the merits of their Establishment Clause claim.

2. Irreparable Harm for which there is no Adequate Remedy in the Law

The inquiry, however, does not end here. The court must weigh the likelihood of success on the merits against the allegation of irreparable harm to the Plaintiffs that might yield from the challenged conduct. Anyone observing the demeanor and testimony of the Plaintiffs at the hearing would easily discern that the Plaintiffs will suffer irreparable harm if the production goes forward. It is equally clear that because this case involves deeply rooted spiritual beliefs and personal sentiment that there is no adequate remedy at law should a constitutional violation exist. Thus, plaintiffs have demonstrated a substantial likelihood of irreparable harm.

3. Balance of Interests

The balance of interests addresses the remaining two elements of the preliminary injunction inquiry: the irreparable harm the non-moving party will suffer if the injunction is granted balanced against the irreparable harm the moving party will suffer if the injunction is denied as well as the interests of non-parties. As the court indicated above, the consequences of erroneously denying injunctive relief are great in that the Plaintiffs will, without question, be irreparably harmed. In turn, the consequences of erroneously granting such relief are equally great in that the court would be requiring the Defendants to curtail the free speech rights of one of its students thereby causing irreparable harm.

There is likewise a threat of substantial harm to the public and local community should the court enjoin the Play's performance. The public has an interest in participating and viewing this controversial speech and in the free exercise of thoughts and ideas which this case implicates. This is of particular concern here given the slim chance Plaintiffs have of succeeding on the merits and so this factor, in addition to the harm to the Defendants if an injunction is granted, tends to weigh in favor of denying injunctive relief.

4. Application of Sliding Scale

Having analyzed each of the factors which must be established for issuance of a preliminary injunction, on balance, the court concludes that the Plaintiffs cannot prevail on their request for a preliminary injunction. Applying the flexible "sliding scale" as the court must, the court's preliminary view of the merits points strongly in favor of the Defendants and is counterbalanced by the irreparable harm to be suffered by the Plaintiffs. However, when the substantial risk of irreparable harm to non-parties and the public is factored into the equation, the balance tips in favor of denying the injunction.

CONCLUSION

The Plaintiffs' motion for preliminary injunction is DENIED.

AXSON-FLYNN v. JOHNSON
151 F. Supp. 2d 1326 (D. Utah 2001)

CAMPBELL, District Judge.

This case involves the scope of First Amendment protections of the Free Exercise of Religion and Free Speech. Plaintiff's suit, brought under 42 U.S.C. § 1983, rests on the contention that Defendants' Acting Program curricular requirements that she use language that she found objectionable amount to a constitutionally impermissible infringement of her rights to Free Exercise and Free Speech. This matter is before the court on Defendants' motion for summary judgment. For their part, Defendants argue that Plaintiff's Free Exercise and Free Speech claims fail as a matter of law. Defendants further argue that Plaintiff's Hybrid Rights claim also fails as a matter of law, and that, if any of these claims do not fail as a matter of law, Defendants are nevertheless entitled to qualified immunity.

For the reasons set forth below, Defendants' motion is GRANTED.

Background

For the purposes of their summary judgment motion, Defendants have accepted Plaintiff's alleged facts as undisputed and therefore the court will recount the facts accordingly. (See Def.'s Reply to Pl.'s Mem. in Opp. to Def's Mot. for Summ. J. at ii.)

In 1998, Christina Axson-Flynn ("Axson-Flynn" or "Plaintiff"), a member of The Church of Jesus Christ of Latter-day Saints ("LDS" or "Mormon" herein), applied for and was accepted into the Actor Training Program ("ATP") at the University of Utah. Before her acceptance, Plaintiff attended an audition conducted by Defendants Barbara Smith, Sandra Shotwell, Jerry Gardner, and Sarah Shippobotham (collectively "Defendants"), instructors in the ATP program. At the audition, Plaintiff was asked if there was anything she was uncomfortable doing as an actor. In reply, Plaintiff informed the Defendants that she would not take her clothes off, take the name of God or Christ in vain (i.e., using those words as profanity), or say the word "fuck."

Although it is not clear from the record whether she told her instructors the reason for her objections at the time, Axson-Flynn subsequently explained that her refusal to use the words "God" or "Christ" as profanity is based on one of the Ten Commandments, which prohibits believers from taking "the name of the Lord thy God in vain...." Exodus 20:8. Plaintiff has also explained that her refusal to say the word "fuck" is due to the fact that it is religiously offensive to her because she finds that it vulgarizes what Plaintiff, as a Mormon, believes is a sacred act, appropriate only within the bounds of marriage.

Subsequent to her matriculation, many of the Defendants (except Gardner, who plaintiff has dropped from this action) apparently suggested that she "get over" her objection to using the language outlined above because not doing so would stunt her development as an actor. Defendants apparently believe, and include as a central tenet of the ATP, that it is an essential part of an actor's training to take on difficult roles, roles which sometime make actors uncomfortable and challenge their perspective.

Nevertheless, while participating in the program, Plaintiff omitted—without approval of or notice by her instructor—words and phrases that she found objectionable from one of her required performances and still received a high grade. However, when Plaintiff's professor, Defendant Smith, discovered the fact that Plaintiff had omitted the language in her earlier performance, she pressed Plaintiff even harder to use the language that Plaintiff found offensive. Ultimately, because she refused to use the language, on at least one assignment Plaintiff received a lower grade and was told that her grades would be lowered if she refused to comply with curricular requirements in the future. For the rest of that semester, however, Defendant Smith apparently acquiesced and allowed Plaintiff to omit the language that Plaintiff found offensive from her performances for that class.

At the end of her first semester, Plaintiff attended her oral semester review. At that review, Defendants Smith, Shippobotham, and Shotwell confronted Plaintiff about her refusal to use the language that she found offensive and told her that she would "no longer be given an allowance on language." They also suggested that she would have to find another place to study acting if she did not modify her stance on the use of such language. In response to the comments at her review, Plaintiff took her concerns to Defendant Xan Johnson, the ATP's coordinator, but Johnson informed her that he supported the other Defendants' position on the matter.

At the beginning of her second semester, Defendants Shotwell, Smith, and Shippobotham again suggested that Plaintiff participate as required in the program, using the language that she found offensive. Plaintiff, wishing to be certain of ATP's position on the matter, then went to talk with Defendant Shotwell, the program's director. Shotwell informed Plaintiff that the ATP would not change its position. In response, Plaintiff, while not asked to leave the program, left before the end of her second semester, apparently believing that it was a foregone conclusion that she would be forced to leave the ATP.

Analysis

The United States Supreme Court has held that the "first inquiry in any § 1983 suit... is whether the plaintiff has been deprived of a right secured by the Constitution and laws" and that the subsequent inquiry requires that such deprivation occur under color of state law." Baker v. McCollan, 443 U.S. 137, 140, 99 S.Ct. 2689, 61 L.Ed.2d 433 (1979) (internal quotations omitted); see also Gunkel v. City of Emporia, 835 F.2d 1302, 1303 (10th Cir.1987). The rights at issue in this case are the First Amendment protections to Free Exercise of Religion and Free Speech. Plaintiff's § 1983 suit rests on the contention that Defendants' curriculum, which required her to use language that she found objectionable, deprived her of her rights of Free Exercise of Religion and Free Speech.

Conceding that they are state actors, Defendants seek summary judgment in this case, arguing that Plaintiff's Free Exercise and Free Speech claims fail as a matter of law. Defendants further argue that Plaintiff's Hybrid Rights claim (an apparent subspecies of a Free Exercise cause of action) also fails as a matter of law, and that, if any of these claims do not fail as a matter of law, Defendants are nevertheless entitled to qualified immunity. After outlining the proper standard of review, the court addresses each of these assertions in order....

B. Free Exercise

The First Amendment to the United States Constitution provides, in part, that Congress shall make no law "prohibiting the free exercise" of religion. U.S. Const. amend I. As with all guarantees of the First Amendment, the Free Exercise clause applies to state and local governments by incorporation through the Fourteenth Amendment to the United States Constitution. See Cantwell v. Connecticut, 310 U.S. 296, 60 S.Ct. 900, 84 L.Ed. 1213 (1940). Plaintiff's Free Exercise claim squarely confronts the central tension in Free Exercise jurisprudence—for this is a case in which acting in accordance with a facially neutral policy incidentally directs a citizen to act counter to her religious beliefs. Put bluntly, Plaintiff, a Christian, was instructed, even if indirectly, to break the Second Commandment in order to conform to the facially neutral and generally applicable policies of the University of Utah's ATP curriculum. Indeed, this case involves the tenuous balance between the rule of law and the rule of conscience, a balance upon which civil society necessarily depends. Under binding precedent from the United States Supreme Court, the requirements and incidental burdens that the ATP curriculum put on Plaintiff's right to Free Exercise of Religion do not violate the Constitution of the United States.

With regard to the scope of the Free Exercise Clause's protection of religiously motivated activity, "as a general proposition, a law (or policy) that is neutral and of general applicability need not be justified by a compelling governmental interest even if that law incidentally burdens a particular religious practice or belief." Swanson v. Guthrie Indep. Sch. Dist. No. I-L, 135 F.3d 694, 697-98 (10th Cir.1998) (citing Church of the Lukumi Babalu Aye, Inc. v. City of Hialeah, 508 U.S. 520, 531, 113 S.Ct. 2217, 124 L.Ed.2d 472 (1993)). [T]he Tenth Circuit has determined that this standard of review is appropriate for the purpose of assessing whether school policies are in conformance with Free Exercise protections. See Swanson, 135 F.3d at 697-98.

Plaintiff was required to comply with facially neutral and generally applicable policies and course requirements of the ATP. These provided that all students must participate in the curriculum as structured by their professors. The curricular requirements are generally applicable to all students and are facially neutral; indeed, Plaintiff pointed to no written policy or course description that suggested otherwise. Finally, Plaintiff has pointed to no reference in curricular policy, guidelines or course descriptions themselves where a system of exemptions are extended to students for religious or other reasons. Plaintiff [thus] has failed to meet her burden of demonstrating a dispute of material fact necessary to withstand Defendants' motion for summary judgment. The burdens that the facially neutral and generally applicable curriculum put on Plaintiff are in conformance with the First Amendment's protection of Free Exercise rights, and Defendants are therefore entitled to summary judgment on Plaintiff's Free Exercise claim.

C. Free Speech

This case presents a novel question with regard to the regulation of speech in the educational forum: does required participation in a University's curriculum constitute compelled speech such that a student's action of refusal to participate, thereby subjecting her to a lower grade, is an action from which the University is barred? This question here posed is actually twofold—whether: 1) Plaintiff's requirement to participate in class constitutes, under the facts of this case, coerced speech subject to First Amendment protection; and, 2) whether Defendants possessed the authority to require complete student participation in the ATP as a prerequisite for accreditation from the program. The second issue is dealt with below in the court's treatment of Plaintiff's "hybrid rights" claim.

With regard to whether the curricular requirements amount to a constitutionally impermissible instance of coerced speech, it must first be noted that, of course, students do not "shed their constitutional rights…at the schoolhouse gate." Tinker v. Des Moines Indep. Community Sch. Dist., 393 U.S. 503, 506, 89 S.Ct. 733, 21 L.Ed.2d 731 (1969). Indeed, Defendants concede the unremarkable principle that university students have First Amendment rights. See Defs.' Reply Memo. at 8.

The relevant test to determine whether compelled speech is constitutionally impermissible is: 1) whether, as a threshold matter, the speech is compelled, and 2) if so, whether such compulsion "invades the sphere of intellect and spirit which it is the purpose of the First Amendment to our Constitution to reserve from all official control." There is no federal court case which has precisely defined the bounds of the "sphere of intellect and spirit" thus reserved, but [there are cases that] stan[d] for the proposition that a student may not be forced to espouse an ideological point of view on behalf of the State.

Defendants acknowledge that Plaintiff will be required to use the language that she finds objectionable as part of her curricular requirements as a student in the ATP. This, as an initial matter, amounts to a degree of compulsion. The relevant question is therefore whether this requirement "invades the sphere of intellect and spirit which it is the purpose of the First Amendment to our Constitution to reserve from all official control."

[In this case,] the ATP faculty are not requiring Plaintiff to espouse an ideological position at all; they merely asked her to read some lines which she finds offensive. She is not being asked to bear an ideological message or accept as her own an ideological proposition of the State in this instance. Defendants are correct in pointing out that Plaintiff is not being asked to be an instrument for, or adhere to, an ideological point of view at all. She is being asked to participate in a classroom exercise. Were this a First Amendment violation, then a believer in "creationism" could not be required to discuss and master the theory of evolution in a science class; a neo-Nazi could refuse to discuss, write or consider the Holocaust in a critical manner in a history class. Indeed, a Catholic law student could not be required to make an argument in favor of capital punishment during an in-class exercise designed to enable law students to argue cases they find unsympathetic. Just as it is reasonable for law school faculty to find that such an ability is necessary for competent would-be lawyers, so is it reasonable for an acting program faculty to use such exercises to foster an actor's ability to take on roles of persons they might find disagreeable. None of the hypothetical situations outlined above involve a citizen being called upon to espouse an ideology on behalf of the State—something that the constitution, as discussed above, certainly proscribes. Rather, these scenarios merely illustrate the fact that learning in a University setting involves the ability to discuss and take on other points of view in a serious manner. These exercises do not ask one to accept or espouse such positions for their truth; they merely foster the understanding and competency necessary for obtaining accreditation from a University degree program. Because she is not being asked to espouse an ideology that is not her own, Plaintiff's Free Speech claim fails as a matter of law, and Defendants are entitled to summary judgment on this claim.

D. Plaintiff's "Hybrid-Rights" Cause of Action

Plaintiff also asserts that, because her § 1983 cause of action invokes both the right of Free Exercise and to Free Speech, she has a "hybrid" cause of action which requires the ATP curricular policy to be evaluated under a heightened scrutiny test. [Accordingly,] the court here must determine whether Defendants of necessity have the authority to require student participation in the ATP as a prerequisite for accreditation from the program, such that these requirements do not impermissibly infringe Plaintiffs hybrid rights.

[I]t must be initially noted that the Supreme Court has a long history of deferring to the judgment of educators, especially involving matters of curricular requirements. In the academic context, the Court suggests that judicial intervention in any form should be undertaken only with the greatest reluctance. See, e.g., Regents of Univ. of Mich. v. Ewing, 474 U.S. 214, 226, 106 S.Ct. 507, 88 L.Ed.2d 523 (1985) (declaring federal courts unsuited "to evaluate the substance of the multitude of academic decisions that are made daily by faculty members of public educational institutions"). Indeed, the Court has clearly noted that the federal judiciary is ill-equipped to evaluate the proper emphasis and content of a school's curriculum. See Board of Curators of Univ. of Mo. v. Horowitz, 435 U.S. 78, 89-91, 98 S.Ct. 948, 55 L.Ed.2d 124 (1978). This judicial deference to educators in their curriculum decisions is no less applicable in a clinical setting— as in this case with the ATP's practical acting curriculum; evaluation in a practice setting "is...an 'academic' judgment because it involves observation of...skill and techniques in actual conditions of practice, rather than assigning a grade to...written answers on an essay question." Id. at 98, 98 S.Ct. 948 (Powell, J., concurring).

With this deference in mind, the Court has held that pupils may be expelled if they will not read from the Bible, so long as the Bible is only used as literature, and not taught as religious truth. See Sch. Dist. of Abington v. Schempp, 374 U.S. 203, 224-25, 83 S.Ct. 1560, 10 L.Ed.2d 844 (1963). It has also held that curricular requirements may be imposed upon students even when those requirements directly counter a student's religious belief. See Hamilton v. Regents of the Univ. of Cal., 293 U.S. 245, 265-67, 55 S.Ct. 197, 79 L.Ed. 343 (1934) (Justice Cardozo in concurrence noting that compelling military education for students whose religious beliefs make military service anathema does not violate First Amendment protections). Indeed, the Court has even gone so far as to hold that it violates the Establishment Clause to tailor a public school's curriculum to satisfy the principles or prohibitions of any religion. See Epperson v. Arkansas, 393 U.S. 97, 106, 89 S.Ct. 266, 21 L.Ed.2d 228 (1968).

The curricular requirements of the ATP program are more than reasonably related to the University's special competency of assuring that its graduates are proficient in their field of chosen study. Indeed, with regard to the question of whether determining University curricula is within the competency of the state, as discussed above, courts uniformly recognize that it is within the academy's singularly special competence to determine the propriety of its own degree requirements and to determine whether students have satisfied those requirements. Courts are loath to meddle in such determinations. This is so because they have long recognized that educational requirements are within the special competency of State educational institutions. The Tenth Circuit Court of Appeals recognized this to be the case when it recently noted: "when judges are asked to review the substance of a genuinely academic decision,...they should show great respect for the faculty's professional judgment." Gossett v. Oklahoma ex rel. Bd. of Regents for Langston Univ., 245 F.3d 1172, 1181 (10th Cir.2001) (quoting Ewing, 474 U.S. at 225, 106 S.Ct. 507.) This is the case because universities are licensing institutions. They of necessity determine the competency necessary for obtaining accreditation from their own degree programs. Given this, there is more than a reasonable relationship between ATP's purpose of assuring that its graduates are competent to take on challenging roles, and the ATP's curricular requirements.

Because there is more than merely a reasonable relationship between the ATP curricula and the purpose of ensuring that ATP graduates have sufficient competency in their chosen field, Defendants have shown that Plaintiff's hybrid rights claim fails as a matter of law and that Defendants are entitled to summary judgment on this claim.

E. Qualified Immunity

Defendants have also raised the defense of qualified immunity. The Supreme Court has held that government officials are entitled to some immunity from suits for damages. See Nixon v. Fitzgerald, 457 U.S. 731, 102 S.Ct. 2690, 73 L.Ed.2d 349 (1982). The Court has recognized that "where an official's duties legitimately require action in which clearly established rights are not implicated, the public interest may be better served by action taken 'with independence and without fear of consequences.'" Harlow v. Fitzgerald, 457 U.S. 800, 819, 102 S.Ct. 2727, 73 L.Ed.2d 396 (1982) (quoting Pierson v. Ray, 386 U.S. 547, 554, 87 S.Ct. 1213, 18 L.Ed.2d 288 (1967)).

As discussed above, Defendants did not violate Plaintiff's First Amendment rights. Also as discussed above, Defendants are entitled to summary judgment on Plaintiff's hybrid rights claim. Consequently, the Court finds that the Defendants are entitled to qualified immunity and summary judgment on all of Plaintiff's claims.

For the reasons set forth above, Defendants' motion for summary judgment is GRANTED.

Notes

1. Can *Boring, DiBona,* and *Linnemeir* be reconciled? If you had been the judge in these cases, how would you have ruled?

2. The facts in *Axson-Flynn* presented the court with a difficult choice: let the plaintiff stay and effectively dictate the instructional program, or allow her to be dismissed because she chose to follow her deeply-held religious beliefs. Did Judge Campbell make the right decision? Of course, where a student presents a bona fide threat to faculty members or other pupils, a dismissal becomes much easier to uphold. *See, e.g., Pacifico v. Playwrights Horizons Theatre School,* 623 N.Y.S.2d 474 (Sup. Ct. 1994) (plaintiff's enrollment was properly terminated after he left inappropriate messages on instructor's home answering machine and later accused her of plotting murder and mind control).

3. The United States Supreme Court has held that participation in high school extracurricular activities can be made contingent on agreeing to submit to random drug testing. *See Vernonia School District 47J v. Acton,* 515 U.S. 646 (1995), and *Board of Education of Independent School District No. 92 of Pottawatomie County v. Earls,* 536 U.S. 822 (2002). In both *Acton* and *Earls,* the school districts had sought to test only those participating in sports. Although the language in the opinions (particularly *Earls*) appears broad enough to also cover students involved in theater productions, the Pennsylvania Supreme Court has held otherwise:

> Were the suspicionless drug and alcohol testing in this case confined to student-athletes and students with driving/parking privileges, the question obviously would be closer. Policy 227 [of the defendant school district], however, captures students involved in all extracurricular activities. Students in the band, chess club, drama club, or academic clubs simply do not pose the same sort of danger to themselves or others [as do student athletes and those with driving/parking privileges].

Theodore v. Delaware Valley School District, 836 A.2d 76, 92 (Pa. 2003). Do you agree?

4. In February 2003, the editors of *The Heights,* an independent student newspaper at Boston College, rejected an ad for a campus production of "Good: A Tragedy," which concerns Nazism, because it featured a swastika. Professor John H. Houchin, the plays's director, then submitted a revised ad that deleted the symbol but included the following notice: "There was to have been a swastika in this space, but *The Heights* refused to print it." This ad also was rejected. Eventually, the editors agreed to run an ad with this message: "There was to have been a swastika in this place, to emphasize that this play takes place in Nazi Germany." Megan Rooney, *Sense and Censorship,* Chron. Higher Educ., Mar. 7, 2003, at A8. If you had been the editor of the paper, which version would you have printed?

5. In January 2004, a Fort Lauderdale high school troupe performing "The Children's Story" was expelled from a countywide theater competition after cutting up an Ameri-

can flag on stage. Written during the Cold War by James Clavell, the play is intended to be a warning against mindless political indoctrination; the destruction of the flag occurs as part of the "re-education" of a group of third graders following the defeat of the United States by a powerful (and presumably Communist) enemy.

In disqualifying the troupe, the competition's judges cited Florida Statute § 876.52, which makes it a first-degree misdemeanor to "publicly mutilate, deface[] or trample[] with intent to insult any flag...of the United States." When word of the decision reached the public, a heated debate broke out between pro-speech and pro-flag advocates. *See* Peter Bernard, *Drama Over the Flag*, S. Fla. Sun-Sentinel, Jan. 30, 2004, at 1A. If you had been counsel to the competition, what advice would you have given the judges?

6. For a further look at the clash between artistic freedom and educational policy, see, e.g., *Lacks v. Ferguson Reorganized School District R-2*, 147 F.3d 718 (9th Cir. 1998), *cert. denied*, 526 U.S. 1012 (1999); *Patterson v. Masem*, 774 F.2d 251 (8th Cir. 1985); *Seyfried v. Walton*, 668 F.2d 214 (3d Cir. 1981); *Bell v. U-32 Board of Education*, 630 F. Supp. 939 (D. Vt. 1986); *Webb v. Lake Mills Community School District*, 344 F. Supp. 791 (N.D. Iowa 1972).

Problem 28

"The People's Liberation Theater," an organization known for having strong political and social views, intends to stage a play next weekend to raise public consciousness regarding the homeless. As its venue, it has chosen a busy downtown shopping mall. Fearing the worse, the property's managers have moved for an injunction. In the past, however, they have allowed private and public groups to use the premises. Given these facts, how should the court rule? *See Horton Plaza Associates v. Playing for Real Theatre*, 228 Cal. Rptr. 817 (Ct. App.), *vacated*, 726 P.2d 1287 (Cal. 1986), *and dismissed*, 736 P.2d 319 (Cal. 1987).

Appendices

APPENDIX A
AGREEMENT TO JOINTLY WRITE A PLAY

Agreement Made by _____, residing at _____, City of _____, State of _____, and _____, residing at _____, City of _____, State of _____.

Witnesseth:

The parties desire to collaborate in the writing of a play (herein called the Play) provisionally entitled _____. They are members in good standing of the Dramatists Guild, herein called the Guild.

Now Therefore, in consideration of the mutual undertakings herein contained, the parties agree as follows:

1. The parties undertake to write the Play jointly.

2. The copyright in the Play shall be secured and held jointly by the parties. All receipts and returns from the Play, as well as from any and all subsidiary rights of every kind therein, whether specifically herein enumerated or not, shall be divided as follows:

To _____, _____ percent

To _____, _____ percent

3. All contracts pertaining to the production of the Play shall be on the form recommended by the Guild at the time.

4. Each party shall keep the other fully informed of the progress of all negotiations had in connection with the lease of the Play for production or the disposition of any subsidiary rights therein. No contract for the production, presentation, or publication of the Play, or for the disposition of any subsidiary rights therein, shall be valid without the signature of both parties. However, either party may grant to the other a power of attorney setting forth the specific conditions under which the same may be exercised. For services rendered under this power of attorney, whether in conducting negotiations or consummating a contract, no agency fee or extra compensation shall be demanded by the attorney-in-fact.

5. Signed duplicate contracts concerning the initial production of the Play shall be given to each party, and shall contain a special provision stating that all moneys, as and when due, shall be paid to the parties at their respective addresses above stated. All sub-

sequent contracts pertaining to the Play or any subsidiary rights therein shall also be in duplicate, and shall whenever possible provide for direct payment to each party of any and all moneys due.

6. The agent, if any, selected to handle the Play shall be mutually agreed on. The agent shall make all payments direct to each author.

7. In making contracts for the production of the Play, the parties shall use their best efforts to secure the insertion therein of clauses providing that in all programs, billings, posters, advertisements or other printed matter used in connection with the production of the Play, the names of the parties, in the sequence in which they appear at the head of this agreement, shall be equally announced as joint authors. In no event shall either name appear without the other.

8. After the completion of the script of the Play, neither party shall make any change or alteration therein without the other's written consent. Such consent shall not be unreasonably withheld. A consent shall be deemed to be for a specific revision unless it states that permission is given for general revision.

9. If either party wishes to sell, pledge, lease, assign, or otherwise dispose of or encumber their share in the Play or in any of the subsidiary rights therein, such party (herein called the Offeror) shall give to the other (herein called the Offeree) written notice thereof by registered mail, with full particulars. The Offeree shall thereupon have an option for a period of _____ days to purchase such rights in the Play as may be offered, at the price and upon the terms stated in the notice. A copy of the notice shall be sent to the Executive Secretary of the Guild. If the Offeree fails, within the aforesaid period of _____ days, to exercise this option in writing, or if, having exercised the option, fails to complete the purchase upon the terms and conditions stated in the notice, the Offeror may sell such rights to any other person at the price and upon the terms stated in the notice, and a copy of the contract for the sale of such rights shall be sent to the Offeree forthwith.

10. All expenses which reasonably may be incurred under this agreement shall be mutually agreed upon in advance, and shall be shared according to the percentage of interest of the parties. This shall also apply to any tax or assessment made by the Guild on the Play.

11. The parties do not form, nor shall this agreement be construed to constitute, a partnership between them.

12. The term of this agreement shall be co-extensive with the life of the copyright in the Play and any renewals thereof. If either party dies during the existence of this agreement, the survivor shall have the sole right to make changes in the Play, negotiate and contract with regard to the disposition of it and rights in it, and act generally with respect thereto as though they were the sole author thereof, except that (a) the name of the decedent shall always appear as co-author, and (b) the survivor shall cause to be paid to the estate of the decedent the decedent's share of the proceeds of the Play and of subsidiary rights therein, and furnish to the decedent's estate a true copy of all agreements pertaining thereto.

13. Any claim or dispute arising under this agreement or concerning the Play shall be submitted to arbitration before three arbitrators in _____ (unless the parties agree upon some other place) under the rules then obtaining of the American Arbitration Association, except as otherwise provided herein.

(a) The arbitration shall be initiated by the filing with the Guild of a written complaint setting forth the claim or dispute to be arbitrated, and mailing a copy thereof to the other party.

(b) Two arbitrators shall be appointed by the President of the Guild or the ranking officer thereof, within five days after the filing of a request for arbitration with the Guild.

(c) The two arbitrators so chosen shall appoint a third arbitrator from a panel or list submitted by the American Arbitration Association within _____ hours after the submission of such list.

(d) The hearing may be held on _____ hours notice.

(e) Any decision made by the arbitrators shall be binding on the parties, and judgment upon the award rendered may be entered in any court having jurisdiction thereof.

14. This agreement shall inure to the benefit of, and shall be binding upon, the executors, administrators, and assigns of the parties.

15. This agreement shall be signed in triplicate, and a duly executed counterpart shall be forwarded to the Dramatists Guild.

In Witness Whereof the parties have hereunto set their hands and seals this _____ day of _____, 20__.

Signature of Collaborator

_____

Signature of Collaborator

_____

[Acknowledgments]

APPENDIX B
AGREEMENT TO TURN A NOVEL INTO A PLAY

This Agreement made by _____, of _____, City of _____, State of _____, herein called the Author, and _____, of _____, City of _____, State of _____, herein called the Dramatist, and _____, of _____, City of _____, State of _____, herein called the Manager.

Witnesseth:

The Author is the author and copyright owner of a book entitled _____ (herein called the Book), which was published by _____ on _____. The Book was duly registered for copyright in the United States Copyright Office on _____, Entry No. _____. The Dramatist desires to write a stage play based on the Book, and the Manager desires to produce the play.

Now Therefore, in consideration of the premises and of the mutual promises and undertakings hereinafter set forth, the parties agree as follows:

1. The Author grants to the Dramatist the sole and exclusive right to write a full-length stage play (herein called the Play) based on the Book.

2. The Dramatist shall proceed forthwith with the writing of the Play. The Author shall not be obligated to collaborate therein nor to render any services whatsoever in connection therewith. However, s/he may elect, if requested, to examine drafts prepared by the Dramatist, confer with him/her, and make suggestions. Such voluntary assistance on the Author's part shall not be deemed a modification of the provisions of this clause 2.

3. The Dramatist shall complete the Play and deliver complete manuscripts of it to the Author and Manager not later than _____. If s/he fails to do so, all his/her rights hereunder, as well as all the Manager's rights, shall cease and terminate in all respects and for all purposes, and the Author shall thereafter be free to make such arrangements for dramatization as s/he may desire, for his/her sole benefit.

4. When and if the Play is completed as aforesaid, the Manager shall have the right to produce and present it in the United States of America, Canada, and elsewhere, subject to the provisions below set forth.

5. The Manager shall, within _____ days after receipt of the complete manuscript of the Play, enter into a contract for its production in the form recommended by the Dramatists Guild (herein called the Production Contract). The Production Contract shall be deemed incorporated in this agreement as though fully set forth herein. The terms and provisions thereof shall apply in all matters and instances having to do with the Play not specifically covered and provided for in this agreement. In the event of a conflict between any of the provisions of this agreement and those of the Production Contract, the provisions of the Production Contract shall prevail.

6. On or before _____, the Manager shall produce and present the Play on the regular speaking stage under his/her own management for a consecutive run as theatrically understood (other than try-out performances), in a regular evening bill in a first-class theatre in the United States, in a first-class manner, with a first-class cast, and under a first-class director.

7. If the Manager fails to enter into the Production Contract on or before _____ as required under clause 5, or fails to produce or present the Play on or before _____ as required under clause 6, all the Manager's rights in the Play shall cease and terminate in all respects and for all purposes, and the Author and the Dramatist shall thereafter be free to make such arrangements as they may wish for the production of the Play by another manager, for their sole benefit.

8. Simultaneously herewith the Manager has paid to _____, of _____, City of _____, State of _____, as agent for the Author and the Dramatist, the sum of $ _____ for the Author's account, and the sum of $ _____ for the Dramatist's account, as advances against their respective shares of the royalties which they are to receive on the Play under the provisions of clause 9. These advances shall in no event be returnable to the Manager.

9. The Manager shall pay the following royalties on the Play:

_____ percent of the first $ _____ of gross weekly box office receipts; and in addition

_____ percent of the next $ _____ of gross weekly box office receipts; and in addition

_____ percent of all gross weekly box office receipts in excess of $ _____. All payments of royalties shall be accompanied by box office statements for each and every performance.

10. The foregoing royalties, as well as the "playwright's share" of all other revenues and proceeds from the Play and from the sale or other disposition of any subsidiary or other rights therein (as more fully set forth in the Production Contract) shall be divided equally between the Author and the Dramatist.

11. All sums of money due and payable to the Author and the Dramatist hereunder shall be paid to _____, as their authorized agent, who shall be entitled to receive a commission of _____ percent thereon.

12. In all paid advertising, promotion, programs, announcements and notices, the Play shall be announced as follows:

[Name of Play]
By [Name of Dramatist]
Based on [Name of Book] by [Name of Author]

The Author's name shall in every instance appear in the same size type as the Dramatist's name and with equal prominence.

13. The Author shall have equal voice with the Dramatist in the exercise of any and all rights vested in the playwright under the provisions of the Production Contract.

14. The world motion picture, radio, and television rights in and to the Book shall be merged in the world motion picture, radio, and television rights in the Play when and if, and only when and if, the Play is completed, produced, and presented as elsewhere herein provided, in full compliance with the conditions set forth in the Production Contract. All book and other publication rights in and to the Book shall remain the Author's sole and exclusive property, and shall not be in any way limited, impaired, or affected by this agreement.

15. The Manager's rights hereunder are personal to him/her, and shall not be assignable by any act or by operation of law without the written consent of the Author and the Dramatist first obtained.

16. No waiver of a breach of, or a default under, any provision hereof shall be deemed a waiver of such provision or of any subsequent breach or default of any kind or nature.

17. Any dispute arising out of or in connection with this agreement shall be heard in the City of _____ by a single arbitrator appointed by the American Arbitration Association under the rules of the Association then in force. The hearing shall be held within _____ days after the appointment of the arbitrator. If a party fails to appear, the arbitrator shall have the right to proceed, take testimony, and make a determination on the basis thereof. Any award rendered by the arbitrator shall be final, binding, and conclusive, and judgment may be entered thereon in the highest court of the forum (state, federal, or otherwise) having jurisdiction.

18. This agreement contains the entire understanding of the parties. There are no representations, warranties, promises, covenants, or undertakings other than those herein expressly set forth.

In Witness Whereof the parties hereto have hereunto set their respective hands and seals this _____ day of _____, 20__.

_____
Signature of Author

_____
Signature of Dramatist

_____
Signature of Manager

[Acknowledgments]

APPENDIX C
AGREEMENT TO PRODUCE A PLAY

Agreement made in the City and State of New York, as of the _____ day of _____, 20__, between and among the parties signatory hereto.

Witnesseth:

Article I
Representations and Warranties

The General Partner represents and warrants to the Limited Partners that—

A. He has entered into, or has duly acquired by assignment, a production contract (herein called the Production Contract) with the author of the Play referred to in paragraph I of the annexed Exhibit A in the form prepared for such contract by the Dramatists Guild which incorporates the Minimum Basic Agreement of the Dramatists Guild. Except as otherwise specified in paragraph I of Exhibit A, the terms of the Production Contract are no more favorable to the author than the minimum terms set forth in the Minimum Basic Agreement.

B. He has acquired and now owns (1) the full and unencumbered right to produce the Play in the United States and Canada, and (2) an interest in the subsidiary rights in the Play to the fullest extent permitted by the Minimum Basic Agreement, subject only to such conditions and limitations, if any, as may be set forth in paragraph II of Exhibit A.

C. The total cost of opening a first-class production of the Play in New York City, including all theater deposits and all cash deposits (or the amount of obligations given in lieu thereof) required by Actors' Equity Association or similar organizations, and including all production expenses and the cost of an out-of-town try-out run, will not exceed the sum set forth in paragraph IV of Exhibit A as the estimated production requirements.

D. The only sums, as of the date of this agreement, expended or obligations incurred by the General Partner for which he is to be reimbursed under any provision of this agreement are the items set forth in paragraph VIII of Exhibit A.

E. The General Partner will receive no payments, directly or indirectly, from the Partnership other than (1) the cash office charge, (2) the items (if any) set forth in paragraph IX of Exhibit A, and (3) the share of profits hereinafter provided for.

F. The General Partner has not entered into any contracts under which any person employed by the Partnership will receive a percentage of the gross box office receipts, other than those set forth in paragraph X of Exhibit A.

Article II
Definitions

Whenever used in this agreement—

1. The term "the Play" shall mean the Play described in paragraph I of Exhibit A.

2. The term "contributions of Limited Partners" shall mean the amount that each Limited Partner shall set forth opposite his signature hereto, including any amount that may be paid by giving an obligation pursuant to Article III, clause 6 hereof, or which may be or may have been paid in advance as provided for in such clause.

3. The term "aggregate limited contributions" shall mean the aggregate of the contributions of the Limited Partners.

4. The term "sinking fund" shall mean the sum set forth in paragraph III of Exhibit A.

5. The term "estimated production requirements" shall mean the sum set forth in paragraph IV of Exhibit A.

6. The term "cash office charge" shall mean the sum set forth in paragraph V of Exhibit A.

7. The term "net profits" shall mean the excess of gross receipts over all production expenses, running expenses, and other expenses, all as below defined.

8. The term "gross receipts" shall mean all sums derived by the Partnership from the presentation of the Play and from the exploitation of its rights in the Play, and from the liquidation of the physical assets of the Partnership upon the conclusion of the run of the Play.

9. The term "production expenses" shall mean the total expenses, charges, and disbursements of whatsoever kind actually and necessarily incurred by the Partnership in connection with the production of the Play preliminary to its New York City opening, including (without limitation) the fees of designers, director, production assistant, production secretary; the cost of sets, curtains, drapes, costumes, properties, furnishings, and electrical equipment; premiums for bonds and insurance; cash deposits with Actors' Equity Association and other similar organizations that require such deposits to be made; rehearsal charges and expenses; transportation charges; cash office charge; reasonable legal and auditing expenses; theater costs and expenses; out-of-town losses (if the Play is presented out of town); advance publicity; preliminary advertising; advance royalties; taxes of whatsoever kind or nature; and expenses for replacement or substitution of any of the foregoing items.

10. The term "running expenses" shall mean all expenses, charges, and disbursements of whatsoever kind actually and necessarily incurred in the course of running the Play, including (without limitation) author's royalties; director's royalties; salaries and other compensation of the cast, general manager, company manager, business manager, production assistant and production secretary; salaries of orchestra and stage employees; theater rentals and other charges; transportation charges; cash office charge; reasonable legal and auditing expenses; advertising, publicity, and promotion expenses; rentals of equipment and properties; miscellaneous supplies; and taxes of whatsoever kind or nature other than the income taxes of the individual Partners.

11. The term "other expenses" shall mean all expenses of whatsoever kind or nature, other than those referred to hereof, actually and necessarily incurred in the course of the Partnership's business, including (without limitation) commissions paid to agents; moneys paid or payable in connection with claims for plagiarism, libel, or negligence; and the like.

12. If there is more than one author, the term "author" shall be deemed to be used in the plural.

13. If there is more than one General Partner, the term "General Partner" shall be deemed to be used in the plural.

14. All pronouns shall be deemed to refer to the masculine, feminine, neuter, singular, or plural, as the identity of the person or persons, firm or firms, and corporation or corporations may require.

Article III
Agreement

1. Partnership: The parties hereto hereby form a limited partnership (herein called the Partnership) pursuant to the provisions of the Partnership Law of the State of New York, for the purpose of producing, presenting, and managing the Play, and exploiting the rights of the Partnership in it, and for no other purpose.

2. Partners: The General Partner shall be the person who executes this agreement as such. All the other parties affixing their signatures hereto (including the General Partner if he also signs as a Limited Partner) shall be the Limited Partners.

3. Name of Partnership: The Partnership shall be conducted under the firm name set forth in paragraph VI of Exhibit A.

4. Location of Partnership: The location of the principal place of business of the Partnership shall be as set forth in paragraph VII of Exhibit A. Upon notice by the General Partner to the Limited Partners, the location may be changed to another place in the Borough of Manhattan, City of New York.

5. Contribution of General Partner: The General Partner shall contribute to the Partnership, by due and proper assignment, (a) all his rights in the Play, including those acquired or to be acquired by him under the Production Contract, and (b) all other rights acquired or to be acquired by him in connection with the Play.

6. Contributions of Limited Partners: Each Limited Partner shall contribute to the capital of the Partnership, at the time specified in clause 7 of this Article III, the sum set forth as his contribution opposite his signature hereto.

(a) If a Limited Partner indicates on the page of this agreement bearing his signature that he will give or cause to be given to Actors' Equity Association or any other similar organization an obligation acceptable to it in lieu of any cash deposits otherwise required from the Partnership by such Association or other organization, stating the face amount thereof and the organization to which it will be given, then the amount specified in such acceptable obligation, when given, shall be deemed equivalent to the making by such Limited Partner of a cash contribution to the Partnership in that amount.

(b) If the Play closes before the repayment in full of the principal amount of the Limited Partners' contributions, and all or any part of such obligation has been satisfied by action of the Partnership, then immediately after such action each Limited Partner who has furnished such an obligation shall pay to the Partnership in cash the full principal amount originally stated in such obligation (less any amount or amounts that he may have previously paid thereunder as his capital contribution), and such cash payment (plus such previous payments) shall thereupon and thereafter represent the capital contribution of such Limited Partner to the Partnership to the extent formerly represented by the amount originally stated in the obligation.

(c) Any prospective Limited Partner may, at the time of executing this agreement, pay to the General Partner all or part of his agreed contribution, and may authorize the General Partner to expend all or part thereof for production expenses as defined in clause 9 of Article II hereof.

(d) In such event, the General Partner shall, upon or before the filing of the Certificate of Partnership hereinafter mentioned, assign to the Partnership all the benefits derived from the expenditure of such funds for production expenses, and pay any unexpended balance of the funds into the Special Account referred to in clause 19 of this Article III. When the Partnership receives, in cash, the balance, if any, of the agreed contribution of such Limited Partner, the Partnership shall thereupon be deemed to have received, in cash, the full agreed contribution of such Limited Partner.

(e) If the Partnership does not come into being, the General Partner shall return the full sum so paid to them, without interest, to such prospective Limited Partner, unless otherwise agreed in writing between them at the time such contribution is paid to the General Partner. In no event shall any other Limited Partner be in any wise liable in connection with any such transaction.

If so provided in paragraph XII of Exhibit A hereof, but not otherwise, each Limited Partner shall, on the written demand of the General Partner, make an additional contribution in cash equal to such percentage of his original contribution as is set forth in paragraph XII of Exhibit A. Each Limited Partner shall pay such contribution promptly after receipt of a written notice from the General Partner requesting such payment.

7. Payment of Contributions of Limited Partners: As soon as aggregate limited contributions equal to the estimated production requirements have been agreed to be contributed (by actual signatories hereto) pursuant to the provisions of this agreement, the General Partner shall notify each Limited Partner in writing to that effect. Upon receipt of such notice, each Limited Partner shall forthwith pay to the Partnership the full amount of his agreed contribution, less any amount previously paid by him to the General Partner on account thereof.

(a) All such contributions shall be deposited and kept in a special bank account, and shall not be used for any purpose of the Partnership until the aggregate limited contributions in full have been so paid in.

(b) If the aggregate limited contributions are not received within _____ days after the sending of such notices, the General Partner shall, within _____ days after the expiration of such _____-day period, return all contributions to the Limited Partners, and the Partnership shall not be formed nor come into being. In such event no Limited Partner shall be under any liability in connection with the Play, provided however that if, during the second _____-day period, the General Partner procures signatures hereto from other persons as limited partners, and obtains from them contributions as limited partners equal in the aggregate to the contributions of limited partners that were not received during the initial _____-day period, the Partnership shall come into effect as and when provided for in clause 8 of this Article III.

8. Duration of Partnership: The Partnership shall commence on the day upon which, pursuant to the New York Partnership Law, the Certificate of Limited Partnership is duly filed in the office of the Clerk of New York County, and shall continue until terminated as in this agreement provided. Such Certificate shall be filed immediately after (but in no event prior to) the date on which the aggregate limited contributions (including any additional contributions obtained and paid pursuant to the provisions of clause 7 hereof) have been actually paid in.

9. Provisions as to Contributions: Until the aggregate limited contributions have been paid in, any Limited Partner may at any time agree, by writing endorsed hereon, to increase or decrease the amount of the contribution set opposite his signature, and any additional person or persons (including the General Partner) may become Limited Partners by signing this agreement as such and specifying the amount to be contributed to the capital by them. After the aggregate limited contributions have been paid in, any additional persons who desire to become Limited Partners as in this clause provided may do so upon complying herewith, but such additional persons shall not be entitled to any compensation with respect to their contributions as Limited Partners, or to any

share in the net profits of the Partnership, except by special agreement with the General Partner, and then only out of the General Partner's own share of the net profits.

10. Production Expenses in Excess of Estimate: If the actual production expenses of the Play, as defined in Article I, clause 9, exceed the estimated production requirements set forth in Exhibit A, Paragraph IV, the General Partner shall, either by making a cash contribution himself as a Limited Partner, or by obtaining contributions from other Limited Partners, make available to the Partnership such sums as shall equal the excess. However, such additional contributions shall not have the effect of reducing the share of net profits payable to the original Limited Partners.

11. Force Majeure: If by reason of an act of God, fire, flood, war, strikes, governmental order or regulation, or any other extraordinary event beyond the General Partner's control, the cost of opening the production of the Play in New York City is increased above the estimated production requirements, the General Partner shall not be obligated to contribute or obtain additional contributions made necessary by any such event, but he shall exert his best endeavors to do so.

12. Abandonment of Production: Anything herein to the contrary notwithstanding, the General Partner shall have the right, in his sole discretion, to abandon the production of the Play at any time prior to its New York opening for any reasonable cause other than his inability or failure to contribute, or to obtain contributions as provided in clause 10 of this Article III. In the event of such abandonment, the production shall be forthwith liquidated, and all funds then held in the special bank account or accounts, as well as all gross receipts as defined in Article II, clause 8, shall be distributed to the same persons and in the same manner as set forth in clause 18(c) of this Article III.

13. Announcement: The production of the Play shall be announced as set forth in paragraph XI of Exhibit A hereof.

14. Termination of Partnership: Subject to the foregoing provisions, the Partnership shall continue until the death of the General Partner, or until all rights of the Partnership in the Play have terminated. Upon such termination the General Partner shall liquidate the affairs of the Partnership as provided in clause 18 of this Article III.

15. Distribution of Net Profits: The net profits (as defined in Article II, clause 7) that may accrue from the business of the Partnership shall be distributed to, and divided among, the General and Limited Partners as follows:

(a) Each of the Limited Partners shall receive such proportion of fifty percent (50%) of the net profits as his contribution bears to the aggregate limited contributions, excluding however all persons who, pursuant to the provisions of clause 9 of this Article III, may be entitled to compensation with respect to their contributions as Limited Partners only from the General Partner's share of the net profits, and excluding from such aggregate limited contributions the contributions made by such persons.

(b) The Limited Partners so excluded shall receive such proportion of the other fifty percent (50%) of the net profits as the General Partner may have agreed to pay them from his share of the profits.

(c) The General Partner shall receive the remaining net profits.

16. Losses of Partnership: The losses shall be borne as follows:

(a) Until net profits have been earned, the losses suffered or incurred by the Partnership, up to but not exceeding the aggregate limited contributions, shall be borne entirely by the Limited Partners in proportion to their respective contributions.

(b) After net profits have been earned, then to the extent of such net profits the General Partner and the Limited Partners shall share such losses pro rata in the same percentages that they are entitled to share in net profits under clause 15 of this Article III.

(c) No Limited Partner (other than a Partner who is both a Limited and a General Partner) shall be personally liable for any debt, obligation, or loss of the Partnership in any event, except (1) from the capital contributed by him hereunder, and except (2) to the extent of his obligation to repay his capital contribution or profits actually received by him, as provided in clause 18(f) of this Article III.

17. Return of Contributions: The cash contributions of the Limited Partners shall be returned to them as follows:

(a) At such times (after the opening of the Play in New York City) as the Partnership has a cash reserve not less than the sinking fund specified in Exhibit A, paragraph III (plus a reasonable amount for initial expenses if the original company is sent on tour), after the payment or provision for the payment of all debts, liabilities, taxes, and contingent liabilities. All cash received by the Partnership in excess of such cash reserve shall be paid monthly to the Limited Partners until their total cash contributions have been fully repaid.

(b) Each such Limited Partner shall receive that proportion of each such repayment as the amount of his capital contribution bears to the total amount of the capital contributions.

(c) If any Limited Partner has given an obligation to Actors' Equity Association or any similar organization, then at the time of each such repayment, the Partnership shall set aside a sum equal to the amount of such obligation, until a sufficient sum is accumulated to release the liability of such Limited Partner, and thereafter the Partnership shall hold such Limited Partner harmless from any liability under such obligation. If, upon the termination of the run of the Play the amount so accumulated has not been used, it shall revert to the funds in the Partnership's special account for distribution as provided in clause 18 of this Article III.

18. Distribution of Net Profits: The time and manner of distribution of the net profits of the Partnership shall be as follows:

(a) After the payment (or the making of reasonable provision for the payment) of all the debts, liabilities (direct and contingent), and taxes of the Partnership, and after making the payments provided for in clause 17 of this Article III, such part of the net profits of the Partnership as can be paid in cash and still leave the Partnership with a cash reserve not less than the sinking fund (plus a reasonable amount for initial expenses if the original company is sent on tour) shall be paid to the Limited Partners and the General Partner in accordance with the percentage provisions set forth in clause 15 of this Article III.

(b) Solely for the purpose of determining whether or not any contributions are to be repaid or net profits are to be distributed to the Limited Partners and the General Partner under this clause 18 (but not for any other purpose), the monthly financial report prepared by the accountants for the Partnership shall be conclusive.

(c) Upon the closing of all companies presenting the Play under the management of the Partnership, and the abandonment of further plans for its presentation, the assets of the Partnership shall be liquidated by the General Partner as promptly as possible, and the cash proceeds shall be applied as follows, and in the following order of priority:

(1) To the payment of all debts, taxes, obligations, and liabilities of the Partnership, and the necessary expenses of liquidation. If there is a contingent obligation or liability, a reserve shall be set up for it, and if and when the contingency ceases to exist, the moneys, if any, in such reserve shall be distributed as herein provided.

(2) To the repayment of the capital contributions of the Limited Partners (if any then remains unpaid) in proportion to their respective contributions.

(3) The surplus, if any, shall be divided among all the partners in the same proportion that they share in net profits under clause 15 of this Article III.

(d) In liquidating the assets of the Partnership, all saleable physical assets shall be sold at public or private sale, as the General Partner may deem advisable. No assets other than physical ones need be sold. The General Partner or any Limited Partner may become a purchaser at such sale.

(e) At any time after the completion of the run of all companies presenting a first-class production of the Play under the management of the Partnership, the General Partner shall have the right to sell or otherwise dispose of the production rights and the Partnership's interest in the subsidiary rights other than the motion picture rights. The General Partner or any Limited Partner may become a purchaser at such sale provided the amount paid is fair and reasonable. The signatories hereto agree that _____, or a person who shall at the time be acting in the capacity that _____ now holds with the League of American Theatres and Producers, Inc., may pass upon the fairness and reasonableness of the amount of the proposed purchase price, and the judgment of _____ shall be final and binding upon all the parties.

(f) If any sums by way of repayment of contributions or distribution of profits have been paid prior or subsequent to the termination date of the Partnership, and if at any time thereafter there are any unpaid debts, taxes, liabilities, or obligations of the Partnership, and the Partnership does not have sufficient assets to meet them, then each Limited Partner and the General Partner shall be obligated to repay to the Partnership forthwith, to the extent required and up to the amount of capital so returned or profits so distributed to each, in the following manner:

(1) The Limited Partners and the General Partner shall, to the extent necessary, first repay any profits theretofore distributed to them. Such repayment shall be made in proportion to the amount of the profits theretofore distributed to each of them respectively.

(2) If such distributed profits are insufficient, the Limited Partners shall, to the extent necessary, repay contributions of capital previously repaid to them. Such repayment by the Limited Partners shall be made in proportion to the amount of capital contributions theretofore repaid to each of them.

(3) All such repayments by the Limited Partners shall be made promptly after receipt of a written notice from the General Partner requesting such repayment. Such notice shall contain a statement of (i) the aggregate amount so to be repaid, and the amount so to be repaid by each Limited Partner and by the General Partner respectively, and (ii) an explanation of the necessity for such repayment. Repayments by the General Partner shall be made by him at the time of sending of such notice to the Limited Partners.

(g) The obligations set forth in the foregoing subdivision (f) shall be in lieu of the obligations imposed under the Partnership Law of the State of New York insofar as such obligations are imposed, and in addition thereto insofar as they are not imposed.

19. Special Account: Forthwith upon the commencement of the Partnership, the General Partner shall, in the name of the Partnership, open and maintain in New York

City a special bank account or accounts, in which shall be deposited all the capital and all the gross receipts of the Partnership, and no other funds. The funds in such special account or accounts shall be used solely for the business of the Partnership.

20. Books and Records; Statements: At all times during the continuance of the Partnership, the General Partner shall keep or cause to be kept full and faithful books and records of account that shall fully and accurately reflect each transaction of the Partnership.

(a) All such books of account shall at all times be open to the inspection of the Limited Partners or their representatives.

(b) The General Partner shall likewise have available for the inspection of the Limited Partners or their representatives, at any time, box office statements received from the theater (or theaters, as the case may be) at which the Play shall be shown.

(c) Not later than _____ days after the opening of the Play in New York City, the General Partner shall deliver to the Limited Partners a complete statement of Production Expenses duly audited.

(d) As long as the Play is being presented as a first-class production by the Partnership, the General Partner shall also deliver to the Limited Partners a monthly statement of operations duly audited.

(e) The General Partner shall also deliver to each Limited Partner all so-called information returns required by the Federal and State governments showing the income of the Partnership and of each Partner.

(f) Within _____ days after the close of all companies presenting the Play, the General Partner shall deliver to each Limited Partner a final detailed statement of the operations of each company.

(g) Within _____ days after such close, the General Partner shall deliver to each Limited Partner a final detailed liquidation statement.

All such statements and reports shall be prepared by a certified public accountant experienced in the theatrical business, upon proper audit of the Partnership's books.

21. Control and Management: Subject to the rights of the author of the Play, and except as otherwise herein provided, the General Partner shall have complete control of the production and presentation of the Play, and of the exploitation of all rights therein, including, without limiting the generality of the foregoing, making changes in the script and the title of the Play, choice of cast, directors and designers, properties, sets, price of tickets, the fixing of the opening and closing date of the New York City company or any other company, and organizing and arranging for additional companies as provided in clause 23 of this Article III.

(a) The General Partner shall, in connection with the Play, render such services to the Partnership as are customarily rendered by theatrical producers, and shall devote as much time thereto as may be necessary.

(b) The General Partner shall not, on behalf of the Partnership, enter into any contract or make any commitment other than those that may be reasonably necessary for the production of the Play and the exploitation of the subsidiary rights therein.

(c) So long as he duly performs his duties and obligations hereunder, the General Partner may engage in other businesses, including other theatrical productions.

22. Office Facilities: The General Partner shall furnish to the Partnership, from the date hereof, office facilities that shall include office space, local telephone, stationery,

secretarial, and like facilities, but not a press department or legal or auditing services. For such facilities the General Partner shall receive the cash office charge specified in clause V of Exhibit A, and no more, for each week that the Play is rehearsed and presented as a first-class production, plus one week after the close of the run. If there is more than one company presenting the Play at the same time, a separate cash office charge shall be payable for each additional company for a like period.

23. Additional Companies: If the General Partner desires to organize an additional company or companies to present the Play, or to take any other action which would involve the use or investment of the Partnership funds (other than for the original production of the Play or for the acquisition of foreign rights thereto), he shall send written notice thereof by registered mail to each Limited Partner.

(a) Such notice shall state the aggregate amount that the General Partner desires so to use or invest, and the proportionate share thereof of each Limited Partner.

(b) If within _____ days after the sending of such notice the General Partner receives written objection to such proposed action from any Limited Partner or Partners, the General Partner shall have the right to take such action for his own benefit and that of the Limited Partners who do not so object in writing, and to use for such purpose such portion of the Partnership funds then or thereafter on hand as does not include the share of any Limited Partner or Partners so objecting.

(c) The Limited Partner or Partners so objecting shall have no interest whatsoever in such additional company or companies, or in any such other action; and the share of the Limited Partner or Partners so objecting in the net profits or assets of the Partnership shall not be reduced by any losses caused by or arising or accruing from any such additional company or companies, or from any such other action.

(d) In the event of such written objection from any Limited Partner or Partners, and in the further event that by reason of such written objection the portion of the Partnership funds that, pursuant to the foregoing provisions of this clause 23, may nevertheless be used or invested by the General Partner for such additional company or companies, or for such other action, is less than the aggregate amount stated in the written notice as the aggregate amount so to be used or invested, the General Partner may not organize such additional company or companies, nor take such other action, unless he procures other persons to become additional Limited Partners and to agree to pay any contributions as Limited Partners equal in the aggregate to the portion of Partnership funds that would have been available for such use if the objecting Limited Partners or Partner had not so objected.

(e) In lieu of procuring such additional Limited Partners, the General Partner may obtain the necessary funds in any reasonable manner he may deem proper, but in doing so he shall not, on behalf of the Partnership, enter into any agreement, obligation, or commitment whereby any amount of cash held for distribution to such objecting Partner may be used.

(f) In no event shall such additional funds (whether obtained from additional Limited Partners or in any other manner) be obtained on any basis that will reduce the share or interest of the non-objecting Limited Partner or Partners in such additional company or companies or in such other action, below that which such non-objecting Limited Partner or Partners would have had if no Limited Partner had so objected.

(g) If any such additional company or companies is organized or any such other action taken, the Partnership's books of account shall be kept in such manner as to reflect the foregoing provisions of this clause 23.

24. Road Rights: Notwithstanding anything contained in the foregoing clause 23, the General Partner shall have the right in his discretion to make arrangements to license the road rights in the Play to any other party or parties, provided (1) the Partnership receives reasonable royalties or other compensation therefor, and provided (2) the Partnership will not be involved in any loss, expense, or liability in connection therewith.

(a) Neither the General Partner nor any of the Limited Partners shall be disqualified from participating in the licensee's venture by investment of their personal funds or otherwise, but in such case the reasonableness of the royalties or other compensation payable by the licensee to the Partnership shall be passed upon by _____ or a person who shall at the time be acting in the capacity in which _____ is now acting with the League of American Theatres and Producers, Inc.

(b) In such event the General Partner shall have the right to render services to the licensee in the exploitation of the road rights.

(c) No road rights shall be licensed to any entity organized or controlled by the General Partner, or in whose financial affairs the General Partner has an interest, (1) unless the General Partner causes such entity to offer by registered mail to all Limited Partners a reasonable opportunity to participate in the licensee's venture at least to the same proportionate extent and upon terms at least as favorable as the participation of such Limited Partners hereunder, or (2) unless the time for the acceptance of such offer shall have expired.

(d) The "reasonable opportunity" above referred to shall be deemed to have been given and expired if, within _____ days from the date of mailing of the notice of offer, the Limited Partner to whom it is addressed fails to send his acceptance to the licensee by registered mail.

25. Second Company; Foreign Company: Neither the General Partner, nor any entity organized or controlled by him or in whose financial affairs he may have an interest, shall present a second company or a foreign company of the Play (or participate in doing so or in the benefits therefrom), unless the Limited Partners are given the same reasonable opportunity to participate therein as is secured to them under clause 24 with respect to licensing.

26. Assignee of Limited Partner: No assignee of a Limited Partner shall have the right to become a substituted Limited Partner in the place of his assignor.

27. Death or Disability of Partner: The following provisions shall apply:

(a) If a Limited Partner dies or becomes disabled, his executors or administrators or his committee (as the case may be) shall have the same rights that the Limited Partner would have had if he had not died or become disabled, and the share of such Limited Partner in the net profits and assets of the Partnership shall, until the termination of the Partnership, be subject to all the provisions of this agreement as if the Limited Partner had not died or become disabled.

(b) The Partnership shall terminate upon the death or disability of the General Partner.

28. Cash Return: Unless agreed to in writing by all the Partners, the Limited Partners shall have no right to demand and receive property other than cash in return for their contributions.

29. Power of Attorney: Simultaneously herewith each Limited Partner has executed a Power of Attorney, in the form hereto annexed as Exhibit B, authorizing the General Partner to make, execute, and file a Certificate of Limited Partnership. The authorization contained in the Power of Attorney shall not be effective until and unless the aggregate contributions of the Limited Partners have been paid as provided in clauses 7 and 8

of this Article III. The Certificate of Limited Partnership shall be substantially in the form of Exhibit C hereto annexed.

30. Execution in Counterparts: This agreement may be executed in counterparts, all of which taken together shall be deemed one original. One original of this agreement (or a set of original counterparts) shall be held at the office of the Partnership, as well as a counterpart original of the Certificate of Limited Partnership filed in the office of the County Clerk of the County of New York. There shall be distributed to each Partner a conformed copy of this agreement and of the Certificate of Limited Partnership.

31. Exhibit A: Exhibit A shall be deemed incorporated herein and is hereby made a part hereof.

Article IV
General Provisions

1. Arbitration: Any dispute arising under, in connection with, or in relation to this agreement, or any breach thereof, shall be determined and settled by arbitration in New York City, pursuant to the rules then obtaining of the American Arbitration Association. Any award rendered shall be final and conclusive upon the parties, and a judgment thereon may be entered in the highest court of the forum, state or federal, having jurisdiction.

2. Construction: This agreement has been made with reference to, and shall be construed in accordance with, the laws of the State of New York.

3. Modification; Waiver: No waiver or modification of any of the provisions hereof shall be binding unless in writing and signed by all the Partners. No waiver of a breach of any provision hereof or of any default hereunder, and no failure to insist, in one or more instances, upon the strict performance of any provision hereof, shall be deemed a waiver of such breach or default.

4. Addresses of Partners: Unless otherwise specified in writing, the address of each party shall for all purposes be that set forth next to his signature at the end of this agreement.

5. Agreement Binding: This agreement shall inure to the benefit of, and shall be binding upon, the parties hereto and their respective heirs, executors, administrators, distributees, successors, and assigns.

6. Entire Agreement: This agreement constitutes the entire agreement of the parties.

In Witness Whereof the parties hereto have hereunto set their hands and seals as of the day and year first above written.

_____

General Partner

[Address of General Partner]

As Limited Partners

[Here insert names, addresses, cash amount to be contributed, and percentage of profits to be received by each limited partner]

Exhibit A

I. The Play is a dramatic composition tentatively entitled _____, written by _____. The author has warranted the Play to be wholly original.

[If the terms of the Production Contract of the play are more favorable to the author than the minimum terms set forth in the Minimum Basic Agreement, so specify here.]

II. The conditions and limitations of the General Partner's right to produce the Play and in all subsidiary rights in the Play are as follows: _____.

III. The amount of the sinking fund shall be _____.

IV. The amount of the estimated production requirements is _____.

V. The amount of the cash office charge shall be _____.

VI. The firm name of the Partnership shall be _____.

VII. The address of the Partnership shall be _____.

VIII. The only sums expended by the General Partner, as of the date of this agreement, in connection with the Play, and for which he is to be reimbursed hereunder, are as follows: _____.

IX. [If the General Partner is to receive compensation for services other than the cash office charge, or if he is to receive payment for rights or property, set forth here the amount of such compensation or payments.]

X. The only contracts entered into that provide for the payment to any employee of a percentage of the gross box office receipts are the following: _____.

XI. The production shall be announced substantially as follows: _____.

XII. The amount that each Limited Partner agrees to provide as additional contribution shall be _____ percent of the amount of his contribution as set forth after his signature hereto.

[XIII. Here insert any special or additional arrangements.]

Exhibit B
Power of Attorney

Know All Persons By These Presents:

That the undersigned make, constitute, and appoint _____ of _____, the true and lawful attorney for the undersigned, and in the name, place, and stead of the undersigned, to make, execute, acknowledge, and file the Certificate of Limited Partnership of _____, a limited partnership under the laws of the State of New York, and to include therein all information required by the laws of the State, and also to make, execute, acknowledge and file a Certificate of Conducting Business under an assumed name, as required by the laws of the State of New York.

Witness the hands and seals of the undersigned this _____ day of _____, 20__.

[Signatures]

[Acknowledgments]

Exhibit C
Certificate of Limited Partnership

[Here insert a form of certificate that complies with the requirements of the Partnership Law of the State of New York and reflects the provisions of the Limited Partnership Agreement.]

APPENDIX D
AGREEMENT TO HIRE A
DIRECTOR-CHOREOGRAPHER

[Date]

[Name and address of Director-Choreographer]

Dear _____:

The following will constitute the agreement between you, in your capacity as director-choreographer, and me, in my capacity as producer, in connection with the dramatico-musical production now entitled _____ (hereinafter referred to as the "Play").

I hereby engage you as the sole and exclusive director and choreographer of the Play. Dance rehearsals for the Play shall commence on or about _____, 20__. In the event that the aforementioned dance rehearsals are delayed not more than _____ days, then, subject to your availability, you agree that your exclusive services will be available to me under this agreement and I agree to continue to so engage you. You hereby accept such engagement subject to the terms and conditions herein contained.

1. You hereby grant me the right to your exclusive services from rehearsals to the New York opening hereunder. Your services are to commence no earlier than _____, and terminate no later than the official Broadway opening of the Play. Upon _____ days written notice to you of the commencement date of rehearsals, you shall make yourself available and commence the services required hereunder. It is agreed that rehearsals shall be held in New York City and continue for a period of not less than _____ weeks. You further agree to remain with the Play during its out-of-town try-out performances and its preview performances in New York City prior to the New York opening and until the opening of the Play in New York City. It is understood and agreed that my exclusive rights to your services hereunder shall automatically terminate if I am not the producer or co-producer of the New York production of the Play.

You further agree that if you are in New York City and it will not conflict with your other commitments, you will from time to time witness performances of the Play for the purpose of checking and rehearsing the members of the cast and any replacements and to do whatever is necessary to maintain the artistic level of the performances. You will have the right of approval of cast, scenic designer and costume designer, production secretary, and two dance assistants (one of which will be the dance captain), and you will be consulted on the selection of the orchestrator and conductor, in respect of those companies directed by you.

You hereby approve of _____ as scenic designer; _____ as costumer; _____ as orchestrator; and _____ as conductor.

2. As full compensation for your services hereunder you shall be entitled to and I agree to pay you the sum of _____ Thousand Dollars as follows:

(a) _____ Thousand Dollars upon the execution of this agreement.

(b) _____ Thousand Dollars on _____.

(c) _____ Thousand Dollars on _____.

(d) _____ Thousand Dollars at the start of the first week of rehearsals.

(e) _____ Thousand Dollars at the start of the third week of rehearsal.

(f) In addition to the compensation hereinabove provided, I further agree to pay or cause to be paid to you, provided you have directed and choreographed the New York production of the Play, the following:

(i) _____ percent of the gross weekly box office receipts of the original company presenting the Play in the United States or Canada, with or without cast changes. For the purpose of this agreement, the following shall not be included as part of the gross weekly box office receipts:

(1) Any federal or other admission taxes;

(2) Commissions paid in connection with theatre parties, benefits, automated ticket distribution or remote box offices, but not ticket brokers;

(3) Any moneys paid to the pension and welfare funds of the theatrical unions;

(4) Subscription fees;

(5) Receipts from Actors' Fund Benefit performances; and

(6) Any other deductions which may be agreed to by League of American Theatres and Producers, Inc. and The Dramatists Guild, Inc.

(ii) _____ percent of the net profits of the limited partnership formed to produce and present the Play (the "Partnership"). "Net Profits" shall be as defined in the same manner as set forth in the Partnership's limited partnership agreement, and such Net Profits shall be paid to you at the same time, in the same manner, and subject to the same terms and conditions, as are applicable to each of the limited partners of the Partnership, and shall be accompanied by accounting statements in the form furnished to the limited partners, but nothing herein contained shall constitute you a limited partner. The limited partners alone shall exercise the rights of limited partners as set forth in the Limited Partnership Agreement.

(g) Provided you have directed and choreographed the New York production of the Play, should I undertake by myself or in association with another manager or on a lease basis, to form any first-class road companies of the Play for the United States or Canada, you shall have the irrevocable option to perform your services hereunder for each such road company. I agree to give you in writing at least _____ weeks notice of the formation of any contemplated road company, and you shall have _____ weeks from the receipt of said notice in which to exercise your option hereunder. In the event you perform your services for any road companies as provided for herein, I shall pay you the sum of _____ Thousand Dollars for each and every company for which you perform your services. Said payments shall be made to you as follows:

(1) _____ Thousand Dollars upon your exercise of such option.

(2) _____ Thousand Dollars at the end of the first week of rehearsal of the Play.

(3) _____ Thousand Dollars on the day said company presents its first paid public performance of the Play.

(h) Provided you have directed and choreographed the New York production of the Play, should you exercise your option to perform your services as a director-choreographer for any of the aforesaid contemplated United States or Canadian road companies, I shall pay you _____ percent of the gross weekly box office receipts of each such company. However, if you elect not to direct and choreograph any of the aforesaid contemplated companies, I shall nevertheless pay you _____ percent of the gross weekly box office receipts of each such company for which you do not perform these services, provided further that if you do not direct and choreograph any such road company or road companies you will receive no fee.

(i) Any touring company, as aforesaid, which presents performances of the Play in the United States, Canada and/or the British Isles, during the existence of my production rights under the Dramatists Guild contract with the authors of the Play (hereinafter referred to as the "Authors"), regardless of whether the production rights for such company are licensed by the Authors, shall be deemed to be a company, as to which the foregoing provisions of this paragraph shall apply, provided, however, that the foregoing provisions shall not apply if the production rights licensed by the Authors are such rights as are properly termed in the theatrical industry as "stock or amateur rights," in which I am entitled to share in the proceeds derived from the disposition thereof. With respect to any performances of any so-called "bus and truck tours" company, the receipts upon which your royalties shall be based shall be the gross receipts to me or my production company, or of such other company which produces the tour (if it is produced by another company) from such performances (i.e., all receipts from guaranteed or fixed fee bookings and the company's share of all percentage bookings) inclusive of my share, royalty, or fee, but after deducting the booking fees payable to the booking organization which books the tour. If the Authors' royalties are computed on any larger base sum, then your royalty is likewise to be computed on such larger base sum.

It is understood that a "bus and truck tour" of the Play may be either a first-class or second-class production or a stock operation, depending on factors other than the mode of transportation and such other facts will determine whether the provisions of sub-paragraph (g) hereof with respect to your being given an opportunity to direct a "bus and truck tour" is relevant to the provisions hereunder.

(j) If I require your services out of New York, it is further agreed that I shall provide you with round-trip transportation during the run of the Play out of New York and at any time that you are required to render your services hereunder outside of New York in connection with the New York company or any road company of the Play. I further agree to pay you the sum of _____ Dollars a day for hotel and living expenses for each and every day you are required to be out of town with the Play.

3. Great Britain Companies: Provided you have directed and choreographed the New York production of the Play, and should I undertake by myself or in association with another manager, or on a lease basis with another manager, to form any company or on a lease basis with another manager, to form any company or companies of the Play in Great Britain, you shall have the irrevocable option to have the right to perform your services hereunder for each such company or companies. I agree to give you in writing at least _____ weeks prior notice of the date of rehearsals and you shall have _____ weeks from the receipt of said notice in which to exercise your option hereunder.

(a) In the event you perform your services for any British company or companies as provided for herein, I shall pay you the sum of _____ Thousand Dollars for each such company or companies, and said payments shall be paid to you as follows:

(1) _____ Thousand Dollars upon your exercise of such option;

(2) _____ Thousand Dollars at the end of the first week of rehearsals of the Play.

(b) In addition to all other compensation herein provided, I further agree to pay you the sum equal to _____ percent of the weekly gross box office receipts from each such British company or companies.

(c) Provided you have directed and choreographed the New York production of the Play, and in the event you do not elect to choreograph and direct said British company or companies as provided for herein, I shall nonetheless pay you _____ percent of the gross weekly box office receipts of each such British company or companies for which you do not perform these services, but if you do not choreograph and direct any such British company or British companies, you will receive no advance or lump sum payment in addition to the royalty.

(d) In the event such British company or companies are formed as herein provided and in the further event you elect to direct and choreograph such company or companies, I agree to furnish you with economy-class round-trip air transportation from New York to London (except that if I furnish first-class transportation to any person connected with the Play, then I shall furnish you with such first-class transportation), and further to pay you _____ Pounds per day for living expenses during the time commencing _____ days prior to rehearsals of the Play through the earlier of the day after the official opening of the Play, or abandonment.

(e) The obligations to you under this paragraph 3 with respect to British companies which you elect to direct shall be subject to all applicable British taxation, currency exchange control and other laws, permissions, and regulations and to you obtaining all necessary passports, visas, labor permits, and union memberships. I agree to secure all such passports, visas, and labor permits, and you agree to cooperate with me fully therewith.

4. Billing: Provided you have directed and choreographed the New York production of the Play, I agree to provide you with billing in all theatre programs and whenever and wherever any person connected with the Play receives billing credit, except that I shall be entitled to accord credit in all advertising and publicity to only the name of the theatre, title of the Play, critical quotations, or any combination of the foregoing. Your billing credits shall appear in the following manner:

Directed and Choreographed by _____

The aforementioned billing credits shall appear on a single line and shall appear on the bottom line of all such advertising and publicity.

Said billing shall be in size, type, color, boldness, and prominence equal to not less than _____ percent the size of the title, but in no event less than the size of the Authors' billing. The name of no person connected with the Play shall appear in size and prominence of type greater than that used for your name. With respect to each company performing the Play under my management or authority in the United States and Canada and/or Great Britain, you shall be billed in the same manner, provided you direct and choreograph such company. If you do not direct and choreograph any such additional companies, you shall receive billing as follows (unless waived in writing by you) wherever and whenever and in the same manner as I am required to afford you billing in connection with productions and presentations directed and choreographed by you: "Original New York Production Directed and Choreographed by _____."

If billing is accorded in a billing box, then the relationship of the size of your credit shall be governed by the size of the letters in the billing box.

In the event that there are special sizes or prominence accorded to the design of the title of the Play, then I shall be entitled to make appropriate changes to reflect said special design.

The provisions for size, prominence, order, and requirements of credits shall not be applicable with respect to use in any medium of quotations from published reports, critics' reviews, or award announcements in advertising or other publicity.

You shall not receive the aforementioned billing credit on the front cover of the original cast album of the Play unless billing credit (other than the title of the Play) is accorded any individual directly connected with the Play and such billing credit appears on the aforementioned front cover.

5. I agree to employ, at my sole expense, a production secretary selected by you and approved by me, for your exclusive use, starting _____ days prior to dance rehearsals and continuing until the official opening of the Play, at a salary of $ _____ per week. During the time that the production secretary is out of town with the Play for the out-of-town tryouts, I shall furnish the aforementioned production secretary with economy-class transportation from and to New York City and $ _____ a day for living expenses.

6. I agree to employ, at my sole expense, two dance assistants selected by you and approved by me, to be available to you beginning _____ days prior to the first day of dance rehearsals and continuing through the official New York opening of the Play. One such assistant shall be paid a salary of $ _____ a week and the second assistant shall be paid a salary of $ _____ per week; such second assistant's obligations shall also include serving as dance captain and performing in the Play. In addition, each of the aforementioned dance assistants shall receive $ _____ a day as per diem living expenses during the time they are with the Play for the out-of-town performances of the Play and I shall furnish them with economy-class transportation from and to New York City.

7. It is further agreed between you and me as follows:

(a) I shall provide you with a dance rehearsal pianist selected by you and approved by me commencing _____ days prior to dance rehearsals and ending on the official New York opening of the Play. Should said pianist be required to arrange any of the dance music, he or she shall do so and all of his or her arrangements shall be subject to the composer's approval. Such pianist, if he or she also arranges any of the dance music, shall enter into an "employee-for-hire" agreement vesting in the Authors, as their interests may appear, all rights in his or her contributions.

During the time the pianist is with the Play for the out-of-town tryout performance of the Play, I shall furnish such pianist with economy-class transportation from and to New York City and $ _____ a day living expenses.

(b) I shall not make any changes in your work after the Play opens officially in New York City without your written approval, not to be unreasonably withheld.

8. For each New York City performance of the Play including theatre parties, benefits, or similar performances, I shall make available to you _____ pairs of House Seats in the fifth to the tenth rows of the center section of the orchestra (but only one pair on benefit performance evenings), to be held available at the box office for you, or your designee, to purchase at the box office price. Such tickets shall be so held until 6:00 p.m. of the day prior to the performance for evening performances,

and until 12:00 Noon of the day prior to the performance for matinees. For the New York City opening you will be entitled to purchase _____ pairs of orchestra seats in the center section of the orchestra and _____ pairs in the center of the mezzanine or balcony.

9. All rights of every nature and description in and to the direction and all choreography and all other ideas and suggestions you may make or give for the Play shall be the sole property of the Authors with full rights of use and disposition in perpetuity and throughout the world, without claim on your part. The Authors shall be deemed the "employers-for-hire" of your contributions and shall be entitled to secure copyright thereon, during the initial term of copyright and all renewals and extensions thereof in their names, as author at law, as their respective interests may appear. However, anything herein contained to the contrary notwithstanding, reference is hereby made to the agreement of like date between you and the Authors with reference to certain participations in the subsidiary rights of the Play.

10. I acknowledge that you have employed and designated _____, of _____, as your sole and exclusive Agent and have authorized and directed me to pay all moneys due or to become due to you hereunder to and in the name of said Agent and to accept the receipts of said Agent as full evidence and satisfaction of said payments. All notices to you shall be sent to you in care of your said Agent.

11. Any claim, controversy, or dispute arising hereunder, related hereto, or connected herewith, shall be settled and determined by arbitration in accordance with the then current rules of the American Arbitration Association. Such arbitration shall be held in the City of _____. The decision and award of the arbitration tribunal shall be final and binding upon the parties and judgment thereon may be entered in the highest court of the forum, state or federal, having jurisdiction.

12. I shall have the right to transfer this agreement to any limited partnership in which I am a general partner or to a corporation controlled by the undersigned provided said partnership or corporation assumes my obligations hereunder in writing.

13. All payments due you based upon the gross weekly box office receipts shall be paid not later than the dates upon which I am required to make payments to the Authors under the Dramatists' Guild contract and shall be accompanied by duly certified box office statements.

14. As and to the extent that the Authors and I agree to take a reduction in or entirely waive the royalties for any week or weeks, then you agree to simultaneously take a reduction in or waive your royalties for a comparable period of time and to a like extent.

15. This agreement shall inure to the benefit of and be binding upon the parties hereto and their respective successors and assigns. It may not be waived or modified except by a writing signed by the parties. It shall be construed, performed, applied and governed by the laws of New York.

Very truly yours,

_____

[Signature of Producer]

Agreed to and Accepted:

_____

[Signature of Director-Choreographer]

APPENDIX E
AGREEMENT TO HIRE AN ACTOR OR ACTRESS

Agreement made, effective as of the _____ day of _____, 20__, by and between _____, of _____, City of _____, County of _____, State of _____, referred to in this agreement as Manager, and _____, of _____, City of _____, County of _____, State of _____, referred to in this agreement as Artist, a member in good standing of Actors' Equity Association, referred to in this agreement as Equity.

1. Employment of Artist. Manager engages Artist to play the part of _____ [if appropriate, add part or parts for which Artist is required to understudy] in the play _____, referred to in this agreement as the Play, and Artist accepts such employment on the terms set forth in this agreement.

2. Term. The term of employment under and pursuant to this agreement shall be the run of the Play during the _____ season, which season is the period between _____, and the evening performance on _____.

3. Opening Date; Rehearsals.

A. The first public performance of the Play shall be on _____, or no later than _____ days after such date.

B. Artist shall begin employment under this agreement at the beginning of rehearsals, which shall commence on a date not earlier than _____ weeks prior to the date of the first public performance of the Play as specified above.

4. Continuous Employment. Continuous employment of Artist is of the essence of this agreement. The calculation of all sums due or benefits accruing to Artist pursuant to this agreement shall be made on the basis of continuous employment, and Manager guarantees that under this agreement Artist will have _____ weeks' continuous employment, beginning on the date of the first public performance, as specified in Section 3 of this agreement.

5. Compensation. In consideration of Artist's services under and pursuant to this agreement, Manager shall pay Artist, on _____ of each week, commencing with the date of the first public performance as specified in Section 3 above, or on the first day on which the Play is actually performed and any admission fee is charged, whichever is earlier, $ _____ each week during the run of the Play, until this agreement is terminated.

6. Rehearsal Expenses and Other Payments. In addition to the compensation set forth in Section 5 of this agreement, Manager shall pay Artist rehearsal expense money and all other sums agreed to be paid or required to be paid by Equity rules.

7. Reduction in Compensation. No reduction of the compensation to be paid to Artist under and pursuant to this agreement shall be binding on Artist without the prior, express, and written consent of Equity.

8. Compensation on Termination. If the run of the Play terminates before _____, this agreement shall automatically terminate, and Manager shall pay Artist promptly for all services already rendered, and all other sums to which Artist is or may be entitled under Equity rules.

9. Arbitration.

A. Any controversy or claim arising out of or relating to this agreement or the breach of this agreement shall be settled by arbitration, in accordance with the Rules of the American Arbitration Association, except as otherwise provided in Equity's rules, and judgment on the award rendered may be entered in any court having jurisdiction.

B. The provisions of this section shall, with respect to any controversy or claim, survive the termination or expiration of this agreement.

C. Nothing contained in this agreement shall be deemed to give the arbitrators the authority, right, or power to change any of the terms and conditions of this agreement in any way.

10. Rules of Equity.

A. Manager has notice that Artist is a member of Equity and must obey its rules, and has notice of all Equity rules applicable to the standard run-of-the-play contract. Manager shall abide by such rules and shall require Artist to do likewise.

B. Manager expressly covenants that at all times all members of all Manager's companies shall be members in good standing of Equity and that Manager shall not require Artist to work in any company unless all members of such company are members in good standing of Equity and unless Manager has fully performed and is fully performing all the terms of the employment contracts entered into or to be entered into during the term of this agreement with all the members of all the companies operated by Manager.

C. No riders, changes, or alterations of this agreement shall be made or agreed to by Manager and Artist without the prior, express, and written consent of Equity.

D. The following Equity rules are hereby made a part of this agreement as though set out in full in this agreement, and all of such rules are of the essence of this agreement and may not be waived or changed without the prior, express, and written consent of Equity: [specify here the rules to be incorporated].

11. Notice. Any notices required or permitted under this agreement shall be in writing and shall be deemed to have been duly served if delivered in person to the party for whom such notices are intended, or if delivered at or sent by registered or certified mail to the business address of the person for whom they are intended, as specified in this agreement.

12. Partial Invalidity of Contract. If any of the provisions of this agreement shall contravene, or be invalid under, the laws of the State of _____, such contravention or invalidity shall not invalidate the entire agreement, but it shall be construed as if not containing the particular provision or provisions held to be invalid, and the rights and obligations of the parties shall be construed and enforced accordingly.

13. Governing Law. It is agreed that this agreement shall be governed by, construed, and enforced in accordance with the laws of the State of _____.

14. No Waiver. The failure of either party to this agreement to insist upon the performance of any of the terms and conditions of this agreement, or the waiver of any breach of any of the terms and conditions of this agreement, shall not be construed as thereafter waiving any such terms and conditions, but the same shall continue and remain in full force and effect as if no such forbearance or waiver had occurred.

15. Entire Agreement. This agreement shall constitute the entire agreement between the parties and any prior understanding or representation of any kind preceding the date of this agreement shall not be binding upon either party except to the extent incorporated in this agreement.

16. Modification of Agreement. Any modification of this agreement or additional obligation assumed by either party in connection with this agreement shall be binding only if placed in writing signed by each party or an authorized representative of each party.

17. Assignment of Rights. The rights of each party under this agreement are personal to that party and may not be assigned or transferred to any other person, firm, corporation, or other entity without the prior, express, and written consent of the other party.

18. Attorneys' Fees. If any action is filed in relation to this agreement, the unsuccessful party in the action shall pay to the successful party, in addition to all the sums that either party may be called on to pay, a reasonable sum for the successful party's attorneys' fees.

In witness, each party to this agreement has caused it to be executed at _____ on the date indicated below.

[Signatures and date(s) of signing]

APPENDIX F
AGREEMENT TO RENT SCENERY

Dated _____

[Name of Producer]
[Address]

Dear _____:

You wish to rent certain scenery (herein called the Scenery) from us, and we are willing to rent it to you on the following terms:

1. The Scenery consists of [here describe Scenery generally and enumerate the items].

2. The Scenery is presently located at our warehouse at _____, City of _____, State of _____.

3. You have inspected the Scenery, and have satisfied yourself that it is in good and useful condition. We make no representation or warranty as to it, except that we own it and have the right to rent it to you.

4. The Scenery is to be used by you in connection with the production of [name of play, dance series, etc.], by [name of author, etc.], that you are to present at the [name of theater], herein called the Theater, located at _____, City of _____, State of _____, for a contemplated run of _____ weeks.

5. The run is to commence on _____.

6. We are to deliver the Scenery to you at the Theater at least _____ hours before the commencement of the run, and are to remove it not later than _____ hours after the completion of the run.

7. You are to have the right to make such minor repairs and adjustments to the Scenery as may be necessary.

8. You are not to make any alteration in or addition to the Scenery without our written consent. Any such alteration or addition is to be deemed our property and we are not to be obligated to reimburse you for the cost thereof.

9. You are to use the Scenery in a careful and proper manner and to comply with all the laws, ordinances, rules, and regulations pertaining thereto.

10. Upon the completion of the run, you are to surrender the Scenery to us, together with all improvements thereon and additions thereto, in satisfactory condition, ordinary wear and tear excepted.

11. You are to insure the Scenery at your expense against loss or damage from any cause in the principal sum of $_____ for our benefit.

12. In consideration of the rental of the Scenery you are to pay us—

(a) A rental charge of $ _____ for the contemplated run of _____ weeks;

(b) Transfer charges from our warehouse to the Theater and from the Theater to our warehouse;

(c) If the run is extended, a rental charge of $ _____ for each additional week or part thereof.

(d) If the run is terminated before the contemplated _____ weeks, you are to be nevertheless liable to us for the charges mentioned in subdivisions (a) and (b) above.

(e) You are to notify us promptly if the run is to be terminated before the expiration of _____ weeks, or if it is to be extended, so that we may make the necessary arrangements for the pick-up of the Scenery.

13. As an advance against the charges above specified, you have paid us the sum of $ _____ simultaneously herewith, receipt of which we hereby acknowledge. The balance is to be paid within _____ days after the actual end of the run.

14. The Scenery is and will at all times remain our property, and you will have no rights with respect thereto except as herein expressly set forth.

15. This is our entire agreement.

If the foregoing correctly sets forth our understanding, please so indicate below.

Very truly yours,

[Name of Scenery Owner]

By_____
Authorized Officer

Approved and Accepted:

Dated_____

_____
Signature of Producer

APPENDIX G
AGREEMENT TO LEASE A THEATER

WHEREAS _____ ("the Licensor") is the owner of the _____, located at _____ ("the Theater"),

AND WHEREAS _____ ("the Licensee") wishes to use the Theater to present the stage play _____ (hereinafter "the Play"),

NOW THEREFORE the parties have entered into the following agreement ("the Agreement"):

1. Grant of License. The Licensor grants to the Licensee a license ("the License") to use the Theater to stage the Play. The Licensee may not use the Theater for any other purpose or business without the Licensor's prior written consent. No legal title or leasehold interest in the Theater is created or vested in the Licensee by the grant of the License.

2. License Period. The License shall commence on _____ and continue until _____ ("the License Period").

3. Assignability of License. The License is personal to the Licensee and may not be assigned. Any attempt to assign the License shall automatically terminate it.

4. License Fee. The Licensee shall pay to the Licensor the amount of $ _____ ("the License Fee"). The Licensor acknowledges that the Licensee has to date paid the sum of $ _____ towards the License Fee. The Licensee shall pay the remaining $ _____ on or before _____. The Licensee may not occupy any part of the Theater until both the License Fee and the Damage Deposit (see paragraph 5 below) have been paid in full.

5. Damage Deposit. In addition to the License Fee described in paragraph 4 above, the Licensee shall provide to the Licensor the sum of $ _____ as a damage deposit (hereinafter "the Damage Deposit"). The Licensee shall submit the Damage Deposit to the Licensor on or before _____. The Damage Deposit shall be kept in a non-interest bearing account and shall be returned to the Licensee within _____ business days after the end of the License Period to the extent that the Licensee has complied with paragraph 15 below.

6. Late Charges. All late payments shall be subject to a _____ percent late charge.

7. Licensee's Use of the Theater. During its use of the Theater, the Licensee shall comply with all applicable federal, state, county, and municipal laws, ordinances, rules, and regulations.

8. Union House. The Licensor has contracted with various unions to operate and maintain the Theater. The Licensee agrees to abide by and fully comply with all such contracts.

9. Personnel. Except as otherwise required by paragraph 8 above, the Licensee shall engage and provide at its own expense any and all personnel required to stage the Play, including but not limited to cast; director; choreographer; musical director; scenic, lighting, and costume designers; and stage manager.

10. Stage Equipment. The Licensee shall at its own cost and expense provide any and all stage equipment required to stage the Play, and shall secure any and all licenses or permits required for the use of such equipment.

11. Box Office. Except as otherwise required by paragraph 8 above, the Licensee shall have sole responsibility for, and control over, the box office, and shall also have sole responsibility for, and control over, any and all outside ticket agents, services, or vendors.

12. Concessions. At each performance of the Play: (a) the Licensor shall have the exclusive right, but not the obligation, to operate coat check, parking, and refreshment stands, and (b) the Licensee shall have the exclusive right, but not the obligation, to operate souvenir stands at which it may sell posters, t-shirts, sheet music, original cast albums, souvenir books, novelties, published texts of the Play, and the like. Revenues earned as a result of the foregoing shall be for the sole benefit of the party authorized to provide same.

13. Publicity. The Licensee agrees to prominently mention the Theater in all materials related to the Licensee's staging of the Play, including but not limited to advertising, credits, programs, and throwaways. In its sole discretion, the Licensor may include the Play in its releases, mailings, or other promotional materials.

14. Use of Trademarks. Except as provided in paragraph 13 above, the Licensee shall not use the Licensor's name, trademarks, or logos in its advertising or promotional materials without the prior written consent of the Licensor.

15. Surrender of Premises. Within _____ hours after the end of the License Period (see paragraph 2 above) or the termination of the License (see paragraph 18 below), whichever occurs first, the Licensee shall remove all of the Licensee's property from the Theater and shall surrender possession of the Theater to the Licensor in good order and repair to the satisfaction of the Licensor, normal wear and tear excepted.

16. Indemnity. As a condition of being granted the License, the Licensee waives all claims against the Licensor for any damage in, on, or about the Theater, and for any injuries to persons in, on, or about the Theater, from any cause arising from the Licensee's use of the Theater. Further, the Licensee agrees to defend and hold the Licensor harmless from and on account of any damage or injury to any person or property arising from (a) the Licensee's staging of the Play (including but not limited to claims of libel, defamation, slander, or infringement of copyright), (b) the Licensee's use of the Theater, or (c) the Licensee's failure to keep the Theater and surrounding areas clean and in good condition. The Licensee agrees to pay for all damage to the Theater, as well as all damage to any person or property, caused by the Licensee's misuse or neglect of the Theater.

17. Insurance. The Licensee agrees to maintain in full force during the License Period, at the Licensee's own expense, a policy of comprehensive liability insurance, including property damage liability, which will insure the Licensee and the Licensor against liability for injury to persons, damage to property, and death of any person occurring in, on, or about the Theater. The insurance shall be not less than $ _____ per occurrence and not less than $ _____ in the aggregate. The Licensee shall provide the Licensor with a copy of the Certificate of Insurance certifying that coverage as required herein has been obtained and naming the Licensor as an additional insured at least _____ business days prior to the commencement of the License Period. All insurance must be primary and not contributing. In addition, all insurance providers must have a Best's Key Rating of "A" or better.

18. Termination; Default; Liquidated Damages. This Agreement may be revoked at any time by the Licensor upon written notice to the Licensee delivered or mailed to the address specified in paragraph 23 below. In the event of such revocation or cancellation, the sole obligation of the Licensor shall be to refund a pro-rata share of the License Fee and the Damage Deposit paid by the Licensee; provided, however, that the Licensor shall not be obligated to refund any portion of the License Fee or Damage Deposit in the event such revocation or cancellation is due to a breach of this Agreement by the Li-

censee. In case of cancellation by the Licensee, the Licensor shall be entitled to keep both the Licensee Fee and the Damage Deposit as liquidated damages and not as penalties.

19. Force Majeure. If at any time during the term of the License the Theater becomes unusable as a result of fire, earthquake, hurricane, flood, strike, work stoppages or other labor disturbance, riot, civil commotion, terrorist act, or other calamity or government order, whether lawful or not, which is beyond the control or authority of the Licensor, the Licensor may terminate this Agreement and shall not be responsible for any damages sustained by the Licensee. The Licensee shall be entitled to a pro-rata return of the License Fee and the Damage Deposit.

20. Severability. The terms of this Agreement are severable such that if any term or provision is declared by a court or arbitration panel of competent jurisdiction to be illegal, void, or unenforceable, the remainder of the provisions shall continue to be valid and enforceable.

21. Arbitration. This Agreement shall be governed by the laws of the State of _____, and the County of _____ shall be the exclusive forum for the resolution of any and all disputes arising from or incident to this Agreement. Disputes that cannot be amicably resolved shall be submitted to binding arbitration before, and in accordance with the then current rules of, the American Arbitration Association. Judgment on the award may be entered in any state or federal court having jurisdiction.

22. Attorneys' Fees. If any legal or arbitral action or proceeding arising out of or relating to this Agreement is instituted, the prevailing party shall be entitled to receive from the other party, in addition to any other relief that may be granted, the reasonable attorneys' fees, costs, and expenses incurred in the action or proceeding by the prevailing party.

23. Notices. Any notice to either party hereunder must be in writing and shall be served either personally or by registered or certified mail addressed as follows:

To the Licensor at: _____

_____

_____

To the Licensee at: _____

_____

_____

24. Entire Agreement. This Agreement, including the following Exhibits and Schedules [insert list here], constitutes the entire agreement between the Licensor and the Licensee relating to the License. Any prior agreements, promises, negotiations, or representations not expressly set forth in this Agreement are of no force and effect. Any amendment to this Agreement shall be of no force and effect unless it is in writing and signed by both the Licensor and the Licensee.

Done this _____ day of _____, 20__ by the following duly-authorized representatives:

FOR THE LICENSOR:

_____

_____

_____

FOR THE LICENSEE:

_____

_____

_____

APPENDIX H
AGREEMENT TO BOOK A ROAD SHOW

This Agreement made by _____, a _____ corporation with a place of business at _____, City of _____, State of _____, herein called the Owner, and _____, with offices at _____, City of _____, State of _____, herein called the Manager.

Witnesseth:

Owner is the owner of the _____ Theatre, herein called the Theatre, located at _____, City of _____, State of _____. The Manager has heretofore presented a first-class production of a certain play entitled _____, herein called the Play, by _____, on the Broadway stage in New York City. The Play has concluded its Broadway run and will commence a tour throughout the United States on _____. The parties desire to book the Play into the Theatre for the period and on the terms and conditions hereinafter set forth.

In consideration of the foregoing, and of the mutual promises and undertakings herein contained, the parties agree:

1. The Theatre: Owner shall furnish the Theatre, lighted, heated, and cleaned, with the scenery and equipment therein contained, janitor, ushers, ticket-sellers, doorkeepers, and tickets, for a period of _____ week[s] commencing _____ and ending _____, inclusive, for an engagement of the Play comprising regular evening and matinee performances, and holiday matinee performances.

2. The Play: The Manager shall furnish the complete production of the Play for presentation in the Theatre, and shall cause performances thereof to be given hereunder in a proper and creditable manner.

(a) Unless otherwise agreed in writing, the Manager shall provide (i) the complete cast, (ii) a stage manager, assistant stage manager, company manager, and other personnel (herein called the company staff) required under the applicable collective bargaining agreements of guilds or unions, (iii) all costumes, (iv) all scenery and stage props, and (v) all spots, floods, and other electrical equipment not already installed as part of the permanent lighting equipment of the Theatre.

(b) At least _____ weeks in advance of the engagement, the Manager shall also furnish (i) scene and property plots, (ii) the music parts, if any, for the orchestra, (iii) photographs of the principal members of the cast, and (iv) press material, advertising mats, and cuts in sufficient quantity to promote and advertise the performances to be given hereunder.

The Manager represents that he has full authority to arrange for a road tour of the Play. The Manager shall have full responsibility for, and shall pay, whatever compensation the author is entitled to receive with respect to the performances to be given hereunder.

3. Owner's Undertakings: The Owner shall:

(a) Furnish _____ local stagehands and _____ apprentices to assist at the performances;

(b) Allow not less than _____ hours immediately prior to the opening of the Play to carry in, set up, and hang the sets and effects thereof;

(c) Allow not less than _____ hours immediately after the closing of the Play to take down and remove such sets and effects; and,

(d) Cause the Theatre to duly comply with the rules set forth in the annexed Exhibit A pertaining to the maintenance of safe and sanitary working conditions for performers.

4. Manager's Undertakings: The Manager shall:

(a) Not permit, without the Owner's written consent, the star or any featured member of the cast of the Play to appear or perform at any theatre, cabaret, or place of amusement within a radius of _____ miles of the Theatre, or at any other place or occasion (including clubs or benefits) patronized by the public within such radius, regardless of whether or not a charge is made by such places, during a period commencing _____ weeks prior to the scheduled engagement of the Play at the Theatre, and _____ weeks after the closing thereof. In the event of the violation of this provision, the Manager shall pay to the Owner, as liquidated damages and not as a penalty, the sum of $ _____ and in addition thereto the Owner shall have the right to seek injunctive relief.

(b) Carry liability and compensation insurance covering members of the cast of the Play and the company staff. Upon the Manager's failure to do so, the Owner shall have the right, but not the obligation, for the term of the engagement, to purchase such insurance, and to deduct the cost of the premiums from the first moneys due the Manager hereunder.

(c) Cause all the scenery of the Play and paraphernalia connected with it to be fireproofed according to law prior to the engagement.

(d) Post a bond guaranteeing the payment of the Owner's out-of-pocket expenses in the event that the Manager is unable to fulfil this engagement.

(e) Cause each and every member of the cast and the company staff to abide by the reasonable house rules of the Theatre. The Manager shall be liable to the Owner for damage to Theatre property caused by any member of the cast or the company staff.

5. Division of Gross Receipts: The gross receipts of the Play during the engagement shall be divided as follows: _____ percent to the Manager and _____ percent to the Owner.

(a) The gross receipts shall be the aggregate moneys paid by the patrons of the Theatre to secure admission to view performances of the Play. No deductions shall be made therefrom except as herein expressly provided.

(b) The admission prices that the Owner shall charge, as well as the free admissions, if any, except to the local press, shall be fixed by mutual consent.

(c) In making its settlement with the Manager, the Owner shall credit the Manager's share with an amount equal to _____ percent of the Equity payroll (as below defined) of the cast of the Play for the period of the engagement. The Manager shall furnish the Owner with a detailed statement of the Equity payroll. This provision applies only to the first _____ dollars of the salary of any member of the cast. The term "Equity payroll" means so much of the payroll as is subject to the provisions of the Manager's collective bargaining agreement with the Actors' Equity Association.

6. Taxes: Any taxes imposed on gross theatrical receipts by the federal government or by the tax authorities of any state or municipality shall be deducted from the gross re-

ceipts of the Play at the conclusion of each performance and all calculations hereunder shall be made on the basis of the gross receipts less such taxes.

7. Advertising: The local advertising of the Play during its engagement shall rest in the Owner's discretion. The Manager shall not arrange for any promotion or advertising without the Owner's consent. Unless the parties otherwise agree in writing, the cost of any local advertising placed by the Owner shall be borne wholly by it, and the cost of any local advertising placed by the Manager shall be borne wholly by him.

8. Incidental Material: The Owner shall have the sole right to sell or cause to be sold sheet music, phonograph records, candy, and refreshments in the Theatre during the engagement of the Play there. The Manager shall have the sole right to sell or cause to be sold souvenir programs or booklets of the Play in the Theatre during the engagement, subject to the usual _____ percent commission to the house concessionaire.

9. Force Majeure: If the Theatre is destroyed by fire, flood, or any other calamity, or if by reason of strikes, lockouts, or any other cause beyond the Owner's control, the Owner is unable to make the Theatre available for the Play hereunder, the Owner shall not be liable to the Manager for any damages caused thereby.

10. Closing of Theatre: If any scheduled performance of the Play at the Theatre is not given because it is found that further rehearsals of the cast are necessary or for any reason attributable to the Manager's fault, the Manager shall pay to the Owner, as and for the rental of the Theatre, and in addition to any other expenses that the Owner may necessarily incur as a result thereof, the sum of $ _____ for each day that the Theatre is closed.

In Witness Whereof the Owner has caused these presents to be signed by its duly authorized officer and its corporate seal to be hereunto affixed, and the Manager has hereunto set his hand and seal this _____ day of _____, 20___.

[Corporate Seal]

Witness as to Owner _____

By _____ (Authorized Officer)

Witness as to Manager _____

Signature of Manager _____

Exhibit A
"Provisions for Safe and Sanitary Places of Employment"

1. All stages shall be clean and properly heated.

2. All dressing rooms shall be properly heated and shall have adequate lights, mirrors, shelves, and wardrobe hooks for the actors' make-up and dressing equipment. Floors shall be washed or vacuumed at least once each week and dressing rooms cleaned at least once each working day.

3. All dressing rooms shall be maintained in a clean and sanitary condition and painted as necessary. Peeling paint and loose plaster shall be repaired.

4. Treads on backstage stairways shall be maintained in a safe condition, with adequate lighting and adequate handrail supports.

5. Alleyways leading to stage doors of theatres shall be accessible and properly lighted.

6. Each dressing room shall contain at least one washstand with hot and cold running water for each six actors assigned thereto.

7. Toilet facilities shall be maintained in good working order and kept clean and sanitary, and shall be on each dressing room floor.

8. All theatres that house musical productions shall provide separate showers for men and women within a reasonable distance from the dressing rooms.

9. Ventilation of the dressing rooms and of all change rooms that are usually found in the basement shall meet the standards set by municipal health codes.

APPENDIX I
AGREEMENT TO ALLOW AN AMATEUR GROUP TO PERFORM A PLAY

Dated _____

[Amateur Group]
[Address]

Dear _____:

We are the sole agents for the licensing of the amateur (non-professional) production rights of a certain play entitled _____ (herein called the Play), written by _____. We hereby authorize and license you to present _____ amateur performances of the Play on the following terms and conditions:

1. The performances shall be given on _____, 20__ under the auspices of your group at the _____ in the City of _____, State of _____.

2. The license fee shall be $ _____ for the first performance and $ _____ for each successive performance.

3. The total license fee must be paid to us at least _____ days before the first performance. In the absence of such payment, this license shall be of no effect.

4. We have available play books containing the text of the Play, a diagram, a photograph of the stage set, and a list of the requisite stage props. We shall be glad to provide copies of these play books to you for $ _____ a copy.

5. On all theatre programs and on all advertisements of the Play under your control you shall cause proper credit to be given to _____ as the author of the Play. In addition, the theatre program shall carry the following statement: "Presented by arrangement with _____ [Amateur Licensing Agency]."

6. The Play shall be presented in the form set forth in the play book. Except for such omissions as may be necessitated by the orders, rules, or regulations of the local authorities, no changes, additions, or cuts shall be made in the text without first obtaining our written consent.

7. We shall not license any amateur group to present the Play within a radius of _____ miles of your city during the _____ weeks preceding your first performance and the _____ weeks following your last one.

8. This license shall be of no effect until and unless you sign and return to us the enclosed copy of this letter.

Very truly yours,

[Amateur Licensing Agency]

By _____
Authorized Officer

Accepted:

Date _____

[Name of Amateur Group]

By _____
Authorized Representative

Index

AUDIENCES
See also Houses
Generally, 327
Characteristics, 337
Disabled patrons, 289-92, 293-94
Etiquette, 349-51
Expectations, 152
Injuries, 161-64, 289-92, 339-49, 350, 352
Playbills and programs, 339-43, 350, 389
Tickets
  Cost, 152, 337
  Group sales and parties, 298-302
  Nature and rights, 327-32, 337-38
  Photographing and taping prohibited, 351-52
  Refunds, 338-39
  Re-sale and scalping, 332-37, 338
  Show times, 350-51

CAST
Generally, 10, 77-78, 193, 209-10
Agents, 232-43, 244
Animal performers, 209
Career characteristics, 77-78, 209-10, 226
Child performers, 208-09
Compensation, 37, 210-21, 226-27, 227-28, 232-38, 383-87, 389, 403-09, 410, 490-92
Cross-over from movies and television to theater, 152, 197-200
Firing
  Due to age, 183
  Due to audience reaction, 195-97
  Due to availability of better talent, 208
  Due to incompetence, 77-78, 133-35
  Due to insubordination, 210, 457-63
  Due to political activities, 197-200
Hiring
  Generally, 490-92
  As breach of existing contract, 206-07, 209
  Auditions, 200-05, 208
  Difficulty of finding suitable replacement for star performer, 208
  Financial considerations, 208, 383-87
  Refusal based on race, 193-95, 207-08
Illness, 159-61, 208, 338-39
Injuries, 167-69, 210, 222-26, 227, 255, 379-81
Training, 457-63
Understudies, 36-37, 77, 208, 338-39
Unionization, 228-38, 243-44, 383-87, 389
Workers' compensation, 222-26, 227

CRITICS
Generally, 353, 360-61
Abuse of power, 359-60
Banned from theaters, 381
Business expenses, 361
Compensation, 353-56
Ethical obligations, 356-59
Gifts and gratuities, 354-55, 358-59
Importance of reviews, 360
Suits against, for unflattering commentary, 361-81
Suits by, to defend reputation, 381

Training, 353-56, 359

DESIGNERS, MUSICIANS, AND CREW
  Generally, 10, 245, 254
  Compensation, 255, 257-58, 275, 387-89, 399-403
  Copyrightability of designs, 258-71, 275
  Costumes, props, and sets, 152, 245-55, 257-58, 275-78, 293, 493-94
  Hiring and firing, 251-54, 255-56, 271-75
  Injuries, 278-83
  Loss of work due to computers, 255, 387-89
  Unionization, 274-75

DIRECTORS AND CHOREOGRAPHERS
  Generally, 10, 171
  Compensation, 179-82, 183, 483-89
  Copyrightability of stage directions, 184-92
  Duties, 171-73, 182, 183, 483-89
  Hiring, 173-79, 483-89
  Training, 451-57
  Unionization, 171-73, 182-83

HOUSES
  See also Audiences
  Generally, 10, 285
  Accessibility by the disabled, 289-92, 293-94
  Concessions, 308-09
  Dangers, 293
  Design, 10, 285-88, 292-93, 294
  Fire and fireproofing, 288-89, 293
  Injuries
    Audence, 161-64, 289-92, 339-49, 350, 352
    Cast, 167-69, 222-26
    Designers, Musicians, and Crew, 278-83
  Insurance, 161-64, 294
  Leases, 298-309, 396-99, 409, 495-98
  Names, 294-98, 360
  Operations, 417-31
  Preservation and renovation, 309-25
  Trademarks, 325

NON-PROFIT PRODUCTIONS
  Generally, 411, 434
  Censorship, 436-64
  Fundraising, 417-31, 434
  Licenses, 435-36, 503-04
  Tax-exempt status, 411-31
  Used to develop commercial properties, 431
  Volunteers
    Duties and liabilities, 432-35
    Rights, 251-54

PLAYWRIGHTS
  Generally, 10, 39, 409
  Co-authored works, 47-58, 62-63, 465-67
  Compensation, 63-67, 80-81, 114-20, 121, 390-96
  Moral rights, 67-80, 81
  Plagiarism, 39-47, 62, 83-95, 112
  Training, 39-42, 78-80
  Unionization, 63-67, 80-81
  Works made for hire, 58-62, 63

PRODUCERS
  Generally, 123, 169
  Advertising and promotion, 43, 131-33, 164-67, 374-79, 389-90, 463
  Compensation, 123-30, 154-59, 170, 471-82
  Dealings with theater owners, 161-64, 302-07, 308
  Disputes among, 169-70
  Duties to investors, 133-35, 138-41, 150-51, 152-53, 471-82
  Methods used to raise money, 123-33, 138-41, 151-52, 431, 471-82
  Sharing of profits and losses, 30-33, 135-38, 153, 471-82
  Tax liabilities, 154-59
  Title as bargaining chip, 128, 167-69, 170
  Training, 170
  Underwriting of productions, 7-9, 131-33, 431

RIGHTS HOLDERS
  Generally, 83, 112, 114, 468-70
  Agencies, 34-35

Authority to grant permission, 95-97, 112-13
Fair use, 97-106
Musical rights (grand and small), 113
Non-profit productions, 435-36, 503-04
Piracy, 83-95, 114-19, 120-21
Refusal to grant permission, 207-08
Retention of rights, 119-20, 121
Right of publicity, 106-12, 113, 295-96, 403-09
Royalties, 7-9, 27-30, 114, 121
Taxes, 154-59

THEATER
See also Theater Lawyers
Generally, xvii, 3
Awards, 3-7, 21
Censorship, 22, 23, 81-82, 364-74, 436-64
Collaborative nature, 10
Competition from movies and television, xvii, 390-96
Costs, 7-9, 123-33, 141-50, 152, 383-90, 431
Depicted in movies and television, 21, 22-23, 170, 182, 208, 244
Elements, 10
Etymology, 9, 20
History, 9-23
Masks, 21
Popularity, xvii, 337
Similarities between theater and law, 36-37
Symbols and traditions, 16, 21, 209-10, 350, 360
Terminology, 35, 37, 209-10
Types
  Generally, 9, 20
  Alternative, 20
  Broadway, 13-20, 21-22, 152, 431
  Burlesque, 11
  "Bus-and-truck" tours, 389
  "First-class," 7-9, 20, 389
  Improvisational, 11-12
  Legitimate, 20
  Musical, 9
  "One man," 3-7
  Political, 9, 364-74, 442-51, 464
  Regional, 12, 130
  Religious, 9
  Repertory, 12
  Second-class, 389
  Summer stock, 12-13
  Vaudeville, 10-11
  Workshop, 7-9, 130
Use of arbitration to resolve disputes, 35, 244, 271-74

THEATER LAWYERS
Advertising, 23-27
Career opportunities, 34-35
Client characteristics, 35-36, 113
Conflicts of interest, 27-30, 141-50
Fees, 30-33
Number, 33-34
Research sources, 35
Similarities between actors and attorneys, 36-37
Training, xvii, 35

TOURING COMPANIES
Generally, 383
Advertising, 374-79, 389-90
Bookings, 396-99, 409, 499-502
Costs, 383-90
Working conditions, 399-403, 410